The Samuel Gompers Papers

THE
Samuel Gompers
PAPERS

VOLUME
2
The Early Years of the American
Federation of Labor, 1887-90

Editor
Stuart B. Kaufman

Associate Editors
Peter J. Albert
Elizabeth A. Fones-Wolf
Grace Palladino
Dorothee Schneider

Contributing Editors
Dolores E. Janiewski
Ileen A. DeVault

UNIVERSITY OF ILLINOIS PRESS
Urbana and Chicago

This book is printed on acid-free paper.

Library of Congress Cataloging-in-Publication Data
(Revised for volume 2)

The Samuel Gompers papers.

Bibliography: v. 2, p.
Includes indexes.
Contents: v. 1. The making of a union leader, 1850-86
—v.   2. The early years of the American Federation of
Labor, 1887-90.
1. Trade-unions—United States—History—Sources.
2. Labor and laboring classes—United States—History
—Sources. 3. Gompers, Samuel, 1850-1924—Archives.
I. Gompers, Samuel, 1850-1924. II. Kaufman, Stuart Bruce.
HD6508.S218   1987   331.88'32'0924   84-2469'
ISBN 0-252-01350-6 (vol. 2)
ISBN 0-252-01138-4 (set)

To
Wesley Reedy

CONTENTS

INTRODUCTION

"A struggle is going on in all the nations of the civilized world," the American Federation of Labor noted in its first constitution, "a struggle between the capitalist and the laborer, which grows in intensity from year to year," threatening "disastrous results to the toiling millions." This ongoing battle shaped the trade union strategy espoused by the AFL and influenced its leaders' conclusion that only combination "for mutual protection and benefit" might secure the rights of labor in an increasingly hostile world. If trade unions appeared to be, as Samuel Gompers put it, "the best and natural form of working-class organization" in response to the concentration of capital, the tasks of organizing national unions and establishing a permanent federation still proved formidable. This second volume of the *Samuel Gompers Papers* attests to the complexities of these tasks and documents Gompers' determined efforts to create a federation capable of fostering working-class unity and stable enough to survive the periodic assaults of organized capital and competing labor organizations.[1]

Although the structure and strategies adopted by the AFL owed much to the experience of British trade unionists, they also reflected the intricate reality of American working-class life. Nineteenth-century wage earners proved to be a diversified lot, and the varied pace of mechanization and organization increased this diversity. Workers were not only divided along lines of skill, ethnicity, race, and gender, but also by experience, opportunity, aspiration, and ideology. Native-born, skilled employees in well-organized trades like railroads, for example, viewed the industrial system from a vantage point far different from that of an immigrant cloakmaker or textile worker, and workers' strategies reflected that difference. The AFL, forced to cope with problems raised by the constantly shifting composition of the workforce, attempted to define an ideology and construct an organization that would serve the needs of this heterogeneous constituency. The correspondence, speeches, and writings that detail this development not only illustrate the variety of working-class experience but also demonstrate Gompers' efforts to federate these diverse components and forge, as he put it, "the strongest human force—a voluntary association united by common need and held together by mutual self-interests."[2]

Creating a foundation for such an association proved an arduous task, and Gompers well remembered that the early AFL seemed more like "a rope of sand" than a disciplined army of labor. "There was not that subtle atmosphere of permanence," he explained, "that is a strategic element today." The AFL, however, possessed strong prospects for permanence almost from its inception: its constitution established a sound dues structure, provided for a salaried, full-time president, and created a five-member Executive Council to administer the Federation. But if the constitution furnished a blueprint for a viable organization, the AFL, as Gompers put it, still "had to be given reality by making it a force in industrial affairs." The strength and effectiveness of the AFL as an organization depended on its ability to organize, attract, and retain affiliated trade union and central labor bodies.[3]

As the only full-time executive in the AFL's employ between 1887 and 1890, Gompers assumed responsibility for promoting the Federation, urging national unions to affiliate, and advising workers on their efforts to organize local and national unions. He not only corresponded with a wide range of labor activists and almost single-handedly produced the AFL's short-lived journal, the *Union Advocate*, but he also traveled extensively, lecturing on behalf of the AFL and organizing what he called "the local shock troops of trade unionism." On his first major trip in 1888, for example, Gompers visited some thirty midwestern cities where, he remembered, he sought out the active labor men, those he could rely on "to stand stanchly [*sic*] for trade unionism."[4] Such organizing trips, usually underwritten by the local labor movement, enabled Gompers to build up a national network of trade unionists and to appoint hundreds of organizers who agreed to work only for expenses. With the AFL barely able to cover Gompers' salary and provide modest office space and supplies,[5] the Federation relied on Gompers' ability to identify and recruit this corps of supporters who donated time and energy to the trade union movement.

Designing a workable structure was essential in building a permanent federation, but Gompers and his colleagues recognized that structure alone could not consolidate the various elements of the working class. Searching for an issue that all workers could support, leaders of the AFL revived the eight-hour movement at their 1888 convention and targeted May 1, 1890, for the inauguration of the shorter work-day. The eight-hour campaign became the centerpiece of Gompers' trade union strategy in this period, allowing the AFL to focus on those immediate economic goals and political demands that, Gompers contended, commanded wide support among workers. "In the whole history of the labor movement," he reported to the 1889 convention, "there has not been any question upon which the thoughts of the civilized world have been so thoroughly centered."[6] With the AFL serving as the conduit for funds and services for the campaign, Gompers capitalized on the Federation's increased visibility and utilized the movement not only to further the goal of shorter hours, but also to promote his theory of economic organization and vision of trade unionism.

Although the eight-hour movement attracted a wide range of labor organizations to the AFL's cause, it failed to gain the support of the KOL, a rival national organization that claimed some 700,000 members in 1886. While affiliates of both labor bodies often cooperated on the local level, competition on the national level intensified during the late 1880s. KOL trade assemblies contested for jurisdiction with trade unions—often affiliated with the AFL—and local clashes, stemming from dual memberships in both organizations, frequently resulted. The documents pertaining to these struggles, and to the personal antagonism that pitted Gompers against Knights' leader Terence Powderly, illustrate the complex competition that colored Gompers' vision and influenced his conception of a workable trade union strategy. Despite the fiery rhetoric that emanated from both sides, however, by 1890 the conflict between the Knights and the AFL was of diminishing importance as the KOL suffered a precipitous decline in membership and its leaders turned their attention away from trade assemblies to promote an alliance with the Populists.

While the AFL and the KOL contested the trade union terrain, Gompers also found himself embroiled in another conflict, one between trade unionists "pure and simple" and socialists favoring the formation of an independent labor party. Although similar struggles occurred in many industrial centers, Gompers' fight with members of the New York City SLP had significant ramifications for the development of the AFL. In New York City factional fights following the 1887 electoral campaign divided the labor movement, and the SLP emerged as Gompers' most severe critic. Such factionalism and the bitter recriminations that resulted reinforced Gompers' adherence to nonpartisan politics, and he led the AFL toward a political program that emphasized lobbying for state and federal legislation favorable to labor. He attempted, for example, to persuade New York state legislators to support the Saturday half-holiday, a mechanics' lien law, a state bureau of labor statistics, and the regulation of child and convict labor, and he joined the New York Working Women's Society's campaign for a factory inspection law. On the national level he lobbied Congress for the regulation of alien contract labor and for support of the eight-hour day. Because he contended that effective lobbying required a nonpartisan stance, he adamantly opposed the SLP's participation, as an organization, in Federation affairs. When the New York City Central Labor Federation accepted the SLP as an affiliate and then attempted to join the AFL, Gompers withheld the charter, pending a decision by the 1890 convention. Although the convention upheld Gompers' nonpartisan position, the issue inaugurated a debate over the political direction of the American labor movement that continued well into the next decade.

By 1890 the Federation had not accomplished all its goals, but it had developed significantly in size and stature, and had achieved a measure of permanence — no mean feat given the hostility that generally faced organized labor and the diversity of the working class itself. Confronted by political opposition and organizational competition, the AFL, with Gompers at the helm, realized financial and structural stability,[7] launched a moderately successful lobbying campaign, and attained national visibility through the eight-hour movement. "Everywhere I am meeting with the greatest success," Gompers reported from the road in early 1891. "Our movement has at last taken a firm hold on the hearts and minds of the wage workers and has their confidence as well as the respect of the people at large."[8]

ACKNOWLEDGMENTS

This project has benefited immeasurably from the help of Wesley Reedy, a leader in the Bakery and Confectionery Workers International Union for more than two decades and assistant to the secretary-treasurer of the AFL-CIO from 1955 to 1982. Strongly interested in preserving the history of the labor movement, he located and made available to the project Gompers-era records held by the AFL-CIO. Further, he provided valuable counsel and assistance to our efforts to secure the Federation's permission for us to publish its records and to arrange for vital financial support from the trade union movement. It is hard to conceive of what the early years of this project would have been like without Wesley Reedy's understanding and cooperation, and it is with that in mind that we dedicate this volume to him.

Leaders of the AFL-CIO have provided invaluable cooperation in the form of permission to photocopy and publish the records of the Federation from the Gompers era, as well as in providing annual grants since 1982. We are particularly grateful to President Lane Kirkland, Secretary-Treasurer Thomas R. Donahue, Assistant to the Secretary-Treasurer James J. Kennedy, Jr., and the members of the Executive Council.

The support of the labor movement has been especially important in today's difficult economic climate for the financing of humanities research. In partnership with the University of Maryland and federal agencies, many national and international unions have joined the AFL-CIO Executive Council in granting funds to see our work to completion. The project has received financial contributions from the AFL-CIO Executive Council, the Joseph Anthony Beirne Memorial Foundation of the Communications Workers of America, and the following unions: the Associated Actors and Artistes of America, the Bakery, Confectionery and Tobacco Workers International Union, the International Brotherhood of Boilermakers, Iron Ship Builders, Blacksmiths, Forgers and Helpers, the International Union of Bricklayers and Allied Craftsmen, the International Brotherhood of Electrical Workers, the International Union of Electronic, Electrical, Technical, Salaried and Machine Workers, the United Food and Commercial Workers International Union, the Glass, Pottery, Plastics and Allied Workers International Union, the American Federation of Government Employees, the Laborers' International Union of North America, the National Association of Letter Carriers, the International Longshoremen's Association, the Mechanics Educational Society, the Newspaper Guild, the International Union of Operating Engineers, the International Brotherhood of Painters and Allied Trades of the United States and Canada, the United Paperworkers International Union, the United Association of Journeymen and Apprentices of the Plumbing and Pipe Fitting Industry of the United States and Canada, the Brotherhood of Railway Carmen of the United States and Canada, the Service Employees International Union, the United Steelworkers of America, the International Brotherhood of Teamsters, Chauffeurs, Warehousemen and Helpers of America, the International Alliance of Theatrical Stage Employes and Moving Picture Machine Operators of the United States and Canada, and the Amalgamated Transit Union. In addition, we continue to draw on the records of many labor unions who have granted us access to their files and permission to copy and publish pertinent material.

Two federal agencies have provided major financial support as well as advice and encouragement in this important undertaking. Without the support of the National Historical Publications and Records Commission (NHPRC) and the National Endowment for the Humanities (NEH), a project of this scope would not have been possible. We have consulted closely with Frank G. Burke, Richard A. Jacobs, Roger A. Bruns, and George L. Vogt of the NHPRC and Helen Aguera and Kathy J. Fuller of the NEH. Sara Dunlap Jackson and Mary A. Guinta of the NHPRC have provided research assistance in the records of the National Archives. Outright grants from each agency, as well as matching grants from the NEH, have been the backbone of our funding.

The Samuel Gompers Papers is located at the University of Maryland, which provides office space, financial support, and other forms of aid as sponsor of the project. At every level of the campus leadership we have received strong moral and practical support consistent with the University's commitment to humanities research. We are particularly indebted to President John S. Toll, Chancellor John B. Slaughter, Provost Shirley Strum Kenny of the Division of Arts and Humanities, and History Department Chairman Emory G. Evans. We have continually drawn on the resources and staff of McKeldin Library, where our project is housed, and have utilized the services of the University of Maryland Foundation in connection with our fundraising efforts.

Aiding us in the search for and reproduction of documents and research information have been the staffs of many libraries, archives, and repositories. Among the most important in helping us assemble material for *The Early Years of the American Federation of Labor* were the Catholic University of America, the Library of Congress, the National Archives, the State Historical Society of Wisconsin, the Tamiment Collection of the Bobst Library at New York University, and the U.S. Department of Labor Library. The Library of Congress has for several years provided the project with an office for the purpose of carrying on our extensive annotation research.

A work of this nature requires the talents of many people. Patrick McGrath worked with us in translating German documents and refining the translations in accordance with modern editorial standards, Carlotta Anderson shared with us information from her own research on the career of Joseph Labadie, and George E. Pozzetta from his work on Cuban cigarmakers. Mary Ann Coyle, the project's research assistant, worked closely with us in the later stages of preparing this volume. University of Maryland graduate students Frederick Augustyn, Lizette LeSavage, Harold Eugene Mahan, Diane Miller, Katherine Kidd Morin, Nora Oakes, Elizabeth Robertson, Kevin Swanson, and Richard Wilkoff, and undergraduate students Margaret Rauner Brodnick, Deona Dichoso, and Tonya Little spent months in annotation work, proofreading, and other tasks requiring accuracy, discipline, and a dedication to the overall objectives of the project. Many other graduate students contributed through assignments they undertook in connection with the University of Maryland's historical editing seminar. Our secretary, Celia Ramos Gray, carried the burden of transcription with professionalism and good humor and bore with us through our many drafts and amendments of text and annotations. In total, the contributions of these people can be measured not simply in the project's productivity but also in the genuine enjoyment the editors have experienced in working with dedicated and sympathetic colleagues.

Our work has benefited from the critical reading of members of our board of editorial advisors. Those who have been able to take time out from their own work to read and comment on our volume include David Brody, Philip Foner, Herbert Gutman, Louis Harlan, Maurice Neufeld, and Irwin Yellowitz. We have sharpened our own perspective and made numerous changes in response to their suggestions. Of course the current editors take full responsibility for the ultimate shape of the volume. In this respect it is important to note that the Samuel Gompers Papers remains a group project, whose every aspect is shaped by the give and take among the various editors in their regular discussions and as they work together. In a profession dominated by the solitary scholar, we have shared in the rare experience of an ongoing creative group enterprise.

Notes

1. AFL, *Proceedings*, 1886, p. 3; SG to P. H. Donnelly, Apr. 23, 1888, below.
2. SG, *Seventy Years*, 1:333.
3. Ibid., pp. 333, 341, 327; the Executive Council consisted of a president, two vice-presidents, a secretary, and a treasurer.
4. Ibid., pp. 336, 328. In December 1887, the AFL convention voted to abandon publication of the *Union Advocate* after a six-month trial on the grounds that it drained the officers' time and the Federation's resources.
5. At first the CMIU provided the AFL with a rent-free office in the "tenement" where the union's own headquarters were located. According to a description in the *New York Sun*, it was "a little room about ten feet by six, lined with shelves and pigeonholes. A $3.50-a-week boy works at a pine table directing circulars, and runs errands. By the one window of the room is a cheap desk. There Mr. Gompers works. There are files full of letters along the walls and a stand behind him. The whole furniture of the room might be worth $14, and the value of the old paper lying around would bring it up to $15." When the Gompers family moved to 171 East Ninety-first St. in January 1888, the front room of the apartment, originally designed

as an office, became the AFL's headquarters. Federation business continued to grow, however, "until it seemed that my family would be crowded out," so Gompers moved the Federation's office to 21 Clinton Pl. about December 1888, where the AFL paid $16 a month for three rooms. Not long afterward the Executive Council authorized him to buy a secondhand typewriter and hire a typist and stenographer to relieve him of the burden of carrying on the Federation's increasing correspondence in longhand (*New York Sun,* June 19, 1887; SG, *Seventy Years,* 1:329).

6. AFL, *Proceedings,* 1889, p. 14.

7. The organization's revenue increased from $2,100 in 1887 to $24,714 in 1890. In the year preceding the 1890 AFL convention some twenty-eight central labor unions and about an equal number of national and international unions contributed the greater part of the AFL's receipts. In addition, hundreds of directly affiliated locals (unions of single trades in which there were no national unions) and federal labor unions (bodies that accepted local workers from more than one trade) contributed substantially to the AFL's income.

8. SG to P. J. McGuire, Feb. 11, 1891, reel 4, vol. 5, p. 435, SG Letterbooks, DLC.

SYMBOLS AND ABBREVIATIONS

A and PLpS	Autograph and printed letter, letterpress copy, signed
AD	Autograph document
AFL	The American Federation of Labor
ALpI	Autograph letter, letterpress copy, initialed
ALpS	Autograph letter, letterpress copy, signed
ALS	Autograph letter, signed
CMIU	The Cigar Makers' International Union
DCU	The Catholic University of America, Washington, D.C.
DLC	The Library of Congress
DNA	The National Archives of the United States, Washington, D.C.
FOTLU	The Federation of Organized Trades and Labor Unions of the United States and Canada
HLp	Handwritten letter, letterpress copy
HLpS	Handwritten letter, letterpress copy, signed
HLpSr	Handwritten letter, letterpress copy, signature representation
HLSr	Handwritten letter, signature representation
KOL	The Knights of Labor
MiDW	Wayne State University, Detroit, Mich.
OFH	Rutherford B. Hayes Presidential Center, Fremont, Ohio
PD	Printed document
PLSr	Printed letter, signature representation
SG	Samuel Gompers
SLP	The Socialistic or Socialist Labor party
T and ALS	Typed and autograph letter, signed
T and HD	Typed and handwritten document
TLc	Typed letter, carbon
TLp	Typed letter, letterpress copy
TLpS	Typed letter, letterpress copy, signed
TLpSr	Typed letter, letterpress copy, signature representation
TLS	Typed letter, signed
WHi	The State Historical Society of Wisconsin, Madison

SHORT TITLES

AFL, *Proceedings,* 1886

AFL, *Proceedings of the First Annual Convention of the American Federation of Labor* (1886?; reprint ed., Bloomington, Ill., 1905)

AFL, *Proceedings,* 1887

AFL, *Official Report of Proceedings of the Second Annual Convention of the American Federation of Labor, Held at Concordia Hall, Baltimore, Maryland, December 13, 14, 15, 16, 17, 1887* (1887?; reprint ed., Bloomington, Ill., 1905)

AFL, *Proceedings,* 1888

AFL, *Report of Proceedings of the Third Annual Convention of the American Federation of Labor, Held at St. Louis, Missouri, December 11, 12, 13, 14, 15, 1888* (1888?; reprint ed., Bloomington, Ill., 1905)

AFL, *Proceedings,* 1889

AFL, *Report of Proceedings of the Ninth Annual Convention of the American Federation of Labor, Held at Boston, Mass., December 10, 11, 12, 13, 14, 1889* (1889?; reprint ed., Bloomington, Ill., 1905)

AFL Records

Peter J. Albert and Harold L. Miller, eds., *American Federation of Labor Records: The Samuel Gompers Era,* microfilm (Sanford, N.C., 1979)

The Making of a Union Leader

Stuart B. Kaufman et al., eds., *The Samuel Gompers Papers,* vol. 1, *The Making of a Union Leader, 1850-86* (Urbana, Ill., 1986)

SG Letterbooks

The Letterbooks of the Presidents of the American Federation of Labor, 1883-1925, Library of Congress

CHRONOLOGY

1886	Jan.–1887 Jan.	SG serves as president of the New York State Workingmen's Assembly (NYSWA)
1886	Dec. 8-11	Founding convention of the AFL held in Columbus, Ohio, elects SG president
1887	Jan. 18-21	Twenty-first annual convention of the NYSWA meets in Albany
	June–Dec.	Publication of the AFL's monthly journal the *Union Advocate*, under the editorship of SG
	Aug.	United Labor party convention meets in Syracuse; excludes SLP delegates
	Nov. 11	Execution of Haymarket defendants George Engel, Adolph Fischer, Albert R. Parsons, and August Spies
	Dec. 13-17	Second annual convention of the AFL held in Baltimore
1887	Dec. 17–1888 ca. Mar. 10	SG's first major organizing trip for the AFL
1888	Dec. 11-15	Third annual convention of the AFL held in St. Louis, launches eight-hour campaign
1889	Feb. 14	Meeting between representatives of the AFL, the KOL, and the railroad brotherhoods at Bingham House, Philadelphia
	Aug. 29	Meeting between representatives of the AFL and the KOL in Philadelphia
	Oct. 14	Meeting between representatives of the AFL and the KOL at Girard House, Philadelphia
	Dec. 10-14	Fourth annual convention of the AFL held in Boston
1890	May 1	AFL's official target date for the eight-hour campaign on behalf of the United Brotherhood of Carpenters and Joiners of America
	Dec. 8-13	Fifth annual convention of the AFL held in Detroit rejects affiliation of New York City Central Labor Federation

Documents

An Address before the New York State Workingmen's Assembly[1]

[January 18, 1887]

THE PRESIDENT'S ADDRESS.

Delegates to the Twenty-first Annual Session[2] of the Workingmen's Assembly of the State of New York—
Co-workers:

In accordance with the laws and customs of our organization, it becomes the duty of its officers to render you an account of their stewardship. In my address I shall endeavor as succinctly as possible to report the laws enacted in the interests of labor, the progress of the labor movement and organization, and such other matters as may have occurred during the past year which are deemed of sufficient importance to call your attention to. I take pleasure at this time in welcoming you to the twenty-first annual session of this organization.

In presenting this address I shall mention the subjects in the order that I deem their importance merits, with such comments or recommendations upon them as in my judgment are both practical or necessary before entering upon another theme.

LABOR LEGISLATION.

I am gratified to be enabled to report to you that more laws of a beneficial character to labor were enacted at the last session of the Legislature than in any previous year. While this is a gratifying result, yet there are many matters of which we have to complain. It behooves us to so shape our legislation as to obtain the best possible results this year. We should formulate our wants in presentable shape and keep a close scrutiny of the conduct of our legislators upon our various measures, so that we may *remember* them when they appeal to us at election time upon their "labor record."

CHILD LABOR.

A law was passed by the last Legislature prohibiting children from being employed under the age of thirteen years.[3] I am of the opinion

3

that the law should be amended to fourteen years. Surely in our time, this age of steam and electricity, it is both unwise and unmerciful to permit children at such a tender age to work in our stores, factories, workshops, mills, etc., etc. There is no sentiment about this question; it is one of primary importance, and is probably the one in which is centered the greatest concern for the prevention of the deterioration of our species, the perpetuation of our manhood, the continuation and improvement of the institutions of our country and our civilization.

TWELVE-HOUR LAW FOR RAILROAD EMPLOYES.

The last Legislature enacted a law by which the railroads operating in and holding charters from the State were prohibited from exacting more than twelve hours' labor from their employes in any one day.[4] Soon after the passage of the law the corporations obtained a decision from the Railroad Commissioners,[5] which declared that while the law prohibited more than twelve hours' labor per day, yet the hours of labor need not be consecutive. In other words the law was so construed that the railroad corporations could alternate the hours of labor of the railroad employes, thus covering the entire twenty-four hours of the day.

How a Commission created at the instance of a popular demand could make so outrageous a decision in violation of the plain spirit of the law cannot be explained except upon the theory that a potent factor is at play in that august Commission of which the corporate interests as against those of the masses is no meagre part. I recommend that this Convention demand from the Legislature the passage of a law to not only make the hours of labor of railroad employes consecutive, but to reduce them to ten per day.

CONTRACT CONVICT LABOR.

The question of the method of employment for the convicts in our State prisons and reformatories is still unsettled. The people have decided at the polls that the contract system must go. Yet the Legislature has thus far failed to provide a permanent method by which the convicts might be employed. There seems to be an evident design to postpone the settlement of this subject until a period of less vigilance on the part of the labor organizations shall set in, and then re-establish the abominable contract system.

At the last session of the Legislature a commission was appointed to investigate and report upon, at this session of the Legislature, a system other than the contract system. Upon this subject your decision should go forth in no unmeaning tones. The Legislature should at this session decide upon a just and equitable system and abolish the commission. To continue it is but a subterfuge to postpone action upon the subject. There is as much information now at hand as could probably be obtained a year hence.[6]

ARBITRATION.

The principle of arbitration has been recognized by our State in the enactment of the law creating a State Board of Arbitration, by which matters in dispute between working people and their employers may be amicably settled.[7]

I am of the opinion that the law should be amended so that the Board may have *original* authority instead of as now being a mere appellate body (what good has been accomplished by the Board was done by the assumption of this function). The question whether arbitration in trade disputes can be practically applied by the State will then be better demonstrated. One thing must not be lost sight of, and that is that successful arbitration is only possible when the labor organizations are sufficiently strong so as to command the respect of the employers by being prepared at any time to defend themselves against unjust aggression.[8]

THE LABOR BUREAU.

The demand of our last convention to increase the powers of the Bureau of Statistics of Labor was acceded to by the Legislature,[9] and the results already obtained by the Bureau in having their blanks more generally filled out and returned, and their questions answered, prove the wisdom of the adoption of this measure. I am of the opinion that the Bureau should not be hampered by a niggardly policy of keeping the appropriation so low that its labors cannot be properly prosecuted.

MECHANICS' LIEN LAW.

I regret to be compelled to report that, notwithstanding the many years of effort to secure the wages of workingmen from unscrupulous employers and contractors, that result is almost as distant as the day the first "Mechanics' Lien Law" was adopted.[10] The law should be amended to not only make it general, but clear and comprehensive, and the blood money drawn from workingmen by robbing them of their meagre wages earned can and should be stopped.[11]

Labor Day.

A bill passed the Legislature declaring the first Monday in September of each year a legal holiday to be known as "Labor Day." Through the careless manner in which the bill was drawn the Governor[12] felt constrained to withhold his signature. I recommend that the measure may be again introduced and become a law at this session.[13]

Constitutional Convention.

The people of this State have ordered a convention to revise or amend the present Constitution.[14] The workingmen certainly contributed largely to the success of the proposition, and since it has been admitted that all interests should be represented at that convention it behooves this Assembly to voice its desires upon this matter, and to take such action to secure a fair representation of labor's interests in that body of delegates from our ranks.

Boycotting and Conspiracy.

This year has witnessed judges on the bench so construing the conspiracy law as to send men to our State prisons (as common felons) and jails for no other reason than that they refused to patronize and induced their fellow-workmen to withhold their patronage from avowed enemies to organized labor — employers who refused to even give the slightest consideration to the almost picayune request that their workmen be not compelled to work more than twelve hours a day.

Such trials, convictions and construction of the laws only tend to bring them into discredit and contempt. It had been supposed that long ago the laws of conspiracy were in no way applicable to men in labor organizations having for their object the matter of regulating wages and hours of labor. If, as has now been decided, that the law of conspiracy still obtains in this question, the sooner it is repealed the better. Surely if monarchial England can afford to expunge obnoxious laws from her statutes, the Empire State of the Union can.

Trades-Union Incorporation.

I regret to say that much to our discredit a law for the incorporation of trades-unions as such is not yet upon our statute books.[15]

Tenement Houses.

In our large cities we find dwellings of the workingmen, women and children, rearing their chimneys skyward to such a height as to almost daze a contemplative observer. Devoid of the commonest sanitary conditions, and built of the flimsiest material, filth being the prevalent surroundings, hundreds of thousands of our fellow human beings are eking out a miserable existence and brought to an untimely and premature death in them. That vice and crime take possession of a large number is not to be wondered at, rather is it that any escape from its baneful influences. Add to this the fact that thousands of men, women and children eat, drink, sleep and work in these modern Lazar houses, making cigars and clothing, and there can scarcely be formed a fair conception of the true conditions. Surely, the commonest instincts of humanity should prompt our law makers to do something to remedy this monstrous wrong. For a proper description of the condition of these pest-holes, commonly known as tenement houses, I refer you to the report of the Commissioner of the Bureau of Labor Statistics for the year 1885.[16]

STATE PRINTING.

There can be no question that it is a blot on the fair name of our State that its printing is done in an office, the proprietors of which notoriously discriminate against members of the typographical union, for no other reason than that they dare be union men.[17] It is time that this state of affairs should cease, and we should reaffirm our resolution calling upon our legislators to create a State printing office, where the work can be done more efficiently and economically.[18]

FACTORY INSPECTORS.

This Convention should insist upon the Legislature increasing the number of factory inspectors to five at least. One thing is certainly obvious to any one, and that is, that two inspectors is an insufficient number in this great State.[19]

APPOINTMENTS.

Immediately after the passage of the three bills requiring labor representation, the Governor requested me to call upon him and offered to appoint me as the labor member upon the State Board of Arbitration. I declined the offer (for reasons which I shall speak of in another way) and suggested the name of the present member of the Board, Mr. F. F. Donovan.[20] When I came to Albany at that time I found a number of men who were here for some time in anticipation of the passage of these bills and already applicants for the offices. To say the least, such actions are not calculated to throw much credit upon our organization, and have a tendency to prevent the passage of laws in the interest of our fellow-workers. I recommend that an amendment to our constitution may be adopted at this session prohibiting any officer of the State Workingmen's Assembly from accepting a public office from the State. In his address to the Convention last year, President Walter N. Thayer[21] said: "Let not personal ambition or jealousies enter into your work and your organization will gather strength each day. Avoid seeking office in connection with labor measures and you will have the respect of all fair-minded men." I am in entire accord with that advice, hence make the above recommendation.

JURY DUTY.

Under this caption I desire to call to your attention that in parts of this State (I am not aware that it is general) a workingman is never placed on a jury. I hold that the genius of the institutions of our country and State is against such a practice. There should be no duties without rights; no rights without duties. Let the workingmen once learn that they are a "class" discriminated against, and they will lose all respect for the law that is administered by a "class" that discriminates against them. The only qualifications for a juror should be that he is honest, intelligent and unbiased, as against the one of "How much is he worth?"

SECRETARY'S RESIGNATION.

In the early part of the year the Secretary, Mr. George A. Perry,[22] tendered his resignation in consequence of his business requiring his removal from the State. Upon examination of the constitution I found no provision for filling vacancies. I assumed the authority, and appointed Mr. James Malley.[23] I recommend that a provision be made in the constitution to fill vacancies. In this instance it was trivial; at some future time it may be important.

FULLER & WARREN BOYCOTT.

In accordance with instructions from the last convention, the firm of Fuller, Warren & Co., not having come to a satisfactory settlement with their employes, I issued a circular to all labor organizations asking them to withhold their patronage from said firm. I am pleased to report that the boycott was entirely successful.

THE POLITICAL BRANCH.

The question of the political branch of this organization seems to me to be still unsettled. At its last session (which I attended), at

Syracuse,[24] it assumed equal functions with this, the parent organization, in *initiating* legislation. The resolutions passed at the last session of this body are entirely unsatisfactory in their workings, especially the last.[25] If it is not the duty of the officers of the political branch to *acquaint themselves* with the measures passed by this body, then there is no necessity for its existence. I shall make no recommendations upon this subject, remembering the manner [in which] those of my predecessor were defeated, but simply state the facts as I find them, leaving you to find the remedy to bring back the political branch as subordinate to, and not the equal and independent of, this State Workingmen's Assembly.

LABOR'S FRIENDS.

It becomes my duty to refer to a man in public office who has been so pronounced in the measures in which we feel so deep an interest as to merit special mention in this address. Governor Hill has in every way suggested and aided in the passage of laws in the interest of labor, signed and executed them in their spirit as well as their letter, and did all that a man in his position could do to advance the interests of the workingmen and women of this State. We are also indebted to several members of the last Legislature, both Republican and Democratic, for their interest manifested in our measures. The Legislative Committee will undoubtedly refer to this subject more in detail, to which I invite your attention.

POLITICAL ACTION.

We have witnessed in the recent elections quite a political upheaval among the workingmen and those who sympathize with labor to take independent political action. Whether this has resulted from a deep settled conviction of the workingmen to sever their connection with the two dominant parties or a demonstration of disgust at and a protest against the corruption prevalent among so many of our public officers, the future must determine. The policy of the Workingmen's Assembly has been briefly this: To elect labor men to offices wherever and whenever an opportunity presented itself. Where it did not, then to stand by the men who stood by our measures and defeat those who opposed them. It would have been a neglect of duty not to mention the above facts in view of recent events.

GROWTH OF THE ORGANIZATION.

It is with evident pleasure that I am enabled to report, and as you can readily see, that the growth of our organization has been very large within the past year. The representation at this Convention is larger than at any previous session in the history of the Assembly, and in

CONCLUSION

I desire to say that much of the influence and prestige this organization can exert and attain will be largely due to the manner in which we deport ourselves. Let us so devote ourselves to the business before us as to deserve the confidence of our constituents and friends, and the respect of our opponents. I trust that our deliberations may be harmonious, speedily performed, and that the result of our labors may redound to the best interests of our fellow-workers.

New York State Workingmen's Assembly, *Report of the Proceedings of the Twenty-first Annual Convention of the State Workingmen's Assembly* (New York, 1887), pp. 4-8.

1. SG was elected for a one-year term as president of the New York State Workingmen's Assembly (NYSWA) in January 1886. He had served as first vice-president during the previous year.

2. The twenty-first annual convention of the NYSWA was held in Albany, Jan. 18-21, 1887.

3. Chapter 409, Laws of 1886, also prohibited minors under eighteen years of age or women between eighteen and twenty-one from working more than sixty hours a week.

4. Chapter 151, Laws of 1886, applied to street surface and elevated railroads in cities with over half a million inhabitants.

5. The New York Railroad Commission (1882-1907) consisted of three commissioners appointed by the governor to monitor railroads and make recommendations regarding their regulation. It lacked enforcement powers.

6. In 1884 the New York legislature abolished convict contract labor. In the summer of 1888 the legislature passed a bill that prohibited the use of machinery for the employment of prisoners and provided that convicts could only be employed making items for use in prisons and other state-run institutions. The question of how to effectively employ prisoners, however, remained the subject of a continuing debate.

7. Chapter 410, Laws of 1886, provided for the voluntary submission of labor disputes to local arbitration boards composed of five arbitrators, two each selected by the employees and employer, and the fifth by the other four. It empowered the governor to appoint a state Board of Arbitration to serve as an appeals body, consisting of one arbitrator from each of the two major political parties and a third representing the labor organizations of the state.

8. The legislature amended the act creating the Board of Arbitration, changing its name to the Board of Mediation and Arbitration (Laws of 1887, chap. 63, 65) and giving it original jurisdiction to mediate in cases of strikes and lockouts.

9. Chapter 205, Laws of 1886, amended chapter 356, Laws of 1883, which established the Bureau of Statistics of Labor. The amendments required firms to grant the commissioner of the bureau access to their premises for inspections and to furnish statistical and other information, and provided penalties for noncompliance.

10. Chapter 342, Laws of 1885, allowed persons who supplied materials or labor

for construction projects to secure payment by placing liens upon the premises of such projects.

11. In 1887 the legislature amended the mechanics' lien law, giving the liens of workers priority over those of subcontractors (Laws of 1887, chap. 420).

12. David Bennett HILL was Democratic governor of New York from 1885 to 1892.

13. Chapter 289, Laws of 1887, designated the first Monday in September as the Labor Day holiday.

14. In May Governor Hill vetoed the bill authorizing a constitutional convention for 1887. The state did not hold such a convention until 1894.

15. In 1871 the legislature provided for the incorporation of trade unions only as benevolent organizations (Laws of 1871, chap. 875). The 1895 membership corporation law (Laws of 1895, chap. 559) allowed trade unions to incorporate without this restriction.

16. New York Bureau of Statistics of Labor, *Third Annual Report* (Albany, 1886).

17. Weed, Parsons and Co., a firm that did not employ union printers, had held the state printing contract from 1866. In June 1887 state officials awarded the printing contract to the Troy *Press* Co., a union shop.

18. A bill to establish a state printing office failed passage during the summer of 1887.

19. In 1887 the legislature amended the factory act, which had provided for an inspector and an assistant inspector, to authorize the factory inspector to appoint eight deputy inspectors (Laws of 1887, chap. 462).

20. Florence F. Donovan.

21. Walter Nelson THAYER, a leader of International Typographical Union (ITU) 52 of Troy, N.Y., was president of the NYSWA in 1884-86.

22. George A. P. Perry, a compositor and in the early 1880s a member and officer of ITU 15 of Rochester, N.Y., was elected secretary of the NYSWA in 1886.

23. James Malley, a Rochester, N.Y., shoemaker, represented KOL District Assembly 63 at the 1886 session of the NYSWA.

24. The fifth annual session of the Political Branch of the NYSWA met in Syracuse, N.Y., Sept. 14-15, 1886.

25. SG is probably referring to the resolution of the 1886 NYSWA providing that the executive officers of the assembly and its political branch cooperate in formulating and lobbying for legislation. These activities were to be subject to the approval of both bodies.

A Translation of a News Account of the 1887 Convention of the New York State Workingmen's Assembly

Albany, 19. Jan. [1887]

THE SESSION OF THE WORKINGMEN'S ASSEMBLY.

When the session of the State Workingmen's Assembly opened this morning, all delegates were present, including the nine women delegates who are here as representatives of the Order of the Knights of Labor. As had been reported on the wires yesterday, a "lively" session was expected, and it was evident that this expectation was not without foundation when the secretary[1] read the minutes of yesterday's proceedings and objections were raised from several quarters. After lengthy debate, the minutes were adopted but not without the intentional omission of some important points and false information concerning passage or rejection of certain resolutions. When this was finished, a delegate who had just stepped into the hall announced that he and other delegates coming from the meeting of the credentials committee at the mayor's office had been attacked by several hoodlums in the waiting room; he said an elderly man had been badly beaten. The latter then stood and said it was a disgrace that a man of his age should be subjected to such treatment. This caused great excitement and President Gompers said: "This is not the first such act of intimidation. I have heard from other members of the convention that they have been attacked or threatened. There are a number of men, or, better, people who would like to be men, participating in this convention who are prepared to go as far as fistfighting in order to get their way. People have not only threatened to abuse me physically but to shoot me. (Several delegates laughed out loud here.) This laughter is worthy of people who utter such threats and carry out such attacks. Let me say one thing, gentlemen: I have no fear. I know my duty and I will not be deterred from carrying it out by threats and attacks from those who have come to divide this convention. I will defy the most brutal attack of the most vicious human being in the state."

The convention then adjourned until the afternoon, and when the meeting was opened again the committee on credentials handed in a majority and a minority report on the undecided credentials. The majority report recommended excluding all delegates not yet admitted, approximately 30 in number, who came from the vicinity of Cohoes, West Troy, and Amsterdam. Some of these towns, which have less than 10,000 inhabitants, sent 30 delegates. There are many women among them who had no credentials yesterday but were furnished with them today. At first the majority report was accepted, but then a terrible uproar began. The opponents threatened the delegates who had voted for it with all sorts of horrible things and succeeded in having the vote reconsidered and, finally, in admitting all delegates, even the infamous Syracuse scab, John J. Junio,[2] who came to the convention with his boss, a scab for Barton.[3] During the afternoon, one delegate stated that a certain delegate[4] from Troy was a scab; the latter pulled out a revolver and was about to shoot the man who had made the accusation when the entire assembly rose to its feet; at this point more weapons appeared. Gompers rushed between the two men and took the revolver away. After the excitement had died down somewhat, the session was adjourned until tomorrow morning.[5]

The convention has been in session for two days now, and still has not even been fully organized.

New Yorker Volkszeitung, Jan. 20, 1887. Translated from the German by Patrick McGrath.

1. Joseph R. Mansion was a stovemounter from West Troy, N.Y.
2. John J. JUNIO, a Syracuse, N.Y., cigarmaker active in KOL District Assembly 152, apparently helped to organize workers at William E. Barton's shop into KOL Local Assembly (LA) 6085 during a CMIU strike.
3. CMIU 6 of Syracuse, N.Y., supported by KOL LA 1809, struck manufacturer William E. Barton in December 1885 after he rejected the union's new price list. Barton continued to operate with workers organized in KOL Florence Assembly 6085.
4. John Brophy was a stovemounter from Troy, N.Y., and secretary of KOL LA 3275.
5. SG appointed an equal number of KOL and trade union delegates to the credentials committee, choosing George W. Perkins to act as its chairman. It became deadlocked over trade unionist challenges that some credentials carried assumed names or were from defunct KOL assemblies. The dispute was not resolved until the convention's last day, when KOL and trade union representatives agreed to refer the unresolved business of the convention to a new executive board with balanced trade unionist and KOL representation.

A News Account of the 1887 Convention of the New York State Workingmen's Assembly

Albany, N.Y., Jan. 20. [1887]

STATE WORKINGMEN'S ASSEMBLY.

The State Workingmen's Assembly convened on Tuesday, in the City Hall, with President Gompers in the chair. Representatives of all the large trades from all parts of the State, 200 in number, were present. In the morning session there was a struggle between the trade unionists and an organized opposition to the Cigarmakers' International Union.[1] The same scenes ensued which have been so often enacted in the New York Central Labor Union when the same elements came in contact. First came a wrangle as to whether the Committee on Credentials should be appointed by the President, as the custom has been, or elected by the convention, and it ended, amid turmoil, in the appointment being made by President Gompers, who delivered his annual address to the convention when the committee was out. But the wrangling referred to was as a storm in a teapot compared with that which ensued when the credential committee reported in the afternoon and held the credentials of about 25 or 30 delegates, because of protests.

The second day's proceedings of the convention (Wednesday) were very much like those of the first. There was nothing done, but wrangle constantly over the reception or rejection of credentials. The scenes in both open and executive session were such as to make the cooler heads ashamed of the proceedings. There were threats of violence, and one delegate to whom objection was made rushed to the platform and drew a pistol, which, however, was taken from him.

There is a long list of resolutions and bills, upon as many subjects connected with the Labor movement, for presentation, which are being held back till the questions of credentials are settled. It has usually taken three days, in the most peaceable times, to finish business before the Assembly. Two days are already spent in organizing.

In the evening of Wednesday the K. of L. delegates representing the opposition to President Gompers, who represents the trades union element, held a caucus, and laid their plans for the morrow. The former resolved to strive to throw out a lot of the delegates who are objectionable to them, and, at the session which is about to open for to-day, the Knights of Labor, who are acting under direction of the "Home Club,"[2] expect to secure full control of the State Trades Assembly.

Whatever be the result, the body must get to business to-day, or else the whole of its proper business will be left topsy-turvy.

After much wrangling about the credentials of delegates, in which the Knights and Trades Unionists took opposite sides, with the former in the majority, a resolution to appoint a harmonizing committee of ten (five from each side) was offered by Delegate McKenna,[3] K. of L., and carried, after which the body adjourned till 2 in the afternoon. There is now good assurance that the proceedings will move along in an orderly way, till the close.

The Albany politicians are watching the convention as closely as they are the caucuses of the Republicans on the Senatorial fight, and the outcome of the session will affect even the small crumbs of legislation that may fall from the politicians' table.

John Swinton's Paper, Jan. 23, 1887.

1. The CIGAR Makers' International Union of America.

2. The Home Club emerged in the early 1880s among socialist elements of KOL District Assembly (DA) 49. Its inner circle consisted of nine men, including the leaders

of the district assembly. DA 49 and the Home Club played an important role in the KOL General Assembly and actively pursued a policy of opposing autonomous trade unions in New York City in the name of organizing all workers under its leadership.

3. Michael F. McKiernan, a Troy, N.Y., bookkeeper, represented KOL Local Assembly 3275.

To Frank Roney[1]

New York. Feb 14th 1887

Frank Roney Esq
V.P. I.M.U of N.A.[2]
Dear Sir

Your interesting and welcome letter came duly to hand and am pleased to have you believe that there was no neglect in my silence upon your previous letter. My time is entirely taken up with the official position in the Federation. You are right in your surmise of the end of that little paper.[3] It enjoys the "Rest of the just" and as you say from "The customary causes."

I very much regret and did so at the time, that you were unable to attend the Columbus convention. It certainly would have aided the men there assembled to have a man of your advanced views[4] present.

While agreeing with you in many, in fact most all things you write about yet I differ with you in taking so gloomy a view of the entire outcome of the convention. It is true probably that more would be desirable but we must look at things as they really are and not as we would have them or wish them to be. There is unquestionably a better feeling and comprehension of the identity of the interests of all trades among the Unionists of the country and that it will be necessary for all to work more earnestly and zealously to advance the interests of any one trade when affe[c]ted by trade trouble. The Federation which is now but in its infancy will, in my opinion, be thorough and permanent and in time based exactly upon your views, but because it has not yet attained that degree of perfection we desire, is no reason to describe it as "Impotent." I am convinced that after you have had an opportunity to look at the proceedings beneath the surface, you will agree that the foundation for a great movement has been laid by the Federation. Of the matters of legislation demanded you will be able to judge better from a perusal of the proceedings which I shall mail you in a few days. Hoping to hear from you often. I am

Yours Fraty   Samuel Gompers.

ALpS, reel 1, vol. 1, pp. 77-78, SG Letterbooks, DLC.

1. Frank RONEY was vice-president of the Iron Molders' Union of North America (1886-88) and a founder and president of the Representative Council of the Federated Trades and Labor Organizations of the Pacific Coast (1885-87).

2. The IRON MOLDERS' Union of North America.

3. Probably the *Picket*.

4. Roney believed that the trade union movement should be governed by a single set of laws that would make it mandatory for all local unions to form trade assemblies or central labor unions. He also believed that any federation of trade unions should be led by a powerful executive officer.

The AFL and the KOL, 1887-90

"There is no conflict necessary between the trades unions and the Knights of Labor," Samuel Gompers told delegates to the 1887 AFL convention. That same year Terence Powderly claimed that he had been "wilfully misrepresented as a bitter opponent of trades unions" and assured textile union leader Robert Howard that he intended "to have every thing that man can do done to heal up the breach between the trade organizations and the K. of L."[1] Gompers and Powderly both maintained that as long as the Federation and the Order confined themselves to their own distinct areas of endeavor, the labor movement could be well served by the two organizations operating simultaneously.[2]

Such expressions of harmony, and the fact that in some communities Knights and trade unionists cooperated in local political campaigns and in efforts to build state and local labor organizations, masked the deep-rooted tensions that separated the AFL and the KOL. Not only did the Federation differ significantly from the Order in objectives and strategy, but a bitter personal antagonism marked relations between Gompers and Powderly. The conflict between the two organizations—a conflict that grew out of the trade unionist–KOL struggle that had been a factor in the founding of the AFL in 1886—was exacerbated further by the steady growth of the AFL, the organization of national trade unions, and the ensuing competition between these unions and newly organized KOL trade assemblies for affiliates.

The Order itself was deeply divided on the issue of trade unions. Some Knights urged the formation of national trade assemblies within the KOL, and cigarmakers, shoemakers, miners, and glass blowers, among others, established such organizations and contested for jurisdiction with national trade unions. The Order's national leaders, on the other hand, opposed anything that smacked of trade unionism, a sentiment often echoed at the district level. They envisioned the future of the KOL in terms of mixed assemblies, asserting that the exclusiveness and narrowness of trade divisions fragmented and weakened the labor movement. Between these two positions stood Knights who advocated a peaceful coexistence between the KOL and trade unions. Many workers continued to retain membership in both the

17

union of their trade and the Order, and this dual membership led to repeated local clashes such as those involving steelworkers at Mingo Junction, Ohio, boot and shoe workers in Worcester, Massachusetts, and beer brewers in Philadelphia.

While Powderly agreed with such KOL leaders as T. B. McGuire, William Bailey, Thomas Barry, and Frederick Turner that trade unions were retrogressive, he initially sought to mute anti–trade union sentiment and to overcome resistance to the formation of national trade assemblies. Nevertheless, the ambivalence, if not outright hostility, of KOL leaders toward trade assemblies within the Order forced many Knights to conclude that their position in the KOL was untenable. In 1888, for example, Henry Skeffington, master workman of shoemakers' National Trade Assembly (NTA) 216, was outraged when the KOL General Executive Board refused to allow local assemblies of shoemakers to leave a mixed district assembly and join his organization. Going before the Board where he "delivered his remarks in a loud tone of voice & accompanied them with violent gestures such as throwing down chairs etc," he warned the leaders of the Order, "You have driven more men into Trades Unions by these acts than by anything else, more than anything that has ever taken place in my trade. . . . I never was a Trades Unionist I am not a Trades Unionist and I don't propose to join Trades Unions if I can stay in the K. of L." The following year, however, he led the shoemakers out of NTA 216 and into affiliation with the AFL as the Boot and Shoe Workers' International Union.[3]

From Gompers' point of view, however, the Order was a key impediment to the AFL's growth. He believed that the trade union was the natural organization of wage workers and that the KOL was an aberration that admitted employers, failed to support strikes and wage demands, refused to recognize trade autonomy, and organized dual unions. He accused the Knights of fighting trade unions "with much more vigor and bitterness than they do unscrupulous employers." His hostility toward the Order was supported by the 1887 AFL convention, which amended the Federation's constitution to allow bodies leaving the KOL en masse to join AFL unions more easily and which refused to seat representatives from the Washington, D.C., Federation of Labor because they represented an organization that "was not fully in sympathy with the trades-union movement, as it was overwhelmingly composed of Knights of Labor Assemblies."[4]

By mid-1888 Gompers was able to report with satisfaction to Auguste Keufer that "the American Federation is growing stronger and the Knights of Labor are growing weaker every day."[5] Many factors played a role in the decline of the KOL. In addition to internal conflicts with trade unionists, the Order was torn by factionalism within its national leadership. In 1888, for example, the General Assembly expelled General Executive Board members Thomas Barry and Albert Carlton and such other prominent Knights as Joseph Buchanan. Splinter groups including the Improved Order and, in 1889, the Founders movement drew additional members away from the KOL. Other Knights became disgusted with the strife and intrigue among their officers, especially as they faced bitter opposition from employers and competition from trade unions. As a consequence, Knights left the Order by the thousands. Membership declined precipitously from a high of 700,000 in 1886 to stabilize well below 200,000 in 1890.

In the face of the growing friction between the KOL and the AFL, leaders of the two organizations conducted a series of negotiations during 1889 concerning the creation of a more unified labor movement and the promotion of the AFL's 1890 eight-hour drive.[6] The meetings were inconclusive, and 1890 was punctuated by the continuing conflict between the trades unionists and the Knights, and between Gompers and Powderly. The rivalry between the Federation and the Order diminished in importance, however, with the decline of the KOL and with Powderly's growing emphasis on an alliance with the Populists.

Notes

1. AFL, *Proceedings*, 1887, p. 10; Terence Powderly to Robert Howard, Sept. 3, 1887, Terence Vincent Powderly Papers, DCU.

2. See, for example, Powderly to P. J. McGuire, Mar. 22, 1889, below; SG to Henry Skeffington, May 24, 1889, below.

3. Minutes of the KOL General Executive Board, Feb. 9, 1888, Powderly Papers.

4. SG to McGuire, Feb. 26, 1887, below; AFL, *Proceedings*, 1887, p. 8.

5. SG to Auguste Keufer, July 18, 1888, below.

6. "A News Account of a Meeting between Representatives of the AFL, the KOL, and the Railroad Brotherhoods at Bingham House, Philadelphia," Feb. 15, 1889, "A Report of a Circular Issued by the Unity Conference Held at Bingham House, Philadelphia," July 11, 1889, "A News Account of a Conference between Representatives of the AFL and the KOL at the KOL Office, Philadelphia," Aug. 31, 1889, and "A News Account of a Conference between Representatives of the AFL and the KOL at Girard House, Philadelphia," Oct. 15, 1889, below.

Charles Merritt[1] to Terence Powderly[2]

Denver, Feb. 15. 1887.

T. V. Powderly, G.M.W.:
Dr. Sir & Bro.

Your esteemed favor of January 27.[3] in answer to the resolutions[4] passed by L.A. 2327. was duly received and submitted to the Local. In reply thereto we most respectfully submit the following:

The resolutions to which you refer were passed by this Local on account of the fact that the order in this section has been greatly injured by the fight made by the General Assembly and the General Executive Board on the Cigarmakers International Union. Many of our best, strongest and ablest men in this section are trades unionists and are bitterly opposed to any war between legitimate labor organizations, and it became necessary to publicly announce that the order was not and is not in sympathy with any such fight. If the fight in New York between D.A. No. 49 and the Cigarmakers Union was brought on entirely by the cigarmakers, it was in our judgment no cause for the action of the General Assembly,[5] advocating as our order does unity of action between all branches of honorable toil.

The unwise or even the dishonorable action of the general officers of the Cigarmakers union was not any just cause for our order to make an attempt to break up their union, which has done much valuable service in forwarding the cause of all people who earn their living by honorable toil, and of yourself this Assembly expected much to promote the cause of harmony between the various organizations of the land, as we have always looked upon you as at least one of the most wise and honorably conservative men that the labor movement in America had developed. We were, therefore greatly disappointed to find that under any circumstances, no matter how much to blame the cigarmakers were that you would lend your influence and aid to further any scheme that would disrupt and retard the work of any organization of working people. Eighteen months ago the time seemed near at hand when all the organized labor of the country would be enrolled under the banner of our noble order. Now a feeling of hostility is manifest which threatens destruction to one or perhaps both, and this Assembly feels confident that the influence of the members of our General Executive Board, if used in the interest of harmony and unity between our order and other labor organizations, could have averted at Richmond and since the unfortunate state of affairs that now exists. The above were and are our reasons for censuring the members, of our General Executive Board and for calling upon them to immediately take some action to undo the great wrong and blunder that has been made in this matter.

You desire proofs of your "belligerent attitude towards trades unions" and of your showing "antagonisms toward trades unions." When things are so much matters of general notoriety as are these, "proofs" so-called are superfluous. Yet we respectfully refer you to the following points:

First—The circular issued by the Executive Board regarding the cigarmakers.[6]

Second.—The new proposed proposition blanks, in which you inferentially, in large type, insist upon persons who join the Knights of Labor yielding any other obligation they may have taken to other *labor* organizations to this order.

Third—The printed report of the conference between the Knights of Labor and the trades unions, to be found in the "Carpenter" for January, 1887. which certainly shows not only antagonism, on the part of the Knights of Labor committee, but antagonism that verges upon excessive rudeness.[7]

Permit us to differ with you in the apparent bileif that you have "built up the trades unions." and that "no sooner were they on their feet through the efforts of men like myself [yourself][8] than they began to try and tear down," etc. Trades unions are a logical and natural development. Neither you nor any other man built them up nor can tear them down. They preceded the Knights of Labor and even yet form its least class of membership. They built up the Knights of Labor, meaning that it should be the educational branch of the labor movement. By unwise leadership, by unnecessary interference, by the admission of "scab" unionists as members (*vide* report of Columbus committee.[9] Mr. Fitzpatrick's[10] testimony), by a want of knowledge and experience in strikes and boycotts, by a yielding to outside clamor and influence the management of the Knights of Labor has undoubtedly fostered the antagonism spoken of and done much to damage the cause of labor.

As for your being "foully belied and villified" by the report made to D.A. 89, of the proceedings of the Richmond Assembly,[11] we beg leave to call your attention to the fact that an explanation and refutation was demanded officially by a local attached to D.A. 89 of you regarding such proceedings and an opportunity given you to explain yourself. The only answer received and months have elapsed, is silence.

It is not the wish of our Assembly to "have the order made a catspaw by other organizations." For this reason we desire the Home Club investigated and the facts of the case reported in full to every member of the order.[12] It is not our wish "that it should be "prostituted to base uses by other organizations" or men. We therefore desire an official statement made of the reasons that, it is openly alleged, induced you to give more weight to the dicta of Father Flannigan than to the entreaties of the 25,000 men then on strike at Chicago.[13] We have heard no explanation of this matter and months have passed. We do not desire to "have the order made an open field for the dissemination of every doctrine but the *real* doctrines of the Knights of Labor," and therefore we strenuously object to it being used by the General officers or any body else as the capitalistic press is used, to denounce radical labor ideas. Radicalism meaning truth is the real doctrine of the Knights of Labor and vague denunciations of it come with but poor grace from men who pretend to be intelliget and honest.

But above everything else we object to your present course — on the cigarmakers question, for instance — because it has an imperialistic tendency. You occupy your place as our servant and not our master. We pay you thirteen dollars a day to execute our will, and not the will of any body else. Your law is and should be the strict letter of our constitution. You of all men ought not to overstep it an inch. If we want the policy or statutes of our order changed we are the ones to change it, not you. If you do not want office as our servant you are not bound to remain in your place. But if you believe that any large proportion of those people who have joined the Knights of Labor to work out from the slavery of a class, will gladly now embrace the slavery imposed by any clique or caucus, then, in our opinion, you will find yourself mistaken. You ask us for full information. If this letter is not full enough we feel amply competent to add to it on many other points.

We are in the full belief that we have herein stated the honest convictions of nine-tenths of the order.

Fraternally Yours.   L.A. 2327.

Chas L Merritt.

R.S.

ALS, Terence Vincent Powderly Papers, DCU.

1. Charles L. Merritt, a Denver printer, was recording secretary of KOL Local Assembly (LA) 2327.

2. Terence Vincent POWDERLY, a machinist, was grand master workman (1879-83) and general master workman (1883-93) of the KOL.

3. Reel 21, Terence Vincent Powderly Papers, DCU.

4. On Dec. 27, 1886, LA 2327 of Denver—a printers' assembly—adopted resolutions condemning the officers of the KOL and of various national trade unions for fomenting the antagonism between them, denying that the Order's rank and file was hostile to trade unions, and urging the KOL General Executive Board to heal the breach. It called on other KOL assemblies to pass similar resolutions.

5. The KOL General Assembly that met at Richmond, Va., Oct. 4-20, 1886, passed a resolution introduced by District Assembly (DA) 49 of New York City requiring cigarmakers and packers who were members of the CMIU either to withdraw from the union or to leave the Order.

6. *The Order and the Cigar-Makers* (Philadelphia, 1886).

7. Under the title "Report of Committee of Conference with the Committee of the Knights of Labor" (January 1887), the *Carpenter* printed the report of the trade union committee of the 1886 AFL convention at Columbus, Ohio. The convention's official proceedings also printed the committee's report (AFL, *Proceedings,* 1886, pp. 17-18). It summarized the committee's meeting on December 10 with a delegation from the KOL.

8. These brackets are in the original.

9. The trades union committee of the AFL's 1886 convention at Columbus, Ohio, consisted of P. F. Fitzpatrick, chairman, Chris Evans, Edward Daley, P. J. McGuire, and Adolph Strasser.

10. Patrick Francis FITZPATRICK was president of the Iron Molders' Union of North America from 1879 to 1890.

11. Joseph R. Buchanan, district master workman of Denver's DA 89 (established in 1885) and a founding member of LA 2327, attended the October 1886 General Assembly in Richmond as a representative of DA 89. His report to the district on Nov. 28, 1886, gave particular attention to General Assembly decisions involving the inner circle or Home Club of New York's DA 49: the rejection of the credentials of Home Club critic John Morrison, the dropping of the investigation of the Home Club, and the approval of DA 49's resolution forcing cigarmakers in the Order to choose between membership in the CMIU or the KOL. Buchanan depicted Terence Powderly as taking a compliant role in these decisions.

12. The special session of the KOL General Assembly held in Cleveland May 25–June 3, 1886, appointed a committee to investigate charges and rumors that the Home Club was attempting to gain control of the KOL. Its hundred-page report to the Richmond General Assembly concluded that the Home Club's purposes were educational and beneficial and that it was innocent of all charges. Buchanan's report to DA 89 on the proceedings of the Richmond General Assembly, however, complained that the investigating committee was stacked in favor of the Home Club and that the Order's general officers had withheld the committee's report from the delegates.

13. Patrick M. Flannigan, pastor of St. Anne's Roman Catholic Church in Lake, Ill., wired Powderly from Chicago on Oct. 16, 1886, appealing to him to halt the Chicago packinghouse strike. Powderly denied that Flannigan influenced him, claiming not to have read the telegram until Nov. 25, fifteen days after he ordered an end to the strike.

To P. J. McGuire[1]

Feb 26th [188]7

P J McGuire Esq
Sec'y &c
Dear Sir

Enclosed please find letter of Mr. Marden[2] to which I have written a pretty strong one, not in response but stating from reports contained in the public press. They (the Lasters Protective Union)[3] really posess fine fighting qualities and certainly understand when they are antagonized either by the manufacturers or false friends.[4]

What do you think of the contests of the Amalgamated Asso of Iron & Steel Workers[5] and the K of L?.[6] Many of their members (the former) thought they were free and exempt from the attacks of the Knights and believed it was a "cigar makers fight" they now know the warfare of the Knights. They fight labor Unions with much more vigor and bitterness than they do unscrupulous employers. To the former they give no quarter if they can. In the latter their saying is "If you won't accept our terms, we will yours."

Fraty yours   Saml Gompers,
Pres.

ALpS, reel 1, vol. 1, p. 104, SG Letterbooks, DLC.

1. Peter James McGuire was secretary of the Brotherhood of Carpenters and Joiners of America (subsequently the United Brotherhood of Carpenters and Joiners of America) from 1881 to 1901. He served as secretary of the AFL from 1886 to 1889, second vice-president from 1889 to 1890, and first vice-president from 1890 to 1900.

2. William Henry Marden was treasurer of the New England Lasters' Protective Union.

3. The New England Lasters' Protective Union.

4. In January 1887 boot and shoe manufacturers in Worcester County, Mass., determined to deal with their employees only as individuals. On Jan. 26 District Assembly (DA) 30 of the KOL and the New England Lasters' Protective Union went out on strike. The strike continued until June when, after an unsuccessful appeal to the Massachusetts State Board of Arbitration, DA 30 announced that it was no longer able to provide financial assistance to the strikers. It ordered its members back to work on June 20, and the Lasters' Union followed one week later.

5. The National Amalgamated Association of Iron and Steel Workers.

6. The _New York Sun_ of Feb. 25, 1887, reported that KOL General Executive Board member William H. Bailey had called upon the Knights to take the place of members of the National Amalgamated Association of Iron and Steel Workers (NAAISW) who were on strike in a dispute over the breaking of mill rules at the Laughlin and Junction Steel Co. works at Mingo Junction, Ohio. From the point of view of KOL board member John Hayes, the NAAISW caused the trouble when it "organized one of their branches out of our Local and then ordered a Strike until their committee was recognized by the company" (Hayes to Terence Powderly, Feb. 19, 1887, Terence Vincent Powderly Papers, DCU). Bailey claimed that the KOL's agreement with the mills required the Knights to keep the works open, and "if we back down, that kills our order in all Iron Mills as it proves that we are unable to take care of their interests" (Bailey to Powderly, Feb. 20, 1887, ibid.). This was the latest in a series of struggles between the two labor organizations following the decision of the Amalgamated not to join the KOL at Powderly's invitation in 1886. The inability of the Knights to operate the Mingo Junction plant led the management to settle the strike with the Amalgamated after ten days. As a result of the conflict, the delegates to the 1887 NAAISW convention resolved that after Apr. 1, 1888, members of their union could not belong to the KOL.

To P. J. McGuire

March 3rd [188]7

P J McGuire Esq
Sec'y &c.
Dear Sir,

Your letters dated Feb 28th and March 1st reached me simultaneously to day.

I have written[1] to Mr Miller[2] in reference to the *Tagablatt* matter[3] and shall be on hand on time.

I do not wish in the remotest desire to question your vote upon the matter of the publication of our official organ on the 15th[4] but desire to say something about the reasons you assign.

To day I recieved a letter from Mr Strasser[5] in which he says that Mr Fitzgerald[6] of the Iron Moulders in a letter to him asks "What has become of the Federation?"

Shall we in view of this state of affairs to allow the whole movement to slumber? Must we not do something to keep alive the interest?. Is it not a fact that this can be best acco[m]plished through the issuance of our paper? I maintain that we should be up and doing, even by assuming a risk, which I am sure you place at too high a figuire. To day *official* notice reached me that the Cigar M.I.U. has endorsed the A.F.L. and I am sure that we will be successful if we have the courage to go on.

It is my intention to ask Unions which have no *Journal* of their own to use our columns and by that means make [it] not only interesting but pecuniarily successful.

The proceedings should be in the hands of the members. Keep pushing the binders for them.

We will be able to talk over matters in Phila on Monday more fully.

Yours Fraty   Saml Gompers
Pres.

N.B. I shall go to Hartford to attend that Trade Union Convention[7] if I have to pay for it out of my own pocket. This should not be neglected.

S. G

ALpS, reel 1, vol. 1, pp. 117-18, SG Letterbooks, DLC.

1. SG to Hugo Miller, Mar. 3, 1887, reel 1, vol. 1, p. 115, SG Letterbooks, DLC.
2. Hugo A. MILLER was secretary of the German-American Typographia from 1886 until 1894.
3. In early 1886 compositors on the *Philadelphia Tageblatt* refused to set type for an editorial attacking their union, German-American Typographia 1. When the *Tage-*

blatt replaced them with members of the Gutenberg Bund, the Typographia and the International Typographical Union instituted a boycott. In the Philadelphia Central Labor Union (CLU), German unions supported the Bund and prevented the CLU from condemning the *Tageblatt*. This triggered the withdrawal of a number of English-language unions, which founded the Philadelphia Building Trades Council. SG and McGuire arbitrated the dispute in March 1887, deciding that the compositors had no right to interfere with the freedom of expression of the *Tageblatt*, that the Typographia should admit the new compositors to membership, and that the unions should cease boycotting the paper (SG and McGuire to Whom It May Concern, Mar. 7, 1887, reel 1, vol. 1, pp. 130-31, SG Letterbooks, DLC). See "Minutes of a Meeting of Members of the Executive Council of the AFL," Apr. 10, 1887, below.

4. The constitution adopted by the AFL's founding convention in December 1886 authorized the president to publish a monthly journal. The Executive Council approved issuance of a journal by a vote of 4 to 1, with McGuire in the negative.

5. Adolph STRASSER was president of the CMIU from 1877 until 1891.

6. Patrick Francis Fitzpatrick.

7. On Mar. 9, 1887, a convention at Hartford, Conn., organized the Connecticut State Branch of the AFL.

To the Executive Council of the AFL

March 14th [188]7

To the Ex Council.

Fellow-Workmen.

I find that a large part of my [time] is taken up with running errands, which time could be put to much better advantage.

If I were authorized to hire a Boy to do this, he could also write the addresses on the wrappers for mailing our Journals, which would in itself be a great saving. The wages of the Boy would not exceed three and a half dollars per week and I believe would be a wise expenditure.

I therefore ask you to return your vote[1] to me upon the above proposition at your earliest convenience, as haste is necessary, and oblige.

Yours Fraty   Saml Gompers,
Pres.

ALpS, reel 1, vol. 1, p. 141, SG Letterbooks, DLC.

1. The Executive Council approved SG's request by a vote of 3 to 1, and SG hired his son Henry.

P. J. McGuire to Gabriel Edmonston[1]

Philadelphia, Pa. March 18/87

Friend Gabe: —

Thanks for receipt for $10.00. This A.M. at 8 o'clock, I was at Post Office and no check from Gompers for that printing That is no way to do business! That check should have been here on the 14th or 15th. The job was cheaply done under the understanding it was to be a cash job. Gompers signed the voucher for the money. I counter-signed it, and he had no business to ask you to send him the check, payable in his name. There is no rule to require it. It is sufficient for the Treasurer to pay all bills. Had the money come to me I would have paid the bill, and sent you a receipt for it, while Mr Gallagher's[2] bill I would have sent receipted to Mr Gompers.

When he was here March 7, he asked me if we could not "put off" Gallagher for a couple of months. I told him I would see about it, but that for the credit of the Federation I preferred to have cash payments. — If the check is not here tomorrow night I will advise you. — I am opposed to issuing the Federation journal until we see our way clear financially first, and we ought to have $400 on hand to start with. The expenses, salary journal postage, etc. will reach nearly $200.00 per month and require the regular monthly payment of tax from 40,000 men. First let us "catch our hare before we cook it" — Let us be sure of 50,000 to 55,000 men, for whom tax will be paid before we rush into expenses regardless of the "wherewith." I have written Gompers this again and again, but he is over sanguine or else lacks business tact. — Would it not be well for you to write to Smith[3] & Harris[4] about this and let the four nearest ones — members of the Ex Council — have a meeting soon in this city to arrange plans and instruct Gompers? — I have asked Gompers to issue the Consti-tution of the A.F.L. — 10,000 copies in English & German — in cheap leaflet form, also a printed circular address to all Trades Unions before issuing the paper. This request was made 2 months ago and repeated again and again but to no effect — What is being done I don't know. I cant see anything more than could be done a few hours each eve-ning — a few letters. This thing galls me, to think the Federation is not pushed. The finances we now have would easily cover cheap leaflets and if we are to get the various unions to join us, a favorable sentiment must be worked up by sending documents to the Local Unions. That is my idea, I may be wrong but I am earnest in this matter.

Enclosed is duplicate receipt as desired for charter fee. The original was made payable to Welsh, if you will remember, at and by your request.

Yours   P J McGuire

ALS, Papers of Gabriel Edmonston, reel 1, *AFL Records.*

1. Gabriel EDMONSTON was a founder and the first president of the Brotherhood of Carpenters and Joiners of America (1881-82) and from 1886 to 1888 served as treasurer of the AFL.
2. Daniel J. Gallagher was a Philadelphia printer.
3. James W. SMITH was second vice-president of the AFL from 1886 to 1887.
4. George HARRIS was first vice-president of the AFL from 1886 to 1887.

To J. P. McDonnell[1]

New York, March 21st 1887

J P McDonnell Esq
Dear Friend.

You will no doubt be surprised to recieve this note from one who to all appearances had not the "courtesy" to answer a very friendly letter. Let me plead (which I assure is a fact) that my official duties are taxing my entire time and energy. You may readily form an idea of the truth of this when I tell you that I have not had the pleasure of partaking of afternoon or evening meals (Sunday included) with my family for months and that although my aged parents live within a quarter of a mile from my "residence" I have been to their house but twice in six months and then only on a flying visit.

I can readily understand how galling it is to a sincere man who has been in the labor movement for years devoting his whole life with whatever little pleasure one can draw from life, to the cause of the emancipation of his fellow-man, to see fellows who were never seen when they were necessary or when danger was at hand, now attempting to dictate to the bone fide labor organizations how they shall conduct themselves. Yes more than that, dispute their very right of existence. These things may last for a time, false issues and sophistry have in times gone by held a brief sway but *truth* has always conquered in the end and so will it be with the Trades Unions, they may may be opposed by the capitalistic class or pseudo friends in the labor movement, but they will continue to grow stronger and mightier — perhaps by reason of this very opposition — because they are the natural organization of the toiling masses brought into life by conditions of our present system of society.

A few days ago I sent you a report of the proceedings of the Columbus session of the American Federation of Labor Did you recieve it? Copies of the bill you wrote for can be obtained by writing to Commissioner C F Peck[2] of the N.Y. Bureau of Labor Statistics, Albany, N.Y. I haven't one.

We are about to issue an official Journal, *The Union Advocate*[3] in about a week. Won't you contribute a something—say a few lines—for its first issue?

Wishing you and your noble *Standard* the success a life of devotion deserves, I am

Yours Sincerely Saml Gompers

ALS, Joseph Patrick McDonnell Collection, WHi.

1. Joseph Patrick McDonnell was editor of the *Labor Standard* from 1876 until his death in 1906. He helped organize the New Jersey Federation of Trades and Labor Unions in 1883 and served as its chairman until 1897.

2. Charles Fletcher Peck was chief of the New York Bureau of Statistics of Labor from 1883 to 1893.

3. SG published the *Union Advocate* monthly, from June to December 1887, when the second AFL convention, concerned about the journal's drain on Federation funds, discontinued it.

P. J. McGuire to Gabriel Edmonston

Philadelphia, Pa. March 21/87

Dear Gabe:

Thanks for check of $64.25 for printing Bill of D. J. Gallagher's. I will pay it tomorrow and send you a receipted bill and send Sam Gompers a duplicate. I can't understand how Gompers kept the check for a week and then returned it to you, and thus delayed payment to no purpose.

Enclosed are vouchers I received today from Gompers. I can not sign them until I first know if there is money to pay them and secondly I think he is going too fast According to Const of Federation, Page 5 of Proc. last line, The Const. went into effect Mch 1/87 consequently the salary of $1,000 per year went into effect then. That would make a little over $19 per week of 52 weeks or $83 ⅓ for each calendar month. He has already drawn I believe $25 for Salary and now wants to draw $50 more, and only 19 days of the month have expired.— Next there is a bill of $22.50 for 2000 Constitutions, while our Brotherhood[1] Const. 32 Pages only cost $11.50 per 1000—and the

Feder Const are about 4 Pages, to cost $22.50 for 2,000. Matters must be looked after more economically, or we can't stand it.

Gompers writes me he has already sent $80.00 to you. He sends out a circular for vote of the Ex Council and pleads for a Boy, I shall vote *No.* until I see some work done and some results He says he has "an enormous correspondence to attend to and in a few weeks an extensive financial system." In the matter also of organizing State Federations I favor it, but vote *No,* against admitting them to our Federation, for it is not allowed by the Constitution,[2] and it means dual representation and double tax for the 6 Carpenters Unions of Connecticut and all other Unions with Nat heads,[3] one tax to State Feder, another tax through the B. or through their Nat Union. This is running it too far and bound to harm the movement.

I favor a meeting of the Ex Council here in this city next month to pass on the needs of the Federation, and to fix rules for financial transactions and to lay out a policy of action for the future.

I have just written Gompers to send out a circular for that purpose. Thanks for $4 Receipt for Copywriting

Yours   P. J McGuire

ALS, Papers of Gabriel Edmonston, reel 1, *AFL Records.*

1. The Brotherhood of CARPENTERS and Joiners of America.
2. The 1887 AFL constitution granted one vote to each state federation represented at the annual convention.
3. That is, a local chartered by a national or international union.

John McBride[1] to Terence Powderly

Pittsburgh, Pa. April 2nd. 1887.

T. V. Powderly Esq.
Philadelphia, Pa.
Dr Sir & Bro.

You have probably noticed the war which is now being waged between the "Miners Federation,["]²[2] and D.A. 135.[3] This war will result, if continued, in the complete demoralization of our miners. After years of hard labor we have finally secured the cooperation of a large majority of coal mine operators and our joint meetings and mutual agreements have placed us and our affairs in a much better position than ever before. If harmonious relations can be maintained between miners and operators, and I think they can be if proper care is exercised, the future is full of promise to us. The great danger

confronting us today is that of a division of our own forces. As you
are aware it is many years since I became a member of the Knights
and until of late my loyalty to the order has never been questioned.
I am still anxious to remain a member and assist in securing the
establishment of the orders principles. To do this peace must be
restored between the two miners unions. I am fully satisfied that D.A.
135 cannot of itself control and adjust mining matters, and, under
the present condition of things, neither can the Federation. There is
a way however in which both organizations may unite and be of great
good to our Miners.

I sometime ago suggested this through the *"Labor Tribune"* and
while there is some slight opposition heard from both sides the great
majority have expressed in favor. My suggestions were ["]1st. The
Executive board of the Federation and D.A. 135 should meet to
consider means for consolidating theire forces. 2nd They should draft
a code of laws to govern mining affairs, and, amongst the provisions
should be a law requiring all officers of the Joint organization to be
members of the K of L. — and such officers shall be elected in general
conventions where representatives of each organization shall have
voice and vote: A per capita assessment, per month, shall be levied,
for the maintainance of the organization, upon all members alike:
The levies to be paid into the same treasury."

The above is simply an outline, and yet it will give you an idea as
to whether or not you can favor it. It would not interfere with D.A.
135's officers, but would prevent them from interfereing with mining
affairs. It would remove all open opposition from the fact that the
provisions I suggest would remove Federation officers. It would undoubtedly increase the membership of the Knights and decrease that
of the open union, yet there would be sufficient of the latter to prove
a valuable auxillary to the former. The order would soon control
matters and the aid from outside would insure success in nearly all
our undertakings. If something of this kind can be agreed upon every
official of the Federation will not only cease their opposition but work
with a will for the order.

Organization is wanted—and personally I care not whether it be
in one form or another, so that it be a good one. I must either secure
harmonious relations between our forces, or quit both in disgust.
What do you think of my suggestions? Can you suggest anything
better? We cannot have harmony with two sets of officers in the field—
There will be a conflict of authority—This we must guard against.
It is officers and not members that cause the trouble.

I shall remain in this city until we have settled the "Coke region" arbitration case,[4] hence would be pleased to hear from you while here. If convenient address me at *St James Hotel.*

If you can approve the plan suggested—urge members of 135 to assist in bringing it about.[5]

With kind regards I am Yours,

With respect   Jno. McBride

ALS, Terence Vincent Powderly Papers, DCU.

1. John McBRIDE served as president of the Ohio Miners' Amalgamated Association from 1882 to 1889 and in 1885 became first president of the National Federation of Miners and Mine Laborers (NFMML).

2. The National Federation of MINERS and Mine Laborers.

3. NATIONAL Trade Assembly (NTA) 135 was the KOL miners' assembly. Soon after its founding in May 1886, it became involved in a series of jurisdictional disputes with the NFMML and its constituent bodies. In 1886 the NFMML voted against allowing NTA 135 to participate in joint conferences between miners and mine operators and claimed sole jurisdiction over all mineworkers. The two bodies negotiated separately with the mine operators in March 1887 and were in open conflict at the time of McBride's letter.

4. The Miners' and Mine Laborers' Amalgamated Association of Pennsylvania chose McBride to represent its members in arbitration proceedings with the mine operators concerning a wage increase. The umpire's decision on Apr. 22, 1887, concluded that the miners should not receive any wage increase until the price of coke had also advanced.

5. Powderly indicated in reply that he would consult with William H. Bailey, master workman of NTA 135 (Apr. 4, 1887, Terence Vincent Powderly Papers, DCU).

A News Account of an Address in Baltimore

[April 7, 1887]

SAMUEL GOMPERS SPEAKS.

Mr. Samuel B. Gompers, president of the American Federation of Labor, delivered an address on "Trades-Unionism" at Rechabite Hall last night, under the auspices of the Federation of Labor. Prof. Joseph Ebert's[1] band played concert music at the opening. Mr. Gompers said: "I do not speak to arouse any enthusiasm, but to develop ideas. I shall speak of questions as they occur to me. Many men, failing to understand the methods by which the trades-union movement grew, fail to understand its destinies or objects. The unions are not organizations that have been agitated into existence. They are the outgrowth of our system. Many may say that they existed before the present capitalistic or free labor system. Trades-unions existed long before the present system, but that was when employers themselves formed the guilds in feudal times. They inscribed upon their banners 'Labor shall be free to work or not, as the individuals see fit.' Free for what? To starve, to compete for work, to fight for the bone offered for labor performed. With the invention and application of steam the laborers were so frequently thrown out of work that they became criminals and paupers. To prevent them from becoming such the unions protected themselves by paying weekly dues to assist those out of work. The trades unions afterwards discussed other questions besides enforced idleness, and the full-fledged form was produced. They cannot be argued out of existence. They will not, by the abuse heaped upon them by their opponents cease to be prominent in the body politic. The unions were the pioneers of the labor movement. Time was when to be known as a president of a union or strike committee meant to suffer on the gallows. And many, many men, good and true, have sacrificed their lives to the cause. It is a fact that the employing class, however much we may deplore it, endeavor to get the greatest amount of labor for the smallest wages for which they can get employes. On the other hand, the workers have always endeavored to get the greatest amount of money for the smallest amount of work. Under these conditions it is impossible for capitalists and laborers to have common interests. To preach otherwise an unpalatable truth, or to cry peace where there is none, is like the ostrich, who hides his head in the sand. There is quite a difference in the matter of capital and labor, between which there is an identity of interest. Then the trades unions are the natural organizations of working people, for none others than those interested in the craft can be admitted to their ranks. I can see but little benefit resulting to the world and country when the foreman, who is often a spy, and the boss, who is antagonistic, may become members. How many of us would care to discuss a grievance in an organization of which the employer and foreman are members? I would say in all frankness, I would myself draw it mildly in a body where my employer was a member. A protective organization that admits both is not natural.

[‘’]At the Columbus trades union convention the chairman of the Knights of Labor committee was a millionaire of Massachusetts. If he is permissible to be a member of labor organizations, what is the difference between him and Jay Gould? In the last few years the Knights of Labor have arrayed themselves on the side of the opponents of trades unions. It lies in their declaration that the K. of L. is not a mere trade union. The unions have gone before. They have made it possible for men to go on and achieve their rights. I have said before that the Knights of Labor is a body capable of immense good. It could, in harmony with the trades unions, do anything under the sun. Hence it is as improper to say we are not mere trades unions, as it would be for unionists to say we are not mere Knights of Labor. I was for 12 years a true K. of L., but when they would force upon me what I would not permit my employer to do it was time for us to part. How many of you, if your employer said you should not belong to a labor union, would accept his dictum? The Knights have assumed a function that we would not submit to from our employers' hands, and it seems that they are receiving an application of the same doctrines from employers, with this exception — the Knight leaves the order and the unionist remains in the union. The Knights have formed an organization for educational purposes, but the union is the body that fights the battles between capitalist and employe. Far be it from me to widen the breach. The lines are not drawn by the unionist. They have been made by the K. of L. because they have made outlaws of men who dared to be union men.

["]We find that the union and Knights are opposed to strikes. The union, however, does not denounce strikes. If they go in for one they strike hard to win. The Knights, who denounce strikes, have the largest strikes and the most failures. I am opposed to strikes, but if the workers denounced strikes and swore not to engage in one, their employers would do the striking for them. I believe the best method of preventing them is to prepare for them. The employer who knows the men are prepared will always think twice before he enters a battle on equal terms. If he knows they are not prepared he will enter a race for a contract to underbid other contractors, as he knows he can cut the laborer's wages. I believe in men having principles. An organization that calls or orders men on strike should furnish bread to maintain the strikers. It is easy to issue an edict to put 1,000 men or women on strike, but they must, if they have principle, at least furnish the commonest necessities of life. I don't know where our boast of principle can come in when our strikers' wives and children ask for bread. It is all very well that the assemblies pass resolutions of sympathy, but sympathy without relief is like mustard without beef. I am not in favor of that autocratic principle of ordering on strikes. I don't believe that one or two or a half a dozen men are intelligent or good enough to direct a strike. A union ought to come together and vote to strike after discussing a grievance without finding a remedy, and they themselves ought to decide when to go back, and not be ordered back. If the working-people are ordered, they strike half-hearted; if they resolve to strike, they will fight for the abolition of grievances, as the volunteer is always better than the conscript.

["]The trades-unions have surrounded themselves with benevolent features, such as traveling, sick, endowment and insurance benefits. Some ask why this is. The union can and will do what any other beneficial bodies will do. You have all noticed the great booms in unions when business is good and disintegration when trade is dull. The beneficial union does not lose members in such time because they have too much at stake in the way of subscriptions and benefits. When an era of prosperity sets in, nearly the whole time is lost by reorganizing. Those unionists who have maintained strength are the first to reap benefits from returning prosperity. As much as you may argue against it, there will be crises and depressions that will rack the organizations to the centre, and I want men to be united. Having been a delegate to the Columbus labor convention, I heard the complaints against over-zealous Knights of Labor. The time was some years ago when if one said the workers would be organized as one man against the whole capitalistic class, even if the worst came to a conflict, he would have been roughly dealt with, and one man who stood up then and organized the Amalgamated Association of Mine Laborers.[2] The Knights of Labor set up a counter organization. It was the same with the carpenters. The barbers had reduced their 96 hours of labor by 15 hours a week, the Knights of Labor turned around and organized the scabs and the bosses who had refused to recognize the union. The carpet-weavers were treated likewise.

"You all know what the cigarmakers have to complain of. I repeat that no seven men as in the executive board of the Knights should direct. I think no tailor or baker should say how many bricks a bricklayer should lay in a day. The American Federation thinks that each trade should direct its own affairs. If any of these have trouble we believe in assisting them, but not while giving five cents give $100 worth of direction. There are general interests of labor. We believe they can be best conserved in a central federation. The people of the country have heard many reports of strife between the Knights and trades-unionists, and look for the day when they shall fight like Kilkenny cats. Out of all this conflict will come more intelligent organization than exists today. The struggle will be for labor's emancipation from thralldom."

Mr. Gompers announced himself ready to answer questions at the close. Mr. Luke[3] asked who the millionaire Knight was, was answered Jno. W. Howes, of Massachusetts. Mr. Culp then asked if there was not a millionaire in the Amalgamated Association of Steel Workers, a trades-union. Mr. Gompers said no, and Mr. Culp said Andrew Carnegel[4] was, as were also Messrs. Drexel[5] and Childs,[6] members of the typographical union.[7] A number of other questions were asked, and the closing of the meeting was very lively. The majority present were unionists. Profs. Richard T. Ely[8] and John H. Wright,[9] of Johns Hopkins University, were in the audience.

Baltimore Sun, Apr. 7, 1887.

1. Joseph W. Ebert was a Baltimore musician.
2. The National Federation of Miners and Mine Laborers.
3. Possibly Charles Luke, a cooper and member of KOL Local Assembly 7537.
4. Andrew Carnegie was a steel manufacturer.
5. Anthony Joseph Drexel was a Philadelphia financier and banker.
6. George William Childs was the publisher of the *Philadelphia Public Ledger.*
7. The International TYPOGRAPHICAL Union.
8. Richard Theodore ELY was an economist at the Johns Hopkins University.
9. John Henry Wright was a professor of classical philology at the Johns Hopkins University.

Minutes of a Meeting of Members of the Executive Council of the AFL

Philadelphia Pa April 10th 1887

Pursuant to a resolution of the E.C. of the A.F of L. the Eastern members of the E.C convened on the above date at 476 N 6th St present G Edmonston, P J McGuire and Saml. Gompers.

The minutes of the previous sessions were read and approved.

Resolved that the President open a Bank account if possible with the German Exchange Bank.

Resolved That the President shall be allowed to retain $100.00 in his posession.

Resolved that to simplyfy the financial system all moneys should be forwarded to the President and at the end of each month the President submit a financial statement and forward to the Treasure all money above the $100.00 above provided.

Resolved that the President have power to fill vacancies in the Executive Board should any occur.

Resolved that the President attend to all conventions of National Trades Unions whenever possible particularly the I.T.U convention[1]

Resolved that the President prepare a circular of how to join the American Federation of Labor, also setting forth its objects and purposes.

Resolved that the application of the Ind. Clothing Cutters[2] for a charter be referred to the next convention of the A.F of L.

Resolved that when the Mutual Musical Protective Union[3] be furnished with documents in reference to the A.F of L.

The German American Typographia[4] having laid the matter of their trouble with the Phila *Tagablatt* in the hands of two members of the Ex Council (McGuire & Gompers) for adjudication. The Ex Council accepted the responsibility and secured the acquiescence of the Publishers of the *Tagablatt*. The Executive Council met and decided the case a copy of which was served on both parties and one retained on file and in letter "copy book.["]

The Tagablatt publishers manifested a desire to avoid compliance with the decision. The G.A Typ'a having sent in notice of their acceptance, It was

Resolved that the E.C. call upon the publishers and demand a compliance.

The committee (E.C) returned and were reported that *Tag't* will probably comply.

Reso[l]ved if they comply the President write a letter in the name of the E.C. to the GA Typo's to be somewhat lenient with the men working in the office and named in the decision.

Resolved that the matter of publishing of the official Journal lay over for future consideration.

Resolved. That when no objections are made to the issuance of a charter to applicants the President have power to issue the same without the vote of the EC.

AD, Minutes of Meetings, Executive Council, AFL, reel 1, *AFL Records.*

1. Although represented at the first AFL convention in 1886, the International Typographical Union (ITU) failed to pay its per capita tax. SG addressed the ITU convention at Buffalo, N.Y., on June 7, 1887, where the delegates raised objection to taking a charter as a subordinate to the AFL. The delegates also learned that the ITU was in a state of financial embarrassment due to misappropriation of funds by its secretary-treasurer. The AFL changed its constitution at its December 1887 convention to allow affiliation by means of a simple certificate of affiliation, and the AFL and ITU resolved the question of ITU indebtedness to the Federation the following year. The AFL issued a certificate of affiliation to the ITU on Dec. 31, 1888.

2. There is no indication that the AFL issued a charter to the Independent Clothing Cutters Union of New York.

3. Beginning in 1887, the AFL regularly asked the National League of Musicians (NLM) to join the Federation, but the League consistently rejected affiliation. The Mutual Musical Protective Union of New York, the largest and most influential of the unions in the NLM, contended that musicians had little in common with other workers or other unions and would suffer a loss of dignity and prestige by affiliation with the AFL. In response, the AFL undertook to charter local musicians' unions of its own, hoping eventually to gain a sufficient number to charter a national union.

4. The German-American TYPOGRAPHIA.

P. J. McGuire to Gabriel Edmonston

Phila Pa Apr 18 1887 10 P.M.

Dear Gabe:

Sam Gompers came here today as by appointment with Mr Crowell[1] of the Boss Brewers. We went to see Mr Crowell in company with the Journeymen Brewers,[2] and the result is that by next Wednesday the whole matter will be settled favorably to the men.[3] Last Friday Mr Crowell came to see me and after many hours talk I "got him to come over". Hence it was agreed to meet today and Wednesday we will meet again to sign an agreement favorable to the men.

I talked with Sam Gompers tonight and find nothing has been done towards getting out a circular or preparing an address as ordered at meeting of the Ex Council.[4] In fact nothing has been done in the way of even writing to each society represented at Columbus. I asked Sam if he wrote to the Iron Molders, etc, and urged them to join the Federation. He said: No, he had a circular partially composed on the subject, but not yet ready. He tells me he has not got a cent from any organization since we met, nor has he had any applications for a charter. He finally ended by saying he expected he would soon have to look for another job, and go to work at cigar making. I submit this for your own consideration. Consequently I write this for your information. When we meet next Sunday we will talk further on the subject. I fear the 6 cents capita tax per year, or ½ cent per month[5] has killed the Federation and Sam is not energetic enough in correspondence. I would suggest you write him and urge him to work. I have done so verbally to him today I would hate to see the Federation drop. But I must say it looks very discouraging for the Federation unless more push is shown.

Yours   P J McGuire

P.S. — In John Swinton's Paper,[6] I note this item this week:

National D.A of Carpenters[7] — Assemblies composed of house carpenters or joiners are invited to correspond with C. T. Dant,[8] Box 429 Washington D.C. with a view to organizing a National District of the craft — Try and find out who Dant is? Let me know

ALS, Papers of Gabriel Edmonston, reel 1, *AFL Records.*

1. Henry P. Crowell was secretary of the Philadelphia Lager Beer Brewers' Association.

2. That is, representatives of the BREWERS' National Union (BNU).

3. Both the BNU and KOL District Assembly (DA) 1 were negotiating for Philadelphia brewery workers who struck on Dec. 30, 1886, against a reduction of wages. SG and McGuire conferred with employers in Philadelphia on Apr. 18 on behalf of

the BNU. In June the employers signed a one-year agreement with DA 1 and KOL loca! assemblies 7086 and 7087 of Philadelphia.

4. See "Minutes of a Meeting of Members of the Executive Council of the AFL," Apr. 10, 1887, above.

5. The AFL's 1886 constitution stated that "the revenue of the Federation shall be derived from International, National, District and Local organizations, which shall pay into the treasury of the Federation a per capita tax of one-half cent per month for each member in good standing." The 1887 convention lowered the per capita to one-quarter cent (AFL, *Proceedings*, 1887, p. 11).

6. John SWINTON published the influential New York City labor reform newspaper *John Swinton's Paper* between October 1883 and August 1887.

7. In 1887 KOL carpenters led by Ira B. Aylsworth of Baltimore attempted to form a carpenters' national trade assembly. The KOL called a convention to meet in Cleveland on Mar. 6, 1888, for this purpose, but postponed it and the national trade assembly did not materialize.

8. Clements T. Dant was a Washington, D.C., carpenter.

To the Editor of the *Craftsman*

April 19th [188]7

To the Editor of *The Craftsman*
Dear Sir

It is with considerable surprise, I must confess that I read the article under the caption "Something To P[on]der" in your issue of the 9th inst.

It is something we are getting accustomed to see in many papers to have the position of labor organizations and labor men maligned but to find the same course persued by labor papers is something we do not expect. Hence the surprise.

Is it a fact as you insinuate that the American Federation of Labor is officered by men, who are more eager to "down" their fellow workingmen known as the K of L. than to wring from the relentless taskmasters a slight increase of labor's poor requittal? Have the men who are the officers of the A.F. of L. not been tried and true champions of labor's cause? Have they not become known and earned the confidence of their fellow-workingmen because of their consistent and unrelenting endevours to wring from relentless taskmasters an increase of labor's poor requittal?.

While admitting the great wrongs that have been committed by "bad or foolish men of the Order" against the Trades Unions. In a self satisfying manner you assure your readers that better counsel will prevail hereafter. I hope and believe so. But would it not be just to say to what this change of front will be attributable. If it comes to pass at all?

Up to last December, when the Federation was re-formed at Columbus Ohio, not only was the attitude of the Knights antagonistic to Trades Unions but even Trades Assemblies were frowned down upon. Their formation discouraged and denied.

It is only since the American Federation of Labor was organized that "the authorities in the Order" have had any forbearance and have in some instances *allowed* the Trades Unions to exist in peace. That this is not entirely so can be seen by "the authorities in the Order" advertizing for "scabs" to take the places of the Iron & Steel Workers Association's members at Mingo Junction and other instances of a like character too numerous to mention.

You say that the press of the closing week (the 9th[?]) heralded forth that the Federation was formed to fight the Knights, which you without any hesitation accept as gospel truth and then proceed to deliver a homily to the men who through no fault of their own and against their inclinations are the officers of the A.F. of L.

The advisability of the I.T.U sending delegates to the next session of the Federation is certainly one that interests that organization vitally and is one deserving all the attention that can be given to it. *The Craftsman* being the official organ of the I.T.U it is but proper that the attention of the members should be called to it, yet in discussing so important a subject it seems to me to be unnecessary to stoop to vituperation and abuse of the officers of the organization.

In connection with the discussion of this subject you should not loose sight of the fact that in framing the laws of (as you say) "somwhat loosely-jointed body" the delegates of the I.T.U took an active part.

The closing paragraph of your article (except the last sentence where you stop reasoning and commence abuse) is a complete refutation of all that you say otherwise throughout the article and I take pleasure in quoting it as being exactly the principles governing the conduct of the officers of the A.F. of L.

"It is formed, as we understand it, for the advancement of the Labor cause, for the definition and settlement of the rights of different trades associations, for the securing of closer co-operation with the Knights of Labor, and with a view to prevent in future, by fair, honorable, and conservative means, a recurrence of encroachments by the latter on the rights of National Trades Union[s.]"[1]

Trusting that you will publish this statement and that the *labor papers* which anxiously and prominently copied your article will do the same with this. I have the honor to subscribe myself

Yours Fraternally   Samuel Gompers.
President American Federation of Labor.[2]

A and PLpS, reel 1, vol. 1, pp. 191-94, SG Letterbooks, DLC.

1. The quoted matter is a clipping affixed to the page; the quotation marks, however, are in SG's hand.

2. Because the *Craftsman* did not publish SG's letter, SG published it in the June 1887 issue of the *Union Advocate*.

To Gabriel Edmonston

April 22nd [188]7

G Edmonston Esq
Treas &c
Dear Sir.

Money is coming in very slow in fact so slow that it is very discouraging. Expenditures must be made some bills are coming in. I ought certainly recieve something for putting my whole time into the work. If I only had the means I wouldn't care a straw but as it is I will have shortly to decide upon giving up the position, take a job at my trade or starve. If the Unions of the Country don't want a Federation, then they don't and that settles it. If they do they ought to pay a little for the protection its very existence it affords and should not insist upon doing what we protest aganist employers doing, i e exacting work without pay. There can be no question that I did a good deal of that in my long connection with the labor movement and am willing to do so again if I get a chance to get back at my trade, but with a large family depending upon me for support I can not give my *entire time* without recompense.

You have some money on hand and I request you to forward me One Hundred dollars and accept my reciept for the same (which please find enclosed) until the end of the month, when I will send the regular warrant with "statement" as ordered at our meeting in Phila. When you can return to me the reciept and I will send you another in place of it.

Fraternally yours   Saml Gompers.
Pres.

ALpS, reel 1, vol. 1, pp. 201 and 200, SG Letterbooks, DLC.

To Louis Herbrand[1]

April 29th [188]7

Louis Herbrand Esq
Sec'y N.B.U.
Dear Sir

The action of the Ex Council of the American Federation of Labor in the matter of the difficulty of the Brewers Union and the Employing Brewers has been to endevour to obtain victory for the men out of the jaws of defeat. When however our work was nearly completed the Boss Brewers in collusion with the representatives of the K of L refused to permit the representatives of the A.F. of L to have a voice in the matter. While feeling keenly the humiliation we resolved to bear it providing it would do any good to the men involved, instead however we see the result. It has been decided therefore that before further action be taken by the Ex Council in this matter to insist that in any future conference and settlement the representatives of the Ex Council of the American Federation of Labor must be a party to it. Hoping to hear from you as early as possible so that we take decided action upon your application I am

Fraty yours   Saml Gompers.
Pres. A.F. of L.

ALpS, reel 1, vol. 1, p. 211, SG Letterbooks, DLC.

1. Louis HERBRAND became secretary in 1885 of the New York Brewers' Union, a KOL local assembly, and served as national secretary of the brewers' national union from 1886 to 1888.

To the Officers and Members of Organizations Represented at the 1886 Convention of the AFL

New York, April 30th 1887

To the Officers & Members of Organizations represented at the Columbus session of the American Federation of Labor.
Fellow-Workmen!

Since the adjour[n]ment of the convention little or nothing has been heard of the action of several organizations there represented, In the matter of their affiliation with the American Federation of

Labor. Applications for a charter, the payment of the per capita tax towards defraying the expences of the organization (That it may prosecute its work), the purchase of copies of the printed official proceedings or subscriptions for the official Journal "The Union Advocate".

If the principles for which the Federation was organized to contend for are of any moment at all, they are worth paying a trifle for. Each Trade Union, National, International or Local should decide upon these important matters and inform the undersigned of the result. Trusting to hear favorably from your organization at an early day. I am

Yours Fraternally   Samuel Gompers,
President American Fedn of Labor
332 E 8th St New York N.Y.

Attest

P. J McGuire Sec'y

N.B. Per resolution of the Ex Council all communication and money's are to be forwarded to the President at the above address.

S. G.

ALS, Papers of Gabriel Edmonston, reel 1, *AFL Records.*

Gompers and the Political Labor Movement in New York City, 1887-89

Although Gompers had actively participated in Henry George's New York City mayoralty campaign in 1886, his commitment to nonpartisan political action subsequently led him to dissociate himself from George's United Labor party (ULP) and other efforts to create a workingmen's party in New York. The ULP was organized in January 1887 by a coalition of George's supporters in the New York City Central Labor Union (CLU), the SLP, and the KOL in the aftermath of their candidate's impressive but unsuccessful showing in the 1886 elections. The party was torn by internal divisions, however, and its August convention in Syracuse expelled SLP members. The socialists responded by organizing the Progressive Labor party (PLP), and both the ULP and the PLP ran slates of candidates in the city's fall elections. Gompers and most trade unions in the CLU refrained from endorsing either party, and at the polls neither the ULP nor the PLP came close to George's tally in the 1886 race.[1] The two parties disintegrated in the aftermath of the election, and the quarrels between the various political factions in the New York labor movement became muted as a large cigarmakers' strike during the late winter and the brewery workers' lockout in the late spring occupied much of the energies of organized labor.

For the remainder of the decade Gompers continued to maintain his neutral position, refraining from supporting any of the existing political parties and stressing that building effective trade unions must take priority over the organization of labor as an independent political force.[2] He advised union leaders not to participate in the 1888 election campaign in their official capacities, and in 1889 and 1890 declined Democratic and Republican overtures to nominate him as a candidate for political office.

Notes

1. See "Labor Politics, the Henry George Campaign, and the United Labor Party," in *The Making of a Union Leader*, pp. 429-30, and "An Interview in the *Leader*," July 25, 1887, below.

2. See "A Translation of an Excerpt from an Article in the *New Yorker Volkszeitung*," Dec. 3, 1888, below.

An Interview in the *Leader*[1]

[July 25, 1887]

THE PLATFORM

WHAT ARE THE PRINCIPLES TO BE PROCLAIMED AT SYRACUSE?[2]

. . .

VIEWS OF SAMUEL GOMPERS.

Mr. Samuel Gompers, President of the Federation of Trades, said:
"The Labor movement, to succeed politically, must work for present
and tangible results. While keeping in view a lofty ideal, we must
advance towards it through practical steps, taken with an intelligent
regard for pressing needs. I believe with the most advanced thinkers
as to ultimate ends, including the abolition of the wage system. But
I hold it as a self-evident proposition that no successful attempt can
be made to reach those ends without first improving present conditions.
This, you may say, is the standpoint of trades unionism; but it is not
a narrow one, for we can see from it that nothing is impossible.
Organization is the requisite of progress, and is more readily effected
as the first object in view is more clearly perceived. This object once
attained, others are seen which previously lay beyond the ordinary
range of vision. It is, therefore, of the utmost importance to have a
well-defined object in view from the start—something that everybody
can see—because the hope of reaching it facilitates organization,
through which the final aim, however dim to the perception of many,
is steadily advanced. For instance, the great political outburst of last
fall was the result of previous organization in the economic field. The
same thing will be true of all future movements."

"In your opinion, then, the platform of the party should essentially
deal with reforms already studied and demanded by Organized Labor
with a view to immediate improvement?"

"Exactly so. Immediate relief with future aims. The Labor movement
may be trusted to work out its own logical outcome. No intelligent
observer can fail to perceive its natural tendency. Continual
improvement, by opening new vistas, creates new desires and develops
legitimate aspirations. It makes men more dissatisfied with unjust
conditions and readier to battle for the right. The poor, the hungry,
has not the strength to engage in a conflict even when his life is at
stake. Organization itself is a result and evidence of improvement."

"Some time ago," continued Mr. Gompers with evident feeling, "I
heard a mother say she wished her sick child were dead. She lived

in a pestilential tenement house, and her misery **was** such that this was, indeed, the most merciful wish her circumstances could inspire. But give this mother a ray of hope; improve her condition ever so little; and mark the change in her speech! Yes, I believe in immediate relief. It is not in degradation that men aspire most to get out of it. Were it so the Chinese would be at the head of modern civilization."

"What do you think of a single tax upon land values as the first and foremost plank of the platform?"

"I have a great regard for Henry George, and cannot speak too highly of his work as a public educator. Had he done nothing more than to awaken thought and compel discussion, I would still consider his achievements as unparalleled in the history of the Labor movement. But in making a platform for the party of 'United Labor,' you should bear in mind that it is the views of the masses that must be considered and brought into a coherent form, and not those of one man, however representative he may be of the aspirations of his time. As many of us understand it, Mr. George's theory of land taxation does not promise present reform, nor an ultimate solution."

"Why does it not promise present reform?"

"While his views have been received with considerable enthusiasm in New York and other places, it is doubtful that they would soon unite a sufficient number of people to gain for the Labor Party that commanding position in the law-making bodies which it must secure in order to carry them out. They will even divide those who are now united on the necessity of other measures if it appears that a single land tax means free trade. Granting the correctness of his position, a work of enlightenment must be undertaken that will consume much time, during which measures intended for immediate relief and improvement will suffer unnecessary delay."

"Why does it not promise an ultimate solution?"

"Private land ownership is unquestionably wrong. But if George's theory be right as to land it is right also as to every kind of property acquired under a system of profit-making. The mere taxation of land values cannot settle the questions between capital and labor arising from the wage system and the progress of machinery; and a Labor Party cannot ignore those questions."

"Do you mean that the effects of machinery under the wage-system should be made a prominent feature of the platform?"

"Yes; and practical measures, readily applicable even under the present conditions must be suggested, tending to correct those effects— that is, tending to render them beneficial, as they should be, instead of hurtful, as they are. It should be well understood that the aim of capital has been to make the worker a constantly greater producer;

whereas the aim of the Labor movement is to make him a greater consumer also."

"And what measures would you suggest?"

"The most important of all is the reduction of the hours of labor, so that machinery may be in fact what it is in name — 'labor-saving.' Secondly, prohibition of the employment of children under 14 years of age; for such employment is the perversion of man's inventive genius to the basest end of avarice — the degradation of the race. Thirdly, and upon the same ground, restriction and regulation of female labor. These are the demands in the support of which Organized Labor is thoroughly united. If we can enforce them by independent political action, the working classes will derive from the success of their party an immediate and substantial improvement, that will enable them, as I said before, to advance further in economic and moral education, and in their perception of ultimate ends."

"In conclusion," observed Mr. Gompers, "let the party be as radical or conservative as it may please in the statement of its final aims; but let it declare that it is a Labor party, organized by and for Labor. Give us a workingman's platform, not a professor's; and insist on the three demands I have just spoken of, for they are calculated to unite all our forces, and they lead in a straight line to the ultimate ends of the Labor movement."

. . .

Leader, July 25, 1887.

1. The *Leader* began publication in the fall of 1886 to support the New York City mayoralty campaign of Henry GEORGE. The paper came under the editorship of the socialist Sergius E. Shevitch in January 1887 and became the voice of socialists within the United Labor party (ULP), an organization established that month to continue the work of the coalition that had supported George.
2. The ULP's convention was held in Syracuse on Aug. 17.

Terence Powderly to Charles Litchman[1]

Scranton Pa. July 29 1887.

My dear Charlie: —

It was an associated press dispatch that said you had given an opinion as to the question of Mellen's right to a seat in the G.A.[2] I saw it in several papers.

List of secretaries received all right.

Make up your article for the Journal on the "Decline and fall of the Knights of Labor" and write up the "Conspiracy" in a double leaded or double shotted article. I believe it should go out in a short time. Before publishing anything concerning it secure the willing consent of the exposer to shoulder his share of the burden of proof when they say "your's another" in reply to the exposure.

Our opponents are right in asserting that we are violent enemies of trades unionists. I tried to instill a feeling of good will toward trades unions in the minds of those around me and I must confess that I didn't make much of a success of it. Bailey[3] started away from my presence once with the threat warm on his lips to "Do everything in his power to antagonize trades unions and to break them up, to make war on them from this time forth." I never favored that policy nor did I ever favor the policy of telling right out in meeting what we intended to do with the trades unionists. It always happens that when a fellow tells another fellow what he is going to do with him, the other fellow won't be there promptly on time to be attended to and the scheme fails. We might just as well make up our minds to the inevitable, the trades men of the present day are a generation removed from the day when trades unions were organizing in this country and they must have the same experience that we have had. The trades must have certain laws to govern them that others do not want and they must in all fairness be allowed to manage their own business so far as that business relates to trade matters purely. I have a plan for the regulation of that but I dare not mention it for fear of having it jumped on and yet we want the trades men with us. How can we hold them unless we allow them to manage some part of their own business. Do not accuse me of being a trades unionist for I am not and never will be again. I want to see those who are now tending that way educated away beyond the trade union point and they cannot be taught except by experience.

I shall write up my plan for the regulation of trade Assemblies and publish it in the Journal before the G.A. It is in brief as follows.

Each trade to be allowed to have a national district in which matters pertaining to the trade alone are to be attended to, Assemblies of that trade to be attached to that N.D.A.

State Assemblies to be organized in every state and territory each one to have jurisdiction over the Assemblies of the State in all matters not relating to trade affairs. State Assemblies to be composed of all Assemblies in the state whether trade or mixed and to hold an annual convention for the purpose of passing on national legislation for the good of the Order and for the election of representatives to the G.A. At said annual convention all Assemblies whether trade or mixed, to have an equal right and voice in the election and selection of representatives. The National Trade Assemblies to have exclusive control over trade matters but to have no right to representation in the G.A. All representatives to the G.A. to be elected by the State Assembly and while members of trades Assemblies stand the same chance of election to the G.A. from the State A. yet no trade shall, as such, be represented in the G.A. That body to be composed of Knights who know no trade, creed, country or color, and to legislate for the general welfare of the whole Order.

In the matter of strikes no trade Assembly to enter upon a struggle until the Assemblies of the N.T.A. has voted upon the matter and no assistance to be extended from the Order until the request for such aid has been submitted to the G.E.B. and passed upon by the Order.

Where Assemblies, trade or mixed, meet four times a month, two meetings of each month shall be devoted exclusively to the discussion of the separate parts of the preamble of the K. of L. and a separate book to be kept for the entry of the minutes of the discussions on questions relating to the declaration of principles.[4]

We may talk as we please about the trade Assemblies doing nothing in their meetings except to talk of trade matters but our mixed Assemblies do exactly the same, they talk of equally as foolish things as the trade Assemblies do. We must lead them all out of that rut and when we recognize the right of the trade to run its own affairs we take the whip out of the hand of the trade union leader and place it in the hand of the tradesman himself who if he has a half an ounce of brains will see that the two meetings in which no trade matters are touched upon are the best.

I will be down Tuesday.

Write out a temporary commission for W. P. White to be used for one time only.

As ever yours,   Terry

TLpS, Terence Vincent Powderly Papers, DCU.

1. Charles Henry LITCHMAN, a shoemaker, was general secretary of the KOL from 1886 to 1888.

2. James H. Mellen, editor of the *Worcester Daily Times*, represented District Assembly 30 at the 1887 KOL General Assembly and was the Massachusetts State Assembly's delegate to the 1888 KOL General Assembly. The *Boston Globe* (July 22, 1887) identified Mellen as an "anti-administration" delegate.

3. William H. BAILEY, a miner, served as a member of the KOL General Executive Board (1884-87) and was master workman of the miners' National Trade Assembly 135 (1886-87).

4. The KOL General Assembly in October adopted a modified version of Powderly's plan.

To P. H. Donnelly[1]

Aug. 20th [188]7

P H Donnelly Esq
Sec'y Ill Miners Prot Asso'n
Dear Sir

Your of the 15th enclosing Money [Or]der for $19.45 came duly to hand, for which please [find] a reciept inclosed.

Am exceedingly thankful for the information contained in your letter in reference to 135[2] and deem your course of the stenographic report of discussion not only a happy that [thought?] but a wise forethought which must accrue to the advantage of the Miners Federation.

If possible I shall be at your National Convention at Indianapolis on Sept 6,[3] at least I shall make an attempt to get there.

In answer to your inquiry I will state that Henry George and John Swinton are *out*, and so far as the laboring forces pulling together is concerned, if you mean politically I must confess that it looks somewha[t] hazy. There are new developments every day and the keenest thinkers can't tell what will turn up "to-morrow" In the economic field the Trades Unions are a unit with every prospect of remaining so if both sides of the political movement (Henry George vs the Socialists) can be kept outside of the Unions.

With best wishes and hoping to hear from you soon and often. I am

Yours Fraternally   Saml Gompers,
Pres.

ALpS, reel 1, vol. 2, pp. 40-41, SG Letterbooks, DLC.

1. Patrick H. DONNELLY was secretary of the Coal Miners' Benevolent and Protective Association of Illinois from 1885 to 1888.
2. KOL National Trade Assembly 135.
3. The third annual convention of the National Federation of Miners and Mine Laborers of the United States was held in Indianapolis, Ind., Sept. 6-8, 1887. SG apparently did not attend the convention.

The Campaign for Clemency for the Convicted Haymarket Anarchists

Following the Haymarket Square bombing in Chicago, eight anarchists were tried and convicted of murder; seven of them received the death sentence and one a long prison term.[1] Gompers' opposition to capital punishment and his belief that an injustice had been done led him to take a public stand for clemency in 1887. At the same time, members of KOL District Assembly 49 like James Quinn, Frank Ferrell, and Martin Hanly defied warnings from the Order's General Executive Board and, together with representatives from the New York City Central Labor Union (CLU), campaigned openly for more lenient sentences. Gompers and his customary antagonists jointly sponsored a public appeal to workingmen on behalf of the condemned men and held a mass meeting on October 20, 1887, at which they denounced the verdict and the lack of a fair trial. On November 9, Gompers, Quinn, Ferrell, and Edward King went to Illinois as representatives of the New York City CLU to present Governor Richard J. Oglesby with a petition calling for the commutation of the sentences. The governor converted the sentences of two of the seven condemned men (Samuel Fielden and Michael Schwab) to life imprisonment. Of the others, Louis Lingg committed suicide before his execution, and George Engel, Adolph Fischer, Albert R. Parsons, and August Spies were hanged on November 11, 1887. On June 26, 1893, Governor John P. Altgeld pardoned Fielden and Schwab, along with Oscar W. Neebe, who had been sentenced to a fifteen-year term in prison.

Note

1. See "The FOTLU, the KOL, and the Eight-Hour Campaign of 1886," in *The Making of a Union Leader*, p. 277.

A Circular Protesting the Sentencing of the Haymarket Defendants

New York, September 16, 1887.

APPEAL ENDORSED BY THE CENTRAL LABOR UNION AND DISTRICT 49, K. OF L.

Fellow Workingmen:

You are aware of the decision rendered by the Supreme Court of Illinois confirming the verdict of the lower court in the so-called Anarchist cases,[1] and fixing the day of execution of the prisoners for November 11th of this year.

As citizens who stand united on the broad platform of human rights and equal justice to all, irrespective of political or social opinions, we now appeal to you to do all in your power to secure a modification of the above-mentioned decision.

Liberty, free speech and justice impartially and fearlessly meted out to friend and foe, are the only safeguards and the primary conditions of a peaceable social development in this country.

Under the misguiding and corrupting influence of prejudice and class-hatred, those men have been condemned without any conclusive evidence as accessories to a crime, the principle of which, as well as the motives which may have actuated the same, are unknown.

The execution of this sentence would be a disgrace to the honor of our nation, and would strengthen the very doctrines it is ostensibly directed against.

The undersigned appeal, therefore, to you as representatives of Organized Labor, the foremost champion of our rights and liberties, to immediately take such steps as may save our country from the disgrace of an act that can be considered in no other light than as a judicial murder, prompted by the basest and most un-American motives.

This is an issue on which all Patriotic Citizens ought to stand united. No factional differences ought to divide us when the fundamental principles of American liberty are at stake.

Leaving to you to decide as to the most efficient method to be adopted, we would suggest that a call should be issued by all the representative labor organizations of this country for great public demonstrations to be held simultaneously in this and in all other cities of the Union on or about the 20th of October.[2]

Hoping that you will consider this our communication in the spirit in which we address it to you, we remain,

Yours in the cause of Justice and Humanity,

Samuel Gompers.   Tom O'Reilly.[3]

Jas. E. Quinn.[4]   John D. Dunn, Syracuse.

Martin A. Hanly.[5]   Geo. H. McVey.[6]

Frank Ferrell.[7]   A. G. Johnson, Jr.[8]

Edward King.[9]   Matthew Barr.[10]

Everett Glackin.[11]   Fred. Haller.[12]

Henry Emrich.[13]   Michael J. Kelly.[14]

PD, Edward A. Wieck Collection, MiDW.

1. The eight men tried and convicted of murder in connection with the Haymarket incident: George ENGEL, Samuel FIELDEN, Adolph FISCHER, Louis LINGG, Oscar W. NEEBE, Albert R. PARSONS, Michael SCHWAB, and August SPIES.

2. Various meetings were held on Oct. 20, 1887, to call for clemency for the Haymarket defendants. In New York the Central Labor Union (CLU) and KOL District Assembly (DA) 49 organized a meeting at Cooper Union where Thaddeus B. Wakeman, the Progressive Labor party candidate for attorney general, Daniel DeLeon, P. J. McGuire, SG, and others spoke. (See "A Translation of a News Account of an Address at a Mass Meeting in New York City," Oct. 21, 1887, below.)

3. Thomas O'REILLY was elected president of the Brotherhood of Telegraphers in 1885 and in 1886 became master workman of KOL DA 45, the telegraphers' trade assembly. He was an editor of the *Journal of the Knights of Labor* from 1889 to 1893.

4. James E. QUINN, a bookbinder, was a leader of the Home Club of DA 49 and was active in the New York City CLU and the United Labor party (ULP).

5. Martin A. HANLY, a grocery salesman, insurance agent, and a superintendent in Jersey City, N.J., was master workman of DA 197 in 1887.

6. In 1887 George H. McVEY was president of the United Piano Makers' Union and financial secretary of the New York City CLU.

7. Frank J. FERRELL was a prominent black trade unionist, socialist, and member of the KOL. He worked as a machinist and stationary engineer in New York City into the twentieth century.

8. A. G. Johnson, Jr., possibly Alexander G. Johnson, a New York City paperhanger, represented the Union Industrial League in the New York City CLU in 1887.

9. Edward KING was active during the 1880s in the New York City CLU and was a supporter of both trade unionism and independent political action on the part of the workers.

10. Matthew BARR was a walking delegate and president of the Tin and Sheet Iron Workers' Union in 1887 and a member of the New York City CLU Board of Trustees in 1886 and 1887.

11. Everett Glackin, a printer living in Brooklyn, was president of International Typographical Union 6 in New York from 1886 to 1888. Active in the New York City CLU, Glackin was involved in the ULP in 1887 and ran against John Swinton for state senator from the Seventh District.

12. Frederick HALLER, a leader of the Cigarmakers' Progressive Union and the New York City CLU, was active in the Henry George mayoralty campaign.

13. Henry EMRICH served as secretary of the International Furniture Workers' Union between 1882 and 1891 and was treasurer of the AFL in 1888 and 1889.

October 1887

14. Michael J. Kelly was a New York City shoemaker and master workman in 1887 of DA 91, the Sons and Daughters of St. Crispin.

To James Smith

Oct 13th [188]7

James W Smith Esq
2nd Vice President A.F of L
Dear Sir

Your very welcome letter came duly to hand and contents noted. Many thanks for information given. It is hardly necessary for me to assure you that I have no desire and that it is furthest from my purpose to involve the American Federation of Labor in any political broil, embroglio or party, but I wanted to know from what source the letters and circulars emenated.

I regret to learn what you say in reference to the feeling in Chicago. I am not aware of what they complain hence cannot make a denial. That I express my opinion as an individual in reference to proceedings in the trial and affirmation of the decision of the lower Court by the Supreme Court of Ill is true, but never have I used the name of the Federation. I abhor anarchy but I also abhor injustice when meted out, even to the most despicable being on earth. I am opposed to the hanging of the seven chicago anarchists for several reasons among them the following are most important. They are not charged with committing murder. No person assumes to know who threw the fatal bomb. Consequently no connection was or could be proven between the party who threw it and the seven condemned men who are charged with inciting some "person unknown" to throw it. So long as capital punishment is part of the laws of our States and Country if it should be enforced no discrimination should be indulged in favor of one nor the law strained to shield another class. Then again apart from any other reason if these men should be executed it would place a halo of martyrdom around them which would lead many to the violent agitation we so much deplore. In the interest of the cause of labor and the peaceful methods of improving the condition and achieving the final emancipation of labor I am opposed to their execution. It would be a blot on the escutcheon of our country. Pardon my voluibility and hoping to hear from [you] at an early day. I am

Yours Fraternally   Saml Gompers.

ALpS, reel 1, vol. 2, pp. 65-66, SG Letterbooks, DLC.

A Translation of a News Account of an Address at a Mass Meeting in New York City[1]

[October 21, 1887]

THIS MUST NOT BE ALLOWED!

. . .

SAMUEL GOMPERS

was greeted with loud applause and began: "I don't know what our chairman[2] means in saying that he wants to get even with the preceding speaker[3] through me. This is not the time to draw attention to the quarrels among workers; rather, we should do everything in our power to forget those quarrels.

"I am no friend of anarchism," he said, "but although I am radically different from those people in my thinking, I still say: Honor to those who assembled in front of McCormick's factory after the murders of the Pinkerton men. The presence of the wives and children of the condemned men shows clearly that these people did not intend to throw bombs. Carter Harrison,[4] whose political views I do not defend in the least, was dropped by his political cronies because he swore in accordance with the facts that he had told Inspector Bonfield[5] the meeting was a peaceful one. We have not come to defend criminals, but to prevent a crime that is being planned by the officials of the state of Illinois. Anarchism will never be eradicated by executing these people. Ideas based on truth have never been eradicated by violence, but false ideas have at times been elevated to a certain importance by the violence used to suppress them. Freedom of speech is the safety valve of society; if it is obstructed, there will be an explosion somewhere. It is dangerous to tamper with this right of ours.

"Nowhere else in the entire world do we have conditions as in the state of New York. If a 'mob' assembles somewhere, even for illegal purposes, people should be asked to go home before being attacked with clubs. We should have a riot act. In 1874 people were driven like rats into a trap; every avenue of retreat was cut off and then they were beaten to the ground.[6] (Hissing and Groaning.) I have just heard that the mayor of Chicago has forbidden any meeting of workers to protest the execution of the anarchists. Imagine! a mayor, not a horse! (Laughter.) Evidently an ass! (Shout: "a cockroach!" Applause.) To me he looks like an animal of prey. Imagine! a mayor giving orders on his own authority, that *this* is all right, and *that* isn't. We shall not let our voices be suffocated; the people will rise up in its majesty and protect its rights."

. . .

New Yorker Volkszeitung, Oct. 21, 1887. Translated from the German by Patrick McGrath.

1. The New York City Central Labor Union and KOL District Assembly 49 called the meeting to protest the sentencing of the Haymarket defendants.
2. Isaac Wood of the Pressmen's and Feeders' Union.
3. Courtland Palmer, a New York City lawyer.
4. Carter Harrison, the owner of the *Chicago Times*, served as Democratic mayor of Chicago from 1879 to 1887.
5. Inspector John Bonfield led the contingent of policemen at the Haymarket Square meeting.
6. On Jan. 13, 1874, New York workers organized a demonstration at Tompkins Square against unemployment and for increased public works. The police forcefully dispersed the crowd, injuring hundreds.

An Editorial by Samuel Gompers in the *Union Advocate*

[October 1887]

The capitalistic, no less than the aristocratic class, is responsible for the stupid and wicked policy that has turned many of the fairest lands of the world into huge military camps, and has deluged every continent in blood for the aggrandisement of their own countries, and to force upon the conquered peoples the products which their makers cannot consume in consequence of the lowness of their wages. The working-class, although its ignorance has sometimes made it the tool of politicians, cannot fairly be charged with any part of this guilt and folly. The wealth, greatness and glory of any nation have meant very little for the working-class. Rather, they have delayed its emancipation. It is the highest interest of every worker that he should concentrate his attention upon the Labor question. To the working-people it is of very little consequence whether the United States have a fleet of ironclads or whether the Republican, Democratic, or any other party are successful in their struggles for office, loaves and fishes; but it is of very great importance that they have a fair share of the products of their skill, of their brain and muscle; that the necessaries and comforts of life be within their reach; that they be not herded like brutes in poisonous tenements; that their children be spared the slavery of the coal bunkers and factory, and be permitted to acquire the

best possible education; that their noble feelings of human dignity be
not outraged by the arbitrary regulations of an irresponsible and
immoral capitalistic class. We, in this generation, by means of our
Trade Unions, have challenged the capitalistic policy, and we will not
cease our efforts until all workers regardless of creed, color, or nationality, are united in the fraternal bond of one grand federation,
making war and robbery forevermore impossible.

Union Advocate, Oct. 1887.

To Richard Oglesby[1]

New York, Nov 7th 1887

To His Excellency John R Oglesby
Govenor of Illinois
Dear Sir.

In the name of mercy, in the name of humanity, the undersigned
in behalf of the American Federation of Labor, composed of more
than half a million heads of families, bread winners earnestly implore
you to excercise your sovereign prerogative with which you are clothed
by the constitution of the great State of Illinois.

The organization I have the honor of representing is not anarchistic
but on the contrary looks upon that theory and movement as per-
versive of the best interests of labor.

Because of this opposition to the doctrine of anarchy I ask your
intervention to prevent an impetous being given that movement,
which it would unquestionably recieve with the execution of the condemned men.

In the name of true Order and progress, of the great State of
Illinois, of our common Country, Our people, of humanity I ask you
to extend clemency to August Spiess, Albert R Parsons, Samuel Fielden, Michael Schwab, Adolph Fischer, Geo Engel and Louis Ling and
commute the sentence of death pronounced upon them.

Grant this prayer and you will be blessed by the living and the
countless thousands yet unborn and incur the everlasting gratitude
of

Yours most Respectfully   Samuel Gompers.
President. American Federation of Labor.

ALS, Executive Clemency Files, Illinois State Archives, Springfield.

1. Richard James Oglesby was a Republican governor of Illinois (1865-69, 1873,
1885-89) and U.S. senator (1873-79).

A News Account of a Hearing to Consider Executive Clemency for the Haymarket Defendants[1]

Springfield, Ill., Nov. 9. [1887]

APPEALED TO FOR MERCY.

. . .

THE AFTERNOON AUDIENCE.

At the afternoon session the crowd was larger than ever. A program had been arranged at a meeting at the Leland Hotel, and George Schilling[2] was put in charge. He introduced the speakers. The first ones were William Bailey[3] and John Campbell[4] of Quincy, who presented a petition signed by 1,000 or more workingmen of that city. Both gentlemen urged commutation on the ground that it would tend to allay the feelings of the workingmen. William Urban,[5] representing the Central Labor Union of Chicago,[6] read the resolution passed by that body and published some time ago. President Oliver[7] of the Amnesty Association[8] made only a short talk. He said that petitions signed by 41,000 people in all parts of the country were presented. These did not include those sent from New York. Thirty-two thousand of the names had been obtained since the decision of the United States Supreme Court was rendered, showing that public feeling was just becoming aroused. The Governor asked if any of the names had been duplicated, to which Mr. Oliver replied he thought not. Mr. C. G. Dixon[9] read the petition of the United Labor party, which he followed with a very few words in favor of Executive clemency on the theory that the belief was general among the workingmen that the misguided Anarchists had got into trouble in their cause. Charles Schulenburg spoke for the Detroit labor societies, insisting that public policy and the peaceful accomplishment of social evolution demanded commutation. He was followed by Edward Goettache of the Chicago Platt Deutsche Gilde, who simply read a petition from that organization.

By far the best speech of the afternoon was made by Samuel Gompers of New York, President of the Federation of Trades of the United States and Canada, and one of the delegates from the New York trades assemblies. The Governor listened very carefully to the representative of that great organization and plainly showed by his questions that he was anxious to hear how the labor men in general regard the Anarchists. Mr. Gompers began by saying that a large field had already been gone over and fully covered by other gentlemen in presenting this case. He felt peculiarly situated in coming here and asking for executive clemency to men under sentence of death — peculiarly for more reasons than one. One was the fact that these men and he had differed all their lives. He continued as follows:

["]Because we have differed, because we may have been opponents and fighting for labor upon different sides of the house, I know of no reason why I should not raise my voice and ask you, sir, to interpose and save their lives from the gallows. The execution, I think, would be an execution not of justice, not to the interest of the great State of Illinois, not to the interest of the country, not to the interest of our fellowman. I come to you as a representative of the Central Labor Union of New York, besides as President of the American Federation of Labor, an organization extending throughout the country; an organization opposed to anarchy; an organization that seeks to improve the condition of workingmen by legal, peaceable, and honorable means and methods. In 1883 the Federation of American Trades and Labor Unions held a convention in the City of Chicago,[10] and there resolved, if possible, to reduce the hours of labor. It had been recognized by workingmen's organizations all over the country that it was necessary that the hours of labor be reduced in order to find employment for the unemployed. The 1st of May, 1886, the eight-hour rule went into effect wherever it was possible. The workingmen of Chicago were largely connected with that, and the reason of the struggle in Mc-Cormick's factories may be attributed in the main to the agitation of that question. There a man was killed, and if you will remember, sir, the meeting which was called in the haymarket square was called to protest against the killing of that one man. I want to say to you, sir, that I am not desirous of going into the details of the question. I don't believe I am competent to do so, but I believe that in some measure, however remote, the police of Chicago have been somewhat responsible for this trouble. I ask myself what good can come to the people of the State of Illinois; what good can come to the people of our country; what good can be added to the good name of our country and people if these men are executed? Are we not strong enough and intelligent enough to protect our lives and our interests as a people without the execution of these men? If these men are executed it would simply give an impetus to this so-called revolutionary movement which no other thing on earth can do. These men would, apart from any considertion of mercy, of humanity be looked upon as martyrs. Thousands and hundreds of thousands of laboring men all over the country would consider that those men had been executed because they were standing up for free speech and free assemblage. We ask you, sir, to interpose your great power and prevent so dire a calamity.

If this great country could be great and magnanimous enough to grant amnesty to Jeff Davis it ought to be great and magnanimous enough to grant clemency to these misguided men.["]

Gov. Oglesby — Did you say that in 1883, when the plan to organize the laboring men of the country, to organize a great National movement to reduce the hours of labor to eight instead of ten and twelve, and did you say that was intended by all the laboring men of the country to be a peaceable effort?

Mr. Gompers — Yes, sir.

Gov. Oglesby — That the laboring men desire to bring about that change in the hours of the day's labor by persuasion, by reason, by presenting themselves to the employers and the public, and in no other method was it contemplated to gain the object desired?

Mr. Gompers — Yes, sir. And permit me to add that the Secretary of the Federation, who was then Mr. William H. Foster,[11] and I, your humble servant, who was then ex-President, had blanks printed which were to be presented by the working men and women asking the consent of the employers to reduce the hours of labor. These blanks were filled with the signatures obtained.

Gov. Oglesby — The purpose of the laboring men of the country, so far as you know, was an honest effort to reduce the hours of labor?

Mr. Gompers — Yes, sir.

Mr. Gompers closed by saying the throwing of the bomb had destroyed the eight-hour movement.

Edward King and James E. Quinn of New York also made brief speeches, and the public reception was closed by a brief speech by George Schilling, representing Districts Nos. 25 and 57, Chicago. He said the idea was getting abroad that the poor man obtained very little consideration under the law and that the rich man did as he pleased. This could be proved a false idea by the commutation of the sentence. This closed the public reception, and the Governor went into his private office to receive the women relatives of the condemned men.

Chicago Tribune, Nov. 10, 1887.

1. On Nov. 9, 1887, Governor Richard J. Oglesby convened a public hearing on the issue of executive clemency for the Haymarket defendants. At the morning session Captain William P. Black, defense attorney, Cora V. Richmond, a spiritualist from Chicago, Elijah H. Haines, former Speaker of the Illinois house, and state Senator A. J. Streeter, among others, offered appeals to the governor. Labor representatives dominated the afternoon session. Altogether, some 300 supporters attended the hearing.

2. George Adam SCHILLING, a Chicago cooper and publisher associated with the anarchist and socialist movements, represented KOL district assemblies 24 and 57.

3. William Bailey represented the Quincy, Ill., Trades and Labor Assembly.

4. John Campbell was a Quincy, Ill., molder.

5. William Urban, a Chicago printer, was president of International Typographical Union (ITU) 9.

6. The Trade and Labor Assembly of Chicago divided in 1884 and its more radical members organized the Chicago Central Labor Union, which continued until 1896.

7. Lucien S. Oliver worked as a painter in Chicago.

8. Supporters of the Haymarket defendants founded the Amnesty Association to circulate petitions for a pardon.

9. Charles G. Dixon, a carpenter, businessman, and politician, was a leader of the United Labor party.

10. The FOTLU held its fourth annual session in Chicago, Oct. 7-10, 1884.

11. William Henry FOSTER, a typographer, was secretary of Philadelphia's Central Labor Union; he was elected as FOTLU Legislative Committee secretary in 1881, 1882, and 1885.

To William Cremer[1]

Nov. 19, [188]7

Mr Wm R. Cremer, M.P.
Grand Central Hotel, New York City
Dear Sir:

The American Federation of Labor charged with the solemn duty of defending the interests of the working people of this vast continent fully recognises that human activity in all ages and in all countries has been chiefly exhibited in two radically different forms, the one military, the other industrial, — or in other words, in fighting and in working — and that the former has invariably declined in an exact ratio to the growth of the latter Therefore we hail with deep satisfaction the arrival of an embassy from our mother country charged with the noble duty of proposing a treaty of perpetual peace between the two great political divisions of the English-speaking people.[2] We sincerely hope that your exalted mission will prove successfu[l] beyond your most sanguine expectations. We feel and know that the aspirations of your delegation and of the A.F. of L. are identical. The voice of the workers will never be heard in all its strength, grandeur, pathos, and infinite delicacy until war's rude trumpet shall be stilled.

For this we bid you welcome to the New World, and believe us our welcome is heartier because one, at least, of your delegation is by birth and education of that social class to which we belong; of that class which has the most profound interest in the establishment of peace.

Furthermore, we feel that it would be a public calamity if your delegation should return without hearing the voice of the workers organized in trade unions. The A.F. of L. has issued a call for a convention of delegates from all Local, National, and International Trades Unions to be held in Baltimore, Maryland, December 13, 1887.[3] The representation in this convention will be on the basis of five delegates from every thirty-two thousand men organized in the union of their trade. Therefore, we would respectfully request you to delay your departure until the representatives of organized labor are in convention assembled.

Hoping that you and your honorable associates will favorably consider a request which I shall have the happiness to forward you to address this convention of the muscle, and I might say, the mind and conscience, of the American people, I am,

Yours fraternally,   Saml Gompers.
President, American Federation of Labor.

HLpSr, reel 1, vol. 2, pp. 97-99, SG Letterbooks, DLC.

1. William Randal Cremer (1838-1908), a leading proponent of international arbitration, was a member of the Amalgamated Society of Carpenters and Joiners. He was secretary of the British section of the International Workingmen's Association in 1865, and in 1871 formed the Workmen's Peace Association, later renamed the International Arbitration League, serving as its secretary until his death. In 1885 he was elected to Parliament on a Liberal-Labour ticket and retained his seat until 1895.

2. In October 1887 a delegation of members of the British Parliament presented to President Grover Cleveland a memorial signed by 234 Members of Parliament favoring a treaty of arbitration between Great Britain and the United States. Cremer, originator of the memorial, addressed the AFL's 1887 Baltimore convention. Following Cremer's speech, SG introduced a resolution favoring international arbitration that the convention adopted. The two countries did not sign an arbitration treaty until 1914.

3. The 1887 AFL convention was held in Baltimore, Dec. 13-17.

A Series of News Accounts of the 1887 Convention of the AFL in Baltimore

[December 13, 1887]

LABOR MEN HERE NOW.

Mr. Samuel Gompers, president of the American Federation of Labor, is now in the city. To an *American* reporter yesterday he said: "When I was in Baltimore and addressed the Federation I had the pleasure of a visit to the Johns Hopkins University with Messrs. Charles P. Oyler[1] and Samuel B. Hasson,[2] and I look back with pleasure to that pleasant interview with Prof. Richard T. Ely, when that gentleman so courteously gave us his views on economic subjects, and explained his plan of study. I would like to have Prof. Ely address the American Federation. In my position, as president of such a great body of workingmen, I have felt deeply the importance of a calm and proper comprehension of all labor questions and the way out of the difficulties that beset our people. To that end, I try to study all I can in the little time I can spare from my duties as president and editor of the journal of the organization, the *Union Advocate*. I find that my editorial duties assist me in this study. With a view to post myself, I have studied German that I may the better examine for myself German writers on economic and social subjects, and thus be able to digest more satisfactorily the German school of political economy. In my study of the labor situation in this and other countries I find that there is a growing international exchange of views by correspondence between the trades unions of different nations. Thus, for instance, far-distant Australia sends to the rest of the world circular statements from the carpenters' unions warning carpenters not to come there under the false impression of hoping to get big wages, for prices are as low there as $1 to $1.20 a day, while many skilled workmen walk the streets. So also correspondence comes from Belgium, France and England in regard to the state of trade. Our Cigarmakers' International Union often admits members on its books direct from Germany and other countries. So the brotherhood of man becomes worldwide."

When asked about the outlook for his organization he replied:

"We have in the American Federation of Labor about forty-five national and international trades unions, besides some local organizations, and we represent a large membership. It is hard to get at the exact numbers. The growth has surprised me. I think there will be a good attendance of delegates to-morrow. I have to travel a great deal. The Milwaukee Trades Council[3] have just arranged for me a program of a series of meetings throughout the Western country, and I expect to make the trip.[4] I will arrange to travel from point to point in a continuous course, so as to save expense, for we boast that we run everything as economically as possible. I receive no extra pay for these lectures or addresses in the cause of labor. I find that mass meetings and addresses are a great means of building up our organization. Our boast is, both among our general officers and locals, to have just as little red tape as possible. Immediately after the close of the session of the American Federation here I will start on my trip through the states. On the 19th I speak at Binghamton, N.Y.; 20th,

Buffalo; 21st, Rochester; 22d, Saratoga; 23d, Troy. After New Year's I speak in other cities in New York until January 20, when I speak in Cleveland, O., and after that go on the trip through the West, which has been marked out for me by the Milwaukee trades union.

"The newspapers treat us very fairly nowadays. You see, they and the people are beginning to recognize the fact that organized labor is not composed of a wild set of fanatics, but it is a business organization, like any other, for the protection of common business interests."

A Call on Mayor Latrobe.[5]

In the afternoon at two o'clock Messrs. M. J. McHenry[6] and W. J. T. Cooney,[7] of the Baltimore Federation of Labor[8] reception committee, escorted President Gompers and the delegates then present — which included all who had arrived at that hour — from headquarters, room 166, Eutaw House, to call on Mayor Latrobe at the City Hall.

The following were the delegates: S. Barend,[9] of the Central Labor Union of Brooklyn and vicinity;[10] Hugh McGregor,[11] clerk of the American Federation; Edward J. Boyle,[12] organizer Oyster Shuckers' National Union, of New York; J. Pender,[13] delegate Oyster Shuckers' National Union; S. Goldwater,[14] of the Trades Council, of Detroit, Mich.;[15] ex-Mayor Daniel McLaughlin,[16] and now member of the legislature of Illinois, representing the Federation of Miners and Mine Laborers, of Braidwood; John Morrison, president of the National Organ Makers' Union,[17] of Warren county, New York; Charles H. Mettee,[18] of the Paperhangers' Union, of Baltimore, and G. Edmonson, of Washington city, of the National Organization of the Brotherhood of Carpenters and Joiners.

Mayor Latrobe, when introduced, expressed his pleasure at meeting the president and delegates of the American Federation of Labor, and said: "Gentlemen, I am much pleased to see you in this informal manner; but, I believe I am to have the pleasure of paying you a formal visit to-morrow morning at the Concordia Opera House."

To this President Gompers replied that they expected to have that pleasure.

Mayor Latrobe, in a pleasant conversational manner, said: "I like to see labor organize, for I do not know what it could do, or what would become of it, without organization. Organization is necessary to labor; that it may be properly represented, just the same as through our Congress the whole people are represented in the making of their laws. Organization is necessary to protect your interests, for individuals can do nothing. They must act through their representatives, and that means organization."

President Gompers, who is a short, alert and strongly-built man, continued the conversation by looking up to the tall form of Mayor Latrobe and smilingly, but earnestly, saying: "I consider that organization is a natural thing, evolved from circumstances. Our object in organization is rather to have one based on common sense, in which we can bring the experience of the past to settle difficulties in the present, rather than to have a pet theory of any man. We try to have a straight organization, based on business principles."

IT IS NO SMALL BODY.

Mayor Latrobe asked Mr. Gompers how many men the American Federation of Labor represented, and said he supposed several hundred thousand.

President Gompers replied: "It is hard to say what are the exact numbers; but, just to illustrate: Here we have a few delegates, and these gentlemen here represent about 250,000 members of their respective national organizations. Here is Mr. McLaughlin, of the coal miners, [who] represents 45,000 men. The typographical union represents 33,000. The cigarmakers, [of] which I and two others are the representatives, have 29,000 members. The Brotherhood of Carpenters and Joiners have 42,000 members. The Central Labor Union, of Brooklyn, has 80,000 [8,000?]; the Detroit union, 6,000. Here is the oystermen's union, a growing body, represented by my young friend Boyle. He has only been a year in a labor union; but during that year he has done a big work organizing the oyster shuckers, and he deserves credit for it. He has worked for the best interests of his craft. He wants to assist in organizing the oyster shuckers of Baltimore, and he deserves the sympathy and active cooperation of all."

Mayor Latrobe then took up the conversation, and said: "There is no class in Baltimore, connected with the oyster business, that ought to meet with more sympathy than the unfortunate fellows who are taken on as dredgers. Heavenly pictures are drawn of the joys and pleasures of an oyster dredger's life, and they are 'shanghaied' into service on the oyster dredgers."

Mr. Boyle, of New York, made the remark that he read about it, and that a stop should be put to it. Such a thing could not happen in New York.

The Mayor continued: "A poor fellow came here the other day and wanted transportation back to Philadelphia, and the city furnished it. They had charged him $9 from Philadelphia, and all his employer had paid him was fifty cents. Poor fellows, there is no one to protect them, and they need protection. The captain of the schooner does not bring them back to Baltimore; but, in this case, the poor fellow, having injured himself in some way, so he could not work, was put ashore down the country, and had to make his way here. I think the Federation of Labor ought to look after their case."

Mr. A. J. King,[19] having come into the room, said: "The poor fellows, when asked how they got caught in such a trap, said they were so hungry that they had their mouths open, and were caught with hook and line." This caused a little laughter.

Then all, pleased with the trip, shook hands and left.

A Trip to the Crescent Club.

Mr. M. J. McHenry then invited President Gompers and the delegates to pay a visit to the Crescent Club and inspect that building. They did so, and there met and engaged in pleasant conversation with Police Commissioner A. J. Carr[20] and Clerk of the City Court Henry A. Schultz. The delegates expressed themselves as much pleased with what they saw at the Crescent Club. One of the delegates, while reclining in one of the handsomely upholstered chairs in the drawing-room, laughingly remarked that it almost equalled his parlor.

The American Federation opens to-day at nine o'clock in the concert hall of the Concordia Opera House, and at ten o'clock Mayor Latrobe will deliver an address. The delegates and their friends appeared to enjoy themselves yesterday at the headquarters, at the Eutaw House.

. . .

Baltimore American, Dec. 13, 1887.

1. Charles P. OYLER served as seventh vice-president of the CMIU from 1888 to 1890.

2. Samuel B. HASSON was president of the Baltimore Federation of Labor from 1888 to 1889.

3. The Milwaukee Federated Trades Council was organized in 1887.

4. See "To the Executive Council of the AFL," Feb. 28, 1888, below.

5. Ferdinand Claiborne Latrobe served seven two-year terms as Democratic mayor of Baltimore between 1875 and 1895.

6. Michael J. McHenry, a glassblower employed by the Baltimore health department, was a member of KOL Local Assembly (LA) 1233.

7. William J. T. Cooney, a Baltimore printer, was a member of KOL LA 1233, served several terms as president of International Typographical Union 12, and was president of the Baltimore Federation of Labor from 1885 to 1887.

8. The Baltimore Federation of Labor was organized in 1883.

9. Simon Barend was a member of CMIU 132 of Brooklyn and secretary in the late 1880s of the Brooklyn Central Labor Union (CLU).

10. The Brooklyn CLU was organized in 1884.

11. Hugh McGregor, a jeweler, served as SG's secretary during the late 1880s, directing the AFL office during the president's absence.

12. J. P. Boyle was involved in organizing oystermen for the AFL.

13. Edward J. Pender, president of Oystermen's Union 1 of New York City, was active during the late 1880s in organizing oystermen's unions in Maryland and Delaware.

14. Samuel Goldwater was a founder of the Chicago Trade and Labor Council, was twice president of the Detroit Trade and Labor Council, and helped organize the Michigan Federation of Labor.

15. The Detroit Trade and Labor Council was founded in 1880.

16. Daniel McLaughlin served as first vice-president of the AFL for one term (1887-88). He helped organize the National Federation of Miners and Mine Laborers in 1885, serving as its treasurer from 1885 to 1888, and was a founder of the National Progressive Union of Miners and Mine Laborers in 1888.

17. The United Association of Organ Makers.

18. Charles H. Mettee was a member of the Baltimore Paperhangers' Union.

19. Andrew J. King was clerk to the mayor of Baltimore.

20. Alfred J. Carr, a lawyer, was treasurer of the Baltimore Board of Police Commissioners in 1887.

[December 14, 1887]

LABOR MEN IN COUNCIL.

The American Federation of Labor met in annual session yesterday morning at 10 o'clock in the new annex hall of the Concordia, with President Gompers in the chair. After a welcome from Mayor Latrobe and by President N. B. Talbott,[1] of the local Federation, a reply from Mr. Gompers and the appointment of the credential committee the delegates adjourned to meet at 2:30 P.M. During the afternoon session the credentials of all were accepted except the delegates of the Washington Federation of Trade and Labor Unions.[2] Committees were appointed on constitution, resolutions, rules, finance and reports. President Gompers read his annual address, and the body adjourned to meet at 9 o'clock this morning. The men as a body are fine looking, and their powers of debate were brought out in the first fight of the day, upon the admission of the delegation from the Washington Federation. The delegates showed themselves masters of parliamentary usage, and of some two dozen who took the floor all were ready and ingenious speakers. President Gompers is a careful and decisive chairman, and has to know his business thoroughly among the trained parliamentarians he must face. The strained relations of the Unionists toward the Knights of Labor assumed form at the outset in the dispute about the Washington delegation, who represented but three unions and nineteen assemblies of the Knights of Labor. There was a large

element desiring harmony, even at the expense of nagging a point.
The powerful opposition of P. J. McGuire, after having first spoken
favorably to the admission of the Washingtonians, did the work, however, carrying the convention against them by a vote of 37 to 7. There
was general applause also at the portion of President Gompers's address where he says there is no cause for discord.[3]

. . .

It was moved by Delegate John S. Kirchner,[4] of the International
Cigarmakers, that the report[5] be accepted, but that the Washington
Federation delegates be excluded. He made a lengthy speech, saying
that the delegates represented nothing that was favorable to trades-
union principles. He then asked what was the complexion of the
Washington body.

Mr. Oyster[6] said: "Its complexion is black and white and represents
nineteen assemblies of the Knights of Labor, nine of which are building trades. It represents three trades-unions—the Typographical,[7]
Bricklayers[8] and Carpenters, No. 1."[9]

Mr. Kirchner said the Washington Federation's motives, as well as
the delegate's, were insincere. He was rapped down for personality,
but continued, saying the Knights in the Washington body owed allegiance to the Knights of Labor and could not be loyal to the Federation. The Federation also had a body tributary composed of carpenters who were expelled from the Brotherhood of Carpenters.

The discussion was fought upon the question of the carpenters'
union, and several delegates spoke for their admission, faint applause
on both sides manifesting itself.

Mr. Ogden,[10] of the Typographical Union, made a speech for admission and general harmony, which brought out strong applause.

Secretary McGuire said that notwithstanding the defection of the
Brotherhood of Carpenters in Washington and other matters, if Mr.
Oyster could bespeak the loyalty of the Washington body to the Fed-
eration, he would vote for them.

After several others had spoken, some favoring and others opposing,
Mr. McGuire said the more he thought of the matter the more he
became convinced that the Washington Federation should be excluded. He said: "Here is a body, 19 tributaries of which are loyal to
the K. of L. alone. Of its three trades-unions one is already represented
here, one was expelled from its national body for transgression of
law, and had since thrown everything in the way of progress of the
Brotherhood of Carpenters, and the other union, the bricklayers, had
never asked their national body to attach itself to the American Federation. What right had that federation in Washington to boycott

union labels and oppose Mr. Edmonston, who stood by his little Brotherhood Union when the other carpenters went over to the K. of L.? It's a question if they could prove their loyalty to us. And as to allegiance, I'd like to know if District 66[11] does not control the Washington body. I don't believe in fighting the Knights of Labor, but when they touch us we would be poor men indeed if we did not defend ourselves." He also alluded to the "machine on Broad street."[12] This carried the convention, and the Washingtonians were disposed of. . . .

Baltimore Sun, Dec. 14, 1887.

1. Nicholas B. Talbott was president of International Typographical Union (ITU) 12 of Baltimore in 1887 and later served as president of the Baltimore Federation of Labor (June 1887–January 1888, February-August 1889).

2. In 1881 KOL assemblies helped form the Washington, D.C., Federation of Labor; the KOL controlled the organization through the 1890s. The Federation sent delegates to the FOTLU conventions, but the 1887 AFL convention refused to seat its delegate, contending that the Washington organization "was not fully in sympathy with the trades-union movement, as it was overwhelmingly composed of Knights of Labor Assemblies" (AFL, *Proceedings,* 1887, p. 8). The Federation remained the District's dominant central labor body until the organization of the Washington, D.C., Central Labor Union in 1896.

3. Gompers said, "There is no conflict necessary between the trades unions and the Knights of Labor" (ibid., p. 10).

4. John S. KIRCHNER was secretary of CMIU 100 of Philadelphia (1881, 1884-90), CMIU fourth vice-president (1885-87), and an organizer for Pennsylvania.

5. That is, the report of the credentials committee.

6. Edward W. Oyster was a member of ITU 101 of Washington, D.C.

7. ITU 101.

8. District of Columbia local 1 of the Bricklayers' and Masons' International Union of America.

9. A division among organized carpenters in Washington, D.C., developed in 1886 when local 1 of the Brotherhood of Carpenters and Joiners of America (BCJA) refused to pay its dues in protest against the Brotherhood's equalizing or redistribution of the funds of all locals on a per capita basis. It opposed the BCJA's use of funds to support a benefits system, wanting to reserve its treasury for organizing purposes and the securing of a standard wage. The BCJA expelled local 1 as of Oct. 1, 1886, and organized a new local, number 190, which elected Gabriel Edmonston president. Most of local 1's members joined the KOL, and although the local itself remained independent it cooperated closely with KOL Local Assembly 1784. The two carpenters' unions fought bitterly for control of the city's carpentry trade.

10. Harry M. Ogden was a member of ITU 3 of Cincinnati.

11. KOL District Assembly 66 was organized in late 1883.

12. The headquarters of the KOL was located on Broad St. in Philadephia.

THE LABOR CONVENTION.

. . .

The members yesterday stirred quietly the first breeze of intestine politics, the main point being, of course, the presidency. The majority seem to favor Mr. Gompers's re-election, but John McBride, of the Ohio miners,[1] who presided to the great satisfaction of all at Columbus, was spoken of, and the Western delegates may try to elect him.

It was said that McBride could not be tempted to take the position at $1,000, as he is already getting $1,200 as the president of the Ohio miners, but when the constitution was altered to increase the president's salary to $1,200 it was regarded by some as a bid for McBride.

Jno. S. Kirchner, of the Cigarmakers' Union, it is said will also be a candidate. Kirchner is a very young man with very mature judgment. He has spoken on almost every question before the convention, and is a very hard man to overcome. He uses very correct, not to say direct, language, and carries points more by force of argument than by magnetism.

McBride is a tall, well-formed man, of polished manners, with pleasant, smiling face. He is exceedingly calm in debate, clear in diction, and is a thorough analyst; being in this something like Kirchner, but without the latter's thrusting qualities. His words carry more weight possibly than those of any other man in the body.

P. J. McGuire will serve no longer as secretary, his duties in the Brotherhood of Carpenters requiring all his time. Who will be secretary no one is saying, and there will probably be no fighting about it, as there is nothing but hard work and no pay.

. . .

Baltimore Sun, Dec. 16, 1887.

1. The Ohio Miners' Amalgamated Association.

OF INTEREST TO LABOR.

. . .

At the afternoon session, which met at 2:30 P.M., the whole time was spent in discussion of amendments to the constitution, and, after extending the time of adjournment to seven o'clock, the work was not completed when that hour arrived.

During the discussion Mr. McBride, of the Miners' Association, created some amusement by emphatically objecting to wasting time which he said should be devoted to business, and not to unnecessary quibbles over the phraseology of sections of the constitution.

The important work of the afternoon was to define the absolute position of the body as a trade union organization entirely distinct from the Knights of Labor. The discussion developed the fact that while some of the delegates were inclined to widen the breach between trades unions and the Knights of Labor, there were fully one-half of the delegates who were directly or indirectly connected with that order. This line of discussion was developed on the proposition to strike out the words "and labor" in the preamble, so as to make it read "trade unions of America." This was carried.

It was claimed that labor would apply to unskilled workmen, and the admission of unskilled workmen had been the cause of trouble in the Knights of Labor, and the source of power against trade unions, which was greatly the source of the trouble between the two organizations. Mr. Kerschner, of the Cigarmakers', urged that they wanted to keep the autonomy of the trades by getting rid of the system adopted by the K. of L., by which one trade had power over another.

Mr. McBride, of the Miners' Association, made a telling speech in favor of accepting the report of the committee on the constitution, and not tearing their work to pieces, saying it was impossible to have it perfect.

Delegate Ogden, of [the] Typographical Union, said there were a number of delegates on the floor who were directly or indirectly connected with the Knights of Labor, belonging to both unions and assemblies.

SKILLED AND UNSKILLED LABOR.

A delegate said if they drew a line between skilled and unskilled labor, they would lose membership, as the Knights of Labor had done. He said: "Take unskilled men in, and then they will stand by you in a strike, and not take your places."

President Gompers saying, "It has been well said, where will we begin to draw the line between skilled and unskilled labor. I am here to-day in the interest of labor. It is hard to draw the line; for instance, my friends of the Typographical Union spoke about distinctions. In the Typographical Union there are unskilled workmen. In my union there are packers, rollers, bunch breakers, strippers and selectors, and every man working in the trade is eligible. So the iron and steel workers take in their helpers. What we want is to take in those who work at manual labor—not with mind only, mark you. If we excluded unskilled labor we would exclude organizations of hod-carriers just about to join this Federation. All have to learn. I hope you will define clearly what you mean by skilled and unskilled labor, if the amendment passes."

This amendment was carried: "We, therefore, recognize the necessity for the existence of organizations based upon the trade union form of organization."

Mr. Kirschner, of the Cigarmakers', then proposed this amendment: "But no organization shall be entitled to representation unless the application for a charter has been received a month previous to the time of meeting of the convention."

Mr. Burt's[1] resolution settled the question by being carried. The issue was made upon denying local unions admission to the Federation.

Mr. Burt's resolution provided that a local or district trade union, not connected with a national, could join "providing that this does not imply that a local or district trade union, not connected with, or having a national or international head, affiliated with this federation, shall not have a vote in the national convention."

ACTION ON SECEDED ORGANIZATIONS.

Then came up the discussion of section 2 of article 4. This section was as follows: "No organization which has seceded from any local, national or internationl organization shall be allowed a representation or recognition in this federation."

Mr. Burt proposed to strike out all this section. He said: "My opposition hangs on the word 'seceded.' I am convinced before the year is out organizations which have seceded from another organization will apply for admission into the Federation, and they can't come in under that section."

President Gompers suggested that they strike out the word organization and substitute "trade unions."

Mr. Miller,[2] of Philadelphia, of the Textile Workers,[3] said they expected to take in District Assembly 126[4] of Philadelphia Textile Workers, which had been expelled from the Knights of Labor, and if they did the amendment would exclude him and his organization.

Mr. McBride's amendment to insert "connected with this Federation" was carried, and the section then read as follows: "No organization which has seceded from any local, national or international organization connected with this Federation shall be allowed a representation in this Federation."

Mr. John Elliott,[5] of the Painters,[6] offered a resolution that the Federation and all central bodies be required to elect delegates, not already elected, to the American Federation by national organizations. It was referred.

The following resolution was passed: "Resolved, that no central organization, hostile to this organization, or with any organization connected with the Federation, be admitted, etc."

Mr. Burt, of the Wheeling, W.Va., Trades Federation,[7] opposed this, saying: "Reverse that, and see how it will work. I decline to vote for it, for the Ohio Valley Trade Assembly might at any time be appealed to by the Cigarmakers' Union at Barnesville, Ohio,[8] and they might be denied admission. Our assembly is declared eligible to get a charter, with seventeen Knights of Labor assemblies; and yet, this is about the same condition of the Federation of Washington, which is denied representation here. It is a poor rule that won't work both ways."

McBride here said: "We don't say you must take in, but that you must keep out."

President Gompers here announced that the father-in-law of the chairman of the reception committee had died, and that Mr. J. M. McHenry would take his place.

General Secretary McGuire here proposed to substitute for the *Union Advocate,* the organ which cost from $850 to $950 a year, and entailed much labor on the president, a monthly circular.

After a long debate, in which Delegate Holland[9] said the *Union Advocate* was what brought him to the Federation, they decided to issue quarterly numbers instead of monthly, or quarterly circulars as they decided upon.

PRESIDENT'S SALARY INCREASED.

On the amendment to increase the president's salary to $1,200, Mr. Miller, of the textile workers, voted against the increase, saying that too high salaries was a cause of trouble in the Knights of Labor, and his organization had ordered him not to vote for any increase. The increase was carried. The question of assessments, not over five cents per member, but to be obligatory and not voluntary, then came before the body.

Mr. McBride said forced assessments meant the ruin of the Federation. "It would be the rock on which we would split."

Mr. Daily,[10] of the New England Lasters' Association, opposed assessments to aid strikes. He said: "We don't want the world to get the idea that we are a great striking machine, like they had of the K. of L. We have seen 65,000 men out on a strike because they thought 600,000 were back of them to sustain them with five cent assessments."

The sentiment seemed to be against assessments, and seven o'clock having arrived, it was laid over, and the Federation adjourned until to-morrow morning.

Baltimore American, Dec. 16, 1887.

1. Joseph H. Burt (variously Burtt), a glassworker from Wheeling, W.Va., was a member of American Flint Glass Workers' Union 53. He served as a general organizer for the AFL in the late 1880s and unsuccessfully challenged SG for the presidency of the AFL in 1891.

2. Isaac B. Miller, a Philadelphia weaver, represented the Textile Workers' Progressive Union.

3. The TEXTILE Workers' Progressive Union of America.

4. The KOL organized National Trade Assembly (NTA) 126 of carpet weavers in early 1886. By the end of that year, however, the Knights had suspended NTA 126 over a controversy concerning trade autonomy.

5. John T. ELLIOTT helped organize the Brotherhood of Painters and Decorators of America in 1887 and served as its secretary until 1900.

6. The Brotherhood of PAINTERS and Decorators of America.

7. Probably the Ohio Valley Trades and Labor Assembly, founded in 1882, which moved from Ohio to Wheeling, W.Va., in 1885.

8. CMIU 284.

9. Thomas Holland of St. Louis represented the Horse Collar Makers' National Union.

10. Edward L. DALEY was the general secretary of the New England Lasters' Protective Union from 1885 to 1895.

[December 17, 1887]

LABOR'S COUNCIL FIRE.

. . .

The day opened in lively style with a labyrinthine entanglement on the assessment question. Mr. Martin[1] offered a resolution, to be engrafted on the "voluntary contribution" clause for strike and boycott support, so as to make "contributions" mandatory "assessments" upon the call of the general officers of the American Federation, the sum not to exceed five cents per week from each person in the tributary unions throughout the country, the assessment to continue until the settlement of the trouble. This was strengthened by an addition that any organization not complying shall be suspended until full payments are made.

Union rights, or autonomy, exactly the same question as States' rights in federal affairs, was the great point upon which all such questions hinged, and, as in national affairs, the object of the American Federation was to concentrate the greatest power possible for the general labor welfare, and at the same time make good the guarantee of unrestricted freedom for each primary union. This, it will be remembered, was the foundation, which differs so greatly from that of the Knights of Labor, and which was the tacitly understood principle of the original confederation of national trades at their first convention, last year.

Hence the word "autonomy" was heard almost as many times as "Mr. President."

To settle this question it was relegated to the referendum system by the following clause, which was passed: "Resolved to refer these sections to popular vote in all organizations affiliated with the Federation, the same to be decided by a two-thirds vote and to be acted upon at the next convention."

The word boycott was omitted at first, but Delegate Kirchner said: "I believe in boycotting all obnoxious employers who deny the rights of labor and oppress the working people when it is clearly proven they have been unjust. I don't believe in mincing matters like the Knights of Labor, who have, when occasion suited, said they would not boycott, would not strike, and would not, in fact, do anything."

Delegate Emrich said: "I concur in that idea. Just so long as employers victimize men who have been active in labor organization, blacklisting them and hounding and boycotting them from shop to shop and from town to town, we will boycott." This was followed by applause, and in the Federation "boycott" will hereafter be the word.

President Gompers evidently did not think so on Wednesday, for he appointed a committee on "withholding labor's patronage from employers inimical to organized labor." This terminology alone, if telegraphed from the convention to all the daily papers, would cost about $5,000 more than the simple word "boycott," and so it is a boon for which newspapers may thank Mr. Kirchner. But how about Jay Gould?

The body then reduced the per capita tax from the former rate of one-half cent to one-quarter cent per month, with the admission fee of each State and mixed trade federation to be $25. The tax is reduced, therefore, from six to three cents a year.

The remuneration of the executive council and of organizers and speakers on duty was put at $3 a day and expenses.

It was decided that "when one or more trades belong to a national or international union, they may organize a central federation, but must exclude any union that is outside of its national or international body, if such exist."

Delegate Edmonston proposed that the executive council should have the power to increase the president's salary to $1,500 when the finances permitted. It was snowed under.

Delegate John S. Kirchner proposed that an organizer should be elected annually. McGuire opposed it on the ground that the increase of salaried officers was dangerous; tending to cause a struggle for

offices, which feature had caused so much corruption at the K. of L.
Minneapolis convention.

The last section of the constitution, requiring a two-thirds vote for
ratifying amendments, was reported by the committee, with the omission of the clause "And must be ratified within six weeks thereafter
by a majority vote of the members of societies composing this Federation." Again the referendum question broke out.

It is a darling principle of socialism that democracy can only be
subserved by referring all questions back to the people, and the well-
known socialists in the convention stoutly defended this sheet-anchor
of democracy. The vote for striking out the section was 35 to 19.
This was not a two-thirds vote, as already required by the constitition.
Somebody called for Gompers's vote, and he voted to strike. This
left it two-thirds of one vote short of a necessary two-thirds erasure
vote. McBride bobbed up to the rescue. He said: "This don't require
a two-thirds vote. This is not to change the constitution. It's only to
accept the committee's report.["] Mr. Gompers had a little spar with
McBride, which resulted in his refusing to preside pending the question. Just then Dr. Richard T. Ely was escorted into the room.

The referendum was stricken out at last, the chief objection being
that many of the organizations had no machinery to return a popular
vote result to this body. Then the old constitution was stricken out
and the new one adopted, the dying year suggesting probably, "Ring
out the old, ring in the new." It is possible, however, that the constitution is not yet adopted, because the law in force when the change
was made is still the old constitution which demands the referendum.

· · ·

AFTER THE KNIGHTS AGAIN.

"The attitude of the Knights of Labor towards many of the trades-
unions connected with the American Federation has been anything
but friendly, and while their declaration of principles advocates assistance to trades-unions, their practices in many cases have been
entirely foreign to those principles. While we agree that a conflict is
not desirable on our part, we also believe that the party or power
which seeks to exterminate the trades-unions of this country should
be met with unrelenting opposition, whether that power consists of
millionaire employers or men who title themselves Knights of Labor.
The Knights of Labor during the last four years have constantly and
persistently declared that the trades-unions must go. Yet the absolute
failure of that declaration is clearly seen in the almost unanimous
demand among their own members for trade charters. We recommend

the utmost resistance on the part of the Federation to all encroachments upon its constituent bodies, irrespective of the quarter from
which they come."

This was declared passed unanimously by a rising vote, but one
member at least did not rise.

"The wonderful numerical expansion of the Federation of Labor
in the past year is due to workingmen joining bodies under self-control,
defections from the K. of L., and desire for open organization."

Mr. Gompers moved a resolution, which was unanimously passed,
declaring that as [the] American Federation was intrusted with American labor interests, which can only be secured by universal peace,
the body hails the English delegation on arbitration, and thanks Wm.
R. Creamer, M.P.

To this was added, by Joseph Wilkinson,[2] (Tailors')[3] "And we also
extend our sympathies to the people of Ireland in their struggle for
self-government, and condemn the present policy of the British government in their coercion of the Irish people."

ELECTION OF OFFICERS.

The election of officers was carried on harmoniously, with the following result: President, Samuel Gompers, International Cigarmakers;
first vice-president, Daniel McLaughlin, Ohio Miners; second vice-
president, Wm. Martin, Amalgamated Iron and Steel Workers; secretary, P. J. McGuire, Brotherhood of Carpenters; treasurer, Gabriel
Edmonston, Brotherhood of Carpenters. Three ballots were taken on
the place of the next convention, which resulted in St. Louis. Chicago,
Toronto and Pittsburg were also considered, and when Holland, the
jolly horse-collar man, from St. Louis, heard the decision he gave a
groan of relief that made the floor tremble and raised a general laugh.

McGuire was not going to run, but as bad feeling was manifested
against Flint-Glass-Worker J. H. Burt on account of supposed K. of
L. proclivities, McGuire said he would accept. Burt did not want the
place, and was only forced to an acceptance when the unpleasantness
occurred. There was no opposition to any candidate. Edmonston was
elected by a rising vote on account of circulars assailing him distributed
late in the evening by E. W. Oyster, the rejected Washington delegate.
John S. Kirchner objected to statements made by delegates to a *Sun*
reporter and published that he had presidential aspirations.

. . .

Baltimore Sun, Dec. 17, 1887.

1. William MARTIN was secretary of the National Amalgamated Association of Iron

and Steel Workers from 1878 to 1890 and a vice-president of the AFL from 1886 to 1890.

2. Joseph WILKINSON was secretary of the Journeymen Tailors' National Union of the United States from 1884 to 1887.

3. The Journeymen TAILORS' National Union of the United States.

An Editorial by Samuel Gompers in the *Union Advocate*

[December 1887]

WORKING WOMEN.

The press of New York City are just now engaged in an investigation into the condition of working women, and as a final remedy for their miseries are using their best endeavors to have them organize into trade unions.

If the reports of these papers are only half true it more than bears out what we have all along maintained and demonstrated before several legislative investigations. The time when Hood[1] wrote the "Song of the Shirt," is not only outdone but is scarcely applicable in describing the real misery existing. In no other country does such conditions prevail. In no place except in *civilized* nations are women so burdened with the helplessness of despair as is by them reported. In a recent issue of the *Sun*, it publishes a poem descriptive of these poor women, one stanza of which runs thus:

> None need wonder if, despairing,
> They should loose their hold on heaven,
> Saying, "Why should I be living?
> What is life that I should choose it?
> Only endless toil and sorrow,
> Joyless, rayless, helpless, hopeless!"
> Yet they labor, worn and woeful,
> From the sunshine to the sunset,
> From the sunset on to midnight,
> Getting for the ceaseless striving
> Just enough to keep them toiling,
> Only that, and naught beyond it.[2]

Union Advocate, Dec. 1887.

1. Thomas Hood (1799-1845), a British poet, published "Song of the Shirt" anonymously in the 1843 Christmas issue of *Punch*.

2. This is the third stanza of a four-stanza poem entitled "At the Needle" that was printed in the *New York Sun*, Nov. 16, 1887.

To William Martin

January 16, [188]8

Mr Wm Martin—
Second Vice-Pres't A.F. of L.
512-514 Smithfield St., Pittsburg, Pa.—
Dear Sir:

Have received yours of the 14th, together with marked copy of *Nat. Labor Tribune*. I thank you for the sentence in the *Tribune* of the 7th inst.—"We want the A.F. of L. to grow in numbers and prestige, and it is the duty of every arm and limb of the grand trunk to push forward such growth."

Have secured apartments to the advantage of the Federation, but at a considerable sacrifice to the comfort of my family. Having the office and family under the same roof[1] will however prove a great convenience to me when I am in the city. I start this P.M. for Albany to attend the N.Y. State Convention A.F. of L[2] and from thence will start on my Western trip, which may extend as far as Denver, Colo.

With best wishes, I remain

Yours fraternally   Saml. Gompers
Pres't A.F. of L.

HLpSr, reel 1, vol. 2, p. 163, SG Letterbooks, DLC.

1. SG and his family moved to an apartment at 171 East Ninety-first St. in January 1888 and Gompers used the apartment's front room as the AFL's office.
2. The New York state convention of the AFL met Jan. 17-20, 1888, in Albany, N.Y., and officially organized the New York State Branch of the AFL.

A News Account of an Address in Denver

[February 10, 1888]

THE LABOR QUESTION.

. . .

THE SPEECH OF THE EVENING.

Mr. Gompers' appearance was greeted with hearty and prolonged applause. He said:

Mr. Chairman, Fellow-workmen, Women and Children of Denver—I can scarcely find words in which to return thanks for the compliments paid me and to express my sense of gratitude for the hospitality extended to me since my arrival in your growing city. I am heartily alive to the fact that while I have been so welcomed personally it is also a mark of distinction for the high office I have the honor to hold and to the grand organization I have the honor to represent. In what I have to say I will be as brief and as lucid as possible. I thank you, indeed—the governor[1] of your state, the mayor[2] of your city and the citizens generally—for your words of welcome.

I do not propose to lecture, but to address the men and women of Denver on the labor question and more especially on the necessity of organization. The rights of labor and the wrongs of labor have been long and widely discussed in the press, in the pulpit and from the rostrum. While these things have been discussed from so many standpoints there is another question of far greater importance. It is well to assert the rights of labor and to point out the wrongs which labor suffers, but it is of far more importance to tell the workingmen what they shall do to secure those rights and to remedy those wrongs. It is of vital importance indeed to consider the question "What shall we do to be saved?" It is necessary to lay down a truthful basis to arrive at a truthful conclusion. I shall to-night deal with the practical rather than the theoretical, the concrete rather than the abstract.

LABOR THE CREATOR OF WEALTH.

We often hear it asserted that labor is the creator of all value. We all admit this. But I have sometimes seen laboring men unable to maintain it against those skilled and trained in the sophistry of the schools and the colleges. I shall try to show the truth and soundness of this maxim. Labor is the creator of all wealth. Let us see how this is. Take the most precious of all stones, the diamond. Is that of value to mankind in its natural state? Is it not the labor required to discover it, to separate it from the worthless surrounding stones, to transport it and cut it, that makes its value when it shines upon the bosom or sparkles from the ear of the more fortunately situated of the women of the world? So of the gold and the silver. Are they of any value to the human family till they have been discovered, the ore dug out of the mine, and the metal extracted from the ore and then converted into coin or articles of ornament? So the tree that stands out in its beauty and its symmetry is of no value till it is cut down and made into joists and boards. So of the wool upon the sheep, the coal in the mine, the iron, the lead and the copper in the ore, they are of no value until there has been expended upon them a certain amount of human force, which we call labor.

If labor is the creator of wealth I often ask myself how is it that the laboring men are not the ones who enjoy the wealth? (Applause.) I often ask how it is that those who spin the wool, who make the lace, who polish the diamonds, who make the golden articles or ornament and who delve in the mines, are not the ones that enjoy the products of labor. I often ask how it is that those who raise the wheat and who fatten the ox so often suffer for the necessities of life? In a community in which these things exist there is something wrong. The question of the proper distribution of the products of labor has been a question of valid importance and absorbing interest in every civilized country in all ages.

SOME PRACTICAL QUESTIONS.

Having said this much on the underlying principles affecting this question, I will now proceed to the more practical aspects of the case.

Many men toil on year after year with no apparent prospect of bettering their condition. The employers are ever inclined to encroach upon the employed. There of course are exceptions to this. But we must in this matter deal with the rule. We cannot consider individual cases. We find that where an employer is committed to any special political views he seeks to draw his employes over to the same opinion. He has the power to discharge any employe, even though he may be a man of family, with children to support and educate. He can thus reduce him to want and drive him to crime. It is this absolute power of discharge that gives him his political power.

WOMAN'S WORK.

There is another aspect of the labor question to which I desire to call attention. It is the labor of women. I will not ask you to take my word. I can refer to the statistics. Thomas Hood's "Song of the Shirt" does not half depict the real miseries of the working woman. A writer of these times has referred to the work of the woman as more slavish than that of the convict. The discipline of the factories is often more cruel and severe than that of the penitentiary. The wages of women in manufactures are often less in proportion than the amount appropriated by the state for the support of convicts in the penitentiary.

CHILD LABOR.

Another form of labor to which I would call your attention is child labor. I hope you have nothing of it in this state. If you have not, do not ever allow yourselves to be drawn into its recognition or tolerance. I have seen tender children in the factories tending dangerous ma-

chinery, parts of which seemed to be constantly reaching out for their
delicate limbs. This may seem necessary. But in this age of steam and
electricity, and of rush after wealth, there should be a halt called
somewhere. The children's bones should not be ground into money
to enrich the monopolist. There once existed among a certain people
a religious belief, which taught that when a man died his soul lived,
was separated from his body and passed into some child just being
born, just coming into the world. This doctrine could not apply to
the man who employs child labor. For when he is born, no human
being dies.

I want to say something on this point to the working men. Some
of you may be tempted to send your children out to work. A little
fellow will bring home a dollar at the end of the week. That may
seem a very grateful addition to the income. But don't you know that
the child is employed because its labor can be had cheaper than that
of a man. He becomes a competitor of his father. And if the father
is not discharged some other child's father often is. In this competition
the rates of labor are often so reduced that the combined wages of
the father and child are less than the father's wages alone before. So
I say, leaving out all other considerations—all considerations of pa-
ternal duty, of humanity and patriotism—it is bad from an economic
point of view to send young children out to work. How can the child,
whose first memories and all whose experiences [are] of toil be educated to the duties of good citizenship? There is often as much need
to a child of protection from the selfishness of ignorant parents as
from the avarice of grasping, cruel employers.

THE DRONES OF SOCIETY.

If labor is the creator of all wealth, then those who do not work
must live on the labor of some one else. If many live without labor
then those who do labor cannot receive a just share of the products
of their labor. It matters not how it comes, whether from an internal
revenue, a tariff, a land tax or the interest on a bonded debt, what
goes to those who do not labor comes from those who do. Every man
or woman who lives without work is supported by the labor of others.
The bees in a hive at a certain time refuse to give any more honey
to the drones. It would perhaps disturb things too much for us to
refuse absolutely any more honey to those who do not work—to the
drones of society. But we should begin by allowing them a little less
honey, and keep on allowing them less and less until we allow them
none at all and compel them to go to work to get their own honey.
The English innkeepers of the olden times used to put out peculiar

signs. Sometimes they would bear significant allegorical pictures. Sometimes they would present very excellent political maxims. At one time, under the rule of a tyrannical king an innkeeper painted on his sign four figures. The first was a workman kneeling on the ground. On his shoulder was a priest, on the priest's shoulder was a king and on the king's shoulder was a soldier. From the mouths of each issued a sort of streamer on which there were printed words telling what each did. From the mouth of the soldier came the words "I fight for all." From the mouth of the king, with his scepter in his hand, issued the words "I rule all." From the mouth of the priest, with his ministerial robes about him, came the words "I pray for all," while from the mouth of the poor working man, in his worn garb, streamed the words "I pay for all." So it is with labor. It pays for all.

HOURS OF LABOR.

I now come to another point, the hours of labor. Is it not strange that those who work the largest number of hours a day in the most disagreeable employments live in the most miserable condition; that those who labor only a few hours live better, and that those who do not work at all live the best. Reduction in the hours of labor should not make a reduction of wages.

Those who work the most hours cannot for various reasons live well. Stand at any point on the streets of your city and watch those who go to work at six o'clock, those who go at seven and those who go at eight, and see if those who go last are not the best dressed. Again, stand at the same place at night and watch the working men as they go home. Those who go at five are better dressed than those who go at six, and the latter in turn are better clothed than those who go at seven. The man who works fourteen or fifteen hours a day has no wish to dress well. He has no time to dress well; and lastly, he has no dress. Again, those who toil so long hours have no time to think how they can get into a condition that will enable them to dress better. This is the great point. Give a man $20 a day and make him work sixteen hours and his condition will not be changed. He will have no time to think of the way in which he can improve his condition and improve himself. He will have no time to enjoy anything, no time to cultivate his tastes. The man who spends less time in work will cultivate new tastes. These tastes in time will become necessities, and a man's necessities cannot be taken from him. These he will have. It is their necessities that determine the condition of the people. With long hours of labor there is no time for improvement no time for development. If the development of the press depended on those who work fourteen hours a day, they would never be able to make an affidavit of circulation. Ask the ones who toil through the long hours, which is the greatest charter of liberty, the state or national constitution; ask them which is the best, the statute or the common law, ask them what the tariff is, or what is the difference between absolute free trade and free trade with incidental protection; ask them the difference between the two parties — though I don't know as they ought to be taken to task for this — and they will be unable to tell you. They will be informed on no questions that affect them or their interests. The men who work only seven or eight hours are not the men who can be bought.

THE UNEMPLOYED.

In the practical sense, of the men who work in the various trades and callings, many will be out of employment. So when the working man applies for an advance of wages, the employer will tell him he can go, that his place can be easily filled. It is the great army of the unemployed that brings us to terms. The appropriation of the labor of the world ought to be such among the human family who want to work that all will have work. When we ask for shorter hours of labor, the employers tell us that we don't want to work. They forget that those who are idle can't eat. As long as there is a man or woman seeking work who cannot find it, the hours of labor are too long.

All people who possess wealth in the common sense of the term place their own valuation on it. The laboring man is the only person the valuation of whose wealth is fixed by the purchaser. The possessors of other forms of wealth, if they cannot exchange it at their own price, can hold it. But the possessor of labor must sell it at the price fixed by the purchaser or lose it. We hear of the law of supply and demand. That is all very well. But we also hear of corners. Men combine to get control of the wheat or corn of the country, and hold it until they get their own price for it. Is not this an interference with the law of supply and demand?

THE NEED OF ORGANIZATION.

What I would say is let us combine our forces, so as to control the law of supply and demand of labor in our own interests. We need organization, combination. The rule that everybody should rely upon himself is not a good one. It is good neither for individuals nor for society. Society is an organization. Government is an organization. Working men talk much of organization, but don't effect it. Wild horses when they are assailed by wolves or other beasts will collect with their heads together, their heels on the outside, and kick at their enemies. The working men seem to reverse this; they arrange their heads on the outside, and then kick like thunder at each other.

There has been of late, among laboring men, more progress toward civilization, and a better conception of their rights, than ever before. This has resulted from organization. Some employe[r]s seem to think the acme of good times is cheap labor. If this is so, China should be the happiest and most prosperous country in the world. In the countries where labor is the highest, there is the most liberty and the most happiness. In those in which labor is the lowest, there is the most tyranny and misery. In countries where labor is low there are large standing armies. In countries where wages are high there are small standing armies, because the laboring men are an army unto themselves. "Ill fares the land where wealth increases and men decay."

A LABOR CRISIS.

I believe we are on the eve of an industrial crisis. I do not know when it will come. You know we have had real estate booms, mining booms and general business booms. These seem to come periodically. Is it not about time for a labor boom?

I am often asked if I favor strikes. I will say that I am opposed to strikes. But I must be excused from denouncing them. They have been denounced so often and so vehemently that I must be excused from joining in the clamor. I would not say we will never have any strikes. You know a certain great organization declared against them and then soon had the greatest strike of the generation on its hands. I believe we should organize and prepare for the necessity of strikes should it come. There is no so sure preventive of strikes as organization with a full treasury behind it. Organization is not worth much without a treasury. Employers will hesitate at the prospect of a strike when they know that the laborers are organized and are prepared to hold out for a time. In the best organized trades there are the least strikes. The unions that have the fullest treasuries have the fewest strikes.

ARBITRATION.

Do I believe in arbitration? I do. But not in arbitration between the lion and the lamb, in which the lamb is in the morning found inside of the lion. I believe in arbitration between two lions or two lambs. When a man puts a pistol to my head and tells me to deliver, there is no arbitration. There can be arbitration only between equals. Let us organize: then we will stand on an equal footing with the employers. We can say to them let us arbitrate, you who can inflict so much injury on us and we who can inflict so much injury on you. Then we can arbitrate. Organization is the best means to prevent strikes and protect people from their ruinous effects. In strikes where there is no organization there occur the greatest violations of law. Trades unions are the conservators of peace. Where there is no organization the strikers lose. Where there is organization the strikers win. Employers fear the power of organized labor.

How to Organize.

You should organize on trade lines. I do not believe that a tailor should be allowed to go into a printing office and order a strike. No one should be allowed to interfere outside of his own trade. I am opposed to ordering strikes; they should be by vote. The men should vote on the question of striking and the majority rule. Then they should in case of a strike vote to return if they choose, and not be ordered back like a herd of cattle. There should be no sovereignty in unions. None should be so high that they can look down on the others. The government should be a pure democracy—the rule of the majority. The masses are safer than any individual ruler. Leading minds may be helpful, but the masses are the rock of safety.

I am often asked what a trades union is. It is an organization of trade people working in any trade or calling, skilled or unskilled. It is the natural outcome of our economic system. It develops as naturally as the flower from the bud. I do not believe in general organization. It should be in the groups of the trades and callings. The men in each calling know each other, and they know whom to trust. They know the sycophants and the traitors. The movements of the confederated organization will be like those of a properly organized army. An army of 5,000 men, 2,000 infantry, 2,000 cavalry, 1,000 artillery men, each arm separate, can be moved and operated effectively as one body. But let the different branches be mixed together promiscuously and it is an unwieldy, helpless mob. The dividing lines indeed should be so narrow that each can feel the touch of his brother's elbow, and if any are attacked all can come to the rescue.

Rocky Mountain News (Denver), Feb. 10, 1888.

1. Alva Adams, a Democrat, served as governor of Colorado from 1887 to 1889 and 1897 to 1899.
2. William Scott Lee was Republican mayor of Denver from 1887 to 1889.

To J. McWilliams

Feb'y 16, [188]8

Mr J. McWilliams
Rec. Sec'y Car Builders Union,
Allegheny City
Dear Sir:

Your communication of Jan. 21st has received my careful consideration, and you will make allowance for the time that has elapsed when I inform yo[u] that I have been on the road speaking and organizing since the middle of Dec. last. In the first place, I ask you to accept my thanks for your breif history of your organization and strike, and would remark that as the painters and carpenters acted so should act all working men. I know full well tha[t] we cannot place much reliance upon the promises of employers to advance wages; nevertheless I regret to learn that you are receiving such low wages. In regard to your next and positive statement that you "will strike in the spring," allow me to say that my province is to advise and not to dictate. Therefore I will give you the benefit of my best judgement based upon extensive observation, and consider it to be my duty to acquaint you with the conclusions at which I have arrived which are as follows: — Unless present appearance are very misleading strikes of any character will not be successful for some time to come, especially when the strike is for an advance of wages. As a matter of fact, the tendencies of the present situation are in an opposite direction largely owing to a powerful combination of the employers. We should therefore exert all our energies to the task of holding our own and preventing a further reduction and other encroachments upon our rights. In the next place, since you have the company afraid of you, it seems inadvisable to risk the chance of a strike in which you have much to los[e] and little to gain under the present gloomy prospects. My advice is, bide your time until you ca[n] take practical action; strengthen your organizatio[n] by all means at your command in the full belief that your time will come if you have the courage [to] wait. Lost strikes break up more organizations than any other cause. The laws of the A.F. of L. herei[n] enclosed with other documents accompanying it wi[ll] explain the rights, duties, and benefits devolving upo[n] and binding upon all unions affiliated. Remember the A.F. of L. is young. Think how far ¼ of one cent a month would go in support of an extended strike. Hopin[g] to hear from you soon, I remain

Yours fraternally
Pres't A.F. of L

HLp, reel 1, vol. 2, pp. 278-79, SG Letterbooks, DLC.

To the Officers and Members of the
New York Stereotypers Association

[ca. Feb. 23-27, 1888]

To the Officers and Members of the N.Y. Stereotypers Ass['n]

Fellow Workmen:

It is with a feeling of regret that I realise my inability to grasp your hands on the occasion of your annu[al] dinner and respond in person to the toast of the "American Federation of Labor" with which you have had the kindness to associate my name. My regret, however, is softened by the consciousness that my absence from your fraternal reunion is in consequence of the performance of a special duty imposed upon me by the delegates of the united trade unions of this wide country who in December last assembled in Convention at Baltimo[re.]

From the evening of the adjournment of that memorable convention I have been almost continually on the road. In the performance of this duty I have travers[ed] the continent from beyond the Ohio to the great lakes and from the extreme East to the foot of the Rockies.

During this extended tour, now only partially accomplished, I have addressed many thousands of representatives of the productive working cl[ass,] not a few municipal and other officials, together with numbers of earnest men engaged in the performance of other necessary social functions, and who by reason of not being wage-workers are, by a wise policy, excluded from membership in our great and rapidly growing federation. Recognising the existence, and appreciating the services, of special classes distinct from that class which constitutes the main body of the people, I have never addressed my audiences in any exclusive spirit, or striven to embitter the strained relations now existing between the capitalistic and laboring classes. While I have endeavored to impress upon my hearers the desirability of a more compact and perfect organization of the class I love and am therefore proud to serve to the full extent of my ability, I have ever striven to maintain a sympathetic spirit for all who are honestly striving to perform their duty according to their light; I have ever striven to keep before my own and their mind's eye the supreme importance of the aspiration for the unity and brotherhood of man.

I address myself specially to the working class because I believe that in the organization of the working class upon the natural, historic basis of the trade union will be found the practical means of regulating the anarchy of the present industrial system, and of conserving and developing the best interests of our country and race.

It is a grave mistake made by many of our public men when they suppose that it is a mere question of wages, of dollars and cents, that is now convulsing every country of the civilized world, and that is nerving the miners and heroic women of the Lehigh and Anthracite coal regions of Pennsylvania to stare starvation in the face.[1] There is a deeper trouble, and a nobler aspiration agitating the working class. The workers in all lands, where industry, science, and art have reached any considerable development, feel that full justice is not done to their class and to their social position. They feel that Capital has it[s] duties no less than its rights, and it is to secure the recognition of this truth that every working class movement is directed as a means to an end.

At the outset of industrial life when each man worked his little bit of land with the rudest tools, and lived in the most complete isolation possible, even then, when industry was most exclusively personal in it[s] mode of excercise, each stroke of work he performed was laying the foundation of that important instrument called Capital. Thus Capital is the product of the whole past industrial efforts of the human race. And as Capital can always command the services of the workman, and bring him into co-operative relations with the Machinery which day by day is ever assuming a more important part in production, it becomes a vital necessity that normal permanent relations between capitalists and laborers should be established. Capital, by common consent, is concentrated in individual hands in order the better to develope its efficiency as an industrial instrument. The capitalist therefore stands in the dignified position of a trustee of the capital placed in his hands. Consequently, when the capitalist diver[ts] any portion of this common heritage from its destined purpose and uses it for selfish purposes, whether in ostentatious luxury or in the payment of armed police he commits the most flagrant crime the mind of man can conceive.

The total product of Labor has first of all to maintain and conserve, and in some degree develope the the indispensable instrument, capital; and then to provide for all the other needs of society. The wages of the workers can never be considered as a paymen[t] of the value of the work performed. Wages are simply the provision of the daily or weekly wants of the workman and of his family. The necessities of every family must be provided for, even when the members of the family are unable to work. This provision must be made, not as charity, but as a measure of justice and true wisdom. The capitalist does not starve when business is slack, nor even when it is tota[lly] suspended; and the capital which furnishes subsis[tence] to the one must do the same for the others.

And now in conclusion, wishing you each and all a good evening's enjoyment, and again expressing my regret at my enforced absence from your hospitable board. I remain

Yours fraternally   Saml Gompers.
Prest A.F. of L.

HLpSr, reel 1, vol. 2, pp. 295-300, SG Letterbooks, DLC.

1. On Sept. 10, 1887, 20,000 miners in the Lehigh anthracite region of Pennsylvania went on strike in support of a demand by the Miners and Laborers' Amalgamated Association of Pennsylvania and the KOL for a wage increase and union recognition. By January 1888 the strike had merged with one by miners in the Schuylkill region, employed by the Philadelphia and Reading Railroad, who refused to dig coal to be shipped on the Reading because the KOL railway workers were on strike. Despite appeals for financial aid on their behalf by the AFL and the Knights, the miners gave up the strike and returned to work in late February and early March.

To the Executive Council of the AFL

New York, Feb'y 28, 1888.

To the Executive Council, A.F. of L.—
Gabriel Edmonston, Treasurer—
Dear Sir:

From the evening of the adjournment of the Baltimore Convention I have been, with the exception of two slight intermissions of a few days duration, continually on the road in prosecution of the trip sanctioned by the Executive Council. During this extended journey I have addressed many thousands of organized and unorganized working people, together with many representatives of other classes, all of whom have tendered me most flattering receptions and assured me that my addresses had given them greater enlightenment on the subject of trade unions than they had before possessed. Thanks to your sanction, I have had the opportunity of advocating the unity of labor in Syracuse, Rochester, Buffalo, Boston, Albany, Troy, Cleveland, Columbus, Cincinnati, Indianapolis, Louisville, Evansville, Maysville, Connersville, Peoria, Quincy, St. Louis, Springfield, Kansas City, Fort

Scott, Denver, Lincoln, Omaha, Sioux City, Minneapolis, St. Paul, Milwaukee, Chicago, South Bend, Grand Rapids, Lansing, East Saginaw, and Detroit. This extensive tour has been arranged, and carried out, in the most inclement season, without expense to the American Federation, and will, if my health and strength permits, be completed on the same advantageous basis. After visiting Cincinnati, Pittsburg, Harrisburg, York, Baltimore, and Philadelphia I expect to return to my home in New York, from which I have been so long seperated, about the 10th of next month. During my journey, the success of which has far surpassed my expectation, I have found the unions in a healthy and active condition, and full of enthusiasm for the success of the common cause. The name of the "American Federation of Labor" is becoming as familiar as a household word, and I flatter myself I have succeeded in arousing general interest in its methods, and making its objects known in a most effective manner. Certainly, such a work of propaganda cannot but redound to the furtherance of the general cause and the strengthening of the various organizations affiliated to the A.F. of L. With hopeful greeting I remain

Yours fraternally   Saml Gompers.
Pres't A.F. of L.

HLSr, Papers of Gabriel Edmonston, reel 1, *AFL Records.*

To the Executive Council of the AFL

New York, March 1, 1888

To the Executive Council, A.F. of L.—
Mr. Gabriel Edmonston, Treasurer.—
Dear Sir & Brother:

In accordance with a suggestion made by a member of our body that the issuance of the "small quarterly report" be deferred until the next quarter, in consideration of the short time that has elapsed since the Baltimore convention, and in view of the fact that the receipts of most organizations are more or less light for a period following their conventions, and also that private circulars give no security against a copy thereof falling into the hands of some weak union man or K. of L. who might argue therefrom that the A.F. of L. exhibited financial weakness. Therefore, I make the following proposition and hereby submit the same to the vote of the Executive Council: "That the publication of the next financial statement of the A.F. of L. be deferred until May 31, '88.["] You are respectfully requested to cast your vote upon the above proposition and transmit the same to this office at your earliest convenience.[1]

Yours fraternally   Saml Gompers.
Prest A.F. of L.

HLSr, Papers of Gabriel Edmonston, reel 1, *AFL Records.*

1. The 1887 AFL convention had amended the Federation's constitution to require the president to publish a quarterly financial report. In 1888 the AFL issued its first report, for the six months ending May 28.

To Gregory Weinstein[1]

March 15th [188]8

Gregory Weinstein Esq
Dear Sir

In reply to your favor of the 14th inst permit me to say that though the time between your invitation and the address is very short I shall still endeavor to present labor's side of the question "Home Industry as applied to the Manufacture of Cigars", before the Young Men's Society for Ethical Culture[2] on Monday Evening March 19th.[3]

Will you kindly call at this office on Sunday morning between 9 and 12 to see me upon an important matter?

You have not stated in your letter where the Y.M.S. for E.C. meets.

Convey to Professor Adler[4] my kindest regards and thanking you for your fraternal expressions of solicitude. I am

Yours Sincerely   Saml Gompers.

ALpS, reel 1, vol. 2, p. 365, SG Letterbooks, DLC.

1. Gregory Weinstein, a Russian-born printer living in Brooklyn, N.Y., was secretary of the Russian-American National League, an organization that attempted to create a favorable climate of opinion in America for Russian revolutionaries. He was active in the New York City Central Labor Union as well as in civic affairs, particularly education reform.

2. The Young Men's Union for Ethical Culture, connected with the Workingmen's School of the New York Society for Ethical Culture, held Sunday evening discussions in which SG often took part.

3. SG spoke in response to an earlier speech by Morris S. Wise.

4. Felix ADLER, a philosopher, educator, and social reformer, founded the New York Society for Ethical Culture.

To Thomas Purdy

March 16, [188]8

Mr Tho. Purdy—
Sec'y Stone Masons' Union, No 1,[1]
11 Yates Terrace, Syracuse, N.Y.—
Dear Sir:

Your favor of the 14th inst., containing application for a certificate of affiliation to the A.F. of L. with the specified fee, has been received. You will please find enclosed receipts for the sum forwarded, and your application will receive prompt attention.

In reply to the point raised by your honored colleagues you will permit me to explain as follows: Any seven or more persons working for wages, and having organized themselves by electing officers and providing for holding regular meeting in any city or place in America, may make application for a certificate of affiliation to the A.F. of L. If such application is endorsed by a union already affiliated to the A.F. of L. and approved by the President a certificate will be then granted. Bodies composed of persons working at different trades and callings are designated as "Federal Labor Unions." Bodies composed of persons working at one special trade or calling are designated as a "Local Union" of such trade or calling. All aforesaid bodies are required to pay a Capita Tax of ¼ of one one cent per month for each of its members in good standing directly to the President of the A.F. of L. But when a suffcent number of Local Unions of a certain trade or calling are organized they are required to form a National or International Union of their trade or calling. When a National or International Union is organised the Local Unions composing it are required to surrender their certificates of affiliation to the President of the A.F. of L. and work under one certificate which is granted to the officers of such National or International Union. With the surrender of its certificate a Local Union ceases to pay Capita Tax directly to the A.F. of L. Upon the organization of, or the granting a certificate to, a National or International Union the Secretary of the same is required to pay the Capita Tax of each and every member of such Union to the President of the A.F. of L.

With regard to State Branches:—When the various unions—Federal Labor Unions, Local Trade Unions (whether having a National or International head or not), Central Labor Unions or Trade Assemblies—,organized in any state of the United States or in any Province of the Dominion of Canada, desire to establish a State organization, for the purpose of securing legislation in th[e] interest of the working people according to the laws of that State, they call a Convention, elect officers, and provide the means to carry out their object by levying a special tax upon the Unions represented in such Convention. This special or State tax is altogether independent of the Capita Tax of the A.F. of L. The Capita Tax of the A.F. of L. is ¼ of one cent per month, and the Capita Tax of the New York State Branch[2] is ⅛ of one cent per month These two Capita Taxes are entirely distinct and seperate, and the only revenue derived from any of the State Branches by the A.F. of L. is $5.00 as a State Branch certificate fee, and $25.00 per year.

Hoping I have made the matter sufficently clear, and that you will freely ask any question which may remain in your minds after a study of the constitution, I remain

Yours fraternally   Saml Gompers
Pres't A.F. of L.

HLpSr, reel 1, vol. 2, pp. 371-73, SG Letterbooks, DLC.

1. Stonemasons' Local Protective and Benevolent Union 1 of Syracuse, N.Y.
2. The New York State Branch (NYSB) of the AFL was organized in January 1888. Unlike its rival, the New York State Workingmen's Assembly (NYSWA), which was formed in 1865, the NYSB did not allow KOL assemblies to affiliate. The KOL also had its own state assembly, and, during the 1890s, rivalry among the three groups handicapped labor lobbying. In 1897 the growing weakness of the KOL removed the main source of conflict, and the NYSB and the NYSWA amalgamated to form the Workingmen's Federation of the State of New York. In 1910 it changed its name to the New York State Federation of Labor.

To Samuel Goldwater

March 20th [188]8

Samuel Goldwater Esq
Dear Sir & Friend.

Owing to the large call made upon us for reports of the proceedings of the Baltimore session of the American Federation of Labor we have but a few copies on hand. I regret so much that a larger edition was not printed so that I might be enabled to supply all who desire copies. However we shall know better in future.

In the matter of the *Union Advocate* time only more truly confirms my opinion that a blunder was committed in suspending its publication. Had it been in existence to-day, many of the attacks now made upon our organization by pretended friends would never be dreamed of or if so not put into execution. There is one thing papers do not like and that is to have their falsehood, hypocrisy or shallowness exposed by a fearless defender of truth.

I suppose you are aware that I have returned home safe from my trip through the country, which by the way I would say was successful beyond my most sanguine expectations or those of our friends in the places I visited.

Since my return home a copy of *The Advance* of your City[1] has been sent to me. In its issue of the 18th inst I find a report of a meeting in which "The Mistakes of Gompers" were discussed.

Of course my lecture was a public one and properly the subject of criticism, favorable or otherwise is immaterial[,] it must lead to thought on the subject.

It is evident however that those who discussed my lecture at the meeting of K of L Assembly are such superficial thinkers and have so little experience in labor movement or more properly speaking learnt so little from their own experience and the experience of others that an answer would be superfluous. "To argue with a man who has renounced his reason, is like giving medicine to the dead". My lecture is part of my record and upon it I am willing to stand or fall. With *The Advance*'s position it is different however.

In the same issue in which they publish "The Mistakes of Gompers" they say editorially " "The Mistakes of Gompers" lies more in what he did not say, than in what he did say" and as if to show the utter ridiculousness of their statement as conspicuously as possible they will [then ask?] (again Editorially and in the same column) exactly what I contended for and which formed the burden of my argument, namely, *A reduction in the hours of labor.*

Had some high sounding titled personage given expression to the same sentiments I think it would have been "all right" "Noble" &c &c. but as it was a *mere Trades Unionist* why it's all a "mistake"

The movement towards the *bona fide* organization of the working people is going on. The Trades Unions are full of life and vigor. The American Federation of Labor is progressing in a natural way and is experiencing a healthy development, the opposition of their combined enemies to the contrary notwithstanding.

With best wishes for the movement which seeks to improve the condition of and finally emancipate labor. I am.

Yours Fraternally   Samuel Gompers.
President. American Federation of Labor.

ALpS, reel 1, vol. 2, pp. 391-93, SG Letterbooks, DLC.

1. Detroit.

To Edward Finkelstone[1]

March 30th [188]8

Ed[']d Finklestone Esq
Pres't J.B.N.U.[2]
Dear Sir

With this I mail to your address a letter from Indianapolis Ind which was enclosed in one to me. The sender did not know your address.

In his letter to me Mr Farnham[3] says he wishes to organize a Barbers Union and desires to place himself in communication with you. Will you please promptly attend to this matter.

A few days ago a letter reached me from Mr Berger[4] President of the Muskegon, Mich. Barber's Union in which he complains of the inactivity of the National Officers of your Union. The importance of maint[ain]ing what has already been accomplished in securing a nationalization of the Barbers Unions cannot be over-estimated and it behooves you to do all in your power to see that the movement does not retrograde.

I understand that you are kept busy with local matters but many of them can and must be forgone in the interest of your national organization. This is not the only word in this matter that has reached me or I would not mention the subject.

I trust you will accept this advice in the spirit in which it is penned.

Will you please call at this office on Saturday between 10 and 12, There are matters over which I wish to have a talk with you.

With best wishes I am

Yours Fraternally   Saml Gompers
Pres AF of L

ALpS, reel 1, vol. 2, pp. 428-29, SG Letterbooks, DLC.

1. Edward FINKELSTONE was the first president of the Journeymen Barbers' National Union, serving from 1887 to 1888.
2. The Journeymen BARBERS' National Union.
3. Milton G. Farnham, an Indianapolis cigarmaker, held several offices in the Indianapolis Central Labor Union, including the presidency, between 1885 and 1888. He became an AFL organizer in 1888.
4. Frederick L. Berger, a barber in Muskegon, Mich., was an AFL organizer.

To P. J. McGuire

April 6th [188]8

P J McGuire Esq
Sec'y A.F of L.
Dear Sir

I regret very much that I failed to meet you at the office to-day when you called.

Last night I was in Washington N.J. in the interest of the Piano & Organ Makers and arrived home about an hour after you left.

I do not know what kept Mr McGregor from the office to-day but presume it must be in consequence of his Wife's sickness, of which he spoke in the early part of the week.

By my letter of the 4th you will see that I attended the Yonkers meeting.

The matter I desired to talk to you about is, that to my mind not only the interest of your Brotherhood but the labor movement of this City and Country demand that you plant the Brotherhood in this city.

The United Order by an overwhelming vote decided to affiliate with the B of C & J of A[1] and a few schemers in league with the worst elements in the ranks of labor have concocted plans not only to thwart the expressed desire of the members but also encompass the defeat and ruin (if possible) of nearly every other Union.

You will understand that this is written in no spirit of dictation but a suggestion arrived at after a mature consideration of all the circumstances attending and surrounding the movement here for the past year.

Hoping to hear from you upon this and other matters at your earliest convenience. I am

Yours Fraternally,   Saml Gompers.
Pres't AF of L.

ALpS, reel 1, vol. 2, pp. 457-58, SG Letterbooks, DLC.

1. The United Order of American Carpenters and Joiners apparently derived from an organization founded in 1872 that declined during the depression of 1873 and was revived toward the end of the decade. It developed lodges in New York City, Brooklyn, New Jersey, and Connecticut and effectively excluded the Brotherhood of Carpenters and Joiners of America from organizing in the New York City area through the refusal of its members to work with members of the Brotherhood. After a period of intense struggle, the two organizations merged on May 13, 1888, to form the United Brotherhood of Carpenters and Joiners of America. Three New York City lodges refused to join the Brotherhood and affiliated instead with the KOL as local assemblies 2410, 2531, and 2588, and independent United Order lodges were still

coming into the Brotherhood in the late 1890s. Most of the United Order's lodges accepted the Brotherhood's constitution and benefits program but even some of these continued using the name United Order of American Carpenters and Joiners for several years after the merger.

A Translation of an Excerpt from a News Account of a Mass Meeting at Cooper Union

[April 20, 1888]

A HUGE MASS MEETING.

. . .

Samuel Gompers, the president of the Federation of Trades & Labor, delivered a speech in which he said he could find no words strong enough to condemn the shameless conduct of the brewery bosses,[1] who have thrown 5000 good, hard-working, peaceful workers out into the streets, merely because they belonged to a workingmen's organization and because other organizations had decided no longer to drink any beer from breweries whose owners did not recognize the union of the brewery workers. He said the bosses claimed that the union "tyrannized" its workers and that the workers would be happy to be free of the union dictatorship. He declared emphatically that this was not true! That the bosses only wanted to destroy the union, so that they could force the workers once again to work 14 to 18 hours a day for $6 to $8 per week! Gompers then became sarcastic and advised the workers of New York not even to think of breaking the law; boycotting was, of course, against the law, so no one was going to "boycott" anybody, but since there was no law telling the citizens to drink certain kinds of beer, it would thus surely not be against the law, not to drink a certain kind of beer, Pool beer, even if Mr. Seifert,[2] the "famous" secretary of the bosses, was threatening to prosecute all "boycotters." These remarks of the speaker were attended by much applause and general amusement, whereas the crowd hissed vehemently at the mention of Seifert's name. Gompers also ridiculed with biting sarcasm the decree of the bosses by which workers are forbidden "to obey anyone" but the brewery pool if they want to have work again. In issuing the commandment like the so-called "Merciful Father in Heaven" that their workers should have no other god before the Pool, the bosses, Gompers said, had done like the frog who burst in trying to inflate himself to the size of an

ox. He said the bosses weren't frogs, of course—rather more like
oxen—but burst they would! (Great demonstrative applause.) The
time would come, he continued, when the bosses would no longer
dare to shut down their shops, because the workers would no longer
allow them that right. (Thunderous applause.) The bosses, said Gompers, should go right on fighting against the workingmen's organizations; the only result would be that the workers would make ever
more radical demands and finally win full economic freedom. In any
case, he said, it was now the most sacred duty of all workers to help
the brewery workers to win and to break the shameless Pool! (Roaring
applause.)

. . .

New Yorker Volkszeitung, Apr. 20, 1888. Translated from the German by
Patrick McGrath.

1. In April 1888 the U.S. Brewers' Association declared a nationwide lockout that
almost destroyed the National Union of United Brewery Workmen of the United
States. On Apr. 8, in response, the New York City locals instituted a boycott against
the New York City brewers' organization, the Lager Beer Brewers' Board of Trade
of New York and Vicinity (LBBBT), which was referred to as the "Pool." SG represented the brewery workers before the New York State Board of Mediation and
Arbitration that met on Apr. 26 to investigate the lockout. The employers, however,
refused to arbitrate, and the workers continued to demand that the union be recognized and the locked out men be reinstated. Although most of the workers returned
to the breweries on a nonunion basis, the New York City struggle continued for the
next fourteen years. During that time the Brewery Workmen, the KOL, and the AFL
made repeated attempts to negotiate with the Pool, but to no avail. During the late
1890s, the boycott became more effective primarily because of the assistance of the
Boston Central Labor Union and the New England workers. Finally, in 1902, New
York employing brewers, tiring of the loss of the northeastern market and facing a
reinvigorated labor movement, signed a contract that ended the boycott and lockout.
2. Albert E. Seifert was secretary of the LBBBT.

To P. H. Donnelly

April 23rd [188]8

P H Donnelly Esq
Dear Sir & Friend.
    Pardon lateness in replying to your favor of the 16th I have been
flitting in [and] out of the City since my return from my long trip
and this is the first opportunity to attend to my accumulated mail.
    You ask me for an opinion upon the attempt to collect $75,000.00
from the K of L by their G.E.B. well they say that it is for "education"[1]

I am won't do anything to prevent their "education" There is no doubt *they sorely need it.* The only question that seems to me to deserve consideration is that their teachers themselves lack Knowledge except in their experimental attempts to disrupt Trades Unions.

It is my honest conviction that many of these presumptious teachers could learn much from the masses, to learn their necessities, their wants, desires, hopes, aspirations and suit their action accordingly.

Yes, Friend the Unionists will have to be watchful and for that reason as much as another I appointed so good a one as yourself to do what you can to aid us in this holy mission of defending the best and natural form of working-class organization, Trades Unions.

Let me assure you that their efforts will prove futile

The Trade Unions are made of sterner stuff. They have been compelled to withstand greater opposition than the K of L can ever hope to launch against them and they have always emerged stronger, better and stauncher to struggle for the improvement in the condition and final emancipation of Labor.

You will understand me I hope, that I would not have you infer that you would be less active without the appointment as Organizer but it will be a souvenior for those that may come after you to look back to the honest, clean and noble record of their ancestor.

With best wishes for future successes I am

Yours Fraternally   Saml Gompers,
Pres't

ALpS, reel 1, vol. 2, pp. 547-48, SG Letterbooks, DLC.

1. In the Mar. 31, 1888, issue of the *Journal of United Labor* Terence Powderly asserted that education was more effective than strikes in improving workers' conditions. He asked the membership to vote on a proposal that the Order support lecturers to teach the principles of the KOL. On May 26, after the KOL endorsed the idea, Powderly called for a voluntary assessment of 15¢ per capita for the education fund.

To C. J. Bartow

April 24, [188]8

Mr. C. J. Bartow—
Rec. Sec'y B'th'd Carpenters L.U. No 231
400-17th St., Birmingham, Ala.
Dear Sir:

The American Federation of Labor has received an application for a charter from Mr Jos. G. Starr[1] 1712 First Ave., Birmingham, Ala.

and others who were formerly organized as an assembly of the Knights of Labor; and as it is the invariable rule of our Federation to enquire strictly into the labor antecedent of the applicants for a charter, before granting the same, Mr P. J. McGuire, your worthy Gen. Sec. and Sec'y of the A.F. of L. has recommended you as a fit and capable member of the Federation to report upon the facts of the case. Should you in your judgment consider Mr Jos G. Starr and the persons he represents to be honest, *bona fide* workingmen having the interests of their class at heart, and favorably disposed toward the trade union movement, as understood by yourself and your fellow members of our great and rapidly increasing federation, you will please so report to this office.

Should you, however, find that they are in anyway desirous of making political capital by the possession of a charter from our body you should, in the best interest of labor, state so frankly and fearlessly. You should also enquire if they have been good members of the K. of L. and are clear of all indebtedness to that body; because we hold that men who have not fulfilled their obligations to one body will in all probability prove derelict to ours. Relying upon your good judgement in this matter and assuring you that your report will be held strictly confidential. I am,

Yours fraternally   Saml Gompers.
Pres't A.F. of L.

HLpSr, reel 1, vol. 2, pp. 553-54, SG Letterbooks, DLC.

1. Joseph G. Starr operated a book and stationery establishment. He became president of Federal Labor Union 2479, which received its AFL certificate of affiliation in late April 1888.

Gompers and European Labor Conferences

Although Gompers was influenced by the ideas and practices of European trade unionists during the 1870s and 1880s, his correspondence with the French trade unionist Auguste Keufer marks the first documented exchange between the president of the AFL and a representative of a European labor movement. Keufer, head of the Fédération française des travailleurs du livre, played an active role in attempts to unite French trade unions in a national federation during the 1890s. He proved to be Gompers' most regular foreign correspondent during the late nineteenth century.

Other European labor leaders also sought contact with Gompers and the AFL during this time. In 1887, when the Trades Union Congress of Great Britain proposed a conference to lay the groundwork for an international trade federation, it invited the AFL to participate in the meeting, which was to be held in London in the fall of 1888. Although Gompers recommended that the AFL send two delegates, the Federation's 1887 convention voted this down on the grounds that it was "wiser to first unite the labor organizations of America, before trying to unite with the workingmen of Europe."[1] When the London conference endorsed efforts to organize political labor parties, most British delegates opposed the move because they feared it would entangle trade unions in the European socialist movement.

The position of the AFL's 1887 convention together with that of the London meeting on labor parties may have persuaded Gompers not to recommend to the Federation's 1888 convention that it send a representative to the next international labor congress, which was to be held in Paris in the summer of 1889. Because the French socialist movement was split and the organizers of the 1889 conference were unable to reconcile the differences between moderate and radical factions, two opposing groups eventually convened in Paris in July. The so-called possibilist meeting consisted of trade unionists and reform socialists from England and France; small delegations from the KOL and the International Typographical Union also attended. The other congress, which became the founding meeting of the Second International, was attended by Marxist socialists from Britain, France,

105

Germany, Austria, and Holland, and a small delegation of New York socialists. No official AFL delegates attended either meeting, but Gompers sent Hugh McGregor as a personal representative to Paris to transmit a letter from the AFL, which was read at both conferences. Although no copy of this message survives, Gompers apparently excused the AFL's absence by its preoccupation with the eight-hour movement in the United States; he also urged the unification of the two congresses. G. F. Kirchner, a delegate representing the United German Trades in New York, reported on the AFL's activities to the Marxist conference, but for the most part the AFL received little attention from either congress. Both meetings considered the AFL's call for an eight-hour day and passed resolutions of support.

Note

1. AFL, *Proceedings*, 1887, p. 26.

To Auguste Keufer[1]

April 25, [188]8

Mr A. Keufer,
Sec'y, Central Committee,
Federation Française des Travailleurs du Livre,
15 Rue de Savoie, Paris, France.
Dear Sir & Brother:

Your letter of April 6th, in recognition of the resolution of the Baltimore Convention to establish fraternal relations between the workers of Europe and America, came duly to hand. The A.F. of L. thanks you and your respected Union for your cordial acceptance of our expressions of good will, and for your generous efforts to make our aspirations known to the organized working people of Paris, of France and her colonies, and to those of Europe generally. We thank you for the copies you have sent of the List of the correspondents of your several Sections, or Local Unions; and hope that you will send us the address of the Secretary or President of the Central Executive of the United Syndical Chambers of France,[2] if there is such an organization in existence.

In my letter to you of January 27 I neglected to inform you that by an amendment to the Constitution made by the Baltimore Convention, the *Union Advocate* was was discontinued. I very much regret that action and am fully convinced that it was an unwise step, as it has deprived the Federation of a very valuable means of propaganda.

Since the date of my last letter many organized and persistent efforts have been made by the capitalists to destroy the power of the trade unions. The Brotherhood of Locomotive Engineers[3] have been badly defeated in a strike[4] undertaken to maintain the old rate of wages. This strike was lost in a large measure by members of the Knights of Labor taking the places left vacant by the engineers on strike. The Coal Miners of Pennsylvania have also been defeated. These Miners were members of the K. of L. but that "Order" failed to support them, and the A.F. of L. issued the enclosed appeal in their behalf. And now the employing Brewers have locked-out their employees in order to break upon the Union. A very vigorous resistance to this attempt is now being made in this and adjacent cities by means of the "boycott," and is spite of the immense amount of capital arrayed against them the workingmen stand a good chance of winning the fight. The "boycott" is a great power in the hands of honest and determined men, for the working people may be forced to work against their will by the pressure of poverty, but they can very seldom be compelled to buy any article they do not want to buy.

And now in conclusion I would express the hope that you will write soon and frequently, and receive for yourself and colleagues the salutation of

Yours fraternally   Saml Gompers.
Pres't. A.F. of L.

HLpSr, reel 1, vol. 2, pp. 566-69, SG Letterbooks, DLC.

1. Auguste KEUFER was general secretary of the Fédération française des travailleurs du livre, the French typographical union, from 1885 to 1920.

2. The French Union des chambres syndicales was formed in 1880 and sought gradual reforms within a republican framework. It called for the legalization of unions, the ten-hour day, state pensions, and aid to cooperative associations. By the late 1880s, the Union was overshadowed by trade unions committed to revolutionary socialism.

3. The Brotherhood of LOCOMOTIVE Engineers.

4. On Feb. 27, 1888, the Brotherhood of Locomotive Engineers (BLE) and the Brotherhood of Locomotive Firemen struck against the Chicago, Burlington, and Quincy Railroad, demanding the end of a classification system under which workers were paid different rates according to their experience and a fixed mileage rate whether for trips on the main or branch lines of the railroad. The Brotherhood of Railroad Brakemen and the Switchmen's Mutual Aid Association supported the strike, and on Mar. 23 the switchmen unofficially joined it. A conflict between the BLE and the KOL, however, enabled the railroad to replace the strikers with KOL men. In the past the brotherhoods had refused to cooperate with the Knights, and during a KOL strike against the Philadelphia and Reading Railroad just two months earlier, members of the BLE had taken the places of striking Knights. Unemployed former Reading engineers and firemen now retaliated by replacing the Burlington strikers, despite an appeal by Terence Powderly (*Journal of United Labor*, Mar. 3, 1888). The brotherhoods officially called off the strike on Jan. 3, 1889.

To David Hill

May 3rd, [188]8

David B. Hill—
Governor of the State of New York—
Honored Sir:

The Bill passed by the Legislature to amend the law known as the "Saturday Half Holiday Law" so that its present provisions shall be inoperative for nine months in the year is now before you awaiting your signature or disapproval.[1]

As the chief executive officer of the American Federation of Labor I deem it my duty to protest against the Bill becoming a law; and respectfully call your attention to a few of the reasons I think are of sufficent weight to warrant your disapproval of the proposed change

It is admitted by all observers that in no part of the civilized world are the people harder worked than in the United States, and that the climatic influences are so severe a tax upon the physical energies and mental systems of our people as to call forth the warning cry to the American people for "relaxation" from the eminent authority Herbert Spencer.[2]

The tendency of the times is to give to Sunday its old puritanical character, to make it a day of rest and religious observance. Surely, then, a half holiday on Saturday devoted to amusement, excercise, and recreation should be afforded the working people

It cannot be claimed that the productivity of labor is diminished by this half holiday. The industries of England (where the Saturday Half Holiday[3] has been the rule for years) bears the best testimony to the reverse being the result.

It is asserted that the State of New York is at a disadvantage with other States by reason of this Law. If we recognise the beneficent effect upon the health and comfort of our people then the so called disadvantage is an argument not worth consideration.

It is doubtful if any useful legislation over which the several States have absolute control can or will b[e] adopted simultaneously, one must lead the van, and there is no good reason why the Empire State should not be the first

To repeal the law now would only have the effect of deterring other States from adopting a similar law

I am aware that compliance with the law so far as private employment is concerned is entirely voluntary, but it must be remembered so is Independance Day. The fact, however, that the law may be permitted to exist will tend to act as an example so that the time will not be far distant when all will observe it.

It can be readily appreciated by all, that the purposes of those seeking this law's repeal are to have no legal holidays at all, if that could be attempted with any degree of safety. Those having any day in the year or the entire year as one continuous holiday have no need for any one day or half holiday stated by law. They have all they want. But the working men of this State who have had a taste and have felt the beneficent effects of a few hours relaxation from the drudgery of the week are loth to part with it.

It lies in your power, dear sir, to prevent this wrong and injustice being consumated, that you will is the earnest wish of,

Yours Very respectfully,   Saml Gompers
President, American Federation of Labor.

HLpS, reel 1, vol. 2, pp. 589-92, SG Letterbooks, DLC.

1. The New York legislature passed a Saturday Holiday Act on May 6, 1887; compliance was not compulsory except for banks and public offices. During the following year it met considerable resistance from the business community and the legislature attempted to amend it to apply only during the summer months. Governor Hill vetoed the amendment on May 7, 1888, asserting that the law had not been given a thorough trial. In 1889 and 1892, SG opposed further attempts to alter or repeal the law.

2. Herbert Spencer, an English philosopher, helped elevate the concept of economic competition unrestrained by governmental interference to the stature of a natural law in society. Since it was analogous to Charles Darwin's hypothesis that unrestrained genetic competition allowed species to adapt and survive in nature, this philosophy was known as "Social Darwinism."

3. In 1850 England passed an act that required women and children working in textile mills to cease working at 2 P.M. on Saturdays. The Factory Act of 1867 extended the mandatory Saturday half holiday to most industries. Not until 1908 did Parliament attempt to regulate the hours of male workers, though as early as the 1870s building trades, engineers, and textile unions in London had by their own efforts secured the Saturday half holiday.

To the Executive Council of the AFL

May 8th [188]8

To the Executive Council. AF of L.
Gentlemen.

Some time ago a letter reached me from Mr Geo W Appell[1] Secretary of the *Metal Workers Union of North America*[2] in which they claim that a Cornice Makers Union of Philadelphia, Pa[3] should be compelled to join the M.W.U of N.A or the *Tinners National Union*[4] recently formed.

It was also claimed that this Cornice Makers Union was previously suspended from the M.W.U of N.A for non-payment of *per capita* tax.

I wrote to Mr Appell inquiring how far he claimed jurisdiction for the M.W.U of NA as in previous conversations with him, he claimed jurisdiction for his organization over all Metal Workers, Gold, Silver, Steel, Iron, Brass, Copper, Tin, in short, all. His answer is Marked I

We have a Union of Architectural Sheet Iron Cornice Workers at Phila which I suppose was meant and recieved an indignant reply from them. Marked II

I reproved them for the tone of their answer and informed them that I wanted a formal answer to the complaint in response to which I recived letter Marked III

It is but proper that I should mention a few facts that have come to me in connection with my official duties and that may tend to assist you in determining the subject matter under consideration.

The M.W.U of N.A reported a membership for the past three months of 4.00.=424=424 respectively.

The correspondence held with the AT & S.I Cornice Workers before they recieved their Charter proves conclusively that they were Knights of Labor and not affiliated with the M.W.U of N.A.

The M.W.U of N.A through their officers have informed me that they claim jurisdiction over all Metal Workers. The sentiments or principles upon which they are organized is repugnant to a large class of Trades Unionists.

I should not fail to mention that the *National Tinners Union* is not affiliated with the A.F of L. The question to be voted upon by the E.C. is as follows.

"Shall the Architectural Tin & Sheet Iron Cornice Makers Union N 6 of Philadelphia be ordered to surrender its Charter to the A.F of L. and compelled to affiliate with the Metal Workers Union of North America".[5]

Each member of the E.C. will forward this letter and enclosed papers to the member of the E.C in rotation as it appears on this letter head. Each member returning his vote upon the question direct to

Yours Fraternally   Saml Gompers.
Pres't A.F of L.

N.B. When these documents reach Secretary McGuire he will forward them with his vote to this office. Vote & forward promptly.

S. G.

ALpS, reel 1, vol. 2, pp. 607-9, SG Letterbooks, DLC.

1. George W. APPEL was general secretary of the Metal Workers' National Union of North America between 1886 and 1889.
2. The METAL Workers' National Union of North America.
3. The Architectural Sheet Iron Cornice Workers' Union of Philadelphia.
4. The TIN, Sheet Iron and Cornice Workers' International Association.
5. The Executive Council voted against the proposal.

To the Executive Council of the AFL

May 10th [188]8

To the E.C. AF of L

Gentlemen.

Affixed to this you will find a declaration of the objects of the Metal Workers Union of N.A. It is clipped from their official Journal *The Hammer,* and published as a Preamble to their Constitution.

While the purposes and motives may be lofty and praiseworthy, it seems rather premature and artificial.

If there is to be a Federation of all Metal Workers it will evolve out of the organization of each Branch in that industry. But a body of 400 or 500 men to claim jurisdiction over all Metal Workers Unions is both unnatural and must fail.

Fraternally Yours   Saml Gompers.
Pres't AF of L

ALpS, reel 1, vol. 2, p. 622, SG Letterbooks, DLC.

A Circular Issued by the
Executive Council of the AFL

New York, May 10, 1888.

To the Affiliated Unions of the A.F. of L. and the Working People of America:

Greeting:

For the first time in its history, the American Federation of Labor appeals to you for financial aid in support of one of its affiliated unions.

More than a quarter of a century ago the boss brewers of this country succeeded in making a combination of the nature of what is now known as a "Trust," or "Pool."[1] Since that period, the comparatively insignificant capitals which were then employed in the brewing business have swollen into gigantic accumulations, rivalling the revenues of many European princes. The mean and temporary structures which were then used as brew-houses have been replaced by solidly constructed and palatial edifices. Every device that boundless wealth could extort from the fertile brains of chemists and other special scientists have been employed by the members of this "Trust" to reduce the cost of their product, regardless of the consumers' health or the welfare of the community, while the selling price of the product has been by them most jealously maintained. Not satisfied with the exorbitant profits accruing from the exercise of their special industry, the brewers have still further ravaged the community by the manipulation of every legislative body, and by reducing to a state of economic vassalage, by force of bond and mortgage, unnumbered thousands of heretofore independent business men. And now the ambition of these insatiate upstarts, ever growing greater by what it feeds upon, has risen to such a pitch of insane frenzy that they actually conspire to crush the union of their workmen under the false, hollow and shameful plea that their workmen hold different political opinions than themselves.

In view of the actual situation, it becomes the duty of the executive of the A.F. of L. to briefly state the facts of the present phase of the struggle for your information as follows:

That before the brewery workmen were organized wages ranged from $40 to $55 per month, and the hours of labor were from fifteen to eighteen hours per day for six days in the week, and from five to six hours on Sunday.

That since the brewery workmen organized their union wages range from $15 to $18 per week; that the hours of labor have been reduced to twelve per day (two of which are devoted to meals), making the hours actually ten for six days in the week and not more than two hours on Sunday.

That an agreement was made and existed the past two years between the Boss Brewers' and the Journeymen Brewers' Unions.

That the agreement contained a clause providing that all questions of difference arising should be submitted to a board of arbitration.

That the said board of arbitration consisted of five persons, three of whom were members of the Boss Brewers' association and two of the Journeymen Brewers' Unions.

That of all the matters of difference brought before the attention of the said board of arbitration by the Journeymen Brewers' Unions, some twenty in number, all except one were decided in favor of the Journeymen.

That the Journeymen Brewers' Unions have lived up to and have not violated any of the provisions of the agreement with the Boss Brewers.

That the agreement above referred to expired on April 1st, 1888.

That, as was customary, notice was sent to the Secretary of the Boss Brewers' Association[2] by the Secretary of the Journeymen Brewers' Unions[3] asking when it would suit the pleasure of the former to receive a committee of the latter, at which the provisions of an agreement for another year might be considered.

That an answer was received from the Secretary of the Boss Brewers' Association which enclosed a circular containing a resolution adopted by the said Association that no new agreements be entered into at the expiration of those then existing.

That, while the circular alleges that the Journeymen Brewers' Unions were too dictatorial, and that the bosses would thereafter "run" their own business, the terms of a new agreement had not yet been presented when the said circular was issued, thus showing that the Boss Brewers' Association were determined upon their present course of action regardless of the terms of a new agreement.

That as the circulars and other public utterances were made by the representative of the Boss Brewers' Association alleging that they were suffering from annoyances, grievances, etc., etc., at the hands of the Journeymen Brewers' Unions, at the request of the latter a committee was appointed by the New York Central Labor Union, who visited the Boss Brewers, all of whom admitted that they were satisfied with their workmen and the rules and conduct of the Unions.

That when said committee asked these Boss Brewers whether they would be willing to discuss an agreement for another year and submit to arbitration, they were referred to the office of the Boss Brewers' Association.

That the said committee wrote a letter to the Secretary of the Boss Brewers' Association asking when and where they might meet the committee to discuss, and if necessary arbitrate, any difficulty between the interested parties.

That an answer was received from the Secretary of the Boss Brewers' Association stating that no trouble of any kind existed "which required arbitration."

That on April 16, without a word of warning, the brewery workmen, some 5,000 in all, employed by members of the Boss Brewers' Association, were locked out.

That there existed no justification for locking out the brewery workmen upon the pretence of grievances, as any such matters could have been referred to the Board of Arbitration, a majority of whom were members of the Boss Brewers' Association.

That a number of Boss Brewers were willing to make an agreement with the Journeymen Brewers' Union, but refrained from so doing by threats of other Boss Brewers—members of the Boss Brewers' Association—to ruin their business if they agreed with their workmen.

In consideration of the above stated facts, and upon request of the Journeymen Brewers' Union, I now issue this appeal for financial aid

in support of said regularly affiliated Union, in harmony with Article
VII., Sections 3 and 4, of the Constitution,[4] and the unanimous approval of the Executive Council A.F. of L.

Yours fraternally,   Sam'l Gompers, Pres.

P. J. McGuire, Sec.

Daniel McLaughlin, First Vice-Pres.

William Martin, Second Vice-Pres.

Gabriel Edmonston, Treasurer.

N.B. — All contributions should be sent direct to Louis Herbrand, 213
Forsyth street, New York City.

Labor Leader, May 26, 1888.

1. The U.S. Brewers' Association (USBA), was a national interest group of lager beer brewers founded in 1862.
2. Richard Katzenmayer was secretary of the USBA from 1867 to 1898.
3. Louis Herbrand.
4. Article VII, sections 3 and 4 of the AFL's 1887 constitution provided that the Executive Council could solicit voluntary financial aid from the Federation's affiliates for unions involved in justifiable boycotts, strikes, or lockouts.

To George Appel

May 22nd [188]8

Geo W Appell Esq
Sec'y. MWU of NA
Dear Sir.

The matter of your letter written to me some time ago in reference to the Cornice Makers Union of Philadelphia has, as I informed you been referred to the Executive Council of the AF of L together with the letters upon the same subject of the Union referred to.

The E.C have decided not to compel the Cornice Makers Union of Phila to join either the Metal Workers National Union of N.A. or the Tinners National Union at present. The reasons the members of the E.C give for their decision are many among which the following may be noted.

Upon investigation it is shown that the Cornic[e] Makers Union is not the body you refer to, inasm[uch] as they never belonged to the Metal Workers Union of N.A and consequently never did secede from it nor owed it any *per capita* tax for which it could be suspended.

That at present it would be inadvisable to force *all* Tin, Sheet Iron, and *all forms of Metal Workers Unions* into your Organization. That it would be more advisable to have the various branches of Metal Workers organized in their respective Unions and finally to endeavor to bring about a general amalgamation of all Metal Workers Unions into one grand Organization.

The Tinners National Union is not affiliated with the A.F of L.

It is of course unnecessary for me to add that it is the desire of the E.C to aid your organization all in its power, but inasmuch as the Cornice Makers are endeavoring to bring about a National Organization of their trade it is deemed unwise to frustrate their purpose in its inception.

With best wishes, I am

Yours Fraternally   Saml Gompers.
President AF of L.

ALpS, reel 1, vol. 2, pp. 667-68, SG Letterbooks, DLC.

To the Officers and Members of the Netherlandisch Isralitiche Sickefund[1]

May 22nd [188]8

To the Officers & Members of the Netherlandisch Isralitiche Sickefund.

Gentlemen.

Information has reached this office that Mr John Klein a monumental Marble and Granite Cutter whose place of business is situated at 20th Street and 9th Avenue, Near Greenwood Cemetery, Brooklyn is dealing unfair with his workingmen.

Employers in this industry generally pay their Employees $3.50 per day for nine hours work. He contrary to that rule refuses to pay more than $3.00 for ten hours work.

The Granite Cutters National Union[2] is a body of workingmen whose skill and devotion to duty is well known and have been made to feel the meanness and averice of this unfair employer.

Then again other Employers are placed at a great disadvantage. They say that either Mr Klein should be required to pay the same wages as they or they will be compelled to reduce wages to his level.

I am aware that the members of your honored Society are chiefly workingmen who frequently find themselves in a like position, and those who themselves are not workingmen are sympathizers with the honest aspirations of labor to prevent a deterioration in their condition. Hence I assume that if you can in any honorable way assist the Granite workers, your fellow men in obtaining not only justice but assist in bringing this unfair Employer to a sense of his duty to his workmen, you will gladly do it.

It is well known that Mr Klein's business depends largely upon the patronage of the members of Benevolent Societies such as yours and I kindly ask you to let Mr Klein know by letter, Committee or otherwise that you would regard it to his interest and your continued good will and patronage to deal fairly with his Employees.

Trusting that you will not regard these suggestions as improper and comply with the above request. I [am] asking you to accept the kind wishes of

Yours Respectfully & Fraternally   Saml Gompers.
President American Federation of Labor.

ALpS, reel 1, vol. 2, pp. 669-70, SG Letterbooks, DLC.

1. SG sent similar letters to the United Brethren Benefit Society and the Hebrew Mutual Benefit Society on June 22, 1888 (reel 1, vol. 2, pp. 772-75, SG Letterbooks, DLC).
2. The GRANITE Cutters' National Union of the United States of America.

A Circular Issued by
the Executive Council of the AFL

Headquarters: 171 E. 91st St., New York, June 4, 1888.

To all Local, National and International Trade Unions in America—Greeting.

It is now generally admitted by all really educated and honest men that a thorough organization of the entire working class, to render employment and the means of subsistence less precarious by securing an equitable share of the fruits of their toil is the most vital necessity of the present day.

To meet this urgent necessity, and to achieve this most desirable result, efforts have been made, too numerous to specify, and too divergent to admit of more than the most general classification. Suffice it to say, that those attempts at organization which admitted to membership the largest proportion of others than wage-workers were those which went the most speedily to the limbo of movements that won't move; while, of the surviving experiments, those which started with the most elaborate and exhaustive platforms of abstract principles were those which got the soonest into fatal complications, and soonest became exhausted.

In the face of so many disastrous failures to supply the undoubtedly existing popular demand for a practical means of solving the great problem, the query naturally suggests itself to many: "Which is the best form of organization for the people, the workers?"

We unhesitatingly answer: "The organization of the working people, by the working people, for the working people, that is, the Trades Union."

The trade unions are the natural growth of natural laws, and from the very nature of their being have stood the test of time and experience. The development of the trade unions, regarded both from the standpoint of numerical expansion and that of practical working, has been marvelously rapid. The trade unions have demonstrated their ability to cope with every emergency—economic or political—as it arises.

It is true that single trade unions have been often beaten in pitched battles against superior forces of united capital, but such defeats are by no means disastrous; on the contrary, they are useful in calling the attention of the workers to the necessity of thorough organization, of the inevitable obligation of bringing the yet unorganized workers into the union, of uniting the hitherto disconnected local unions into national unions, and of effecting a yet higher unity by the affiliation of all national and international unions in one grand federation, in which each and all trade organizations would be as distinct as the billows, yet one as the sea.

In the work of the organization of labor, the most energetic, wisest and devoted of us, when working individually, cannot hope to be successful, but by combining our efforts *all* may. And the combined action of all the unions when exerted in favor of any one union will certainly be more efficacious than the action of any one union, no matter how powerful it may be, if exerted in favor of an unorganized, or a partially organized, mass. The Brotherhood of Painters has, within a little more than one year, gained nearly one hundred subordinate local unions, and it has been largely enabled to achieve this remarkably rapid growth by the assistance of the Brotherhood of Carpenters, the Tailors, the Cigar Makers and other affiliated unions of the American Federation of Labor. Thus, furnishing another proof, if any further proofs were needed by union men, that "in union there is strength."

We assert that it is the duty, as it is also the plain interest, of all working people to organize as such, meet in council, and take practical steps to effect the unity of the working class, as an indispensable preliminary to any successful attempt to eliminate the evils of which we, as a class, so bitterly and justly complain. That this much desired unity has never been achieved is owing in a great measure to the non-recognition of the autonomy, or the right of self-government, of the several trades. The American Federation of Labor, however, avoids the fatal rock on which previous organizations, having similar aims, have split, by simply keeping in view this fundamental principle as a landmark, which none but the most infatuated would have ever lost sight of.

The rapid and steady growth of the American Federation of Labor, arising from the affiliation of previously isolated, together with newly-formed, National Unions; the establishment of local unions of various trades and callings where none before existed; the spontaneous formation of Federal Labor Unions, composed of wage-workers following various trades in places where there are too few persons employed at any particular one to allow the formation of local unions of those trades, thus furnishing valuable bodies of auxiliaries and recruits to existing unions upon change of abode, this steady growth is gratifying evidence of the appreciation of the toilers of this broad land of a form of general organization in harmony with their most cherished traditions, and in which each trade enjoys the most perfect liberty while securing the fullest advantages of united action.

And now, in conclusion, you will permit us to express our acknowledgement of the very moderate amount of governing which has fallen to the lot of those who have the honor to address you. While much of this good fortune must be attributed to the nature of the federal form of our organization, our task has been immeasureably lightened by the assistance of a body of organizers, who, without hope of reward, except the consciousness of performing a sacred duty to their fellow workmen, have carried the propaganda of trade unionism into the remotest parts of the Continent. Much of our burden has been also eased by the generous co-operation of the Executives of National and International Unions, both affiliated and unaffiliated, the latter of whom have doubtless so acted from a conviction that within the lines of the Federation will be fought to the bitter end the fast-coming grand struggle between Capital and Labor, involving the perpetuation of the civilization we have so laboriously evolved. Deeply grateful, as we are, for your fraternal support, we should be negligent of the duty we owe to each and all did we not urge the Local, National and International Unions who have not yet joined the American Federation of Labor to do so without further delay.

Yours fraternally,   Saml Gompers. President.
P. J. McGuire, Secretary.
Daniel McLaughlin, First Vice-President.
William Martin, Second Vice-President.
Gabriel Edmonston, Treasurer.

PLSr, Papers of Gabriel Edmonston, reel 1, *AFL Records.*

To John Elliott

June 11, [188]8

Mr John T. Elliott—
Sec'y B'th'd Painters, etc.,
1314 North Fulton Ave., Baltimore, Md.—
Dear Sir:

Yours of the 9th inst. enclosing Money Order for Capita Tax to hand. Please find enclosed receipt for same. The 1st semi-annual report (financial) of the A.F. of L. is in press, and will probably reach you within one week from date. In the matter of arranging an exchange of working cards, I have spoken with Archibald[1] to very little effect. The feeling of the officers of the various organizations of Painters here is very antagonistic to the Brotherhood. The Protectives have notified the Building Trades Section of the C.L.U. that they will not recognise the cards[2] of the Brotherhood on they ground that they have admitted to membership expelled members of other organizations. I do not think that the Brotherhood will have much influence here until the Carpenters' make a breach in the Chinese wall around this city.

Saml Gompers.
Pres't A.F. of L.

HLpSr, reel 1, vol. 2, p. 711, SG Letterbooks, DLC.

1. James Patrick ARCHIBALD, a paperhanger, was an officer in the New York City Central Labor Union (CLU) and district master workman of paperhangers' National Trade Assembly 210 from 1888 to 1890.

2. During the 1880s and 1890s the painting trade in New York City was badly splintered; at one point thirteen organizations of painters existed. Despite SG's intervention, the Brotherhood of Painters and Decorators of America had difficulty translating its affiliation with the AFL into a general recognition of its working cards by the New York City CLU's Building Trades Section and the Board of Walking Delegates.

To Frederick Haller

June 11th [188]8

Fred Haller, Esq
Pres't. New York S.B. AF of L.[1]
Dear Sir

In the New York *Sun* of the 9th inst I read a letter signed by W C Parker "Vice President of the American Federation of Labor".[2] In this letter Mr Parker assumes the title to an office he does not posess and discusses subjects foreign to the purposes and spirit of the American Federation of Labor.

We are about to enter the era of excitement consequent upon a Presidential election and we should use the utmost caution to prevent any man from dragging our organization into the meshes of such an imbroglio or trailing its fair name in the dust.

Party politics and the questions upon which the opinions of our affiliated organizations and members diverge so much and upon which they might be arrayed against each other must be eschewed by the Officers of the Federation, at least in their official capacity. The man who seeks to act otherwise must be seen to in time before it is too late.

I am aware that Mr Parker is a Vice President of your State Branch and believe he had no authority to use its name (If that is what he intended by using the title of the AF of L.) in his letter.

I call upon you to see to it that Mr Parker is prevented from using his office for the purpose indicated or be compelled to give up the office he holds.

Hoping to hear from [you] in reference to this matter at your earliest convenience. I am

Yours Fraternally   Saml Gompers.
Pres't AF of L

ALpS, reel 1, vol. 2, pp. 723-24, SG Letterbooks, DLC.

1. The New York State Branch (NYSB) of the AFL.
2. William C. Parker, a Brooklyn printer, was first vice-president of the NYSB. In his letter to the *New York Sun* (June 9, 1888), he challenged claims in the Republican press that the tariff would protect American workmen from cheap European labor and argued that unrestricted immigration was overcrowding almost every trade.

The Executive Council of the AFL to the Trade and Labor Unions of San Francisco

New York, June 13, 1888

Labor Omnia Vincit

To the Trade & Labor U[n]ions of San Francisco—
Fellow Workmen:

The fact is being fast forced upon the consciousness of the wage-workers of this continent that they are a distinct and practically permanent class of modern society; and, consequently, have distinct and permanently common interests.

The recognition of this fact by the more advanced members of the working class has resulted in an organized movement to render employment and the means of subsistence less precarious by securing an equitable share of the fruits of their toil. The proof of the existence of a popular demand for a practical means of alleviating and finally abolishing the misery and degradation resulting from the present industrial system may be found in the marvelous growth of trade unions[,] of the formation of numerous National & Internatio[n]al Unions[,] by the incorporation of numberless Loca[l] Unions, and in the establishment of Trade & Labor Councils and Federations in almost e[very] industr[ial] centre. Hand in hand with this numerical growth and concentration of power has proceeded a more general recognition of the trade union methods of transacting business and the trade union policy of autonomy or self-government in all trade affairs.

This encouraging progress infuses us with hope that the day is not far distant when the unity of the working class will be achieved and when a successful attempt made be made to eliminate the evils of which we, as a class, so bitterly and justly complain. That this desirable and inevitable working class unity should be delayed by a few Local and yet fewer National Unions holding aloof from the general movement would be a misfortune to be deplored.

Therefore, we, the Executive Council of the American Federation of Labor call upon all Local, National & International Trade Unions, in general, to unite their forces while preserving their indisputable right to self-govenment; and upon the local Trade & Labor Unions of San Francisco, in particular, to join the Trade & Labor Federation of the Pacific Coast[1] in order that their special, no less than their general, interests may be fully represented in the rapidly developing movement which we have the honor to serve.

The rapid aggregation of wealth in the hands of a few unscrupulous men; the unity of Capital, demands the unity of Labor. This great necessity is the dominant fact of the present age. We must recognise the facts, or the facts will crush us.

Yours fraternally   Saml Gompers.
P J McGuire
Daniel McLaughlin
William Martin
G. Edmonston

HLpSr, reel 1, vol. 2, pp. 732-34, SG Letterbooks, DLC.

1. The Representative Council of the Federated Trades and Labor Organizations of the PACIFIC Coast.

To Gabriel Edmonston

New York, June 14th 1888

Gabriel Edmonston Esq.
Treasurer AF of L.
Dear Sir.

Enclosed you will please find a Bill[1] that requires introduction in Congress pursuant to a resolution of the Baltimore Convention and the Executive Council of the AF of L at its recent session.

It seems to me that it would be advisable to have it introduced simultaneously in House and Senate (For which purpose please make another copy) I suggest Mr O[']Niell[2] of the Labor Committee in the former and Senator Blair, or Hiscock[3] or some other prominent Republican in the latter as pretty good men into whose hands you could place the Bills for introduction.

On Saturday I leave here for the East and shall be gone about a week or ten days.[4] Upon the completion of the trip I shall come on to Washington.

Have the Bill introduced regardless of its chances.

Fraternally Yours   Saml Gompers,
Prest

ALS, Papers of Gabriel Edmonston, reel 1, *AFL Records.*

1. The bill, providing for the regulation of vessels engaged in domestic commerce (S. 3216, 50th Cong., 1st sess., 1888), required that each ship should have a master who had passed an examination to establish his qualifications. It was introduced on June 25, 1888, by Senator Henry Blair, and was referred to the Committee on Commerce; the bill was never reported out of committee.

2. John Joseph O'Neill of Missouri was a Democratic U.S. congressman for five terms (1883-89, 1891-95). He gained a national reputation for the introduction and passage of a bill providing for the arbitration of labor differences involving railroads that affected interstate commerce.

3. Frank Hiscock of New York was a Republican U.S. senator from 1887 to 1893.

4. SG left New York City on June 16 to make an organizing trip through New England.

A Translation of an Interview in the
New Yorker Volkszeitung

[June 18, 1888]

DECLINE OF THE CIGAR INDUSTRY.

. . .

Samuel Gompers, the president of the American Federation of Labor, was also asked about the contribution of the *Staatszeitung*[1] by a reporter from the *Volkszeitung*.

"Yes," he said, "the cigar trade in New York—only in New York, you understand—has declined. In 1886 it had blossomed here to its fullest extent. This was the year in which there were the most union shops in New York, especially among the big factories, and in that year there was also the greatest demand on the part of the manufacturers for the union label. In 1887 the trade was already declining because there were no longer as many union factories and shops. The union label and its phenomenal use had provided the manufacturers with the great business upswing of 1886. In the first quarter of the current year a decline was again recorded in comparison to the first quarter of 1887. This is a result of the most recent action of the manufacturers, by which the use of the union label was reduced once again. In the quarter from January 1 to April 1 of this year 20,000,000 fewer cigars were made in New York than in the same quarter of last year.

"To be sure, other factors contributed to bringing New York cigars into discredit nationwide. The reintroduction of the tenement-house system in New York has become known throughout the country as has the introduction of machines. The tobacco plant is extremely sensitive to fat, oil, or any other impurities, and without oil machines absolutely will not work.

"The statement of the *Staatszeitung* that the union demands absolutely equal payment for its members for both good and bad work is simply ridiculous. The wages are without exception piece wages and significantly higher for good work than for the poorer grades of cigars. The manufacturer is at complete liberty to give his best workers the best work, whereby they then have the opportunity to earn proportionately more. Actually the union establishes only a minimum wage, below which none of its members may work, but leaves it up to each manufacturer to pay higher wages to the better workers. Naturally they very seldom make use of this freedom.

"The manufacturers say in the *Staatszeitung* that wages have risen from $2 to $5 per thousand as a result of the union agitation a few years ago. This is true. Naturally wage increases of $5 per thousand have occurred very seldom; those of $2 happened significantly more often, but the earlier wages were literally starvation wages.

"For 30 years experiments have been made with the use of machines. The bunching machine was the final result of these experiments. I gladly admit that their introduction was a consequence of wages that were still too high from the standpoint of the manufacturers. Where the exchange value of human labor sinks to the lowest possible level, the introduction of machines is, of course, unnecessary from the standpoint of the manufacturer. But China, where these conditions do prevail, certainly isn't the happiest country under the sun, is it?

"It is still an open question whether this bunching machine is really of advantage in the cigar trade. As soon as the world finds out that only tobacco scraps can be processed with the machine, people will no longer buy cigars produced with it. Such a cigar is only a cheap substitute for a pipe. Good cigars with long 'fillers' can simply not be produced by means of the machine.

"The machines have put a lot of workers out of work. The manufacturers know this as well as we do. And still they complain in the *Staatszeitung* about the shorter workday won by the union? Where is the consistency here? Is this not simply ridiculous?

"The manufacturers further admit that New York's trade in the better grades of cigars probably has increased rather than decreased. Well, the dealers know that machines and tenement-house work cannot be used for these cigars. This is why the aversion against this type of New York work is not yet as great as in the middle grades. Moreover, the manufacturers who make such products have union shops and the union label.

"When Mr. Haas from Kerbs & Spies says he could teach a girl in six weeks to make cigars with the machine, this might perhaps be so. In any case he cannot teach her to make a good cigar. That is impossible. Even a good cigarmaker cannot produce a good cigar with the machine.

"George Lies[2] and his business partners think that the reduction of wages would bring the industry back to New York. Despite the reduced wages, the workers would then be better off than before and would have steadier work. This is illogical. The introduction of machines will not bring the trade back to New York; on the contrary, it will drive it out more and more. Where is the steadier work supposed to come from?

"As far as competition in the country is concerned, I can assure

you that everywhere in the country towns (with the exception of
Binghampton and other small towns, which the bosses are constantly
referring to) the wages are higher than in New York. If the union
has done its utmost to raise wages in New York, it has done so in
order to achieve a balance of wages, to bring the wages in New York
to the same level as is common throughout the country. We would
certainly not react with alarm if the cigar trade were driven out of
New York. We know that for the same cigars, which would perhaps
no longer be made in New York, higher wages are paid elsewhere in
the country than here. Naturally we would prefer to see the trade
stay here, since our members are, after all, here and in any case would
like to stay; however, the same wages as elsewhere would have to be
paid.

"Mr. Haas says that he tried for two years to work in cooperation
with the union but that the competition from Binghampton had forced
him to abandon this system. But he told me recently that it was not
the competition from Binghampton but that of the New York tenement-house manufacturers that forced him into abandoning this system. So, what is true?

"The contention of Messrs. Lies & Co., that the union does not
allow its members to work in factories where machines are used, is
untrue.

"As far as the competition from Binghampton is concerned, it simply
does not exist. Only two factories there produce good cigars, and
these pay appropriate wages. Furthermore, rubbish of the very lowest
kind is produced there. And even for this, the wages there are just
as high as those paid here for the same rubbish, whose production is
now being introduced in New York and which is destroying the hitherto good reputation of the products here. In short, for good products,
wages in the country are at least as high or higher than in New York,
and for rubbish the same pitiful wages are paid here as anywhere else
in the country."

New Yorker Volkszeitung, June 18, 1888. Translated from the German by
Patrick McGrath.

1. On June 11, 1888, the *New Yorker Staats-Zeitung* published an article on the
decline of New York City's cigar industry. It featured interviews with several cigar
manufacturers who contended that the CMIU had raised wages to such a degree that
cigars made by machines and by cheaper labor outside the city had taken over the
market.

2. George P. Lies was New York City's second largest cigar manufacturer in 1888.

To the Executive Council of the AFL

New York, June 29, 1888

To the Executive Council, A.F. of L.

Gentlemen:

I am in receipt of a letter from a prominent delegate to the Baltimore Convention, saying:—

"The Ex. B'd, K. of L. is working hard to get the appointment for the new Dep't of Labor.[1] I believe that if the Dep't is to be of any value to organized labor it must not fall into the hands of politicians; and I therefore hold that the Ex. Co. A.F. of L. ought immediately consider what steps are necessary to secure that Dep't in labor's interest."

In connection, I would state that Brother John McBride of Ohio has informed me that he is a candidate for the position, and requests me to write a letter to President Cleveland[2] stating that his appointment would be satisfactory to labor. Will you give me authority to comply with his request?

I suggest that you nominate three (3) persons whom you may consider fittest to perform the functions of Commissioner of the Department of Labor, and forward such nominations by telegraph to this office.

I will upon receipt of your nominations prepare a letter to President Cleveland suggesting a selection from the list of names.

I would particularly request that no member of the Ex. Co. should be nominated. Let us take no part in the unseemly struggle for office.

Yours fraternally,   Saml Gompers.

Pres't, A.F. of L.

HLSr, Papers of Gabriel Edmonston, reel 1, *AFL Records.*

1. The Bureau of Labor was created within the Department of Interior in 1884, with Carroll D. Wright appointed the first U.S. commissioner of labor. In 1888 Congress made the bureau an independent subcabinet-level agency and renamed it the Department of Labor (DOL); Wright headed the new department. The DOL achieved cabinet level status in 1913.

2. Grover Cleveland (1837-1908) was a Democratic governor of New York (1883-85) and president of the United States (1885-89, 1893-97).

To Louis Hartmann[1]

June 30, [188]8

Mr Louis Hartmann—
Gen. Organizer, A.F. of L.
490 Wood St., Chicago, Ill.—
Dear Sir & Brother:

In reply to yours of the 27th you will permit [me] to say that while I feel bound by the letter of the Constitution I trust I shall never cease to be guided by the spirit thereof. Art. IX, Sec 3[2] is most specific in its terms, and leaves me no liberty as to whom I shall grant certificates to. I feel the necessity of organizing the entire proletariat, and will ever strive to realise this much to be desired result. That much progress has been made to this end we must all acknowledge. The name of an organization of which you are Secretary is an evidence of progress—Trade & *Labor* Assn. In my address to the Baltimore Convention I took occasion to state that the name of this organization is the American Federation of *Labor*. Again, the feature of F.L.U's[3] is an innovation in trade union organization. I regard it as a most progressive step, and as such fraught with possibilities for good or evil. It opens the door to an immense number who previously could not identify themselves with the labor movement proper. Therefore, it is necessary that all who desire progress should jealously conserve and ardently defend this advanced post known as Federal Labor Unions. Too much vigilenc[e] cannot be excercised in this direction. Consequently, I reiterate my statement of the 16th instant:[4]—The *applicants* must be wage-workers.

Hoping that you will consider this a suffcent answer to your question, and relying upon your good sense and devotion to the bonafide movement of the working class.

I remain,

Yours fraternally,   Saml Gompers
Pres't, A.F. of L.

HLpSr, reel 1, vol. 2, pp. 797-98, SG Letterbooks, DLC.

1. Louis HARTMANN, a cigarmaker, was secretary of the Illinois State Federation of Labor and the Trade and Labor Assembly of Chicago.
2. Article IX, section 3, of the AFL constitution stated that any seven wage earners not already affiliated with the AFL could form a federal labor union, with the endorsement of "the nearest Local or National Trades Union officials connected with this Federation" (AFL, *Proceedings*, 1887, p. 4).
3. Federal Labor Unions.
4. To Hartmann, reel 1, vol. 2, pp. 757-58, SG Letterbooks, DLC.

P. J. McGuire to Gabriel Edmonston

Phila. July 2 1888

Bro Edmonston
Dear Friend:

I am in receipt of a letter from S. Gompers dated June 29 in regard to the new Dep't of Labor. I have answered it and told him as I now I tell you that I am of the opinion our Executive Council should not meddle with the subject at all, for I am credibly advised that there will be no change at all, as the Com of the Labor Bureau becomes the Head of the new Dep't—one being merged into the other. If we should favor any one let us favor Mr Carroll D. Wright, the present incumbent, as he has done his work well and is favorable to the Labor interests.

Yours   P. J McGuire

P.S. O[']Brien[1] letters recd Thanks. Will notify you in case Altvater appeals.

ALS, Papers of Gabriel Edmonston, reel 1, *AFL Records.*

1. Patrick L. O'Brien, an early member of Brotherhood of Carpenters and Joiners of America local 1 of Washington, D.C., was one of those who led the local at the time of its expulsion from the Brotherhood in 1886. During 1888 he attempted to organize a KOL national carpenters' assembly.

To the Members of the CMIU

New York, July 7, 1888.

To the Members of the C.M.I.U.:
Greeting:

The appeal of Mr. Goodacre[1] as well as the position he assumes upon the question, I confess, surprises me. To maintain that a member of a trades union can retain his standing while acting in direct opposition, yes antagonism, to the purposes of that organization requires a peculiar and wonderful stretch of imagination.

The appellant not only opposed the enforcement of the resolutions of the Convention, but went specially out of his way to have his opposition aired in the public press, which at nearly all times is happy when anything can be published against the action of a union. He not only antagonized and acted against the interests of the International Union, but he called upon the members to act in direct opposition to the expressed will of the legislature of the Cigar Makers' International Union, viz: the Convention. He says that the resolutions are not binding because the members did not vote upon them. If this is so then no resolution whatever of the Convention is binding. Not even those which direct the officers to agitate against the tenement-house system of cigar making, the Chinese coolie system, etc. If the resolutions of the Convention are not binding upon the members, they certainly cannot be binding upon the officers, yet what would be said if any officer would ignore and act in opposition to a resolution directing him to do a certain thing. For instance, the Cincinnati Convention[2] passed a resolution that the office of the International President should be more centrally located. (This was not voted upon by the members.) Supposing the International President had moved the office instead of "more centrally" to Massachusetts or Maine, and claimed that the resolution was not binding upon him. What would the appellant have said? "Outragious, he ought to be impeached!" And had he done so he certainly should have been. The delegates to the Convention, coming right from the midst of their respective constituencies, were certainly supposed to know their wants upon an important matter, whose emergency required immediate and pronounced action, and they exercised their heretofore undisputed right.

I am not one who will attempt to deprive a member of his opinion, but to my mind a member, if in the minority, should endeavor within the legitimate limits of the union, to make his minority opinion transferred to the majority, and until that is accomplished, abide by the decision of the majority, his opinion to the contrary notwithstanding; failing in this he ceases to be a union man. A member cannot and should not be permitted to act against the interests of the union under any pretense. The appellant's pretense is of the flimsiest.

Yours Fraternally,   Samuel Gompers,
Second Vice-President.

Cigar Makers' Official Journal, Supplement, July 1888.

1. James J. Goodacre of Hartford, Conn., was a member of CMIU 42 as well as a KOL organizer and member of KOL Local Assembly 1977. In January CMIU 42 voted against endorsing a resolution passed by the 1887 CMIU convention favoring the retention of the internal revenue tax on cigars. When Adolph Strasser refused to publish a report of local 42's action in the *Cigar Makers' Official Journal*, Goodacre protested in a letter to the *Hartford Times*. Strasser instructed the local to expel Goodacre from the union, calling his public statement an invitation to "open rebellion" (*Cigar Makers' Official Journal*, Supplement, July 1888). The CMIU Executive Board upheld Strasser's expulsion of Goodacre.
2. The convention met in Cincinnati, Sept. 21-30, 1885.

To Thomas O'Dea[1]

July 7th [188]8

Thomas O'Dea
Sec'y Bricklayers International Union[2]
Dear Sir.

I regret very much to be compelled to write you upon the subject in mind viz complaints that reach me from several points wherein Bricklayers belonging to your organization are working not in harmony but in direct opposition to the efforts of Union Hod Carriers[3] and Masons helpers and tenders.

You are aware that the purposes of the American Federation of Labor holds as one of its cardinal principles the autonomy and independence of each Trade Union and that I am not at all desirous of interfering with your organization or involve them into any trouble even if I could, but your attention is respectfully called to the fact that organized workmen can be engaged in better work than antagonizing their fellow–Trades Unionists.

I am aware that you cannot by an "order" prevent this from occurring but much can be done by the officers of Trades Unions to cultivate fraternal feelings among their members for their fellow toilers.

In the hope that the causes for complaint may soon cease to exist, that the Trades Unionists of the country may act in harmony for the best results and wishing the Bricklayers International Union every success. I have the honor to subscribe myself.

Yours Fraternally   Saml Gompers.
Prest AF of L.

ALpS, reel 1, vol. 2, pp. 836-37, SG Letterbooks, DLC.

1. Thomas O'DEA served as secretary of the Bricklayers' and Masons' International Union from 1884 to 1887 and from 1888 to 1900.

2. The BRICKLAYERS' and Masons' International Union of America.

3. SG on several other occasions had to settle disputes between hod carriers and bricklayers. The HOD Carriers did not organize their own international until 1903.

Adelbert Dewey[1] to Terence Powderly

Philadelphia, July 10 1888 11:55 P.M.

Dear Brother Powderly:

Just as we were about to go to press last week Bro. Hayes[2] handed me your dispatch directing me to let the Department of Labor at

Washington alone. The enclosed editorial[3] was in the paper, but I took it out. What's the matter? If there is anything in the wind let me know it, and I will govern myself accordingly.

My reason for writing the enclosed article was this: I have learned that great political pressure is being brought to have Cleveland appoint Sam Gompers to that position as a campaign move for the labor vote in New York State. I would sooner see *the Devil himself* in that position than Sam Gompers. Wright has made a good commissioner, and I do not know of any one of the applicants so well qualified or more willing to serve labor interests than Carroll D. Wright.

Thanks for your compliments to *Journal*. I think myself that it looks well. Circulation has increased nearly 1000 this week. With kind wishes,

Yours very truly, A. M. Dewey,

Let me hear from you if convenient about the Wright matter. We go to press on Monday next with our big edition of 100000 copi[e]s. Got my story all right yesterday. Will send your proof of Coxe article tomorrow. If you have anything you want to get into the big edition, please let me have it by Friday night if possible.

Yours, Dewey.

ALS, Terence Vincent Powderly Papers, DCU.

1. Adelbert M. DEWEY, a printer, was editor and manager of the KOL organ, the *Journal of United Labor,* from 1888 to 1889.

2. John William HAYES, a grocer, was a member of the KOL General Executive Board from 1884 to 1916, serving as KOL general secretary-treasurer (1888-1902) and general master workman (1902-16).

3. The editorial endorsed Carroll D. Wright to head the Department of Labor.

Terence Powderly to Adelbert Dewey

Scranton Pa. July 11 1888.

My dear Dewey:—

There is nothing particular in the wind concerning the Labor Department that I would care to entrust to paper. I heard a week ago that you were to write, or would be requested to write, an editorial for the Journal favoring Wright, hence my telegram to Hayes. Take my advice and if any one wishes to have the Journal say a word for any one let that one do so over his, or her own signature. As one of the Trustees I object to booming any one in the paper. So far as Gompers is concerned you may rest easy, he will not be appointed. I don't think there is any disposition to remove Wright and if there is it will be time enough to take up his cause when the battle is opened. I shall explain more fully when I see you but if my advice is worth anything do not write anything in favor of any one for that position. If any one else wishes to do so let it be done over the signature of that person. We can dictate something in relation to the future policy of that department if we don't go off half cocked in favor of some one before being asked. The one who suggested that department to the president and who had the most to do with the bill in its infancy should have some say in the matter, don't you think so.

As ever Fraternally yours,

TLc, Terence Vincent Powderly Papers, DCU.

To Auguste Keufer

July 18, [188]8

Mr A[']te Keufer—
Delegate Fed. Francaize des Travailleurs du Livre,
15 Rue de Savoie, Paris, France—
Dear Sir & Brother:

Your esteemed favor of May 18 came duly to hand, but the pressure of business has been so great that an earlier reply thereto has been preclude[d] We thank you very much for the list of National Uni[ons] of Typographers in Western Europe and the central organizations of workingmen in France; and will be thankfull for any other addresses that you may send The subscription (l'abonnement) to the *Carpenter,* th[e] same as the majority of the official organs of Trade Unions in America, is not optional (facultatif), neither is there any special fund (caisse special[)] for printing. The Brotherhood of Carpenters is composed of 450 local unions with varying numbers of members, some unions having not more than 7 members, while other unions have several hundre[ds] of members. Union No. 8 located in Philadelphia havi[ng] 539 members in good financial standing, No. 33 in Bost[on] has 864 members, No. 56 in Los Angeles, California, has 785 members. Each Union collects, holds, and expends its own funds; and each union must reserve regularly each month a certain proportion of its receipts for special purposes, such as strikes and benevolence. Each Union must pay a fixed tax, called *per capita* tax, to the General Secretary, P. J. McGuire, for each of its members in good financial standing. This tax yeilded, for the month of May last, the sum of

$3,074.65, the number of members, in good standing, being 27,805. From this tax (mainly) is paid the general expenses of the Union or Brotherhood, among which is a *per Capita* tax of ¼ of one cent per month for each of the members of the Brotherhood paid to the American Federation of Labor amounting to $68.21, and 28,000 copies of the *Carpenter* costing for printing $185.00. Each Union is supplied with as many copies of the *Carpenter* as it has members in good standing. The Union then supplies each of its good members with one copy free of cost.

You ask, how will the struggle between the A.F. of L. and the K. of L. terminate? We reply, the American Federation is growing stronger and the Knights of Labor are growing weaker every day. At the end of the first year of its existence, Dec. '87, the A.F. of L. had 2,421 local unions with a total membership of 600,340 members in good standing, the total receipts for the *year* being $2,100.34. We do not know how many members we have to-day, but the total receipts for the *six months* ending May 28 were $2,047.28, being an increase of nearly 100 per cent. The following shows the decrease of the Knights of Labor—

July 1, 1886 — Members 729,677
     ″ ″,   '87 —   ″   548,229
     ″ ″   '88   ″   348,672

A loss of 50 per cent in two years.

Two of the affiliated unions of the A.F. of L. have successfully resisted lock-outs since my last letter. The Flint Glass Workers' National Union[1] have won a victory. The employers, threatened to crush the Union. The struggle began December 11, 1887, involving 8,000 men. The Union had a fund of $90,000, and in its struggle of five months duration spent $145,000. The defeat of the employers was complete! The Iron & Steel Workers' Union, numbering 55,000 men are now locked-out, but the employers are fast conceding the demands of the workmen, which were for the scale of wages of the previous year[2]

The American Federation of Labor has resolved not to send delegates to the International Trade Union Congress which will meet in London next November,[3] and will only be represented by letter. We hope, nevertheless, that the Congress will have a grand success, and that it will devise some means by which the trade unions of Western Europe may form a Federation. We know that the divergent views which exist among workingmen is a terrible obstacle to unity. We know that education is necessary to unity, but we hold that organization is as necessary for the sake of education, as education is necessary for organization. Education and organization march side by side.

Enclosed you will find a copy of an Appeal lately issued by the Federation.

Thanking you very much for your last letter, and wishing you every success, I remain

Yours fraternally   Saml Gompers
Pres't A.F. of L.

HLpSr, reel 1, vol. 2, pp. 852-55, SG Letterbooks, DLC.

1. The American FLINT Glass Workers' Union of North America.
2. On June 30, 1888, members of the Western Iron Association of Manufacturers, after refusing to sign the National Amalgamated Association of Iron and Steel Workers' (NAAISW) wage scale, closed all union mills, locking out over 100,000 workers. The NAAISW successfully fought the lockout and during the first two weeks major firms, such as Jones and Laughlin and Carnegie, signed the scale. On July 18 victory was assured when the Western Iron Association, weakened by defections, released its members from their pledge against signing the union scale.
3. Organized by the Trades Union Congress of Great Britain, the International Trade Union Congress opened Nov. 6, 1888. It adopted resolutions endorsing the eight-hour day and calling a workingmen's international congress for Paris in 1889.

To George Suter[1]

July 25th [188]8

George J Sutter, Esq
Dear Sir:

Your favor of the 24th came duly to hand and assure you that I share your regrets at our failure to meet and have a talk upon the subject in mind while I sojourned in Washington. I recognize that as good an understanding cannot be arrived at through correspondence as by conversation but trust we shall do as well as we can.

Permit me to say the same as I stated to Mr O'Brien[2] last Friday. That while in Baltimore I was approached and the deplorable situation and antagonism which existed among the Carpenters and Joiners of Washington and their position towards the organized Carpenters and Joiners of the Country as represented by the Brotherhood was gone into. Several men called my attention to the fact that a member of the Brotherhood had gone to your city obtained employment and because he deposited his travelling card with the recognized local he was dis-charged from his employment at the instance of members of your Union.

I was asked to intervene or rather endeavour to use my good offices to aid in bringing about a better understanding, harmony & unity if possible between your organization and the Brotherhood. As this is in line with my duties I promised to do what I could and trust my efforts may not be in vain. I am certain they will not if we but enter this matter with a sincere purpose to accomplish it and the co-operation of good men can be secured.

It is not my purpose to enter into a long detail of byegones. I prefer if that is possible to relegate the past into oblivion and see if through correspondence we cannot arrive with your organization at some general or specific understanding which I may lay before the Ex Board of the Brotherhood and urge its adoption.

It is superfluous for me to dilate upon the desirability of Union in the National organizations of our respective trades with one so well equipped as yourself with that knowledge. all I desire to mention upon it is, that a matter of small consequence should not stand in the way of obtaining so great and desirable results in organization and Unity of the carpenters and Joiners of the country.

You are aware no doubt that practically the United order of carpenters of New York and Vicinity[3] are affiliated with the Brotherhood. If your organization were in full fellowship with it also the few straggling carpenters not within its fold would soon be brought into line through the wonderful influence of organization.

Will you kindly inform Mr O'Brien that this letter is intended for his purusal as it would be entirely unnecessary to write seperately to two men so nearly associated with each other as you and he are upon the same subject.

Let me say further that you may make whatever use you desire of this letter and would esteem it a favor if you will read it to the meeting of your Union. Let us act open and above board in this matter and we may be rewarded with success.

Trusting that the unity may not be far distant that I may hear from you and your Union at an early day and my lot may not be the common one of the peacemaker, kicks from both sides, I am.

Yours Truly   Saml Gompers.
Pres't AF of L

ALpS, reel 1, vol. 2, pp. 873-75, SG Letterbooks, DLC.

1. George J. Suter was a leader of the Washington, D.C., independent carpenters' local 1.
2. Patrick L. O'Brien.
3. The United Order of American Carpenters and Joiners.

To J. P. McDonnell

July 26th [188]8

J P McDonnell. Esq
Dear Friend.

In the past few weeks I made the acquaintance (by correspondence) of a man by the name of Mr J H Fitzgibbon,[1] his correspondence was of such an impressive character that I appointed him Organizer. Immediately or thereafter he organized a Union of Lumbermen[2] who sent in their application for a charter. His letters pulsate with enthusiasm for his new work. He was a K of L, discovered the cause of their failure i e interfering with trade troubles of which they knew little or nothing and destroyed a good movement of his fellow-workmen. Today he is a good out and out Union man. He is now engaged in making estimates of the timber lands of which he seems to be an expert and indispensable to the employers. He will devote a day or more each week to organizing purposes and as he travels from place to place you can see his services may prove invaluable.

In his last letter he says that the work being in the interior papers are seldom if ever seen, and if some labor paper (and I say you) could send him a few sample copies it would do a great good in the first instance and more than repay any publisher of any Union paper (you) than can be imagined.

I have informed him that I would write to a publisher and I now do make this statement to you so that you may act upon it as seems most advantageous. Of one thing I again assure you that his correspondence bears the imprint of sincerity.

If you decide to acquiece, let me suggest that you accompany the paper with a brief letter stating that *you* are sending the papers in compliance with his request. Keep sending the papers for a few weeks and await results.

With best wishes I am.

Yours Sincerely   Saml Gompers.

Address. Box S Marinette, Wisconsin.

N.B. Last week while in Washington in the interest of labor legislation, I saw your Senator Bloadget[3] (elected by K of L votes) vote *against* the Bill for the payment of government workmen who worked more than eight hours. Certainly Leon Abbet[4] should be defeated by K of L men for such a man.

S. G.

ALpS, reel 1, vol. 2, pp. 884-85, SG Letterbooks, DLC.

1. James H. FITZGIBBON was president of the Menominee River Laboring Men's Protective and Benevolent Union and editor of the Marinette, Wis., *Laborer.*
2. Fitzgibbon organized a union of lumbermen in Sturgeon Bay, Wis. On July 27, 1888, SG sent this union its certificate of affiliation as Federal Labor Union 2705.
3. Rufus Blodgett was superintendent of the New York and Long Branch Railroad between 1884 and 1910 and served as a Republican U.S. senator from 1888 to 1892.
4. Leon Abbett, a lawyer, served as a Democrat in the general assembly (1865-67, 1869-71) and senate (1875-78) of the New Jersey legislature and as governor of New Jersey (1884-87, 1890-93).

To Lawrence Banford[1]

Aug 11th [188]8

L H Banford. Esq
Dear Sir & Friend.

In answer to your telegram let me say that I am billed to speak at Grand Rapids, Michigan on Labor Day but owing to Bronchitis which I have contracted in my travels and public speaking I doubt my ability to even keep this engagement.

Physicians inform me that this may trouble me for a long time perhaps for life. I trust however that I may soon be in good form to speak and accept some of the invitations that so constantly are tendered. Let me hear from you often.

With best wishes I am

Yours Fraternally   Saml Gompers.

ALpS, reel 1, vol. 2, p. 928, SG Letterbooks, DLC.

1. Lawrence H. BANFORD, a cigarmaker, was a general organizer for the AFL and was elected treasurer of the New York State Branch of the AFL in 1888.

To William McKinney[1]

Aug 11th [188]8

Wm H McKinney. Esq
Reading. Pa.
Dear Sir.

Permit me to thank you for the lucid manner and statement of the case of the Bricklayers and Masons Union of your city[2] in your favor of the 8th inst.

Succinctly the case is. The Union was part of the International Bricklayers Union, that body decided that nine hours should constitute a days work. All Unions affiliated with it enforced that law and demand except the Reading Union. They were given a years grace to enforce it, after the expiration of that time, rather than make an effort to secure that reduction in their hours of labor and live up to the law they surrendered their charter.

They now wish to connect themselves with a National organization and wish to know whether the American Federation of Labor will grant them a Certificate of Affiliation.

Let me say in answer (not to you but to them) emphatically *No.*

I recognize that the I.B.U is not one of the most advanced of Trade Unions and they are not doing right in so many instances holding themselves aloof from the general labor movement, but this is no reason why they should not be aided in every legitimate attempt to gain advances for their craft. There is no reason why the AF of L should encourage a rebellious faction against the regular authority.

In all matters connected with trade affairs and the conduct of business belonging to the Trade Unions the American Federation of Labor has proclaimed and means to stand by and defend the principle of independence and autonomy.

Thanking you for the interest you have taken in this matter and asking you to advise that local organization to obey the general law and become affiliated with the I.B.U.—their first natural allies, and hoping to hear from you often. I am

Yours Fraternally   Saml Gompers.
Pres't AF of L

ALpS, reel 1, vol. 2, pp. 929-30, SG Letterbooks, DLC.

1. William H. McKinney, a molder, was a general organizer for the AFL and president of the Trade and Labor Council of Reading, Pa.

2. The Bricklayers' 1886 St. Louis convention approved an amendment making the nine-hour day mandatory for all locals beginning May 1, 1886. All but six complied; Union 4 of Reading, Pa., was one of those that did not. The Bricklayers' Executive Board gave the six an extension, and shortly afterward the Reading local said it had achieved the nine-hour day. The 1888 convention, however, granted the Reading union a dispensation for the season to work ten hours on the grounds that the local could not enforce the nine-hour day because the majority of bricklayers in Reading were nonunion.

To Henry Bacon[1]

August 17 [188]8

Mr H. J. Bacon
Treasurer Conn. State Branch A.F. of L.,
31 Newton St., Meriden, Conn.—
Dear Sir & Bro:

Please find enclosed receipt for $2.00 Delegate Tax.

In answer to your enquiry would state that each State of this United States has its seperate Constitution and body of Statutes.

The theory of the law, of the English-speaking peoples, is that if any number of subjects, or citizens, desiring to combine for any purpose, not in conflict with the fundamental law, they may so do by permission of the legislature expressed by a special act, or a general act, under whose provisions they are recognised as one body, and as such can sue or be sued under their corporate name. This theory of the law generally prevails in practice; but, both the practice, and eventuaally, the theory of the law is modified to conform to altered social circumstances. So we find New York Civil Justice Steckler[2] holding the Treasurer of an un-incorporated society of workingmen responsible for the funds placed in his care. Other judges swayed perhaps more by the spirit of equity than the letter of the law have decided that any officer receiving any kind of compensation for his services from any society is as responsible to that society as if it were a single person. A few years since the officers of many National Trade Unions conferred concerning the advisability of having their Unions incorporated, and concluded against so doing, on the ground that if they rendered themselves liable to be sued (by incorporation) they would be speedily broken up.

In short, my opinion is that your Branch cannot be sued. The A.F. of L. is not an incorporated body; if it were, its headquarters would be located in Washington or one of the Territories, if chartered by the Federal government. And if it was incorporated by the State of New York and the headquarters was moved to another State it would require to be incorporated afresh. But all these remarks are wide of the mark—I do not know the law of Connecticut; but I beleive that the Conn. State Branch, A.F. of L. can neither sue nor be sued.

Fraternally
Prest A.F. of L.

HLp, reel 1, vol. 2, pp. 942-43, SG Letterbooks, DLC.

1. Henry J. BACON was a carpenter.

2. Alfred Steckler was elected to a twelve-year term as judge of the Fourth Municipal District Court in 1880.

To James Fitzgibbon

August 18, [188]8

M J. H. Fitzgibbon—
Dear Sir & Bro:

Accept my best thanks for the interesting details contained in yours of the 10th inst. and for the excellent work you are doing. I know how difficult it is to organize by writing and that personal contact with men is necessary. But this is not a fact to be deplored It is conducive to solid growth. The most enduring woods are not those which attain their maturity the soonest. If the object of the A.F. of L. was simply to drag the largest possible number of men under its banner in the shortest possible space of time, regardless of the quality of the recruits and their subsequent education, then it would have adopted the policy of the K. of L. and would probably share its fate. That the A.F. of L. is guided by different motives can be judged by the fact that it started with a Capita Tax of one-half of one cent per month for each member in *good standing*, and only asked $10.^{n}/$_{100}$ per annum from central bodies such as Central Labor Unions, Trade Assemblies, and State Branches, containing many thousands of members each; and at the end of the first year of its existence it reduced this Capita Tax one half, that is, to $\frac{1}{4}$ cent. Now, this tax produces just sufficent to maintain a very modest office with a limited amount of printing; and does not yeild sufficent to pay travelling expenses. Yet I have during the present year spoken in every considerable city from Maine to the Rockies, & from the Lakes to Dixie. This has been rendered possible by voluntary effort on the part of the Local Unions. In short it may be said that the power of the A.F. of L., or rather its Executive, is as limited as that of the Federal government was at the time of the adoption of the Constitution, and stands out in sharp contrast to that of the K. of L., which more closely resembles that of some European military monarchy. The A.F. of L. has deliberatly chosen the Federal system, and appeals to the higher motives in human nature as a means of propaganda. When this becomes clearly understood, as it will be in time, the A.F. of L. will not lack agents to accomplish its grand mission.

If you can come to Milwaukee on Labor Day, I will cross over from

Grand Rapids and confer with you. I have decided to print the Manual[1]
as the labor has become almost insupportable. Best wishes.

Prest A.F. of L.

HLp, reel 1, vol. 2, pp. 944-45, SG Letterbooks, DLC.

1. The AFL commonly sent the *Manual of Common Procedure,* along with traveling
cards, working cards, and the seal of the union, to newly affiliated unions.

An Item in the *New York Press*

[August 21, 1888]

WHEN MR. GOMPERS WAS SOBER.

General Master Workman Powderly of the Knights of Labor stopped
in the city only a few hours yesterday, going back to Philadelphia
almost immediately after testifying before the Ford Investigating Committee.[1] When asked as to the trouble in District Assembly 49, he
said to a *Press* reporter: "You New York newspaper men know a great
deal more about that matter than I do. You are here on the ground
all the time, and from my experience you don't let a great deal of
news of any importance go by you."

As Mr. Powderly was leaving the room where the investigation is
being held he saw President Samuel Gompers of the American Federation of Labor. Since the General Executive Board of the Knights
of Labor issued a circular about two years ago, in which they made
the statement that they "had never had the pleasure of seeing Mr.
Gompers when he was sober,"[2] there has not been a great deal of
love lost between the heads of the two big labor organizations. When
Mr. Powderly saw Mr. Gompers, however, he went over to him smilingly and held out his hand. Mr. Gompers took it rather gingerly, and
the two men went to the back part of the room. After a little talk
the president of the American Federation tackled Mr. Powderly about
the obnoxious circular.

"I have never done you a wrong, Mr. Powderly," said Gompers,
"and so I think it came with bad grace from you to make a statement
that you have never seen me sober, which you must have known was
not the truth. You nor any other man ever saw me any other way
than sober."

"When you appeared before the General Executive Board at the
Astor House in regard to the cigarmakers' troubles some two years

ago, I would not be willing to swear you were sober," responded Mr. Powderly.

"Well, I would," said Gompers quickly.

"What can I do to make the thing right?" asked Mr. Powderly.

Mr. Gompers was willing to let the matter rest if Mr. Powderly was willing to retract the statement, and the two great men shook hands and separated.

New York Press, Aug. 21, 1888.

1. In August 1888 the House Select Committee to Inquire into the Importation of Contract Laborers, Convicts, Paupers, etc., of the Committee on Investigation of Foreign Immigration began hearings on the contract labor system. SG and Powderly both testified before the committee, which was chaired by Melbourne H. Ford.

2. See "The General Executive Board to Members of the KOL," July 2, 1886, *The Making of a Union Leader*, p. 410.

To David Boyer[1]

Sept 8th [188]8

David P Boyer, Esq
Dear Sir & Friend.

Your favor of August 31st reached this office in due time but owing to the fact that I had been on a lecture tour though Michigan (Grand Rapids on Labor Day [. . .]) arriving home this morning an earlier answer was impossible.

In reply to your request for advance "copy" of my Columbus speech[2] let me say that heretofore I have never written out a speech all having been delivered *ex tempore*. If I find time however I shall depart from this rule and write it.

Should I do so however I shall send it on by mail per Registered letter to your address where you can deliver it to Mr Stephens[3] in time. The "copy" *must be preserved* and not "cut up" as it must be read from the Ms. and not from printed sheets.

Will you see Mr Dorn[4] and have him send me a copy of his last two Reports, also please let me have a copy of the Report of your State "Bureau of Labor"[5] I shall want to use both for reference for my speech.

Of course another thing I shall insist upon, i e That the speech shall not be published as what I "will say".

Will you please inform me about what time in the day I shall be expected to speak. Also as near as possible a programme of the days proceedings.

Hoping I have not imposed too much upon your good nature, that you will find it convenient to comply with my requests and that I may hear from you at an early day I am

Yours Truly   Saml Gompers

ALpS, reel 1, vol. 2, pp. 975-76, SG Letterbooks, DLC.

1. David P. BOYER was chief organizer of the International Typographical Union from 1885 to 1888.

2. SG addressed workers in Columbus on Sept. 24, 1888, as part of the Ohio centennial celebration.

3. Possibly Luther P. Stephens, Columbus correspondent for the *Cleveland Leader.*

4. Henry Dorn.

5. The Ohio State Bureau of Labor Statistics.

To the Members of the CMIU

[September 1888]

OUT OF WORK BENEFIT.

To the Members of the C.M.I.U. of A.:

It is quite some time since I have written anything for our *Journal*, due to my multifarious duties in the American Federation of Labor, and this would not, or could not, be written except that the notes were taken while traveling on the road, prompted by reading the discussion now going on upon the proposed "Out of Work Benefit." I am not aware that I can add much to what has already so ably been said upon this subject, but believing that the proposition to insure our members against absolute starvation when out of employment is so immeasurably important to our well-being that I will venture to ask the indulgence and consideration of our members for what follows. As a rule the workers form or join unions for the protection it affords them against unfair and avaricious employers and to shield themselves from the otherwise fearful effects of our competitive system. The first condition that presents itself to the union is the maintenance or increase of wages and a reduction in the hours of labor. To achieve success in these matters brings other reforms and improvement in the worker's condition as a logical and natural consequence. If this statement of the first purposes of the union and its results is correct, we should bend our every energy to secure its attainment. That an "Out of Work Benefit" would largely be instrumental in accomplishing that purpose I more than believe — I am convinced.

One need take but a cursory view and he will find that those unions having the benevolent and protective features are less subject to the fluctuation of their membership than those without these benefits. The wages and other conditions of the members of the former are less affected by dull time.

Almost any kind of a union can protect their members during busy or so-called prosperous seasons, but to maintain such conditions during dull seasons is far more important to the welfare and progress of the working people.

When dull times overtake us we find the organizations that have no beneficial features losing their membership fast. There is nothing which binds them to the union.

The only reason for their joining being to protect themselves in their wages and their hours of labor. They find that the union fails to give them that protection. They leave in disgust and become an easy prey to the caprice and avarice of employers. Now mark the contrast.

A union which is based upon the protective and benevolent plan, during the same dull times we will say are defeated in the first struggle to maintain wages, hours of labor and other fair conditions. Does it not appear plain that the other benefits have the effect of retaining their membership in the union? Being provided with a sick, out-of-work, traveling, strike, death and even other and more benefits they lose too much by leaving the union and don't leave.

The very fact that the workers remain organized, ostensibly only for the "benefits," is all important, inasmuch as their organization is always a lever to protect them from all the wrong and injustice successfully practiced upon the unorganized.

These "benefits" do more than even maintain fair conditions during dull times, for upon the recurrence of fair or busy trade the toilers who maintained their union are among the first to share in the fruits of a general revival, while those who deserted their unions must devote the major portion of these periods in re-organizing their forces before they can share in it. How many defeats, how many heartaches, how much poverty have been caused and golden opportunities lost by reason of the want of permanency in our organizations is incalculable. Upon this subject in making my report to the Baltimore convention of the American Federation of Labor, I took occasion to say:

"It is noticeable that a great reaction and a steady disintegration is going on in most organizations of labor that are not formed upon the basis that the experience of past failures teaches, namely, the benevolent as well as the protective features in the unions. There are times when the labor organizations are in no position to take a decisive stand in defence of the toilers, and, apart from any considerations of humanity, the fact that the benevolent features or organization keep the members within the union, is all important to the permanency of the unions and the consequent protection in all times that organization affords. I can scarcely find language strong enough in which to impress this fact upon your minds."

I am more convinced than ever of the truth and importance of that statement. There is in my judgment no benefit so necessary and beneficial to the interests of workingmen as an "out-of-work benefit." The world looks with sympathy upon the man who is sick and seems sometimes willing to aid and assuage his sufferings, but the man out of work seldom, if ever, is he regarded as otherwise than shiftless. While this may be true in isolated cases I believe, but that the rule is through no fault of their own I am certain. Yet the belief prevails that "he can get work if he wants to," leads them to look on with cold indifference. The whole world seems to have their hands raised against the man out of work, and labor organizations that have no "out-of-work benefit," are no exception to that cruel thought and act, protest loud as they may against the implication. That our members may rise to the great opportunity and vote in favor of the "out-of-work" amendment proposed by Union 144,[1] which, when adopted will place our organization upon a humane and permanent basis— the road to prosperity and success—and will tend as an incentive for other unions to follow in our wake, is the sincere wish of yours fraternally,

Samuel Gompers.

Cigar Makers' Official Journal, Sept. 1888.

1. Local 144 proposed that the CMIU amend its constitution to include an out-of-work benefit of $3 a week for as many as six weeks for members who had belonged to the CMIU for at least one year. The proposal was defeated by referendum in 1888. In 1889 the convention approved a similar amendment, which was proposed by SG, and the membership sustained the decision by a small margin.

To P. M. Arthur[1]

Oct 9th [188]8

P. M. Arthur, Esq.
Grand Chief. Bro'd Locomotive Engineers.
Cleveland, Ohio.
Dear Sir.

Upon the approach of the annual convention of your respected organization I venture to address you upon a subject of vital importance both to your organization and the labor movement in general, i e. the affiliation of the Brotherhood of Locomotive Engineers with the great family of Trade Unions of our country under the banner of the American Federation of Labor.

I am well aware that the past policy of the Brotherhood has been to "affiliate with none", and I am not prepared to say that in the then chaotic condition of the labor movement, the crude ideas prevailing as to the rights and autonomy of the Trade Unions, that your declaration was not justifiable. But, Sir, to-day we find the conditions changed. The Trade Unions of the country are all advancing, Keeping abreast with each other, all affiliated for the general welfare and the advancement of our general interests, yet withal each organization jealously guarding its rights to settle and determine its own affairs in its own way uninterefered with by Any person or officer of any other organization regardless of how high sounding his title.

On all hands we see the employing class combining and concentrating their forces to crush out the spirit of independence by their attempts to disrupt our organizations, to heap odium upon us when we attempt to maintain our rights and to construe our perfectly conservative methods to protect our interests into acts of conspiracy. When climax or how far this tendency will reach depends more upon the action of the Workingmen of our country than upon any other agency.

If we remain unorganized, or if organized isolated, we shall be an easy prey to their averice and their well concocted plan, organized and affiliated with each other presenting a solid phalanx of organized workmen "Distinct as the billows, yet one as the sea" we shall not even be required to exert the power of our organizations. The influence of our organized condition will restrain the employing class from carrying out their scheme.

Several of our organizations can honestly lay claim to superiority in their basis and strength over ot[her]s. This however would hardly be a good reaso[n why?] they should not co-operate to protect the in[terests] of each other and defend each other against the encroachments of those who seek their downfall.

On the contrary it seems to the ordinary mind that our own best interests demand are conserved when we help those that are weak to attain a fair degree of power, more especially when such help in no way injures ourselves, for in so doing we increase our own power and influence in the same ratio.

Of course in one letter I can scarcely point out all the advantages that would accrue to the bona fide labor movement—the Brotherhood of Locomotive Engineers included—from an affiliation of all the National and International Trade Unions with the principles, purposes and methods of the American Federation of Labor as the guiding star.

That the labor movement h[as] suffered from the attacks of persons and organizations who have signally failed to comprehend the purposes and mission of the Trade Unions I think we all admit. That a federation of the Trade Unions to protect themselves from this series of onslaughts is necessary and prevent them is obvious

In view of all the interests involved, In the holy name of labor, In the spirit of the mission the Trade Unions are called upon to fulfill I ask your favorable consideration of this matter. To engraft its purposes in your address to your forthcoming convention and to lay this letter or its purport before your delegates.[2]

That your convention may be eminently harmonious and successful and the best possible results to your craft attend your efforts is the sincere wish of

Yours Fraternally.   Sam'l Gompers.
Pres't American Federation of Labor

ALpS, reel 2, vol. 3, pp. 64-67, SG Letterbooks, DLC.

1. Peter M. ARTHUR served as grand chief engineer of the Brotherhood of Locomotive Engineers (BLE) from 1874 to 1903.
2. The 1888 BLE convention, which met in Richmond, Va., Oct. 17-Nov. 2, took no action on SG's appeal.

To Florence Kelley Wischnewetzky[1]

Oct 17th [188]8

Mrs. Florence K. Wischnewetzky.
Dear Madam.

I hope you will pardon the apparent neglect in answering your favor, but in truth I have been out of the city most of the time and while home almost unable to do any work.

In reference to the matters upon which you write first let me say that I sincerely regret that Doctor Wischnewetzky[2] was so seriously ill and also my ignorance of it, but glad to learn that he will recover his usual health. Kindly remember me to him when you write.

A few days ago I had a conversation with a gentleman in reference to the Pamphlet "Free Trade".[3] He said he could not or did not feel at liberty to touch it just at this time as any one who did would be thought working for the Democratic Party and in its pay by workingmen. Mr Derossi of this city wrote me last upon the same subject and so informed him.

The[n] again the political parties are distributing so much literature upon the tariff question gratuitously that it would be difficult to sell a pamphlet at 25¢. I concur in your view of the death [of] young Marsh.[4] I caused a letter to be sent to Newark in reference to that matter urging action.

Your translation of Engel's "Condition of the working Class in England"[5] you sent me some months ago, and although I had read it some fifteen years ago I enjoy it better in English. There is one thing that strikes me as rather a peculiar omission in the "Preface" and "Appendix". While Engels speaks of the labor movement in America the great "Eight Hour" upheaval of May 1886 and the great preparations made fo[r] it, he never so much as mentions the Federation which inaugerated it and was by resolution and common consent the leader in the movement, while the Knights of Labor which antagonized it (Because the movement was inaugerated by the Federation and not the K of L. This is now in proof by the best authority. A member of the Ex Board of that Order) is held forth as *the* Organization of the proletariat of America

[When?] Engels was in England, the bluster the K of L m[ade was?] heard by him as well as by others, while the business-like manner without unnecessary ostentation of the Federation went by and goes by unnoticed. I am realy surprised at it from so keen an observer as Engels. There is no doubt that his observations need amending.

I learned a few days ago that Mr Engels was here for a few months *incog.*[6] Did you see him? I would have given much to have had the pleasure of a conversation with him.

With sincere wishes for your welfare and the Docters speedy recovery and return. I am

Truly yours   Saml Gompers.

ALpS, reel 2, vol. 3, pp. 87-89, SG Letterbooks, DLC.

1. Florence KELLEY Wischnewetzky was a prominent reformer and suffragist.

2. Lazare Wischnewetzky, a Russian-born socialist and physician, married Florence Kelley in 1884. They moved from Switzerland to New York City in 1886 where he established his medical practice and both joined the SLP. The couple divorced in 1892.

3. Under the title *Free Trade: A Speech Delivered before the Democratic Club, Brussels, Belgium, January 9, 1848* (Boston, 1888), Florence Kelley Wischnewetzky published a translation of an address given by Karl Marx; Friedrich Engels wrote the preface for Wischnewetzky's edition. Marx's talk condemned the disastrous effect free trade would have on the working class's standard of living, but supported it in the expectation that it would break down nationalism and heighten the antagonism between the proletariat and bourgeoisie, thereby hastening the advent of revolution.

4. Albert Marsh, a twelve-year-old boy employed by the Union Rubber Co. of Newark, N.J., was killed on Sept. 7, 1888, while emptying a naptha tank. No one witnessed the accident, and Marsh's absence was not noticed until some time after his death. The *Newark Advertiser* (Sept. 8, 1888) maintained that the boy suffered from epilepsy and had probably had a seizure while emptying the tank.

5. Friedrich Engels (1820-95), Karl Marx's collaborator, wrote *The Condition of the Working Class in England in 1844* based upon his experiences while working as a clerk in his father's firm in Manchester, England. The book described the deteriorating conditions faced by textile workers in Manchester at the same time that the textile industry was rapidly increasing its productivity through mechanization and the development of the factory system. Translated into English by Florence Kelley Wischnewetzky, the book predicted that the declining economic condition of English workers would lead to a proleterian revolution. Engels wrote a new preface for Wischnewetzky's edition.

6. Engels traveled in North America from Aug. 17 to Sept. 20, 1888, visiting New York City, Hoboken, Pittsburgh, Boston, Montreal, and Toronto.

To Emmett Lake[1]

Oct 22nd [188]8

E. J. Lake, Esq.
Dear Sir & Friend.

Owing to absence from this City an earlier reply to your favor of the 17th was impossible.

The Horse Car R.R. Employees are not affiliated with the A.F. of L. except in some localities through the Central Labor Unions of the place.

I would advise the Men of your City to organize and form a part of the National organization of their calling D.A. 226[2] K. of L. It is the only National Union of Surface R.R. employees and deem the above suggestion in the interest of all concerned. There is no doubt in my mind that that organization will in a short time be what it is now only in embryo a Trade Union.

In the matter of your application for my endorsement, let me say that in a previous matte[r] of the same description the Ex. C. decided not to interfere i[n] such matters. Hence I am not at liberty to comply with your request.

Fraty yours   Saml Gompers.

ALpS, reel 2, vol. 3, p. 104, SG Letterbooks, DLC.

1. The AFL commissioned Emmett J. LAKE, a Troy, N.Y., carpenter, as its first general organizer in 1888.

2. The KOL chartered National Trade Assembly 226, composed of surface passenger railroad employees, in 1887.

To the Mass Meeting at Clarendon Hall,[1] New York City

Oct 26th [188]8

To the Mass-Meeting of Organized-Labor. Clarendon Hall. NY City. Fellow-Workingmen.

A previous and important engagement to address the working people of Newark N.J. prevents my attendance at your meeting this evening.[2] Owing to the important character of your meeting I made an endeavor to have the one at Newark postponed but without success.

Let me assure you that the objects of your meeting meet my unqualified sympathy and the means resolved upon by the Troy convention[3] my earnest support.

The Law of conspiracy as well as the old "common law" construction of conspiracy as applied to the labor organization in their endeavor to secure improved conditions for the toiling masses must be abolished.

More than twenty years ago the last vestige of this relic of barbarism was expunged from the statutes of monarchical England.[4] It is time, the latter eigthth of the nineteenth century, [th]at the Empire State of Free America should follow suit.

The men and women of labor who dare raise their voices against the oppression and wrong heaped upon their fellow toilers, who demand "more" of the result of their labor, who believe that in the terms "the progress of civilization" something more than an indiscriminate scrimmage for office is meant, should not have the iron doors of a Jail gaping to recieve them, a standing menace to cur them into a humiliating servitude.

I would advise you to take such action as will bury beneath the avalance of your votes every aspirant for office who fails to stand up manfully in defence of our inalienable right to work out our own emancipation, And squelch by the overpowering weight of our scorn and contempt those who desire to make our movement a failure.

The conspiracy law so far as it applies to labor organizations peacefully endeavoring to obtain better conditions must go! All who stand in the way of its achievement, whether open enemy or pseudo-friend must go with it.

With best wishes for the success of your meeting and the movement to which again I pledge you my undivided support I am

Fraternally yours   Samuel Gompers.
President American Federation of Labor.

ALpS, reel 2, vol. 3, pp. 117-19, SG Letterbooks, DLC.

1. On Oct. 25, 1888, a mass meeting of workingmen at Clarendon Hall in New York City protested against the courts' interpretation that the state's conspiracy laws made striking and boycotting illegal. The meeting called for increased political pressure on state legislators to change the laws and vowed to oppose candidates in the next election who did not publicly endorse the changes.

2. Apparently this letter is misdated, as the meeting occurred on the evening of Oct. 25.

3. One hundred delegates participated in a labor convention held in Troy, N.Y., Sept. 17-18, in support of amending New York's industrial conspiracy laws. The convention appointed a committee to agitate for amendments to the conspiracy law sections of the state penal code and resolved that workers should refuse to vote for legislative candidates who did not publicly support the amendments.

4. By the Conspiracy and Protection of Property Act of 1875 Parliament exempted trade unions from prosecution as conspiracies in restraint of trade as long as the activities in which they engaged were not of themselves of a criminal nature. Unfavorable court rulings later weakened the immunity granted by this act.

The Executive Council of the AFL to the Officers and Delegates of the International Trade Union Congress, London

October 27, [188]8

To the Officers & Delegates of the International Trade Union Congress in London assembled—
Companions:

The American Federation of Labor in the name of its 3,000 self-governing local Trade Unions with an aggregate membership of more than 600,000 working people sends you fraternal greeting and congratulates you upon the happy auspices under which you assemble as the true representative body of the proletarian class That your deliberations may be harmonious, and that they may result in strengthening the impetus toward republican institutions and social guarantees against idleness with all its concomitant misery & crime is the earnest prayer of the workers of the land of Washingto[n] and John Brown.

We would be glad to be represented in your body by a delegate of our own, but the work at home requires the active presence of all our available men.

The late war of slave emancipation has added to the ranks of our class more than 4,000,000 people who stand in direst necessity of organization and education. With the emancipation of the slaves has arisen a fervent aspiration for the establishment of equitable and normal relations between the possessers of the implements and means of industry and the main body of the people. You are no doubt cognisant of the many attempts that have been made to unite the toilers of this broad continent and realise that aspiration. You are also probably aware of the small measure of success which has attended those efforts, and will readily believe us when we state [t]hat the failure to unite the workers is direc[t]ly traceable to the lack of ability on the part [o]f pseudo leader[s] to grasp the historical and social importance of the trade union.

That the trade union is the historic and natural form of working class organization is becoming day by day more evident to the minds of our people. And the conviction is slowly but surely gaining ground that by the organization of the workers upon the basis of their trades and callings and the federation of the various unions in a grand universal union, with the autonomy of each guaranteed by all, will be found the practical realization of the aspiration voiced by our lamented President, Abraham Lincoln, in the memorable sentence— "The government of the people, by the people, for the people."

Having declared our unswerving fidelity to the trade union as the best method of organization among the workers in the more industrially advanced countries; you will permit us to state that, in our opinion, the most efficaceous means of removing the obstacles to free combination of the working people would be the establishment of a permanent Bureau whose function should be the compilation and dissemination of trade union statistics and literature with the [object?] of forming a healthy public opinion on the subject of the organization of labor.

Upon the subject of the limitation of production by means of the reduction of the hours of labor, you will allow us to say that we do not favor any limitation of production while any human being is lacking food and shelter. But in view of the fact that the application of steam machinery and the minute subdivision of the of the processes of industry are continually throwing large numbers of our fellow [workingmen?] out of employment, and that the permantly unemployed class is rapidly increasing—so that in this country, where the natural opportunities are so vast, more than five per centum of the population are doomed to a fate worse than death—we should make a strenous effort to reduce the hours of labor to such a point as would afford to all the opportunity to labor; that is to say, to the means of life.

Concerning the desirability of the State regulation of the hours of labor, we hold that in the face of actual social conditions the State should be urged, in the name of humanity, to regulate the hours of labor of children under 18 years of age. For ourselves we are chary of invoking State interference, for we are convinced that when the right to free combination is definitely assured we shall be able to work out our own salvation as a class, and ultimately achieve that grand social transformation for which the whole efforts of our ancestors in toil and suffering has been one long and arduous preparation.

Under another cover you will recieve a few copies of a pamphlet published by this body containing a brief sketch of the present standing of the National and International Unions of America.

Again wishing you every success, and regreting our enforced absence from your councils, We are

> Yours fraternally,   Saml Gompers. President,
> Daniel McLaughlin 1st Vice-Pres.,
> William Martin 2nd   "   " ,
> G. Edmonston Treasurer
> P. J. McGuire Secretary

HLpSr, reel 2, vol. 3, pp. 127-32, SG Letterbooks, DLC.

To Ida Van Etten[1]

Nov 5th [188]8

Miss Ida M. Van Etten.
Dear Madam.

In reply to your note which just came to hand permit me to say that I fully concur in your views as expressed therein.

There is no doubt that in the performance of the multifarious duties attending your office you need some assistance at least for a time.

But it should be paid for by the girls and women themselves and above all they must choose who it shall be, some one in whom *they* have confidence, some one they have a right to find fault with, some one they dare kick if necessary.

If the rich ladies desire in reality to bear the burden, let them make the donation to the Society[2] every month in advance not for the payment of a Secretary but for general purposes and let the responsibility and honor? of choosing their officers remain with those most interested.

You remember I stated it as my conviction that as soon as an industry is partially organized you even should [divest yourself of as much work and responsibility?] in connection therewith as possible. If the working women and girls of different trades or callings begin to organize you cannot attend to it all yourself. In fact should not if you could. They must become self reliant and develop an adaptability to perform their own work. If you do it all they will never learn. A child may stumble and hurt itself in learning to walk but that is even preferable than that it should never learn to walk at all.

With best wishes I am

Yours Fraternally   Samuel Gompers.

N.B. How did the trouble at Cohnfeld's[3] terminate? Let me know by mail.

S. G.

ALpS, reel 2, vol. 3, pp. 168-69, SG Letterbooks, DLC.

1. Ida M. VAN ETTEN helped organize the New York Working Women's Society in 1888 and for several years was a leading figure in organizing women workers in New York.

2. The New York Working Women's Society, organized in 1888 by middle-class and working-class women, sought to organize women workers into trade unions, promote the passage and enforcement of laws for the protection of women and children in factories, and educate consumers on working conditions. In 1890, as a result of its efforts, New York passed a law providing for women factory inspectors. The Society helped establish the National Consumers' League.

3. In November 1888 women feather workers in New York City, in response to a wage reduction at Cohnfeld's shop, organized the Feather Workers' Union and negotiated a union scale. Three months later, however, the feather manufacturers repudiated the agreement and the workers went on strike. The struggle ended unsuccessfully on Mar. 20, 1889.

To Florence Kelley Wischnewetzky

Nov 9th [188]8

Mrs. F. K. Wischnewetzky
Dear Madam.

I hope and know you will pardon my apparent neglect in not answering your favors before this when I assure you that the pressure of business just now in preparing for our forthcoming St Louis Convention[1] is so great as to leave but very little time for anything but the most important matters. Not that I regard your letters as unimportant but there are other matters more so.

Permit me to say that the Federation proper was organized November 1881 in Pittsburg Pa[2] and that it was but re-named in 1886. In 1884 at the Chicago convention the resolutions to prepare for the enforcement of the "Eight Hour" workday on May 1st 1886 was adopted by the Federation. At the next (Washington) convention[3] the resolutions took practical shape to place the movement into operation.

The movement did take place, did a wonderful good, was initiated and conducted by the Federation. I repeat that the omission of these facts in the book by Mr Engels is almost unpardonable. If done by a man less acquainted with the details of the labor movement of the world it would not be worth a notice. But in Mr Engels (if I had less respect for him) it almost seems wilful.

It affords me pleasure to learn that you will aid the ["]Eight Hour" movement by your new book,[4] which by the way I wish you every success in. I regard the achievent of this boon as the greatest for the *near* future and one upon which every well wisher of our class should concentrate their efforts and subordinate everything else to.

I regret to learn what you say of Mr McGuire but there is a likelihood of some misunderstanding in the matter, perhaps the note gone astray. He is not a man to treat a correspondent as you say he has you. Mr J S Kirchner 543 Dillwyn St Phila. is a friend of mine and one who would no doubt aid you in your project for labor legislation. In a month or two a Penna. State Labor convention will be held and will no doubt prove a live body.

Mr Bayard[5] informs me that no such inv[it]ation has ever been extended to this Government by the government of Switzerland.[6] I shall ascertain the truth.

Write to J P McDonnell, Paterson Labor Standard for information in reference to Albert Marsh. He is most likely to know or inform you who does.

Many thanks for your suggestion in reference to the question of child labor. It is a subject upon which I have strong convictions and never lose an opportunity to present the subject in all its hideous shape before the notice of the world.

Have you read my letter to the International Labor Congress which convened in London Nov 6th.[7] The labor papers publish[ing?] it in the issue of the 10th inst. *N.Y. Volkszeitung* of Sunday the 4th.

About two weeks ago while in Phila I desired to call on you but hesitated and finally decided not to in consequence of your present surroundings. Under the circumstances I did not know I would be welcome. "You're all right" but —

I am pleased to learn of Dr Wischnewetzky is soon to come back entirely recovered.

With best wishes I am

Yours Very Truly   Saml Gompers.

ALpS, reel 2, vol. 3, pp. 185-87, SG Letterbooks, DLC.

1. The AFL held its third annual convention in St. Louis, Dec. 11-15, 1888.
2. The FOTLU held its first annual convention in Pittsburgh, Nov. 15-18, 1881.

3. The FOTLU held its fifth annual session Dec. 8-11, 1885, in Washington, D.C.

4. Wischnewetzky was working on a study of child labor and subsequently published a pamphlet entitled *Our Toiling Children* (Chicago, 1889).

5. Thomas F. Bayard, a Democrat, was secretary of state in Grover Cleveland's first administration, from 1885 to 1889.

6. In June 1888 the Swiss Federal Council proposed to call an international conference to discuss the passage of uniform international legislation regulating the employment of women and children, establishing minimum hours of labor, and abolishing Sunday labor. In September 1888 SG corresponded with the U.S. Department of State and the Swiss government inquiring whether the United States had been extended an invitation. In March 1889 Switzerland formally invited thirteen European countries to the conference to open in May 1890, but withdrew the invitations because Emperor William II of Germany issued an invitation for a similar congress. The German congress took place in Berlin in March 1890.

7. See "The Executive Council of the AFL to the Officers and Delegates of the International Trade Union Congress, London," Oct. 27, 1888, above.

To the Executive Council of the AFL

New York, Nov 19th 1888.

To the Executive Council A.F. of L.
Colleagues.

For quite a time there has been a matter of deep concern to me which I desired to evade and avoid because it affected my personal interest and effected me solely, but I cannot refrain from mentioning the matter to you so that you may decide what ought to be done.

You remember that at the begining of the present term arrangements where made by several organization throughout the country for me to address meetings. The arrangement was that each locality should pay a proportion of travelling, hotel and incidental expenses. When I reached several places they where without or had sent it to the gentleman? who attended to the management of the trip and from whom I never got a final accounting though the matter has been a subject of correspondence without eliciting an answer from him. I had travelled in mid-winter nearly 10.000 miles, made about 50 speeches with the greatest success, and came home about $90.00 out of pocket.

About three month ago at the invitation of the Boston C.L.U.[1] I went there to deliver an address. A gentleman there stated that arrangements had been made for me to speak in several places for which my expenses—travel, hotel and incidental—were to be paid. There were but three meetings but so far were the evenings apart that it took me two weeks. For this I received in all $5.00. I returned $45.00 out of pocket.

You will observe by the financial report that there is not an item of one cent or more for car fare or other incidental expenses for me and I assure you it has been quite an item although I will not charge for it.

I submit however that my salary is not large enough to admit of me standing the loss of the amounts stated above and I have no private means upon which to draw.

It is true that you resolved that I should accept the invitations and upon my motion "providing it be at no expense to the Federation" I could not forsee what happened.

I would have waited to submit this matter to the E.C. meeting in St Louis, but if you authorize the payment of it I want it published in this quarterly report so that all may see it before the convention meets and exactly know how the money has been expended.

Will you kindly return your decision or vote upon this matter at your earliest convenience and oblige

Yours Fraternally   Saml Gompers.
Prest

N.B. The balance at end of this quarter will show over $600.00 on hand

S. G.

HLSr, Papers of Gabriel Edmonston, reel 1, *AFL Records.*

1. The Boston Central Trades and Labor Union.

To Wilhelm Liebknecht[1]

New York, Nov 22nd 1888

W. Liebknecht. Esq.
Borsdorf-Leipzig. Germany.
Dear Sir

Your letter and circular requesting the privelige of using my name to a call for an International Congress of Workingmen to be held in the Autumn of 1889 in Switzerland[2] came duly to hand. Permit me to say that an invitation was extended to the Trade Unions of America through the American Federation of Labor, by the Trade Union Congress of Great Britian to participate in and be represented at the International Labor Congress just closed in that Country, and that the A.F. of L. took the view that the movement in our country had not yet sufficiently developed, that the work of organizing the toilers of this country had not yet been sufficiently advanced to permit us to be represented by a delegate there.

You will readily see that the expression of the convention of the organization is binding upon its president and since no distinction can be made between my functions as president and my individuality I am constrained by my sense of duty to decline the honor you wish to confer.

> Very Respectfully Yours   Sam'l Gompers.
> President American Federation of Labor.

ALS, Institut für Marxismus-Leninismus, Berlin, German Democratic Republic.

1. Wilhelm Liebknecht (1826-1900) was a German socialist leader and journalist. Exiled in Switzerland and England after participating in the revolution in Germany in 1848, he became an ally of Karl Marx and Friedrich Engels. He returned to Germany in 1862, became a member of the Reichstag in 1867, and in 1869 cofounded the Sozialdemokratische Arbeiterpartei (Social Democratic Workingmen's party; SDAP) with August Bebel, thereafter serving as editor of its organ, *Der Volksstaat*. After spending two years in prison (1872-74) for his opposition to the Franco-Prussian War, he was again elected to the Reichstag, serving until his death. He participated in the merger of the SDAP and the Lassallean Allgemeiner Deutscher Arbeiterverein (General German Workingmen's Association) at Gotha in 1875 to form the Sozialistische Arbeiterpartei Deutschlands (Socialist Labor Party of Germany; SAPD), becoming its leading spokesman. Liebknecht subsequently led in reorganizing the SAPD as the Sozialdemokratische Partei Deutschlands (Social Democratic Party of Germany) and became editor of the party organ, *Vorwärts*.

2. After the disbanding of the International Workingmen's Association in 1876, various groups attempted to establish a new international socialist organization. The proposed Swiss conference was not held; instead, socialists and trade unionists held two congresses in Paris in July 1889.

To Gabriel Edmonston

New York, Nov 23rd 1888

Dear Friend Gab

I scarcely know how to express my sincere gratitude at your generous offer, but either the A.F. of L. will bear the expence or I will. The money I can borrow from some friend and pay it off gradually upon returning to my trade at the close of the St Louis convention. My name is good for that amount and I know I can obtain it as a loan, but as a gift no, not even from so valued a friend as yourself.

Of course you had no occasion to say that the offer was not intended to be a charitable act. I am confident you would not insult me by even harboring such a thought, but all the same I can't accept it.

Yes, My Boy, If I was only little more like most men and have more "business principle" about my life, I think I should be a little better off than I am, but I can't, "I ain't built that way". Call me foolish if you will but I can get back at you by saying "So are you". How much have you not sacrificed for our noble cause? More than I have, for I never had anything. I only did not get things that I might have got. While you sacrifice things you had.

However let it go, every man has his hobby. I have mine in devoting my humble efforts to the amelioration and emancipation of my class and to speak frankly I have no desire to be cured of it until we shall [have] arrived at our goal.

With sincere wishes for your welfare and again thanking you for your offer I am as ever

Yours Sincerely   Saml Gompers.

ALS, Papers of Gabriel Edmonston, reel 1, *AFL Records.*

A Translation of an Excerpt from an Article in the *New Yorker Volkszeitung*

[December 3, 1888]

FOUR QUESTIONS.

1. What are the underlying causes for the collapse of the political labor movement during the past year?

2. Do you think there is a possibility of a revitalization of this movement and is this desirable at the present time?

3. If so, do you consider any of the existing labor parties capable of focusing the political activities of the workers within the scope of their present organization? If so, which party and why?

4. If not, in what form and based on what principles could you envision the beginnings of a reorganization? Should it be purely political, or should it emerge from existing union organizations, and what are the chief demands that a successful party should include in its platform?

. . .

SAMUEL GOMPERS,

the president of the American Federation of Labor, responded to the above questions for a reporter from the *Volkszeitung* as follows: As to the first, "I do not think this question is sufficiently delimited. The political labor movement throughout the country must be viewed as having made advances; in various states the workers have managed to elect several of their own candidates. The local political labor movement of New York City, however, did not collapse this year, but shortly after the elections of 1886, when a self-appointed executive committee had the impudence to take the leadership of the movement out of the hands of the Central Labor Union in order to control it itself. Since that time, after the movement was wrested from the hands of the organized workers, I have wanted nothing more to do with it.

"I want to answer the first half of the second question by saying that I do not consider it probable that a revitalization of this movement will be possible for some time to come, at least not before the sharp edges of disappointment and hurt feelings, resulting from the last elections, have been smoothed over. Also, new, more honest men will have to appear on the scene; then one circumstance or a series of circumstances will suffice to start a new movement. As far as the second half of this question is concerned, it has already been answered in my response to the first half."

Gompers responded to the third question with the following words: "My personal opinion is that none of the political labor parties presently in existence is capable of focusing the efforts of the workers." To the fourth question he responded as follows: "If independent labor politics are to be pursued, they will have to come either directly or indirectly from the industrial labor organizations. The next movement will probably not originate in New York, as happened last time, but outside this city, since otherwise a concentrated movement would probably not come about. I must admit that although I have acted and voted independently of established parties all along, I believe that workers can achieve greater success in improving their moral, political, and economic conditions if, as workers, they keep themselves out of politics and concentrate all their efforts first on organizing their trades and then on producing a uniform ideology. The essential point is that we should create a healthy public opinion about our interests. I believe that all labor organizations, industrial or political, which can rightfully call themselves labor organizations and want to achieve real results, must make achieving an immediate improvement of the workers' position in industry the basis of their demands. Once this improvement has been made, there is then no reason not to make additional demands, especially since these will carry greater weight because of the success already achieved."

Asked whether he thought that the convention of the American Federation of Labor in St. Louis might provide the impetus for a political labor party, he smiled and explained that it would be impossible to say what would or would not be proposed there. He said he would recommend that the delegates apply all their energies toward implementing the eight-hour day as the norm, because he considered its importance far greater than usually perceived.

New Yorker Volkszeitung, Dec. 3, 1888. Translated from the German by Patrick McGrath.

The Campaign for Eight Hours

One of the AFL's major achievements was the revival, in 1888, of the eight-hour campaign. Strategically, the shorter workday was a particularly attractive issue for the Federation. It not only promised tangible benefits to working people, and as such was an issue that all workers could support regardless of ethnic or political differences, but it also provided the AFL with a forum to publicize and promote its program. On Gompers' recommendation that it set a day "when the working people of the entire country shall be called upon to simultaneously demand the enforcement of eight hours as a day's work," the convention designated May 1, 1890, for the inauguration of the eight-hour day.[1]

During 1889 the AFL Executive Council called for simultaneous, nationwide, mass meetings on George Washington's birthday, Independence Day, and Labor Day to publicize the movement; in all, according to Gompers' report to the 1889 AFL convention, nearly a thousand meetings were held. In addition, the AFL published and distributed eight-hour pamphlets by George Gunton, Lemuel Danryid, and George McNeill, and utilized the efforts of general organizers and newly commissioned special organizers who worked throughout the country in behalf of the movement. The Federation also invited KOL participation, but the 1889 General Assembly voted to provide only moral support. Nevertheless many KOL local assemblies joined in the shorter workday campaign.

Recognizing that not all the Federation's affiliates were prepared to enforce the eight-hour day by 1890, the 1889 convention authorized the Executive Council to choose one or two trades to lead the movement; it further provided that the Council should collect a per capita assessment of 10 cents a week, beginning no later than March 1890, to assist those trades. On Mar. 17, 1890, the Council named the United Brotherhood of Carpenters and Joiners of America to spearhead the campaign, with the United Mine Workers of America (UMWA) to follow the Carpenters, and by April carpenters in a number of cities were on strike. While the AFL's circulars and other public statements may suggest the existence of a cohesive national movement, the drives to attain shorter hours were largely local affairs in their

163

planning and execution.[2] These local campaigns, however, were quite effective. By May 1, according to P. J. McGuire's report to the 1890 Carpenters' convention, some 46,000 carpenters in 137 cities had achieved shorter hours.

The UMWA, however, did not take up the movement. It first postponed its effort to May 1, 1891, a decision the 1890 AFL convention endorsed. Following the convention, Gompers and other trade union leaders gave widespread publicity to the miners' anticipated campaign. Then, on April 28, 1891, the UMWA, weakened by a prolonged strike and internal dissension, cancelled its plans entirely.

The AFL's role in the movement for the shorter workday changed significantly after 1891. The Federation sponsored campaigns in 1896 and 1900, but these efforts apparently did not attract the same attention as earlier ones. Subsequently, although the AFL continued to support eight hours through education and agitation, it was left for the most part to individual unions to achieve this objective.

Notes

1. AFL, *Proceedings*, 1888, p. 10.
2. See "To a Mass Meeting of New York Carpenters," Apr. 9, 1890, and "An Excerpt from an Article in the *New York Sun*," Apr. 29, 1890, below.

A Series of News Accounts of the 1888 Convention of the AFL in St. Louis

[December 10, 1888]

THE FEDERATION OF LABOR.

The coming session of the American Federation of Labor, which will convene in this city to-morrow at 12 o'clock, will in all probability be the most largely attended and important session yet held by the organization. It is claimed that the association now represents about half a million workingmen in the United States. The carpenters are said to have the largest representation, having a membership of about 66,000. The cigarmakers, iron-molders and printers come next, with a representation of about 40,000 each. Numerically, it is the strongest labor organization in the United States. The meetings of the present session will be open to outsiders, unless there arises some question which the membership deem best to discuss in private. Among the more important measures to be discussed, the much mooted eight hour law will come up for its share of consideration, and it is thought that measures will be arranged for a general attempt to enforce the law.[1]

Another measure which will probably engage the attention of the session is the question of raising a fund for the maintenance of members during strikes. Hitherto the national organization has taken no part in the settlement of intricate questions between employer and workmen, but this measure was broached at the session last year, and it has been studied by some of the unions composing the organization since that time. Should this measure be adopted, it will be necessary to increase the per capita tax of members; but in case it is not approved, circumstances will admit of a reduction of the per capita tax, as a surplus is arising from even the present low rate of ¼¢ per month, from each member.

Another measure that will probably be considered will be the propriety of affiliating with the World's Congress of Labor, the biennial session of which was recently held in London. The feeling of the body on this point can not yet be anticipated.[2]

In regard to the election of officers, which will occur on the last day of the session, it is thought that Samuel Gompers, the present incumbent, will be retained in the capacity of president. The same may also be said of Secretary J. J. McGuire.[3] Both have held the respective offices since the organization of the order—two terms—and both have proved to be efficient officers.

The only delegate that has arrived in the city thus far is Frederick Haller, of Buffalo, N.Y., one of the delegates of the International Cigarmakers' Union. Regarding the eight-hour law, Mr. Haller said that it had been generally enforced among the cigar workers of the Eastern States, and that it was working satisfactorily to both employers and employes. None of the officers have yet arrived, but President Gompers and Secretary McGuire are expected this morning. It is also thought that many other officers and delegates will arrive by the morning trains.

St. Louis Globe-Democrat, Dec. 10, 1888.

1. On Dec. 15, 1888, the AFL convention passed a resolution condemning the practice of forcing government employees to labor ten hours a day in violation of the eight-hour law and endorsed the bills before Congress to enforce the shorter day and secure back pay.

2. The International Trade Union Congress that met in London in November 1888 called for an international workingmen's congress at Paris in 1889. SG maintained that it would be "inexpedient" for the Federation to send a representative to the meeting, and the St. Louis convention endorsed this position (AFL, *Proceedings*, 1888, p. 17. See SG to Auguste Keufer, Jan. 10, 1889, below).

3. P. J. McGuire.

[December 14, 1888]

STRIKE ASSESSMENTS.

. . .

REPORT ON THE PRESIDENT'S ADDRESS.

The committee on the president's report then being ready, their report was read and acted upon in sections. The different features of their work were approved until the important question of the proposed strike assessment, which had been referred back to them on Wednesday, was reached, when a long and lively discussion followed, this matter evidently being a grave problem for the federation to solve. Delegate Kirchner led the favorers of the assessment idea with great vigor, making a stirring speech advocating the necessity of the federation's always being ready to assist any of the unions in a struggle. Secretary McGuire, while believing that this should be the principal duty and object of the organization, urged the advantages of voluntary contributions, stating repeatedly that the assessment feature was the rock upon which the Knights of Labor had split, and was one of great danger to the federation.

STRIKE ASSESSMENT PLAN ADOPTED.

The report as approved by the committee was finally adopted, however, and recommends an assessment of 2 cents per head for the establishment of such a fund, the matter to be decided by a popular vote to be taken immediately after the adjournment of this convention, and the returns made within six months. The fund, if raised, is to be subject to the orders of the executive council, who can use it in assisting any union on strike as they may consider necessary. If the fund is exhausted and a union still needs financial assistance, the executive board is empowered to levy a weekly tax of 2 cents per head for a period not to exceed five weeks, and if two trades-unions call for assistance at the same time the funds raised by such a tax shall be divided equally between them.

EIGHT-HOUR MOVEMENT.

Considerable interest appeared suddenly in the faces of all the delegates when the special committee on the eight-hour movement was called on to report, but died away upon the announcement by the secretary of that committee that they would submit the report at the morning session to-day.

. . .

St. Louis Republic, Dec. 14, 1888.

[December 15, 1888]

FIRST OF MAY, 1890.

. . .

EIGHT-HOUR MOVEMENT.

The special committee of seven was then called on for their report on that portion of the president's address concerning the eight-hour movement. Chairman Kirschner[1] of the committee announced that it was ready and that it would be read by Committee Secretary Wm. J. Dillon.[2] A dead silence of expectancy fell over the convention, and every delegate leaned forward in his chair as Mr. Dillon advanced to the stage bearing the document which embodied in its pages the most important work of the present convention of the American Federation of Labor. The reading of the report was begun in such a low tone that it failed to penetrate all portions of the hall, and impatient cries of "louder!" rose from every side, in response to which the secretary cleared his voice and began anew. The committee began its report

by indorsing fully and unqualifiedly the president's suggestions regarding the eight-hour movement, its necessity for the workingman
owing to the invention and development of machinery applied to the
industries, and submitted the following for the consideration of the
convention:

First — That for the purpose of agitating the eight-hour movement,
causing its full meaning to be understood and enlisting all the laboring
masses in its favor, the convention in indorsing it appoint the following
dates upon which simultaneous mass-meetings of labor all over the
country should be held and the movement advanced: Washington's
Birthday, February 22, 1889; Independence Day, July 4, 1889; Labor
Day, first Monday in September, 1889; Washington's Birthday, February 22, 1890.

Second — That the executive council of the American Federation
of Labor gather statistics as to the number of hours constituting a
day's work for the different trades, the number of unions and men
affected by the movement, and the financial resources of all affiliated
unions in order to be able to report at the next annual meeting in
December, 1889.

Third — That the executive council prepare printed circulars and
issue the same to all the manufacturing firms of the United States,
inviting them to meet labor representatives for conference, with a
view to arriving at a friendly settlement of the eight-hour question.

Fourth — That the executive council also issue a pamphlet on the
eight-hour movement, fully explaining its objects and aims, which
shall be disseminated among the unions for the purpose of full instruction.

Fifth — That, being unable to agree upon any certain fixed date
upon which the demand for the establishment of eight hours as a
day's work should be simultaneously made, the committee refer that
question to the convention for settlement.

At the conclusion of the reading of this report a perfect storm of
applause arose, showing that the unhesitating indorsement of the
movement by the special committee was in thorough accord with the
spirit of the convention.

"Gentlemen," said the presiding officer with an enthusiastic ring in
his voice, "you have heard the report of the committee, What action
do you take on it?["]

THE DEBATE OPENED.

On motion, it was decided to consider the report seriatim, but as
developments showed, it would have been undoubtedly accepted

unanimously as a whole, the different sections being approved as soon as submitted, without debate, until the fifth was reached, in which the question of the eventful day upon which the movement would be enforced, was referred to the convention.

Delegate Blackmore[3] moved that the American Federation of Labor name June 1, 1890, as the day for the general demand for eight hours as a day's work. Delegate La Vine[4] of Chicago moved that the movement be concentrated on the building trades, and the Federation use its power towards securing eight hours for those different unions in the building trade.

Delegate Perry[5] offered an amendment that the question be referred to the affiliated unions for a vote to be taken, returns of which should be made within six months.

A MILWAUKEE MAN'S AMENDMENT.

Delegate Appelhague[6] of Milwaukee submitted an amendment that the convention name as the day upon which the great movement should be made as May 1, 1890, and there being no further motions offered, President Gompers declared discussion of those already before the house in order. Delegate Emrich led off in a speech against the establishment of a certain day, and urged that agitation of the movement be kept up, and the date settled at the next annual convention.

PRESIDENT GOMPERS SPEAKS.

President Gompers sprang to his feet and began a vigorous speech in favor of naming the day at once. "This convention," he said, "must set the day, or else its work amounts to nothing, and the eight-hour movement is no further advanced than it was last year. We cannot agitate without an objective point. By saying that on a certain fixed date the voice of labor shall demand the establishment of eight hours as a day's work, we fix the attention of the world on the movement, and give it a prominence and a character that cannot be done in any other way. At the mass-meetings which are to be held, if the day was not fixed, the movement would be uncertain, wavering, there could be no definiteness in it. We would have the same sort of crowds as heretofore, the same speakers, no accessions, no enthusiasm and no progress. When those meetings are held we must be able to point to a certain day and say: 'At that time the demand will be made.' By the time of our next convention it will be thoroughly under way. Our executive council will be perfectly posted as to the strength and financial resources of the federation, the affiliated unions will be prepared, and everything possible for the success of the movement will have been done. There is no good reason for deferring action, and it is of vital importance that this convention take the decisive step and fix the day." The president's remarks were received with enthusiasm.

Delegate Ives[7] of the International Typographical Union then said that a concession of two hours per day was a tremendous one, and that, perhaps, it would be wiser to gain it by degrees. If they could secure the establishment of nine hours as the working day, it would be a great victory.

Several other delegates spoke on the question some of them taking the ground that it was unwise to name the day at this time, as there was no way of knowing whether all the unions were ready for the movement, and it might be best to thoroughly ascertain the fact before taking such momentous action as was proposed.

SECRETARY M'GUIRE.

Secretary McGuire said that all these arguments had been used in Chicago in 1884, to prevent the naming of May 1, 1886 as the date for the previous eight-hour movement to be put into execution. It had been proved by that experiment that the fixing of the day resulted in a strengthening of the different unions, one having gone into that movement with 7,000 members and come out of it with 26,000. As to confining it to the building trades, that would result in failure, as the other unions would not have the proper interest in the fight. It should be made a general demand, as universal as the field of labor itself. Make it definite by naming the day. Courage will come, and the federation be stronger by the agitation, a fact proven by the experience of the Chicago carpenters, who struck for eight hours with 600 members, won the fight, and came out with 5,000 members. Boston with 106, which increased to 2,400. Here in St. Louis the carpenters flourished during that movement more than ever before or since. The K. of L. have it in their platform. It lies there, it sticks there, and it will stink there, as they are afraid of enforcing it. We have strength now that we did not have in 1886. The National Association of Master Builders[8] are with us, and they were against us then, and public sentiment is on our side. During the last campaign, Jas. G. Blaine[9] insisted that the eight-hour question was the coming issue. If we set the day now our next convention reports will show that we are ready for the contest."

THE STRIKE OF 1886.

Delegate Kirschner said that conditions were more favorable now than in 1886. At that time there were no trades working eight hours, while now there were several, and they will be a force to draw from, as they will not be on strike. The cigar-makers' union, the master builders, the German typographical unions all had won the eight-hour fight, and consequently the movement of 1886 had not been a failure. Eight million hours of labor had been saved by it.

Delegate Emrich thought that it was dangerous for any organization to commit itself to a policy not fully indorsed, and that for this reason it was unwise for the Federation to go to the length of naming the day. On the 1st of May, 1886, the movement in New York had been sold out. Powderly issued his famous circular, the building trades settled on nine hours and the movement was weakened. Delegate Kliver[10] of Chicago said the strike of 1886 had partially failed because the heavy hand of jurisdiction had been laid upon it, but in Chicago it had succeeded, and nearly 24,000 workingmen were now working only eight hours daily and getting better wages than they did formerly for ten hours work.

Delegate Dillon of the Flint-glass Workers' Union figured that with 100 men working eight hours only there was a saving of 20 per cent. of labor, which created that much increased demand for the unemployed labor. Delegate Shields[11] wanted to know how a man could agitate when he had no date to agitate on, and argued that the fixing of a certain day was a necessity and that there was nothing accomplished by this convention unless that was done.

POWDERLY'S POWER BROKEN.

Delegate Haller of New York said there was no danger in naming a day. They had no Powderly now. His bull had no terrors for the laboring classes. His power is broken, and two years ago by issuing his circular he burnt his own house. Working people have no faith in such documents coming from such a source.

Delegate Johnson[12] of the Miners' Union spoke in favor of the movement and of naming the day for its enforcement. Several years ago the miners used to work not 10 or 12 hours, but all hours, and now their working day is fixed at nine hours.

Delegate Perry spoke against the setting of the day, which would be simply telling their antagonists when the blow would be given and allowing them to prepare for it.

Delegate Foster[13] of Boston said that this movement was for the benefit of the labor organizations, as it gave them an aggressive force, an active principle and a definite point to look to.

Several other delegates indorsed the movement and the naming of the day it should be inaugurated, and then President Gompers announced that voting on the various amendments and the original motion would be proceeded with. It being apparent that the majority of the convention favored May 1 as the date to be fixed, Delegate Blackmore changed his motion to read May 1, instead of June 1, 1890, which did away with Appellagen's amendment.

THE DAY NAMED—MAY 1, 1890.

The amendments of Delegates La Vine of Chicago and Perry of Brooklyn were lost, and on motion of Delegate Dillon, the ayes and noes were taken on the original motion that the 1st of May, 1890, be named.

Thirty-eight delegates answered "Aye" when their names were called, and eight responded "No," three of the eight being members of the International Typographical Union, the list of those voting in the negative being as follows: Delegates Bauer[14] of the Boilermakers' Union,[15] Emerich of the Furniture Workers,[16] Archie[17] of the Granite Cutters, Taylor,[18] Lake[19] and Ives of the International Typographical Union; Perry of the Central Labor Union, Brooklyn, and Reinhardt[20] of the St. Louis Waiters' Union.[21]

"The motion is carried," said President Gompers in a loud voice, advancing to the front of the step, "and I now announce that this convention of the American Federation of Labor has named as the day upon which workingmen will demand that eight hours constitute a day's work, May 1, 1890."

This important announcement was received with applause that shook Central Turner Hall, and the Federation had taken the step which will inaugurate the most momentous labor movement since 1886.

. . .

St. Louis Republic, Dec. 15, 1888.

1. John S. Kirchner.
2. William J. DILLON was secretary of the American Flint Glass Workers' Union from 1886 to 1893.
3. Henry H. Blackmore was corresponding secretary for St. Louis local 4 of the Brotherhood of Carpenters and Joiners of America (BCJA) in 1887 and represented the Brotherhood at AFL conventions from 1888 to 1891.
4. John W. La Vine, a cigarmaker, represented the Trade and Labor Assembly of Chicago.
5. James H. Perry, a Brooklyn house carpenter, was district secretary of the United

Order of American Carpenters and Joiners in 1887 and chairman of the Brooklyn Central Labor Union Committee for Eight Hours.

6. Emil Applehagen was secretary of CMIU 25 of Milwaukee (1885-89) and a founder and president (1887-89) of the Milwaukee Federated Trades Council. Moving to Duluth, Minn., in 1889, he was elected president of the city's Trades and Labor Assembly and served as district organizer for the AFL.

7. Eben C. Ives, a St. Paul printer, was active in International Typographical Union (ITU) 30, serving as its president in 1887. He represented the ITU at the 1888 and 1889 AFL conventions.

8. Delegates from construction firms in twenty-six cities organized the National Association of Builders of the United States of America in March 1887. Initially directed toward eliminating labor agitators and walking delegates, it adopted a more conciliatory strategy in February 1888, approving the establishment of arbitration committees in each city with representatives from trade unions and construction companies, and becoming more receptive to the trend toward shorter working hours.

9. James G. Blaine (1830-93) was a leading figure in the Republican party in the decades following the Civil War. He served in the U.S. House of Representatives (1862-76) and Senate (1876-81), ran unsuccessfully for president (1884), and was secretary of state (1881, 1889-92).

10. William H. KLIVER, a Chicago carpenter, was first vice-president of the Illinois State Federation of Labor and fifth vice-president of the United Brotherhood of Carpenters and Joiners of America.

11. William J. SHIELDS was general president of the BCJA from 1886 to 1888.

12. Alexander Johnson of Nelsonville, Ohio, served as vice-president of District 10 of the National Progressive Union of Miners and Mine Laborers in 1889.

13. Frank Keyes FOSTER, a Boston printer and labor editor in the 1880s and 1890s, was active in the ITU, the KOL, and the FOTLU. In 1887 he helped found the Massachusetts State Federation of Labor and during the same year he established the *Labor Leader* in Boston, which he edited until 1897.

14. Robert Bower was a Chicago boilermaker.

15. The International Brotherhood of BOILER Makers.

16. The International FURNITURE Workers' Union of America.

17. David Archie was a St. Louis stonecutter.

18. Charles F. Taylor was a member of ITU 10 in Louisville.

19. Obadaiah Read LAKE of ITU 8 of St. Louis was master workman of KOL District Assembly 17 in 1889.

20. Ernst Reinhardt was a St. Louis waiter.

21. The German Progressive Waiters' Union of St. Louis.

To Auguste Keufer

January 10, [188]9

Mr. Au[gust]e Keufer—
Deleg[ate Fed] Française des Trav. du Livre
15 [Rue de] Savoie, Paris, France
Dear Sir & Bro.:

You[r we]lcome letter of Dec. 6th '88 to hand and contents car[efull]y noted.

I am pleased to hear that you were a delegate to [the] International Congress in London. Thus far we have [rec]eived no official notification of the business transacted by [said] Cong[ress] but by the reports in the journals we [are] led to [believe] that it was practically a failure. That it was a [fa]ilure does not surprise us. Before an International [Congre]ss can be a success a long and very arduous [prepa]ration is necessary. The workers of the world must [be] better educated in social matters, and that education m[ust] be based upon real history instead of pseudo-phi[los]ophical vagaries. In the meantime, however, we [need] not combat the visionaries, [the] red-flag men. We have a positive work to perform and [we can] only demonstrate the superiority of our meth[od by] practical experiment. Let us use our utmost [effo]rts to organize the working people so that they may [be able to ass]ist each other in all the accidents of life, [to protect ea]ch other in sickness and in idleness, and thus main[ta]in the highest possible standard of life for all.

It [is for s]uch or similar reasons that the St. Louis Convention [of] the A.F. of L. resolved to send no delegates to either [of the] Congresses to be held this year—Zurich[1] and Paris. Th[e p]revailing opinion in America is that the Trade Union move[m]ent in Continental Europe must have more opportunity [to] develop before any thing like successful results [may] be expected.

There [has ta]ken place a very serious division[2] in the [ranks of the] Knights of Labor and a rapid disintegratio[n of] that powerful organization is very probable The [main cause] of the [dec]line of the K. of L. is the low [mo]ral [deve]lopment [of the] Executive Officers.

Hoping to hear from you soon and that you will please inform me of the time & place of the Paris Congress

I remain,

Yours very fraternally   (per Hugh McGregor,)
Pres't A.F. of L.

HLp, reel 2, vol. 3, pp. 369-70, SG Letterbooks, DLC.

1. The conference scheduled for the fall of 1889, about which Liebknecht and SG corresponded in November 1888 (see SG to Wilhelm Liebknecht, Nov. 22, 1888, above).

2. Probably a reference to the Founders' Order of the KOL, a secret offshoot of the Knights organized after the 1888 KOL General Assembly. Its leaders were determined to return to the original principles of the Order.

To Lee Hutchinson[1]

Jan 17th [188]9

L. A. Hutchinson Esq.
Gen'l. Sec'y. National Building Trades Council.[2]
392 Crawford St. Detroit Mich.
Dear Sir & Bro.

In reply to your favor of the 15th inst permit me to say that the suggestions I made to the St Louis convention of the American Federation of Labor in reference to and under the head of "Industrial Divisions"[3] is in exact line with your National Council, with this addition that each Trade Organization as well as industrial division should to be affiliated in one common bond through the A.F. of L. This I deem the most common sense as well as scientific form of organization of the working people.

With this I mail to your address a copy of the proceedings of the St Louis convention to which I invite your attention. The subjects under consideration I have marked, with blue pencil.

The matter will recieve the attention of our E.C. shortly and I earnestly hope for your co-operation. Hoping you will write often I am.

Yours Fraternally   Saml Gompers
Pres't.

ALpS, reel 2, vol. 3, p. 425, SG Letterbooks, DLC.

1. Lee C. Hutchinson, a Detroit carpenter, was secretary-treasurer of the National Building Trades Council (NBTC).
2. The Amalgamated Building Trades Council of Chicago founded the NBTC at a convention held in that city on June 28, 1887, in response to the formation of the National Association of Builders by employers.
3. At the 1888 AFL convention, SG had proposed a reorganization of the AFL: the trade unions would organize into divisions by industry to deal with their special interests, and these industrial divisions would be represented by delegates to the AFL conventions and representatives on the Executive Council. The convention referred the proposal to the Executive Council, which took no further action.

To Elizabeth Morgan[1]

Jan 17th [188]9

Mrs Elizabeth Morgan
Dear Madam.

Your highly interesting letter of the 15th as well as clippings[2] and "ordinance" came duly to hand.

There is no doubt in my mind in reference to the truth of the accounts given. The "White" modern slave is a product of our economic conditions and to secure a beneficent change should command our best efforts.

But I am not desirous of dealing in generalities however and will not attempt to enlarge upon this subject more especially to one with whom upon this subject at least I agree with so well as I do with you. I prefer if possible to make a practical suggestion if that is possible.

In your letter I notice that you propose to have the present law so changed so as to have five Women of the twenty Inspectors now provided. Let me suggest that instead of doing this, rather have it changed to have five *addiotional* Women Inspectors. In the first instance by your proposition you admit that there are *too many Male* Inspectors, which I don't think you intend and in the second you are likely to encourage the antagonism of the whole twenty who are at present in office. Not one knowing who might be supplanted should your amendment prevail. You will pardon the suggestion. I am far from the field of operations and my vision may be dimmed thereby, but that is how it occurred to me and thus frankly state it.

There is no doubt that you are engaged in a noble work to uplift the poor Women and Girls who are ekeing out a miserable existence by their long hours of drudgery and unrequited toil and frequently the degradation resultant therefrom and no employment at all, and I have never allowed an opportunity to go by whenever I could arouse a feeling and action against the iniquity. I am indeed proud of the record of Federal Labor Union 2703[3] and to count the noble women who constitute its members as my comrades in this our great cause I appreciate as an honor.

With best wishes for success and hoping to hear from you as often as convenient. I am Dear Madam—

Yours Fraternally. Saml Gompers.
Pres't. A.F. of L.

ALpS, reel 2, vol. 3, pp. 423-24, SG Letterbooks, DLC.

1. Elizabeth Chambers MORGAN was a founder of AFL Ladies' Federal Labor Union (FLU) 2703 and of the Illinois Women's Alliance.
2. Possibly from the *Chicago Times* series called "City Slave Girls" that appeared in the late summer of 1888, describing the poor working conditions of women in factories and shops. Its revelations led FLU 2703 to join with other women's organizations to form the Illinois Women's Alliance on Nov. 2, 1888. On July 25, 1889, as a result of pressure from the Alliance, the Chicago City Council passed an ordinance authorizing the commissioner of health to employ five female sanitary police to inspect factories and tenements.
3. The AFL chartered Ladies' FLU 2703 of Chicago in June 1888. It was one of several all women's FLUs chartered by the Federation and included clerks, bookbin-

ders, candy makers, typists, gum makers, music teachers, and other female workers. It organized local women's craft unions for the AFL and agitated for the improvement of working conditions of women and children.

To James Perry

Jan 22nd [188]9

James H Perry Esq.
Chairman Com. Eight Hour Agitation, C.L.U.
293. S. 3rd St. Brooklyn. E.D. NY.
Dear Sir & Friend—

In reply to your favor of the 21st, in which you enquire whether organizations represented in the Brooklyn Central Labor Union are required by the resolutions of the St Louis convention of the American Federation of Labor, to *strike* for the enforcement of the Eight Hour workday May 1st 1890, whether "preppared for it or not" permit me to say that I have carefully examined the proceedings of the convention upon the subject of the Eight Hour agitation and movement and in no place do I discover even a reference to a "strike". I am surprised that anyone should for a moment harbor the thought that the A.F. of L. would favor a strike whether the working people are "prepared for it or not".

The number of improvements in the toilers condition that were enforced *without a strike* is more than can be told, but that they are numerous all agree.

There is no good reason why we may not be able to enforce the Eight Hour workday May 1st 1890 if we bring about the same conditions that enforced other demands of labor. 1st By agitation to enlighten public opinion, 2nd By organizing our forces so that the employing class as an advantageous alternative will concede the Eight Hour rule rather than risk the loss consequent upon a possible strike for it.

I desire to call your attention to one of the resolutions of the St Louis convention upon this subject which will dispel from the mind of any one the fear that the A.F. of L. has the disposition to do anything foolhardy or illy-considered. It Says: "The Executive Council shall also prepare printed circulars which are to be issued to all manufacuring firms in the country, requesting them to meet representatives of this organization in conference, so that a friendly arrangement of a reduction in the working hours may, if possible, be effected."

The working people are entitled to a reduction in their hours of labor to Eight per day and the A.F. of L. will endeavor to help them enforce it.

Trusting that the Brooklyn C.L.U. will co-operate heartily with us in the movement to enforce the Eight Hour workday May 1st 1890 without a strike if possible or to that end that we may place the organizations of the entire country in the condition that they will be "prepared for it".

Fraternally Yours   Sam'l Gompers.
President A.F. of L.

ALpS, reel 2, vol. 3, pp. 457-58, SG Letterbooks, DLC.

P. J. McGuire to Officers of the AFL, the KOL, and the Railroad Brotherhoods

Philadelphia, Pa. Jan. 26. 89

Confidential
T. V. Powderly Esq.
Dear Sir:—

After mature deliberation in conference with Mr. T. V. Powderly, of the Knights of Labor & with his approval, I do hereby invite you to have one or more of the Chief Officers of your organization to attend an informal conference to be held at the Bingham House Market St Cor 11th Philada. Pa on Thursday Feb'y 14. 1889 at 10 AM.

The object of the conference is to effect, if possible, an amicable & harmonious understanding between all the various labor organizations of the Country. It is not intended to form any new organization to embrace all, as that is probably neither desirable or practical. But the American Federation of Labor, the Knights of Labor & the various organizations of Railroad Men, ought to, if nothing else—have an annual conference of their chief officers, collectively to exchange views, and though they may differ in details & methods, they could present to the world at least an apparent bond of interest & tolerance, that would soon dissipate the prevalent public notion, that the labor organizations are at war with one another and over which the corporations and trusts have so much reason to exult.

Hoping your worthy organization will be represented on the above occasion and awaiting an early reply I Remain[1]

Yours Fraternally   P. J McGuire

P.S. This communication is sent to all the Chief Officers of the Organizations above mentioned.

ALS, Terence Vincent Powderly Papers, DCU.

1. See "A News Account of a Meeting between Representatives of the AFL, the KOL, and the Railroad Brotherhoods at Bingham House, Philadelphia," Feb. 15, 1889, below.

To John Kirchner

Feb'y 7, [188]9

Mr John S. Kirchner—
Gen'l Organizer, AF. of L.—
355 N. 4th St. Phila., Pa.—
Dear Sir & Bro:—

Under another cover you will receive a letter of invitation & blank Credential to Conference of Trade & Labor Unions of Phila.[1] Fifty similar letters & credentials are mailed herewith to the Unions of your city that are affiliated to the A.F. of L., also several of a somewhat different tenor to non-affiliate Union. In this I have done my best for the resuscitation of the Phila. Central Labor Union[2] to the prejudice of much other work of a very pressing nature, but nevertheless I shall feel that we are well paid if the proposed Conference [is] successful. With best wishes for your success in this matter I remain,

Yours fraternally,
Pres't A.F. of L.

HLp, reel 2, vol. 3, p. 530, SG Letterbooks, DLC.

1. Under the auspices of the Philadelphia Central Labor Union (CLU), Kirchner invited all trade unions and KOL assemblies of that city to send representatives to a Feb. 26 conference to discuss forming a unified central organization. Two hundred delegates representing sixty organizations attended. At a second meeting on Mar. 12, delegates from Philadelphia's labor organizations formed the United Labor League of Philadelphia.

2. The Philadelphia CLU was organized in 1885 as an offshoot of the Philadelphia Central Short-Hour League; it had been declining since 1887.

To the *Carpenter*

New York, Feb. 7th 1889.

To the Carpenter:

A letter reached me a few days ago, in which I was asked how it was possible for Mr. P. J. McGuire to act as Secretary of the American Federation of Labor, while holding the office of General Secretary of the United Brotherhood of Carpenters and Joiners of America. I was further asked whether he receives any salary as Secretary of the A.F. of L. The letter contained remarks that reflected no credit upon the writer.

Believing, however, that possibly the same erroneous impression may lurk in the minds of other members of your organization, and for the purpose of setting this matter right at once by disabusing their minds, I avail myself of your columns to answer the writer of the letter referred to, as well as any other who may be laboring under the same impression.

First. While it is true that Bro. P. J. McGuire is Secretary of the A.F. of L., the position is merely an honorary and advisory one, entailing little, if any work certainly not of a character to interfere with his duties to the U.B. When any letters, or other matters connected with the A.F. of L., are sent to him, (which are few) he encloses them in an envelope and mails them to this office to be attended to.

Second. He does not receive any salary, either directly or indirectly, as Secretary of the A.F. of L.

Third. Frequently, against his urgent requests and earnest protestations, he has been elected to the office of Secretary of the Federation.

The delegates to the conventions of the A.F. of L. have always desired to honor the Brotherhood, and manifested it by electing one of its most prominent and devoted members to a position of honor. Why an objection should be raised by any member of the U.B. because of it, is more than I can understand, except that some people will always find fault, whether cause for it exists or not.

Trusting that this may meet the eye of my correspondent, that he and others may be convinced of their error, and with best wishes for the continued success of your grand organization. I am

Yours fraternally,   Saml. Gompers,
President American Federation of Labor.

Carpenter, Feb. 15, 1889.

A News Account of a Meeting between Representatives of the AFL, the KOL, and the Railroad Brotherhoods at Bingham House, Philadelphia

[February 15, 1889]

LABOR MEN IN COUNCIL.

A meeting of the representatives of various labor organizations was held yesterday at the Bingham House to discuss measures to secure harmony among and co-operation between associations of working men throughout the country.

Among those present were General Master Workman Powderly and General Secretary-Treasurer Hayes, of the Knights of Labor; Samuel Gompers, President, and P. J. McGuire, Secretary, of the American Federation of Labor; Harry Walton,[1] of the Executive Committee of the Brotherhood of Locomotive Engineers; Jeremiah J. Leahy,[2] of the Executive Committee of the Brotherhood of Locomotive Firemen,[3] and G. M. Bailey,[4] of the Brotherhood of Locomotive Switchmen.[5]

The meeting was organized by the election of Mr. Bailey as Chairman, and Mr. Leahy as Secretary. Letters expressing sympathy with the objects of the meeting and approval of whatever might be done to secure harmony were received from Grand Chief Engineer Arthur, Grand Chief Conductor Wheaton,[6] Grand Master Fireman Sergeant,[7] Grand Master Brakeman S. E. Wilkinson[8] and Wm. A. Simscott,[9] General Secretary and Treasurer of the Switchmen's Mutual Aid Associations of North America. A resolution, offered by Mr. Powderly and seconded by Mr. Gompers, was adopted providing for an exchange of the Constitutions of the organizations represented.

The following resolution, offered by Mr. McGuire and seconded by Mr. Powderly also prevailed:

"Resolved, We hold that the interests of all classes of labor are identical, and hence all organized labor should work together in harmony, and we believe the time has come when trades' unions, knights of labor and all others should clasp hands and march together for the advancement of the working classes."

Messrs. Gompers, Powderly and Walton were appointed a committee to prepare an address setting forth the purpose of the meeting, the need of organization, etc., to be sent throughout the country.[10]

Philadelphia Public Ledger, Feb. 15, 1889.

1. Henry WALTON was a member of the Brotherhood of Locomotive Firemen (BLF) Grand Executive Board from 1885 to 1894.

2. Jeremiah J. LEAHY was a member of the BLF Grand Executive Board from 1886 to 1890.

3. The Brotherhood of LOCOMOTIVE Firemen.

4. George S. Bailey was a member of St. Louis Lodge 37 of the Switchmen's Mutual Aid Association (SMAA).

5. The SWITCHMEN's Mutual Aid Association of the United States of America.

6. Calvin S. WHEATON was grand chief conductor of the Order of Railway Conductors from 1880 to 1890.

7. Frank Pierce SARGENT was grand master of the BLF from 1885 to 1902.

8. Stephen Edward WILKINSON helped organize the Brotherhood of Railroad Brakemen (name changed to Brotherhood of Railroad Trainmen in 1890) and served as grand master from 1885 to 1895.

9. William A. SIMSROTT helped organize the SMAA in 1886 and served as its grand secretary and treasurer from 1887 until 1894.

10. See "A Report of a Circular Issued by the Unity Conference Held at Bingham House, Philadelphia," July 11, 1889, below.

To Emil Applehagen

Feb 16th [188]9

Emil Applehagen Esq.
P.O. Box 1023. Duluth. Minn.
Dear Sir & Friend.

Owing to absence from this city an earlier reply to your favor of the 11th inst was impossible.

You ask my opinion upon the establishment of Trade Schools[1] and its effect upon the working people. I am frank to say that the matter cannot be treated fully in a letter that I have time to write at present being too much engrossed in the Eight Hour movement which is of paramount importance. I will however say this much upon the subject. The organizations of labor should not only refuse their endorsement to any such scheme as tends to form "Trade Schools" but should oppose them at every step. Wherever the "Trade Schools" have been established they have proved themselves the breeding pen for unfair men who rush to take the places of men made vacant by a lock-out or strike to prevent further encroachments upon our wages, hours and other conditions of labor. I am aware that there [are] some well intentioned people who favor all sorts of schem[e]s and believe they are doing good. Of them I have nothing more to say than that they are mistaken. But of the vast majority who contribute either money or their moral support to the formation of such schemes as the "Trade

Schools" I unequivocally assert that they are prompted from a well designed purpose to undermine the very objects and aims for which the working people organize.

Does it not seem strange that some of these people who pretend to display such a solicitude for the "welfare of the poor Boys" yet at every opportunity turn their backs upon, and make the conditions of workingmen worse and harder to bear?

It is untrue that ["labor? org]anizations deprive the Boys from learning a trade." The facts are that they insist that not any one trade shall be over-run in the first instance and in the second that Boys when taken by Employers to learn a trade, shall be regularly apprenticed for a term so as to become competent workmen and not "botches". That they may earn a livlihood by their trade upon attaining manhood and not curse themselves and everyone connected in the wrong which has prevented them from obtaining a mechanical education in the only practical College of labor, the Factory and Workshop.

There are many things I would like to add to the above but time forbids.

Trusting that the above will suffice however I am

Yours Fraternally   Saml Gompers.
Pres't.

ALpS, reel 2, vol. 3, pp. 581-83, SG Letterbooks, DLC.

1. Beginning in the early 1880s, manufacturers helped establish trade schools as a substitute for the apprenticeship system, the traditional vehicle for training skilled workers. They contended that mechanization had rendered apprenticeship obsolete and that such schools were necessary to keep trades from deteriorating. Furthermore, trade schools enabled manufacturers to bypass union apprenticeship rules, which limited the number of workers in each craft.

To P. J. McGuire

Feb 19th [188]9

P. J McGuire Esq.
Dear Pete.

By this time you know that the first meeting of the Eight Hour conference was a decided success. Twenty five Unions sending delegates. I have no doubt more will respond for the next meeting, Thursday 21st. It was a pretty good stroke to make after the C.L.U. failed to take action.[1] The conference was called and the machinery for the mass-meeting were put into good working order all in less than three days. You know that the meeting will be held at Cooper Union and I do hope you will try and be on hand as early as possible. Ingersoll,[2] McNiell,[3] McDonald,[4] Pryor[5] and others have been invited to address the meeting — Of course you, myself and King[6] — Taking things all in all we anticipate having a good gathering. The meetings of the Com. are far apart from each other and I am not authorized to act in the matter of inviting any speakers. I certainly would like to have Foran[7] and if I had thought of it I certainly would have suggested his name. I will consult a few men and probably wire you to-night to have him come anyway.

Yours,   Saml Gompers.

ALpS, reel 2, vol. 3, p. 587, SG Letterbooks, DLC.

1. On Feb. 15, 1889, a New York City conference of trade and labor unions appointed a committee consisting of SG, Sergius E. Shevitch, and Robert Crowe to arrange and publicize meetings in support of the AFL eight-hour campaign. The following day the committee issued a call for a Washington's Birthday mass meeting at Cooper Union on Feb. 22. On Sunday, Feb. 17, the New York City Central Labor Union failed to support the eight-hour demonstration, but a separate conference of delegates meeting on the same day endorsed the plan.

2. Robert Green Ingersoll was an orator widely known for his outspoken agnosticism. He supported Henry George's 1886 New York City mayoralty campaign and worked on behalf of the Haymarket defendants.

3. George Edwin McNEILL, a Boston printer, was an eight-hour advocate, labor leader, and labor editor.

4. J. P. McDonnell.

5. Roger Atkinson PRYOR, a lawyer, had defended New York City eight-hour strikers in 1886 and in 1887 represented the Haymarket defendants before the U.S. Supreme Court.

6. Edward King.

7. Martin Ambrose FORAN was a Democratic congressman from Ohio from 1883 to 1889.

A Translation of a News Account of an Address at a Mass Meeting in New York City

[February 23, 1889]

EIGHT HOURS!

. . .

SAMUEL GOMPERS,

who was introduced at this point by the chairman[1] and greeted with applause, said, among other things: "When the representatives of the *bona fide* labor organizations of this country discussed in St. Louis whether it would be advisable to set a date on which the 8-hour day should be introduced, they were of the unanimous opinion that the time had come to shorten the workday. Whatever our views might be with respect to other things, in this we are all agreed, that the workday must be shortened. (Loud applause.) Many objections have been raised against this idea. One of the objections of our opponents is that if we workers had more free time, we would spend it at the saloon and throw our money away. Now, many of the people who hold this view are troublemakers and spendthrifts themselves, who are afraid that they will have fewer luxuries if we have more time for ourselves; thus their argument is not honest. (Applause.) The reduction of work hours that we workers demand will improve us physically, morally, and intellectually, not degrade us. Nations that have shorter work hours produce more than those with longer hours. If the people who work the longest were the smartest, then China, where workers earn 6 cents a day, would be marching at the front of civilization! But this is not the case; Chinese industry cannot compete with ours. Nevertheless, as long as the current long work hours continue, the coolies will be able to come here from China and underbid us on the labor market. Economists agree that people who work too long are not capable, in the long run, of acquiring the skills necessary to be successful in the field of industry. Our entire public life would not have become so thoroughly corrupt if the citizens did not have to work too long and could, instead, concern themselves with their public servants and with politics. It is often argued that we workers are lawless and violent. I need only allude to the last strike of the horse car drivers, whose purpose was to uphold the laws of the state of New York. Yes, my friends, I tell you, the worst scofflaws and anarchists are the railroad corporations of our country. The bosses maintain that they force no one to sign contracts promising not to join a labor organization, but what do they mean when they tell a worker: 'You cannot work for us unless you sign our contract.' Isn't this the worst coercion, the vilest slavery imaginable? The countries with the longest working hours have the lowest wages and vice versa. Such is also the case with the different branches of industry. The workers who earn the highest wages have the shortest workday. And this is only natural; a person who has time for relaxation, thought, and schooling can produce more and better than one who only sweats and strains without pause. A shortening of the workday is not, as many mistakenly believe, linked to a wage cut; rather, as soon as the workday is shortened, the wages will begin to rise and business will improve." At this point the speaker began to talk about the movement of 1886 and pointed out that the eight-hour movement had reaped progressively more advantages for the workers and improved their condition. Then he explained more precisely the purpose of the present agitation—being carried on by means of concurrent mass meetings throughout the country—and announced that as soon as the impact of these mass meetings was felt, a circular will be sent to employers, in an attempt to get the eight-hour day by peaceful means. He said that if all workers did their duty as agitators until May 1, 1890, success could not be long in coming.

. . .

New Yorker Volkszeitung, Feb. 23, 1889. Translated from the German by Patrick McGrath.

1. Daniel HARRIS, president of CMIU 144 in the late 1880s.

To P. J. McGuire

Feb 26th [188]8 [9]

P. J. McGuire Esq
Sec'y A.F. of L.
Dear Sir & Friend.

Your favor of 25th duly to hand and contents noted.

I protest emphatically against you entertaining the idea of resigning the Secrataryship of the Federation. What will the enemies of labor and of our movement particularly say? Do you think for a moment that they would believe that your resignation was caused by the peurile grumbling of a small minority, yes, one dissatisfied member here and there, in the Br[other]hood?. It would be heralded forth that "McGuire & Gompers Are Out" "The Federation's Split" "McGuire Deserts the Federation" &c &c and then the spicy stories columns long in which will be told of our "contests, bickerings &c". An obituary on the Eight Hour movement would be written, everything in fact said and done to destroy our organization and movement. I know and assure you I can appreciate what you have to contend against. But I am satisfied, and experience has taught me that if men desire to find fault with the officers of their organizations in the labor movement they will continue to in spite of the desire to please or placate them. You may rest assured that if you would resign, flushed with what that faction would consider a victory (By resigning you tacitly admit that their complaint is true and justified) they would raise some other issue and fight harder and crowd you closer than they can ever hope [u]pon the issue that "you are Secretary of Federation a[t th]e same time being Secretary of the Brotherhood." [This is?] no time to resign Pete, and you must not. [You ar]e too devoted to it, to allow anything to interfere with [the s]uccess of our movement so auspicously begun.[1]

Kirchner left here last even[ing in g]ood condition. I suppose you saw him to-day.

I shall follow your suggest[ion in] the matter of that item of expenditure.

How about the per capita of the U.B? The report will go to press on Thursday.

With best wishes for the success of your meeting to night I am

Yours. Saml Gompers.

ALpS, reel 2, vol. 3, pp. 609-10, SG Letterbooks, DLC.

1. McGuire retained his position as secretary. His proffered resignation may have been linked to the issue SG addressed in "To the *Carpenter*," Feb. 7, 1889, above.

To John Kirchner

Feb 28th [188]9

John S. Kirchner. Esq.
Gen'l. Organizer — A.F. of L.
Dear Sir & Friend

Your favor with clippings of Phila papers giving an account of your conference came duly to hand. I assure you that I read them with great interest. It certainly seems that your movement will meet with success if you follow the advice contained in my telegram which by the way I am pleased to learn was well recieved. Go far but not too far. Remember there are many of our fellow workers who are not advanced as far as we and it is inadvisable to promulgate declarations of principle which may tend to divide you from those you seek to co-operate with. It does not convert nor convi[n]ce. It merely creates antagonism and opposition

Eight Hours is the cry which can unite all forces at least for the present and will check the indifference and want of confidence too prevelant to day. Other questions can be taken up as they develop and arise.

With best wishes for the success of your movement I am

Yours Fraternally. Saml Gompers.

Pres't.

ALpS, reel 2, vol. 3, p. 633, SG Letterbooks, DLC.

To P. J. McGuire

Feb. 28th [188]9

P. J. McGuire Esq.
Sec'y A.F. of L.
Dear Sir & Friend.

The question of our Eight Hour pamphlet has given me considerable trouble and the following is the result of my thoughts.

That we request Geo. E. McNiell to write a pamphlet of about 24 to 32 pages, pay him $50.00. down and a royalty of about one cent on each copy sold. We could sell them for 10¢ and cover our expense and give it the widest circulation just at this time.

Let me know your opinion on this upon reciept and I will submit it to the E.C. for approval.

A thought occurred to me before this of writing a circular letter to about ten or fifteen men inviting articles of about 500 words upon the subject but then there is no doubt that it would be a repitition of the one idea with the only difference the language employed. Hence I abandoned it.

Then again it must be borne in mind that this is a great opportunity to get out something that will live in history and should not be lost by republishing old matter.

If you deem it necessary I will run over to see you on Monday talk the matter over and return the same evening.[1]

Yours Truly   Saml Gompers.
Pres't.

ALpS, reel 2, vol. 3, pp. 634-35, SG Letterbooks, DLC.

1. The AFL commissioned George McNeill to write *The Eight Hour Primer*, George Gunton to write *The Economic and Social Importance of the Eight-Hour Movement*, and Lemuel Danryid to write *History and Philosophy of the Eight-Hour Movement*. By the end of 1889, the Federation had distributed about 60,000 copies of these pamphlets.

To Jefferson Wade[1]

March 2nd [188]9

J. D. Wade. Esq.
Sec'y. Balt. Federation of Labor.
Dear Sir

Your favor of the 1st came duly to hand and contents noted.

You ask my judgment upon the trouble between the Balt. Fed. of

Labor, Washington Fed. of Labor and the Firm of I. Hamburger and Sons.[2] I admit that a man who only hears one side of a case may decide justly yet not fairly and consequently who must decline to decide it unless both parties agree to make a statement of the case and agree to be bound by my decision. I am satisfied however that the W.F. of L. will not consent to such a proposition owing no doubt to the complexion of that body and the refusal of the Balt. convention of the American Federation of Labor to admit their delegates to seats in that body in 1887.

You should procure incontro[v]ertable proof that the committee from the W.F. of L. stated that they would "prefer the cutting to be done by unorganized labor in Washington rather than by organized labor in Baltimore". If this is true that they made such a declaration I am of the opinion that the statement or declaration should be printed and sent to every labor organization in Washington and also a number of active labor men. If you make an honest and fair settlement with a firm with which you had an equal or dominant jurisdiction and you find that firm living up to the conditions, you should give them all the aid you can to protect them from unjust or illy-considered action from any quarter.

I trust that you will take proper and timely action for the next Eight Hour meeting, July 4th

Can't your Organization prevent that "Stuff" from cheating his unfortunate piano makers by paying them off in orders on "Pluck-me-Stores".[3] If there is no law upon the Statute Books of Maryland the sooner you seek its enactment the better and in the meantime let him know that labor is alive and intends making the facts known.

Anticipating the pleasure of reading Pro. Ely's[4] address which you promise to send me and wishing the movement and yourself the greatest success, I am

Yours Fraternally   Saml Gompers.
Pres't.

ALpS, reel 2, vol. 3, pp. 643-44, SG Letterbooks, DLC.

1. Jefferson Davis Wade, a member of International Typographical Union 12 and of the KOL, later served as chief of the Maryland Bureau of Industrial Statistics (1898-1900).

2. At a conference with the Washington and Baltimore Federations of Labor in February 1889, I. Hamburger and Sons, clothiers, agreed to hire only union workers at its operations in the two cities. The Washington federation, however, boycotted the firm, refusing to recognize the agreement because it did not compel Hamburger to employ a cutter in the nation's capital.

3. During a February 1889 meeting of the Baltimore Federation of Labor, a delegate from a lodge composed of piano makers accused a large Baltimore piano-making firm of instituting a form of trucking system. Under this system, the delegate explained,

The AFL Executive Council in 1890

Samuel Gompers

P. J. McGuire

William Martin

Henry Emrich

Chris Evans

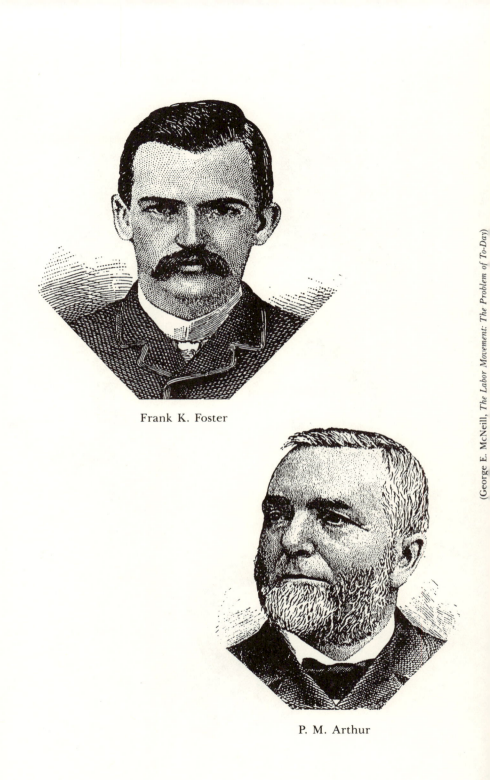

Frank K. Foster

P. M. Arthur

(George E. McNeill, *The Labor Movement: The Problem of To-Day*)

Pages from the AFL Account Book, 1887 (George Meany Memorial Archives, AFL-CIO).

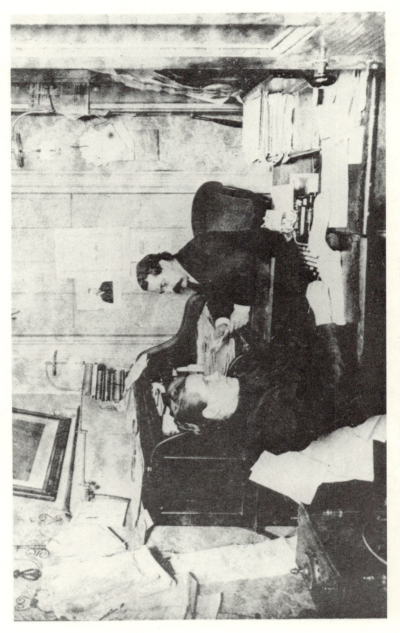

AFL office, New York City, late 1880s (*American Federationist*, 1950).

American Federation of Labor.

◄ EXECUTIVE ✦ COUNCIL. ►

President—SAMUEL GOMPERS, 171 East 91st Street, N. Y. City.

First Vice-President—DANIEL McLAUGHLIN, Box 26, Braidwood, Illinois.

Second Vice-President—WILLIAM MARTIN, 512-514 Smithfield Street, Pittsburg, Pa.

Treasurer—GABRIEL EDMONSTON, 805 Eleventh Street, N. W., Washington, D. C.

Secretary—P. J. McGUIRE, P. O. Box 884, Philadelphia, Pa.

Gabriel Edmonston Esq.   New York, June 14th 1888

Treasurer A F of L.

Dear Sir.

Enclosed you will please find a Bill that requires introduction in Congress pursuant to a resolution of the Baltimore Convention and the Executive Council of the A F of L at its recent session.

It seems to me that it would be advisable to have it introduced simultaneously in House and Senate (For which purpose please make another copy) I suggest Mr O'Niell of the Labor Committee in the former and Senator Blair, Hiscock or some other prominent Republican in the latter as pretty good men into whose hands you could place the Bills for introduction.

On Saturday I leave here for the East and shall be gone about a week or ten days. Upon the completion of the trip I shall come on to Washington Have the Bill introduced regardless of its chances.

Fraternally Yours

Saml Gompers, Prest

Samuel Gompers to Gabriel Edmonston, June 14, 1888 (George Meany Memorial Archives, AFL-CIO).

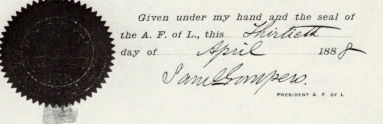

Gabriel Edmonston's AFL organizer's commission, 1888 (George Meany Memorial Archives, AFL-CIO).

Labor Day parade, Union Square, New York City, 1887 (Museum of the City of New York).

Pennsylvania miners' strike, 1888 (*Harper's Weekly*).

John W. Hayes (Library of Congress).

Henry W. Blair (Library of Congress).

David B. Hill, 1888 (*New York Daily Graphic*).

LET THEM FIGHT IT OUT.
THE LABOR CONVENTION IN SYRACUSE.

A cartoon of the United Labor party convention at Syracuse, 1887 (*New York Daily Graphic*).

A cartoon depicting the movement for clemency for the Haymarket anarchists, 1887 (*Frank Leslie's Illustrated Newspaper*).

Building barricades on 10th Avenue, New York City, during the streetcar strike, 1889 (Bettmann Archive).

Der Arbeit Siegeszug.

"Labor's Victorious Advance," a cartoon supporting the 1890 eight-hour campaign. (The labels on the dragons read "Exploitation" and "Ignorance of the Masses.") (*New Yorker Volkszeitung*).

Samuel Gompers, 1890 (George Meany Memorial Archives, AFL-CIO).

Gompers and the Struggle between the Central Labor Union and the Central Labor Federation in New York City

In the late 1880s internecine struggles deeply divided the New York City Central Labor Union (CLU) and led to the creation of a rival central body, the Central Labor Federation (CLF). This conflict eventually opened the way to a major challenge to Gompers' political philosophy.

In January 1889 the *New Yorker Volkszeitung* published reports that accused a number of CLU delegates of accepting pay from brewery owners and undermining the brewery workers' union. The accused delegates were, as it happens, members of the KOL and had supported non-socialist candidates in recent elections. The bribery scandal and the clumsy attempts of the CLU to investigate it led to a split in the organization. About thirty trade unions, mostly German-speaking and socialist, withdrew and formed the CLF; the unions that remained in the CLU were almost exclusively Anglo-Irish and many were local assemblies of the KOL. In March the CLF applied for membership in the AFL, and Gompers, after attempting unsuccessfully to negotiate reunification, granted them a charter in early June.

This fracturing of the central organization weakened the labor movement in New York. Neither the CLU nor the socialists were able to stage more than feeble electoral campaigns in the fall of 1889 and the organization of the eight-hour movement in the city lagged badly. Recognizing that neither central body had gained much from the split, the CLF dissolved and merged back into the CLU in December. The conflicts that were at the root of the original rupture, however, had not healed, and disagreements between socialists and followers of other political parties continued to plague the CLU.

In May 1890 the socialist *Workmen's Advocate* and *New Yorker Volkszeitung* published reports that James Archibald, secretary of the CLU, had been on the payroll of the Democratic party. When Archibald and his adherents denounced the accusations and banned journalists of both papers from the CLU's meetings, supporters of the socialists in the central labor body resurrected the CLF in late June. About forty labor organizations sent delegates to the CLF; the large majority of these represented German unions, although a few KOL assemblies also sent representatives. At its second meeting the CLF voted unanimously to admit delegates of the SLP as regular members.

Soon after its reorganization the CLF became active in a variety of labor causes, including the cloakmakers' struggle[1] and, in cooperation with the SLP, the revival of the eight-hour movement in the city—both campaigns that were close to Gompers' heart. It also sought reaffiliation with the AFL. Gompers, however, advised Ernest Bohm, the secretary of the CLF, that he could not reissue the old charter of the organization and suggested that it might not be eligible for a new one because it had accepted delegates from the SLP. The CLF lodged a formal complaint against the decision not to return its old charter, but the AFL Executive Council upheld Gompers. In September the CLF decided to apply for a new charter.

Clearly aware that the decision on the CLF's charter application would be of great importance for the future political direction of the AFL, Gompers declined to act on it alone, nor did the Executive Council make a decision. Instead, Gompers took the unusual step of putting the matter before the Federation's 1890 convention. The CLF chose Lucien Sanial, one of its delegates from the SLP, to present its case to the convention and urged all AFL unions affiliated with the CLF to send representatives to the meeting; five delegates from unions affiliated with the CLF attended. The CLF's appeal to the convention was unsuccessful, however, as that body, acting on Gompers' recommendation, rejected the application by a vote of three to one.

Later in the decade the CLF temporarily joined the Socialist Trade and Labor Alliance, a competing body to the AFL; in 1899 it merged with the CLU to form the Central Federated Union. The new body affiliated with the AFL.

Note

1. See "A Translation of an Excerpt of a News Account of a Mass Meeting at Cooper Union," July 11, 1890, below.

A Translation of a Circular Addressed to the Organized Workers of New York City

THE EIGHT-HOUR LEAGUE.

The committee appointed by the eight-hour league in Clarendon Hall has issued the following call:

To the organized workers of New York City.
Fellow workers:

The present state of organized labor in this city is a particularly sorry sight to behold! Without some common ground upon which a remedy for the workers' hardships can be planned, unified action in the interest of labor is totally impossible.

Half of the workers and their organizations are being opposed by the Central Labor Union, the other half, by the Central Labor Federation. Bitterness, fighting, disunity, and hostility are common. Given these conditions we ask: What are our duties? The advancement of the labor movement, the hope of the working masses, with eyes open and hearts beating together, calling on our manliness and honor to find neutral ground upon which all can unite and forget their disagreements at least for the time being, so that we can concentrate all our energy on agitating for the eight-hour movement and introducing the eight-hour workday on May 1, 1890.

With this aim in view, without desiring in any way to be a social labor organization, the eight-hour conference, which convened the huge and successful eight-hour mass meeting in Cooper Union on February 22, resolved to appoint itself as a permanent organization for the advancement of the eight-hour movement. We therefore appeal to you, irrespective of your particular affiliation in the labor movement, to be represented in this eight-hour league. Elect three delegates to attend the next meeting, which will take place on Thursday evening, March 11, at 8 o'clock in Clarendon Hall. We request the officers of those organizations that will have no meeting by this time to appoint delegates until the members may decide otherwise.

In future the meetings will probably be held weekly; delegates may be sent at any time.

Appealing again for your support and assistance in this movement, we remain

Fraternally yours,   Robert Crowe
Geo. G. Block[1]
B. O. Ricker
Committee.
Samuel Gompers, Chairman

New Yorker Volkszeitung, Mar. 10, 1889. Translated from the German by Patrick McGrath.

1. George G. BLOCK, secretary of the Journeymen Bakers' National Union from 1886 to 1888, was a founder of the New York City Central Labor Union and a leader in the Henry George 1886 mayoralty campaign.

To P. J. McGuire

March 11th [188]9

P. J. McGuire Esq.
Dear Sir & Friend.

Your favor of the 6th inst enclosing circular adopted at the recent conference of the Executive officers of several Labor Organizations at Philadelphia Pa. come duly to hand.

[Fr]om the day of our conference until a few days ago I was delighted with the result, but to my surprise and chagrin I saw an article in the *Journal of United Labor* (the official Organ of the K of L) which not only places the statements contained in the circular outside [of][1] the pale of truth, the sentiments of the conference at naught, but is an encouragement of that series of guerrilla war and antagonism to the Trade Unions which called forth the contests and bitterness our conference sought to allay.[2]

If the Trade Unions through their representatives are supposed to dis-arm while allowing the same weapons in the hands of those who sought to destroy them before and are keeping up their fire during a truce or treaty of peace I shall not be a party to it. Under [suc]h circumstances I prefer to sound a warning cry to the Trade Unions to defend themselves at all hazards. The American Federation of Labor was organized to defend and protect the Trade Unions and as its President I shall not lull them into a fancied security to prove an easy prey to their "pretended" friends or avoued enemies.

For the above reasons I shall not submit the circular to the Executive Council of the American Federation of Labor until I recieve some official assurance from Mr Powderly that the article in question and the thoughts it promulgates is disapproved by him and the methods advocated will not be tolerated by his Order.

Fraternally Yours   Saml Gompers.
President

ALpS, reel 2, vol. 3, pp. 675-76, SG Letterbooks, DLC.

1. In the original, "of" is inserted above the line, positioned to read "outside the of pale of truth."

2. An article entitled "A Significant Straw" (*Journal of United Labor,* Feb. 28, 1889) claimed that "there is no privilege enjoyed or protection afforded by a distinctive trade union which is not enjoyed or afforded to as great or greater degree by a District Assembly of our Order." It also expressed the belief that "there is no good reason why every trade organization in existence at the present time should not within the next five years become a Trade District of our Order."

To Ernest Bohm[1]

March 14th [188]9

Ernest Böhm Esq.
Sec'y C.L.F. of NY.
202 E 57th St.
Dear Sir.

Your application for a Certificate of Affiliation from the American Federation of Labor came duly to hand. It becomes my duty to inform you that several protests have been lodged against its issuance. Among the protestants is the New York Central Labor Union and I have concluded to request both bodies to select a committee to meet me at this office in reference thereto.

You are therefore requested to have a committee of three delegates of your organization at this office Friday Evening March 22nd at 7.30. O'clock and oblige

Yours Fraternally   Saml Gompers.
President American Federation of Labor.

N.B. It may be necessary for your Committee to subsequently meet representatives of the other organizations protesting against your recieving a C. of A.

S. G.

ALpS, reel 2, vol. 3, p. 701, SG Letterbooks, DLC.

1. Ernest BOHM was secretary of the Central Labor Federation of New York City from 1889 to 1899.

To Frank Green

March 14th [188]9

Frank O. Green Esq.
Dear Sir.

Your letter and Postal to hand. It is imposible to recount in a letter all the good the Unions have accomplished for the working people or in fact to yet give more than a glimpse of the revolution wrought in the condition of the whole people by the organizations of labor — the Trade Unions.

With this I mail to your address a few papers which may aid you in arriving at a fair idea of the work and mission of the Unions. In this I shall merely make a few statements which are incontrovertable.

Herbert Spencer says, It is the "remnant" which saves society from demoralization and preserves the liberties for the people. By the nature of things tyranny is always exerted upon the non-posessing class. The working people form that class to-day and all attempts to abridge rights and priveleges fall inevitably upon the them. It necessarily follows that their action is directed to prevent encroachments upon, and to extend their rights and priveleges, and since their rights and priveleges cannot be extended without according the same to all others, the benefits of their action is felt by all Inasmuch as organized effort accomplishes more than individual effort in any given direction. The working people are the "remnant" and the labor organizations the machinery to maintain past achievements and further our advancement and our civiliza[tion]

In any Country where the organizations of labor ar[e] strongest there the moral and material condition of [the] whole people are highest and best. Look at C[hina?,] Africa, India, Russia, Italy, Spain, Germany, Franc[e,] England and America or any other.

In any State of these United States where [the] Organizations of labor are strongest there the moral and material condition of the whole people are high[est] and best. Look at Mississippi, N. Carolina, Georgia, Indiana, Ohio, Illinois, Michigan, Pennsylvania, Massachusetts and New York or any other.

In any Industry of any Town, City, State of ou[r] or any Country where the working people are best organized there can be seen the highest and best moral and material conditions of all the people Follow this all the way through and you will find the same results. Even taking any industry of which there are several Branc[h]es or Divisions and the same results can be seen, that the best organized branch is socially, morally and m[at]erially superior. Yes, take these matters for instance.

The same Branch of Industry in different Cities or in Factories of any one city and no deviation from the invariable rule will be found. Let me say a few words in reference to the late Street Car Strikes.[1]

Before the Employees on the Surface R.R. were organized they were recieving from $1.00 to $1.68 per day and were required to work from 14 to 18 hours a day. The Union secured for them $2.00 per day of 10 hours work inside of 12 consecutive hours. Even though their second strike was lost, yet the fear of the influence of what the Union might do compels the Companies to abide by the wages and hours enforced by the Union. The Bakers & Brewers, are exactly in the same position. While in the Building Trades, for instance, with a large number of unemployed, wages and hours of labor are the same as for the past year. Many more instances could be cited but these are sufficient. Nor can it be said that it was pure philanthropy which prompted the employers to grant these concessions. Every one was wrung from them. Last year the members of the Amalgamated Association of Iron & Steel Workers of the U.S., also the members of the National Lodges American Flint Glass Union, both affiliated with the American Federation of Labor[,] were on strike and locked-out respectively to maintain wages and other fair conditions of labor. Both were victorious after a struggle lasting one ten weeks and the other twenty-eight weeks against the greatest combinations of capital in any industry.

I could go on reciting the wonderful benefits the Unions of labor have conferred upon all mankind. Our very life our progress our standing and advancement puts to shame the opposition to the Trade Unions.

All interests are organized. Chambers of Commerce, Boards of Trade, Builders Exchanges, Iron & Steel Manufacturers, Doctors, Lawyers and all the others too numerous to mention. This is all right, for — Capital and the Professions? Save the mark. But for the working men and women to organize to protect their only posession, their power to labor. It is monstrous! Trusting you will convert your opponents from the error of their ways, I am,

Yours Very Resp'y,   Saml Gompers.

ALpS, reel 2, vol. 3, pp. 695-98, SG Letterbooks, DLC.

1. An estimated 6,000 street railway workers in New York City and another 800 in Brooklyn struck in late January and early February 1889. The New York City workers were affiliated with division 1 of KOL National District Assembly (DA) 226, those in Brooklyn with DA 75. In New York the strike protested the employers' refusal to negotiate a contract, while in Brooklyn the workers demanded a wage increase, shorter hours, and reduced use of part-time workers. The companies turned down the state Board of Mediation and Arbitration's offer to mediate the disputes and

introduced strikebreakers under police protection. The strikers subsequently returned to work.

Terence Powderly to P. J. McGuire

Scranton Pa March 16, 1889.

P. J. McGuire Esq.
Philadelphia, Pa.
Dear Sir and Bro.

Enclosed you will find the address sent by John Devlin,[1] member of our Board; the others have been awaiting the return of the members of the Board to their homes and will be sent on as soon as reached.

I shall prepare an article to appear in our Journal side by side with the Address when it is published and in that article speak of the entire absence of any desire to "conquer or gobble up" at the conference, and will state, in vigorous terms, that no such inference or idea must be gathered from any of our future meetings or actions.

Do me the favor to give me the address of the officer who refused to sign the address, because of that article in the Journal of United Labor, and I will at once write him fully explaining the situation; do this as quickly as possible and I am satisfied that I can secure his co-operation.

Should you communicate with Mr. Gompers in the near future I would ask that you request him to caution Henry Abrahams,[2] of Boston, against interfering in the affairs of the Knights of Labor; he is endeavoring to influence the shoemakers to leave our Order[3] and in some way has given out the impression that he is acting for the Federation in the matter. I do not know that he is connected in any way with the Federation but he is a member of the Cigarmakers Union and Mr. Gompers has an influence over him there; I think a line from him will settle the matter.

With kindest regards, I remain,

Fraternally yours,   T. V. Powderly.

TLpS, Terence Vincent Powderly Papers, DCU.

1. John DEVLIN was a member of the KOL General Executive Board from 1888 to 1893.

2. Henry ABRAHAMS, a Boston cigarmaker, was president of the Massachusetts State Branch of the AFL from 1889 to 1890.

3. On Mar. 9, 1889, Abrahams wrote Leon Jaquith, secretary of KOL shoemakers' National Trade Assembly 216, urging him to join other shoemakers in organizing a new union. Abrahams concluded, "Is not your place by their side in this momentous

struggle. Or are you again to be beguiled by promises which if the K. of L. would they could not perform" (Terence Vincent Powderly Papers, DCU).

P. J. McGuire to Terence Powderly

Philadelphia, Pa., March 20, 1889

T. V. Powderly:

Dear Sir:—

Yours of 16th at hand, and will file the copy of address as signed by John Devlin.

I am satisfied with your proposition to publish an article in the Journal side by side with the address when the latter is ready to be published. I think that will fill the bill.

The person who refuses to sign the address until he secures an explanation as to that article in the Journal is Mr Samuel Gompers, President of the A F.L. 21 Clinton Place New York. I believe if you will write him and assure him of your disapproval of that unfortunate "break", and that for the future all desire or effort at "gobbling" will be suppressed or "sat down" on by you, that he will be satisfied. I am sure Mr Gompers is acting in good faith to establish fraternal relations between all branches of organized labor, but that Journal article riled him.—

I have wrote Mr Gompers to see what can be done in regard to Mr H. Abrahams of Boston.

Yours   P. J. McGuire

ALS, Terence Vincent Powderly Papers, DCU.

Terence Powderly to P. J. McGuire

Scranton Pa. March 22, 1889.

P. J. McGuire Esq.

Box 884. Philadelphia Pa.

Dear sir and brother:—

I am very much surprised to learn that it was Mr. Gompers who objected to the signing of a document, which he assisted in drawing up, because a party who knew nothing of the matter wrote an editorial differing in sentiment from the spirit and tone of the deliberations

of the conference. Does it not strike you as though Mr. Gompers had
a very poor case on which to base his refusal to sign? The A.F.L. was
represented by its chief officers at the conference, they know what
the intentions of all present were and it is also well understood that
communications intended for an officer of a labor organization, unless
personal in their character, go through the secretary of the same. I
wrote the secretary of the A.F.L. and explained to his satisfaction that
the editorial in question was not authorized and that it was in direct
opposition to my wishes;[1] did not that communication reach Mr. Gompers? I was unfortunate enough to have a little misunderstanding with
Mr. Gompers during the trouble between the cigar makers union and
the K. of L. some time ago and in the report of the transaction his
name appeared in a rather unfavorable light. He felt aggrieved, but
then he had his revenge when he retaliated by perpetrating a wrong
against me at the last session of the St. Louis meeting of the A.F.L.,[2]
and when that was over I expected that he would consider the matter
as square between us. I certainly do not intend to allow my personality
to stand in the way of the success of the labor movement, I was and
am sincere in wishing to have all labor organizations on a friendly
basis and do not stand in the way of the accomplishment of that object.
I have plainly and candidly stated my position to you, and to Mr.
Gompers through you, and the only one who now holds back is one
of the men who drew up the manifesto. This is very strange to me,
I certainly do not want to see the K. of L. attempt to absorb the
trades unions, I will oppose such a thing with all the strength of my
being for I consider their interests can best be served while acting
separately but in harmony with each other. I wish to promote that
harmony but will not yield to any childish whim which will require
an unnecessary act. I have the dignity of the order of the Knights of
Labor to maintain and while maintaining it will never, if I can prevent
it, allow a trade union to be wronged by the K. of L. neither will I
intrigue or in any way connive at the absorbing of a trade union. I
have prevented several attempts lately and have refused positively to
allow more than one trade union to become a part of the K. of L.
since the first of January. I do not want them in the K. of L. while
they have the A.F.L. to attend to their affairs and would rather see
them come to us as individuals in mixed Assemblies. While we have
National Trade Assemblies in the Order we will aid and protect them
to the best of our ability and allow them that autonomy which will
permit them to manage their own trade affairs independently, but so
far as seeking to bring in the trade unions, such is not, and never
was, my intention. There is room for the great mass of laboring men
in the K. of L. where they can manage their economic and political,

non partisan, affairs; there is room for another organization to take care of purely trade matters and if the drift is that way I do not think that either Mr. Gompers or any one else should set his or their individuality, or personal opinions, up before the good of the many.

I have written plainly, I will carry out to the best of my ability the agreement to effect unity and harmonious relations which was tacitly entered into at our conference, but I will not attempt to make explanations where I have already made them and where they are in reality not necessary.

I have stated my position fairly and will work earnestly to have the manifesto do its work among all workingmen. It should not be delayed and most assuredly not by one of those whom the working men of the nation appointed to assist in drawing it up. Tell Mr. Gompers not [to] pay heed to trifles. If the official organ of the A.F.L. editorially stated that that organization would gobble up the whole Order of the Knights of Labor in five years, or five months, I would not mind it for it could not be done, and I would have no fears that would cause me to hesitate about still keeping step with Mr. Gompers and yourself in the great work of allaying the differences of the past.

With kind wishes I remain

Sincerely and fraternally yours,   T. V. Powderly,
General Master Workman. Knights of Labor.

TLpS, Terence Vincent Powderly Papers, DCU.

1. Powderly to McGuire, Mar. 7, 1889, Terence Vincent Powderly Papers, DCU.
2. In his presidential address to the 1888 AFL convention SG said he had met with Powderly in Philadelphia a few months earlier to discuss relations between the KOL and AFL. SG maintained that they agreed to meet again a week later to reach a tangible settlement prior to the KOL General Assembly but that Powderly initially pretended to be detained by out-of-town business and then subsequently did not contact him.

To August Delabar[1]

[ca. March 26, 1889]

Mr. August Delebar.
Sec'y Journeymen Bakers Nat'l Union[2]
Dear Sir

In conformity with the resolutions adopted at the St Louis Convention of the American Federation of Labor to request the labor organizations to give unlimited support to your National Organization

and particularly Bakers Union 49 of Chicago Ill. against the unfair
and so-called independent Bakers Union No 1[3] of said city I have
had a correspondence with the Secretary[4] of the Illinois State Branch
of the A.F. of L.[5] His attention was called to the circumstances connected with their organization and their antagonism to your Union.
Today a letter reached me from Mr Beckler, their Secretary above
referred to in which he says that the Central Labor Union of Chicago
has been suspended from the State Branch of the A.F. of L. "until
such time as they either suspend Independent Bakers Union or it
becomes part of the Journeymen Bakers National Union"

In the hope that the persons composing the unfair organization
may be brought to a realization of their errors and success attend
your Nat'l Union I am.

Yours Fraty.	Saml Gompers.
President

ALpS, reel 2, vol. 3, p. 731, SG Letterbooks, DLC.

1. August DELABAR was secretary of the Journeymen Bakers' National Union
(JBNU; after 1890 the Journeymen Bakers' and Confectioners' International Union)
from 1888 to 1892.
2. The Journeymen BAKERS' National Union of the United States.
3. In late 1886 the Chicago local of the JBNU split over support of the Haymarket
defendants. Those sympathetic to the anarchists formed Independent local 1, and
the JBNU rechartered the rest of the Chicago bakers in February 1887 as local 49.
The 1888 AFL convention resolved to give unlimited support to local 49 in its struggle
with the independent union. In December 1891 the Chicago unions merged.
4. George H. BECKLER, a cigarmaker, was an officer of the Illinois State Federation
of Labor from 1888 to 1890.
5. The Illinois State Federation of Labor was organized in 1888.

To Alfred Fuhrman[1]

Mch 28th [188]9

Alfred Fuhrman Esq.
Cor. Sec'y. Fed. Trades & Labor C. of the P.C.
Dear Sir.

Your favor of the 20th came duly to hand and contents noted.
Permit me to call your attention to the fact that your Organization
has acted exactly as was expected. Did you not see upon the "Manuals"
the instructions to organizations giving them the right to suspend the
formula? We all know that there are a number of our fellow-working
people, who, through lack of experience do not understand how to

proceed with business at meetings and it was (as the inscription plainly states) formulated especially to aid them, and to inculcate a spirit of cohesiveness and fraternity among them. I am sure that if you were to organize a Union having no National head and would give them and have them work according to the "Manual" it would not appear quite so ridiculous to them. Another consideration. Supposing a traveller would have come to your city and would inform you that the Federation had a "Manual". Is it not likely that your organization would have regarded it as a slight or an exhibition of lack of confidence in you, not to have sent you a copy at least for your information, and it is for the latter reason they were sent to you.

I assure you that I am keenly alive to the fact that the workingmen and women have serious work enough to do without wasting time in "tomfoolery", but it must also be borne in mind that we must learn the Alphabet before Grammar and the denomination of numerals before Geometray or Mathematics. To aid our less advanced fellows the Manual is intended.

It is a little more than a week that I have issued a circular[2] in which I laid particular stress upon the Brewers troubles and in the Financial Report their matter is mentioned.[3] Enclosed please find copy of each. In a day or two I shall have a conference with Mr. Kurzenknaabe,[4] Sec'y of the Brewers Nat. Union and may decide upon some course of action for the near future. It would certainly prevent the Boss Brewers concentrating their fight upon one place if bothered a little at different places. With best wishes and hoping to hear from you often I am.

Yours Fraty   Saml Gompers.
Pres't.

ALpS, reel 2, vol. 3, pp. 740-41, SG Letterbooks, DLC.

1. Alfred FUHRMAN, a brewer, was secretary of the Representative Council of the Federated Trades and Labor Organizations of the Pacific Coast from 1889 to 1890.

2. The circular solicited donations in support of the brewers' strike.

3. The 1888 AFL convention pledged financial support to the National Union of the United Brewery Workmen of the United States (UBW), which lost about two-thirds of its membership during that year due to lockouts in ten cities.

4. Ernst KURZENKNABE was national secretary of the UBW from 1888 to 1899.

To P. J. McGuire

April 15th [188]9

P. J. McGuire Esq.
P.O. Box 884. Philadelphia Pa.
Dear Sir—

Owing to business of importance connected with the A.F. of L. which has kept me flitting hither and thither I have been unable to reply earlier to the letter of Mr Powderly to you and which you enclosed for my perusal.

Mr Powderly in his letter deals so much in personalities that I think those portions of it neither becoming to him, nor deserving of an answer from me.

The plain question is, that having agreed upon a circular, the basis of which breathed the spirit of peace and a desire for more harmonious relations among the labor organizations of the country. In the next issue of the Official Journal of his Order appeared an Editirial, flagrantly violating the *entente cordiale* upon which I supposed we had entered. That Editorial sounded the watchword along the line of the K. of L. to renew the war upon the Trade Unions as of yore, to rekindle the internecine strife in the labor Movement our conference sought to allay.

Mr Powderly says that it will not occur again. I beg to assure you that the Editorial has already done its work. It has been acted upon and the spirit of it is being carried out by those high in the councils as well as the lay members of the Order.

Protests have come to me from all over the country against my agreement with Mr Powderly unless he shall give some tangible evidence of stopping the attempts to undermine the Trade Unions. Several instances are cited of, not only unfraternal actions of Knights of Labor since our conference, But treacherous methods that have been adopted. Methods that all labor men abhor regardless to which organization they may owe allegiance.

Supposing I were to sign the circular declaring to the world we are at [peace.] Then view the co[nsequ]ences of the Editorial that Mr Powderly says some party wrote who new nothing of our agreement. Don't you think that the working people and the public generally would deplore the innocence of Mr Powderly and the ignorance of Mr Gompers?

Mr Powderly says he has "the dignity of the Knights of Labor to maintain" let me say that I have the rights and interest of labor to defend, whether Trade Unions or Knights of Labor.

You know how anxious I was for the success of the conference and with what pleasure I regarded the results of its deliberation. Need I say that I feel keenly disappointed that anything should have arisen to render the influence the circular might exert, impossible for the present. I do think, However, that our meeting need not be wholly nugatory.

Let me ask you to suggest to Mr Powderly that he might name a time, conveniently near, when we can meet either in Philadelphia or in this City. We might talk the matter over and probably arrive at an understanding by which the matters complained of can be amicably adjusted.

Hoping to hear from you and Mr Powderly [at the ear]liest convenience of both I am

Yours Fraternally   Saml Gompers.
President American Federation of Labor.

ALpS, reel 2, vol. 3, pp. 792-95, SG Letterbooks, DLC.

To William Trant[1]

May 16th [188]9

Mr William Trant.
Gotham, near Broadview. Assiniboia. N.W.T. Canada.
My Dear Sir & Bro.

I have the honor to acknowledge the reciept of your favor of the 11th inst., which I perused with keen interest and surprise. In my mind I coupled you with the busy throngs of old England, and to be suddenly awakened by your voice emanating from the far, unsettled North Western Territory of Canada was indeed a surprise.

Yes. The American Federation of Labor has republished part of your book on "Trade Unions"[2] and I believe the wide notice it has recieved among our fellow-working people has largely contributed to the current knowledge of the subject. While it is a fact that there is a nominal charge of ten cents for the work ($500 [$5.00?] per 100 copies) in its American shape, It is also true that it has been anything but a profitable venture, in a pecuniary sense, for the A.F. of L. Thousands of copies have been distributed gratuitously as is the case of all official publications of labor organizations. As a consequence the publication has not brought in the return of the money expended on it. However, Since I do not belive that filching of a man's mental production any more justifiable than his physical. I shall lay the request in your letter before the Executive Council of the A.F. of L. advising action upon it. You may feel assured that you will hear from me as soon as a decision has been arrived at, which by the way, must be by correspondence.

So far as I am concerned, I assure you that, perhaps, with the exception of Prof. Thorold Rogers' book, "Work & Wages"³ I have never read a work with greater pleasure and interest than your original book a few years ago, and I know that this is the universal sentiment of all who have read it.

With this I mail you a copy of our work, together with a pamphlet on "Eight Hours"⁴ written specially for our organization and bearing upon our present movement. I shall take pleasure in sending you a copy of all our publications from time to time. With sincere wishes for your success in your new home reciprocating your kind words and hope in the triumph of our cause, I am, Dear Sir, [. . .]

N.B. I regret very much that we did not meet when you were here. Som[e] day?

S. G.

ALpI, reel 2, vol. 3, pp. 839-40, SG Letterbooks, DLC.

1. William Trant, an English-born journalist and author, published *Trade Unions, Their Origin and Objects, Influence and Efficacy* in 1884. In 1889 he emigrated to Canada, later serving as a public official in Saskatchewan.
2. P. J. McGuire published selections from Trant's *Trade Unions*, with his own history of the AFL appended, in the *Carpenter* between Oct. 15, 1887, and July 15, 1888. McGuire turned the plates used in the printing over to the AFL, which republished the work as a pamphlet in 1888 and kept it in print throughout SG's tenure in office.
3. *Six Centuries of Work and Wages: The History of English Labour* (New York, 1884). James Edwin Thorold Rogers was an English economist and professor at King's College, London, from 1859 to 1890.
4. Probably *The Eight Hour Primer* by George McNeill, which had been published by April 1889.

To the Executive Council of the AFL

May 21st [188]9

To the Ex. Council. A.F. of L.
Fellow-Workmen.

The Central Labor Federation of this City¹ some time ago applied for a Charter from the A.F. of L. The Central Labor Union which had been organized in this City for a number of years (and from which the organizations forming the C.L.F. seceded upon the ground that the latter body was corrupt) protested against the issuance of the Charter. I endeavored to secure a reconcilliation between the two contending organizations without avail the feeling against each being too severe. There were several hearings had before me upon the above subject but there was more feeling than evidence adduced. I then requested both parties to submit statements which you will find enclosed.

I deem it my duty to call your attention to the fact that the C.L.U. has been in existence since 1880 and has never made any attempt to affiliate or co-operate with the A.F. of L. or the old Federation. That there is but one organization in it that is affiliated (through its National Union, the Granite Cutters) with the A.F. of L. and that a large number of the organizations in the C.L.F. are affiliated with the A.F. of L. The exposition of the corruption of the C.L.U. by the seceeding organizations which formed the C.L.F. has caused the former to re-organize itself completely and keep out of its meetings a number of the corruptionists. It is necessary to add that the K. of L. Assemblies control the C.L.U. The Secretary of the Granite Cutters Nat'l Union, Mr Dyer[2] has protested also against the issuance of the Charter but gives no grounds upon which he bases it.

I submit this application with the papers to the E.C. and asking them to vote upon it. The 1st Vice President will forward the papers to the Second Vice President, He to the Secretary, He to the Treasurer who will forward them with his vote to this office. Each member of the E.C. will forward *his vote direct to this office* at his earliest convenience and oblige.[3]

Fraty yours   Saml Gompers,
Pres't.

ALpS, reel 2, vol. 3, pp. 885-86, SG Letterbooks, DLC.

1. New York.
2. Josiah Bennett DYER was secretary of the Granite Cutters' International (later National) Union from 1878 until 1895.
3. The Executive Council voted in favor of chartering the Central Labor Federation.

To Henry Blaskovec

May 23rd [188]9

H. Blaskovec. Esq.
Sec'y. Cig Makers Union 97.[1] Boston Mass.
Dear Sir.

Will you kindly furnish me with a full report of the action of the K. of L. authorities—both general and local—in the case of your

Union and Naughton's Cigar Factory and the circumstances of the formation of the K. of L. Assembly of unfair men to antagonize the efforts of Union 97.?[2]

It is very important that this information should reach this office not later than Tuesday Evening the 28th

In making the report I ask you to omit the mention that it is in response to this letter. If you have any matter printed in reference to it, please send it on also.

Asking your compliance with the above request at your earliest convenience I am.

Fraty Yours   Saml Gompers.
Pres't. A.F. of L.

ALpS, reel 2, vol. 3, p. 890, SG Letterbooks, DLC.

1. CMIU 97 of Boston.

2. Members of CMIU 97 struck the Norton, Sleeper and Co. cigar factory in February 1888 to protest a reduction in wages. The men who replaced the strikers formed KOL Local Assembly 80 in 1889. According to local 97, these men worked for wages below the union rate.

To Henry Skeffington[1]

May 24th [188]9

H. J. Skeffington. Esq.
Sec'y-Treas. Boot & Shoe W.I.U.[2]
Dear Sir.

Your favor of the 23rd containing complaint of the conduct of the Knights of Labor in the matter of the difficulty between the members of your Union and Arthur R. Jones & Co of Whitman Mass. and also in the difficulty in the Commonwealth factory,[3] came duly to hand.

In reply permit me to say, that from the information before me, it is evident that the war on Trade Unions by the K. of L. is again revived The honest efforts of the Unions to maintain fair wages, hours and conditions of labor is to be frustrated if the Knights can succeed and the autonomy and independence of the Unions interfered with and over-ridden.

It seems that the K. of L. have learned little from their experience in past endeavors in these matters and it is likely that the American Federation of Labor will find it necessary in defending the Trade Unions to teach the Knights that it is wrong & against their interests to unwarrantably interfere with our business.

The American Federation of Labor has no antagnism to the K. of L. On the contrary it would aid and encourage it in their mixed assemblies. But, it denies them the right to hamper hinder or interfere in the organization and development of the Trade Unions or upon the adjustment of the question of wages and conditions of employment between Union men and their Employers.

To my mind it appears that the Employers will live to regret the attempt to enter into agreements with persons who do not represent their Employees for the purpose of avoiding or evading the latter's just demands. Stand by your organization and your rights, And you will defeat the machination[s] of unfair Employers though they be in league with presumptious and untrue labor men.

You may rest assured that this matter will recieve the attention it requires at the earliest possible moment.

With best wishes for success I am

Yours Fraternally   Saml Gompers.
Pres't American Federation of Labor.

N.B. If my health permits I shall be at your convention June 3rd[4]

S. G.

ALpS, reel 2, vol. 3, pp. 893-95, SG Letterbooks, DLC.

1. Henry J. SKEFFINGTON was secretary-treasurer of the Boot and Shoe Workers' International Union (BSWIU) in 1889, and both general secretary and general treasurer from 1890 to 1894.
2. The BOOT and Shoe Workers' International Union.
3. The BSWIU complained that the KOL accepted as members workers who took the places of strikers at the Commonwealth Boot and Shoe factory in Whitman, Mass.
4. The BSWIU held its first convention in Boston, June 3-5, 1889; SG attended.

To P. J. McGuire

May 28th [188]9

P. J. McGuire Esq.
Dear Sir & Bro.

In reply to your favor of the 27th I desire to repeat what my letter of last week clearly stated. That I will be pleased to meet Mr Powderly to discuss the matters upon which we corresponded. In fact I am anxious to.

You say, that Mr Powderly felt badly miffed and expressed his feeling very strongly to Mr Barret[1] because I failed to meet him in Phila.[2] I assure you that no one regrets our failure to meet more than I. But, after the telegram and letter explaining that I was ill and confined to my bed, It seems to me a little sympathy instead of resentment should have taken posession of him. This is the first time in my life that I had to plead sickness as an excuse for not performing a duty and apparently it is discredited. Shall I furnish him with an affadavit or the address of my attending Physician, so that he may be convinced?

By a letter which you will recieve a few hours after this, you will see that in all probabi[li]ty I shall be in Boston for a few days next week. Would therefore not be able to meet Mr Powderly in the early part of it. I am willing however to make it June 5th or 6th or other later date in Phila.

Unless the E.C. whose servant I am and whose instructions I shall obey—orders me, I refuse to go to Scranton to meet Mr Powderly.[3] I am satisfied to have the meeting in your office, the K. of L. office or this, but to Scranton, for the above purpose of my own free will: Never.

If we succeed in meeting Mr Powderly, He will be convinced I have not raised *imaginary* objections.

Enclosed find a letter which by mistake was addressed to this office and belongs to you.

Thanking you sincerely for your kind wish in regard to my health which is improving, hoping to see you next week and anxiously expecting a favorably response from Mr Powderly, I am

Yours   Saml Gompers.

N.B. When do you start for Denver?[4]

S. G.

ALpS, reel 2, vol. 3, pp. 905-6, SG Letterbooks, DLC.

1. William H. Barrett, a Philadelphia shoe cutter, was a prominent member of the Philadelphia Shoecutters' Mutual Beneficial Association and a founder of KOL District Assembly 70, a trade assembly of shoemakers. He edited the *Labor World* in the late 1880s.

2. McGuire had arranged a meeting between SG and Powderly for May 22, 1889, at the carpenters' headquarters in Philadelphia. SG wished to discuss the trade unions' complaints against the Knights with Powderly before signing the harmony address drafted at the Feb. 14, 1889, meeting.

3. Powderly lived in Scranton, Pa.

4. See "To P. J. McGuire," June 7, 1889, n. 5, below.

To the Editor of the *New Yorker Volkszeitung*

May 29th [188]9

To the Editor of the N.Y. Volkszeitung.
Dear Sir.

Some time ago you published an account of a meeting, in which my name appeared as accepting an office in an organization of a political nature. This report was republished in many papers and distorted into such inconcievable shapes that one would realy believe I was guilty of the most treacherous conduct.

Of course, I can not attempt to follow up every false rumor or inaccurate report that is circulated or published about me, but I respectfully ask you to publish this explanation which I believe will disabuse the minds of fair minded men as to my action in this matter.[1] I confess that I entertain no hope to convince the maliciously inclined who have siezed upon a pretext to vilify and abuse me.

A few months ago two young men came to this office and stated that they were to meet opponents to the Eight Hour question in a public discussion. They asked for material and information for the affirmative side. I aided them in their purpose. They subsequently informed me that they won the day and were highly elated with their success.

A few weeks after I recieved a letter stating that they had formed a Social and Debating Club of young men, That they appreciated the service I had been to them and asked me to accept the honorary office of Vice President. Assuring me that their Club was non-political.[2]

Evidently they wrote to others and that is the way my name and theirs became connected.

In my letter to them I expressed regret should the Club not exert itself "to secure the amelioration in the condition and aid in the emancipation of sufferring, down-trodden humanity" This is the extent of my offending. To gain a hearing for, and continually using every means and opportunity to bring the wrongs of labor to the notice of the world.

I have never attended any of their Club's meetings, I have never seen any of its members, except the two above mentioned and that was bef[ore] the Club was formed and am not a member.

It seems that the whole trouble rests upon the fact that the young men (I hear that not one of them is over twenty years of age) chose the name, "George Washington Club" had it been any other, it would have been just as inoffensive, "smelled just as sweet" and probably would never have been known outside of its own narrow circle.

Trusting that this explanation will set this matter at rest and those who have circulated and published the false and distorted version, will give this as wide publicity. I have the honor to subscribe myself

Yours in our holy cause   Samuel Gompers.

President American Federation of Labor

ALpS, reel 2, vol. 3, pp. 912-14, SG Letterbooks, DLC.

1. The *New Yorker Volkszeitung* published SG's letter on May 30, 1889.

2. According to Arthur D. Cochrane, who wrote Terence Powderly requesting that he accept a similar honorary position with the club, "it is in no sense political but rather aims to inspire a feeling of pure patriotism and love of honest government which shall rise above politics and corruption and act with the idea that an Americans highest earthly allegience is due to Our Country" (Cochrane to Powderly, Apr. 24, 1889, Terence Vincent Powderly Papers, DCU).

To P. J. McGuire

June 7th [188]9

P. J. McGuire Esq.
Sec. A.F. of L.
Dear Sir & Bro:

I arrived from Boston yesterday, from the Shoe Makers Int U. convention where I was in attendance. It was a very good gathering and believe that my presence was opportune. When about leaving the train (from Fall River to Boston) I turned around and saw Mr Powderly and Hayes. We had a short talk. I explained my inability to meet him (the former) on account of sickness. He promised to call here at the end of this week and would wire me the date. Neither spoke of our respective missions, but it was plain that we went to attend rival conventions of the Shoemakers.[1]

By the *Boston Globe* which I sent you, you can tell, about, the result of the visit.[2] To me it appears that we have the prospect of a good movement in that industry. A good foundation has been laid.

During my stay in Mass. I have learned of matters that the K. of L. have been engaged in, that throws some of their previous unfair actions completely in the shade. If Mr Powderly will call here I shall take pleasure in submitting some of the documents in my posession to him for his consideration, And if he can either explain them satisfactorily or agree to remedy the wrongs charged against the Order I will gladly sign the "address". I hope to show them to you shortly and am satisfied you will be surprised.

Later letters from Messers Lake[3] and Ogg[4] lead me to the same conclusion you have arrived in reference to the I.T.U. I am afraid that your non-attendance at their convention will leave them, under a misapprehension, to adopt some resolution on the Eight Hour question which will be anything but agreable reading.[5]

Will you give me the address of some reliable Union man at Johnstown Pa.? A number of Unions have made inquiries from me so that they may be enabled to send their appropriations direct to their suffering comrades. We have an excellent directory of Trade Union officers which this morning I compared with the list of survivors published by *The World* and find that our comrades are among the dead or missing in that awful calamity.[6]

Thanks for your action in reference to Union #12. Have written to *Buchdrucker zeitung*.[7]

Will you make any suggestion in reference to the Editorial sent. I believe that my suggestion *recommen*[*ding*] a general amnesty would have borne good results. It wa[s] the first of a series of "strategetic" acts I had in mind. But I suppose like the obstinate Juror who thought his eleven colleagues mistaken, I think my suggestion should have been adopted.

In the matter of the application for a Charter of the CL. Fed. of this city, the E.C. has voted in favor of granting it.

As soon as Mr Powderly calls here or I see him I will inform you and advise you of result.

Yours Fraty   Saml Gompers.

ALpS, reel 2, vol. 3, pp. 932-34, SG Letterbooks, DLC.

1. The first convention of the Boot and Shoe Workers' International Union and the third annual convention of KOL National Trade Assembly 216 met simultaneously in Boston.

2. The *Boston Globe* of June 4, 1889, carried three articles on the two conventions.

3. Obadaiah R. Lake.

4. Robert Y. Ogg was master workman of KOL Local Assembly 901 in 1884, president of International Typographical Union (ITU) 18 of Detroit in 1885, and was elected as a Labor Republican to the Michigan legislature in 1887 and 1888.

5. ITU leaders were opposing the AFL's eight-hour campaign because they believed it was to culminate in a general strike. SG had asked the AFL Executive Council to endorse sending McGuire to the ITU's Denver convention in June and he wrote ITU leaders to assure them that they were under an erroneous impression about the general strike. The ITU convention passed a resolution that on May 1, 1890, eight hours would constitute a day's work for printers.

6. On June 7, 1889, the *New York World* published a list of survivors of the flood at Johnstown, Pa., which had occurred on May 31.

7. Possibly a reference to German-American Typographia 12 of Louisville, Ky. The *Deutsch-Amerikanische Buchdrucker-Zeitung* was the official journal of the Typographia.

"Vindex" to the Editor[1] of the *Bakers' Journal*

Paterson, June 15th 1889.

SAMUEL GOMPERS.

Editor Bakers' Journal: —

Since Mr. Gompers has been occupying the responsible and honorable position of president of the Federation of Trades, I think few men have been the objects of a wider or deeper interest than he and perhaps no man has a more delicate and difficult position to fill or one which requires more of that peculiar gift which the French denominate *Savoir faire,* urbanity or the entire absence of passion in mingling among men and in dealing with the refractory elements of human character.

I confess that it was with no small amount of solicitude that I saw him called to that position both on his own account and that of the Federation for not only energy and ability are needed to cope with its varied and multifarious duties but tact and an instant insight of character and motives. Mr. Gompers assumed the place knowing well that the success of the labor movement would involve a necessity, that every available force must be used with wisdom and care, that every true and friendly spirit must be kept true by studying their foibles and often yielding something to an erratic and imperious subordinate, while still surrendering nothing of his own authority or dignity.

I had not met Mr. Gompers until quite recently when I went to his office at 21 Clinton Place, New York city on purpose to pay my respects to him. There was at the time a poor woman in the office who had a grievance against some one in her Union and the manner of Mr. Gompers in dealing with the case satisfied me of the fitness of the man to deal with all the problems and vexations of a trying and exacting position. He was as kind and courteous to that poor working woman as to any one and gave her to see that he was thoroughly in earnest to give her all the attention that was her due and to see that no wrong was done in the matter.

The figure and face of Mr. Gompers strongly resembles that of General Sheridan[2] in his prime. He smiles with the same quiet kindly smile that Sheridan used to have and the person to whom he talks has for the time all his attention and it is so given that you feel that the act is spontaneous. He had a kind word for many friends in Paterson and especially for the Baker and its editor and Mr. Sigley of whom he spoke as an unselfish veteran of the cause and he spoke too with calm and evident forbearance of men in other places who have not been in accord with him but in whom he expects yet to see a more fraternal spirit and a striving for harmony and unity within the lines of duty to the cause of Labor.

Vindex.

Bakers' Journal, June 22, 1889.

1. J. P. McDonnell.

2. Philip Henry Sheridan was a U.S. army general most notable for his Civil War service.

From Terence Powderly

Scranton Pa June 18, 1889.

Samuel Gompers Esq.
21 Clinton Place, New York, N.Y.
Dear Sir:—

It is now several months since we drew up the manifesto to go out to the world as the voice of the officers of organized labor, and, up to the present time, it has been withheld in order to obtain your signature. Mr. McGuire writes me that you refuse to sign it because of certain actions, which are not detailed.

Will you do me the favor to specify what they are that I may know exactly the cause for the delay and at the same time take steps, if possible, to remove the cause.

Very truly yours,   T V Powderly

TLpS, Terence Vincent Powderly Papers, DCU.

To Josiah Dyer

June 19th [188]9

Josiah B. Dyer, Esq.
Gen'l Sec'y. G.C.N.U. & G.O. [General Organizer?] AF of L.
Drawer H. Barre, Vt.
Dear Sir & Brother:—

Your very welcome letters together with Charter Application for Polishers[1] and M.O. came duly to hand and contents carefully noted.

In the matter of the Allegheny matter[2] you may rest assured that my record of the autonomy of the Trade Union to regulate its own trade affairs shall not be interfered with if the "court knows itself, and it thinks it does", A few days ago I recieved a letter from Mr Smyth[3] in answer to one of mine in which he says that the men referred to have refused to do the work, are out on strike, but fears that they will ultimately prefer breaking from the Union that [than?] have their work restricted. Have you any later news from your Branch upon the subject?

Under the circumstances I can do nothing but accept your resignation as Trustee,[4] with regret that you had to leave New York City, the centre of capitalism, Unionism, boodleism and civilization? You find fault with me for speaking of Barre, as a "one horse town". Why my dear fellow, it way behind. Here in our glorious city a grand, great and wonderful discovery has been made. The chief Doctor? of the Board of Health has solemnly stated that in the largest and crowded tenements, that is where there are more than a hundred or more people living in one house — there is a lesser degree of mortality than in tenements where twen[t]y people live.[5] You can't boast of such wonderful or par[a]doxical discoveries in Barre I venture to assert. This doctor? is the same who some years ago reported *officially* to the Board of Health that the tenement cigar factories were wholesome and healthy institutions and then issued a *private* book to the Profession detailing the evil effects of the system.

I leave to you the privelege of placing whatever degree of credence upon Doctor? Tracy's official utterances when investigating the condition of the poor. Please bear in mind that owners of modern "Black holes of Calcutta" are generally willing to pay for a plentiful supply of official whitewash. Why Friend Joe! Just think of it. The men, women and children of our great city living with more than a hundred people in a house can boast of living in *the* heal*l*thiest spots on earth, according to this M.ule D.river.

I was much interested by your account of how you spend your leisure time. Merely writing letters, attending your correspondence, Editing Journal[6] seven days in the week and repeating or attending meetings until 11 or 12 evenings for diversion. Do you know that sometimes I think that you labor agitators ought to be made to work?

The Charter for the Polishers I mail with this, but the outfit (the seal has to [be] made) will not be forwarded before Monday. Isn't it superfluous to say how much I appreciate your efforts and devotion in our cause? I regret to learn that the Carpenter's are not up to the mark. But am equally sure you won't let go until you've given them a good shaking up.

The Per Capita of the G.C. is due the last of this month.

Judging by your letter, you won't want the services of the Indian

Doctor or any other I hope for a long time. I am enjoying pretty good health and I thank you for inquiry and wish regarding it.

With sincere wishes for your welfare & success and hoping to hear from you often and anything new about your Town or other topic. I am

Yours Truly   Saml Gompers.

N.B. I also forward cut of Badge. Thanks

ALpS, reel 2, vol. 3, pp. 966-68, SG Letterbooks, DLC.

1. The AFL chartered the organization as Granite Polishers' Union 3723 of Barre, Vt.

2. Probably a reference to the complaint of the Granite Cutters' National Union (GCNU) that two members of Marble, Slate Workers, and Tile Layers' (MSWTL) Union 2711 of Pittsburgh and Allegheny, Pa., were working for lower wages than those paid to members of the local GCNU affiliate.

3. Arthur B. Smyth, longtime secretary of MSWTL 2711, was an AFL organizer and secretary of the National Building Trades Council of Allegheny, Pa. In 1890 he helped found and served as first president of the National Association of the Marble Industry of the United States.

4. Dyer resigned as AFL trustee because the GCNU moved its headquarters to Barre, Vt., in April 1889.

5. In a preliminary report for the Board of Health on mortality in New York City during 1888, Sanitary Inspector Roger S. Tracy asserted that the death rate for the tenement-house population was lower than that of the remaining population. This proved, he contended, that "people do not live under such extremely bad sanitary conditions in the tenements as they have been supposed to" (*New York Times,* June 19, 1889).

6. The *Granite Cutters' Journal.*

To Terence Powderly

New York, June 27th 1889

T. V. Powderly Esq.,
Gen'l. M.W. K. of L.:
Dear Sir:—

I have to-day authorized Mr P. J. McGuire to affix my signature to the manifesto agreed upon by our Conference some time ago at Philadelphia.

In my letter to Mr McGuire I take occasion to mention the fact that you have expressed a desire to rectify any wrongs that may have been done by the K. of L. and endeavor to prevent them in the future, and that I take your word as an earnest of your desire.

Business of great moment prevents me from stating the grievances complained of now, but I shall take an early opportunity of so doing, and trust that in the future neither may have cause of complaint, that we may work together and harmoniously to the end of our great purposes.

Very Respectfully Yours   Saml Gompers.
Pres't A.F. of L.

ALS, Terence Vincent Powderly Papers, DCU.

P. J. McGuire to Terence Powderly

Phila. June 29 1889

T. V. Powderly. Esq.
Dear Sir & Bro:
On my way to Lowell, Mass. I stopped over in New York, on June 27th, visited Mr S. Gompers, and prevailed on him in the interest of harmony to sign the address agreed on by us in the Bingham House, Feb'y 14th.
Today I received the enclosed letter, which you can return at your leisure.
On Monday, I will publish the address with the signatures, and give it to the press.

Yours Truly   P J McGuire

ALS, Terence Vincent Powderly Papers, DCU.

A Report of a Circular Issued by the Unity Conference Held at Bingham House, Philadelphia

[July 11, 1889]

UNITING THEIR FORCES.

One afternoon in February last there came together at the Bingham House in this city a gathering of men representing the great labor organizations of the country, including the Knights of Labor, American Federation of Labor, Switchmen's Union and the two Brotherhoods of Railway Firemen and Brakemen.[1] Interchange of ideas developed the fact that there were no obstacles in the way to the formation of an alliance, offensive and defensive, for future action, and the convention (if such it might be called) adjourned after appointing a committee to draft a circular to the wage-workers of America. After several months the circular has made its appearance, signed by T. V. Powderly, John W. Hayes, Samuel Gompers, P. J. McGuire, Eugene V. Debbs,[2] W. N. Sargeant,[3] W. S. Simcott[4] and George S. Bailey. It is to be earnestly hoped that the suggestions made by the leaders of labor's forces will be heeded by the local officers and the rank and file. The circular reads as follows:

["]For years the opinion has prevailed, because a difference existed in the forms of the organizations of labor, that it necessarily meant opposition and antagonism.

["]While this impression has, to some extent, dwelt in the minds of our fellow-working people it has been utilized by the corporations and trusts to the greatest advantage to themselves, and to the injury of our interests and our cause.

["]Differences of opinion and matters of detail in methods for the improvement of labor's condition were magnified by interested parties into conflicts of the most belligerent and warlike nature.

["]The old ruse of raising false issues to keep the oppressed from uniting was resorted to in every instance—how much to our detriment can probably never be told. That it was and is hurtful to an enormous extent all agree.

["]To disabuse the minds of our fellow-toilers of this false impression, the undersigned have met in conference and issue this circular of warning and advice to the working people of America.

["]We call your attention to the constant and systematic attempts of the employing and speculative classes to prevent you from organizing. They would crush out organization wherever it has demonstrated any power to curb the avarice of unfair employers, and insist upon improved conditions for the toiling masses compatible with our time, our civilization and the institutions of our country.

["]This antagonism to the organizations of the working people should be the best argument in their favor.

["]It is often said that the interests of labor and capital are identical. Whatever arguments may be used against that proposition, there is no denying that the interests of the toilers are identical, and as a consequence they should be brought to a realization of that fact at once. Through compact organization this can be done.

["]The obstacles which have retarded the growth of this sentiment in the past are trivial and should be swept aside. The ventilation given to every trifling dispute between the officers of labor societies has caused unorganized workingmen to look with suspicion on organization generally. Confidence could not be placed in a movement, in which, to use the hackneyed words of the enemies of labor, 'a few leaders were struggling for power.'

["]If through zealous effort in behalf of their separate organizations the officers of the same have appeared to differ with each other, the fact stands that there has never been any real cause for any serious divergence of opinion.

["]That the future may witness no repetition of past misunderstandings, we have assembled to counsel with each other and to demonstrate by our presence at this gathering that between official heads of the organizations of labor there exists no difference of opinion or feeling which will stand in the way of the future welfare of labor generally.

["]We therefore call: First—Upon all organizations of labor to put forth renewed efforts to strengthen and solidify their ranks, and to leave nothing undone to make each society the power for good that it is intended to be.

["]Second—Upon all unorganized workingmen to study the principles upon which organization is based; to meet and consult with members of labor societies in their various localities with the object in view of ultimately bringing within the folds of organized labor every worthy man and woman who toils in America.

["]Thus far have we gone at our preliminary meeting. We hope that the example may be followed in every place where a labor society exists; that the advice we give may be acted on, and that when we meet again in the near future we may be prepared to report that the groundwork has been laid for a plan upon which all societies may become allies in defending the rights of each other.["]

Journal of United Labor, July 11, 1889.

1. The Brotherhood of RAILROAD Brakemen.
2. Eugene Victor DEBS was grand secretary and treasurer of the Brotherhood of Locomotive Firemen (1875-92) and editor-in-chief of its journal, the *Firemen's Magazine* (1880-92).
3. Frank P. Sargent.
4. William A. Simsrott.

A Circular

[July 12, 1889]

AN URGENT APPEAL.

To the Workers of America.

Nine thousand miners in Illinois and Indiana have been on strike since May 1st against a reduction in wages,[1] and now appeal to us for financial aid.

The coals of Northern Illinois, Indiana, Ohio and Western Pennsylvania meet in competition in the Lake and Northwestern markets. To allow each State a share of the markets, a fair relative rate of mining should exist. It was the belief of the National Progressive Union of Miners and Mine Laborers[2] that the rates prevailing in the aforesaid competitive district for the last two years gave to each State a proper relative rate, or as nearly so as it was possible to fix upon and do justice to all interests. The coal statistics of Chicago for 1888 show that since 1886 "Illinois has increased her tonnage 27 per cent., Indiana 57¼ per cent., Ohio 25⅛ per cent., and Pennsylvania has sustained a slight loss." From this showing it is evident that both Indiana and Illinois had an advantage over Ohio and Pennsylvania. Ohio and Pennsylvania have settled prices for the next upon a basis of 2½ cents below last year's rate, and miners of both Indiana and Illinois would have accepted like terms, but their corporations have insisted upon a reduction of 15 cents in Indiana, while the demands of the Illinois corporations, with the condition named, run from 10, 15 and 20 cents. This the miners refuse to accept, and their appeal for financial help should be promptly and generously responded to by the American people, for to them it is evident, or should be, that to increase the advantages in the market of Illinois and Indiana means either less work or low wages to miners and mine laborers of both Pennsylvania and Ohio.

While the striking miners do not all belong to the American Federation of Labor, they are fighting for our interests as well as their own; hence no true member of the American Federation of Labor will hesitate or allow difference in opinion as to methods of organization [to] prevent him from relieving the distress of the families of those who are contending for justice and right.

Let each affiliated Union of the A.F. of L. at once collect money, or provide for its collection at its first meeting, and at each succeeding meeting, until the strike ends, and forward the sums promptly to Patrick McBryde,[3] Lock Box 172, Columbus, Ohio.

By order of the Executive Council A.F. of L.

Sam'l Gompers,
President.

N.B.—The Operative Cotton Spinners, No. 2709,[4] of Kearney, N.J., have succeeded in bringing their employers, one of the proudest corporations in America, to terms. Now let us score another victory for the Miners!

Signal (Indianapolis), July 12, 1889.

1. The coal miners' strike in northern Illinois was substantially ended in September

when the miners accepted the operators' terms. The Clay County, Ind., strike lasted through November.

2. See glossary under National Federation of MINERS and Mine Laborers.

3. Patrick McBRYDE represented KOL National Trade Assembly 135 at the founding convention of the National Progressive Union of Miners and Mine Laborers in 1888, and served as the new organization's secretary-treasurer (1888-90). He was secretary-treasurer of the United Mine Workers of America from 1891 to 1896.

4. Operative Cotton Spinners' Union 2709, which was directly affiliated with the AFL, struck successfully during the spring of 1889 against a 20 percent reduction in wages at Clarks Mills, Kearney, N.J.

To Charles Thomas

July 19th [188]9

C. C. Thomas. Esq.
Sec'y Electrical Union 3696. A.F. of L.[1]
Dear Sir & Bro: —

Your letter enclosing one dollar for pads of letter heads came duly to hand as well as the copies of your By-Laws. I enclose a reciept for the former. As soon as a fresh supply is recieved from the printer I shall mail a pad to your address and kindly ask you to acknowledge its reciept.

I have carefully examined your By-Laws and can find nothing to base a constitutional objection upon. There are two matters though which to mind appears, in the light of my experience, rather impractical. Sec 2 Art 2 provides that "if not more than *two black balls* shall have been cast, the candidate shall be declared elected" In times that may come before the Union you will find that number entirely too low. I don't think that the livlihood of a man should depend upon the vote of three or four men (out of hundreds). If you desire to retain the provision I have no objection. But if you do, I can only say that I hope you will not have the trouble resulting from it which I fear and which I have seen from similar laws in Unions.

Sec 1 Art 10 Makes a rather peculiar provision. In defining the duties of the President. You empower him with the appointment of "his subordinate officers" I think this is investing your President with entirely too much power, one that is both irksome and disagreable at times to an honest, sincere man, and dangerous in the hands of a man not posessed of those qualities.

You will of course understand that I in no wise aim to reflect upon any member or officer of Your Union. The best friends men have are those who dare criticise and show their faults frankly. The man that flatters you, beware of. He has some ulterior purpose to serve.

In the hope that what I have so freely written may be accepted in the spirit it is penned and with best wishes. I am

Yours Fraty   Saml Gompers.
Pres't.

ALpS, reel 3, vol. 4, pp. 20-21, SG Letterbooks, DLC.

1. Pittsburgh Electrical Union 3696, which was directly affiliated with the AFL.

To the Executive Council of the AFL

July 22nd, [1889]

To the Executive Council A.F. of L.
Fellow Workmen:

During my recent visit to Chicago on July 4th,[1] I had an extended conversation with a number of influential labor men. There was discussed among other things a question of holding a convention of representatives of labor organizations and representatives of the employing class for the purpose of discussing the eight hour movement. Our friends there are of the opinion that such a convention or congress could be made entirely successful if held in that City, and say further that if necessary a very large sum of money could be raised to further that project. You will remember the instructions given the Executive Council by the St Louis convention as follows. "The Executive Council shall also prepare printed circulars which are to be issued to all Manufacturing concerns of the Country, requesting them to meet representatives of this organization in conference so that a friendly arrangement of the reduction in the working hours may if possible be effected." In accordance with this I propose that the president be empowered to call a convention, congress or conference of representatives of organized labor and the employing class to meet in Chicago on or by March 1890.[2]

I have made a change in the clerical force in this office and employed the services of a Stenographer and Type-Writer. It will become necessary to purchase a Type-Writing machine, and I ask you to vote upon the proposition, authorizing the President to purchase one. I have a Caligraph Type-Writer in this office. This is a sample of its work, costing $55.00 less 10 per cent. Will you please return your vote upon the above proposition at your earliest convenience, and I request you to regard the first of them as confidential until the matter is made public, if it is made public at all.

Fraternally yours. Saml Gompers.
President. American Federation of Labor.

TLpS, reel 3, vol. 4, p. 34, SG Letterbooks, DLC.

1. SG spoke about the eight-hour movement at a Fourth of July demonstration.
2. The Executive Council voted against calling such a conference.

To Charles Oyler

July 27th, [188]9

Charles P. Oyler Esq.
1015 Forest Place, Baltimore Md.,
Dear Sir:—

In reply to your favor of 25th, inst, Permit me to say, that I am surprised that you should ask me to protest against Tom Furlong's[1] appointment. You know as well as I can tell you, that a position of that kind, The Secret Service[2] men of the lowest instincts, cunning and sharpest practices and unscrupulous as a rule, are those selected. It seems to me that, Furlong possesses these qualities, to a marked degree.

The labor organizations by the principles they advocate, by their honesty, sincerity and straightforwardness of their conduct, is a standing protest, not only against Tom Furlong but the system that permits the employment of such as Tom Furlong by the government.

I regret that at any time I should be compelled to decline to comply with a request emanating from you. But a sense of duty to our cause impels me in this instance.

Fraternally yours. Saml Gompers.
President. American Federation of Labor.

TLpS, reel 3, vol. 4, p. 54, SG Letterbooks, DLC.

1. Thomas Furlong established the first special railroad detective service for the Pennsylvania Railroad in the 1870s and in 1880 went to St. Louis to organize a similar service for the Missouri Pacific Railroad. In 1889 the KOL and trade unions successfully protested Furlong's candidacy for the office of chief of the U.S. Secret Service, citing his role in breaking the 1886 Southwestern railroad strike.
2. The U.S. Secret Service was organized within the Treasury Department in 1865. Its primary responsibility was to deal with counterfeiting, forgery, and the alteration of currency or securities of the U.S. or foreign governments.

To Rutherford B. Hayes[1]

New York, August 10th, 1889.

To the Honorable Rutherford B. Hayes.
Ex President of the United States.
Mentor Ohio.
Dear Sir: —

The American Federation of Labor at its last convention, held at St Louis Mo., adopted a series of resolutions to concentrate and crystallize thought among the people of our Country upon the question of the reduction of the hours of labor, of the toiling masses, to eight per day. Not only in Government, but also in private employment.

It is also proposed that conferences be held by the representatives of the organized working people with representatives of the employers, "so that a friendly arrangement of a reduction in the working hours may, if possible, be effected." This reduction of the hours of labor is intended to be, to eight per day and take effect May 1st, 1890.

We are keenly aware of the responsibility resting upon us and the necessary preparatory work before the final and successful termination of this great question.

It is our purpose before acting finally, to obtain the views upon this momentous subject, from the best informed men in America. Men whose thoughts and utterances are worth recording. Men in public life. Men whose views sway the minds of their fellow-citizens. Hence I respectfully ask you to favor me with an answer to the following questions.

1st, Should the working people of our Country be required to work more than eight hours per day?

2nd, What would, in your opinion, the effect of the general reduction of the hours of labor to eight per day, have upon the manhood, independence and citizenship of our people. — The body politic of our Country?

Asking, Dear Sir, a reply to the above at your earliest convenience. I have the honor to subscribe myself.

Yours, very respectfully. Sam'l Gompers.
President. American Federation of Labor.[2]

Dictated by S. G.

TLS, Rutherford B. Hayes Papers, OFH.

1. Rutherford Birchard Hayes (1822-93) was president of the United States from 1877 to 1881.

2. SG sent this letter to the president of the U.S., the members of the cabinet, forty U.S. senators, seventy-five congressmen of both political parties, former presidents of the U.S., and other prominent individuals.

An Article in the *Critic*

[August 10, 1889]

THE LABOR LEADERS.

Among the various subjects that will agitate the labor unions in the coming few months will be the election of officers of the various national organizations, and as the Knights of Labor and American Federation of Labor are the two most prominent of these, it may not be uninteresting to make a possible forecast of the future of the two.

Mr. Gompers, the present President of the American Federation of Labor is a genial gentleman of Jewish descent, who was elected some two years ago, and at that time was very popular among the trade unionists because of his strong opposition to the Knights of Labor, and the fact that he was a cigarmaker by trade and a member of the Cigarmakers' International Union. In the convention that first elected him there were eight or nine members of that craft from various organizations, and at his subsequent election nearly as many.

Since that time, Mr. Gompers has not proven as radical in his administration of the A.F. of L. as was desired by his adherents, and it is rumored that Mr. Strasser, President of the Cigarmakers' Union, is not only displeased with his action, but positively opposed to his re-election, some going so far as to say that this is caused by jealousy.[1]

It will also be remembered that the Baltimore Federation last year had Mr. Gompers before them for what they considered overstepping his authority,[2] and the feeling in Baltimore is not very favorable to his re-election even among those who most favored him years ago.

The following circular recently issued by him has also created a feeling of distrust in the success of the movement for eight hours inaugurated by him at the last session of the Federation, and many feel that this circular is a sign of weakening, and will be used as a weapon to defeat him for a re-election in December next. This is the circular:

"My attention has been called to an erroneous impression that has gone forth that the resolutions adopted at the St. Louis Convention of the American Federation of Labor implied a simultaneous strike of all the working people of the country for eight hours May 1, 1890.

I beg to assure you that nothing was further from the intention of the convention than adoption of a resolution implying a general strike. I was in continual communication with the committee having that subject under consideration. I presided at the convention during the discussion upon this report, and not one of the advocates uttered a single remark that could bear such an interpretation. The fact of fixing upon a certain date was advocated because it would concentrate the efforts of the working-people about a certain given point, it would crystalize the discussion of this important question and would encourage the workingmen to remain true to and become members of their respective trade organizations. You are no doubt aware of how ardent an advocate I am for the reduction in hours for labor, but I assure you that in the present condition of organized labor no movement looking to a general strike upon so early a date would receive my countenance or support. We want 'eight hours,' and hope to receive their assistance in return at some future time. The end of the labor movement, the end of the agitation for the reduction of the hours of labor, will not end in 1890. So long as there is a wrong in existence, so long as there is one person seeking employment and cannot obtain it, so long there will be work for our organizations. . . .[3]

"Yours fraternally,   Sam'l Gompers,
"President A.F. of L."

As to the rumored resignation of Powderly, it might as well be stated that Powderly is no coward, and notwithstanding what his enemies may say to the contrary he will remain in office until the meeting of the General Assembly at Atlanta in November next,[4] when he may be re-elected or decline to run. He has not lost the confidence to any extent of the Order, and the men who have stuck to the organization and do the work locally in the several States will wait until he gives an account of his stewardship before they express an opinion. At present there is no opposition except in his enemies' minds, and the administration have been doing better educational work in the last year than ever before.

The general opinion now prevails that the work of the next conventions of the Federation and Knights of Labor will have all it can do to settle on a line of action in the eight-hour movement, and the election of new officers.

Mr. Powderly's book, "Thirty Years in the Labor Movement,"[5] is in the press of a Columbus (Ohio) firm, and will shortly be given to the public, and cannot help being a mighty lever in molding public opinion as to the labor cause.

In reference to the stories often going the rounds of the press about the salaries of the labor leaders, it might be well to say that Powderly does not receive $5,000, nor did he ever get that sum as a salary; to the contrary, the reports of the organization show that he not only received less than that amount, but paid all his own traveling expenses and part of his clerk hire out of what he did draw.

Mr. Gompers only gets $1,500, which he could easily have in private life, and the heads of some of the national organizations, such as the Amalgamated Association, Glass Workers, and others get as much, if not more than this.

Critic (Baltimore), Aug. 10, 1889.

1. See "Adolph Strasser to the Editor of the *Critic*," Aug. 17, 1889, below, for Strasser's reply.
2. The Baltimore Federation of Labor was angered by reports in June 1888 that the AFL, without seeking its advice, had chartered a musicians' union in that city. The Baltimore Musical Union had applied for an AFL charter on June 6, but in a July appearance before the Baltimore Federation, SG reported that he had not issued a charter to any group of Baltimore musicians.
3. These ellipses are in the original.
4. The thirteenth annual convention of the KOL General Assembly met in Atlanta, Ga., Nov. 12-20, 1889.
5. *Thirty Years of Labor, 1859-1889* (Columbus, Ohio, 1889).

P. J. McGuire to Terence Powderly

Philadelphia Pa. Aug 14, 1889

Mr. T. V. Powderly
G.M.W. of the Knights of Labor:—
Dear Sir and Bro.—

I am instructed by Mr. Gompers to write you and request an interview with you the next time you come to this city. There are many subjects Mr. Gompers and I would like to talk over with you. And if you have no objections Mr Daley of the Shoe Lasters and Mr Skeffington would also like to be present.

The nature of Mr. Daley's and Mr. Skeffington's business with you I do not know. But I do know that Mr. Gompers and I wish to see you in regard to continuing the work so happily begun at the Bingham House on Feb'y 14th.

Please let me know by return mail what date will you be in Philadelphia?

With best wishes,

Yours Truly.   P J McGuire

TLS, Terence Vincent Powderly Papers, DCU.

Adolph Strasser to the Editor of the *Critic*

Buffalo, N.Y., August 17, 1889.

To the Editor of The Critic:

In your issue of August 10 I noticed the following under the caption of "Labor Leaders:"

"Since that time Mr. Gompers has not proven as radical in his administration of the A.F. of L. as was desired by his adherents, and it is rumored that Mr. Strasser, President of the Cigarmakers' Union, is not only displeased with his action, but positively opposed to his re-election, some going so far as to say that this is caused by jealousy."

Allow me to say that the above is entirely devoid of truth, or even a semblance of it; the circulation of idle rumors of this kind is not creditable to anybody.

Yours truly,   A. Strasser,
Int. Pres.

P.S. — Please publish the above in your next issue.

(While Mr. Strasser may be right as to the *truth of the rumor,* yet *The Critic* distinctly says it was *"rumored,"* and as a matter of news published it, as it does everything else of interest to the workers of America, without allowing any one, of any organization, to dictate what is right to publish or not. We agree with Mr. Strasser in saying that the circulation of *idle rumors* is not creditable to *any body*, but a newspaper is intended as a conveyer of news, and when it publishes an item as a rumor, as *The Critic* did in the above, and leaves the reader to judge for himself as to its trustworthiness, even prejudiced people give it credit for honesty of purpose.

We would say also to Mr. Strasser that we publish his letter for the benefit of our readers in the same spirit as we published the "rumor.")

Critic (Baltimore), Aug. 24, 1889.

A News Account of a Conference between Representatives of the AFL and the KOL at the KOL Office, Philadelphia

[August 31, 1889]

AN IMPORTANT CONFERENCE.

A secret conference which lasted for three hours took place at the headquarters of the Knights of Labor, at 814 North Broad street, on

Thursday,[1] between Samuel Gompers, of New York, President, and
P. J. McGuire, of this city, Secretary of the American Federation of
Labor, on the one side, and General Master Workman Powderly,
General Secretary-Treasurer Hayes and Member of the General Executive Board A. W. Wright,[2] of the Knights of Labor, on the other.
What transpired was not disclosed until yesterday, when a *Public Ledger*
reporter was apprised of the facts. It appeared that the conference
was for the purpose of adjusting a number of matters of difference
between the Knights and the trade unions, but more particularly to
discuss the eight-hour question. This question is now one of absorbing
interest to the leaders of the Federation, inasmuch as the first of next
May has been fixed for its adoption by all the trades attached to the
Federation. It is understood that the officers of the Federation are
desirous of leaving no stone unturned to carry out the instructions
of the Convention adopting the eight-hour resolution, and, therefore,
sought the conference with the Knights so that they could not be
accused of neglecting their duty in that regard.

The Knights May Help.

After disposing of minor considerations, it is said, the parties to
the conference began on the eight-hour question and discussed it
from all standpoints in detail. The result, apparently, was satisfactory
all around, and especially to the Federation men. The Knights, it is
understood, said they had no desire to oppose the eight-hour movement of the Federation, but hoped it would succeed. Mr. Powderly,
it is said, declared that a majority of the local assemblies of the Knights
had already voted in favor of the adoption of the eight-hour day, and
that the question was bound to come before the next General Assembly of the Order, which meets in Atlanta, Ga., next November.
In fact, it is said the Knights went so far as to promise that the local
assemblies should be advised to act upon the question, and they gave
assurance that the General Assembly would have its attention called
to the subject in such a way that an expression of opinion would be
obtained from it. The conference is said to have been conducted in
a friendly manner throughout.

Work of the Federation Men.

The harmony which characterized this conference is regarded as
auspicious for the eight-hour movement. President Gompers, who has
gone back to New York, is the head and front of the movement, and
he looks upon the result of the meeting with no little satisfaction. For
a long time past eight-hour literature has been disseminated from his

headquarters in New York, and not only working-men, but clergymen, professors of political and social economy in the various colleges and elsewhere, have been communicated with on the subject. The result, it is said, has been gratifying. The Federation claims a membership in its affiliated bodies of over 600,000 workers, and some of the trade unions, like the printers, carpenters and cigar makers, have their members under splendid control. The fact that the eight-hour movement begun by the unions failed several years ago has often been laid at the door of the Knights, who then appeared indifferent, and, therefore, the existence of a promise from them to help rather than resist the present movement, is looked upon as a hopeful sign.

To Go to the Conventions.

So far as could be ascertained yesterday the conferees did not presume to bind their organizations, but to see that the conventions had the matter presented to them in proper shape.[3] Whether the eight-hour movement will become a general movement for Knights of Labor and Federation men, therefore, will depend upon the General Assembly of the Knights in Atlanta next November, and the General Convention of the Federation in Boston in December.[4] Even if the Knights decide to keep out of the movement, there is very little doubt, from what members of the Federation say, that it will carry it on alone to a final conclusion in accordance with its own motion. A great many Knights are known to be in favor of eight hours as a working day, but many of them, including some of the leaders, have contended that the time had not yet arrived to demand it. It is therefore probable that, while the Federation may be unanimous upon the point, with or without the concurrence of the Knights, the latter may have a severe contention in their own ranks over it.

Labor Day Agitation.

The fact that the Federation has fixed the time for a general adoption of the eight-hour day makes the question all the more interesting. It has, as it were, served notice on the employers that they can so make their contracts and estimates as to be prepared for a reduction of the workmen's hours in May, 1890. On two days thus far, Washington's Birthday and the Fourth of July, there has been a more or less general agitation of the eight-hour question in consonance with the recommendation of the last general convention. The next agitation is to be on Monday next, which is Labor Day, and the next and last on Washington's Birthday again. The critical time for the agitators of the movement, therefore, will be from the time of the close of the approaching labor conventions and the day fixed for the adoption of the eight-hour day.

A "STIRRING UP" PREDICTED.

Representatives of the Federation say that the movement, while quiet at present, is forging ahead all over the country, and that the indications are that there will be exciting times towards spring. The movement of several years ago was stirred up to a formidable aspect in a very few months, they say, and the chances of success next year are much better than they were then. The reports of meetings arranged for Monday next show that the agitation is to be carried on in many of the large cities all over the country. Buffalo, New York, and Pittsburg are mentioned among the cities where big meetings are to be held. President Gompers, it is announced, is to speak on the eight-hour question in Buffalo on Labor Day, and Secretary McGuire is to speak in Albany in the afternoon, and Cooper Institute, New York, in the evening. Labor Day is also to be celebrated, under the auspices of the United Labor League, in this city, and the eight-hour question no doubt will be discussed.

Philadelphia Public Ledger, Aug. 31, 1889.

1. Aug. 29, 1889.
2. Alexander Whyte WRIGHT, a journalist, was a member of the General Executive Board from 1888 to 1893 and an editor of the *Journal of the Knights of Labor* between 1889 and 1893.
3. Participants at the meeting agreed that the executive bodies of both organizations would meet on Oct. 14 to pursue the matter further.
4. The AFL held its fourth annual convention in Boston, Dec. 10-14, 1889.

To Oscar Seidel[1]

September 7th, [188]9.

Dictated by S. G.
Oscar Seidel Esq
Sec'y of Progressive Textile Workers Union,
Philadelphia, Pa.,
Dear Sir: —

The Press of this City published a statement, that at your convention,[2] held in the City of New-York, you passed a series of resolutions condemning my action in accepting the appointment as a member of the committee "on Site and Buildings" for the Worlds Fair for 1892,[3] because, as it is stated I would have to mix and sit with "capitalists["]!

Having seen no contradiction, or denial of that statement from you, or any other person as to the accuracy of that publication, I assume that the resolution was passed.

Permit me to ask you whether in your opinion, if I was guilty of any conduct unbecoming my position as President of the American Federation of Labor? Would it not have been a wiser and manlier course to pursue, if you had instructed your delegate to the Boston convention of the American Federation of Labor to prefer charges against me, instead of assuming the functions of Judge, Jury and Executioner?

The appointment on the committee I never sought, and is one that will only entail extra labor upon me, but will in nowise interfere with the duties I owe the Federation, on the contrary it seems to me that I would have been false to my trust if I failed to accept the duty involved, and the opportunity afforded to watch, protect and advance the interests of labor that this proposed exposition promises to afford.

I do think that had a little more deliberation and judgement been used in this matter, instead of receiving your unwarrantable and un-justifiable condemnation, my course would and should have received your support and approval.

At any rate whatever action you took, or proposed to take, it seems to me that your readiness to rush into public print, exhibits more of a personal feeling than the desire to benefit the cause of labor.

Fraternally yours.   Saml Gompers.
President American Federation of Labor.

TLpS, reel 3, vol. 4, p. 186, SG Letterbooks, DLC.

1. Oscar G. SEIDEL was secretary of the Textile Workers' Progressive Union of America (TWPUA).

2. The third national convention of the TWPUA began in New York City on Aug. 31, 1889.

3. During 1889 New York was one of the cities actively promoting itself as a site for a world's fair to commemorate Christopher Columbus's discovery of America. SG served on the executive committee to bring the fair to New York City, and also on the committee on sites and buildings. The TWPUA raised its opposition to SG's participation in this effort at the AFL's 1889 convention, which was held in Boston, but that body declined to interfere. On Apr. 25, 1890, President Benjamin Harrison signed into law an act establishing Chicago as the site of the World's Columbian Exposition; the fair was held from May 1 to Oct. 30, 1893.

To Terence Powderly

New York, September 11th, 1889.

T. V. Powderly Esq.
Gen'l Master Workman of the Knights of Labor.
814 N. Broad Street, Philadelphia, Pa.,
Dear Sir: —

I am just in receipt of a letter from Pittsburg, Pa., in which it is reiterated that the unfair Slaters of Pittsburg, Pa., have been granted a charter as a local assembly of your order,[1] and although few in number, they are giving the Slaters Union of that City — affiliated with the American Federation of Labor — no end of trouble, in causing strikes against their employment, side by side with true Union men.

At our conference, held August 29th, you assured me that no charter had been issued to these people. Although I accept your assurance, I respectfully request you to make some statement, in any manner agreeable to you, but which will for all time settle the question to the satisfaction of all concerned.

I learn that it is the intention of your Executive Board to visit Pittsburg during the coming week, and suggest that the opportunity to comply with this request is appropos.

Hoping to hear from you at your earliest convenience, and this matter may receive your attention, I am,

Yours, very respectfully. Saml Gompers.
President, American Federation of Labor.

Dictated by S. G.

TLS, Terence Vincent Powderly Papers, DCU.

1. SG had complained to Powderly that during a strike of an AFL-affiliated Pittsburgh slaters' local the strikebreakers were organized into a KOL assembly (SG to Powderly, July 7, 1889, SG Letterbooks, DLC).

To John Ehmann

September 14th, [1889]

John Ehmann Esq,
138 Fifth Ave., Pittsburg, Pa.,
Dear Sir and Bro: —

Your favor of the 7th inst. came duly to hand and the contents carefully noted. Right upon the heels of your letter came an application for the formation of the Federal Labor Union,[1] under the auspices of the American Federation of Labor, reached me. I think I see your good work united with it, your name is upon the application. I think you could perform a great duty and confer a lasting benefit upon our movement, if you were to compile some such statement upon the formation, growth & officers salaries, an effective work of trade unions of this Country, and I assure you I should be pleased to give you whatever aid lies in my power. I have a book containing the reports of proceedings of the formation of the Federation since 1881, and I will forward it to you by mail or express, if you assure me that it will be returned in the course of a week or two. I would gladly lend it to you if I had a quantity of them, but they are scarce and care must be exercised to retain a continuous history of the movement in this office.

The Tailors National Union pay their Executive Officer $24.00 per week, until last year, $20.00 per week. For four years theretofore, the work was entirely gratuitous.

The Cigar Makers International Union pay their Executive Officer, $25.00 per week. For four years that officer received $250.00 per annum, for four years more $1000.00 per annum.

The Journeymen Bakers National Union pay their Executive Officer $24.00 per week. The Boiler Makers, $5.00 per week. Brewers, $20.00 per week. Brick Layers, $30.00 per week. Carpenters, $35.00 per week. Coal Miners, (I believe) $18.00 per week. Granite Cutters, $20.00 per week. Iron Molders $20.00 per week. Iron and Steel Workers, $30.00 and $40.00 per week. Metal Workers $5.00 per week. Musicians, $30.00 per week. Painters and Decoraters, $20.00 per week. Piano Makers, —— Shoe Lasters, $25.00 per week. Typographical, $30.00 per week.

There are a number of others that I know nothing at all about, as to the salaries they receive, I would suggest that you might prepare a short hectograph letter containing the questions that you desire answered, and mail them direct to the officers of the National organizations and I believe they will answer you promptly and correctly.

With sincere good wishes for your welfare and hoping to hear from you frequently, I am,

Yours fraternally.   Sam'l Gompers
President, American Federation of Labor.
per H. McG.

Dictated by S. G.

TLpSr, reel 3, vol. 4, pp. 208-9, SG Letterbooks, DLC.

1. Federal Labor Union 3792 of Pittsburgh.

A Petition Issued by the AFL

[September 27, 1889]

A TRUE CENSUS WANTED

In the matter of the census, for which preparations are now being made, a brief comparison of what was asked of Congress at its last session with what was granted on behalf of the great masses of the people who are dependent upon their daily, weekly, and monthly wages for subsistence — comprising, as they do, at least four fifths of the men, women and children of our country — will make clear the situation. The two following points will sufficiently cover the case: —

First. — The memorials presented to the Senate ask of the President and Congress that a thorough examination "be undertaken of the condition of the industries of the country and of the employment and idleness of the people — and that reports be made of every person whether he or she be employed or idle, and of the nature and amount of employment during the next preceding or census year."

The response to this prayer is found in the ninth section of the Census Act,[1] which limits the examination to persons living in "dwelling houses" and "places of abode," taking no account of their condition or of their employment or idleness, and rigidly excluding the great multitudes of the houseless and homeless — of those who have neither "dwelling houses" nor "places of abode" — from any and all enumeration or recognization in the census.

The leaving out of the present law the provision of the seventeenth section of the Act of eighteen hundred and seventy-nine,[2] requiring an enumeration to be of the employment or non-employment of the people, appears to betray a continued determination by influential interests, to exclude from all consideration by the Census Office of the two chief and inseparable interests of the people — that of labor and its compensation.

Indeed, the circumstances attending this second denial to the people of a place in the Census that will give a just and complete idea of their condition seem to warrant the conclusion that the controlling influences in those two denials were identical, and justifies the expectation that they will again be used if the opportunity is presented. Upon the first application Congress, without a dissenting voice, granted the place asked for; but the Census Office effectually overruled the action of Congress and suppressed all reference to the matter in its reports; but upon the second application, largely reinforced, Congress itself denied the prayer. This denial it is not yet too late to reconsider.

Second — A request was made that the census be taken in the

winter — at the time when the houseless and homeless are compelled to find shelter in the towns and cities, where they can be easily reached, and when the houses of the well-to-do are open and occupied by the families then at home.

This request is answered in the provisions of the nineteenth section, requiring the enumeration to be taken in the summer — to commence on the first Monday in June — when the armies of houseless and homeless are gone and scattered in every direction, and the occupants of the abodes of comfort have fled and are fleeing, by tens of thousands, from all our larger towns and cities to Europe, to the coasts, to the islands, to the mountains — anywhere, everywhere — leaving their homes in charge of servants, or closed against all occupation.

At the same time the churches are closed, and clergy and laity alike are absent; the schools are in vacation, and both teacher and pupil have escaped. All are away who can get away, and their neighborhoods, to a large extent, are depopulated.

These movements begin in May and continue all through the months of June, July, and August, into September, when the tide turns and sets as strongly homeward until November, at which time every one is supposed to have reached his or her home, and all the functions of society are again set in motion and will continue until a renewed exodus begins the following May.

These conditions were not known forty years ago — they were then impossible, and especially so when the season for census taking was established by taking our first census during a summer of one hundred years ago. At that time the means of transportation that would enable us to flood Europe in a few weeks, and at the same time cover our mountains and crowd our coasts with the population of our towns and cities did not exist. But we have them now in the greatest abundance. During the last twenty years the world's capacity for transportation has increased and been used to an almost limitless extent, and these changed conditions render imperative the necessity of change in census methods to meet them.

The New York City Police Reports show that whilst the number finding lodgings in the station houses of that city in June, 1887, were 5,975, in July 5,748; and in August, 6,310, in December the number was 17,909; in January 13,448; and in February, 13,027; or quite three times greater in the winter than in the summer; and that the cheap lodging houses which, in 1887, were thronged with 3,921,826 lodgers, and in 1888 with the enormous multitude of 4,649,660, were in summer quite deserted. Here the evidence is conclusive that if the policy of government is to have a census taken that, in spite of the best exertions of enumerators and tabulators, will prove utterly un-

reliable if not criminally false, then and in that case the summer is
the season in which to do the work.

The conditions found in the city of New York are also found, in
proportionate extent, in every city and town in the United States.

In the rural districts, also, during the summer months, there are
abnormal conditions which render the taking of an accurate Census
a thing of the utmost difficulty. Indeed, the whole country is then in
a state that makes the obtaining of a true census an impossibility, and
a close approximation a matter of guess—a travesty of statistics.

But from Thanksgiving to Christmas—even to the close of the
holidays, everybody is at home; even the few who in winter are compelled to seek summer skies and milder airs in the Sunny South, defer
their flight until the festivities of the New Year have ended.

With all these self-evident facts before us, the least reflection must
convince all that December is the true month for taking anything like
an accurate census.

The law requires that special return shall be made concerning
corporations of every character—of railroads, express companies,
insurance companies, the telegraph companies, of manufactures of
every nature, of mining, and of every interest representing property
or capital, in production, trade or speculation—and provide for every
great interest an expert at the head of a department created for it.

In the census of agriculture returns are made of the number of
acres under cultivation, the product per acre, and its value; but the
labor employed, and its cost or value, is not considered.

In the production or manufacture of fabrics of cotton or wool the
capital invested, the number of carding machines, and spindles, and
looms used—the amount of cotton or wool consumed and product
produced are given—but the amount of labor employed and wages
paid are not of the elements enumerated.

In mining and in the production of iron and steel the capital invested
and the product produced are the chief elements reported upon; but
the amount of labor employed and wages paid are not returned.
Nothing appears to show the condition of the employes engaged in
the work.

So in everything labor as an element of special or general interest—
its employment or non-employment, its cost or value, is never referred
to and under the law no publication of statistics bearing upon the
idleness of the people, or their condition, can be made in the Census
Reports—these things are specially excluded by its provisions. But
the capital employed is always counted and returned. The people who
are without capital—workingmen, laborers, the wage earners of the
country—do not appear to have any interest that government is

bound to respect or care for. Yet Abraham Lincoln declared our government to be a government of the people, by the people, and for the people.

In the interest of trade, capital, and speculation, Congress proposes to expend six million four hundred thousand dollars in an inquiry concerning their condition and development. But a proposition to expend a sum equal to one-fourth of that amount, out of the eighty millions of surplus now in the treasury, in making inquiries into the "welfare" of the "common people" is sure to meet with the greatest opposition from those very limited classes who have already received the most favorable attention from Congress, whilst "the people" whose condition and interest have never yet, through a census, been examined into or reported upon by our government, includes at least three-fourths of our entire population.

Much anxiety is now shown because of the idleness of the criminals now confined in our penitentiaries for high crime. Is there not far greater cause for anxiety because of the idleness of the people who are not yet criminals.

Dr. John S. Billings,[3] U.S.A. who had in charge the Mortality and Vital Statistics for the census of 1880, and occupies the same position for the Eleventh Census, in his report for the census of 1880, Vol. XI, p. xvi., says:

"The agencies to which great differences in mortality between different locations are chiefly due, are: — (I) poverty; (II) age distribution of the living population; (III) density of population; (IV) race; (V) meteorological conditions; (VI) epidemics."

No class of statistics can have greater value than those which bear upon the health and mortality of the people. When so able a statistician as Dr. Billings finds that poverty is the chief [agent?] of a people's mortality; that density of population, a direct result of poverty, is another chief agent in human destruction; and that epidemics always find their victims most plentiful among the crowded populations of the poor, it becomes a matter of the highest importance that the evidence upon which these facts are based should be gathered with the greatest care, and laid before government and people, in a form that cannot be misunderstood, for their instruction.

What is wanted is a full and complete census of the people, taken at the time and by the means used in enumerating all other matters, showing the real conditions of the great masses of the people, their occupations and the amount of their employment or idleness, as a basis for action in the promotion of the "general welfare," which the Constitution makes the special duty of Congress to provide for.

The census provided for in the law as it stands is in no sense a census of the people. It does not provide for ascertaining the real population of the country, but for only a portion of it. It provides for an enumeration of the "wealth and industry of the United States," but not for the poverty and idleness of the people.

Without an investigation that will give a just and complete idea of the condition of the people no intelligent action can be taken. But with the knowledge which such a census would give in our possession, the evils which now press so heavily upon society would soon disappear. Without it what will be the end?

For the reasons herein before set forth, on our own behalf and on behalf of our fellow wage-receivers, we ask of Congress and the President that they reconsider the action whereby we are denied what should be a common right of everyone living in the United States, and that our number, our condition, and our interests, in the taking of the Eleventh Census shall, by the enactment of the Supplement Act[4] herewith submitted, receive equal consideration and attention with that rendered to the most favored classes of our fellow citizens.

And we now, with this third application for our common rights, and as we will ever most respectfully pray.

Signal (Indianapolis), Sept. 27, 1889.

1. The Act of Mar. 1, 1889 (U.S. *Statutes at Large*, 25:760).
2. The Act of Mar. 3, 1879 (U.S. *Statutes at Large*, 20:473). The 1890 census enumerated both the number of unemployed and the duration of their unemployment.
3. John Shaw Billings was a physician in the U.S. army surgeon general's office.
4. The text of the Supplement Act (H.R. 7172, 51st Cong., 1st sess., 1890) did not appear in the *Signal*, nor did it become law.

A Circular

[October 4, 1889]

To the Workers of America:
Greeting:—

One of the oldest and most faithful unions of the American Federation of Labor—the Journeymen Bakers' National Union—is now grievously suffering from the effects of a general lockout of its members in the cities of New York and Brooklyn,[1] the strain upon its treasury being so great that it is at length compelled to ask for financial aid.

The action of the union of employing (boss) bakers in discharging every workman who refused to sign a degrading and immoral contract binding himself to sever his relations with his union and his fellow-men is an action that should call forth the reprobation of every friend of progress and humanity. The more will the enormity of this high-handed proceeding of the bakers be apparent when we reflect upon the terrible conditions under which the journeymen bakers have la-bored and suffered for so many long and weary years that their lives became almost intolerable—a condition to which the employers would now relegate them.

The first real effort of the journeymen bakers to emancipate them-selves from their slave like condition was manifested in the great strike of June, 1880. On that occasion the New York Union numbered over 5,000 members. All of them quit work on the same day, and assembled at Irving Hall, where the employers had to call and sign an agreement wherein they pledged themselves not to require their men to work longer than twelve hours on six days and fifteen hours on Saturdays, to abolish board—that is, give their men the liberty to board where they pleased—and to engage their men from the union labor bureau instead of at the various drinking houses, called "bakers' homes," where the unemployed journeymen suffered both in pocket and mor-als. After the men had received all they asked for they returned to work.

The New York union thus firmly established, George G. Block, the secretary of that union, concluded to start the Bakers' Journal, with the view of thereby establishing the now existing National Union, and at the same time educate the men of the entire country up to the principles of trade unionism. On the second day of May, 1885, the first number[2] appeared and at once found its way into every bake shop in the land. The bakers of all the leading cities at once organized and held a successful convention,[3] through which all local unions were greatly benefited and enabled to better their condition. The employers displayed great antagonism against all the active workers in the new movement, and went as far as to establish an opposition paper to counteract their efforts. This paper, however, had but a short life, while the organ of the journeymen has now entered upon its fifth year of usefulness, and has for a year past been ably supplemented by another official journal, published in the English language,[4] and edited by the experienced pen of J. P. McDonnell, of Paterson.

The few and struggling unions of 1885 have in the meanwhile increased to upward of eighty disciplined subordinate local unions whose combined efforts enable the Executive council of the Journey-men Bakers' National Union to disburse nearly $1,000 weekly in support of the brave men who are so nobly struggling in defence of trade unionism and progress.

Therefore, by the virtue of the provisions of Article VII of the Constitution of American Federation of Labor, which reads as follows:

Sec. 3. While we recognize the right of each trade to manage its own affairs, it shall be the duty of the Executive Council to secure the unification of all labor organizations, so far as to assist each other in any justifiable boycott, and with voluntary financial help of the organizations connected with the AF of L in the event of a strike or lockout, when duly approved by the Executive Council.

Sec. 4. When a strike has been approved by the Executive Council, the particulars of the difficulty, even if it be a lockout, shall be explained in a circular issued by the President of the Federation to the unions affiliated therewith. It shall then be the duty of all affiliated societies to urge their local unions and members to make liberal financial donations in aid of the working people involved.

I herewith express my desire that contributions be forwarded immediately to August Delabar, Secretary Journeymen Bakers' National Union, Room 52, No. 150 Nassau street, New York city.

Yours fraternally,   Samuel Gompers,
President American Federation of Labor.

Signal (Indianapolis), Oct. 4, 1889.

1. On Aug. 20, 1889, the Bakers' Association of New York and Vicinity, consisting of some twelve of the largest bakeries in New York City and Brooklyn, posted regulations requiring bakery workers to bargain individually with their employers. Employees had to sign the regulations in order to keep their jobs. Workers in fourteen shops in New York City and Brooklyn struck and the employers replaced most of them. The Journeymen Bakers' National Union (JBNU) instituted a boycott against the Bakers' Association.

2. Of the *Deutsch-Amerikanische Bäcker-Zeitung*.

3. The JBNU organized at a convention in Pittsburgh, Jan. 13-16, 1886.

4. The *Bakers' Journal*.

A News Account of a Conference between Representatives of the AFL and the KOL at Girard House, Philadelphia

[October 15, 1889]

THE EIGHT HOUR MOVEMENT.

The conference between the representatives of the Knights of Labor and the American Federation of Labor in regard to the eight hour movement was held yesterday afternoon at the Girard House. The Knights were represented by General Master Workman T. V. Powderly, J. W. Hayes and A. W. Wright, of the Executive Board, and the interests of the Federation were looked after by Samuel Gompers, of New York; P. J. McGuire, of this city; W. Martin, of Pittsburg; Henry Emrick, of New York, and J. B. Lennon,[1] of New York, who acted as a substitute for Daniel McLaughlin, who was prevented from attending by his continued illness.

The conference opened with a discussion of the present condition of the labor organizations in regard to the progress of the eight hour movement, and the delegates alternated in describing what progress had been made in the various Orders.

Mr. Powderly, on behalf of the Knights, stated that it was impossible for their side to take any definite action until after the General Assembly to be held at Atlanta next month; and that the movement of the Knights in regard to the proposed change would be guided wholly by the action of the next Assembly. In order that none of the Assemblies of the Knights of Labor shall misunderstand this question, every means have been taken to keep them informed as to the intentions of the promoters of the object. Circulars have been sent to every Assembly in the Order, and requests made that the movement be fully discussed and the delegates accordingly instructed. Mr. Powderly concluded by saying that the board was heartily in favor of the movement, but its actions will have to depend on the will of the Atlanta Assembly.

Samuel Gompers, representing the Federation side, stated that every endeavor had been made by his organization looking to the success of the object. Since the St. Louis convention letters have been sent to many prominent clergymen, physicians and publishers in all parts of the country asking for expression of opinion on the eight-hour movement. Most of the replies have been favorable. On Washington's birthday two hundred meetings were held; on the Fourth of July three hundred were held, and on Labor day more than four hundred, in all sections of the country, were held and literature circulated containing articles requesting all labor organizations to join in the movement. Mr. Gompers will make an earnest endeavor to attend the next meeting of the Knights of Labor Executive Board and will personally present the plan of the Federation of Labor as decided upon at St. Louis. Mr. Gompers said that harmonious action between the two bodies was what was wanted, and felt convinced that the results achieved would more than repay the trouble and labor of the conference.

Other matters outside of the eight-hour movement were discussed, and on behalf of the Knights a proposition was submitted to secure harmonious action in regard to working cards and labels. Representatives of the Federation then spoke against the trade organizations within the Knights and made requests that such organizations be discouraged in the future.

No time was set for the next conference, but it was decided that the discussion looking to unanimous action between the different orders be continued.

In regard to the plans of the Federation to make the eight-hour movement a success Mr. Gompers said after the conference that it was not their desire to encourage strikes, but that his Order was entirely without sentiment in the matter. The point will be carried peaceably, if possible, but forcibly if necessary.

Philadelphia Inquirer, Oct. 15, 1889.

1. John Brown LENNON was general secretary of the Journeymen Tailors' National Union of the United States (subsequently the Journeymen Tailors' Union of America) and editor of the *Tailor* from 1887 to 1910, and was treasurer of the AFL from 1890 to 1917.

A Translation of a News Account of a Nominating Convention for the New York Seventh Senatorial District

[October 26, 1889]

SAM. GOMPERS NOMINATED.

Yesterday afternoon the senate convention of the County Democracy of the 7th senate district was held in No. 354 Grand St. Approximately 50 delegates were present. The convention was called to order by John H. Carl. A member of the conference committee, who together with the Republicans of the district was supposed to be on the lookout for an appropriate candidate for the office of senator, motioned that each assembly district, one after the other, should be called on to suggest a candidate. The delegates of the third and eighth assembly districts declared that they had no one to suggest. Excise Commissioner William Mitchell,[1] representative of the 10th assembly district, suggested in a lengthy speech "Samuel Gompers, president of the American Federation of Labor" as a candidate for the existing office. He referred to the fact that Gompers, as the representative of labor organizations, had been appointed a member of the world's fair committee and said further that the former mayors Cooper[2] and Grace[3] had highly recommended him to the committee because of his noteworthy abilities. Nathan E. Levy also gave a lengthy speech in support of the nomination. He said that Gompers was held in the highest esteem by the labor organizations of the country so that, in the opinion of these organized workers, nothing of importance got done without his approval. O'Rourke from the 14th district declared he was at first in favor of Fred. W. Diehl for senator but later, however, came to be convinced that Gompers would be a very good candidate for the office. Thomas Baur pointed out that the nomination of Gompers would strengthen the County Ticket of the "citizens" coalition. He praised the working class and asked: "What is a party without it?" Alderman Benjamin[4] also declared himself in favor of the nomination. The vote was then taken, in which all the delegates rose from their seats and showed themselves thereby in favor of Gompers as candidate for the office of state senator. A committee consisting of one delegate from each assembly district represented at the convention was appointed to inform Gompers of the nomination. We hear that Gompers will make the acceptance of his candidacy conditional to the decisions of the Central Labor Federation and the Central Labor Union meetings to take place next Sunday.

In the evening the senate convention of the Republicans from the 7th senate district was held in No. 28, Ave. A. At this convention as well, according to agreement, Samuel Gompers was nominated for the office of senator.[5]

New Yorker Volkszeitung, Oct. 26, 1889. Translated from the German by Patrick McGrath.

1. William P. Mitchell was a leader of the County Democracy from the fourteenth assembly district.
2. Edward Cooper was Democratic mayor of New York City from 1879 to 1881.
3. William Russell Grace.
4. Philip B. Benjamin.
5. See "To the Committee of Notification of the Republican Party of the New York Seventh Senatorial District," Oct. 28, 1889, below.

To the Committee of Notification of the Republican Party of the New York Seventh Senatorial District

October 28th, [188]9.

Messrs. Joseph Mulvey, H. H. Broekmay, Theo. F. Ruhll,[1] Nicholas Fish[2] and Ferdinand Dryer
Committee of Notification the Republican Party of the 7th Senatorial District New-York.
Gentlemen: —
When the Committee of the 7th Senatorial District, formally and

officially notified me, that your organization had unanimously nominated me for Senator in your district, I stated that a formal answer
would be tendered you, and that I would write in substance what I
verbally stated to your Committee.

Before the nomination was tendered me, I stated to the gentlemen
who had in mind the presentation of my name to your convention,
of my determination to make my acceptance of the nomination con-
ditioned upon the consent and approval of my friends and co-workers
in the ranks of organized labor of this City. In making this statement,
I impressed upon the gentlemen referred to, the fact, that I regarded
the good will and the best interests of the organization of the working
people, as paramount to any political advancement, or preferment of
myself.

I have asked the advice of my fellow-workingmen,[3] and they have
answered to the effect, that my services, as President of the American
Federation of Labor, is preferable to them, and to our cause, than
any I can render them as Senator in the Legislature of the State of
New-York. Hence in deference to their judgement, I most respectfully
decline the nomination your organization so generously and kindly
tendered me.

In so declining, it will probably not be amiss to say that, I am not
unmindful of the honor you conferred upon me, and the many kind
things the members of your organization, who I have met, have said
of me. The earnest proffers of aid, and to the intention to zealously
support my candidature, and also the very cordial response, the mention of my name in connection with the nomination, has called forth;
not only from the people in the 7th Senatorial district, but throughout
the entire City.

Permit me to assure that fear of defeat, never entered my mind,
in connection with my determination to decline; for if ever man was
reasonably sure of election to any office, I was. If I would have accepted
the nomination from your organization, and also from the regular
Republican and even the disaffected Republican organization in the
district, almost precluded the possibility of defeat at the polls.

You will therefore understand, that it was not fear of defeat that
prompted me to the determination to decline.

It is probably also appropos to say here, that in all our conversations
and communications, no pledge as to my future course was either
asked or given, and that I would be, if elected, free to exercise my
own judgement. The calumnious statement of interested parties to
the contrary notwithstanding.

Kindly accept for yourself, and convey to your colleagues, my sincere appreciation and thanks for the honor conferred, and compliment implied by your nomination.

Very respectfully yours.   Saml Gompers.

TLpS, reel 3, vol. 4, pp. 290-92, SG Letterbooks, DLC.

1. Theodore Frederick Ruhle was a New York City inspector.
2. Nicholas Fish was a New York banker. He had served as U.S. minister to Belgium from 1882 to 1886.
3. SG consulted the New York City Central Labor Federation at its meeting on Oct. 27 (see "An Excerpt from a News Account of a Meeting of the New York City Central Labor Federation," Nov. 2, 1889, below).

To John Elliott

October 31st, [188]9.

John T. Elliott Esq.
Sec'y B'th'd Painters & Decoraters of A.
1314 N. Fulton Ave., Baltimore, Md.,
Dear Sir and Bro:—

No, dear Jack, I won't write a book. I have not yet reached that point in my life at which I have made war upon my fellow-men; nor have I yet determined to commit hari-kari.

I have not seen the advance sheets of Mr. Powderly's "Thirty Years of Labor" and of course can not judge of its worth, or the truthfulness with which it portrays the doings and characters of men in our movement. You speak of the attack upon you in his book.[1] Need I remind you of the attacks made upon me? I think, however, I have lived long enough to prove their statements false and malicious; and it appears to me that none would more heartily wish that their slanders had never been uttered, than the authors; so do I believe that your opportunity will come.

I want to make this suggestion to you, which you can take for what it is worth. Write a letter to Mr. Powderly, calling his attention to the fact, of which you complain, and ask him to eliminate the libelous matter from his book, before it is given general publicity. Don't write in anger; let your letter be dignified and manly to him; and have it registered in the post office.

It is my opinion that an injunction could be procured in the United States Courts, restraining him or his publisher, from issuing a book containing libelous matter. The question of fact, of course, would be decided by the Court.

If you have any of the advanced sheets of that book, and will kindly send them on, I will return them in the course of a few days.

Do you want me to forward the copies of the "Painter and Decorator"[2] now, or have you any objections to my retaining them for a while?

I have received a letter from our friend, John M. Welter,[3] in which he expresses an earnest desire to be one of the delegates of your organization to the Boston convention. As to his ability I have already spoken to you while in Baltimore. As to the advisability or practicability of his appointment, of course I have nothing to say; that is a matter of your own concern. That your organization will be fully represented at the Boston convention, is my sincere wish.

Enclosed please find receipt for $10.67 cts., paid by your organization as per capita tax, to the American Federation of Labor, on 4468 members.

With sincere good wishes for your welfare; hoping for a successful convention, and anticipating the pleasure of meeting you there, I am,

Yours truly.   Saml Gompers.
President, American Federation of Labor.

Dictated by S. G.

TLpS, reel 3, vol. 4, pp. 306-7, SG Letterbooks, DLC.

1. In the book Powderly accused the Baltimore delegate to the 1882 KOL General Assembly (Elliott) of being drunk and unfit for his duties (*Thirty Years of Labor, 1859-1889* [Columbus, Ohio, 1889], pp. 562, 594-95.)

2. The *Painter* was the journal of the Brotherhood of Painters and Decorators of America (BPDA).

3. John M. WELTER, a charter member of BPDA local 42 of Buffalo in 1887, was secretary of the Buffalo Central Labor Union and the Buffalo Building Trades Council during the late 1880s.

To George McNeill

Nov. 1st [188]9.

Mr. Geo. E. McNiell.
Dear Friend:—

Owing to pressure of work I was unable to answer your favor earlier.

I certainly agree with you in reference to the very obtuse and matter of fact statistical reports many of the Bureau's of Labor issue. The purpose seems to be to becloud a question by a mass of figuires, presented in such a shape to defy investigation; except by an expert. You may rest assured that I will gladly co-operate to secure an improvement in these matters.

It is true that the *whole* fault for a defective Census will not depend upon the law; but it certainly will in reference to one of the most important factors connected with a Census. Let me call your attention to it.

The Law for the taking of the 10th Census (1880) contained a provision for the enumeration of the number of unemployed. This provision of the Law was violated by omission. Not a line, not a figuire having been either as-certained or reported upon it. Before the present Law—for the 11th Census [(]of 1890)—was enacted a protest was made against the omission of the clause, providing for the same purpose. It was omitted however. This was not ignorance but design and betrays an understanding that the violation of the 1880 Census Law was tacitly agreed upon. Does it not strike you that way? Please don't mention this fact to any one for the present, since I intend to have the A.F. of L. take strong grounds upon the subject at the conve[ntion][1] and I don't want our thunder stolen.

Will you let me have a copy or advance copy of your "Industrial Democracies"? I desire to see it and consult with a few men as to the advisability of either purchasing a number of copies, purchasing the plates or probably making some other arrangement in reference to it agreable to all concerned.

The clips I mentioned, if they were not enclosed were lost.

I enclose a list of labor papers as requested. Hoping to hear from you soon and with best wishes. I am.

Yours Fraternally.   Saml Gompers.

N.B. If there is anything you care about writing or suggesting for our convention I should be pleased to have it.

S G

ALpS, reel 3, vol. 4, pp. 314-15, SG Letterbooks, DLC.

1. The 1889 AFL convention recommended that the Executive Council lobby for an amendment to the 1890 census law to provide for the enumeration of the number of unemployed.

An Excerpt from a News Account of a Meeting of the New York City Central Labor Federation

[November 2, 1889]

ORGANIZED LABOR.

Last Sunday's[1] meeting of the

CENTRAL LABOR FEDERATION.

was of great importance for the entire labor movement in this country. The proceedings were highly interesting. A delegate of Millers' and

Millwrights' Union No. 2 presided. There was a very large attendance of delegates. An invitation sent by the Rheinpfallzer Maennerchor to its coming entertainment will be accepted if it be shown that only union help is employed, and union beer and cigars be sold on that occasion.

It was then announced that Samuel Gompers, president of the American Federation of Labor, was present for the purpose of asking the advice of the delegates in an eminently important matter. Mr. Gompers was granted the floor, and he said that what he had to lay before the body might be of great importance not only for the workmen of New York, but of the whole country. He then continued, to state that a political nomination had been tendered him by the united Republicans and County Democrats. He laughed at the idea when the rumor of the contemplated nomination first reached him; but when he was really approached by some politicians he declined to definitely accept, as he desired to consult some friends. He was advised by them not to accept the nomination until he had obtained the opinion of the labor organization of New York. He had been asked what he would do in case he were elected, and his answer had been that he would go to the Senate as a free man, absolutely untrammelled by promises made to any set of politicians; he would pledge himself to nothing but the well known demands of labor. At all events he would only accept if the Central Labor Federation and the Central Labor Union told him to do so. He concluded, saying: "I am not going to make an attempt to influence your decision; you are to decide as you deem fit in the interest of the labor movement. I shall abide by your decision." Mr. Gompers' remarks were warmly applauded.

A lengthy discussion followed. One of the delegates attempted to "puff" the candidacy of one Roesch,[2] the candidate of rotten Tammany in Mr. Gompers' district, but the attempt was nipped in the bud by the chairman. Another speaker declared that the constitution of the Central Labor Federation could not be violated by indorsing the nominations made by any of the old political parties, and, before everything else, "We cannot afford to lose Sam. Gompers just yet!" A third speaker was in favor of leaving Mr. Gompers to decide for himself, while a fourth speaker said: "The president of the American Federation of Labor comes to this body, which is part of the organization he represents, to ask for our opinion. According to my idea our answer ought to be: 'Touch not pitch, lest you be defiled!' From the individual standpoint we ought to thank Mr. Gompers for his sincerity, and we should answer him frankly and honestly. What could he do for us if he were elected? The same parties who have nominated him are the ones who to-day oppress labor. The Senate is but a chamber of prostitution, not to be touched by workmen unless elected upon the labor ticket for the direct purpose of putting an end to such prostitution. Let us tell Mr. Gompers that, if he desires to do his duty, and all other workmen of this city do theirs, New York will soon become the center of a great American Labor Party. The Republicans and Democrats have delivered this country into the clutches of the monopolists, and for this reason there can come no salvation to labor from that side."

Several other delegates followed in the same strain; and only two spoke in favor of Mr. Gompers accepting the nomination, their argument being that this would be a good opportunity of electing a representative of Organized Labor to the State legislature, a feat several times attempted upon a labor platform, but always unsuccessfully.

Mr. Gompers then formulated his question thus: "Does the Federation advise Samuel Gompers to accept or decline the nomination offered him?" The vote stood as follows: 40 against and 8 in favor of accepting; part of the delegates refrained from voting. When Mr. Gompers said, "I thank you for your advice, and I shall, of course, submit to the decision of organized labor," he was again loudly applauded.

. . .

Workmen's Advocate (New York), Nov. 2, 1889.

1. Oct. 27, 1889.
2. George F. Roesch, a Tammany Hall Democrat and member of the New York Assembly (1883, 1885, 1888-89), subsequently won the election in the seventh district and served in the New York Senate from 1890 to 1894.

To Frank Hamlin[1] and Henry Himmelsbach[2]

Nov. 4th, [188]9.

Messrs. Frank D. Hamlin & H. Himmelsback.
Gen'l Organizers A.F. of L.
Brothers: —

Your letter of the 2nd inst. together with application, endorsement and enclosures, came duly to hand and contents noted. The certificate of affiliation will be issued to the Laborers Union of your City, with the number in regular rotation. I am disinclined to issue charters where nationalities are made a distinct feature, and, therefore, issue it in the name of: Laborers Union No. 3849, Rochester, N.Y. If they desire they can make such divisions in their methods of organizing upon lines of differences in language as they themselves decide, but this should not appear upon the charter issued from this office.

The certificate of affiliation is mailed to your address with this, and I enclose a receipt for $10.00, received in payment for the same and for the outfit, which will be forwarded to you in the course of a few days.

Thanking you sincerely for your joint efforts, and asking you to convey to the officers and members of the Laborers Union, my sincere wishes for their success, I am,

Yours fraternally.   Saml Gompers.
President, American Federation of Labor.

Dictated by S. G.

TLpS, reel 3, vol. 4, p. 323, SG Letterbooks, DLC.

1. Frank D. Hamlin, a machinist, was an AFL organizer in Rochester, N.Y.
2. Henry Himmelsbach, a cigarmaker, served during the early 1880s as secretary and president of CMIU 5 and in 1889 was secretary of the Rochester Trades Assembly and an AFL organizer.

To the Officers and Delegates of the General Assembly of the KOL

November 9th, [1889]

To the Officers and Delegates of the General Assembly Knights of Labor in Convention Assembled, at Atlanta, Georgia.
Brothers in labor, greeting:—

In pursuance to a resolution adopted by the Executive Council of the American Federation of Labor, and the suggestions of the General Executive Board of the Knights of Labor, it is my privilege to communicate with you in reference to a question, upon which the attention of the working people has been concentrated and crystallized in the past few years, more than any other one question. A question that strikes deep into the citadel of poverty and demoralization; a question that seeks to raise man from the sloughs of misery and despair; a question easier of solution than almost any other; a question that gives man time and an opportunity to investigate for himself, the underlying principles, for the improvement and the amelioration of the condition of the people, and to secure their final emancipation from the thraldom of injustice—The Eight Hour Question.

You are already aware that the Convention of the American Federation of Labor, held in St Louis, December, 1888 passed a series of resolutions calling upon the working people of America, to agitate, organize and prepare for the enforcement of the Eight Hour Workday, May 1st, 1890.

It is superfluous in this letter to quote the resolutions upon that subject, adopted by the Convention, a copy of which, however, please find enclosed. You will observe, from this document and the resolutions, of which I enclose a copy also, that the movement has been received with acclaim by the working people of our Country, and has steadily grown and developed until the movement may well be regarded as a national sentiment and principle. One that will be carried on with its banner aloft until victory shall finally have perched upon our side.

On February 22nd, 1888, simultaneous mass-meetings were held throughout the entire Country, by the working people, and resolutions of a similar character (a copy of which is enclosed) were adopted by them in more than 240 cities and towns. The second series of simultaneous mass-meetings were held on July 4th, and were participated in, by over 360 cities and towns throughout the Country. On Labor Day September 2nd the number of meetings to agitate the Eight Hour question, held simultaneously, had grown to more than 420.

Nearly 300 General Organizers of the American Federation of Labor have held meetings and delivered addresses in their respective cities and towns, and adjacent places, on this same subject, and several Special Organizers and lecturers have been placed in the field to travel throughout the Country, to address our fellow-working people, upon this important question.

We secured the services of three of the ablest Economic thinkers in the Country, to write a series of Pamphlets on the Eight Hour question, and its effect upon the Economic, Social, Commercial and Industrial affairs of our Country. These Pamphlets have been printed, and editions of more than 50,000 circulated broadcast. More than one-quarter of a million circulars were issued, from time to time, in reference to the same question.

About 1200 personal letters were sent to men in public life, Economists, Manufacturers, Commercial men and Ministers of various denominations, calling their attention to the Eight Hour movement, and asking their opinion upon the advisability of its adoption. (A typewritten copy of these letters, with such alterations as the special case required, is also herein enclosed.) Answers were received from a very large number, nearly all of whom have, more or less, pronounced in favor of the adoption of the Eight Hour Workday.

The Officers of the American Federation of Labor have devoted a large part of their time in public discussion of the subject, and to bring the matter before the business meetings of their organizations, and impressed the necessity of the enforcement of the Eight Hour rule on the day set.

Such in brief, has been the public agitation for the successful termination of this movement, inaugurated by the American Federation of Labor.

Many of the National Trade Unions affiliated to the American Federation of Labor have taken up the question, with a determination for its enforcement, and who are now engaged in taking a vote of their respective memberships, to ascertain the extent to which they are willing to go, to achieve success, and two national trade unions, have resolved to hold special conventions in time to determine upon their course of action, upon this momentous subject.

All of the National Trade Unions are engaged in voting upon a proposition for a Federation Defense Fund, in order to further the movement.

It is our plan to achieve the Eight Hour Workday for all who may be in a position to accomplish it with our aid, and what is of as much importance, to secure the substantial reduction in the hours of labor, of those whose daily toil is inordinately long.

At present it is impossible to say definitely, what action will be necessary to be taken by the working people to secure the Eight Hour Workday. Some have stated that it will be conceded upon the demand of organized labor, that the employers will recognize the necessity of so doing. If not from a spirit of humanity, at least, from a wise discretion. Such permit me to say I hope may be the case. Others again believe that our employers will not manifest such good judgement, and that organized labor will be compelled to resort to a cessation of work to enforce the demand.

It is the policy of the American Federation of Labor, and all bona fide labor organizations, to avoid the harsh measure of a strike whenever possible; but, if we can not obtain justice; if in the light of the immense improvements in machinery as applied to the modern methods of production; if, with all civilizing influence of this latter part of the nineteenth century; we can-not secure a substantial reduction in the hours of labor, so that all may find an opportunity of remunerative employment without a strike, then probably that must be resorted to.

We appeal to you for your co-operation in this movement, because we believe that the interests of the toiling masses are identical. We recognize the necessity for unity of action and purposes in the whole body of organized labor, and spurn with contempt the policy of isolation.

Nor do we attach any more importance to the fact that the American Federation of Labor inaugurated this present movement, and ask your co-operation, than if you had initiated it and asked our organization to aid you.

Some of the movements in the world's history that have had the most humble beginnings have been most far-reaching in their influences, and wrought wonderful changes.

So with our present movement. To what narrow limits it may be confined, or what scope it may take, it is at present, impossible to determine. But of one thing all may rest assured, we have entered it and shall face the coming time with clear heads and stout hearts.

In this movement we ask you to throw your lot with us, without restraint or reservation. If our efforts are crowned with victory, the working people will be proud of those who have stood by and for them.

In any event it behooves us to continue to present a solid front in the van-guard for labor reform, and the toilers emancipation.

Sincerely trusting that you will give this your early and favorable consideration, and asking to be advised as soon as a decision is arrived at. I have the honor to subscribe myself,

Yours very respectfully.   Saml Gompers,
President, American Federation of Labor.[1]

Dictated by S. G.

TLpS, reel 3, vol. 4, pp. 339-45, SG Letterbooks, DLC.

1. The 1889 General Assembly of the KOL, meeting in November in Atlanta, Ga., decided that SG's letter did not contain a plan upon which it could legislate but expressed confidence that Knights would give their moral support to the trades inaugurating an eight-hour drive on May 1, 1890.

To Patrick McBryde

November 18th, [188]9.

P. McBryde Esq.
Sec'y Treasurer Nat'l Prog. Union of M. & M.L.
L.B. 172, Columbus, Ohio.
Dear Sir and Bro:—

Your favor of the 15th inst. enclosing draft and report, came duly to hand and contents carefully noted. In reply to your statement as to the doubts existing to your ability to send a delegate to the Boston Convention of the American Federation of Labor, permit me to say that I would regard the omission of your organization to be represented by its full quota of delegates, as entirely unfortunate.[1]

It seems to me that in view of the present circumstances it is not only policy, but, your bounden duty, to have the Miners and Mine Laborers case properly represented at our Convention. More especially in the view of the recent circumstance of Mr. O'Mally's[2] expulsion from the Gen'l Assembly of the Knights of Labor, because he dare be a member of your organization. You can understand that the effect of this action will be to encourage D.A. 135 and bring a corresponding feeling of depression among members of your organization. This can only be offset if special consideration is given it at our Convention to the encouragement of your Nat'l Union.

Should your organization not be represented it will instill into the Miners the idea that they are entirely isolated from the labor movement of the Country, and it appears to me that scarcely anything worse could occur than to have such an opinion prevail among them.

I trust that you will give this matter your earnest and early consideration, and bring the matter before the notice of the Executive Officers of your organization in order that the matter may be attended to soon.

Enclosed please find a receipt for $70.37 cts. paid by your organization as per capita tax for six months, to the American Federation of Labor.

Again earnestly wishing that the above matter may receive your prompt attention, with sincere wishes for your welfare and hoping to hear from you at an early day, I am,

Yours fraternally. Saml Gompers,
President, American Federation of Labor.

Dictated by S. G.

TLpS, reel 3, vol. 4, p. 355, SG Letterbooks, DLC.

1. Chris Evans, Nial R. Hysell, and David Ross represented the National Progressive Union of Miners and Mine Laborers (NPUMML) at the 1889 AFL convention.

2. Timothy Thaddeus O'MALLEY, a miner, was master workman of KOL District Assembly 38 in the late 1880s. He was expelled by the 1889 KOL General Assembly on charges that he was sympathetic to the NPUMML, a rival organization to coal miners' KOL National Trade Assembly 135.

A Translation of a News Account of a Mass Meeting at Cooper Union

[December 6, 1889]

AN INTERNATIONAL LABOR CONGRESS.

The mass meeting arranged by the delegates of labor organizations for yesterday evening, in support of holding the world's fair of 1892 in the city of New York, did not attract a very large crowd to Cooper Institute; however, there was great enthusiasm for the idea. James P. Archibald chaired the meeting and introduced Samuel Gompers, president of the American Federation of Labor, as the main speaker of the evening. Gompers said he was very much in favor of having the world's fair held in New York since this would, in his opinion, give the labor movement an impetus that it could hardly receive otherwise. He said he viewed the celebration as an opportunity that might never come again. If the world's fair took place here, he said the city would experience such an upswing in every branch of industry that in 20 years New York would be so altered that today's inhabitants would not recognize it. He predicted our tenement-house system would find only disfavor in the eyes of the thousands who would visit the world's fair, and the pressure of public opinion would force the landlords to introduce the improvements that are necessary to make living in these houses endurable for the poor. "We intend," the speaker continued, "to make sure that, if the fair takes place here, the buildings, etc., will be put up by union workers. If this does not happen, the idea will have neither my support nor sympathy and I will treat the fair just as organized labor treats all the products of unorganized labor. We insist and will continue to insist that if the fair takes place here, it will not become a monument to cheap labor and the degradation of man; we are determined to make it a tribute to the dignity of the American man." He said the fair would bring representatives of labor from the entire civilized world to this country, and therefore it was important to take the opportunity to convene an international labor congress here for the purpose of discussing the great labor questions of the day.

Thomas J. Ford, the next speaker, mentioned the advantages that Philadelphia had garnered from the centennial fair of 1876 and that should suffice to convince the people of New York to apply all their energies toward having the fair held here. A fair in any city other than New York would not become a world's fair, he said, but would remain a local undertaking. He said the people of Europe were laughing at the pretentions of Chicago and other inland cities and expected the world's fair to be held here in the great metropolis of the New World. After more speakers, among them Harry Cole and John P. Lennon, had spoken in a similar vein, the following resolution, worked out by the conference committee of labor organizations, was read and unanimously adopted amid great applause:

["]Whereas, it is of the greatest importance and in the interest of organized workers of this country and all other countries, that the international exhibition, which is to take place in New York, should not only show how far business and industry have advanced, but should also give organized workers, whose interests and objectives are the same throughout the civilized world and who have produced the wealth displayed in all the international guest exhibits, the opportunity to tie the bands of unity around the wageworkers of the whole world, and

["]Whereas, during the last world's fair, which was held in Paris, an international labor congress took place, whose discussions advanced the aims of labor organizations in every country represented there, be it therefore

["]Resolved, that we workers and citizens of New York advise the American Federation of Labor, the Order of the K. of L., the Central Labor Federation and the Central Labor Union of New York, and all other labor organizations to discuss whether it would be advisable to convene an international labor convention in the year 1892 during the world's fair in New York and that such a convention be organized in a manner worthy of the American people and the great cause of the emancipation of the worker![."]

It was further decided to appoint a provisionary committee that is to contact the various labor organizations concerning the aims mentioned in the resolution.

New Yorker Volkszeitung, Dec. 6, 1889. Translated from the German by Patrick McGrath.

A Series of News Accounts of the 1889 Convention of the AFL in Boston

[Dec. 11, 1889]

BANQUET OF LABOR LEADERS.

In the long dining hall of the American House, last night, about 150 gentlemen, delegates to the fourth annual convention of the

American Federation of Labor and guests, sat down at 8 o'clock to a complimentary banquet tendered by the organized labor of the city of Boston, by courtesy of the city government. Frank K. Foster presided, and at his right sat President Samuel Gompers. Mr. Gompers is about as well known and popular a labor leader as any man in the country, and he was readily singled out as the conspicuous figure of the occasion. On Mr. Gompers' right sat Senator Robert Howard,[1] and on the left Mr. P. J. McGuire, general secretary of the U.B.C. and J. of A.

The main corridor of the American House was crowded before 7 o'clock in the evening with vari-colored badged figures, that presented quite a formidable array of labor strength. They were stalwart figures for the most part, and they represented many departments of actual industry; and they were surmounted in most cases also by heads that had few silver locks. It was a gathering of strong men in the prime of life — men who impressed the casual beholder with an appreciation of the extensive influence that they wield.

At the dinner President Gompers spoke, in answer to the toast, "The American Federation of Labor," of the earnest spirit that characterized the work of the delegates, and earnestness is the word that gives the most comprehensive and accurate idea of the impression which the manner of delegates conveyed. There was none of the frivolous disposition apparent that is sometimes manifested at convivial gatherings of fraternal organizations.

. . .

Boston Herald, Dec. 11, 1889.

1. Robert HOWARD, a spinner, played a leading role in national organizations of his trade and was elected to the Massachusetts Senate in 1885 and 1886.

[December 11, 1889]

LABOR'S TRIUMPHS

. . .

SPEECH OF PRESIDENT GOMPERS.[1]

"Mr. Chairman, Fellow-Delegates, Friends, Fellow-Workingmen — To respond to the toast, 'The American Federation of Labor,' in adequate terms to do the subject justice, requires too much time and possibly ought to be responded to by some one better qualified to perform that duty. I cannot respond to that toast at all without asking you to accompany me, even for a few moments, over the road that the organized working people of our country have travelled within the past few years, to attain our present proud position. I will not attempt to speak of the early formation, the organization of the trades unions of our country, but merely to say that these trades unions are the natural product of our modern society (applause), and just as much a natural, legitimate product of our economic conditions as it is for the cause to grow under the conditions natural to bring it into existence.

"It is not the first instance or attempt at federating the trades unions of the country. We have had others, we have fought the battle, and though poor, owing to our inherent weakness and the fact that our minds had not sufficiently developed, and that the trades unionists of the country had not yet recognized their own importance, they were not accorded the same honor, the same influence, the power that belonged to them, and as a consequence they went to the wall.

"In 1881, in the city of Pittsburg, the corner stone of our present federation was laid, and there we organized what was then known as the organized federation of the trades and labor unions of the United States and Canada. The organization was ushered in with loud acclaim, with immense numbers, but within the next year, owing to an organized and insidious antagonism based upon superstition and ignorance of the benefits, the tendencies and the purposes of the labor movement, it was sought to crush out the lifeblood of the then new organization. So the time went on, for year after year, and gradually growing weaker and weaker, till in 1884, in the city of Chicago, the representatives of the various trades unions affiliated with the then organization to which I referred, and this was the precursor of the American Federation of Labor, and which, though few in number, sent out hurling through the world the resolution that on May 1, 1886, an attempt would be made to enforce the eight-hour work-day for the people of America. (Applause.)

"That resolution of that small body of men was taken up and echoed and re-echoed from one corner of our country to the other, until it overwhelmed opposition and beat down the plans of those who would strangle the trades unions of our country. And on the day that arrived there were more working people who were benefited by that resolution than any one ever hoped or has ever been done by the working people of the whole world. Pardon me, if for a moment I digress. It is popularly believed that the eight-hour movement of 1886 was a complete failure. I ask your attention just for a moment, to go with me, and I desire to call your attention and demonstrate in a few words how absurd that statement is.

"You know as well as I can tell you and you need but to have your attention called to it. Do you know of any one trade where the working people work as many hours a day as they did before May 1, 1886? Look even now at the skilled, or so called unskilled labor—the car drivers and conductors—and notwithstanding their having been beaten by the corporations, they yet do not work as many hours as they did before May 1, 1886. (Applause.)

"The bakers of whom it was proverbially said they worked as long as they had their eyes open, now since 1886 work at most from 10 to 11 hours and in very few instances 12 hours a day, where formerly their hours were 16 and 18 for six days in the week, and on one day it was nearly 24. Look at the brewery workers, at our street laborers, at our laborers of every kind, at our skilled workmen and you will find, even in commercial houses, the storekeepers themselves do not keep their business places open as late as they did; they close earlier than in 1886. I merely refer to this to demonstrate to you that the movement of 1886 was not a failure, and the small body of earnest, sincere and intelligent trades-unionists, assembled at that convention, did as much for the elevation of the human family as any body of patriots that ever assembled. I am proud to know that in this assembly we have a few friends whom we can shake by the hand, with whom we can affiliate, whom we affiliate with now, and with hope and strength may hope to affiliate until every wrong from which labor suffers is rooted out of our social system. (Applause.)

"All the efforts of combinations, all the efforts and the channels by which falsehood could be transmitted, were used to mislead the minds of the working people as to the probable outcome of that movement, and I say that the credit due to the federation of organized trades and labor of the United States and Canada has not yet been given to it, and history must be written some day and the honor it deserves accorded to it. (Applause.) A cloud passed, and from that time even then it became weak as an organization, until there was one level blow attempted to be struck at the trades unions wholesale, and with a grand response on the part of the men true to their organization a conference was called and the venue changed for the holding of the convention of that organization. And in the city of Columbus, O., in December, 1886, we founded the trades unions outside of the federation, affiliated with the federation finally and the breath of life was placed in the struggling form, and the American Federation of Labor was born into the world. From that time, possibly, the record of the organization is as well known to you as to me. It would be manifestly improper, however, were I not to mention an instance or two.

"At that time we had not $100 in the treasury, but, we laid the foundations of our organization so strong we built immutably, built possibly grander than we knew. (Applause.) The strength of the American Federation of Labor lies in its recognition that the trades unions are the organizations whose mission it is to improve the condition of labor for the present, and to secure its final emancipation in the future. (Applause.) It is the safeguard of today, the germ of society, the hope of our children. We recognize that the trades unions of our country are best qualified to decide upon the questions of trade disputes between them and their employer. We recognize that it is not meet, that it is not intelligence, that it is not progress, that it does not bring the best results, when the grocery store keeper proposes to discuss the question of how many shoes a man shall wear. (Applause.)

"We say, and we proclaim, that we want in trade disputes no pound of advice and a penny's worth of assistance; that if there is anything we advocate, it is a penny worth of advice and a pound's worth of assistance. (Applause.) We believe, and proclaim as strongly as a people can, the identity of interests of all classes of labor. We feel for our brothers and sisters of labor, and hope to be able to assist them, and we expect to build slowly, yet grandly, so that when one member of the family of organized working people is attacked the whole of the grand army of labor shall respond with their sympathy and their dollars. (Applause.)

"Many men have asked me, 'Where will this lead us to?' I can answer this. We are an eminently practical people; we know what we want, and are in a business way going about it to obtain the best possible results. Wherever that may lead us, there we follow. We are not either blessed or cursed by 'isms or 'ists; we believe that the working people are those more intimately interested in the solution of this labor problem than any other people, and recognize that with the elevation and the amelioration of the condition of the working people the whole and all classes of the people are correspondingly benefited.

"Our movement, the eight-hour movement, of which many of you would like to hear something from me upon, and very likely our newspaper friends also—I beg to ask you not to expect me to say anything on at this time, for it would be in anticipation of what I shall in a more formal and official manner give utterance to tomorrow.[2] I ask you trades unionists, representatives of labor organizations, the bona-fide labor organizations of the whole country (applause), to rise up to the standard of what will be expected of you at this convention. (Applause.)

"The eyes of the world are riveted upon Boston this day and this week. It behooves us, as men who have in a measure laid claim to some sincerity of purpose, who have been honored and trusted by our co-laborers, to show that we are worthy of our time, worthy of our movement and honestly represent the interests of our fellow workingmen of today, and shall endeavor to work out their aspirations for tomorrow." (Great applause.)

. . .

Boston Globe, Dec. 11, 1889.

1. Gompers made these remarks at the banquet at the American House.
2. That is, in his annual report to the AFL convention.

[December 14, 1889]

EIGHT! EIGHT! EIGHT!

. . .

Name for Local Unions.

Regarding the change of name of local trade unions, as suggested in the report of the committee, President Gompers, leaving the chair, said that he was a consistent advocate of trade unions. The local unions are a great auxiliary to the national trade union. The president was of the opinion that much good came from local bodies. They are the recruiting camps of the union. He thought the present system of sending delegates needed changing. He was not in favor of decreasing the number of delegates at the convention. He suggested that the various local unions adopt the title of Local Union, American Federation of Labor.

Delegate Kirshner favored the change also in a very forcible argument. The secretary of the committee on constitution said that it was the opinion of the committee that it was unnecessary to change the names of the various local labor bodies. Delegate Lennon arose and said that as the matter now stood, any 10 men could come together, form a union, and send a delegate to the convention. This was not what the delegates wanted. A man coming to this convention should have a constituency behind him.

Delegate Vann[1] said that it appeared to him that if the recommendation of the committee was accepted by the conference, they would have such an unwieldly body that it would be almost impossible to transact the business of the conference. The line should be drawn somewhere.

Delegate Dillon said that he looked at the matter in a different light. It was true that, if the convention saw fit to indorse the recommendation of the committee, the number of delegates would be increased, but the object was to spread the organization.

Another delegate thought that it was unjust to allow 10 men to elect a delegate to the conference while 4000 members of a trades union could only elect two.

President Gompers arose again, and said he did not know of any man coming here representing only 10 men. They could not afford it, and it was foolish to think that they would attempt such a thing. For instance, a union representing 4000 laboring people sent two delegates, and according to the constitution these two delegates had 40 votes in the convention. Continuing, President Gompers advocated the standing of section 1, article 2 of the constitution.[2] It was through the central office of the federation that the various local unions came to learn of each other.

After further discussion the question came up on the amendment, and it was voted down. The motion then came up on the adoption of the recommendation of the committee, but it was lost by a vote of 13 to 44, and the article stands as originally printed in the constitution.

REPORT ON EIGHT HOURS.

The committee on eight hours then made their report through George E. McNeil. The committee reported that the matter of the granite cutters had already been covered in their report.

The committee approved the petition of the unions affiliated with the American Federation of Labor, requesting the same to endeavor to secure the enactment of an eight-hour law in all the States of the Union which shall provide that all employes, whether State, city, county or town, shall work but eight hours per day, whether the work be done by the government or not. The report was indorsed.

The committee reported the expediency of the executive council petitioning Congress to enact a law extending the statute of limitation, so as to enable government employes engaged in the public service from the year 1877 to the year 1882, inclusive, to recover such portion of their compensation as was denied them by reason of the [violation of the] existing national eight-hour law.[3]

The following interesting report was then read and received with deafening applause:

The organized forces of the grand army of labor in all the centres of industry in America, in England and Europe have determined to secure a reduction of the hours of labor to eight per day. And the only question at issue in labor circles is when and how this result shall be reached. Your committee, in canvassing the question of time and method, have come to the conclusion that the suggestions of President Gompers and the action of the federation at its last convention are founded upon historical precedent and logical reasoning. In presenting this report your committee feel it to be their duty to call attention to the fact that the hours of labor have been reduced in some of the industries from 16 to eight per day, with great benefit to the wage workers and the people at large; that in other industries, where large capital is invested and the most improved machinery introduced, the hours of labor were reduced from 14 and 12 to 10 hours per day, resulting in great public benefit. These reductions have occurred not only in this but in other countries, notably in Australia, where the hours of labor were reduced in 1856 to eight hours by some of the trades, and similar action is now intended in most, if not all, of the industries. In England the hours of labor were reduced in the great textile industries as early as 1847 to 10 hours per day, and in those industries, as in all others these reductions have not resulted in stagnation, but, on the contrary, have increased the purchasing power of the day['s] work of those receiving the benefits of increased leisure. If, then, wages have increased with each succeeding reduction of the hours of labor, then the question worthy of consideration in a convention of wage workers, is: How far can these reductions continue and yet produce the same results? The answer to this proposition is not left alone to experiment, but can be foretold in time to avert a great calamity. But, even if left to experiment, the great benefit of successful results is worth all it will cost to try to reach the minimum of working hours and the maximum of wages.

That a reduction of time to eight hours per day would result in increased wages and increased production, without increasing the cost of the product, is evident from the fact that the reduced hours of labor would require an increase in the working force sufficient to produce the same amount as now in 10 hours. The increase in working force would necessitate the increase of the plant, thus attracting into the army of the employed the vast horde of demoralized and

HALF-STARVED UNEMPLOYED.

The increase of the number of permanently employed will extend the market in this country alone to at least 2,000,000 of consumers.

As production is determined by the demand, and demand is governed by the number of consumers and the condition of civilization;

and as civilization is the result of the opportunities of the masses of
mankind to sell their labor or its products, the highest civilization
being in that place where the demand for labor is regular and strong,
then that measure is most productive of common good which will set
more men working and more workers thinking, and which will increase the demand for more and better products.

Invested capital is opposed to the reduction of the hours of labor,
not because capitalists think that wages will be reduced, but because
they know the percentage of profit per dollar and per man will be
diminished through the increased wages that will follow reduced hours.

To try to arrest the natural evolution of the human race by the
unwise policy of keeping down wages is simply a movement to limit
the markets, thus restricting more production. Your committee are
agreed that existing conditions will not in our judgment justify the
hope that at this time all the crafts are prepared to successfully enforce
the eight-hour system on the 1st of May, 1890, although many of the
trades are now ready, and many more will be by the time specified
for the inauguration of this the greatest of industrial reforms. We
therefore recommend that the executive council shall have power to
select such trade or trades from those affiliated with the American
Federation of Labor as shall in their judgment, be the best prepared
to achieve success, and that each union in the federation be requested
to assess their members 10 cents per week for so many weeks as shall
be necessary to

SECURE THE SHORT-HOUR DAY;

payment upon such assessments to commence not later than March
1, 1890.

That all trades affiliated with the American Federation of Labor
not now working the eight-hour day, or between whom and their
employers existing contracts may prevent, shall appoint committees
to confer with their employers, and, if possible, secure a reduction
of the hours of labor to eight per day and that the executive council
shall appropriate for their use, if needed, such a sum or sums as can
be spared from the money received for the trade or trades selected
by the executive council.

During the past year the efforts of President Gompers and the
executive council to forward the eight-hour movement are worthy of
the highest commendation. Through extensive correspondence they
have enlisted the sympathy of business men, manufacturers, professional men, ministers of the Gospel and economic thinkers, and have
endeavored to secure the co-operation of the Knights of Labor in this

movement. President Gompers in his letter to the general assembly of that organization, set forth in an able, clear and comprehensive manner, the position of the federation, and urged them to "throw their lot with us without restraint or reservation."[4] This communication from our official representative was answered by the misrepresentation of our position and an attempt to evade their responsibility, on the plea that no "plan" had been suggested, and while professing their adherence to the eight-hour movement they indorse the absurd and preposterous plan of the general master workman, thus confessing their impotency of power and insincerity of purpose.

Gentlemen of the convention—As the representatives of the organized labor of this republic, and of the continent of America, the supreme duty of success devolves upon us. In this movement toward the emancipation of labor there is no such word as fail. The longing hearts of the underpaid and unemployed beat responsive to our demand. Women weary of life and children robbed of the sweet delights of childhood, groan and cry under the heavy

BURDENS OF REMORSELESS POVERTY.

Age, unduly hastened by ill-requited toil, trembling in want, prays for our success. The monarchial and industrial serfs of Europe look toward these shores with aspiring hopes that here, where men are sovereign in political power, they may be freemen in their economic and social relations. This movement for less hours of toil, more hours of leisure, and more wealth for wealth producers, is co-extensive with civilization. To the trade unionists of Great Britain and Europe, marching shoulder to shoulder with us, we send the exultant shouts of greeting and all hail.

To all who love liberty and are loyal to the principles of free government; to all who look forward to an increased wealth more widely distributed; to all lovers of the human race everywhere; to union men and to those not now under the banner of organized labor, we appeal, in the name of justice and humanity, of increased wealth and diminished poverty, to concentrate their energies upon the single issue of the reduction of the hours of labor.

Edward L. Daley, Chairman.
W. J. Shields, Secretary.
George E. McNeill.
David Ross.[5]
William J. Cannon.[6]
H. M. Ives.[7]
William T. Roberts.[8]

It was voted to transmit a copy of the report of the eight-hour committee to the various labor unions of Great Britain.

. . .

Boston Globe, Dec. 14, 1889.

1. John D. Vaughan was a member of International Typographical Union (ITU) 49 of Denver and a delegate to the Denver Trades Assembly.
2. "The objects of this Federation shall be the encouragement and formation of local trade and Labor Unions, and the closer Federation of such societies through the organization of Central Trade and Labor Unions in every city, and the further combination of such bodies into State, Territorial or Provincial organizations, to secure legislation in the interest of the working masses."
3. Henry Blair presented the AFL resolution to the Senate on Feb. 10, 1889, where it was tabled.
4. See "To the Officers and Delegates of the General Assembly of the KOL," Nov. 9, 1889, above.
5. David Ross of Oglesby, Ill., a miner and subsequently a lawyer, represented the National Progressive Union of Miners and Mine Laborers.
6. William J. Cannon was financial secretary of CMIU local 17 of Cleveland, Ohio.
7. Harry M. Ives was elected president of ITU local 121 of Topeka, Kans., in 1889.
8. William T. Roberts was a vice-president of the National Amalgamated Association of Iron and Steel Workers between 1888 and 1890.

[December 14, 1889]

POWER TO ASSESS

The fifth day's session of the American Federation of Labor was opened at 9 o'clock by President Gompers. The report of the committee on constitution was taken up after roll-call at the point at which it was left last evening. The debate on the report was very animated, and great interest was manifested in the arguments of the several speakers.

The friends of a closer union and improved machinery for handling the strikes which may occur May 1 were out in full force.

The representatives of the International Typographical Union[1] and a number of the printers who come from central organizations were decidedly opposed to the question of assessments to meet the expenses of the expected strikes May 1.

The feeling was decidedly in favor of a closer bond of union, which would give all the compactness and effectiveness of the Knights of Labor, while preserving perfect independence and control of trade matters to the trade organizations.

The contest came over sec. 1, art. 8, of the proposed constitution, as submitted by the committee on constitution. This section reads:

"The executive council shall have the power and are directed to levy a strike assessment of 2 cents a member on the 1st of January, 1890, on all national and international bodies under the jurisdiction of the federation."

. . .

The vote on this was referred to the secretary to compile a vote on the numerical basis provided by the constitution of one vote for each 1000 members in the individual organizations. This vote showed that 1129 votes were in favor of the assessment, and 367 votes were in the negative. The proposition that the executive council shall

Levy an Assessment

when a strike is entered upon for an indefinite period, brought forth another animated discussion, in which the purpose and construction of the federation was clearly brought forth.

The section in full read:

["]In case any national or international body affiliated with this federation shall organize a strike or be locked out, and, by reason of financial distress, it shall become necessary for it to call upon the federation for aid, the executive council, if it deems that such organization is entitled to receive such assistance, shall make an assessment not exceeding two cents a member per week upon every other national or international body so affiliated with the organization.["]

Frank K. Foster, in the course of a lengthy speech, spoke against giving the executive council such unlimited power in the levying of assessments. (Applause.)

H. J. Skeffington rose to reply, and warmly accused Mr. Foster of not properly representing the organization which had sent him there,[2] in the course he was pursuing.

Mr. Foster rose to a point of order.

The chair ruled that Mr. Skeffington had no right to impute that Mr. Foster did not represent his organization.

Delegate Martin said that Delegate Labadie[3] had insinuated that it was not in accordance with liberty to make this assessment. We propose, said he, to handle our own business without the interference of any other body or calling, but we do not want liberty which would see poor little children starving. If we thought that this would be permitted in the American Federation of Labor we would not stay in it a month. (Applause.) The amount is only $1.04 a year.

Delegate Cannon — It is proposed to extend the power of the council without referring it to the organizations affected by it, and it is only one step in an encroachment which will finally reach an unlimited power to levy assessments. I will oppose it. The power that creates is greater than the thing created. (Applause.)

President Gompers: I hope delegates will not applaud. If they do, other delegates have the right to hiss. I hope we shall have neither.

Delegate Cannon — While the local bodies and the international bodies created this federation they

CAN ALSO DESTROY IT,

and the first step in that direction is unlimited power to levy assessments. I am opposed to the principle in toto, and would resort to it only in a case of extreme necessity. The paying of its dues by a society, its initiation and stipulated dues is enough, and assessment should only be resorted to in very extreme cases. Nothing so demoralizes a great organization as assessments. When a man knows he has to pay a fixed sum he is prepared for that, but he never knows when the last of his assessments will be paid.

Delegate McNeill moved that the section be amended by striking out the portion objected to, to giving unlimited power to the executive council, and inserting "assessments for a period not exceeding five weeks." He said: This organization has reached the most serious and critical hour of its existence. It is going back to the experiences which have been the decay and death of the efforts to concentrate the several unions into one federated body. This is a federated union and not an amalgamated union.

The chairman — The hour has arrived when we have to take some action on the invitation of the city government to visit the city institutions.

On the motion of Delegate Lennon it was decided to decline the invitation on account of the want of time, and the city messenger was notified to that effect.

Mr. McNeill, continuing — There are two features to which I wish to call special attention. The first is that this body

HAS ONLY SUCH POWERS

as are conferred on it by the affiliated bodies, and it has no power to take one step beyond the directions given by these bodies. The second is that the message of this motion will bring the entire bulk of the differences upon the federated unions instead of upon the local unions, and just as soon as you make the members of any given trade in this body feel that they are to depend for their success on this body, and the assessments of the federation generally, strikes will multiply indefinitely, and your assessments will not be paid, because while one trade or calling was to pay its assessment to the support of other men engaged in a strike elsewhere at the same time, self interest will dictate that they keep it themselves rather than give it to other trades. I am speaking from experience, and if the history of this movement teaches anything, it teaches that the federation must not step beyond the power given it by the rank and file of the bodies affiliated. I hope the motion as amended will prevail.

(The section had been amended by striking out "such assessments shall remain in force at the discretion of the executive council," and inserting the words "for a period not exceeding five consecutive weeks, unless otherwise ordered by a general vote of all national and international unions.")

Delegate Hysell[4] said the motion left it optional with the council to levy assessments or not as it thought fit. It is only after the council has decided and canvassed the facts of the case that an assessment would be ordered. If it is decided to assess, it is

ONLY TWO CENTS A WEEK

for each member. It could not in any case continue longer than a year, and then where is your unlimited power? It stops at an assessment of $1.04. I am surprised to hear gentlemen talk about unlimited power. I hope this amendment will not be carried, but that the section of the constitution will be adopted as it stands.

Delegate Robert Howard said: There is one thing at which I am very much pleased, and it is that several of the bodies represented here who favor this assessment, never expect to get a cent out of it. The iron and steel workers, the cigar makers and others only want this passed in order to help their fellow men. I was sorry to hear Brother McNeill say it led to ruin in the past. It did nothing of the kind. The labor organizations which were ruined in the past were mere baby shows. They have been defeated in the past for want of proper resources. If this assessment was fixed and it destroyed the association, then the sooner it is destroyed the better. (Applause.) Let them go, and those who are willing to stand for right will keep together. The representative of the granite cutters[5] has opposed the motion, although there was no other body except my own begged as much in support of its members.

President Gompers—That is a reflection on the members.

Delegate Howard—I did not mean it as such, Mr. President.

I Don't Believe It Interferes with Liberty

at all, as Brother Labadie seems to think. It is just the same power as that possessed by the United States toward the different States to levy troops for the army in time of war or for any other dangerous issue.

Delegate Kirschne[r] said: "The rank and file of the organization has, by a popular vote, agreed to the principle of this proposal, and the only question is, shall we establish a fund to tide organizations in distress over their difficulties. I hold that since the rank and file of the federation has agreed upon it, it will only kill the principle involved in this issue to limit it to five weeks. Besides that it will be the means of squandering that much money because the employers have notice in advance that after five weeks they are to be left to themselves, and they say "we have only to hold off for five weeks and the rest of the organization of the country will be bled to that extent, and we will be in a better position to beat the men.["] (Applause.)

The chairman—We have no power to levy any assessment beyond that ordered by all national and international unions. The question was submitted to the organizations of the various unions.

A motion was made at 11.50 by Delegate Emrich to suspend the rule relating to adjournment at noon, and continue the discussion.

President Gompers suggested the postponement of the question till the afternoon session.

Secretary Maguire thought they ought to come to some conclusion on the matter at the present time, after having devoted the greater part of the morning to the discussion of the matter. (Applause.)

The assembly voted by acclamation to

Adopt the Assessment Plan

under discussion.

. . .

Boston Globe, Dec. 14, 1889.

1. Eben C. Ives, Harry M. Ives, Robert Y. Ogg, and John D. Vaughan.
2. Foster represented the Massachusetts State Federation of Labor, an organization he helped found in 1887 and of which he was secretary from 1889 to 1895.
3. Joseph Antoine Labadie, a labor journalist, was president of the Michigan Federation of Labor (1889-90).
4. Nial R. Hysell represented the National Progressive Union of Miners and Mine Laborers (NPUMML). He had served on the executive board of the National Federation of Miners and Mine Laborers (1886-87) and was a Democratic Ohio assemblyman (1888-92).
5. James Grant and John Heffernan, representing the Granite Cutters' National Union of the United States of America, voted against the assessment.

FEDERATION ADJOURNED.

. . .

The special committee appointed to consider the attitude of the federation towards the Knights of Labor submitted the following report:

To the Officers and Delegates of the American Federation of Labor:
Your special committee appointed to issue an address to the working people of the country, upon the attitude of this organization towards the order of the K. of L. has carefully considered that part of the president's report bearing upon the subject, together with the recommendations of the committee on resolutions and other kindred documents; also the correspondence relating to the issue in question in the hands of the general secretary. As a result of this consideration the committee beg leave to report the following:

REPORT OF SPECIAL COMMITTEE.

To the Working People of America, Greeting:
The philosophy of trade unionism is based upon actually existing conditions in the labor world and universally inherent qualities of human nature. The history of the trade union justifies its present existence, and is a guarantee of its future usefulness. Organization to protect the interest of those who are forced to sell their labor for wages, as in relation to the interest of those who speculate in labor as a commodity, is a fully demonstrated necessity. Experience has also proved that the wage earners are the natural and proper guardians of the wage earner's rights; that the most effective defence against encroachments upon these rights can be achieved through the medium of organization upon craft lines.

It thus becomes imperative that the integrity of the trade union form of organization be zealously guarded; that this well-tested bulwark of labor be defended from covert attacks of jealous rivals, as well as from the open antagonism of declared opponents.

The American Federation of Labor desires to establish no monopoly in the sphere of labor organization. It does not seek to establish an autocracy of labor. It does, however, pledge itself to maintain the prestige and authority of its affiliated organizations and to enter its most emphatic protest against the policy of any labor society which permits itself to be used as an ambuscade for the destruction of the trade union movement.

In view of the extended injury suffered by the trade unions of

America at the hands of men who masquerade as Knights of Labor, we deem it necessary to briefly state the attitude of the A.F. of L. toward that order.

We seek no quarrel. We deprecate antagonism in the ranks of labor. We cast no reflection upon the honesty and sincerity of purpose of the rank and file of the order of the K. of L. For years the officers of this organization have sought to establish amicable relations with that order, even at a period when certain of its leaders were seeking the very life of the trade unions. Whatever friction may have arisen in the past between the two organizations, the cause must be looked for in other directions than in that of the federation. Much of the trouble has been occasioned by the organization of national and international trade districts of the K. of L. in crafts where national and international trade unions already existed. Not only has the creation of this dual authority been productive of evil results, but too often the national trade district has been made the dumping ground for men who have been branded as unfair by the trade unions.

With the original educational purpose of the K. of L. as vested in mixed assemblies, the trade unionists of America were and are in sympathy. The evidence of this fact is to be found in the large number of trade unionists who worked zealously for the building up of the order in its early period of growth, but who were forced to leave that organization when ambitious and unscrupulous persons sought to trench upon the rightful prerogatives of the trade unions and subordinate the legitimate labor movement to the aggrandizement of personal ambition.

Since the organized protest made by the trade unions in the spring of 1886 against the continuous onslaught upon the autonomy of the trade organization, conferences have been held between the general officers of the A.F. of L. and the K. of L. For lack of satisfactory results from these conferences and apparent indisposition of the general officers of the latter organization to recognize the rightful authority of the trade unions in trade affairs, we feel that the A.F. of L. should plant itself squarely upon the position assumed by the executive council at the conference, which was held at Philadelphia, Oct. 14, 1889. This position is as follows:

1st. That the Knights of Labor shall discountenance and revoke the charters of all trade assemblies or districts within their order.

2d. That in turn the American Federation of Labor and affiliated trade unions will urge their members and encourage the working people to become members of mixed assemblies of the K. of L.

The time has arrived when the trade unions should claim their own. The trend of organization shows that the wage earners of America are weary of having their interests adjusted by the measure of the huckster or yardstick of the merchant.

The success of the short hour cause is of too vast import to be imperilled by policies of masterly inactivity or acrobatic poising.

The march toward the eight-hour goal must not be halted at the behest of the middleman. Professions of harmony and platitudes of peace are poor recompenses for the attempted weakening of the trade union column.

We therefore assert the natural right of the trade unions to occupy the trade union territory.

When this right is conceded discord will end and organized labor be more closely united.

(Signed)   Christopher Evans,[1]
John T. Elliott,
Robert Y. Ogg,
Charles Kassel,[2]
Frank K. Foster.

This report was listened to with the closest attention, and at the termination of its reading by Delegate Foster the applause was deafening.

The report was adopted by a rising unanimous vote.

. . .

Boston Globe, Dec. 15, 1889.

1. Christopher EVANS, AFL secretary from 1889 to 1894, was secretary of the National Federation of Miners and Mine Laborers from 1885 to 1888.

2. Charles Kassel, a cigarmaker, represented the St. Louis Central Trades and Labor Union.

An Interview in the *New York Sun*

[December 30, 1889]

KNOW WHAT THEY WANT.

The headquarters of the American Federation of Labor is visited daily by representatives of labor organizations seeking alliances with this new and powerful combination of workingmen. The offices are in one of the oldest buildings in Clinton place. Its front doors are dilapidated and broken, and its floors not over clean. An employment agency for women, a tailor shop, and a magic hair restorer share the building with the American Federation of Labor. The President, Sam

Gompers, is assisted daily by a secretary who has been associated with him for many years. This secretary is a Scotchman,[1] and is popular with workingmen because he never agrees entirely in his views with anybody. President Gompers said yesterday that he believed that they would need to increase their clerical force after Jan. 1.

"We'll need probably another man when the money begins to come in from the different organizations paying the 2 cents per member assessment determined upon by our recent Convention in Boston to maintain any of our members whom it may be necessary to order out on strike after May 1 to get the eight-hour work day into working shape," Mr. Gompers explained. "So far I have not heard a discordant note as to the want of wisdom in the organization's demand. For years I have been collecting the sentiments and opinions of public men, speakers, politicians, and preachers, and they all seem to agree upon the wisdom of our demand. Our Executive Council have done all that was possible to sound public opinion, and so far all the objections they have discovered have been the result of past prejudices and a desire not to change the existing condition of things. I am of the opinion, and so is every one of the Executive Council, that in a new country like the United States we will meet with little opposition in bringing about a shorter work day. I am of the opinion that it is only the workingmen who now work long hours and who are shaky as to the success of any effort to shorten the work day that oppose us. Why, I have found employers of thousands of men that are anxious to help forward any shortening of the hours of labor if we only make it general. One employer writes:

" 'I am willing to work only six hours a day, and would gladly do so, were it not for the fact of the great competition in our trade at certain seasons of the year. In very few businesses is it possible to work continously the whole year round. You just go ahead and get your eight-hour work day into ship shape, and everybody will think better of the workingmen in the long run.' ["]

"There is a belief that the action of the Convention on the eight-hour question was a back down from its former position" was said.

"I cannot see that any one can consistently say that," Mr. Gompers replied. "The Convention in 1888, at St. Louis, decided to agitate for an eight-hour work day. They laid down rules for agitation purposes only. Now that it is approaching near to the culmination of the agitation, and the day set for the realization of our hopes, we have set about making arrangements as to what shall be done toward making a complete success of all our work. It was settled by the Convention that the Executive Council shall pick out the trades that shall insist upon an eight-hour work day upon May 1. It is not to be supposed that with our present experience we would serve notice upon the whole country through the press that we wanted an eight-hour work day, and when May 1 came let all the workingmen leave their employment pell mell. It would result in anarchy. We have been taught by experience that it is much better to begin meekly. We are a meek and humble folk any way, and it ill becomes us to assume grand airs. It seems that when we do confusion follows us. It is proposed that we start out with one business, and have that well worked into the eight-hour work day, and then start with another. It has been said that it was more than likely that the Executive Committee would pitch upon the building trades to begin with. I do not know for sure what the Executive Council will do. In some cities now men in the building line work only 8 hours, and some 9 hours, and, generally, of all workingmen they have the shortest hours. It is expected now to kind of level them up. Perhaps the Executive Council may settle upon the workingmen in the building line. There are many unions of them in the Federation; they have little effect upon general trade, and would be a great card, if successful, to the Federation. Whatever we do the public will be certain to suffer little."

"What amount of opposition will other unions make?" was asked.

"There we are all at sea. It depends largely, I think, upon the attention the public gives us in the next few months. We're bound to experience the hostility of certain kinds of labor organizations. I do not know but that this may be a help to us. It surely will should the employers meet our demand in anything like the way I hope they will from their letters and talk. If there is resistance, it may depend upon our leaders as to what hostility is engendered. It is too much to expect that a change of so much real importance to the welfare of mankind should not be opposed."

"It has been said that you have the most radical of workingmen among your members."

"Well, most of the workingmen in unions have some good reason for belonging to them, else they would not go on year after year paying in their money. The officers of the Federation do not know anything as to their individual opinions, whether or not it is to turn Mr. Harrison[2] out of the White House and put Mr. Sergius E. Schevitsh[3] in as Dispenser of Supplies. We shall simply insist upon their contract with us that they shall work for the eight-hour workday. We know what we want, and we hope to get it.

["]Unluckily in past movements, good or bad, to help the workingmen, this knowledge was lacking."

New York Sun, Dec. 30, 1889.

1. Probably Hugh McGregor.
2. Benjamin Harrison (1833-1901) was president of the United States from 1889 to 1893.
3. Sergius E. SHEVITCH was editor of the *New Yorker Volkszeitung* and an important figure in the SLP in New York City.

A Resolution of the AFL in Favor of the Eight-Hour Day

New York, ~~Jan. 14, 1890~~

"Whereas. The wonderful and phenomenal discovery of steam and electricity and the application of these forces to the wealth producing methods of our country, has rendered the time pregnant with the thought and desire that the toil of the masses of our people should be lighter and less burdensome.

Therefore be it

Resolved That it is the sense of the Senate of the United States Congress that the day should be divided into eight hours for work, eight hours for rest, and eight hours for recreation; and we further declare our belief that a general reduction of the working hours to eight per day, would be conducive to the public weal and contribute to the industrial, commercial, intellectual, social and moral advancement of the people."[1]

T and HD, RG 46, Records of the United States Senate, DNA.

1. On Jan. 15, 1890, Henry W. Blair introduced the AFL's petition in the U.S. Senate, which referred it to its Committee on Education and Labor.

A Circular

New York, Jan. 22, 1890.

MASS MEETINGS

To the Working People of America—
Greeting:

> Slaves cannot breathe in this land—yet that boast
> Is but a mockery; when from coast to coast,
> Though fettered slaves be none, her floor and soil
> Groan underneath a weight of slavish toil,

For the poor many, measured out by rules
Fetched with cupidity from heartless schools,
That to an idol, falsely called "The Wealth
Of Nations," sacrifice a people's health,
Body, and mind, and soul; a thirst so keen
Is ever urging on the vast machine
Of sleepless labor, 'mid whose dizzy wheels
The power least prized is that which thinks and feels.

—Wordsworth.

On the 14th of December, 1888, the freely elected representatives of the laboring people of America, in convention assembled in the city of St. Louis, amid enthusiastic applause, decided to commence an agitation for the inauguration for the eight hour workday on the first of May, 1890. The body above referred to, the American Federation of Labor, resolved then and there that their Executive Council should arrange a grand series of simultaneous mass meetings in all parts of the country, the final ones preparatory to the day of action, to be held on Washington's birthday, February 22, 1890.

Therefore the Executive Council of the American Federation of Labor, in pursuance of the solemn duties devolving upon it, now calls upon you to assemble in the most convenient places, adjacent to your homes, on the natal day of the revered founder of this Republic, and give expression to your firm determination to emulate his great deed and found the eight hour workday—"Eight hours for work, eight hours for rest, eight hours for what we will."

And now having performed our immediate duty by notifying you of the date of the next in the series of simultaneous mass meetings ordered by the St. Louis Convention you will pardon a brief review of some important events which have happened since, and have probably been largely influenced by the memorable vote of your representatives on the fourteenth of December, 1888. On the occasion of the hundredth anniversary of the storming of the Bastille a convention of workingmen from all over the world was held in Paris; although that convention was divided in language and political opinion, the influence of the vote of the St. Louis Convention produced such general enthusiasm that all factions became a unit in favor of an agitation for the establishment of the eight hour workday, and America took her rightful rank among the nations. Mark the results! One month had not passed away when one of the most gigantic struggles in the history of our times occurred in London.[1] No sooner had the struggle begun when money in its support poured in like water through a broken dam. Noble Australia telegraphed thousands upon thousands of dollars. In a few weeks upward of a quarter of a million of dollars was given to sustain the soldiers of the grand army of industry who were bravely battling for their rights. John Burns,[2] one of the several devoted chiefs in that great struggle, says: "Within a few months nearly two hundred different trades have gained a considerable reduction in the hours of labor and an advance of ten per cent. in wages. More than 100,000 new members have been enrolled in unions." It is worthy of notice also that in that struggle "there were 5,000 pickets maintained day and night over [lines] thirty or forty miles in extent, by land and water; and the discipline and vigilance of the cordon were as exact as with the Prussians at the siege of Paris." There were one or two important features of that strike which it were well to note:—the police and soldiers were treated by the strikers like brothers; they were heartily cheered on several occasions. Some employers, too, when the strike fund [was] depleted, actually paid their laborers the rate of strike pay. In short a decisive victory in the face of seemingly overwhelming odds has been achieved across the Atlantic, and the fame of "the docker's tanner," like the sound of the musket shot at Lexington, has rolled around the world.

In our own land, too, the agitation during the past year has not been unproductive of results. On every hand there is evidence of encouragement and hope for the success of our movement. Many scores of letters have been received by your Executive Council from all sorts and conditions of men—clerical, judicial, political, professional and commercial—strongly endorsing your claims for more leisure, for a greater share of the products of your toil, and warmly sympathizing with your efforts to achieve a higher degree of civilization. Manufacturers and others who but a year ago were bitter opponents of the eight hour workday, have listened to our arguments, have read the series of pamphlets issued by your Executive Council, and have been converted to our cause. Only yesterday in the Senate and House of Representatives of the United States your claim was endorsed by unanimous consent.

Workers of America! The time is approaching when your courage, your manhood, and the trades unions who have so laboriously evolved may be put to the test. Let it not be said that we have failed in our duty and are unworthy of our sires. Turn out en masse on February 22, and make your demonstrations worthy the memory of him whose birthday we propose to honor by labor's declaration.

Yours fraternally, Samuel Gompers,
President American Federation of Labor.

Signal (Indianapolis), Jan. 31, 1890.

1. The Tea Operatives' and General Labourers' Association initiated the London dock strike on Aug. 14, 1889. Other major riverside unions supported the strike that at its height involved some 100,000 workers. Workers returned to work in mid-September and a formal settlement on Nov. 4 included increases in wages and overtime pay, fixed overtime hours, abandonment of the subcontracting system, and a minimum pay equivalent to four hours of work for workers discharged before the end of the day.

2. John Elliott BURNS, an engineer, was a leader of the 1889 London dockers' strike and a Member of Parliament from 1892 to 1918.

To John Plunkett

Feb 8th [1890]

Mr. James E. Plunkett.[1]
Secretary Granite Polishers Union #3.723. AF of L.[2]
Barre, Vt.

Dear Sir & Bro: —

I am in receipt of a letter and telegram from Bro. J. B. Dyer in which he informs me that it is your determined purpose to strike for a reduction in the hours of your labor and an increase of pay. That you gave notice to your employers that this is to take effect on the first of this month & That your employers are antagenizing and propose to fight you upon it.

It seems to me that you are about to make the same mistake that almost all new Unions generally do, namely, to strike when you are illy prepared for one.

The ills that have crept upon you for years, that you have allowed the employers to exert their power, and probably injustice over you for years without attempting to resist by organizing, you now want to wipe out with one fell swoop. Mark, I do not attempt to say that you are not justified, But there [is] a wide difference between justification and the power to abolish wrong and injustice. It is very easy to go into a strike, it is not quite so easy to come out victorious and I urgently call upon you to mark the chances for victory before you decide upon a strike and then repent of your course at leisure.

The history of labor is littered with the skeletons of organizations done to death because of hasty strikes gone into, for the best of reasons but unprepared. When new Unions are formed and the men go on strike and loose, it is not only that they loose what conditions they have, they loose their organization. The employers then take greater advantage of the men and for years it is almost impossible for them to reorganize. I am not trying to paint a gloomy picture for you. but it is the result of the experience of a life time, which I want you to profit by and think of.

Then again the American Federation of Labor decided that the contest for a reduction of the hours of labor (if contest there must be) shall take place May 1st 1890. Don't you see that you may frustrate the purposes of the whole movement and make it a failure?

Suppose the employers generally look upon your proposed strike as the time to concentrate their efforts and defeat you? Can't you see that they will say that the workmen are defeated in the first contest, that we can't win, that such a defeat will encourage every other employer and correspondingly discourage all other workmen who desire to make a stand for the Eight Hour workday May 1st.

If you have the interest of your craft as well as of all the working people at heart you will not enter this contest at this time, but bide your time, organize, prepare yourselves to make your demands May 1st 1890 and if then they are not conceeded *strike* for then and strike hard and determined to win.

I have written thus fully upon this question because the danger your action may bring to our movement cannot be calculated. Some of the greatest revolutions have had their beginnings in the remotest and most insignificant quarters and I do not want you to underestimate the importance of your actions.[3]

Sincerely trusting that wise counsel and deliberate action will prevail and that success will crown our joint efforts to improve the condition of our fellow-toilers. I am

Yours Fraternally   Saml Gompers.
Pres't. A.F. of L.

ALpS, reel 3, vol. 4, pp. 446-49, SG Letterbooks, DLC.

1. John E. Plunkett.
2. Granite Polishers' Union 3723 was directly affiliated with the AFL.
3. The polishers presented a new price list to the manufacturers on Feb. 1; it called for a 15 percent wage increase, a nine-hour day, and an eight-hour workday on Saturday. The union struck when the granite companies began discharging some of their men. The parties settled the dispute before the end of the month.

A Translation of a News Account of a Meeting of the AFL Executive Council

[February 9, 1890]

PREPARATIONS FOR THE FIGHT.

The Executive Council of the American Federation of Labor held its regular monthly meeting behind closed doors yesterday at No. 21

Clinton Place. All members were present. A number of official communications were read; the responses to the last circular of the Executive Council concerning the preparations for the introduction of the eight-hour day were generally favorable. Many trade unions declared themselves willing to take responsibility for putting their demand through, whether they are designated by the Council to do so or not.

A discussion about the Federation's finances revealed that there would be sufficient funds available on May 1, in case of a strike, to support successfully the unions designated by the Executive Council.

Then a more lengthy discussion took place on the question of which industries should be ordered to strike in an emergency and in which parts of the country a strike would be most successful. No definitive decision was reached; however, it appears that the iron industry and Pittsburg are to be chosen. Vice-President Martin stated in this regard he could affirm with considerable certainty that the branches he represents would emerge victorious from the struggle. President Gompers, on the other hand, seems to think that the building trades ought to lead off and that New York should be chosen as the center for the campaign. However, a final decision on the question was postponed until the next monthly session.

. . .

New Yorker Volkszeitung, Feb. 9, 1890. Translated from the German by Patrick McGrath.

To John Elliott

March 1st 1890.

Mr. John T. Elliott
Sec. Brotherhood of Painters & Decoraters.
1314 N. Fulton Ave. Baltimore, Md.
Dear Friend:—

Your favor, report and cheque came duly to hand.

Mr. Evans informs me that you report as paying $80.00 as strike assessment, and $10.50 for per capita tax making a total of $90.50 whereas the cheque calls for $90.00.

He also informs me that the strike assessment upon your membership would be $84.00 and he holds back the issuance of the receipt

March 1890

for your respective payments until we hear from you in reference to the matter.

I think it superfluous to assure you that I appreciate the enormous work and trouble you have in fighting for your organization and collecting the small stipends for the conduct of the affairs of the organization which protects and advances their interests, but it is the experience of all organizations of labor.

I could have wished that the Brotherhood might have started with a basis of higher dues, for it is the result of my observation that an organization which starts upon a basis of low dues always finds it much more difficult to increase its dues than even an organization that started upon a higher basis.

Men who pay 25 cents a month as a rule in their union make more objection to a raise of 5 cents a month in their dues than organizations which pay 20 cents per week when a raise of 5 cents per week is proposed, and then most people look upon the immediate benefits that union bring them and you know as well as I can tell you that a union can only be of just so much benefit in proportion as the members pay fair dues into it, and when men find that the union does really stand them in good stead and pays them a favorable return they are not so antagonistic when the question presented to them will show that the payment of a few cents more will bring them a still larger return.

However we must do the best we can and hope for good results.

I think I answered your several letters but if there is anything I have omitted I wish you would just repeat the questions and I assure you of their early and earnest attention.

With best wishes I am,

Your True Friend.   Saml Gompers
President.   American Federation of Labor.

TLpS, reel 3, vol. 4, pp. 480-81, SG Letterbooks, DLC.

To the Editor of the *New York Sun*[1]

March 11th 1890.

To the [Editor] of the Sun.
N.Y. City.
Dear Sir:—

In your yesterday's (Monday) issue was published an article by Matthew Marshall[2] upon the Eight Hour question in which while professing so great a regard for the movement to reduce the hours of labor, there is exhibited so remarkable a lack of information and inaccuracy of statement that I am forced to ask you to kindly publish the following answer.

I think the whole basis of Mr. Marshall's errors may be traced to his statement that "Since the product of eight hours labor, everything else being equal, cannot be so great as the product of ten hours there will be one fifth less product of labor to be distributed among consumers, and therefore the same amount of wages will buy one fifth less of everything which the laborer needs than it did before."

I desire to have Mr. Marshall just eliminate from that sentence the four words "everything else being equal" and allow the present to speak of the results of the past, and the future the results of any movement to reduce the hours of labor, and the answer to Mr. Marshall is, I think, complete.

To my mind it seems beyond comprehension how the hours of labor of the toiling masses of the whole country can be reduced from ten to eight hours per day and yet "everything else remain equal." The millions of hours taken from manual labor and given to the toilers for opportunities of leisure and thought would of necessity produce results in the methods of wealth producing never dreamed of even by the inventive geniuses of our own era.

If Mr. Marshall will but compare the latter portion of his article with the first part, he will find how self-contradictory it is.

He speaks of the mechanic twenty years ago having gone into the factory so early in the morning and leaving it so late, and that now the change has come to a lesser number of hours per day. Would Mr. Marshall have the world believe that the mechanic whose hours of labor have been reduced is worse paid, poorer fed, clothed or housed than the mechanic he had in mind. Yet if the reduction in the hours of labor meant so great a sacrifice on the part of the toiler, it certainly would have had the same effect on the mechanic whose hours of labor were reduced from twelve to ten. The truth of the matter is that when the hours of labor are reduced it makes greater consumers of not only those who were previously unemployed, but makes greater consumers of those who have had permanent or regular employment, and thus each in turn giving an impetus to production, it could receive in no other way.

The general belief has been that when the demand for a certain article has become greater, that then the price for the same has become higher, when as a matter of fact this does only apply to such articles that do not depend so much upon human ingenuity and [brawn?] for their production, but in the production of such articles the result of men's minds and muscle the reverse is the truth.

This is demonstrable on every hand that as the demand for articles has increased the methods of production have become better, and the articles produced are sold cheaper to the consumer.

Mr. Marshall has great concern for the unskilled laborers and finds so much to be afraid of on that score. Let me call his attention to the fact that the street car drivers and conductors who frequently worked 14, 16, and 18 hours a day for the sum of $1.20 to $1.60 secured a reduction of the hours of their labor to 12 per day with wages at $2.00 and that though their organization[3] is not as strong as I would wish, yet their movement has secured that benefit to them to this day. The same may be said of the Hod Carriers, of the day laborers, and many other unskilled workmen, or I might refer Mr. Marshall to the 100,000 [dockside?] laborers of London, the Coal Miners of Belgium, and many other instances too numerous to mention, showing that there is yet that spark of human nature which makes the whole world akin, and which when called into play will make the unemployed laborer stand side by side with his employed brother, in the struggle to raise the one from the sloughs of poverty and despair, and the other to a higher plane of civilization.

Mr. Marshall says that he has read all the literature issued by the American Federation of Labor upon the subject of the Eight Hour movement, and I am free to express my surprise that he has not disabused his mind of his "economical and arithmetical fallacies."

It is very likely he has not given them the attention they deserve, and I specially invite his attention to re-read the first one published by the Federation upon that question and entitled "The Eight Hour Primer," as well as some other literature upon the subject and which I shall be pleased to furnish him.

Respectfully Yours.   Saml Gompers
President. American Federation of Labor.

TLpS, reel 3, vol. 4, pp. 502-5, SG Letterbooks, DLC.

1. Published Mar. 13, 1890.

2. Thomas Hitchcock, a New York City lawyer, was associate editor of the *New York Sun* and wrote weekly financial articles under the name Matthew Marshall.

3. Probably a reference to division 1 of KOL National District Assembly 226.

To Adam Menche[1]

March 14th 1890.

Mr. Adam Menche
Genl. Organizer A.F. of L.
1427 South 11th St. Denver, Col.
Dear Sir and Brother:—

Your favor of the 9th inst. to hand and contents noted.

I am pleased to note the various phases of the movement you report.

If you can secure the organizing of the various workmen in the mines and quarries it would be one of the greatest advantages for our movement.

By the way the Drillers and Quarrymen seem to have taken quite a stand for organizing all over the country. Within the past three months we have issued about 8 or 10 charters to drillers & quarrymen and in the near future hope to organize them into a National Union.[2]

Denver would be an important point for such a body.

I think that you possess advantages for organizing our fellow-workers in Colorado over our friends Buchanan[3] or Haskell.[4] Both these worthy men were known to have theories which the people neither appreciated nor understood, and as a consequence created a prejudice, which to insure success in organizing, would have to be overcome first.

Where you although possibly believing in the same end, having the same aspirations, are known as Mr. Adam Menche an earnest, intelligent, and indefatigable worker in the cause of organization and labor reform.

You have no antagonism, or antipathies, or prejudices to overcome in the first instance. I think you will catch my idea more fully now, when I remarked above that you possess advantages over them to organize our fellow-workmen.

I think the course decided upon by your trades Assembly[5] empowering the committee to hold mass-meetings a wise course, and one that should be considered so by all.

The reports to this office indicate that there were more than 500 Mass-Meetings held throughout the country on Feb. 22nd. In New York it was held on the 24th owing to every large hall having been engaged for Washington's Birthday.

In Boston on the 22nd. Tremont Temple was crowded and an overflow. It was the grandest labor demonstration ever held in that city, and all over the country reports of similar character have been received. By the clippings Mr. Vaughan sent me I see that your meeting was a decided success. In all likelihood Mr. Mc-Neil may be sent on the road for about a month just previous to May 1st.

Sincerely hoping that that date may prove a red-letter one in the interest on our great movement I am,

Fraternally Yours   Saml Gompers
President.   American Federation of Labor.

TLpS, reel 3, vol. 4, pp. 512-14, SG Letterbooks, DLC.

1. Adam MENCHE, a cigarmaker, was active in the Denver Trade and Labor Assembly.

2. The QUARRYMEN's National Union of the United States of America.

3. Joseph Ray BUCHANAN was a Denver labor editor and labor organizer in the 1880s and a leader of the People's party during the 1890s.

4. Burnette G. HASKELL, a San Francisco labor leader and founder of the International Workingmen's Association or Red International in 1881, became a leading advocate of the utopian socialist ideas of Edward Bellamy and Laurence Gronland.

5. The Denver Trades and Labor Assembly was founded in 1882.

To Ida Van· Etten

March 19th 1890.

Miss Ida M. Van-Etten
Dear Madame:—

I regret that a continued illness prevents my attendance at the Mass-Meeting to be held at Cooper Institute to-night.

Permit me to assure you that I am in entire sympathy with the purposes of the meeting. It is beyond dispute that to have proper factory inspection a larger number of factory inspectors should be appointed, and that among that number should be some women who alone would be competent to discover such evils as prevail in factories, and which are entirely sealed to the investigations of men.

Some difference of opinion has arisen as to the proper number of women factory inspectors. I am prepared to admit that the largest number obtainable should be demanded, but I am also aware that it requires great efforts to secure a little, hence I believe that a demand for an increase in the number to eight should be insisted upon and expected in the hope that the good results of our agitation will convince our legislators that an increase in the number would be both practical, desirable, and advantageous to all concerned.

In principle no doubt that appointment of the inspectors should rest with the chief of such a department, but the present incumbent[1] who rests his claim of efficiency on the ground that the unfair employers of labor have not objected to his administration of the law is one of the evidences to my mind why he should not have the power of appointing factory inspectors.

There is [a?] provision in the bill for which the meeting was called to enforce the prohibition of women as well as child labor in factories and work shops for more than sixty hours a week.

This proposition meets with the hearty sympathy of all the well wishers of our race, and even from the pretenders to be such.

The tendency of legislation all over the world has been in this direction in the monarchical countries of Europe, and in Germany the Emperor is having the question discussed at this time by his order.[2]

In our state such men as Colonel Ingersoll,[3] David Dudley Field,[4] not only advocate but declare it entirely within the dominion and jurisdiction of constitutional legislation, but the factory inspector James Connolly declares the whole subject matter to be unconstitutional and certainly against such a judgment do we not only protest but denounce. Never in the history of our country has an advocate or sympathizer with a project subject to legislative action questioned the constitutionality of a proposition. It is well known that constitutional inhibits are generally called in question by those who are opposed to the merits of a measure, hence it must fall to the lot of our factory inspector to be known as the enemy of the women and children whose lives are mulcted by the greedy and avaricious corporations and monopolies.

Sincerely wishing the meeting to be an entirely successful one and that the remedial legislation so absolutely necessary be passed[5] I am
Earnestly and Hopefully Yours   Saml Gompers
President. American Federation of Labor.

TLpS, reel 3, vol. 4, pp. 521-23, SG Letterbooks, DLC.

1. James Connolly, New York state's first factory inspector, served from 1886 to 1895. A New York City painter, he was president of the New York State Workingmen's Assembly in the 1870s and active in the KOL in the 1880s.

2. In February 1890 German Emperor William II called for an international conference to standardize protective legislation for women and children so that no country would be at a competitive disadvantage for having adopted such measures. Delegates from thirteen European countries met Mar. 15-29 in Berlin and adopted a series of recommendations including the limiting of the hours of work for women and the outlawing of factory work for children under the age of twelve. The conference's decisions were not binding, however, and had little practical impact.

3. Robert Ingersoll.

4. David Dudley Field was a prominent New York legal reformer.

5. Beginning in 1888 the New York Working Women's Society and a number of individual women campaigned to amend the state factory inspection law. The state factory inspector, James Connolly, strongly opposed a proposal before the New York state legislature that the women inspectors be independent of the state factory inspector's office. After the bill's defeat, SG advised Ida Van Etten of the Working

Women's Society to accept a compromise. The legislature passed a law in 1890 authorizing the appointment of not more than eight women deputy inspectors by the state factory inspector to serve under his authority on the same footing as the male deputies.

To P. J. McGuire

New York March 20th 1890.

Mr. P. J. Mc-Guire
Sec. U.B.C. & J. of A.
124 North 9th St. Phila, Pa.
Dear Sir and Brother:—

Pursuant to instructions from the Boston Convention of the American Federation of Labor to the Executive Council to select a trade to make a demand for the Eight Hour workday May 1st. 1890, I beg leave to inform you that at the meeting of the Executive Council of the A.F. of L. held in the City of New York March 17th 1890 the following resolutions were adopted upon this question.

Resolved That we hereby select the United Brotherhood of Carpenters & Joiners of America to make the movement for eight hours as a day's work on May 1st. 1890, and will sustain them in such localities as the Executive Board of said organization may select to make the movement, and next after that we will sustain the United Mine Workers of America in making a movement to establish the Eight Hour workday on such date as the Executive Officers may select as most advantageous to the interests of their trade, then we will next select and sustain each and every trade in continuous succession as rapidly as they can perfect their organizations, and prepare to make the demand. Permit me dear sir, on behalf of the American Federation of Labor to congratulate your grand and noble Brotherhood upon the proud distinction imparted, conveyed and implied in being chosen as the best disciplined, prepared and determined to lead the movement for a reduction in the hours of labor to eight per day.

There is no doubt in my mind that few of the historians of the great events in the history of the development of our people will accord a higher place of honor and distinction than to the United Brotherhood of Carpenters & Joiners of America.

Sincerely hoping and expecting that success may crown our efforts and that hereafter the wage-workers may be placed upon the same advantageous ground of the Eight Hour workday, so that all may be better prepared for the great struggles yet in store to ameliorate the

condition, and finally secure the emancipation of the working classes
I am,

Fraternally Yours   Saml Gompers
President.   American Federation of Labor.

TLpS, reel 3, vol. 4, pp. 528-29, SG Letterbooks, DLC.

A Translation of a Circular

[March 22, 1890]

Workers of America:

The resolute stance of the American Federation of Labor at the
last convention in St. Louis, proclaiming the eight-hour day, has echoed
throughout the entire civilized world. This step has done away with
the intellectual and moral stagnation that arose through the misman-
agement and resulting collapse of a once powerful organization and
has planted new hopes in the hearts of the pioneers of progress for
a better future. The resolutions made in St. Louis have circulated
throughout the entire country and they resound like a signal to the
fighting men of labor.

Fifteen months have already gone by since that memorable proc-
lamation in St. Louis, and the day of a possible battle is near. Thanks
to the sacrifices of half a million members and the understanding of
the educated, scholars, journalists, and others, and thanks to the
additional support of countless thousands who recognize the great
importance of the American Federation of Labor, the agitation begun
there has taken on the form of a movement that will not cease until
the desired goal is reached. This fact was duly recognized at the
Boston convention and from that convention, held in the town hall
of that proud, old city, there went out to the suffering sons of labor
the assurance that the day for the improvement of their situation was
dawning. The Boston convention made the following resolution:

We, therefore, recommend that the Executive Council shall have power to
select such trade or trades from those affiliated with the American Federation
of Labor as shall, in their judgment, be best prepared to achieve success,
and that each union in the Federation be requested to assess their members
10 cents per week for so many weeks as shall be necessary to secure the
short-hour day; payments upon such assessments to commence no later than
March 1, 1890.

In issuing this appeal we are well aware of the fact that a great many employers will agree to the demand without a contest as we have seen in the case of the plasterers' union. On March 3, 1890, the Operative Plasterers' Union marched with music and banners to Cooper Institute in New York and, amid the sounds of the band, 2,200 of the workers took seats in the hall while all the members of the Employing Plasterers' Association sat down on the platform. After a short discussion an agreement was ratified according to which the workers shall work only eight hours daily at a wage of $4 per day. Several similar cases have come to our attention, but we also know that there are employers who will oppose a reduction in work hours. And in order to be doubly sure of success, we must prepare ourselves financially. We must be constantly aware that the greater the funds at our disposal, the smaller the demand that will be made on them.

I call upon you, therefore, in accordance with the resolution made in Boston, to comply with its spirit and to send all pledged or collected monies for this purpose by "Post Money Order" or "Bank Draft" to Secretary Chris. Evans, No. 21 Clinton Place, New York.

By order,   Saml. Gompers,
President.

New Yorker Volkszeitung, Mar. 22, 1890. Translated from the German by Patrick McGrath.

To P. F. Fitzpatrick

March 26th [1890]

Mr. P. F. Fitzpatrick
Pres. Iron Moulders Union of North America
185 Walnut St. Cincinnati, O.
Dear Sir and Brother:—

There is an apparent attempt on the part of certain Knights of Labor to destroy the efficiency of the trade unions not only the general opposition prevailing through the country but it is especially directed against the trade unions and the trade union movement of this city. Everything is done to hamper the progress of the movement.

I would therefore respectfully request you to write a letter to your local unions of this city urging them to send in their credentials to the Central Labor Union of New York so that the trade unions shall have their proper place in the movement.

The formation of local assemblies by the K. of L. with a membership of 7 or 10 and the sending of a full quota of delegates is being carried on with the greatest unction to work out the schemes of the disruption of our movement, hence the above request.

With sincere good wishes to yourself and Brother Weaver[1] for the movement and hoping to hear from you at your earliest convenience I am,

Fraternally Yours   Saml Gompers.
President.   American Federation of Labor.

TLpS, reel 3, vol. 4, pp. 543-44, SG Letterbooks, DLC.

1. John G. WEAVER was assistant secretary of the Iron Molders' Union from 1886 to 1903.

To Josiah Dyer

March 29th [1890]

Mr. Josiah B. Dye[r]
Sec. Granite Cutters Natl Union U.S. of A.
Drawer H. Barre, Vt.
Dear Sir and Brother:—

Your favor came duly to hand with money order for per capita tax, a receipt for which has already been forwarded to you.

I regret to learn that the National Union Committee were not satisfied with my answer to the question contained in your former letter in reference to the assistance to organizations depending upon the action of the Executive Council.[1]

In all probability I may not have written as fully or sufficiently comprehensive so as to be entirely understood; let me add then that at the Boston Convention of the American Federation of Labor the law was passed for the assessment of each organization to the amount of two cents for each member within the national unions affiliated, and the possible assessment for five weeks of two cents per member.

It was also decided that a trade be selected by the Executive Council to lead in the demand for the enforcement of the eight Hour workday May 1st 1890.

It certainly seems to go without saying that the Convention contemplated that all efforts should be concentrated both financially and morally to achieve victory for the trade selected in making the demand for eight hours.

An organization (The United Brotherhood of Carpenters & Joiners of America) has been selected as the one deemed by the Executive Council to be in the best position and is willing to make the demand in accordance with the resolution of the convention, and as implied by my previous letter that the assistance will depend upon the action of the Executive Council.

That decision has been made at least so far as the immediate resources of the Federation are concerned.

You can readily understand that if the organizations affiliated to the Federation each are assessed a small stipend that all cannot be assisted at the same time, and that it will be necessary to use some discretion and that that discretion must be lodged somewhere.

It would possibly be different if there was a vast accumulated fund but with the meagre resources the assistance should be given to one organization at a time so that the efforts of all can be concentrated upon the one, and when victory is achieved to again concentrate the efforts upon another and so on.

I sincerely hope that this explanation will be satisfactory both to you, your national Committee, and your organization, and that you will look at this in the broad view to the best interests of all concerned.

I am aware that the bosses in your trade have perfected an organization[2] and although you may be met with opposition on their side it seems to me that in the end when the working men are fairly organized it is best to meet and decide upon the question of wages and conditions of labor with the organizations of employers instead of the sporadic and gorilla warfare of the unscrupulous and unfair among them.

I sincerely thank you for your kind expressions for my welfare and personal wishes for my health which it affords me pleasure to say I am regaining.

That you are in your usual robust health is my earnest prayer and that success may attend you and the organization in every undertaking is the hope of

Yours Fraternally   Saml Gompers.
President. American Federation of Labor.

TLpS, reel 3, vol. 4, pp. 548-51, SG Letterbooks, DLC.

1. Dyer had apparently proposed that a conference of executive officers of AFL affiliates, rather than the AFL Executive Council, decide how the AFL would assist organizations participating in the eight-hour campaign. Gompers answered that the Executive Council had decided on Feb. 7 that such a conference would be inadvisable because the Boston convention had given the responsibility to the council and that calling such a conference would be regarded as "an exhibition of weakness and or faltering of purpose" (SG to Dyer, Feb. 8, 1890, reel 3, vol. 4, p. 442, SG Letterbooks, DLC).

2. Probably the Granite Manufacturers' Association of Barre, Vt., which was founded in 1889.

To a Mass Meeting of New York Carpenters

April 9th [1890]

To the Officers & Members of the local Unions of New York United
  Brotherhood of Carpenters & Joiners of America. in Mass-Meeting
  assembled.

Dear Sirs and Brothers:—

I learn that you are to hold an important gathering this evening
for the purpose of deciding upon the all important question that
confronts us at this time namely, the Eight Hour movement, and
further, what action your trade will take May 1st?[1]

I desire to call your attention to the fact of the selection of your
trade by the Executive Council of the American Federation of Labor
to lead in the demand for the enforcement of the Eight Hour workday,
and that all other organizations of labor should concentrate their
efforts to help yours to victory.

I need not mention the very grave importance that your decision
may have in determining the movement in this city and possibly in
the entire country.

I refer you to the bold stand of your fellow members in Chicago
and their determination to make no surrender unless eight hours and
a recognition of their union shall have been an accomplished fact.[2]

I am aware that you have obstacles to contend against in the Building
Trades of this city, but you are not without assistance from some
branches and some very important ones at that.

I learn that the Hod Hoisting Engineers affiliated with the American
Federation of Labor are discussing the advisability of demanding the
enforcement of the Eight Hour workday and I have been assured
that should your organization make the demand they without doubt
would also do so.

The Builders Laborers I have also been informed will hold a meeting
on Sunday afternoon and there determine whether they will make
the demand.

The Plasterers you know already have it, and I am firmly of the
opinion that if your organizations are decided to make the demand
you will certainly be successful and secure the co-operation of several
branches in the building trade who now seem luke warm in the matter.

Sincerely hoping that you will deliberate coolly and give this matter
your earnest consideration with the best results to the trade and the
labor movement in general I have the honor to subscribe myself,

Yours Fraternally   Saml Gompers,
President. American Federation of Labor.

TLpS, reel 3, vol. 4, pp. 597-98, SG Letterbooks, DLC.

1. At a joint meeting of New York City carpenters' unions on Apr. 9, representatives of the United Brotherhood of Carpenters and Joiners of America, the Amalgamated Society of Carpenters and Joiners, and the Progressive Association of Carpenters and Joiners voted to demand the eight-hour day at a wage of $3.50 per day on May 1. A fourth carpenters' union, the United Order of American Carpenters and Joiners, did not support the action.

2. The strike, initiated by the United Carpenters' Council of Chicago on Apr. 7, involved an estimated 5,000 to 6,000 carpenters. It was supported by KOL District Assembly 57. The unions and employers reached a settlement on May 5 that included an eight-hour workday and a wage increase.

To Thomas Talbot[1]

April 15th [1890]

Mr. T. N. Talbot
G.M.M. Natl. Association of Machinists.[2]
16 Whitehall St. Atlanta, Ga.
Dear Sir and Brother: —

In compliance with former letters I again call your attention to what I regard as an essential feature to the success of your organization namely, to eliminate certain objectionable features from the constitution in order to cultivate fraternal relations with the machinists of the entire country.

Hitherto I have mentioned the fact that a number of machinists have given expression to sentiments that were in antagonism to attaching themselves to organizations that discriminate against any wage-workers of the trade.

They say that our employers care very little what nationality or color or previous conditions of life the wage-workers has been or is in so long as he will consent to work cheap.

You are aware that I have used whatever influence I am possessed of to prevent the organization of another national union of machinists believing that the best interests can be served when one organization of a trade has absolute control of all trade matters and that it should have entire jurisdiction of these matters.

I have been unable to induce this union who were the projectors of the movement I refer to to join your National union unless the changes are made as were indicated in my [last] letters to you one of which is here repeated. I also believe that were your organization to affiliate itself with the American Federation of Labor it would not only be performing what would be proper but advance the interests of the machinists of the country, [and] would be performing its duty towards ameliorating the condition of the wage-workers who are engaged in the contest for justice and right.[3]

With this I ship to your address a few documents together with a copy of the constitution of the American Federation of Labor and a blank application for a certificate of affiliation.

Sincerely hoping that your approaching convention may be an entire success and trusting that favorable action will be taken towards the ends indicated and that I may hear from you often and at your earliest convenience I am,

Fraternally Yours   Saml Gompers
President.   American Federation of Labor.

TLpS, reel 3, vol. 4, pp. 615-16, SG Letterbooks, DLC.

1. Thomas Wilson TALBOT was grand master machinist of the National Association of Machinists (NAOM) from 1889 to 1890.

2. The National Association of MACHINISTS.

3. The 1890 AFL convention disapproved of the exclusion of individuals on the basis of race from membership in the NAOM, an organization not affiliated with the Federation. The convention instructed the AFL Executive Council to call a conference to form a new national organization of machinists. SG conferred with NAOM leaders who indicated they could not drop the racial ban immediately but believed the next NAOM convention would comply; he then proceeded to call a machinists' convention and issued a charter to the new International MACHINISTS' Union of America (IMUA) in June 1891. The new organization indicated that it would be ready to amalgamate with the older organization, which had changed its name to the International Association of Machinists (IAM) in 1891, as soon as the IAM abandoned its racial restriction. The IAM dropped the ban from its constitution in 1895, after which the IMUA disbanded. While the IMUA's members could join the IAM on an individual basis, the IAM's racial restriction remained in its ritual and its locals continued to exclude black workers.

An Interview in the *Indianapolis News*

[April 19, 1890]

GOMPERS IN TOWN.

When the C., H. & D. train from Cincinnati drew into the Union Station at 11 o'clock this morning, a man of striking appearance came down the steps and walked briskly to the exit gates. He was below medium height, rather heavily built and with a big head covered with coal black hair worn almost long enough to sweep his coat collar. A fierce black mustache and goatee, and something of a bull dog look of determination about his jaws and mouth, gave him an appearance which made persons meeting him turn to glance at him a second time.

Samuel Gompers, President of the American Federation of Labor, for that is who this gentleman proved to be, was met by officers of the local branches of the Federation at the gate and escorted to the court north of the station. There he found a double line of four or five hundred of the striking carpenters[1] — quiet, sober men — awaiting him and with hat off he passed through. The men cheered heartily and dispersed, and President Gompers was taken to the Spencer House.

He talked unreservedly of the objects of the great order of working men of which he is the head, looking straight into the eyes of the person addressed and speaking with deliberation and force.

"We believe," said President Gompers, "that an eight-hour day will be of advantage to every member of the community, whether he be employe, employer or neither. An eight-hour day would give more and steadier employment to the toilers, and would consequently improve business for the merchant, the farmer, the manufacturer and everyone else, as from the wage-earner must come much of the profits which are made in every kind of business. We believe that employers who oppose the eight-hour day are standing in their own light.

"In order that the conditions surrounding the wage-earner may be bettered, there must be some concessions from every side. We hold that an eight-hour day promises the best results with the smallest amount of injury to anybody. In December, 1888, the American Federation of Labor served notice that it had taken up the eight-hour fight, and that it would make a systematic campaign in favor of it. Since then we have gone on steadily in the direction indicated. We did not want to paralyze industry, and to avoid that result of our agitation, we determined to have one trade inaugurate the eight hour movement throughout the country. The carpenters were the ones chosen for this, and in order to clear ourselves of any charge of unfairness we gave employers notice early in January that on April 15 they must give carpenters an eight-hour day. All other connected trades are as much interested in the outcome as the carpenters are and stand ready to help the cause on by stopping work at any moment that it is thought advisable.

"Some of the employers apparently believe that if they can defeat the carpenters in this strike they will have effectually suppressed the eight-hour movement. They do not comprehend the magnitude of the matter at all. The eight-hour movement has come to stay. A defeat of the demands of the carpenters in Indianapolis, were it possible, would be but a trifle. The sentiment is growing everywhere. Every man of our 360,000 members knows that it is a matter of vital importance to him. We want an eight-hour day made universal among all the trades, and we are never going to waver in this struggle until we get it. The full treasury of the Federation is at the command of the striking men in Indianapolis. There is absolutely no limit to the length of time which the strikers can hold out. The employers should understand this thoroughly. Unless they yield this concession, which is in accord with every sentiment of humanity and justice, and has the approval of the press and public throughout the entire country, their operations must cease indefinitely.

"I want to keep in this work until I have seen the eight-hour day recognized and adopted in every section of the United States, then I will be ready to lay down my arms, for I will have seen accomplished one of the greatest reforms of modern times."

Mr. Gompers will address a mass meeting at Mozart Hall this evening at 8 o'clock, on the "Eight-hour Day." To-morrow morning he will go to Chicago, and from there to Milwaukee, delivering addresses to workingmen at both cities.

Indianapolis News, Apr. 19, 1890.

1. Carpenters in Indianapolis struck on Apr. 14, 1890, to achieve an eight-hour workday and a wage rate of 35¢ an hour. Although contractors at first refused to meet with a committee of carpenters, they settled on Apr. 22 after workers from other building trades threatened to join the strike. The carpenters won eight hours but compromised on wages, agreeing to 30¢ an hour for most workers, with skilled workers commanding more.

A Circular Issued by the Executive Council of the AFL

New York, April 22 [1890]

AN ADDRESS TO WORKINGMEN.

To the wage-workers and sympathizers with progress of America, Greeting:

As you are well aware, in accordance with the resolution of the Boston convention of the American Federation of Labor to select a trade to make the demand for the enforcement of the eight-hour work day, May 1, the Executive Council have decided that the United Brotherhood of Carpenters and Joiners of America shall make the demand.

We had reason to hope from the calm, deliberate, and educational manner in which the agitation for the movement had been conducted, from the timely notice which we gave of our intended movement, so that arrangements and contracts could be made in accordance with the shorter hours' workday, and further, from the decision of the St. Paul convention of the employing builders,[1] that the reduction of the hours of labor to eight per day would have been gracefully conceded without cessation of work or dispute. We are confronted, however, with an evident determination on the part of the employing builders to antagonize by every means in their power the introduction of this most absolutely necessary reduction of the hours of labor. We call upon you to witness the hostile attitudes of the boss builders of Chicago and Indianapolis as evidence of what opposition and treatment we may expect when the general demand is made May 1. No quarter is to be given to labor. We will have to conquer by force of numbers, organization, determination, and discipline, what is not only our just and reasonable right, but even the slightest concession to ameliorate the condition of the toiling masses.

It appears that the wealth, power, and influence of the employing and corporate classes of the country are to be concentrated to defeat the movement, which seeks not only to improve the condition of the employed, but which will find employment, and consequently save from poverty, degradation, and despair the hundreds of thousands of our idle fellow men and women. In view of this situation, it will be necessary for the wage-workers and their friends of America to rally with a greater unanimity of purpose than ever before; to concentrate all their efforts to counteract, and overcome the action of our enemies. Those of our fellow toilers who contemplate taking action to secure concessions in their several trades and callings, we ask to defer action until this great first struggle has been won. If we are successful in this contest—which we shall be, with your aid and co-operation—concessions will be easier attained by all. Should you, on the other hand, diffuse your efforts upon various movements, it will but mean defeat for all; even though an advantage be gained by you, it will be but temporary. It will surely be taken from you, and leave the wage-workers of the whole country in a demoralized and hopeless condition for quite a time.

To meet the combined opposition of the enemies of labor its friends must rally and stand united. They must voluntarily contribute their mites to place at the disposal of the American Federation of Labor a sum of money sufficient to meet all contingencies. Remember that though the funds of the federation and its affiliated unions are large, they may be strained to the uttermost, and though your contributions may be small, when all do the best they can a vast amount will be the result. We desire to be prepared for every emergency which may arise in this movement, and assure you that, should the fund raised not be required to assure victory in the eight-hour movement of the carpenters and joiners, it will be devoted to securing the same beneficent result to the trades and callings selected in their turn to make the demand.

There is a very large number of sympathizers with the labor movement who are not wage workers, and who would gladly financially aid the impending struggle, and an opportunity is here afforded them so to do. In the name of our noble and progressive cause we appeal to all to aid to the extent of your ability and bring improvement and victory to the toilers, honor and advancement to the entire people of our country and the whole civilized world. Send all contributions to Secretary, Chris Evans, 21 Clinton place, New York.

> Fraternally yours, Samuel Gompers,
> President American Federation of Labor.
> Attest: Chris Evans, Secretary.
> William Martin, First Vice President.
> P. J. McGuire, Second Vice President.
> Henry Emrich, Treasurer.

Chicago Inter Ocean, Apr. 23, 1890.

1. The fourth annual convention of the National Association of Builders met in St. Paul, Jan. 27-29, 1890. It decided to leave the question of the reduction of hours to eight per day in the building trades to the discretion of the local builders' organizations.

A News Account of a Mass Meeting in Chicago

[April 23, 1890]

URGING THEM TO STAND FIRM.

More than 3,000 journeymen carpenters and their friends and sympathizers from the other trades gathered at Battery D last evening to listen to the stirring speeches of Samuel Gompers, of the American Federation of Labor, Edward Maher, and C. S. Darrow.[1] The meeting was held under the auspices of the Trades and Labor Assembly of Chicago. It was an orderly, enthusiastic meeting, and showed that the temper of the strikers has not weakened since they quit work. Robert Nelson[2] was chairman, and Judge Altgeld[3] and Henry Lloyd[4] occupied seats on the platform with the speakers. The meeting was called to order by J. W. Le Vine,[5] who introduced Chairman Nelson. After a brief greeting to the assemblage Mr. Nelson in turn introduced the chief speaker of the evening, Samuel Gompers.

It was with more than usual pleasure, Mr. Gompers began, that he addressed this mass-meeting, because in it was assembled the advance guard of the great eight-hour movement which was about to be set in motion by the American Federation of Labor. "We ought to have some justification for our demands," continued the speaker. "We ought to be able to show that our demands rest upon the necessities of the people; that they are but the natural result of a general desire for better conditions, and that we are not actuated by the selfish whim of the moment.

WE CAN SEE IN HISTORY

that the people of all lands in all times have carried on the uncompromising bitter struggle for better conditions, and our present movement is but the continuation of that eternal human struggle for better and higher things. We, the working people, declare to the world, regardless of the calumnies that are heaped upon us, that we are engaged in that holy struggle for better conditions for the human family.

"We want more of the comforts and necessities of life. The inventions of mankind have in less than fifty years increased the power of production more than 100 per cent. We want some of the advantages that have accrued to man by reason of his inventive genius. I am not saying that we are now demanding our just share of this increased production, but we want more of them than we are now getting. While we find this enormous increased production on the one hand, we find on the other a million idle men in America, a million men unable to produce employment. Surely this is an anomalous condition of society, and bears evidence that something in our social fabric is radically wrong. I know that we are frequently charged with being discontented. Now I desire to say very plainly that we are discontented. Discontent is the sign of human advancement. None are so content as the Indians and the Chinese, and should we emulate them? Wherever a people is least discontented there you find civilization the lowest. The only perfectly contented people are the savages.

WHEN I AM ASKED

if this eight-hour movement is my alpha and omega of the labor problem I simply answer, we want more, and when we get it we shall want more, and when we get that we shall want more. I hope the day will never come when the human race will not want more. It will be a time of stagnation, and all progress will have ceased. Ask a hungry man what he wants and he will tell you a meal; that is his conception of more. Ask the laborer who earns $1 a day what he wants and he will answer, a raise of 10 cents a day. Ask the man who gets $2.50 a day, and he will want a 50 cent raise. The man who gets $5 a day will want $6, the man of $5,000 a year wants $6,000, and the millionaire wants all the more millions he can lay his hands on. Man's desire for more is regulated by his economic conditions, and we have no quarrel to-night with the man who wants millions or thousands more, but we do object, and that most emphatically, to these men interfering with our demand for 10 cents more. We want more, and if I read the signs of the times rightly we are going to get more. Those who antagonize this movement are the enemies of their kind, they are those who would stop progress and throw us back into the contentment of the savage.

"The plea is raised by the employers that they cannot afford the eight-hour system; that its enforcement or acceptance by them means industrial and commercial depression, and will divert our trade and commerce to countries where longer hours prevail. Now I believe this question should be argued on a broader basis, but they have chosen the ground, and we are prepared to meet them upon it. Now, if shorter hours means commercial and industrial depression, it naturally follows that longer hours means a better condition of industry and commerce, and if this be true then China and India ought to be at the very

Head of the World's Commerce.

Do not America and England, where shorter hours prevail, sell the products of short hours to countries where long hours prevail? Are not the rich men of countries where shorter hours prevail Croesuses in comparison with those of long-hour countries? The long hours of slavery never produced a millionaire, and even now in America the merchants of the North, West, and East, where shorter hours of labor prevail, compete successfully with the merchants of the South, where longer hours prevail. Men are cheap in lands where the hours of work are long, the men are less intelligent, and there is no machinery."

Mr. Gompers argued the justice and moral nature of the demand for an eight-hour work day from almost every standpoint. Referring to the condition in Chicago, he said: "We find here that the carpenters gave formal notice to their employers that on a certain day they would demand a uniform work day of eight hours, the establishment of a minimum rate of wages, and that all disputes between employer and employe be settled by a board of arbitration. The best writers, thinkers, and economists of the day have agreed that arbitration was the one remedy for these labor differences, and now, when with confidence in their cause, the workingmen come forward and offer to arbitrate their differences, the offer is scorned. Well, let it be so. We know what we want, and we know that the world is with us. We know that our cause is just and right, and we will never compromise on anything less than the eight-hour day. On May 1 the entire resources of the federated trades of America will be thrown open to the carpenters. Meetings of workmen will be held all over Europe to flash across the ocean a greeting and the sympathy of the toiling masses with the striking carpenters. Eight hours is the first step in a long delayed justice, and by standing together, man to man, we will win our battle!"

At the conclusion of Mr. Gompers' address the following resolutions were unanimously adopted:

Whereas, The Chicago Trades and Labor Assembly and the Central Labor Union have decided to hold a demonstration and parade in this city on May 1 in favor of the eight hour movement, therefore be it

Resolved, By the working people in mass-meeting assembled, that we heartily indorse said action and that we pledge ourselves to participate in the parade and do all in our power to make the same a grand success.

Resolved, That this mass-meeting of toilers are in hearty sympathy with the carpenters of this city now on strike, and that we extend to them all aid possible to enable them to successfully carry on their struggle to elevate their craft.

Edward Maher spoke next. He was succeeded by C. S. Darrow. Both spoke briefly, but feelingly and forcibly, and then the meeting was adjourned.

Chicago Inter Ocean, Apr. 23, 1890.

1. Clarence Seward DARROW, a Chicago lawyer active in Democratic reform politics, became corporation counsel to the city in 1890.
2. Possibly Robert Nelson, an iron molder, the district master workman of KOL District Assembly 24 of Chicago in 1887.
3. John Peter ALTGELD was judge of the Superior Court of Cook County (1886-91) and governor of Illinois (1893-97).
4. Henry Demarest LLOYD of Chicago was a noted social activist and reform writer.
5. John W. La Vine.

An Excerpt from an Article in the *New York Sun*

[April 29, 1890]

EIGHT-HOUR PROCLAMATION.

. . .

The peculiar complications of the new labor crusade were not changed yesterday. The local conditions, especially, appear to be much mixed. While the American Federation has set the date for the eight-hour demonstrations at May 1, the men upon whom the actual demonstrating devolves have determined upon May 5, and they say they will positively refrain from taking part in any proceeding until that time. They also say that they are following out plans of their own making, and are in no way under the leadership of the American Federation of Labor [or] any other organization. As was stated in *The Sun* of yesterday, the carpenters and joiners of New York are divided into four bodies, two [of] whom are in the movement for eight hours, while one is neutral, and the other is hostile to [it]. Alfred Ashley, who is the spokesman and walking delegate for the Amalgamated Society of Carpenters and Joiners[1] and Charles E. Ow[e]ns,[2] who holds the same office in the United Brotherhood, were present at a meeting of the Board of Walking Delegates of the various unions yesterday morning. After the meeting Mr. Ashley said to *The Sun* reporter:

"The Amalgamated Order is not associated with the American Federation of Labor, and, while in no way hostile to it, is not acting under any orders from it. You must understand that the carpenters who are in this movement are in it entirely of their own accord. It was their determination to take this step long before anything was said by any other body. We are acting in accord with the United Brotherhood, who are also independent of the American Federation of Labor in this matter. Our act is local, and has no connection with the action [of] bodies in any other city. The Amalgamated Order is an international body, with the [c]hi[ef?] branch in Manchester, England. We have branches in England, Australia, Tasmania, Canada, and throughout the United States. We do not claim 2,000 members here, however, as *The Sun* had it this morning, but really number only 600. In fact, the United Order doesn't number more than [. . .], the United Brotherhood has 3,500, and [the] Progressives don't have more than 150. The United Brotherhood was formed over a year ago, when the large majority of the members of the United Order seceded. The United Order is only a local organization, while the seceders wanted to belong to a national body. We don't believe that many men will be called out in this city, because the bosses are practically agreed in granting our demands. I have spent a large part of the week [in] company with Mr. Owens interviewing the bosses, and all but a few have said that they are willing to call eight hours a working day. Two are opposed to it, and four are holding off. The latter say that they are willing to grant our terms, but that they can't do it now, as they have a number of contracts on hand on which they submitted prices on a nine-hour basis and it would involve loss to change on these. Of course it won't do for us to make an exception [in?] these cases, because that would only open the door for other suggestions of an evasive nature. We made our demands two weeks ago and have been quietly interrogating the bosses ever since. We want to say, too, that we are on very excellent terms with the bosses and no such questions are arising here as in Chicago. We don't stand out for a recognition of our unions, or anything of that sort, because we don't have to. It is only a question [of] hours and we treat with each boss individually. If of half a dozen bosses who hang out one gives in after a strike has been begun we will send the men in his shop right back to work again, without reference to the action of the other bosses. The Amalgamated Order contains the best workmen in the city. Its membership is restricted to the best men under 40 years of age, and the dues are 35 cents a week. We have a full treasury, and can afford to fight, if need be. Besides that, we have the financial support of every branch in the order throughout the world. We sent to England last week for $15,000 to [use?] in case of emergency, but we haven't any idea that we will need it. The United Order is hostile to us simply out of jealousy, but they can't hurt us."

Mr. Owens corroborated Mr. Ashley as to the position of the carpenters. They were desirous of arguing before having recourse to extreme measures, he said, but wherever the bosses refused on May 5 to grant the demands of the men the latter would be called out, and would be kept out until their demands were acceded to. Mr. Owens and Mr. Ashley said that they did not think it would be found necessary to call out more than 300 men on May 5. Clarendon Hall has already been secured as a headquarters for them. Their pay during the strike will be $1 [a] day, so that each striker will suffer a loss of [$].50 for each day that he is out. The carpenters will not participate in any of the parades or meetings of the other trades in favor of eight hours, prior to May 5, but will have a mass meeting of their own in Webster Hall next Saturday night. Mr. Ashley said that while the carpenters have no prejudice against the Socialistic Labor party, they do not propose to affiliate with it in any of its demonstrations.

The officers of [the] Federation deny that the eight-hour demand in this city was not instituted by them. They show by documents that it was suggested [at] a convention of the branches of their order held at St. Louis in the fall of 1888 and sanctioned by the Convention of 1889. The control of [the] present movement was reposed, they said, [in?] the organization which had been selected to start it. President Gompers said that he had [no] idea how many men would actually strike in the United States in the first week of May. He said he had been informed, and firmly believed that no other trades would strike but the carpenters, and he had done everything possible to prevent sympathetic strikes. About 5,000[?] men will make the demand, he thought.

The Socialists got a final and definite promise yesterday of a general permit for their parade on Thursday night.

The employer builders, contractors, and carpenters were silent yesterday, but some of their representatives were not thoroughly convinced that they would submit so quietly to the demand of the carpenters as had been claimed.

"It is all a question," said one of these men, "whether the builders can induce their customers to pay the amounts necessary to make up the difference between eight and nine hours a day. It has been estimated that this would amount on [one] of our large public buildings to about $20,000. The carpenters are really going too far. Nine hours a day for such labor as they do is certainly moderate enough. They go to work at 7 and work until noon. Then they start in at 1 and work until 5. Now they want to wait until 8 before beginning the day. They ought to remember the proverb that it is wise to leave well enough alone."

New York Sun, Apr. 29, 1890.

1. The American District of the Amalgamated Society of CARPENTERS and Joiners.
2. Charles E. OWENS was president of the Grand Executive Council of the United Order of American Carpenters and Joiners.

A News Account of an Address in Louisville

[May 2, 1890]

PRESIDENT GOMPERS' ADDRESS.

. . .

The crowd shouted themselves hoarse and threw their hats in the air when President Gompers arose. His Prince Albert coat was but-

toned up tight, and on the left lapel he wore a rose and the blue
ribbon of the Louisville branch of the International Cigar Makers'
Union.¹ He seemed to feel at home and he talked in a free and easy
manner for nearly one and three quarter hours and the crowd did
not seem to tire of listening to him. He said:

PRESIDENT GOMPERS' SPEECH.

"Fellow-Workingmen, Ladies and Gentlemen: I little contemplated
that I should be required to speak after so eloquent an address delivered by the gentleman whose name stands in the city of Louisville
as the synonym of honesty of purpose. Judge Toney.² (Applause.) This
I ask you not to consider as in any spirit of a mutual admiration society
between the Judge and your humble servant, but as a tribute to one
whom I have learned to be devoted to the cause of the people—to
the cause of progress.

"My friends, we have met here today to celebrate the idea that has
prompted the thousands of working-people of Louisville and New
Albany to parade the streets of y[our city]; that prompts the toilers
of Chicago to turn out by their fifty thousand or hundred thousand
of men; that prompts the vast army of wage-workers in New York to
demonstrate their enthusiasm and appreciation of the importance of
this idea; that prompts the toilers of England, Ireland, Germany,
France, Italy, Spain, and Austria to defy the manifestos of the autocrats
of the world and say that on May the first, 1890, the wage-workers
of the world will lay down their tools in sympathy with the wage-
workers of America, to establish a principle of limitation of hours of
labor to eight hours for sleep (applause), eight hours for work, and
eight hours for what we will. (Applause.)

"It has been charged time and again that were we to have more
hours of leisure we would merely devote it to debauchery, to the
cultivation of vicious habits—in other words, that we would get drunk.
I desire to say this in answer to that charge: As a rule, there are two
classes in society who get drunk. One is that class who has no work
to do in consequence of too much money; the other class, who also
has no work to do, because it can't get any, and gets drunk on its
face. (Laughter.) I maintain that that class in our social life that exhibits
the greatest degree of sobriety is that class who are able, by a fair
number of hours of day's work to earn fair wages—not overworked.
The man who works twelve, fourteen, and sixteen hours a day requires
some artificial stimulant to restore the life ground out of him in the
drudgery of the day. (Applause.)

"You have heard frequently this charge of drunkenness against the laboring class. Now, say there are a hundred men employed in a factory; and when the factory closes down at night ninety-five of these will go home to their wives and families, while the other five will go from the shop, and get drunk at the neighboring saloon. The modern moralist, looking at this factory closed down, will exclaim: 'All of them drunk,' while the fact is that ninety-five out of the hundred have gone to their homes, but are also counted in with the five who have spent their money for liquor. Now, this modern moralist does not contemplate the other class that gets drunk. When they are ready to send him home an electric button is touched, a carriage arrives, and he is driven home; he is undressed and put to bed, and no one has seen him except those who are paid to keep quiet. The modern moralist gets up on the following Sunday morning, casts his eyes to heaven, and prays for the poor drunken devil that he saw yesterday. (Laughter and applause.)

"Now, I don't want to see drunkenness on the part of any one, nor is it my intention to make a temperance speech, but we have outlived the charge made against us that we have devoted our leisure time to drunkenness and debauchery. I ask you where you find your tradesmen and mechanics and other workmen working more hours a day, is it not a fact that there is a larger degree of drunkenness in the community than where they work nine, ten or eight hours? (Applause.) And where the shorter hours have ruled, you find there is a greater degree of sobriety, far surpassing anything that has ever been seen before.

"We ought to be able to discuss this question on a higher ground, and I am pleased to say that the movement in which we are engaged will stimulate us to it. They tell us that the eight-hour movement can not be enforced, for the reason that it must check industrial and commercial progress. I say that the history of this country, in its industrial and commercial relations, shows the reverse. I say that is the plane on which this question ought to be discussed—that is the social question. As long as they make this question an economic one, I am willing to discuss it with them. I would retrace every step I have taken to advance this movement did it mean industrial and commercial stagnation. But it does not mean that. It means greater prosperity; it means a greater degree of progress for the whole people; it means more advancement and intelligence, and a nobler race of people. I would not unsay one word that I have said, except to make it stronger. I would not retrace one step I have taken in my connection with this movement for the eight-hour law. I call on the wage-workers of Louisville and New Albany and the whole world to enforce it. (Applause.)

"They say they can't afford it. Is that true? Let us see for one moment. If a reduction in the hours of labor causes industrial and commercial ruination, it would naturally follow increased hours of labor would increase the prosperity, commercial and industrial. If that were true, England and America ought to be at the tail end, and China at the head of civilization. (Applause.)

"Is it not a fact that we find laborers in England and the United States, where the hours are eight, nine and ten hours a day—do we not find that the employers and laborers are more successful? Don't we find them selling articles cheaper? We do not need to trust the modern moralist to tell us those things. In all industries where the hours of labor are long, there you will find the least development of the power of invention. Where the hours of labor are long, men are cheap, and where men are cheap there is no necessity for invention. How can you expect a man to work ten or twelve or fourteen hours at his calling and then devote any time to the invention of a machine or discovery of a new principle or force? If he be so fortunate as to be able to read a paper he will fall asleep before he has read through the second or third line. (Laughter.)

"Why, when you reduce the hours of labor, say an hour a day, just think what it means. Suppose men who work ten hours a day had the time lessened to nine, or men who work nine hours a day have it reduced to eight hours; what does it mean? It means millions of golden hours and opportunities for thought. Some men might say you will go to sleep. Well, some men might sleep sixteen hours in a day; the ordinary man might try that, but he would soon find he could not do it long. He would have to do something. He would probably go to the theater one night, to a concert another night, but he could not do that every night. He would probably become interested in some study and the hours that have been taken from manual labor are devoted to mental labor, and the mental labor of one hour will produce for him more wealth than the physical labor of a dozen hours. (Applause.)

"I maintain that this is a true proposition—that men under the short-hour system not only have opportunity to improve themselves, but to make a greater degree of prosperity for their employers. Why, my friends, how is it in China, how is it in Spain, how is it in India and Russia, how is it in Italy? Cast your eye throughout the universe and observe the industry that forces nature to yield up its fruits to man's necessities, and you will find that where the hours of labor are the shortest the progress of invention in machinery and the prosperity of the people are the greatest. It is the greatest impediment to progress to hire men cheaply. Wherever men are cheap, there you find the least degree of progress. It has only been under the great influence of our great republic, where our people have exhibited their great senses, that we can move forward, upward and onward, and are watched with interest in our movements of progress and reform.

"I have said this much about the employers and their interest as connected with this question of the reduction of the hours of labor. Now, I want to say a word as to the workingman. There are many people who believe that when the hours of labor are shortened wages necessarily fall. There is no more unsound proposition, politically or socially. We notice that in any country where the hours of labor are longest, not only are the employers the poorest, but the wage-workers are the poorest. It applies not only to countries, but it applies with the same force to States and cities, to different shops in cities, and affects the different industries in any one city. You notice in any of the establishments of Louisville or New Albany, or any other place you have been in, that the people who enter the factory or establishment the earliest in the morning and leave it the latest at night always receive the lowest wages in that establishment. (Applause.) And you notice that those who come latest in the morning and leave earliest in the evening are the best paid. (Applause.) This is no dream; it is a truth. I have another thought to express, if you have patience to listen. First: A man who works eight hours a day can't afford to work as cheap as the man who works sixteen or eighteen hours a day. I will tell you why: The man who works eight hours a day has sixteen hours a day left. He must do something with them. He will go to the theater, read a magazine, or visit a friend at home, and when he does so he must have decent clothes. (The speaker was here interrupted by a committee from the glass-blowers of New Albany, who presented him with a glass cane. The speaker briefly acknowledged the compliment, and resumed.)

"He may take his wife or his best girl to a friend's. If he happens to be married, he takes his wife, and he wants her to be neat and clean and dressed fairly well. When his friend visits him he wants to have, probably, a pretty picture on the wall, or perhaps a piano or organ in his parlor; and he wishes everything about him to be bright and attractive. Take the other working man; he has no necessity for decent clothes—nobody comes to see him; he simply comes home to go to bed. (Laughter and applause.) He does not see his wife except when he returns from his work, and he is too tired to think about pictures and pianos. When he comes home the lamp is turned down ready for him to go to bed. (Laughter.) For books and the study of political economy, or books treating of the condition of the people, or the current news in the newspapers, he has no time. Why, if it depended on him, you would not see the boasting publications of the papers claiming to have the largest circulation in the world. You will always find that the wage-worker who works the longest hours in the day has the least. Take, for example, China. There you will find that he receives six or eight cents a day—enough to pay for his rice and an occasional rat, as a luxury. (Laughter.) You will find in the foreign countries people receiving in wages about as much as will supply them with those degrees of comfort that they are willing to live upon. In France they get enough to buy a square meal and a little wine. In America, workingmen can have a beefsteak much oftener, and perhaps a little better beefsteak, because they demand it. Whenever a man finds that he can live on just so much, he generally finds also that he doesn't get a cent more than what is necessary to get it. If a workingman thinks he can live on a sandwich and a herring, he is pretty apt to find that his employer is going to pay him just enough to get that sandwich and herring. (Laughter.)

"The man who works the long hours has no necessities except the barest to keep body and soul together, so he can work. He goes to sleep and dreams of work; he rises in the morning to go to work; he takes his frugal lunch to work; he comes home again to throw himself down on a miserable apology for a bed so that he can get that little rest that he may be able to go to work again. He is nothing but a veritable machine. He lives to work instead of working to live. (Loud applause.)

"My friends, the only thing the working people need besides the necessities of life, is time. Time. Time with which our lives begin; time with which our lives close; time to cultivate the better nature within us; time to brighten our homes. Time, which brings us from the lowest condition up to the highest civilization; time, so that we can raise men to a higher plane.

"My friends, you will find that it has been ascertained that there is more than a million of our brothers and sisters—able-bodied men and women—on the streets, and on the highways and byways of our country willing to work but who cannot find it. You know that it is the theory of our government that we can work or cease to work at will. It is only a theory. You know that it is only a theory and not a fact. It is true that we can cease to work when we want to, but I deny that we can work when we will, so long as there are a million idle men and women tramping the streets of our cities, searching for work. The theory that we can work or cease to work when we will is a delusion and a snare. It is a lie.

"What we want to consider is, first, to make our employment more secure, and, secondly, to make wages more permanent, and, thirdly, to give these poor people a chance to work. The laborer has been regarded as a mere producing machine, as Judge Toney said, but back of labor is the soul of man and honesty of purpose and aspiration. Now you can not, as the political economists and college professors, say that labor is a commodity to be bought and sold. I say we are American citizens with the heritage of all the great men who have stood before us; men who have sacrificed all in the cause except honor. Our enemies would like to see this movement thrust into hades, they would like to see it in a warmer climate (laughter), but I say to you that this labor movement has come to stay. (Loud applause.) Like Banquo's ghost, it will not down. (Applause.) I say the labor movement is a fixed fact. It has grown out of the necessities of the people, and, although some may desire to see it fail, still the labor movement will be found to have a strong lodgment in the hearts of the people, and we will go on until success has been achieved.

"We want eight hours and nothing less. We have been accused of being selfish, and it has been said that we will want more; that last year we got an advance of ten cents and now we want more. We do want more. You will find that a man generally wants more. Go and ask a tramp what he wants, and if he doesn't want a drink he will want a good, square meal. You ask a workingman, who is getting two dollars a day, and he will say that he wants ten cents more. Ask a man who gets five dollars a day and he will want fifty cents more. The man who receives five thousand dollars a year wants six thousand a year, and the man who owns eight or nine hundred thousand dollars will want a hundred thousand dollars more to make it a million, while the man who has his millions will want every thing he can lay his hands on and then raise his voice against the poor devil who wants ten cents more a day. We live in the latter part of the Nineteenth century. In the age of electricity and steam that has produced wealth a hundred fold, we insist that it has been brought about by the intelligence and energy of the workingmen, and while we find that it is now easier to produce it is harder to live. We do want more, and when it becomes more, we shall still want more. (Applause.) And we shall never cease to demand more until we have received the results of our labor.

"In this connection I am reminded of a fable I once heard of a donkey, who, being worked very hard each day, at the close of his daily labors, was tied by his master to a stake with a rope allowing him only a limited amount of grass on which to graze. The donkey soon became dissatisfied and asked his master for an extension of the rope, which was complied with. The next day, the donkey, enjoying the greater liberty granted him, asked that the rope might be still further extended, which caused his master to be very much provoked, and he addressed him in the following terms: 'You ungrateful donkey, do you not know that your father was contented with a space half as large as that which you demand?' This allusion to his father caused the donkey to hang his head for a moment in shame, but brightening up he said: 'Well, sir, but do you not know that my father was an ass?'

"Now, they tell us that we live so much better than our forefathers; that we are discontented with our lot. Well, as to that, we simply remark that our forefathers were not quite as intelligent as they ought to have been, and if they had demanded a little more than they got it would have reflected more to their credit. We insist that we are entitled to more, and we shall never cease to demand it until we get it. (Applause.)

"Now the question is, 'how to get it.' In December, 1888, the Federation of Labor held a convention in St. Louis, and there we first raised the question in regard to the limitation of working hours to eight hours, and we held simultaneously mass meetings throughout the length and breadth of our country. We had our own speakers to advance the cause. We wrote letters to eminent jurists and men in public life asking them what they thought of it, and they all agreed that the introducton of the eight hour system was a necessity. We have adopted a method in carrying on this agitation that I think will commend itself to all right thinking people. We have selected the Carpenters' and Joiners' to make the first test. (Applause.) We have adopted this plan because we have no desire to stop the wheels of industry. We are citizens of this country, and desire to do the best we can to promote its industries, and in the pursuit of what we conceive to be our rights it is our desire not to injure any of them, or as few as possible." (Applause.)[3]

. . .

Louisville Courier Journal, May 2, 1890.

1. CMIU 32.

2. Sterling B. Toney was judge of the Louisville law and equity court.

3. SG also addressed a group of black workers in Louisville on May 1. He told the *New York Sun* that separate meetings were held in the city "because of the unfortunate race question which is still prominent there" but expressed the hope that "race differences will not last much longer under the civilizing influences of the unions" and the belief that "the gaining of the eight-hour day will help in this direction" (*New York Sun*, Apr. 30, 1890).

To Michael Carrick[1]

May 6th [1890]

Mr. M. P. Carrick
Mc-Maugher St. Alleghany, Pa
Dear Sir and Brother: —

Your favor of the 4th inst. duly to hand and contents noted, and

I desire to express my appreciation for the interest you have taken in the matter upon which you write.

If Mr. O'Shea[2] is a painter and follows that as his avocation he certainly should belong to your Brotherhood. I am not sure however, that he does nor whether he has given up painting.

Will you please advise me upon this subject?

If the Icemen desire to form a union under the banner of the American Federation of Labor and are honest and earnest in that desire I shall do nothing to prevent them accomplishing their purpose.

Of course you understand that it requires no special skill to become an iceman or an ice driver but that is no reason why they should not be permitted to join the Federation.

One of the arguments always urged against the trade unions was that we objected to the organization of unskilled workmen.

While I have been president I have always maintained that a trade union could be organized from all classes of wage-workers of any particular trade or calling whether skilled or unskilled.

I wish you would give this matter all the consideration it deserves and advise me of the result of your observation as to the intent of the people in question.

Fraternally Yours   Saml Gompers.
President   American Federation of Labor.

TLpS, reel 3, vol. 4, pp. 715, 717, SG Letterbooks, DLC.

1. Michael Patrick CARRICK was secretary of Brotherhood of Painters and Decorators 15 of Allegheny, Pa.

2. John E. O'Shea, a leader in Pittsburgh KOL Local Assembly 7482 of ice drivers and helpers, was apparently the individual of the same name who was a painter in Pittsburgh during the 1880s and 1890s. In May 1890 O'Shea's assembly withdrew from the KOL. This is possibly the origin of the federal labor union the AFL chartered about the same time, known as Ice Drivers' and Helpers' Union 5105.

A News Account of an Address
in New York City

[May 6, 1890]

EIGHT HOURS GOES HERE.

. . .

About 1 o'clock, President Samuel Gompers of the American Federation, who returned from Louisville on Sunday, walked into Clarendon Hall. There was not many men present at the time, but he was received with cheers. He said he felt like addressing the men as "Fellow-Chips." He congratulated them upon their success, and upon the substantial successes throughout the country. He continued as follows:

["]We are now in the middle of the swim. We want eight hours, and everything shows, my friends, that we are going to have it. As was well said by your General Secretary, P. J. McGuire, than whom no better friend of the workingman lives to-day, we have got the eight-hour chip on our shoulders and we are not going to let any nine-hour man or any one else knock it off. The eight-hour movement means higher wages for everybody, and work for all. It means more time for self-improvement, for pleasure, more time to spend with your wives and families, and an improved state of affairs for everybody who labors with his hands for a living. I tell you that a man who is not with us in this eight-hour movement is against us. The man who is not in favor of a working day of eight hours is an enemy of ours. I don't care how nice any man may talk in favor of a day of nine hours, it does not matter to me who the man is, no matter how high-sounding his title may be, or how high up he may be in the ranks of any labor organization, the man who talks in favor of nine hours is an enemy to us and to laboring men generally. We are going to establish a working day of eight hours for every man and woman engaged in manual labor in this country. The carpenters were selected by the American Federation of Labor to lead the movement, and another organization has been chosen to follow that lead as soon as the carpenters have succeeded. And I judge you have succeeded, for I have just been informed that seven eighths of the employers in this city have acceded to your demands.

["]We have no "ists" or "isms" in this movement. We all have our hobbies, but these, with our numerous prejudices, are all put aside in this movement, and we are all united for eight hours. In Louisville on May 1 I saw 20,000 men in line, and the bosses saw it was policy to yield. I am glad to see that the bosses here are yielding so rapidly, and it is only a question of a day or two when you will all be at work again. I am pleased to see that there has been no breach of the peace in any of our demonstrations throughout the country. Our movement was endorsed by half a million workmen in Hyde Park, London, yesterday. It is hardly necessary to wish you success, for success is yours and ours already.["]

. . .

New York Sun, May 6, 1890.

To Auguste Keufer

May 9 [1890]

Mr. August. Keufer
15 Rue de Savoie Paris, France
My Dear Sir and Brother:—

In the midst of the confusion and excitement attending our movement I take advantage of a few moments lull to write a few words of greeting to you and through you to our comrades, the proletariat of France.

You have no doubt learned before this of the success with which the advance guard of our Eight Hour movement has met.

At the Boston convention the Executive Council of the American Federation of Labor was authorized to select one of the trades to make the demand for the eight hour workday May 1st. 1890.

After repeated sessions and a collection of information and statistics upon the question and the readiness of the organizations to participate in the movement, the United Brotherhood of Carpenters and Joiners of America was finally selected as the trade to make the demand. I might as well add that that organization numbered 73,000 on the date when the demand was made, and that all through the country there are but very few places of importance whatever where the employers have not acceded to the demand to inaugurate the Eight Hour workday without a diminution of wages.

The members of the national and international trade unions affiliated to the American Federation of Labor assessed themselves two cents per member per week, and the first call has already been forwarded into the funds at this office, and at this writing a further call for four weekly assessments of the same amount is being made.

The solidarity of the working people thus exhibited to the employers has had quite an effect to induce them to act as they have.

The agitation for the Eight Hour movement not only has had the effect of gaining this immense advantage for the Carpenters & Joiners of America, but it has given courage and hope to the working people who for years were disheartened and acting on the defensive against the encroachments of the employing classes.

Every trade and labor union of the country has vastly increased its membership and obtained improved conditions although in compliance with our plan of action many trades are holding back in their demands until they are reached in the order of readiness, discipline, numerical and financial strength to be selected to make the next demand for eight hours in their industry.

In all likelihood the Coal Miners of this country will be the next trade selected to make the demand. As to the date I cannot at this time definitely say owing to many considerations important in their bearing upon the subject at issue.

The demonstrations of the toilers of Europe prove the universality of our movement and is a ray of hope for the attainment of the poet's dream "The Parliament of man, the Federation of the world."

In my letter to both labor congresses held last July in Paris I urged the concentration of all efforts upon one or two questions, and to defer discussion on all controversial subjects, while nearly at the end of the words resolutions of sympathy with the Eight Hour movement were adopted.

I regret to see that there was not a greater degree of unanimity and fraternal regard shown for the movement to which I called attention then and which I not only foresaw but has been verified by subsequent events; however, I have to thank you for your efforts towards advancing the cause of labor, and also for your very many kind expressions for myself.

Let me assure you that I shall always be pleased to hear from you upon any matter coming under your observation and of interest to our movement.

With this I mail to your address a few of the documents issued by the Federation and to which I invite your attention.

With sincere good wishes I am,

Yours With Fraternal Greetings   Saml Gompers.
President American Federation of Labor.

TLpS, reel 3, vol. 4, pp. 726-29, SG Letterbooks, DLC.

To Martin Lauer and Henry Mattill[1]

May 21st [1890]

Messrs. Lauer & Mattill
Managers Publishing House of the Evangelical Association.[2]
265-275 Woodland Ave Cleveland, O.
Dear Sirs:—

Your favor of the 19th inst. in reply to mine of the 13th[3] came duly to hand and contents noted.

You say that there is no reason for grievance on my part whatever and add that the hours of work in your institution are ten per day and that you pay your men for ten hours work.

Does it not seem to you that there is not much "infidelity" in a movement of working people who depend upon their daily wage for their daily bread when they are willing to forego part of the labor they could perform in order to give those who might be out of employment an opportunity to earn the wage which shall support them instead of eating the bread of idleness or charity, or possibly something worse?

You say that the people now in your employ are satisfied with their conditions. Does it not seem a remarkable resemblance to the condition of slavery as it existed not many years ago? The slaves were also "satisfied" with their condition; they had become brutalized and demoralized to such an extent that they knew very little of a distinction between their just dues and their actual condition.

The men who have made the demand of your establishment for the enforcement of the eight hour workday were prompted by a holy and a noble purpose. The Judas Iscariots who turn traitors to the cause of progress and civilization by attempting to defeat them in their just course are "satisfied" because they "know not what they do."

It seems to me a peculiar position for your establishment to occupy when the Press which you stigmatize as "infidel" has conceded the beneficent measure for a reduction in the hours of daily toil, while you with a self satisfied air deny a concession to the laborer which would have a tendency to raise him not only materially, but morally and socially to a higher appreciation of his duties as a man.

At the close of your letter you add that that is all you have to say upon the subject "for the present," indicating that you may have something to add. I certainly should like to know what further you can urge to bolster up so indefensible a position as the one you occupy on this question.

Sincerely hoping that you may soon see the error of your ways and concede the just demands of organized labor and that I may hear from you soon to that effect. I am.

Very Respectfully Yours   Saml Gompers.
President   American Federation of Labor.

TLpS, reel 3, vol. 4, pp. 757, 756, 758, SG Letterbooks, DLC.

1. Martin Lauer and Henry Mattill, Evangelical ministers, were agents for the Publishing House of the Evangelical Association in Cleveland, Ohio.
2. The Evangelical Association, also known as the Evangelical Church, was a religious sect founded by Jacob Albright in Pennsylvania in 1803.
3. SG's letter urged the publishing house to reconsider its opposition to the eight-hour movement.

To David Hill

June 3rd [1890]

Hon. David B. Hill
Governor of the State of New York.
Executive Chamber Albany N.Y.
Dear Sir:—
I am in receipt of a letter from your private secretary Mr. Williams[1] being your answer to mine of May the 31st.[2]

Permit me to say that my informant has no objection to his name being known to you, but apprehends that should it be made known to the prison officials his existence would be made most miserable.

In his letter to me he says that he has communicated with you giving his full name and I merely refrained from using it to carry out his request.

I now inform you that his name is James Wilson, cell 638, sentenced October 30th 1888.

Sections 101 and 102 are the law governing the labor of convicts in the state's prison and provide that convicts of the third grade shall do no work that enters into competition with free labor, and it also provides for the work such convicts shall do.

I am informed that there are a number of convicts of the third grade who are working in the rag department and that there is a larger number than allowed by law working in the shoe department.

Information reaches me that there are other violations in connection with this but they are not specified.

The convict Wilson says that the tasks put to the men to do are so heavy and severe that the present law is looked upon as much worse than the old contract system.

If you can take any action upon this matter and apprize me thereof you will greatly oblige,

Yours Very Respectfully   Saml Gompers
President American Federation of Labor.

TLpS, reel 3, vol. 4, pp. 791-92, SG Letterbooks, DLC.

1. Timothy Shaler Williams.
2. On May 31 SG informed Governor Hill that the warden of the state prison at Sing Sing was violating the Convict Labor Law and asked the governor for a remedy. Hill apparently contacted the superintendent of the prison who reported that the warden denied the charge, but SG considered this "a mere denial by the man who seemed most interested in the matter" (SG to Hill, June 25, 1890, reel 3, vol. 4, p. 853, SG Letterbooks, DLC).

Excerpts from the Proceedings of the National Temperance Congress, New York City

[June 12, 1890]

. . .

THE ATTITUDE OF THE LABOR MEN
TOWARD THE LIQUOR TRAFFIC.

The discussion was opened by Mr. Samuel Gompers, President of the American Federation of Labor, who read the following paper:

Ladies and Gentlemen: I have been asked to address this assemblage upon the topic, "The Attitude of the Labor Men toward the Liquor Traffic," and I desire to say that the invitation was accepted after considerable thought, and with the distinct understanding that entire freedom of expression would be guaranteed me.

In view, however, of the well-known views entertained by most— yes, all of you, I enter upon the task with many misgivings as to the result.

At best, in the short time allotted, a mere assertion of facts can be uttered and only generalizations indulged in, trusting either that they will be found self-evident truths, or that a future opportunity may be found for the demonstration of their justness.

In the first place, permit me to say that, generally speaking, the labor men look with considerable indifference upon the efforts of the Temperance and Prohibition agitations. This is due to several causes, and can be briefly stated thus:

So far as the immediate and tangible condition of labor is concerned, the working people find that Liquor Traffic reformers are only different to other employers of labor in this respect, that they usually treat their employees with a greater degree of unfairness than do other employers; that all legislation to regulate the Liquor Traffic can and does only affect the workingmen when they indulge in liquor (as they must if they want to indulge in liquor at all) over the bars, or as sold to them otherwise in the only way they can buy it—namely, in small quantities, and at such times as they want it; that legislative regulation of the traffic cannot and does not affect the rich or well-conditioned people, who can and do purchase large quantities and use it at will; that many employers of labor have used this argument: that, inasmuch as the Liquor Traffic has been regulated or prohibited in certain localities, and money cannot be expended for liquor, the workers can afford to work for less wages; that the so-called Prohibition of the Liquor Traffic has not prohibited it, but has merely given them worse liquor at higher prices; that you cannot make men more sober or temperate in the use of liquor or make them Total Abstainers by law; that the, only natural and permanent manner in which men become sober, temperate, or Total Abstainers in and from the use of liquor is through the improvement in their habits and customs; that the habits and customs of the people become improved by the improvement in their material conditions and surroundings; that high wages and a reasonable number of hours of labor tend more largely to improve the habits and customs of the working people, hence lead to a greater degree of sobriety and regularity of conduct; that, as a rule, there are three classes in society which habitually get drunk—namely, those who have no work to do because they are too rich, and find the rounds of society life too monotonous, and look for the excitement resulting from the exuberance of the contents of champagne bottles; the second, those who, after having the spirit crushed out of them by their too long hours of daily drudgery, let in too much spirit at night as a substitute; the third, those who have no work to do because they cannot find it to do, and "get drunk on their faces."

There are probably other statements of equal importance and truth, but which lack of time reminds me had better remain unsaid if I desire to make a few remarks on a matter to which your attention should be directed, and which in a large measure determines the course of our people.

There can be no question of difference that in no civilized country on the face of the globe do the changes in the weather occur more often; that in consequence the climatic conditions of our country are of the most trying and exacting upon the human system; that the climatic conditions have undoubtedly tended to work up the nervous systems of our people to the highest possible tension; that this high tension of the nervous system evidently accounts for the quicker movements and work of our people over that of any other on earth; that, as a consequence, the body requires greater nutriment and more rest to maintain anything like an equilibrium, or, in the absence of either, or both, stimulants will be indulged in, even if they do subtly destroy both mind and body.

None know better than do the so-called leaders in the movement for Labor Reform the curse of liquor and the hindrance it is to the better education and activity in that field of operations; but we view this question as we find it, the result of poor conditions rather than the cause. I do not pretend to say that this rule is invariable, but I am sure it is general. Hence we base our operations upon removing the cause of the evil rather than dallying with the result.

The sad refrain of "the Song of the Shirt" is more heartrending, pitiful, and truthful to-day than at the time in which it was written. The pitiless, arrogant, and relentless taskmaster stalks this earth to-day as in the days of yore. The toilers' endless and hopeless and unfairly requited drudgery is almost as bitter now as ever.

It is the "Gospel of Relaxation" and leisure, that results in better material and moral conditions, that we preach and urge you to consider.

Mind, I do not wish to be understood to say that your gatherings and agitations do no good. On the contrary, I hail them as an excellent means to awaken thought and discussion upon an extremely important condition of life.

In the time of the old fire-alarm bell, it was very irksome and annoying to be aroused from our slumbers during the night, but it was far preferable to being roasted alive in our beds. So, say I, with all forms of agitation. They are the danger signals that wrong exists, which require the intelligent action and co-operation of mankind. To me nothing appears more fraught with dire results than a torpid or dormant condition of the people. They are the causes of reaction, and most destructive to the body politic, moral, social, and economic.

I therefore hail you as cranks, as fellow cranks who, knowing that all things are not right merely because they exist, and knowing this, in the face of all opposition, rancorous antagonism and flippant ridicule, dare proclaim and maintain what we believe to be right.

My friends, I trust you will not regard me in any way inimical to your various movements or agitations to regulate the Liquor Traffic. My purpose was to state as truthfully as I perceive and understand the attitude of the Labor Men toward the Liquor Traffic.

. . .

Mr. Thomas[1] said:

I am the son of an iron-worker, and from the day I was eleven years old until two or three years ago, I worked in an iron mill and in coal-mines. Our friend, Mr. Wakeman,[2] said that the Labor question lay across the path of the Prohibition question. I believe that the Prohibition question is the Labor question; and because I believe it is the Labor question, that is the reason I am a Prohibitionist. I look upon Mr. Gompers and Mr. Wakeman as representative workmen. I look upon Charles H. Leitchman[3] as a representative workman. He told the people of Pennsylvania to vote and work for Prohibition. I look upon P. M. Arthur as a representative workman. He said, "Every friend of the workingman will vote against the saloon every time he gets a chance, and close it up, not only upon Sunday, but upon every day of the week." I look upon Ralph Beaumont[4] as a representative workman. He says that to-day, more than all other questions that do not deal with the fundamental principles of political economy, the Liquor Traffic rises up above all things else, the obstacle in the way of the working man. I look upon Terence V. Powderly as a representative workman. He says, "Boycott the saloon, and in five years' time there will be an invincible host working against oppression and tyranny and monopoly."

Strikes have been referred to. I have had a share in them, and I never yet knew an unjust strike started among laboring men that I did not trace the cause of it to the saloon. I have never known a just strike to fail of success that I did not trace the cause of that failure to the saloon. I know our brother Wakeman is not a very ardent advocate of the wage system, anyway. But, brethren mine, the wage system is here, and as long as it is here we have got to deal with it. A workman, before the Senate Committee on Capital and Labor, said, "Drunkards, their impotent and debased progeny, convicts and paupers, born of the saloon, make the wage rates in the labor market, and sober men, intelligent men, have to receive the wages that are made in the labor market by these drunkards and convicts and paupers." Where do you get your convicts? In the saloon. Where do you get your paupers, brothers mine? Again, in and from the saloon. Now, I know it has been said that poverty causes drunkenness, rather than drunkenness poverty. We Prohibitionists have an unfortunate habit of matching theories with actual experience and figures. Our brother Rae,[5] of England, will bear me out in the statement that this question has been examined in the large cities among the working people of England; and, brothers, the men and the women who are sent to the poorhouses, who receive public support and alms as the result of poverty and indigence caused by the liquor traffic, are not the unskilled workingmen, are not the ignorant hand laborers, the poorest paid, but are skilled workingmen, who work short hours and get the largest wages. The actual facts are demonstrated by observation and test in England. I wish to God that our census enumerators would test some of those facts here; but they won't. I just want to say, in parenthesis, here — our brother Parsons[6] suggested that we get the laboring people into the house of God. Amen to that! But, as a laboring man, brothers and sisters, I say, in the name of God, get the house of God to the laboring people!

I am sorry that a good man like our brother Wakeman considers this a religious craze. It is because, I am sorry to say, our brother Wakeman don't come into the Church — he may come into the church building, but he doesn't get into the Church spirit, and the Church spirit doesn't get into Brother Wakeman and his associates. Let him understand us better, and he will know us better. I am glad that our Brother Metcalf[7] alluded to the fact that taxation is caused, in large measure, by the Liquor Traffic, and that the working people of this country pay the taxes. In the name of God, let us put a stop to this tax-maker!

The remaining two minutes of the hour were given to Mr. Gompers, who said:

There is but one thing, ladies and gentlemen, that I desire to say, and that is in regard to one statement of our friend, Mr. Thomas. I think it is a misstatement, based on anything but facts. It is not so, and I deny and defy a contradiction, that in any place on earth there is more drunkenness where wages are higher and the hours of labor are shorter. The very opposite is the truth. Wherever the hours of labor have been reduced, it has resulted in higher wages, and the more leisure given to the people has resulted in more sobriety. You can look to any trade that you please, to any calling that you please, and you will find that the workingmen and women who work eight or nine hours a day are more sober than those who work twelve, thirteen, and fourteen a day. I assure you that the man or woman who works twelve or fourteen hours a day has no spirit left. They have not a proper stomachful of food, and want and will have—I don't know whether they want it, but they will have, a stimulant as a substitute for the spirit that is driven and crushed out of them during the day.

Mr. Thomas: Mr. Goshen,[8] the Chancellor of the Exchequer of England, says that the strike of the dock laborers and others, that resulted in higher wages and shorter hours, brought about an era of prosperity for the workmen of England, and the result has been a rush to the beer barrel, a greater consumption of spirits than ever before, and a greater revenue to the Treasury. There are other facts that might be mentioned.[9]

. . .

National Temperance Congress, *Proceedings of the National Temperance Congress, . . . New York . . . June 11th and 12th, 1890 . . .* (New York, 1891), pp. 282-85, 299-302.

1. John Lloyd Thomas was secretary of the national executive committee of the Prohibition party.

2. Thaddeus Burr Wakeman, a New York City businessman, lawyer, and author, was associated in the early 1890s with the Nationalist movement and the SLP.

3. Charles H. Litchman.

4. Ralph BEAUMONT was a lecturer for the KOL.

5. Robert Rae was secretary of the National Temperance League of Great Britain.

6. Solomon Parsons was pastor of the Prospect Street Methodist Episcopal Church in Paterson, N.J.

7. Henry B. Metcalf was treasurer of the Campbell Machine Co. of Pawtucket, R.I.

8. George Joachim Goschen (1831-1907), chancellor of the exchequer, was a Liberal Member of the House of Commons.

9. See "To the Editor of the *New York Press*," July 12, 1890, below.

From Terence Powderly

New York June 18. [18]90.

Mr. Samuel Gompers
President A.F.L.
New York.
Dear Sir:—

It is the intention of the General Officers of the Knights of Labor to review, and reply to, the numerous charges and accusations which have been made and circulated, by the officers of the American Federation of Labor against the Knights of Labor. The meeting will be held Friday June 20 in Cooper Institute That you may not have to depend upon hearsay or garbled reports of the meeting, I deem it but an act of courtesy to you to invite you to be present and occupy a seat on the platform on that occasion. It will afford me great pleasure to share the platform with you should you desire to reply to anything to which you may take exception during the deliberations.

I have the honor to be

Very truly yours   T. V. Powderly.

ALS, Terence Vincent Powderly Papers, DCU.

To Terence Powderly

New York, June 19th 1890.

Mr. T. V. Powderly
G.M.W. K. of L.
Astor House New York.
Dear Sir:—

I am in receipt of your favor of the 18th inst. in which you say that it is the intention of the General Officers of the Knights of Labor to review and reply to the numerous charges and accusations which have been made and circulated by the officers of the American Federation of Labor against the Knights of Labor, at a meeting to be held at Cooper Union, on Friday evening the 20th inst.

You are courteous enough to invite me to attend the meeting so that garbled reports of the meeting should not reach me, for all of which I desire to express my appreciation. At the close of your letter, however, you add that should I desire to reply to anything to which I take exception, it would give you pleasure to divide the platform with me.

This may not have been intended but certainly is, and will be accepted by the world as a challenge to discuss the question at issue, and so I regard it.

You can readily understand that a challenge, where the greatest efforts have been made to have the meeting entirely composed of your followers, and where there are probably four or five beside yourself who are to address the meeting on your side of the question, is entirely and manifestly unfair. You must also be aware that the time for preparation has been of the shortest character, as far as I am concerned; and that it is now well known that this move has been in contemplation by you and your followers for several weeks, and that I shall be at a disadvantage owing to the fact. However, I waive all this; and will accept your challenge to meet you, not at a remote time, but to-morrow evening June 20th at Cooper Union, but must insist upon the following conditions.

1st. That I shall meet you and you alone as my disputant.

2nd. That the time be equally divided between you and I, and

3rd. That the meeting shall be an entirely free and open one to which the general public shall have free access without the demand of any sign or pass word and that no person be admitted to the Hall until 7.30. P.M.

If these conditions are acceptable to you and are carried out, I can assure you that notwithstanding the short notice of a few hours you will find on the platform,

> Yours Very Respectfully   Saml Gompers.
> President American Federation of Labor.

TLS, Terence Vincent Powderly Papers, DCU.

From Terence Powderly

New York June 20. 1890.

Mr. Samuel Gompers,
President A.F.L.
Dear Sir:—

My letter inviting you to participate in the deliberations of the Cooper Institute meeting to night was not intended as a challenge in any sense of the word. Challenges are usually accompanied by the rules and conditions under which the controversy, or contest, is to be carried on, had I intended my letter as a challenge this would have been done.

Until last Monday evening I had no intention of taking up the subject of the Charges made by the Federation. It is always the rule when the General Executive Board meets at any point to hold public meetings. I expected that the rule would be observed at this session of the G.E.B. and it is owing to the issue of certain circulars from the headquarters of the American Federation of Labor that it has been decided to make the matter a subject for public discussion. In a word this meeting has not been in contemplation by (me or my) followers for several weeks, and since it is the direct result of your own utterances it is safe to assume that you still have in mind the [aims?] and motives by which the officers of the American Federation of Labor was actuated in promulgating the principles enunciated in the manifestoes so recently issued.

There is to be no dispute so far as I am concerned but I cheerfully accede to your request that you shall meet me, and me alone, in the discussion so far as it relates to the American Federation of Labor. I shall talk on other matters but in deference to your wishes will first discuss the subject at issue between us and then allow you the same length of time in which to make answer, after that I shall take up the other matters to be discussed.

You, who were once a member of the Order, must know that private meetings are not called as this has been. It is to be a public meeting. No sign or password will be taken up and all are entitled to admission whether Knights or members of the Federation.

The management of the meeting is not under my control or direction and I am powerless in the matter of keeping the doors closed until 7.30 P.M., this I regret very much but I have no jurisdiction.

Unless I am in error you will not only occupy the level of equality with me to night but will have the the advantage for the discussion will hinge on what you directed, and which as a matter of course must be familiar to you, while I have yet to make the first preparation for the meeting of this evening.

I have the honor to remain.

Very truly yours. T. V. Powderly.
G.MW. K. of L.

ALS, Terence Vincent Powderly Papers, DCU.

To Terence Powderly

New York, June 20th 1890.

Mr. T. V. Powderly
G.M.W. K. of L.
Astor House New York,
Dear Sir:—

In your letter just to hand you very laboriously try to show that your letter of the 18th inst. to me was not a challenge because it contained no provision for rules and conditions. It is this very omission that bears upon its face the complete unfairness of your proposition, and which I sought to supply by the very fair conditions I proposed.

Let us be frank with each other Mr. Powderly; at least I propose to be, and say to you that it is my candid opinion that you never expected that I would accept your challenge, or that if I did, I would be entrapped into a packed meeting for which preparations (I am reliably informed) have been in progress for several weeks.

What if I had declined your proposition, would you and your followers have said, Mr. Powderly did not challenge Mr. Gompers? Would you and they not have declared that the offer from you to "divide the platform with me" was a bold and fair challenge, and that I was too cowardly to accept it? But finding that I am man enough, feel strong and justified enough to reiterate and prove any and every thing that I ever said in connection with your order, you hide yourself behind a subterfuge of words, and say, it was not a challenge. I direct your attention to the Press of this city and of the country for a confirmation of my assertion that your letter was a challenge.

After your attempt at explanation you very ingeniously offer what you do in reference to the discussion of the charges of the Federation's officers, and extend to me equal time to reply, then you and the other members of your Executive Board are to go on in your own discussion. In other words, the whole performance of this evening which has been so broadly and loudly advertised that you would "review and reply to the numerous charges and accusations made and circulated by the officers of the American Federation of Labor" is now to be confined to a mere prologue and you wish me to play a petty character and to die in the first scene; Then you and the rest of your characters are to proceed to the end of your tragedy or farce. Of course you and your colleagues are not to refer to me or the American Federation of Labor after having snuffed me out of existence, Oh no, not even by a word, gesture or wink. How generous.

You say you cannot comply with the conditions I make owing to the fact that you have not the management of the meeting. How is it then that you had sufficient power in the first instance to offer to share the platform with me?

It seems to me that those having the meeting in charge should be willing to forego anything to give you the opportunity with one fell blow to annihilate the American Federation of Labor and its officers.

Mr. Powderly, all through your letter you hum and haw and hedge. You palpably betray the weakness of your position, and will stand before the general public convicted as a pettifogger.

You remind me that I was once a member of your order. I want to call your attention to the fact that so were very many hundreds of thousands of others who learned there the double-dealing methods of you and your confreres.

I desire to add that any accusation ever made by me against any person I have either substantiated or am willing at any time to substantiate, and now within three hours of your proposed meeting I stand ready to meet you under the conditions named in my letter of yesterday.

The meeting hall (Cooper Union) is situated but three minutes from this office, and I shall await your reply here until the commencement of the meeting.

Very Respectfully Yours   Saml Gompers.
President American Federation of Labor.

TLS, Terence Vincent Powderly Papers, DCU.

Excerpts from a News Account of a Meeting at Cooper Union

[June 21, 1890]

POWDERLY'S WARM TALK.

Samuel Gompers, President of the American Federation of Labor, did not meet Master Workman T. V. Powderly, of the Knights of

Labor, in joint debate at Cooper Union last night, and consequently a one-sided indignation meeting was held instead. There was a great crowd, mainly composed of Knights of Labor, but also containing many Federation men, but the latter bore the sledge-hammer blows administered to their leaders without indications of disapproval. The failure of Mr. Gompers to appear and jointly debate the differences between the two labor organizations was due to inability to agree upon the terms of debate with Mr. Powderly. . . .

Although it was generally understood that President Gompers would not be on hand there was a crush at the hall, and at 7.30 o'clock the throng had reached to the curb at the opposite side of Eighth street, and travel on that thoroughfare was blocked. It would have been an impossiblity for a man to have walked down either side of the street.

A platoon of policemen under Capt. McCullough[1] had entered the hall to prevent a rush, while twenty officers were drawn up in front of the doors to keep the crowd from breaking through. At twenty minutes before 8 o'clock the doors were opened one by one and 5,000 men and a few women made a grand rush. Three of the officers' new Summer helmets were crushed down over their heads and fell to join the displaced headgear of about one hundred citizens. Notwithstanding all this, however, order was finally maintained, and besides a few crushed toes and bruised bodies nobody was injured.

In five minutes from the time the doors were opened every seat in the big building was occupied and the crowd rushed down towards the platform, filling up the aisles. Just then Inspector Williams[2] appeared and gave orders that every man leave the aisles and take places at the rear of the hall. The front entrance was then closed, but still a steady stream flowed down the stairway to the back of the big hall, which soon became packed. The people began to leave when they found they could not see and hear all that went on. A few minutes past 8 o'clock there were about three thousand people on the plaza in front of the Union. A big truck was wheeled into the midst of the crowd and two men mounted it. They were Thomas McGuire,[3] a prominent leader of the Knights of Labor, and Mr. Murray, who is at the head of the Cigarmakers' Union and a leader in the Central Labor Union. They were cheered by both factions, which seemed to be pretty evenly represented, and then, much to the amusement of the crowd, they began to talk about each other, saying nice things about their own organization and running down the other to their hearts' content. The crowd asked lots of questions and did all they could to add to the fun, which lasted just as long as the big meeting inside.

Opening the Big Meeting.

Among those who occupied seats on the stage were George Murray,[4] M.W. D.A. 49; William McNaire,[5] Recording Secretary D.A. 49; T. B. McGuire, D.A. 49; Charles Rodgers,[6] D.A. 253;[7] O. D. Culver,[8] Treasurer D.A. 253; John J. Sullivan,[9] Recording Secretary D.A. 253; George Warner,[10] D.A. 253; Henry Grauber,[11] D.A. 197;[12] John Reilly, D.A. 227;[13] James P. Archibald, D.A. 210;[14] Capt. Barry,[15] Sandy Hook Pilots' Association; John Bell,[16] Moulders' Union; M. Ryan, Marble Polishers' Association;[17] Edward Conklin,[18] President of the Progressive Painters;[19] Miss Mary Shea, Co-operative Shirt-Makers;[20] Miss Sullivan, Co-operative Shirt-Makers; John Carson, Treasurer D.A. 49; John O'Connell, President Ale and Porter Brewers' Association;[21] Thomas Reardon,[22] Ale and Porter Brewers' Association; J. Raleigh, Ship Joiners' Association;[23] P. McCord,[24] Amalgamated Carpenters; John McPherson,[25] United Order of Carpenters; Thomas Marron, United Order of Carpenters; John Hameron,[26] United Order of Carpenters; Frederick Huntley,[27] Mystic Tie Association;[28] Master Workman Woods, of the Marble Cutters;[29] James Killarn,[30] Housesmiths; John Holland,[31] Alexander Wright and Thomas Costello,[32] of the General Executive Board; E. O. Culver, Master Workman Progressive Carpenters; John McCounder, Painters No. 1;[33] John Devlin, General Executive Board; P. Reynolds,[34] Stevens Assembly; J. J. Doyle,[35] Vice-President D.A. 49; John O'Reilly,[36] D.A. 220;[37] John Fletcher, P. J. McGuire,[38] John W. Hayes, Executive Board; Henry Hicks,[39] Vice-President D.A. 253; John Gerry, Stairbuilders' Union, and Charles Miller,[40] Clothing-Cutters' Union.

George W. Meyer,[41] of the committee managing the meeting, called it to order and introduced George Warner as Chairman. The Chairman said: "The object of the meeting is to make replies to certain accusations that have been made by a certain association, namely, the American Federation of Labor. It was called by the Knights of Labor of this city and no one else."

Alexander Wright was the first speaker introduced and he said the troubles among the labor organizations were jointly due to following the advice of men who lacked wisdom and the ravings of thoughtless and irresponsible agitators, who falsely claim to represent labor. Mr. Wright explained that he was only killing time while the Master Workman got his breath and then Grand Master Workman Powderly was introduced. He was received with tremendous enthusiasm. Those who were not already standing rose and cheered with vigor. The cheering continued for fully two minutes, during which time Mr.

Powderly stood on the edge of the platform and bowed in response to each successive cheer and each one appeared to be louder than the others. When the enthusiastic applause was ended the speaker was listened to quietly until he began to read the letter from Samuel Gompers, President of the American Federation of Labor. Then the Federation men cheered, but the speaker went on quietly until the end. The Federation men rose again then, and noisily demonstrated their approval of their President's action. The Knights of Labor remained perfectly quiet, but the cheering for Gompers continued for many moments. Master Workman Powderly waited again, and when at last quiet was restored he attempted to go on. A great shuffling of feet and the very demonstrative movements of about 300 men in the front seats, who rose to go out, stopped him though. The Federation men made a great deal of noise as they filed out and their number seemed much larger than it really was as they walked up the aisles. Mr. Powderly lifted his voice above the clatter of feet and chairs and requested all who wanted to go out to do so at once, as there were thousands waiting outside for a chance to get in. The Knights of Labor cheered this and the Federation men hurried. Four or five people rushed for every seat that had been vacated. After that there was no further disturbance, except when the Knights became too enthusiastic. Repeatedly during his address the Master Workman had to stop for a few seconds, because of the applause.

MR. POWDERLY'S SPEECH.

"It is with a feeling of sadness that I stand here to discuss the question I must discuss to-night," Mr. Powderly said. "I would much rather leave it alone and not touch it, as I prefer to go on and fight only for the cause of labor. I am not here to answer for any of our misdeeds or past actions, but to enter in detail into the causes that have led up to the present misunderstanding. It is not a misunderstanding between the American Federation of Labor and the Knights of Labor, but between certain officers of the organizations." He had, he said, respect for an honest foe who fought openly, but not for a cowardly enemy who enters the ranks of labor to breed dissension. The General Master Workman then read President Gompers' letter, as given above,[42] and Mr. Wright explained that the letter had been handed over to the Executive Committee, who had agreed to let the matter rest where it was, as some of the terms employed were not such as they could consistently ask the General Master Workman to reply to.

Mr. Powderly then resumed and said had Mr. Gompers presented himself he would have been treated with absolute fairness. In spite of the fact that he might be charged with reviving ancient history, he said he would read from some old reports. He alluded to the charge that the Knights had stolen their principles from the trades-unions, and said it was true and had never been denied and, moreover, they were proud of it.

"They became ashamed of their child and abandoned it, and we adopted the outcast and reared it to healthy manhood, and are proud of the child of our adoption. We have nursed it and added to it until it stands to-day the foremost declaration of principles of the century." He reviewed the organization's course on the currency and eight-hour movement, and claimed that the Federation tried to spring the eight-hour strikes without making any preparation therefor, and in such a manner that it could shirk responsibility for failure, but still claim credit for success if the movement proved successful. Mr. Powderly said when this movement was started in 1886 the Knights of Labor were not consulted or advised as to the arrangements, and had raised no funds to meet the emergency. Therefore the General Assembly would not order co-operation, and he warned the local assemblies to act considerately, as no general assistance was possible. "Wherever the officers of the Federation of Labor have gone from that day to this they have wilfully and maliciously lied when they said I was opposed to the eight-hour movement. I will not be led blindly by fools," Mr. Powderly said earnestly. "We believe in eight hours for labor and want it, but there is a difference in the methods by which we hope to reach it." He denied that the K. of L. took any part in that eight-hour movement or was in any way responsible for the failure. The Federation was responsible, but it never openly assumed the responsibility, and when the movement failed he said the officers "pulled themselves under the barn and pulled their principles with them." This remark caused some hisses and the speaker said "only two classes hiss, geese and cowards."

After Mr. Wright had read from Mr. Powderly's report on the eight-hour movement of May, 1886, to back up the Grand Master Workman's claim the latter read from a report to show that the Federation's next move was to adopt the Knights of Labor day for agitation and called for mass-meetings all over the country on Washington's Birthday, 1889. He also read a letter from Mr. Gompers stating that the Federation Committee did not agree to a general strike in May, 1890, and saying no movement looking to a general strike met his approval, but he "would aid those who were in condition to take the step."[43] In other words the Grand Master Workman said he "would help those who could help themselves," and he announced that he hoped to receive their assistance in return at some future time. Mr. Powderly next took up the report of the Federation and read a list of organizations claiming to belong to it, footing up a total membership in 1889 of 549,461. He named a number of associations which he said "did not belong to the Federation then, do not now and never will." He also said that the number he named were counted twice or thrice by being listed independently, and also with other organizations of which they were members, and that there were 37,000 miners enrolled with their local organizations who were included in the 350,000 in the general organization. The 8,000 conductors,[44] and 12,000 firemen were wrongly listed, he said. The conductors were pronounced too high-toned. "They include the Brotherhood of Locomotive Engineers, with Brother T. M. Arthur at their head. Why, Brother Arthur has said that he would not have anything to do with any workingman, but Chauncey M. Depew.[45] The man behind Brother Arthur, however, will never sleep with Chauncey Depew whatever Mr. Arthur may do." The telegraph operators[46] were also included in the list, and Mr. Powderly said, "They belong to us." He said the list had been reduced over 100,000 by his eliminations, and there were many doubles and trebles left.

"Not over one hundred thousand men acknowledged allegiance to the Federation. Take the Typographical Union, for instance," he said. "It stands in this position. 'You will, or we won't.' It is held by a rope of sand, maintained by the hope of a few people that the Federation will some day do something for labor. What would you think of Powderly if he said, Go in and win, with 549,461 men behind you with their dollars? What would you think of him if he had lied as these men have? I have travelled all over this country during the past year and spoken under the auspices of trades unions when they were in sympathy with the Knights of Labor, as they should be, and have said when any man does anything to thwart the honest efforts of trades unions he is a dastard and should be suppressed and kicked out. President Gompers," he said, "had pursued a defiant policy, and in all of his speeches had a dagger drawn to strike a blow at the Knights of Labor. You had better attend to your own affairs in future than be represented by men who wilfully misrepresent you," he said. He alluded to an occasion when he had been asked to meet Gompers for a conference, and had replied: "I will meet the devil in the cause of labor," but he was misrepresented on this occasion and in relation to their conference by Mr. Gompers, and falsely accused of being unfriendly to joint action for the general good of labor. The Master Workman requested Mr. Wright to relate the history of the overtures made by the Federation to the Knights of Labor in connection with the eight-hour movement. Mr. Wright spoke of the agreement that the Knights of Labor had offered to enter into with the Federation. "It was a fair agreement," he said, "and one that was for the benefit of workingmen, but the Federation had first questioned it and then refused to sign it.["]

Then Mr. Powderly resumed. He spoke of "scabs," and said that if the Federation, which made much complaint about them, wanted to find scabs it must look in the Federation and not in the ranks of the Knights of Labor. It was ever the Federation men and never the Knights of Labor who worked under price. One cause of complaint that the Federation had against the Knights of Labor was that the Knights had raised the wages of cigar-makers in Pennsylvania. That took work out of the hands of the Federation, for when the price was raised Knights of Labor were willing to work in Pennsylvania. Then Mr. Powderly literally brought down the house by saying, with his hands uplifted, that he did not care who the man was, if he raised the price of labor or shortened the hours of the workingman he was deserving of all the good that laborers could say or think of him. The speaker next turned his attention to the man Harry J. Stephington,[47] who was expelled from the Knights of Labor, and taken into the Federation. In connection with this he said that the action of the Federation threatened the life of labor organizations. The expelled man, he said, was an assassin who would sacrifice any organization or the welfare of a community to further his own selfish ends.

Then Mr. Powderly talked at some length about the benefits of mutual love and brotherly trust. Men should work together for the good of all. He spoke of the necessity of leaders, and admitted that all might make mistakes. Then he offered, if he had not satisfied his fellow Knights of Labor, to step down and go into the ranks, while the organization elected some one else in his place. The audience cheered the generosity and unselfishness of Mr. Powderly's offer until everybody was hoarse, but everybody shouted that Mr. Powderly alone was wanted.[48]

New York World, June 21, 1890.

1. Either John H. McCullough (variously McCullagh) or his nephew, John, both of whom served as New York City police department captains.

2. Alexander S. Williams was a New York City police inspector.

3. Thomas B. McGuire, a marble polisher and truck driver, was a former master workman of KOL District Assembly (DA) 49 and a member of the KOL General Executive Board from 1886 to 1888 and 1892 to 1897. Newspaper accounts also place T. B. McGuire inside Cooper Union during the meeting.

4. George E. Murray, a New York City housepainter, was master workman of KOL DA 49.

5. William MacNair (variously McNair).

6. Charles P. Rodgers (variously Rogers) was a New York City marble cutter active in the New York City Central Labor Union (CLU). He was a delegate from DA 253 to the 1889 KOL General Assembly.

7. Building constructors' KOL DA 253 of New York City was organized in 1887 or 1888.

8. Oscar D. Culver was a New York City carpenter.

9. John J. Sullivan, a roofer, was a member of the Slate and Metal Roofers, probably KOL Local Assembly (LA) 2412.

10. George Warner, a housesmith, was master workman of KOL DA 253.

11. Henry C. Gruber was a New Jersey cigarmaker.

12. KOL DA 197 of Jersey City was founded in late 1886 or early 1887.

13. Actually KOL National Trade Assembly (NTA) 226 of New York City.

14. KOL NTA 210 of Painters, Paper Hangers and Decorators was chartered in late 1886 or early 1887.

15. William J. Barry, a Brooklyn pilot, served as a delegate from KOL DA 49 to the 1886 and 1888 KOL General Assemblies.

16. An iron molder named John Bell was living in Brooklyn beginning in 1888; in the early 1890s he worked as a machinist and a clerk.

17. Possibly the Whitestone Association of Marble Polishers.

18. Edward J. Conklin was active in the New York City CLU.

19. The Progressive Painters' Union, with several locals in New York City, was probably associated with the KOL as LA 2888.

20. The Co-operative Shirtmakers of New York City.

21. The Ale and Porter Brewers' Protective Union (APBPU), KOL LA 8390; it later became local 59 of the International Union of United Brewery Workmen of America.

22. Thomas Reardon (variously Riordan) was the walking delegate for the APBPU.

23. Possibly shipjoiners' KOL LA 7148 of New York City.

24. Possibly William H. McCord, a New York City carpenter, who represented the Amalgamated Society of Carpenters and Joiners at the 1890 meeting of the New York State Branch of the AFL and the 1890 AFL convention.

25. John McPherson was president of the United Order of American Carpenters and Joiners in New York City. While most of the United Order merged with the Brotherhood of Carpenters and Joiners of America in 1888, a faction headed by McPherson joined the KOL in 1890.

26. Possibly John Hamerand, a New York City carpenter.

27. Frederick Huntley lived in New York City and was employed as a blindmaker and a sawyer.

28. The Mystic Tie Association of Sash, Door, and Blindmakers, possibly KOL LA 7643 of New York City.

29. Probably the Reliance Labor Club of Marble Cutters, KOL LA 3973.

30. John Killoran was a member and, in 1891, walking delegate for the housesmiths' union, probably the Housesmiths' Benevolent and Protective Union of the City of New York, organized as KOL LA 2914.

31. James J. HOLLAND, a Jacksonville, Fla., businessman, lawyer, and politician, served on the KOL General Executive Board from 1888 to 1890.

32. John COSTELLO, a Pittsburgh miners' leader, was a member of the KOL General Executive Board from 1888 to 1890.

33. Progressive Painters' Union 1.

34. Probably Patrick Reynolds, a railroad worker and a member of Uriah Stephens Assembly, KOL LA 5214, of New York City.

35. John J. Doyle was a member of the Franklin Society of Pressmen.

36. Probably Thomas J. O'Reilly, a cooper and an active member of KOL DA 220 of Brooklyn.

37. KOL DA 220 of Brooklyn, also known as the Long Island Protective Association, was organized in late 1887.

38. Actually Patrick C. McGuire, a housesmith who was a member of DA 49 in New York City.

39. Henry A. Hicks, a stairbuilder, was worthy foreman of building constructors' KOL DA 253.

40. Charles L. Miller was president of the United Clothing Cutters' Association, affiliated with the KOL as garment cutters' and trimmers' LA 2853.

41. Actually George E. Murray.

42. Earlier in the article the *New York World* had published both an excerpt from SG's letter to Powderly of June 19 and his letter to Powderly of the 20th.

43. Powderly was reading from SG's letter to Edward T. Plank, president of the International Typographical Union, of May 20, 1889, assuring the printers that "nothing was further from the intention of the [AFL] Convention than the adoption of a resolution implying a general strike; . . . we shall try to aid those who are in a condition by May 1st, 1890 to obtain '8 hours'" (reel 2, vol. 3, pp. 875-76, SG Letterbooks, DLC).

44. The Order of RAILWAY Conductors of America.

45. Chauncey Mitchell Depew, a New York Republican politician and lawyer, was president of the New York Central and Hudson River Railroad from 1885 to 1898.

46. The Brotherhood of TELEGRAPHERS.

47. Henry J. Skeffington.

48. The *Journal of the Knights of Labor* presented a full text of Powderly's speech in "Knights of Labor and the Federation," July 3, 1890.

An Interview in the *New York World*

June 22, 1890.

GOMPERS'S BITTER TALK.

Samuel Gompers, President of the American Federation of Labor, was in full war paint yesterday. When *The World* reporter called on him Mr. Gompers had just completed the heading for the speech he delivered last evening at the labor mass meeting in Philadelphia. No newspaper reporter ever found a man better prepared for an interview than was Mr. Gompers. He had a lot of sheets of paper covered with notes, and as he stood beside his table the great labor agitator evidently appreciated the fact that in talking to the reporter he was really speaking to the million and a half of *The World*'s readers.

"In the first place," said Mr. Gompers, "I want to say that Terence V. Powderly deliberately and maliciously uttered a lie when he said the Confederated Labor organization claimed affiliation with the Brotherhood of Locomotive Engineers, the Telegraphers and the Typographical Union. The organization I represent never made any such claim. Our roll of separate organizations, their unions and branches, shows fifty-three bodies, and a total membership of 600,000 members in good standing. These do not include the State branches, Trade and Labor Assemblies, Central Labor Unions, Federal Labor Unions and local unions affiliated with the American Federation of Labor, which did not send delegates to our Boston Convention of last year. We do claim connection with the Amalgamated Railroad Engineers and the International Typographical Union.

"By making these wild assertions Mr. Powderly has created a man of straw. We never claimed the railroad organizations, but our membership is made up without counting them at all. If what Mr. Powderly says in regard to them is true, it is in every way a piece of treachery on his part to expose the weakness of an organization of labor to its employers. If so, Mr. Powderly will know that his exposure is worth a great deal of money to his employers. I am unwilling to enter into a bantering of epithets with Mr. Powderly, and instead of his harsh language towards me I should think he could have been more specific in his utterances. I prefer to be more specific in my reply than he was in his attack, and though I have refrained heretofore, in the interest of the general labor movement, from characterizing the actions of T. V. Powderly and his confessions as they deserve, I now feel that the proper time has come for me to speak in rightful condemnation.

"The utterances of Mr. Powderly at the Cooper Union meeting last evening render it necessary that I should not only recite but prove to his deluded followers and the general public his contemptible conduct to the labor movement in general and the trades unions in particular. Before doing so I want to call attention to the fact that Mr. Powderly said he would devote a little time to the discussion of the charges made by the Federation of Labor against his Order of the Knights of Labor, and then discuss other and general questions. He thus endeavored to make it apparent that our charges were only to be an incident of the meeting, while by his correspondence he made it impossible for me to appear at the meeting with any self-respect. The fact is, that meeting was devoted to a denunciation of the Federation of Labor, the eight-hour movement and myself.

"Let me recite a few incidents showing the unfair and treacherous conduct of the Knights of Labor officers towards trade unions. I will not attempt to recite them in regular order, but just as they occur to me. The Amalgamated Iron and Steel Workers were on strike at

Mingo Junction, Pa., in 1887 against reduced wages and obnoxious mill rules. Suddenly they learned that a member of the General Executive Board of the Knights of Labor had entered into an agreement to furnish Knights to take the place of strikers at the reduced scale. He sent out a call through the Associated Press throughout the country calling on Knights of Labor to take the places of strikers. That man was William H. Bailey. At Brilliant, O., the men of the Amalgamated Association went on strike against reduced wages, when Knights of Labor became scabs and took their places. One K. and L. Association, to whom two scabs belonged, expelled them from the Order. Mr. T. V. Powderly at once wrote a letter ordering their reinstatement as good men in good standing.[1] Jacob C. Bullock[2] of the Amalgamated Iron and Steel Workers in his official report says that Gus Specht and Charles Glasso were expelled from the Order and took an appeal to the Executive Board, who ordered their reinstatement. This I am quite sure of, as I have read the original letter written by Master Workman T. V. Powderly. I here want to call attention to the fact that the difference of price between the Amalgamated Association and the Knights of Labor was $156.90 per 100 tons and $149.53.

"During the lockout of the cigar-makers in New York City the officers of the Knights of Labor organization furnished scabs, who promptly took the places of union men, and subsequently admitted them into full membership of their order. A delegation of cigar manufacturers called on the General Executive Board of the Knights of Labor at that time and used the following words to them:

"'If you do not come to our rescue we will have to submit to the International Union and bend our knees to its officers.' The Knights of Labor did go to the boss manufacturers' rescue by declaring their scab shops as Knights of Labor shops, and granting the use of their trade label for their product. Nearly all these cigar manufacturers were at that time tenement-house employers, and their bill of prices was 13 per cent. cheaper than that of the union.

"I charge that the subsequent reduction of wages for cigar-workers in New York City was the result of the action taken by the Knights of Labor. That Order is responsible for this reduction and the increase is what our cigar-makers are now struggling to obtain. At Syracuse during the forty-days' suspension of charters by the Knights of Labor the cigar-makers in James A. Barton's shop struck against a reduction of wages. Barton, with the assistance of a notorious scab, known as Junio, organized an association of Knights of Labor, and a special dispensation was granted to the organization. The difference in wages was from $1 to $3 per 1,000. In Jacksonville, Fla., and two or three other places the printers went on strike. The Knights of Labor immediately organized the scabs into Knights of Labor associations.[3] But the fact that the printers were editors of the labor papers in those sections compelled the Knights to back down from that position so far as compositors were concerned. An executive officer of the Knights approached one of the proprietors of the Troy *Times*, with whom the local union had been in conflict for a long time and denounced the Union's attitude as improper, offering, if Mr. Francis[4] would consent to take scabs into his employ, to declare them Knights of Labor.

"During the strike of the New York cigar-makers Bob Schilling[5] sent a letter to Thos. B. McGuire offering to send him 500 scabs who could be organized into Knights of Labor assemblies. That letter was published at the time. When the Journeymen Beer Brewers' lockout took place all union workmen were boycotting the product of scabs. But the Knights declared these lockout breweries Knights of Labor producers and even urged the sale of their product. When the strike at the Chicago Stock Yards[6] was made for eight hours Mr. Powderly wanted to deprive the men of their coveted boon. Mr. Powderly actually sent out a despatch ordering them back to work under the ten-hour rule. Bulletins announcing his arbitrary action were posted in the city an hour before the despatch reached the men. That order was accompanied by a threat of a revocation of the men's charter if they failed to obey. While the Southwestern Railroad strike was in progress Mr. Powderly entered into an agreement with Jay Gould by which the most active and best men were blacklisted with his consent. He afterwards excused his position on the ground that Gould had fooled him.

"When the Locomotive Engineers and Firemen struck on the C.B. & Q. system the officers of the Knights of Labor encouraged scabs to take the places of strikers. Mr. Powderly remained silent until nearly all the engines were manned, and then he told the Knights not to do so, but the language employed by him was certainly construed, by every man who could read, as meaning that they were to continue their hostile attitude. During my conference with Mr. Powderly at Philadelphia I entered a protest against the issuance of charters to the scab musicians of Pittsburg. He promised me that these charters would not be issued. I subsequently learned that these charters had already been issued when he was speaking to me. And that Knights of Labor scab assembly is still in existence.

"These undermining tactics have been continued, but in lesser degree, owing to the downward tendency of their organization. But even now the German tailors of Columbus, O., have been on strike for the past four months to aid a number of women who desire better conditions for themselves.[7] The District Master Workman at Columbus is now endeavoring to organize the scabs who took the places of the strikers into Knights of Labor assemblies. When the eight-hour movement was originated by the International Cigar-Makers throughout the country, Knights of Labor worked nine and ten hours a day, and as they filed out of their shops they were hooted at. The Knights of Labor organization is inherently an anti–trade union organization, because it teaches its members that open and public association is a failure, when as a matter of fact, agreeably to the republican institutions under which we live, I claim that there is no necessity for oath-bound organizations.

"Look at the difference in our name and theirs and you will see that ours is American in spirit and meaning, while theirs is purely mediaeval and an imported article. Let me quote a few remarks made to me by prominent Knights of Labor. Frederick Turner[8] said: 'The sooner your trade unions are wiped out the better, and I will do all I can to bring that result about at the earliest moment.' John W. Hayes said: 'Do you expect me to vote in any way to bring a victory to a trade union?['] T. B. McGuire said: 'We have legislated all trade unions out of existence, and so far as we are concerned they do not exist.'

"At Richmond, Va., they first introduced resolutions compelling all Knights to leave trade unions, and afterwards made the rule apply to the International Cigar-Makers' Union. Mr. Powderly speaks of his favorable attitude towards the eight-hour movement. Why did he not say one word in favor of it during that entire contest? It does not matter so much what a man says, but what he does. Is it not strange that during the recent movement, where Knights of Labor were openly opposed to the eight-hour question, we were entirely successful in establishing it? But where they professed to be friendly it only resulted in defeat or a partial victory. On the other hand, where they were openly opposed to eight hours, especially in the case of the New York and Brooklyn contestants, we gained a sweeping victory. In this connection I may cite the Progressive Carpenters, who openly boasted that they would not take part, but the carpenters' movement proved a complete success.

"One of the causes that led the Knights of Labor to oppose trade unions is the fact that employers of labor and storekeepers either fail to understand or appreciate the position of the wage-earners, or the methods by which they are to be improved. I cannot at this time, in view of the great work before us, devote much time to Mr. Powderly's puny cries, or his attempts to build up an organization which has proved to be a failure. In one word, Powderly and his organization has become a back number.

"Since Mr. Powderly now proposes war against federated labor I can only say that we bid him do his worst. The trades unions of this country and all the world have only one mission—to improve the condition of the workingmen and to finally secure their emancipation.'

General Master Workman T. V. Powderly spent all of yesterday in investigating the immigration system. Accompanied by John Hayes, A. W. Wright, James J. Holland, John Costello and John Devlin, the Knights of Labor Executive Committee, he visited the Barge Office. The party was received by Chief Inspector Milholland, and Labor Inspectors Lee and Conkling, and shown on board the revenue cutter Washington, in order that they might see how alien contract laborers are detected and detained at this port. Mr. Powderly was much interested by what he saw. He declined to say anything regarding his controversy with President Gompers.

New York World, June 22, 1890.

1. On Aug. 5, 1887, members of National Amalgamated Association of Iron and Steel Workers Lodge 15 of Brilliant, Ohio, struck the Spaulding Iron and Nail Co. over a wage dispute. The company assembled another crew, including Charles Glasso and Gus Sprecht, both members of the KOL. Glasso and Sprecht's local assembly of the Knights expelled them for working during a strike, but upon their appeal the KOL General Executive Board reinstated them. Following negotiations between the firm and General Executive Board member William Bailey, KOL members began filling other positions at the mill. Lodge 15 called off its strike on Apr. 5, 1888, and the firm rehired all but two of the strikers.

2. Between 1885 and 1886 Jacob C. BULLOCK was vice-president for the fourth district of the National Amalgamated Association of Iron and Steel Workers.

3. Members of International Typographical Union (ITU) 162 in Jacksonville, Fla., struck several newspapers on Apr. 5 and 6, 1886, over wages. When nonunion printers took their places, the union organized a boycott that continued through May. The ITU voted the strikers $500 to show support, but the KOL refused to endorse the boycott since it would only benefit "outside unions." The strikers were successful at two of the papers.

4. Charles S. Francis was proprietor of the *Troy Daily Times,* whose compositors struck unsuccessfully for union recognition in January 1884.

5. Robert SCHILLING was a Milwaukee labor editor. He ran unsuccessfully for Congress in 1888 and served as chairman of the Wisconsin central committee of the United Labor party in 1889.

6. Probably the Chicago packinghouse workers' strike of October 1886 against reinstatement of the ten-hour day.

7. On Apr. 15, 1890, members of Journeymen Tailors' Union 27 of Columbus, Ohio, struck for an increase in wages for women vest and pants makers employed in custom-made clothing shops, and for an equalization of prices paid in all shops regardless of the gender of the tailor. Although the local labor movement supported the strike, it failed in September.

8. Frederick TURNER, a goldbeater and later a grocer, was general secretary-treasurer of the KOL from 1883 to 1886 and was then general treasurer of the Order until 1888.

To Gabriel Edmonston

New York, June 24th 1890.

Mr. G. Edmondston
805 11th St. N.W. Washington, D.C.
Dear Friend:—

I am in receipt of your favor of the 21st inst. and thank you sincerely for your hearty good wishes and words reminding me of certain incidents connected with Mr. Powderly and our Eight Hour movement of 1886. If there is anything that occurs to you, any documents or public utterances published in the press of which you have a copy kindly send it on to me, and also if you have any numbers or a complete file of the "Picket."

Let me assure you that I shall do all I possibly can to check any impetuosity that may temporarily overtake me, and now and then say a thing to him that will cause him to use a "cuss word."

Try to get a copy of the New York "Star" or "World" of Sunday the 22nd. or a Phila. "Ledger" of the 23rd.[1] I shall try to obtain a copy of either for you.

Give my love to Sam[2] and ask him to remain cool himself or he will lose his balance on the bicycle. Tell him that he can understand how pressed I am with work and to excuse me from writing for a while. With best wishes, to you, yours and him and asking you to write frequently to yours truly

Sam.

TLS, Papers of Gabriel Edmonston, reel 1, *AFL Records.*

1. *The World, The Star,* and *The Public Ledger* reported on the exchanges between SG and Powderly.
2. Samuel Julian GOMPERS, SG's son, moved to Washington, D.C., in about 1887. There he worked as a printer, compositor, and clerk.

A Circular

July 2nd [1890]

To the Wage-Workers of all Countries.
Comrades:—

Recognizing the identity of interests of the wage-workers of the world, the great bond of interest and sympathy which should prevail in the hearts and minds of all toilers, and inasmuch as the Government of the United States of America has decided to hold an International Exhibition in 1893 in the City of Chicago to celebrate the 400th anniversary of the discovery of America by Christopher Columbus, and being desirous of further cementing the friendly feeling and the necessary unity of action and concentration of thought for an amelioration in the condition and final emancipation of the toiling masses, I take pleasure in notifying you that an International Labor Congress[1] will be held in the city of Chicago during the time of the holding of the Exhibition.

The object in holding the convention is to formulate and discuss the very many questions affecting our interest and to give a greater impetus to the cause of progress and civilization, and to make known to the world by our unalterable determination, that we insist upon being larger sharers in the world's progress.

We extend to you a kind and fraternal invitation to attend this International Labor Congress, and we appeal to you to hold no other International Labor Congress in any other country during 1893.

It is our intention to have the Congress in a position to discuss the question of labor from a broad and liberal standpoint, embracing as wide a scope of economic thought as the world itself.

A temporary Executive Committee consisting of two from each country and five from America will be appointed in a short time to act until conventions are held.

When each National industrial congress shall meet, we ask them to appoint a committee of two to act as a permanent Executive Committee on behalf of their country. In the United States each National Trade and Labor Union is requested to appoint one at their respective conventions, or if conventions are not held in time, the Executive Officers (if they have the power) are requested to appoint their delegate.

Permit me to assure the organized working men of the world that every thing will be done within our power to make their stay in America both pleasant and interesting, and our Congress a credit to the great Cause we have the honor to represent.

The details of arrangements will be made known to you from [time] to time.

Address all communications to,

Yours Fraternally   Saml Gompers.
President
By Order of the American Federation of Labor.
21 Clinton Place N.Y. City.

TLpS, reel 3, vol. 4, pp. 886-87, SG Letterbooks, DLC.

1. The AFL's 1889 convention met while Congress was contemplating holding a world's fair in 1892 to celebrate the 400th anniversary of Christopher Columbus's discovery of America. The convention approved a proposal by SG to hold an International Labor Congress in conjunction with the fair in whatever city Congress might select. On Apr. 25, 1890, President Benjamin Harrison signed a law establishing Chicago as the site of the World's Columbian Exposition. The Exposition actually took place May 1 to Oct. 30, 1893, to avoid competing with individual state celebrations planned for 1892. The AFL failed to generate sufficient European participation for its international labor congress and its 1892 convention abandoned the effort. In conjunction with the Exposition, however, a World's Congress Auxiliary sponsored a series of international congresses on various subjects. One of these was a general labor conference held Aug. 28–Sept. 4.

To Herman Brockmeyer[1]

July 3rd [1890]

Mr. N. F. Brookmeyer
Sec. Journeymen Barbers Union
165 Allen St. City.
Dear Sir:—

In reply to your favor of the 1st inst. I desire to say that it will be impossible for me to attend and address a mass-meeting of the Barbers on the 10th inst.

While I am anxious to aid in every way in the organizing of our fellow working people I am still of the impression that much injury is done to our cause by the injection of the question of nationality, race or religion. Our employers care very little what we are so long as we work cheap. I urge upon you and the so called Jewish Barbers to drop this particular appellation and to organize as people of that trade.

With best wishes for success I am,

Very Respectfully Yours   Saml Gompers.
President American Federation of Labor.

TLpS, reel 3, vol. 4, p. 888, SG Letterbooks, DLC.

1. Herman F. BROCKMEYER, apparently secretary of the Journeymen Barbers' International Union in 1889-90, was a New York City barber active in the Central Labor Federation.

To Charles Jenney[1]

July 3rd [1890]

Mr. Chas A. Jenney
Special Agent Eleventh Census
58 William St. City.
Dear Sir:—

In reply to your favor of the 1st inst. permit me to suggest the advisability of your representative calling here Monday July the 6th to copy the addresses I promised.

In compliance with your request for suggestions upon the beneficiary features of the Trade Unions and their achievements let me say that the question could cover the following grounds.

What amounts has your union paid to its members in cases of sickness within the past one or ten years?

What amounts has your union paid for death of its members within the past one or ten years?

What amounts has your union paid for the burial of members within the past one or ten years?

What amounts has your union paid for burial of members' families within the past one or ten years?

What endowments has your union paid to member's wife or family within the past one or ten years?

What endowments has your union paid to members out of employment within the past one or ten years?

What amounts has your union paid to members traveling, within the past one or ten years?

What amounts has your union paid to members on strike within the past one or ten years?

What amounts has your union paid for the insurance of tools within the past one or ten years?

What amounts has your union paid in law to defend the interests of its members?

What amounts has your union paid to aged or decrepit members within the past one or ten years?

What amounts has your union paid in donations to the needy within the past one or ten years?*

What were the hours of labor of the members of your craft trade or calling ten years ago?

What were the wages of your craft trade or calling ten years ago?

What are the average hours of labor of your craft trade or calling at the present day?

What are the average wages of the members of your craft trade or calling to-day?

What was the membership of your organization ten years ago?

What is its membership to-day?

What dues do the members of your organization pay?

What assessments do the members of your organization pay?

If there is any other information or additional questions that occur to you kindly suggest them and I will give you my advice.

I desire to say that I share your opinions that much prejudice would be allayed was the public mind cleared from the erroneous impressions previously gained of the purposes of the Trade and Labor Unions.

Very Respectfully Yours   Saml Gompers.
President American Federation of Labor.

*What amounts has your organization paid or donated toward assisting other working people improving their condition in the past ten years?

NB. You can change from 10 to 5 or score [. . .] last years.

S G

TLpS, reel 3, vol. 4, pp. 884-85, SG Letterbooks, DLC.

1. Charles Albert Jenney, longtime president of the Underwriter Printing and Publishing Co., was a special agent for the tenth and eleventh U.S. censuses, dealing with insurance statistics.

A Translation of an Excerpt of a News Account of a Mass Meeting at Cooper Union

[July 11, 1890]

THE MASS MEETING.

. . .

Sam. Gompers was now introduced with great applause. "It seems to me the most recent action of the conspiring Bosses has not had any great effect; this mighty gathering proves that the miserable trick they've just played has only strengthened the resistance, only increased the power and courage of the strikers. The clothing manufacturers who are now attempting to lock out their cutters maintain that the boycott against Benjamin & Co. is the only problem.[1] But why have they selected precisely this moment to settle the matter? Couldn't they have acted earlier? Did they have to wait until just this moment when

the cloakmakers are so close to their victory?[2] There is a conspiracy
here, and it has to be fought with all our might."

The speaker then praised the cloak cutters for their solidarity and
pointed out that the cloakmakers should not make the mistake of
viewing themselves as Jews, as a sect or as a special race, but rather
as American workers. Returning to the recent disturbances, he said
that one should keep calm and cool. But concerning the responsibility
for everything that might very well come, he said it lay with this
despicable band of conspirators that has put thousands on the streets.

Long enthusiastic applause followed Gompers' speech.

. . .

New Yorker Volkszeitung, July 11, 1890. Translated from the German by Dorothee Schneider.

1. Members of the Clothing Manufacturers' Association threatened to discharge
all cutters and trimmers who belonged to labor organizations as of July 12, 1890,
because of a boycott against Alfred Benjamin and Co. instituted by KOL National
Trade Assembly 231 and KOL Local Assembly (LA) 2853. Workers contended that
manufacturers designed the announcement to weaken a newly formed amalgamated
organization, the United Garment Workers' Association, which included LA 2853.
The lockout did not occur.

2. On May 21 two garment manufacturers in New York locked out their cloakmakers, members of the Cloakmakers' and Operators' Union, in anticipation that the
cloakmakers were going to strike for higher wages. On June 2 the United Cloak and
Suit Cutters' Association announced that its members would no longer work alongside
nonunion cloakmakers. In the middle of June, after the failure of arbitration, the
Cloak Manufacturers' Association inaugurated a lockout of about 300 cutters and
5,000 cloakmakers employed by its members. The two unions and the Contractors'
Union formed the Amalgamated Board of Cutters', Contractors', and Cloakmakers'
Unions to resist the lockout. In settlements reached with the unions in July, the
manufacturers agreed to employ none but union workers and the unions agreed to
take in all nonunion workers currently in their manufacturers' employ.

To the Editor of the *New York Press*

July 12th [1890]

To the Editor of The Press . . . .
Dear Sir:—

When I read my paper "The attitude of the Labor Men towards
the Liquor Traffic" at the National Temperance Congress June 16th,
Mr. Thompson in a very emphatic manner went out of his way to
make an attack upon the short hour movement and quoted Mr.
Goschen, Chancellor of the Exchequer of England as his authority
for the statement that the reduction in the hours of labor of the

English Dock Laborers only tended to greatly increase their drinking habit.

Feeling certain that this statement was at variance with the truth, or if the statement were true that the basis of it was conceived from error I wrote letters to Mr. Goschen, and Mr. John Burns (The Leader of the Dock Laborer's Movement) of which the following are copies (I also enclose the originals for your inspection as to authenticity.)

Copy.

June 17th [1890]

To the Right Honorable Mr. Goschen,
Chancellor of the Exchequer.
London, Eng.
Dear Sir:—

I trust you will pardon me for breaking in upon what must be very valuable time to you, but I deem the matter of such importance that I am constrained by a keen sense of duty to do so by asking you a question.

It will be necessary, however, to say in explanation that at the National Temperance Congress held in the city of New York a few days ago I took occasion to speak upon reduced hours of labor as a means to improve the moral as well as the material well being of the wage workers, and added that reduced hours of labor would make the people more temperate in the use of alcoholic beverages.

A gentleman in the audience quoted you as saying substantially as follows. Mr. Goschen the Chancellor of the Exchequer of Great Britain says: "that the increased wages and reduced hours of labor of the Dock Laborers in England has only tended to make them greater drinkers of intoxicants which has contributed largely to the Exchequer of the country."

Scarcely crediting the possibility of such a remark emanating from you I kindly ask you to spare a few moments to affirm or deny that statement and oblige,

Yours Very Respectfully   Saml Gompers.

Copy.

June 17th [1890]

Mr. John Burns
108 Lavender Hill Battersea, London, Eng.
My Dear Sir and Comrade:—

A National Temperence Congress was held in the city of New York a few days ago which I addressed, and advocated a reduction in the hours of labor as a means to improve the moral as well as the material condition of the people, and wean them from the drinking habit.

I was met with the statement by a gentleman at the Congress to the effect that Mr. Goschen the Chancellor of the Exchequer of Great Britain was the authority for the statement that the increase in the wages and the reduction in the hours of labor of the Dock Laborers of London has merely tended to increase their drunkenness and largely contributed to an increase in the treasury from the liquor traffic. Now I am inclined to the belief that Mr. Goschen did not make that statement, or if he did that it was not true, and I have written to Mr. Goschen asking him to answer the question whether he did make the statement, and I now ask you the two questions:

Whether you know that he made the statement or not, and if he did whether it was true that the Dock Laborers have increased their drinking habit since their victory?

I know that there are very many calls upon you to do many things, but this matter is of such vital importance, and so much can be made out of it against our movement that I ask you kindly to answer as soon as possible.

Sincerely hoping that your health may have been restored to you, and with sincere good wishes for the success of our Cause I am,

Fraternally Yours   Saml Gompers.
President American Federation of Labor.

The following replies were received by me June 10th & 11th respectively. They speak for themselves, are a complete refutation of Mr. Thompson's charge and verify in every particular the statements I made to the Congress.

Mr Goschen's Reply
Treasury Chambers. Whitehall. London, June 27th 1890.

Samuel Gompers Esq.
Sir:—

I am directed by the Chancellor of the Exchequer to acknowledge your letter of the 17th inst. and I am to inform you that the statement you mention as being imputed to him that the increased wages and reduced hours of labor of the dock laborers has only tended to make them drinkers of intoxicants is absolutely unfounded. What Mr. Goschen did say in his Budget Speech was that the increased prosperity of all classes in Great Britain during the past years has been accompanied by an increase in the consumption of intoxicating liquors. "All classes" he said "have combined" "to toast the prosperity" "of the country."

I am, Sir,

Yours Faithfully   Clinton E. Dawkins.

Mr Burn's Reply

108 Lavender Hill. Battersea.

Dear Sir: —

The Chancellor of the Exchequer did not say that the increase in wages and reduction of hours of labor of the Dock Laborers of London had merely tended to increase their drunkenness and largely contributed to an increase in the Treasury from the liquor traffic.

His statement was that the increase of 2 millions was due to the fact that the people had been toasting the prosperity of trade in the country. He made no reference to any class but did say that there had been a great increase in the duty from Rum.

I attended a meeting last night of 6000 Dock Laborers and asked those who ought to know what was the effect of higher wages and better conditions and the universal opinion was that the workers of London who have received better wages are more sober than ever they were.

As an abstainer myself I am delighted at the conduct of the Dockers and more than pleased at the diminution not only of drinking but of betting amongst them, due in no small measure to the fact that their leaders: Mems, Mann,[1] Tillett[2] and others are temperance men. The greatest enemies I have in London are the Betting men and Publicans, their enmity is a testimony to this fact that as we ask for reduction of hours so do we concurrently ask the men to use such reductions for more leisure and education, and urge the men to spend their higher wages in home comforts.

In 20 years the amount spent on liquor per head of population has decreased 20 per cent whilst the aggregate has increased through growth of population.

The proposals of the Government, happily defeated, to compensate publicans for extinction of licenses were introduced by the Publican's Government in anticipation of the bankruptcy of thousands of their friends through the growth of the temperance idea and greater reduction in drinking amongst the workers.

In England as elsewhere the short hours movement has always tended to sobriety and increased intelligence of the worker. In my own trade 12 or 14 years ago secretaries have been bribed to transfer the meeting place from the "Pig and Whistle" to the "Brown Bear" so that the publican might have the profit from drink consumed. So great has been the change that the proprietor of the "Brown Bear" will almost give you [£]20 to take the meeting away as the drink consumed does not pay him to have the meeting there. At Boat Races, Beanfeasts, Holiday gatherings etc. the change in the drinking habits is most marked.

Side by side with the demand for shorter hours is also the demand for Free Libraries, Parks and open spaces, Gymnasia, Cricket and Football grounds. Leisure to-day does not mean drinking but the opportunities for thought, education and true thrift which is impossible to men whose long hours make them animals and content with a brutal existence.

The rich man who drinks does so because he has nothing better to do. This means that the poor man who provides him with the means for drinking has to work longer hours than he should and as a consequence often heals the monotony of his toil by bouts of drinking, the cause of which the 8 hour advocates are going to remove by equalizing the labor of both. Thus the lazy man will have something to take an interest in whilst the previously overworked slave will have leisure without which manhood and its best characteristics are impossible.

Yours Truly   John Burns.

Asking you to kindly publish this correspondence so that the wide circulation the charge was given by the press at the time may be counteracted, and the impression made upon the assembled people removed I remain,

Yours Very Respectfully
President American Federation of Labor.[3]

TLp, reel 3, vol. 4, pp. 904-10, SG Letterbooks, DLC.

1. Thomas MANN was president of the Dock, Wharf, Riverside, and General Labourers' Union of Great Britain and Ireland (DWRGLU).
2. Benjamin TILLETT was general secretary of the DWRGLU.
3. The *Press* published Burns's letter to SG on July 14.

Terence Powderly to John Lavery[1]

Scranton Pa July 15, 1890

J. T. Lavery Esq.
R.S. S.A. Alabama.[2]
1st Ave. Bet. 9th & 10th Sts. Birmingham, Alabama.
Dear Sir and Bro.

Accept my very best thanks for the kindly interest you manifest in ascertaining the truth concerning the difficulties between the Knights of Labor and the Federation.[3]

I enclose, herewith, a copy of the Journal containing my Cooper

Union speech, and as it was a public expression of mine there is no necessity for a repetition here. The matter is not a personal one with me and the facts all go to show that I have gone as far as self-respect will permit in the effort to create a friendly feeling between the officers of the Federation and our Order.

No public expression of mine, no secret circular of mine, nor private letter, written either at my dictation or myself, has ever breathed anything but the friendliest of feelings for the Trades Unions of America, but the officers of the Federation did not desire peace and manufactured grievances against our Order when nothing real existed, on the same theory that the wolf who stood up stream complained that the lamb further down the stream had so riled the water that he could not drink.

The Eight Hour strike which Messrs. Gompers and Mc.Guire precipitated on the first of last May turned out to be a failure and they were angry to think that I did not give them some opportunity to find fault, but I refrained from saying one word except to encourage them until the strike was finally settled, and then I discovered that Gompers was busy all the time secretly fighting the Knights, why, he even went so far as to issue a circular every day against us in New York City.

The secret of all this lies in the fact that he was once a member of the Order and was detected, with others, in procuring our labels from Headquarters and then peddling them out to scab manufacturers so that he might have it to say that the Knights of Labor label was being used on unfair goods. When we discovered him in that act we took the Charter away from his Local Assembly and Mr. Gompers stands an expelled member ever since. If he was sincere in the labor movement he would go on building up his own organization and not meddle with ours.

He deliberately lied to their last convention when he told them that he had overtures from employing farmers to join with them for he can not show a solitary line from any such source, and I think it is not the part of manhood to deceive workingmen in any organization by false representation.

The workingmen of Birmingham may be deceived for a while, but you may rest assured that it will be for but a short time and then [they] will see Mr. Gompers in his true light.

I know that he does not represent the rank and file of the Trades Unions in his war on the Knights, for wherever I have had anything to do or wherever I could exert an influence both Knights and Trade Unionists are working in harmony.

What does Mr. Gompers know of you that he should warn the men of Birmingham not to have anything to do with you? Should not common sense dictate to the Trade Unionists of Birmingham that they stand a better chance of gaining their point by presenting a solid front than if they act on his advice and make war on the Knights?

Suppose I wrote to the Knights of Birmingham or anywhere else and told them to fight the Trade Unionists or have nothing to do with them, would I be acting in the interest of organized labor? I hardly think so.

With very best wishes, I remain,

Sincerely and fraternally yours,

TLc, Terence Vincent Powderly Papers, DCU.

1. John T. Lavery, a clerk from Birmingham, was president of the Salesman's Mutual Protective and Aid Association, a member of KOL Local Assembly 5009, and recording secretary and treasurer of the KOL's Alabama State Assembly.
2. The Alabama State Assembly of the KOL was organized in 1887.
3. Lavery wrote Powderly on July 10, 1890, that the Birmingham Trades Council refused to seat him as one of the delegates of his union because he was also a member of the KOL and therefore presumably hostile to trade unions. Lavery challenged the inference and asked Powderly to explain the Knights' attitude toward the AFL.

To George Eby[1]

July 18th [1890]

Mr. Geo. M. Eby.
Sec'y Clerks & Salesmen,
Duluth, Minn
Dear Sir & Bro:—

Your favor of the 13th. duly to hand and contents noted. In reply I desire to say that in the enthusiasm of your great success a little exaggeration as to numbers is pardonable.

There is the matter of forming a National Union of the Clerks and Salesmen[2] that I desire to have you make the next move in.

We have quite a number of Clerks Unions affiliated with the American Federation of Labor which could be immediately communicated with to carry on the preliminary work; and together with the help of the other unions, organizers and the labor press I am satisfied that the movement would be a success. What is required is the active attention of some man who not only is willing but also possesses the ability to do the necessary work. We have a number of good men through the country, notably one in Indianapolis, whom I feel confident will aid you or any one else who will undertake the task.

I wish you would bring this matter to the notice of your Union and get the views of the members upon it and advise me of the result as soon as convenient. You might also consult Mr. Applehagen.

With best wishes I am.

> Yours Fraternally.   Saml Gompers.
> President American Federation of Labor.

TLpS, reel 3, vol. 4, p. 935, SG Letterbooks, DLC.

1. George M. EBY was the first president of the Retail Clerks' National Protective Association of America.

2. The Retail CLERKS' National Protective Association of America was organized in December 1890.

To Gabriel Edmonston

N.Y. July 20th 1890.

My Dear Gabe:—

Your letter of 11. A.M yesterday came duly to hand and I hasten to reply in anxiety to enquire how my Sam is getting on.

I know your consideration for the feelings of others and your desire to allay any alarm. Hence I also know that if you found it necessary to secure the attendance of a Doctor at the time you did (1.30. A.M.) his case must have been, if it is not now, serious.

The only thing that reassures me is the one that he retained some of the milk on his stomach.

Of course I am awfully busy with the work in hand and cannot well afford coming on to Washington unnecessarily, but I hope you will not have either of these in mind if you deem my presence either necessary or advisable.

I am under obligations to you for your kindness to my Boy. Not only in this but also in many other instances. To say to you that I appreciate it and am grateful to you, I think is superfluous.

Convey to him the solicitious injunctions, and best wishes of his Mother, Sisters, Brothers and myself, to take care of himself and the gratitude of all for your devotion to him.

Let me know, by wire if necessary, of any change in his condition.

Ask him to write as soon as he can which, would be gratifying to the folks.

I shall feel in a better condition or moved to reply to your pleasantries when I have better news of him.

> Truly Yours. Saml Gompers.

N.Y. [N.B.] Had no postage and had to use official envelope. Why
don't you write now and then and keep up our correspondence?

> S. G.

ALS, Papers of Gabriel Edmonston, reel 1, *AFL Records.*

To James Cannon[1]

July 21st [1890]

Mr. James Cannon
40 Washington St. Memphis, Tenn.
Dear Sir and Brother:—

In reply to your favor of the 11th inst. which I received through
the kindness of Brother Mc-Guire permit me to say that I coincide
with you indeed that the propaganda of the labor movement has not
received the same widespread attention as that of the other sections
of the country. I believe however that this is largely due to the fact
that the South until recently has not developed its industries, and
that as a consequence organizations of labor are comparatively new.
I have no doubt however, that the near future will see much of a
change for the better.

I should take pleasure in issuing a commission to Mr. J. C. Roberts[2]
as organizer for your city or for the state if necessary, and supply him
with such documents as are published by the American Federation
of Labor to further the purposes of organization, but I desire to call
your attention to the fact however, that while we have several hundred
organizers throughout the country holding commissions not one of
them is receiving any salary or compensation. What they do has been
and is a work of love. There is no one now in the field—that is
traveling from place to place at the expense of the Federation, and
I am not sure that anyone will be within the very near future.

If you think that Mr. Roberts will consent to act in the same capacity
as the other organizers and under the conditions I name, kindly give
his full name and address and as stated already I will take pleasure
in issuing the commission to him.

Kindly advise me upon this matter at your earliest convenience and oblige,

Yours Fraternally　Saml Gompers
President American Federation of Labor.

TLpS, reel 3, vol. 4, pp. 940-41, SG Letterbooks, DLC.

1. James Cannon was financial secretary of United Brotherhood of Carpenters and Joiners of America 394 of Memphis, Tenn.
2. James C. Roberts was a Memphis carpenter. SG appointed him a general organizer of the AFL.

To Ernest Bohm

July 24th [1890]

Mr. Ernest Böhm
202 E. 57th St. City.
Dear Sir:—

I am in receipt of your favor of the 19th inst. in which you make a formal demand for the charter of the C.L.F. of New York and I repeat to you that that charter cannot be returned to your body in consequence of the fact that the C.L.F. of New York ceased to exist last December. This information was not alone communicated to me by Mr. Henry Emrich but by a delegate of the C.L.F. to the Boston convention and many others connected with it.

It seems to me that your statement that upon the "adjournment of the C.L.F. in December 1889 it was tacitly understood that all the property of that body was to remain in the hands of the officers, but that the charter was to be turned over to you (Me) personally for safe keeping" carries with it in the first place the stigma that the unity with the C.L.U. was not made in good faith, and second I desire to say that charters of the American Federation of Labor are in my official and not personal care.

I desire to assure you and your colleagues that I am in no wise in sympathy with the C.L.U. in its conduct of late in matter connected with the labor movement, but this cannot sway my judgement in returning a charter to an organization which surrendered it when the books of this office already show that fact.

You ask me to "act fairly" and return the charter? I believe my record in the movement of labor entitles me at least to the distinction of being fair and if my sense of duty and loyalty to an organization, the interest of which is committed to my care, prevents me from complying with your request I think it does not necessarily follow that I have ever been other than fair in my connection with the labor movement.

Sincerely hoping that this may be taken in the spirit in which it is written I am,

Fraternally Yours.   Saml Gompers.
President. American Federation of Labor.

TLpS, reel 3, vol. 4, pp. 952-53, SG Letterbooks, DLC.

To Mr. Conklin

July 26th [1890]

Mr. Conklin
Room 161 Post Office Building. City.
My Dear Sir:—

I have the honor to acknowledge your favor of the 24th in which you ask me if I would accept the nomination as a candidate for Congress.

In reply permit me to say that under no circumstances will I allow my name to be used in connection with the nomination you speak of at the coming election.

By the way a statement is attributed to some one that at the last election when I was nominated for Senator, Governor Hill secured my withdrawal from the nomination. I desire to say to you, and you have my privilege to say it to any one you please that the statement is without any foundation in fact, and made out of whole cloth.

In my letter to the Senatorial Convention I gave the true reasons for my declination and all others I beg to assure you, are pure fabrications.

Assuring you of my hearty appreciation of the honor implied by coupling my name with the position referred to and thanking you for the interest you have taken in the matter, I have the honor to subscribe myself,

Yours Very Respectfully   Saml Gompers.

TLpS, reel 3, vol. 4, p. 955, SG Letterbooks, DLC.

To John Kirchner

July 28th [1890]

Mr. J. S. Kirchner
437 N. 4th St. Phila, Pa.
Dear Sir and Friend:—

Your favor of the 25th inst. with clipping of our journal came duly to hand and I read it not only with surprise but indignation. I cannot for the life of me account for that editorial comment[1] unless it be that he is dissatisfied with something. In the first instance it is not in accordance with the facts and his own statement is a contradiction in itself. He says "While we do not underestimate the value of agitation and activity, there cannot be and never was a revival of the labor movement in any part of the globe, without a general revival of industry and improvement in the conditions of employment."

I want to call your attention to the fact that he speaks of an impossibility of a revival in the labor movement without an improvement in the "conditions of employment," trying to bring about the improved conditions of employment, except from the revival in the labor movement: it is the condition precedent and not subsequent which he admits. In my opinion the labor movement energetically and earnestly conducted can and does prevent stagnation in business and dullness in trade, hence I also hold that the same causes namely, activity and energy in conducting the labor movement will bring a revival in industry.

I am considering whether I should answer the article, but I am inclined to the belief from the tone assumed in the editorial note that Mr. Strasser is itching for a fight, right or wrong and I would prefer so far as I am concerned, to allow his statement to go by unnoticed rather than [entering into?] a quarrel intentionally provoked which, though I am satisfied I am in the right, would be regarded by our enemies as an internecine strife and redound to the detriment of the whole movement. But supposing that his statement were absolutely true the question that would occur to an ordinary man would be, is there such an awful wrong, mischievous and unwarrantable statement in that part of your letter which he quotes and criticizes as to call forth his antagonism and comment.

I wonder whether Mr. Strasser will deny that the movement to reduce the hours of labor can prolong fair trade and postpone an industrial crisis or stagnation.

At present I am of the opinion that I shall not gratify him by entering into a quarrel through the journal but I would be willing and anxious to meet him and demonstrate the falsity of his position.

[If you?] reply to the article, and I think you should, you have my permission to use the arguments or points in this letter as your own but I request you not to mention my name in connection with it.

I am pleased to see the movement progressing in your city and am gratified if I have in some way been instrumental in aiding it.

Never mind John, you keep straight and stick to the tack and trend in which our movement is going and we shall soon have the satisfaction of seeing the Cigar Makers Int. Union of America in the foremost ranks of our great struggle.

I wish you would write a little more often to,

Yours Truly   Saml Gompers.
President American Federation of Labor.

TLpS, reel 3, vol. 4, pp. 963-65, SG Letterbooks, DLC.

1. In a letter published July 1890 in the *Cigar Makers' Official Journal*, Kirchner attributed the increased strength of Philadelphia's cigarmakers' union to the AFL's revival of agitation for the eight-hour day. He indicated the local would soon strike for a new bill of prices. Adolph Strasser contended that the cigarmakers were better off primarily because of improvement in the cigar trade and cautioned that this made a strike unnecessary. Kirchner did not reply to Strasser's comments.

To Frank Sargent and Eugene Debs

Aug. 30th [1890]

Messrs. Frank P. Sargent & Eugene V. Debbs
Grand Chief & Grand Secretary Brotherhood of Locomotive Firemen.
Fellow-Workmen:—

Your kind invitation extended to me to participate in the Reception to the delegates to your convention[1] and their friends came duly to hand.

Permit me to assure you that I employ no idle words when I say that I exceedingly regret my inability to be with you on that occasion. In acknowledging the compliment implied by your invitation I appreciate the fact that it is tendered not so much to me personally as from the fact of the circumstances that have placed me as one of the representatives of the idea we so much hold in common—Federation.

It becomes our duty and the fulfillment of the mission of the great trade unions of our time and country to realize the fact that in the never ending process and struggle for the improvement in the condition of the wage-workers, that it is necessary to be continually alert in strengthening the weak points in our ramparts to prevent successful attacks and destruction of our defenses by our antagonists of all stripes.

Single trade unions have unquestionably accomplished wonderful results but have too often been beaten in the contest with united and aggressive capital, and to my mind the weak part of our trade union system has been a lack of concerted action when one has been engaged in a struggle to maintain or defend itself or its members, in other words the failure to fully and thoroughly federate the interests of all.

No man appreciates more thoroughly nor would defend more earnestly and relentlessly the autonomy and independence of our trade unions than I, but I believe in the exercise of this autonomy and independence we should voluntarily associate ourselves with our fellow workers, not in centralized autocracy but a federalized democracy.

I am fully aware that all movements towards a progressive and desirable end must take their natural course of proper and healthy development, hence I believe the primary consideration with you should be the federation of all the railroad trade unions. What the ultimate tendency of federation with the organized trade unions of other callings may develop, the common sense of the wage-workers and the future will decide.

The thought that federation among the railroad organizations would provoke and multiply strikes, recent events have dispelled, and removed with one master stroke all reasonable opposition to the attainment of that purpose.

Accept my assurances and well wishes for the harmony and success of your convention and the hope that it will place to its record at least one milestone passed, in the onward movement to the solution of the greatest problem mankind has ever been called upon to solve.

Fraternally Yours   Saml Gompers.
President American Federation of Labor.

TLpS, reel 4, vol. 5, pp. 58-59, SG Letterbooks, DLC.

1. The fifteenth convention of the Brotherhood of Locomotive Firemen took place in San Francisco, Sept. 8-15, 1890.

To Ernest Bohm

Sep. 11th [1890]

Mr. Ernest Bohm
Sec. Central Labor Federation
202 E. 57th St. City.
Dear Sir and Brother: —
I am in receipt of your favor of the 9th inst. informing me that

you were instructed to make application to the American Federation of Labor for a charter.

I beg to inform you that the formal application should contain the names of seven persons in whose names the charter can be made out and to have the application accompanied by the fee of $5.00.

By referring to the list of organizations which you forward I notice the name of "American section, Socialistic Party" and I cannot bring myself to understand how a political Party as such can be represented in a central trade union organization. Of the merits or demerits of the "Socialistic Labor Party" it is not within my province to discuss but the representation of that party or any other political party in a purely trade union central organization is to my mind not permissible. I desire also to ask whether there are any organizations attached to the Central Labor Federation which according to the constitution of the A.F. of L. are not eligible therein.

Enclosed please find a blank application as per above and also a copy of the constitution.

Kindly asking you to bring the matters herein contained to the notice of the C.L.F. for its early consideration I am,

Fraternally Yours   Saml Gompers
President

TLpS, reel 4, vol. 5, p. 80, SG Letterbooks, DLC.

To David Hill

Sep. 18th [1890]

Hon. David B. Hill
Governor of the State of New York.
Albany, N.Y.
Dear Sir:—

A few months ago I took occasion to write you in connection with violations of the law in the matter of the labor of convicts at Sing Sing Prison. Later I forwarded a number of letters by Mr. Ed. J. Kean,[1] that I had received from prisoners. Others came to me since describing a condition of affairs which is horrible and inhuman. They also contain charges of corruption and favoritism which are palpable and easy of demonstration.

As Governor of the State, I make my request to you, to give this matter your early and earnest attention in order that the fame of our penal institutions may not become a by-word and deserving of the condemnation of the civilized world.

If you think that the request is incompatible with your duties, or the interest of the State and decline to act, I kindly ask you to return the letters and enclosures handed to you by Mr. Kean & oblige,

Yours Very Respectfully   Saml Gompers
President American Federation of Labor.

TLpS, reel 4, vol. 5, p. 99, SG Letterbooks, DLC.

1. Edward KEAN, a New York City printer, was chief clerk of the New York Bureau of Labor Statistics between 1885 and 1891.

To George Eby

Sep. 24th [1890]

Mr. Geo. M. Eby
Care Silberstein & Bondy[1]
9-11 W. Superior St. Duluth, Minn.
Dear Sir and Brother:—

Many thanks for your favor of the 17th inst. giving an account of the progress of the labor movement in your city, and I am also under obligations to you for the clippings you enclosed.

Permit me to say that to my mind if the working people would give but one half the attention to the improvement of their economic condition much more will be accomplished than by dabbling in that cesspool of corruption commonly known as party politics. Be the opinion what it may in reference to this, every man has a right as a citizen to act and vote with and for any party as his conscience may dictate, but certainly the organizations of labor should be left unsullied from the pernicious influences and results of party politics.

The working men of your city need but look back one year and note the contrast both in their economic condition and social standing and compare it with that of the present day, when they will be convinced that the methods by which they have attained this enviable position and brought about so remarkable a change is the one to be followed, rather than entering into an agitation and a movement the results of which are highly questionable and a discussion of which has already brought a division not only of opinion but of action in your ranks. Earnestly wishing that a conflict may be avoided and that harmony may be restored to the ranks of the Trade Union movement of your city I am,

Fraternally Yours   Saml Gompers.
President

TLpS, reel 4, vol. 5, p. 112, SG Letterbooks, DLC.

1. Bernard Silberstein and Isaac Bondy operated a dry goods, carpet, and millinery establishment in Duluth.

To Edward Berk

Sep. 26th [1890]

Mr. Ed. Berk
Sec. Journeymen Plummers Union 5130 A.F. of L.[1]
37 Stewart Ave Columbus, O.
Dear Sir and Brother:—

Your favor of the 23rd inst. submitting the rules that the employers desire to enforce came duly to hand.

You ask my opinion of the same and I will be frank enough to say that those that you marked "satisfactory" are sufficient guarantee to the employers that you propose to do right by them.

The proposition to have *overtime* commence at seven o'clock is entirely unfair and improper. In the first instance overtime should be entirely discouraged if it can possibly be avoided. To have overtime commence at seven o'clock merely means that you will work until seven o'clock whenever it suits that fancy of the employers; and you will find that fancy to be, every day that you work.

Overtime should commence immediately after your nine hours work; and if you have been in the habit of having time and a half for overtime and double time for Sunday it should continue in the same way.

Since the employer has the power and the right to discharge any man for carelessness it seems to me that that is sufficient to protect the employer and he should not be privileged to deduct any amount from the wages of a workman as proposed in rule 6. In reference to rule 9, I cannot see any objection being raised since all that is required of the Plummers is to give written orders for what may be required the following day.

You should ascertain who will be required to "charge up" all the material, whether the plummer or the helper. If the plummer, his statement in writing of unused material should be a protection against his being charged with any loss and he should give reasonable care to the safe deposit of all such unused material. If the helper is required to make such a report, it is not the concern of the plummer and consequently he should not be held responsible for it.

I would suggest that you would present these reasons to the employers why you should not be required to submit to them and I am satisfied that a fair presentation of them will convince them that their position is an untenable one.

With kindest wishes and hoping to hear from you soon I am,

Fraternally Yours   Saml Gompers.
President American Federation of Labor.

TLpS, reel 4, vol. 5, pp. 123-24, SG Letterbooks, DLC.

1. Probably Journeymen Plumbers' Union 5180, which was affiliated directly with the AFL.

To Henry Blair

Sep 27th [1890]

Senator Henry W. Blair.
U.S. Senate Chamber. Washington D.C.

The amendment[1] adopted yesterday by the Senate is subversive of the spirit of the Alien Contract Labor Law. Unless Senate improves the law to protect the wage workers of America it were better left unaltered.

Samuel Gompers.
President American Federation of La[bor]

ALpS, reel 4, vol. 5, p. 127, SG Letterbooks, DLC.

1. SG apparently objected to the exclusion of certain categories of immigrants in the bill before Congress to amend the Alien Contract Labor Law of 1885. As enacted in 1891, the amendment (U.S. *Statutes at Large*, 26:551) excluded ministers, professionals, and college professors. It also made port inspectors responsible for reporting suspected cases of illegal immigration to a board of special inquiry, prohibited promises of employment in advertisements abroad, and required immigrants whose passage was paid for by another to prove that they were not contract laborers.

An Excerpt from a News Account of a Meeting of the New York City Central Labor Federation

[September 27, 1890]

ORGANIZED LABOR.

. . .

THE SOCIALIST ISSUE.

It was four o'clock when the special order, "Mr. Gompers' excommunication of the Socialists," was taken up.

Delegate Rosenfelder,[1] Eccentric Engineers No. 3,[2] argued that it was useless to discuss the matter at any length. The Socialists should remain in the C.L.F. and the C.L.F. should waive the charter. Delegate Dougherty stated that he had no instruction from his union and could not speak on the matter.

Delegate Adolph Jablinowski,[3] Cigarmakers' Union No. 90,[4] said that the request for a charter should be pushed, so that Mr. Gompers' position and that of his fellow members of the Executive Committee of the A.F. of L., concerning the Socialists be well defined and remain a matter of record.

Delegate Blumenberg,[5] Carpenters No. 513,[6] claimed that the charter would be of no use to the C.L.F. The American Section should remain represented.

Delegate Hecker[7] of the Custom Varnishers and Polishers[8] was opposed to a charter because the C.L.F. as a local central body could do better without it.

Delegate Fraeber of the Cloakmakers[9] was in favor of forcing the question to an issue by demanding a charter. The Socialists performed more labor for the workingmen than did the officers of the A.F. of L. They fought for all the toilers against the capitalists. We could better dispense with the charter than with the Socialists.

Delegate Simon Gompers,[10] of the Shoe Workers,[11] said that Mr. Gompers was not hostile to the Socialists but on the contrary had always leaned in his views to the doctrine which they professed. As President of the American Federation of Labor, he was compelled to take into account the objections of many to their official representation in the bodies affiliated with the Federation. A charter was not necessary, it could be of no practical benefit, and he, therefore, was in favor of settling the question by not applying for a charter.

The delegate of the Clothing Cutters' Progressive Union said that the Socialists should not only be represented in the C.L.F. but also in the American Federation of Labor. (Applause.) I am not a member of the S.L.P., observed the speaker, but I recognize with other toilers their necessity in the Labor movement. We should not bend our knee to any man. My union believes that the Socialists are just as good as we are and they should remain.

Delegate Sanial,[12] of the American Section, said he had little to add to his statement of last Sunday. The Section had endorsed the utterances of its delegates at the previous meeting of the C.L.F.,[13] as published in the *Workmen's Advocate* for the information of all, and it was now confidently waiting for the action of this body. He would be sorry to see the discussion of such an important matter drift on the inferior plane of personalities; for it was a national issue, involving the tendencies [and] future progress of the labor movement and it should be considered on the highest ground of principle. Let us cast a rapid glance at the economic conditions of the movement. Since the railroad power had reached a high degree of concentration every railroad strike had been a failure. The telegraph operators some years ago were well organized. They thought they had a monopoly of the skill required in their industry and they struck to better their condition. What was the result? A stupendous failure. And why? Because the telegraph industry had reached the highest possible degree of concentration. Again, this year had been one of extraordinary activity in the iron trade throughout the world; to the extent that far from having to fear the competition of English iron in our markets we had for the first time in the history of the United States been able to ship American iron to England. And yet the great Association of Iron workers, which is affiliated with the American Federation of Labor, had not dared to demand from the "masters" any concession. Why? Because the iron industry, though not yet concentrated in the same degree as the railroads and the telegraphs, is sufficiently so to make the advantages that might be gained by a strike of little permanent value as compared with the enormous sacrifices which it would entail.

I might consider every industry and show you, by actual figures, that the helplessness of Labor, so long as it is organized on a purely economic basis, must grow in proportion to the growth of capitalistic concentration, temporary success being still possible in those trades only which, like the carpenters and other builders, the bakers, the cigarmakers, etc., are still to some extent open to the competition of second class capitalists. But here, as elsewhere, the process of concentration is rapidly advancing, and if the lines of the labor movement are not so advanced that Labor may concentrate its political as well as its economic forces, I make bold to predict that the trades unions will be utterly powerless within a few years, owing chiefly, of course,

to the amount of unemployed labor—of "surplus labor"—which
inevitably follows capitalistic concentration. Now, we Socialists represent here this idea, that labor must concentrate all its power, political
and economical, against the common enemy; and with this end in
view we promote by all the means at our command the organization
of trades unions, as the alpha—the first letter in the alphabet of
Labor. It is an idea that the force of circumstances would of itself in
the natural course of events, force into the heads of the working
people, whether they liked it or not.

We believe that they are ready to accept it; that most of them have,
in fact, already accepted it; and that the only obstacle to its being
carried out is the cowardice of so-called conservative leaders, who
while claiming to entertain advanced views, are actually doing their
best to keep alive old prejudices by persisting in a false assimilation
of the Socialist Labor party to the old political parties. It were high
time this humbugology were exposed and repudiated. Let the C.L.F.
stamp it out; let it boldly proclaim that the economic and the political
movements of labor must be one; and that the Socialist Labor party,
as the only representative of this idea, is of necessity the party of
Labor and its only party.

Delegate Vogt[14] said that Mr. Gompers must be judged by the public
effect of his action; and the public impression as to his letter[15] was
that it was aimed against Socialism. That public impression was well
voiced to the delegate shortly after the publication of the letter, when
a prominent politician sneeringly told him of the blow dealt to the
Socialists by Gompers, who had thereby won for himself the sympathy
of the public. Such an effect was to be foreseen and it must be taken
as having been intended. When McMackin[16] in 1887 issued his edict
against the Socialists, he too employed at first the dodge that he meant
the Socialist Labor party as an organization and not the individual
Socialists. At Syracuse he, with George and McGlynn,[17] threw off the
mask and openly entered upon that famous campaign against Socialism, that resulted so disastrously—to its originators. We know that
Gompers *had* socialist leanings, in fact he was a member of the Socialist
party; but we also know that in his public action he has "gone back"
upon his former convictions; we remember his anxiety to accept an
old party nomination for Senator, his open attacks upon Socialism in
the convention of the Cigarmakers' International Union, and thereby
we must measure him. While we have proof that other central bodies
comprising Socialist Labor party sections have been chartered by the
American Federation of Labor, we refuse to predicate our case on
precedent. This movement will not halt in its onward march because
of any precedent. The formation of the Central Labor Federation

was a departure from precedent, a revolutionary step, a declaration of war upon the old tradition of political scabbism in the labor movement. The C.L.F. was founded upon the very principle of unity between the political and the economic organization of labor, upon which the American Section claimed and was logically admitted to representation. What this unity means was demonstrated by the workingmen of Germany in February last, when for a few weeks they laid down their economic struggles, postponed strikes and trades-union work and devoted themselves exclusively to the task of piling up 1,500,000 labor votes at the polls.[18] Hasn't that vote done more to benefit the cause of labor in all its interests than 1,000 strikes? The 68,000 votes cast in New York in 1886 and the large labor votes polled in Chicago, Milwaukee, Cincinnati, made capitalists and capitalistic politicians tremble and platforms began to overflow with promises of labor laws: legislators began to bestir themselves and the power of labor was felt in the land. All that has ceased with the collapse of the independent political movement and in this year, when that movement is considered extinct, the platforms adopted by the old party State conventions do not even refer to the demands of labor, politicians do not even take the trouble of throwing a sop to the disorganized workers. Men who tell you in the face of these facts that you have no business to connect yourselves with a true labor party, are either monumental fools or serving the enemy. Don't consult the enemy as to what will best further your interests, but consult your friends; and as you know and every honest workers knows, your best friends are the socialists.

Delegate G. H. McVey said that he at first had not favored the application for a charter, but since he had heard the able arguments made he was in favor of it. Any other action would be cowardly. We should carry this fight into the Convention of the American Federation of Labor, for the issue involved is of national importance. We must force the Executive Council of the American Federation of Labor to show its hand. He moved that the President of the Federation be notified that the C.L.F. sees no reason to exclude the American Section.

This motion was adopted, all the delegates voting for it, except Simon Gompers, who subsequently explained to the reporter that upon the ground which he had taken and which he still believed to be right, he could not consistently vote otherwise.

. . .

Workmen's Advocate (New York), Sept. 27, 1890.

1. Probably Christian Rosenfelder.

2. Eccentric Association of Engineers' local 3.

3. Ludwig JABLINOWSKI was secretary of Cigarmakers' Progressive Union 1 (subsequently Cigar Makers' Progressive International Union [CMPIU] 90) from 1885 until 1889 and a founder of the New York City Central Labor Federation (CLF).

4. CMPIU 90, an affiliate of the CMIU.

5. Robert Blumenberg was secretary of the CLF's Building Trades Council.

6. United Brotherhood of Carpenters and Joiners of America 513 of New York City.

7. A. Hecker.

8. International Furniture Workers' Union of America 39.

9. Probably Operators and Cloak Makers' Union 1.

10. Simon GOMPERS, SG's uncle, was a shoemaker.

11. Probably Boot and Shoe Workers' Union 117.

12. Lucien Delabarre SANIAL was a prominent leader of the SLP and editor of its organ, the *Workmen's Advocate* (1889-91).

13. Sanial, Hugo Vogt, and others defended the SLP's representation in the CLF at the federation's meeting on Sept. 14.

14. Hugo VOGT, a notary public, was a leader of the SLP in New York City.

15. SG's letter to Ernest Bohm, Sept. 11, 1890, above, appeared in the *Workmen's Advocate*, Sept. 20, 1890.

16. John MCMACKIN, a painter, was a leader in the New York City CLU. He served as special inspector of customs for New York City from 1889 to 1894. As chairman of the New York County Central Committee of the United Labor party (ULP), he ruled on Aug. 5, 1887, that membership in the SLP violated the ULP's constitutional prohibition of membership in another political party, effectively expelling the socialists from the ULP. The ULP state convention held in Syracuse on Aug. 17 upheld McMackin's decision.

17. Edward MCGLYNN was a Catholic priest in New York City. He was excommunicated in 1887 after a conflict with the Church related to his outspoken support of Henry George.

18. Despite the anti-socialist law of 1878 that forced the Sozialistische Arbeiterpartei Deutschlands (Socialist Labor Party of Germany) underground, the party won almost 20 percent of the popular vote in the February 1890 Reichstag elections. The anti-socialist law lapsed in September and the party, renamed the Sozialdemokratische Partei Deutschlands (Social Democratic Party of Germany) in October, became a legal organization.

To William Ferguson

[October 4, 1890]

Mr. Wm. Ferguson
Sec. Typographical Union No. 6
240 William St. N.Y. City
Dear Sir and Brother:—

Enclosed please find decision of arbitrator in the case between your organization and Typographical Union No. 7 in the matter of the dispute in the "Morgen Journal" office.

Assuring you that I have endeavored to perform the duties to the best of my ability and with an earnestness of purpose to arrive at a just conclusion I am,

Fraternally Yours   Saml Gompers
President American Federation of Labor.

Oct. 4th [1890]

In the matter of the rival claims of Typographical Unions No. 6. and No. 7 English and German Unions respectively and which was referred to the undersigned as arbitrator it is but proper to preface briefly the case as presented, and to give the reasons which govern the arbitrator in rendering his decision.

The Proprietor of the "Morning Journal" on or about September decided to issue a German paper to be called the "Morgen Journal."

A member of Typographical Union No. 6. was directed to secure German compositors for the office, and upon learning this state of affairs Typographical Union No. 7 claimed that the German composing department of that paper came under their jurisdiction by reason of various matters herein-after referred to.

Union No. 6 disputed this claim, asserting its right to set German composition and to secure work for its members. The publishers of the paper desired to have their composition performed by union members and rather than have any dispute, preferred that the matter should be left to arbitration, to which both Unions No. 6. and No. 7 acquiesced (the former under protest) and pending the arbitration an equal number of members of both Unions were to be employed, the Publisher and both Unions agreeing upon the undersigned as arbitrator.

It is held by No. 6 that it derives its corporate existence from the International Typographical Union the constitution of which provides that "In it alone is vested the power to establish subordinate Unions of printers" etc, etc, and hence the German Printers' Union has been tolerated rather than a right accorded to it to organize the German Printers.

On the other hand it is submitted that the International Typographical Union made special provision for the organization and recognition of German printers unions by a special, mutual agreement entered into between the conventions of the International Typographical Union and the German American Typographia which provided for cases of the character under consideration.

In the 2nd. section of said agreement the following occurs: "Where there is a German department in an English Union or German Union office, or single members of a German Union are working or vice versa, where there is an English department in a German Union office, or single members of the English Union are employed the members of both Unions shall act in unity in all disputes" etc. etc.

Section 3. of the same agreement also reads that "It shall be the rule that German compositors not belonging to either Union, setting German in an office controlled by the English Union, shall be compelled by the chairman to join the German Union. English compositors in a German office, not yet belonging to either Union, shall be compelled to join the English Union."

From the testimony elicited and a careful consideration of the facts submitted and a personal investigation it is evident that the composing rooms of the "Morning Journal" and the "Morgen Journal" are separate departments, within the meaning of the agreement entered into between the International Typographical Union and the German American Typographia.

Thus, so far as the law and agreement are concerned the claim of the office by Union No. 7 is justified.

During the investigation it was claimed that in consequence of the crowded space in the composing rooms the German compositors are required to use certain material formerly and still used by the English compositors; that the Foreman of the German department is but the Assistant of the Foreman of the English department, that the said Foreman pays salaries of all compositors German and English alike, as well as the Assistant Foreman's of the German department.

From personal investigation and an interview (in the composing rooms) with Mr. Hugh Dalton ex-President of Typographical Union No 6. and present Foreman of the New York "Daily News" office (the proprietors and publishers of which issue a German daily paper called the "Tages Nachrichten") I learn that the same condition of affairs prevails, so far as the German compositors using type that the English compositors sometimes use, that the Foreman of the German department is but the Assistant of the Foreman of the English office, that the latter pays the wages of the English and German compositors as well as that of the said Assistant Foreman; and that notwithstanding these facts there is a recognized German department under the jurisdiction of Typographical Union No. 7, and though the majority of the compositors working in said composing rooms are members of Union No. 6 from all of which the arbitrator respectfully submits that the claim of Union No. 7 to the jurisdiction of the German department of the composing room of the "Morgen Journal" office should be and is allowed.

The arbitrator calls attention that this award in nowise restricts the right of the members of Union No. 6 to set German, and in accordance with the understanding arrived at between both parties the arbitrator's decision applies exclusively to the "Morgen Journal" office.

The arbitrator desires to add that he regrets that any dispute should have arisen between two organizations which have done and still continue to do so much good in protecting and advancing the interests of their members, and to maintain the honor and dignity of the craft, and that his own position in being selected as the arbitrator has been entirely a disagreeable and unwelcome one to himself.

Were the dispute between a Union and the employer it would hardly be as difficult, but between two such organizations he submits to the good will and kind judgement of the disputants, the labor movement in general, and the general public.

He recognizes that if the members of two organizations working upon the same floor run counter to each other an undeserved injury may be inflicted upon a fairly inclined employer. Finding however, that such a result has not been the case in the matter of the "Daily News" and the "Tages Nachrichten" and depending upon the good will, the earnestness and sincerity of the members of both Unions to deal fairly with an employer of union men; he has no hesitancy in declaring his belief that the publishers and proprietors of the "Morning Journal" and "Morgen Journal" will encounter no other inconveniences more [than] would result from the fact which is at present apparent that the composing rooms are much too crowded.

Very Respectfully Submitted.　Saml Gompers.
Arbitrator.

TLpS, reel 4, vol. 5, pp. 144-49, SG Letterbooks, DLC.

To S. R. Holmes[1]

Oct. 8th [1890]

Mr. S. R. Holmes
Care "Sunday Press" Findlay, O.
My Dear Sir:—

Replying to your favor of the 3rd inst. permit me to say that I keenly feel the position in which you are placed by reason of my letter to Mr. Cook.[2] If the Plasterers, not being of a sufficient number to organize a local union, and other wage-workers will organize a Federal Labor Union I see no reason why you and such men as you could not be permitted to become members. The reason upon which I based my decision is as you can readily understand that the line must be drawn somewhere in allowing employers of labor to become active members in the labor movement.

The policy followed by the K. of L. in allowing employers to become members of their order very frequently deterred working men from seeking an improvement in their condition by reason of fear in giving offence to such employers.

The Trade Unions are based upon a different standard. They recognize that while there are men who are employers of labor [. . .] in unison [and] sympathy with the aspirations of the working people, who is to decide where the line is to be drawn. The mere statement of a man being in favor of the labor movement is no guarantee that he will not be among those to take advantage of utterances of his employees when he supposes his interests to be assailed by any act of these employees in their organized capacity.

The American Federation of Labor holds it as a self evident maxim that the emancipation of the working classes must be achieved by the working classes themselves. There is no doubt that men with best intentions outside of the ranks of labor can aid in this movement. We court their co-operation, their sympathy and their advice but cannot give into their hands the direction of the affairs which rightfully belong to and must be exercised by the wage-workers.

If the men of whom you speak have pursued the course you mention it seems to me that at least so far as they are concerned (men who will profess their love for certain principles to-day and the opposite to-morrow) my decision is justified and the stand of the American Federation of Labor a correct one.

I hope you may be successful in forming the Federal Labor Union that you speak of and I ask you to consult Mr. Henry Schelling[3] 522 Washington St. Findlay, O. in reference to the matter.

Reciprocating your kind expressions of good will and hoping to hear from you as frequently as convenient I am,

> Yours (I hope soon fraternally) Sincerely.   Saml Gompers.
> President American Federation of Labor.

NB. You can show Mr Schelling this letter.

> S. G.

TLpS, reel 4, vol. 5, pp. 151-52, SG Letterbooks, DLC.

1. Possibly Shipley R. Holmes, a Findlay, Ohio, real estate agent.
2. About Sept. 29, 1890, SG wrote to John H. Cook, a laborer at the City Gas Works in Findlay, rejecting the Workmen's Protective Association's application for affiliation on the grounds that the AFL constitution excluded employers from membership.
3. Henry Schelling was a Findlay cigarmaker and an AFL organizer.

To the Executive Board of the
United Brotherhood of Carpenters
and Joiners of America

Oct. 24th [1890]

Fellow-Workmen: —

Some two years ago the American District of the Amalgamated Carpenters & Joiners made application for a charter from the American Federation of Labor. The same was referred to the St. Louis convention and by that body rejected upon the objection of the United Brotherhood of Carpenters & Joiners' delegates on the grounds that a dual organization in the trade would be inimical to the interests of the Carpenters. Just prior to the Chicago convention of the United Brotherhood[1] the District Secretary[2] requested an expression of opinion as to whether a charter would be granted to the Amalgamated if an application were made. At that time I referred the matter to General Secretary Mc-Guire who stated that the convention would without doubt take some action and in all probability arrive at an understanding and a mutual agreement. On the 20th of this month I again wrote Secretary Mc-Guire upon the subject. He replied that in consequence of the resolutions adopted at the Chicago convention for a mutual recognition of the cards of the U.B. and the Amalgamated he considered that no objection could be interposed. He suggested however, that Your Honorable Board would be the proper authorities for an official declaration of that character; hence I most respectfully request you to state whether the Executive Board of the United Brotherhood has any objection to a charter being granted to the American District of the Amalgamated Carpenters & Joiners?

Since the time is close at hand for the convention of the A.F. of L. and the constitution of the American Federation of Labor provides that a charter must be obtained thirty days prior to the holding of the convention to entitle an organization to be represented by a delegate at the convention I most respectfully request you to give this matter your earliest attention and advise me thereof and oblige,[3]

Yours Fraternally   Saml Gompers.
President American Federation of Labor.

TLpS, reel 4, vol. 5, pp. 182-83, SG Letterbooks, DLC.

1. The sixth general convention of the United Brotherhood of Carpenters and Joiners of America (UBCJA) was held in Chicago, Aug. 4-11, 1890.
2. George CAVANAUGH of New York City was secretary of the American District of the Amalgamated Society of Carpenters and Joiners.
3. The UBCJA dropped its objection to the chartering of the Amalgamated.

To Hugh Grant[1]

Oct. 28th [1890]

Hon. Hugh. J. Grant
Mayor N.Y. City
Dear Sir:—

I have the honor to acknowledge the receipt of your favor of the 25th. inst. asking me to be a member of a committee to co-operate with the American Committee for the Relief of Famine in Ireland.[2]

In reply permit me to say that my sympathies are so largely in accord with the movement in question for which the Committee has been organized that I willingly accept the appointment and trust I may be in some way enabled to aid in the achievement of the object in question.

Very Respectfully Yours   Saml Gompers.
President American Federation of Labor.

TLpS, reel 4, vol. 5, p. 186, SG Letterbooks, DLC.

1. Hugh John Grant was Democratic mayor of New York City from 1889 to 1892.
2. The American Committee for the Relief of Famine in Ireland was organized in the fall of 1890 to aid Irish potato blight victims. The committee was composed of major statesmen, politicians, businessmen, and other prominent individuals.

To Ernest Bohm

Nov. 7th [1890]

Mr. Ernest Bohm
Sec. Central Labor Federation of N.Y.
385 Bowery N.Y. City
Dear Sir:—

In reply to your favor of Oct. 29th. inquiring what became of your application for a charter, permit me to say that it has been my intention to personally visit one of your meetings and explain the matter, but taking into consideration the fact that your organization was so largely interested in the recent political campaign I deemed it to the interest of your movement to postpone any visit or communication, in order to avoid a discussion which might have a tendency to embarrass you or diminish the votes for your candidates, until after election.

Inasmuch however, as your meetings for the past few weeks have been the stumping ground for a tirade of [undeserved?] abuse and attack upon me, both personally and officially, and having gone to the trouble of giving them publicity in the daily and weekly papers of this city you have rendered it impossible for me to attend your meeting for this purpose with any degree of self-respect.

The Central Labor Federation of New York applied for a charter, and among the organizations composing it is the American Section of the Socialist Labor Party of New York City. I have expressed the opinion that as a political party the American Section of the Socialist Labor Party should not be entitled to representation in a Trade Union body.

You and [I] differ upon that, and I have concluded to refer the entire matter to the convention of the American Federation of Labor to be held at Detroit, Mich. Dec. 8th 1890.[1]

It seems to me that men in the labor movement can honestly differ with each other without finding it necessary to indulge in abuse and I cannot for the life of me understand why an expression of opinion should call forth the spleen manifested by you in your official journals, and which was given out officially by you for publication in the public press.

If you care to send a representative of your organization to the convention of the American Federation of Labor for the purpose of defending your position in the matter, I am satisfied all courtesies will be extended to him for the purpose of presenting his case.

Very Respectfully Yours   Saml Gompers.
President American Federation of Labor.

TLpS, reel 4, vol. 5, pp. 224-25, SG Letterbooks, DLC.

1. The 1890 AFL convention was held in Detroit, Dec. 8-13.

An Article by Samuel Gompers in the *Carpenter*

[November 15, 1890]

THE NEW YORK CENTRAL RAILROAD STRIKE.

Public attention has been attracted to the recent strike of the employes of the New York Central Railroad,[1] not because of the number of employes involved, the causes of the dissatisfaction that culminated in the withholding of their labor by the strike method, or because of the conduct or continuance of that special skirmish in the industrial war.

The strike of the carpenters for eight hours was vastly more important as a fact and as a study; but as that strike was in the direction of progressive civilization directly affecting production and not commercial distribution, it was less startling than the short, impulsive strike of the railroad men.

As men can exist longer without eating than they can without breathing, so the men engaged in the varied business interests, can calmly witness the stoppage of production in any industrial center or enterprise other than their own, while the stoppage of the transmission of news by electricity, or of the transportation of passengers and freight over any of the great avenues of trade, awakens commercial and financial fear endangering a panic.

Wendell Phillips[2] said: "The laborer puts his hand into the cogwheels of the factory, and when the machinery stops the employer asks, What is the matter?" The employes of the New York Central Railroad put their hands into the cogwheels of the intricate machinery of commerce, and the people will not only ask what is the matter, but what is the remedy?

In your letter requesting my views upon some of the questions involved in the New York Central strike, you say: "There are at least three parties interested in every railroad strike: first, the employes; second, the corporation, and third, the general public"; and you add, that "each of these parties has, of course, its interests and rights." As your space and the time at my disposal will not permit an exhaustive essay on so important a theme, permit me to give my views upon the first proposition as stated in your commmunication. "What are the rights of employes?" "Have they the right, after voluntarily striking, to be heard in any grievance either through a committee of their own or through a committee of the organization to which they belong, or through any other representative whom they may select?"

It is now almost unanimously acknowledged that employes have the right to strike, and, having the right to strike, that they have the right to use all constitutional means to make the strike successful. As a strike is the withholding of labor for a better condition of the market, it must be conceded that the laborer has the right to fix the price and conditions upon which he will put his labor into the market. Having the inalienable right to organize for mutual protection and benefit, they have the right of use to all the rights, customs, privileges and immunities of organized bodies. An organized body can speak only through and by its legally constituted representatives, and the members of organized bodies are the only constituted and competent persons to select such representatives.

As the principal is responsible for the acts of his agent in his capacity as agent, it is the duty of the principal to protect the agent when he performs the duties assigned him, and the agent has the right of immunity from responsibilities within certain legal and moral limits. Agents are, and should be, held up to public odium when they, as agents, perform an act that is dastardly, contemptible or cruel, even when such acts are not punishable by courts of justice; but when an agent of an organized body seeks the betterment of his principal, that is, his constituency, by securing by equitable methods a new contract, the man, or body of men, who would maltreat the agent bearing such a commission, would shoot the bearer of a flag of truce on a field of battle. The right of representation by a chosen spokesman will be contended for by organized laborers with all the legal weapons that Nature, art, science and invention can furnish; and he who stands in the way of the speedy recognition of this inherent, inalienable right is an enemy of peace.

Before considering your second division of the question of the right of the employes, permit me to clearly recapitulate some of the rights that are included in the foregoing statement. Employes have the right: first, to organize; second, to strike; third, to prevent the employment of other laborers (within legal bounds); fourth, to divert trade to other parties; fifth, to the protection of the judicial and executive departments of State as against the false representation of facts, the employment of a private armed band, and as against the unwarrantable discharge and black-listing of the members of the organization or their representatives; sixth, the right to know the cause why they are discharged; seventh, the right to be recognized through their representatives; the right to know why wages are reduced, or why they cannot be increased, their hours of labor reduced, and why the sanitary conditions and protective appliances of science and invention are not introduced; ninth, the right to their share in the joint product of the capital invested, the management and themselves.

This last brings us back to the question of interests. You say, "each of these parties (the corporation, the employes and the general public) has its interests and rights." It is the interest of the employe that the management should be economical, that the stocks should not be watered; that a fair remuneration should be paid for the service of management and for the use of money. In brief, the interest of the employes includes the interest of the general public, with this addition, that as regular and full employment at present wages, with hope of better wages as a condition, depend upon a successful business, the interests of the employes to this extent are one with the management. Interests conflict when high salaries or large profits accrue to tall talkers, and low wages and uncertainty of employment accrue to hard workers.

The second division of your question as to the rights of employes relates to the rights of the employes (to put it in your language) after "voluntarily striking." It is held by many, and perhaps by most employers, as well as by many so-called political economists, that a strike is a permanent severance of the relations and interests between the employer and the employes who have struck. Against this proposition I quote the words of George E. McNeil in a recent article on strikes.[3] He says: "A strike is not the voluntarily withholding of labor; it is the compulsory act of intelligent, self-respecting men and women, a method of self-defense." This is true of strikes for less hours of labor and for higher wages as well as strikes against a reduction of wages, discharge of leaders, officers and other representatives, black-listing, shop rules, etc. The wage-worker is a party in interest with his employer in spite of the fact that under the wage system they live in antagonistic relations toward each other. France and Germany continue their commercial and political relations and interests, but do not disband their armies or disarm their defenses. All civilized countries stand prepared for war, and yet they are constantly seeking new treaties (contracts) for mutual benefit. A war between two nations is but a temporary affair (a strike) that will ultimate in a renewal of commercial and political relations, often with enlarged mutual interests. The overthrow of Napoleon the First was not the subjugation of France. Every nation during war, or after defeat, has the acknowledged right of representation in negotiating terms of settlement. A strike is a war between two important factors in industrial or commercial enterprises, and the right to negotiate a settlement is never waived nor vitiated. It is time public sentiment was awakened to the importance of the recognition of this truth.

A strike is an attempt not to destroy the enterprise, but to defeat the administration of the enterprise; in fact to compel a treaty (contract) that will give them (the strikers) greater advantage of conditions and opportunities.

The wage-worker not only has the right to control his time, that is, the amount he will sell, but he has the right to his special skill or adaptability in the position he occupies in any given establishment or enterprise. He has, by continuous employment for an employer, accumulated an equity, that is, an interest, that is lost to him, lost to the employer and the public, if he leaves that employer, except in rare cases when the change is purely voluntary; but it is nevertheless true that as they strike not against their employment but against its conditions, they have an interest in equity in the past and future results of the joint effort of the employers and themselves. The opportunity to labor in the position they occupied at the time of the strike is their capital; it is their situation, their property.

The Constitution of the United States provides that "in all criminal prosecutions the accused shall enjoy the right to have the assistance of counsel for his defense," and in the constitutions of the several States this right to be heard by himself or his counsel is fully provided and guaranteed. However great the crime against persons or property, the United States and the State governments not only permit, but provide for the representation of the accused by counsel. It is only in the relations of the employers and employes that this right is denied. General Butler has said that "the Constitution grows"; it is time that the judges of the courts, men of legal attainments, and the public generally should grow up to the constitutional provisions for the protection of the rights of the wage-workers.

To your question, How shall these rights be secured and maintained? permit me to answer, that as the rights of the people have been obtained in the past by organized, earnest, self-sacrificing effort, it is safe to continue on that line. The effort to obtain a larger freedom is in itself an educator to still grander efforts.

Carpenter, Nov. 15, 1890.

1. On Aug. 8, 1890, members of KOL District Assembly 246 struck the New York Central and Hudson River Railroad after about sixty active KOL members had been discharged. The strikers demanded the men's reinstatement and an increase in wages. Two weeks later locals of the switchmen's association struck in sympathy, but the failure of other railroad unions to support the strikers, the company's use of Pinkerton guards, and the depletion of the district assembly's treasury caused the Knights to call off the strike on Sept. 17.

2. Wendell Phillips, a lawyer, was well known for his support of antislavery, prohibition, women's rights, and the labor movement.

3. Probably "George McNeill on Strikes," an article published in the *Union Printer* on Feb. 12, 1887. McNeill concluded that strikes antedated unions and that unions were the product of strikes, not their cause.

An Excerpt from a News Account of a Meeting of the New York City Central Labor Federation

[November 15, 1890]

ORGANIZED LABOR.

. . .

After a short but lively discussion, in the course of which Mr. Gompers' letter[1] was variously commented upon by the speakers, the said document was received and filed. Successive motions were then made, discussed and adopted, which, taken together, constitute the following body of instructions:

1 — In case of his admission to the Convention of the American Federation of Labor, to be held in Detroit on the 8th of December, 1890, the delegate of the C.L.F. shall urge the necessity of merging into one comprehensive movement the economic and political forces of labor, upon the ground that political power is necessary to the accomplishment of the objects contemplated by the labor movement.

2 — That he shall inquire why the President of the American Federation of Labor has not carried out the principle laid down by the various conventions of that body, to wit: that the open trades unions should be supported against the attacks of the Knights of Labor.

3 — That he shall act in conjunction with such other delegates as may be sent to the Detroit Convention by organizations affiliated with the Central Labor Federation.

4 — That he shall request the Convention to act in conjunction with the labor movement of the rest of the world, by sending delegates to the International Labor Congress, which will be held in Brussels on August 19, 1891,[2] and to so instruct those delegates that they will urge the endorsement, by the Brussels Congress, of the International Labor Congress which it is intended to hold in Chicago in 1893.

5 — That in case he is not admitted to the Detroit Convention, the delegate of the C.L.F. shall call a mass meeting in the said city of Detroit, at which he will publicly state the position of the Central Labor Federation.

. . .

Workmen's Advocate (New York), Nov. 15, 1890.

1. See SG to Ernest Bohm, Nov. 7, 1890, above.
2. The 1891 session of the Second International met in Brussels, Aug. 16-22.

A Series of Accounts of the 1890 Convention of the AFL in Detroit

[December 4, 1890]

PLOTTING AGAINST GOMPERS

All signs point to an excitable time at the tenth annual convention of the American Federation of Labor, when it opens next Monday at

Detroit, Mich. The matter upon which all attention will be centered is the fight of the Socialists against President Samuel Gompers.

The Socialists since they formally declared war against President Gompers have not missed a single chance to obtain a strong representation at the convention, and their emissaries have been doubly active in the cities with large German populations.

The cities of Milwaukee, Cincinnati, Cleveland, Chicago, Buffalo and Brooklyn, and this city will, it appears by the present announcement of delegates, send men pledged against the present Federation leader.

Here is an instance of the way the Socialists are working: The National Brewery Workers' Union at its last convention[1] elected General Secretary Ernest Kurzenknabe a delegate to the Federation Convention. Kurzenknabe is not a good English speaker. The shrewd Socialists therefore last night induced Ernest Boehm, corresponding secretary of the Central Labor Federation, and one of the four walking delegates of the Cloak-makers' Union, to resign as walking delegate of the Cloak-makers' Union, and elected him to Kurzenknabe's places as general secretary and A.F. of L. delegate of the Brewery Workers' Union. Kurzenknabe had resigned beforehand as he was told to do. Boehm is an anti-Gompers man.

The Socialists also scored another victory last night in the election of a delegate by the furniture workers, who was, moreover, pledged beforehand against Gompers. The man elected is Rudolph Braunschweig,[2] the former friend of Anarchist John Most,[3] who defeated Charles Speyer.[4]

The election proceeded by the general vote of all local unions. It was at first supposed that Speyer, who is attached to Furniture-workers' Union No. 7, had been elected, but returns from Brooklyn secured Braunschweig the majority. Furniture-workers' Union No. 7 last night made Braunschweig promise that he would, at the convention, do these four things:

First, protest against the Governor,[5] Lieutenant Governor,[6] Mayor[7] or any other official of the State of Michigan participating in the opening exercises of the convention; second, that the proceedings of the convention shall be conducted partly in German and all reports printed in the same language together with the English reports. Third, to vote for the admission of Lucien Saniel, the delegate from the Central Labor Federation, and fourthly and lastly, to vote against a third term for President Gompers.

There was a rumor abroad to-day that Boehm would not be recognized at the convention, it being claimed he had not been constitutionally elected as secretary of the Brewers' Union. Ex-Secretary

Kurzenknabe was elected on the "referendum" plan, in which every member of every local union connected with the national union could deposit a vote.

So far there are said to be four votes from this city which Gompers will not get. They are those of Delegates Saniel, Braunschweig, Boehm and Delabar.

Last night more trouble was heaped upon President Gompers. The Clothing Cutters' Union, which has received the tender care of Mr. Gompers, had him go before their union and explain if it was really true that he had granted a charter to a K. of L. assembly.[8]

The union also wanted to know if such was the case why he couldn't give the C.L.F. a charter too. Mr. Gompers stated that all his acts throughout his years of service for the Federation were dictated by the constitution, to which he had strictly adhered and always would.

Mr. Gompers is said not to have lost any sleep over the plotting of the Socialists. He has received word from all over the country assuring him that he will come out of the Detroit Convention with colors flying.

New York Daily News, Dec. 4, 1890.

1. The fourth convention of the National Union of the United Brewery Workmen of the United States was held Sept. 8-13, 1889, in Cincinnati, Ohio.
2. Richard Braunschweig, a carpenter in New York City and apparently a member of International Furniture Workers' Union of America 7, was once a follower of Johann Most but broke with him in 1889 to form the Independent Revolutionists of New York City.
3. Johann MOST, a prominent anarchist, was publisher of *Die Freiheit* and a leader of the American Federation of the International Working People's Association—the Black International.
4. Probably Carl SPEYER, a German immigrant and leader of the New York City furniture workers.
5. Cyrus Gray Luce was Republican governor of Michigan from 1887 to 1891.
6. William Ball, a Republican, was acting lieutenant governor of Michigan from 1889 to 1890.
7. Hazen Stuart Pingree was Republican mayor of Detroit from 1890 to 1897.
8. While there was no national organization of clothing cutters at this time, the AFL chartered several local clothing cutters' unions in the latter part of 1890, and SG claimed in December that most of the clothing cutters in New York City and Brooklyn were organized in the AFL.

[Detroit, Michigan, December 8-9, 1890]

SHOULD A CHARTER BE ISSUED
BY THE
AMERICAN FEDERATION OF LABOR
TO THE
CENTRAL LABOR FEDERATION OF N.Y.
WITH THE
SOCIALIST LABOR PARTY REPRESENTED THEREIN?

[Afternoon Session, December 8, 1890]

President Gompers, previous to the convention, suggested to the Central Labor Federation of New York the advisability of sending some person to the convention for the purpose of presenting their side of the demand for a charter, when that subject should come up for discussion.

Mr. Lucian Sanial came to Detroit in response to the invitation. He presented credentials as a duly elected delegate to the convention. The credentials were referred to the committee on credentials, who referred the credentials back to the convention without recommendation.

Upon motion of the convention Mr. Sanial was accorded the privilege of the floor for the purpose of making a statement of his case. He then read the following paper:

LUCIAN SANIAL'S STATEMENT.

So much has lately been said in unfriendly papers concerning the object of the New York Central Labor Federation in sending me as its delegate to this Convention, that, in justice to all, I have deemed it necessary to state my case in writing. I do this in justice to my constituents, that their purpose may not be misrepresented; in justice to myself that I may give a literal account of the performance of my duty; and in justice to you, that your action may not be misunderstood.

And right here let me correct any false impression which may have been created by the organs of a class naturally hostile to Organized Labor, and interested in nothing so much as in its disruption. My mission is not to sow discord, but to tender you the earnest co-operation of a representative and powerful labor body, every member of which is deeply imbued with the idea that union is the necessary fundament of progress in the labor movement.

Without entering into a consideration of the particular circumstances that brought the Central Labor Federation into existence, I shall state that it was first established on the 12th of February, 1889, and then obtained from the American Federation of Labor a charter, for which it paid the usual fee of five dollars. On December 15, 1889, in the interest of unity, the various organizations represented in the Central Labor Federation again sent delegates to the New York Central Labor Union. Then, of course, for the time being, the Central Labor Federation ceased to meet; but no resolution was passed to surrender the charter. Had this been proposed, it is safe to say that it would have met with a strong opposition, for there were many who, while wishing to see the forces of labor thoroughly united in New York and consequently favoring the attempt at reconciliation as an experiment worth trying, looked with mistrust upon the controlling influence of certain K. of L. leaders in the C.L.U. They did not believe that the apparent reconciliation could be lasting. Their worst apprehensions, I am sorry to say, were realized, and in a few months, a number of organizations had, in disgust, withdrawn their delegates from the C.L.U. Under those circumstances the Central Labor Federation resumed its weekly sessions. One of the first acts of its Secretary, Ernest Bohm, was to call upon Henry Emrich, one of its trustees, for the charter, which had been left in his hands for safe keeping. Emrich answered that he had surrendered it to Samuel Gompers, President of the A.F. of L. Mr. Gompers was then called upon, but replied that as the charter had been surrendered he could not return it and an application for a new charter would have to be made. The Executive Council of the A.F. of L. was then appealed to, but confirmed Mr. Gompers' decision. Thereupon an application was made, to which no answer was received for an unusual length of time. When at last it came, it was somewhat indefinite as to the charter itself, but contained a reference to the admission of delegates from the New York American Section of the Socialist Labor party, in terms which meant plainly that Mr. Gompers did not approve of their admission and deemed it sufficient reason to withhold the charter. The body which they represented, he said, was a "political party," and as such should have no place in a central body representative of trades unions. Finally the matter was left for decision to this Convention.

There are two questions involved in the proposition as stated by Mr. Gompers: (1) Is the S.L.P. a "political party" in the sense in which this phrase is understood by us workingmen? (2) Is it true that, because of that part of its character which is political, it is debarred from representation in the central body affiliated with the American Federation? I shall examine them in their reverse order.

In the first place allow me to submit the following letter, which speaks for itself:

["]In 1885, the members of the German Section of the S.L.P. of Baltimore organized the German Central Labor Union[1] of that city. The same Socialist Section, being represented therein by three delegates, moved that the German Central Labor Union be represented in the Baltimore Federation of Labor. The motion was unanimously carried and delegates were elected to and admitted by the said Baltimore Federation, which is a branch of the American Federation of Labor since this organization was formed. I am glad to say that I, as a member of the S.L.P. Section of Baltimore, was representing the German Central Labor Union in the Baltimore Federation for some time, as the minutes of both these central bodies will show.

["]Therefore we have, on the one hand: Socialist Section—German C.L.U.—Baltimore Federation of Labor—American Federation of Labor. And we have, on the other hand: N.Y. American Section, S.L.P.—Central Labor Federation—American Federation of Labor. Where is the difference? When Mr. Gompers refuses to admit the C.L.F., he must also protest against the admission of the Baltimore Federation of Labor.

["]Fraternally,   E. A. Hoehn.["][2]

Here then, is a positive precedent directly against Mr. Gompers' opinion, and I have been told that there were others exactly like this. I shall not mention them, however, for I have not taken the trouble of inquiring. I leave with those who think that precedent is good law the care of investigating this and any other that they may become aware of. As for me, I am willing to place my case upon the far higher ground of principle. Therefore, I come to the first and far more important question, Is the Socialist Labor Party a "political party" in the sense that wage-workers the world over attach to this expression?

Surely it is not so understood in Germany, where every trade union is a creation and practically a branch of the S.L.P. It is not so understood in France, where every *syndicate ouvrier* is a creation and a branch of the S.L.P.; where the municipality of Paris is under the influence of the Socialists—thanks to which the building and kindred trades enjoy higher pay in fewer hours than they previously did—and where the socialist agitation bids fair to carry the eight-hour work-day. It is not so considered in Switzerland, or in Austria, where, thanks to Socialist agitation, the working time has already been reduced and regulated by law, not merely for children, young persons and women, as in England, but for men as well. It is not so understood in England, where in twenty months the Socialists have organized 117 trade unons, with a membership of over 500,000 wage-workers; where they have conducted and won the most gigantic strikes that ever took place;

where they have overcome the antiquated conservatism of more or less corrupt leaders (whose chief business is to bow to this great Liberal or that greater Tory in the lobbies of Parliament); where they have exploded the notion that a wage-slave is a "free" man, and that his liberty to be a slave, worked to death and starved for his pains, should not be interfered with by the legislator; where they have initiated what is now known as the "new trade unionism," and where they will surely—and long before you, at the rate they go—establish the eight-hour normal work-day as a mere preliminary step to still further, higher and nobler ends.

Nor is it so understood by the Central Labor Federation of New York; nor by the labor organizations represented in that body; nor by any man who walks with his eyes open and sees the chasm between an honest, straightforward labor party and a dishonest, bamboozling plutocratic party.

This is neither the place nor time for me to present an argument in favor of independent political action by the working class. Before your Convention I must strictly confine myself to the question, although, in the form in which Mr. Gompers has unwisely put it, I am fairly entitled to some latitude of treatment.

There is this fundamental difference between the old plutocratic parties and the S.L.P., that the former are notoriously the political machines of the employing class, and as essential a part of the whole machinery through which they control, rob and oppress their wage-workers as is their industrial and commercial machinery; whereas the Socialist Labor Party is owned and controlled by wage-workers like yourselves, who are in full sympathy with you upon all the economic principles thus far advanced, or the demands thus far made by the American Federation of Labor, and who use this so-called "political party" exclusively for the advancement of those economic principles and demands. As I speak, it is busy organizing trades, and long before the American Federation existed, its members were busy organizing many of the very unions which are now constituting your force and prestige. When and where did you ever see the Republican party, or the Democratic party, or for that matter any other political party, engaged in such work?

I don't suppose that you are ready to deny any organization in the American Federation—whether it be a central body or a local union—the right to take political action of an independent labor character; and I trust that, on the other hand, you would summarily repudiate any organization that would take political action in alliance with either the Republican or Democratic party. Now, the S.L.P., as I have explained, is essentially a *bona fide* labor organization, which is not more political than any of the unions affiliated with you have a right to be under your constitution. Again, the Central Labor Federation has merely seen fit to declare — by the admission of the delegates of the American Section of the S.L.P., and by sending to this Convention, as its representative, one of those very delegates — its right to take independent political action with this economic labor party, which the members of its constituting organizations own and control; and in taking this step, deliberately and unflinchingly, it has at the same time virtually announced that the time is coming when Organized Labor in all parts of the country must and will recognize the absolute necessity of taking independent political action. It is for you to decide whether, as workingmen and representatives of workingmen, you can sustain Mr. Gompers in his judgment that this is a crime which unfits the Central Labor Federation for affiliation with the American Federation of Labor.

. . .

[Morning Session, December 9, 1890]

. . .

SPECIAL COMMITTEE'S REPORT.

Mr. President and Delegates:

The committee appointed to consider the subject matter of the Central Labor Federation of New York City in its relation to the A.F. of L. has attended to its duty and begs leave to report as follows:

Organization was affected by the choice of W. J. Shields as chairman and Frank K. Foster as secretary.

The committee listened to extended statements by President Gompers, Lucian Sanial, A. Waldinger[3] and Ernest Bohm, and from the evidence adduced and arguments submitted reached the following conclusions:

1. That we recommend the cordial acceptance of the proffered fraternity of the S.L.P. as embodied in the address of Mr. Sanial. The hope and aspiration of the trade unionist is closely akin to that of the socialist. That the burden of toil may be made lighter, that men shall possess larger liberty, that the days to be shall be better than those that have been, may properly be the ideal of those in all movements for labor reform.

2. We recognize, however, that men of different schools of reform thought often seek to arrive at the same end by different roads. This

right of difference must be considered. This is the logical outcome of variation in circumstances, of birth, education and temperament. We affirm the trade union movement to be the legitimate channel through which the wage-earners of America are seeking present amelioration and future emancipation. Its methods are well defined, its functions specialized, its work clearly mapped out.

3. We further hold that the trade unions of America, comprising the A.F. of L., are committed against the introduction of matters pertaining to partisan politics, to the religion of men or to their birthplace. We cannot logically admit the S.L.P. to representation, and shut the door in the face of other political organizations formed to achieve social progress. We are of the opinion that a political party of whatsoever nature is not entitled to representation in the American Federation of Labor. While, therefore, deprecating the necessity which has arisen of refusing to admit those who seek our comradeship, we feel compelled to make the following recommendations:

First—That the credentials of Lucian Sanial, from the Central Labor Federation of New York City, be returned.

Second—That the position taken by President Gompers and the Executive Council in regard to the old charter of the C.L.F. of N.Y. be affirmed on the ground that the C.L.F. did virtually cease to exist and forfeited thereby its charter.

Third—That the decision of President Gompers against granting a new charter to said organization be affirmed, as the decision by this body is in accord with the meaning and intent of our constitution.

Fourth—That the delegates to this convention, while declining to admit representatives from the S.L.P. as a political party, declare themselves tolerant of all phases of the reform movement, and would bar no delegate as an individual, because of his belief, whether radical or conservative.

W. J. Shields,
John B. Lennon,
W. J. Cannon,
Frank L. Rist,[4]
Frank K. Foster. Secretary.

. . .

. . .

PRESIDENT GOMPERS' SPEECH.

Mr. Chairman[6] and Fellow Delegates: In view of the lengthy discussion on the preliminary skirmishes of this question; in view of the
statement made by Mr. Sanial upon the floor of this convention, I
think that it is due to you and that it is due to the trades unions of
this country that you should know something of the side of the American Federation of Labor upon this question.

A statement of facts, or an alleged statement of facts was presented
to you and it seems to me to be wholly within the purview of this
discussion that you should be made acquainted with the other side.
As a matter of fact, the Central Labor Federation of New York grew
out of the troubles of the local organizations; of charges, criminations
and recriminations of the Trade Unionists and Knights of Labor in
the old Central Labor Union. That there was considerable truth and
foundation for the charges and criminations of dishonesty, I have not
the slightest hesitation in saying I believe; that they were all true, I
do not believe. However, in consequence of the turbulent condition
of the C.L.U. of New York, some of the well meaning good fellows
of the labor movement determined that they would secede from the
C.L.U., some of them I said, but not all, because a good many good
men remained behind. When the many good men representing organizations of labor came together and formed what they termed the
Central Labor Federation, they applied for a charter to the office of
the Executive, and in accordance with the constitution I granted it
to them as the C.L.F.

They worked along, did some good work, but owing to the fact
that the factions on either side were warring against each other much
of the good work that both desired to do was defeated and the
movement was rendered nugatory. Owing to this, the well intentioned
men on both sides, together with my urgent appeals, suggested and
urged that committees from both organizations should meet and discuss terms of harmony and reconciliation.

Committees were appointed from both sides and discussed this
question at great length at meeting after meeting, which lasted for
nearly three months.

In the meantime the Central Labor Federation being affiliated with
the American Federation of Labor, selected a delegate to attend the
Boston convention of the American Federation of Labor held last
year. The negotiations for peace and reconciliation were going on,

and on the Saturday of the adjournment of the Boston convention, Mr. Daniel Harris, the representative of the Central Labor Federation of New York declared, in the course of a discussion "that unity in the labor movement in the City of New York had again been secured, and that that *was the last day that the Central Labor Federation of New York would be in existence."* I think the delegates who were in attendance at the Boston convention last year and who are here to-day, will bear me out that that statement was made. The following day the official journal of the C.L.F. announced that the *Central Labor Federation had adjourned sine die,* had ceased to exist and that the old Central Labor Union of New York and Vicinity had changed its name so that it was called thereafter, the "Central Labor Union of New York" and practically, for the purpose of harmony, making it a new organization.

As I say, this was published in the official, or semi-official journals of the Central Labor Federation and the then existing Central Labor Union.

A few weeks after that the former trustee of the Central Labor Federation of New York, called upon me at the office of the American Federation of Labor, and *handed* the *charter of the Central Labor Federation* to me with these words, or something substantially like them, *"The Central Labor Federation having ceased to exist, I am directed to hand over to you the charter of that organization."* This matter was currently known and when this charter was handed to me after the official of that organization left the office, I directed the secretary of the American Federation of Labor, Mr. Evans, to note in his official accounts that the Central Labor Federation had surrendered its charter.

The old dissensions were renewed. The unity did not bring about harmony, and several organizations that formerly constituted the Central Labor Federation, held private meetings for the purpose of discussing the problems or the disputes or the difficulties that were ever present in the Central Labor Union. The Central Labor Union, upon being informed of this, passed a resolution, suspending from that organization all unions affiliated therein, which held clandestine or secret or private caucuses or meetings. When that was passed the delegates who held these meetings declared that they would reorganize the Central Labor Federation of New York.

A few days or weeks, I don't know which, but shortly thereafter, I received a communication from Mr. Bohm, asking for the charter of the Central Labor Federation of New York, that was placed in my hands "for safe keeping." His letter, now that I remember it, says that. You will find the import of this statement a little later on in my remarks. I answered that the Central Labor Federation having gone out of existence and surrendered its charter officially to the president, *that charter* could not be returned. This, evidently, caused discussion by them, and they inquired when the next meeting of the Executive Council would take place and I informed them. Mr. Bohm and Mr. Delabar, who are here, represented that body, before the Executive Council. The statement was gone all over and the Executive Council decided that the charter was finally and formally surrendered to the American Federation of Labor.

Shortly after that the Central Labor Federation applied for a new charter—or rather this. Mr. Bohm wrote me a letter, in which he said he was instructed to make application for a charter; accompanying that letter was a list of the organizations connected with the Central Labor Federation. At the head of that list, I suppose owing to the fact of its alphabetical order, was the American Section of the *Socialist Labor Party.* I, as I reported to you, gave this matter my judgment and best thought, and I concluded that I could not upon constitutional grounds, I could not upon trade-union grounds, consistently grant them a charter, and so informed Mr. Bohm. I told him, or suggested the mode of a proper form of application, which must be accompanied by a regular blank made out, and a fee of five dollars to be forwarded. Mr. Bohm answered that the Central Labor Federation declined to have the American Section of the Socialist Labor Party withdrawn, and insisted upon their demand for a charter from the American Federation of Labor.

At the next meeting of the Executive Council, I laid this matter before them. It was deemed advisable that I should go before the Central Labor Federation, and make an explanation of our position in the matter and try to allay any feeling. During this time, however, the S.L.P. of N.Y. was in a heated political campaign and the organizations in the Central Labor Federation were largely permeated with the same spirit, and were largely affected by it, and as the organs of the Socialist Labor Party said, "Their affiliated unions" were part of the Socialist Labor Party. (They claim them as *affiliated* unions.) I knew if I should enter the Central Labor Federation about that time and present the case as I thought it necessarily should be, it would arouse bitter discussion; and, as at that time there were conflicts going on, to which your attention has been called, between certain trade unions and certain knights of labor assemblies, and which I was endeavoring to do all I possibly could as a union man and as the executive officer of the American Federation of Labor, to allay. The meetings of the C.L.F. were utilized for the purpose of making severe, unwarranted attacks upon me personally and officially, and I was under the impression that to go there during that turmoil, during the campaign and election, would only add fuel to the fire, hence I concluded that

I would wait until after election. Soon after, but before election I received a letter demanding to know what had become of their charter application. I was then, necessarily, compelled to give my reasons for not answering earlier, and I did give them, saying that it was out of consideration for their movement that I did not at that time want to enter into a discussion of their organization which would have, or might have a tendency to decrease the votes polled for their candidates, and further said that I had determined to refer the entire matter to the convention of the American Federation of Labor. I extended an invitation to the organization, suggesting that they might send some one to represent them at this convention to defend their side of the question, and expressed the belief that all courtesies would be extended to him, and I think you have fulfilled and carried out the promise I made, in extending courtesies to Mr. Sanial to make his address yesterday.

Since that time, however, the Central Labor Federation has shifted its position. From the application for a charter it has reverted back to the demand for the old one, and now I hold, immaterial what the causes were, or what the motives were that prompted their action, *that the application for a new charter is a bar to the claim of the old one.* I hold further that any local organization which has ceased to exist and which surrenders its charter to a national organization either verbally, or by letter, with the statement that "the charter is surrendered," that those people if at any future time, in that trade, in that town, desired to form a union, they would have to do so under a *new charter,* and in all probability their number or name would be given out to some other locality. I think the analogy complete.

It has been said that the charter was placed in the hands of Mr. Emrich, an officer of the Central Labor Federation, "for safe keeping," and not to be handed over to the president of the American Federation of Labor. I state that Mr. Bohm and Mr. Delabar, before the Council of the American Federation of Labor, admitted that it was directed to be placed in the hands of the president of the American Federation of Labor. And now my memory is refreshed, I here declare that the second letter from Mr. Bohm contains the statement that the charter was placed in *my* hands and not as claimed by Mr. Sanial and others, that it was placed in the hands of Mr. Emrich.

So much for the facts in the case. I want to say here, by way of personal explanation, that since this subject was pending words were not too beautiful or too forcible when applied to your humble servant. Every motive was ascribed to me, and not alone that, but under the guise of pleasantries, yes, under all these plausible statements, lies the fact that this organization, through its officers, has been attacked in a fearful way. Why, not more than last Saturday I was charged with trying to throw every obstacle in the way of organizations of socialistic tendencies being represented here at this convention. I say here and now, and I challenge any man to prove, or even to stand where he is sitting, and say that in any one instance I have said one word, or written one word, directly or indirectly, which would have a tendency to keep a delegate away from the meeting, and I will wait and pause for a reply. (Pauses.) On the contrary, there is not an organization I heard from that hesitated about sending a delegate to this convention, but that an urgent letter immediately followed asking them to send representatives to this convention. Mr. Delabar, I regret to see that he has just left the room, but I think it necessary to say what I intended notwithstanding, Mr. Delabar informed me that the Executive Council of the National Bakers' Union had decided not to send a delegate to this convention. A letter followed immediately to him, urging him and begging him to impress it upon the officers of the Bakers' National Union that it would be desirable that they should send delegates here. Was that throwing obstacles in the way? (Mr. Delabar has re-entered.) Since Mr. Delabar has returned I wish to repeat what I have said.

Mr. Delabar: I wish you would.

Mr. Gompers: I say that I received a letter from Mr. Delabar, in which he informed me that the Executive Board of the Journeymen Bakers' National Union would not send a delegate to this convention, and that I immediately thereafter wrote an urgent letter to him that he should prevail upon the Executive Board of his organization to be represented at this convention. I am sure that Mr. Delabar does not hold the views in common with me upon this question that is before the convention. Mr. Waldinger, who has been elected, who is a book-keeper by occupation—

Mr. Waldinger: I beg to differ.

Mr. Gompers: I will stand corrected. I do not wish to make any mistake. I understood he was a member of the Bookkeepers' Federation. However, I understand that he has not been a member of the Machinists' Union, but is elected its delegate to this convention.

Mr. Waldinger: Mr. Chairman.

Chairman Daly: Do you desire to say anything?

Mr. Waldinger: I beg to utterly deny that I am not a member of the Machinists' Union. I am a machinist by trade, and if Mr. Gompers, or anyone else, states differently, he states a falsehood.

Chairman Daly: What do you represent?

Mr. Waldinger: I represent the United Machinists of New York.

Mr. Gompers: I do not want to do any man an injustice, but I beg to assure the gentleman that I have been positively informed that the gentleman was not a machinist, and I beg his pardon for making the statement (Applause) if it is not founded upon truth. I want to speak the truth as I know it.

A Voice: You ought to do it then.

Mr. Gompers: Generally if those who charge falsehood were a little more accurate in their own statements and men enough to admit a mistake, I think it would be better for all of us. (Applause.) Well, Mr. Bohm, who is a bookkeeper by occupation and who, until a few weeks ago, or until about November, was secretary of the Socialist Labor Party Campaign Committee, and thereafter manager for the Cloak Makers' Union, is now representing the National Beer Brewers' Union here.

Mr. Bohm: May I explain that I am also secretary of Local Union No. 33,[7] am a member of it. It is a local union attached to the national organization of German Brewers of the United States, and I desire to explain how I came to be elected a delegate to this convention. There is nothing crooked in it.

Mr. Gompers: I do not say that there is.

Mr. Bohm: I desire to have the delegates understand my position. The National Executive Committee of the Brewers' organization at its meeting, decided to send the Secretary of the St. Louis union[8] as their representative, but his organization would not allow him to come to this convention, and the Executive Committee looked around for another person. The National Secretary of the Brewers' Union[9] could not go on account of sickness, and they requested me to come in his stead. I do not think there has been a wrong committed, although the *Daily News* of New York city published an article, in which they said that the Socialists were working hard to fill this meeting, and claimed it was a put up job between Mr. Kurzenknabbe and myself that I should come to this convention and give the socialists a lift. I brand that as a falsehood.

Mr. Gompers: I want to be frank in my statements. I did not charge anything crooked, but what I do urge is this, that in my humble judgment, if this question of the Central Labor Federation's charter was not under consideration—whether, in other words, if it were not the consideration of the recognition of the Socialist Labor party, either directly or indirectly, at this convention of the American Federation of Labor, Mr. Ernest Bohm would not be a delegate to the convention. (A sneer.) You sneer. Well, if you sneer at it shall I prove it to you out of your own mouth. (Pauses.) I assure you I do not speak of these things with any acrimony at all, and without the intention of hurting any one, but I do say that it at least shows that I have not thrown any obstacles in the way of having these organizations represented, but that I have rather urged every one of them to be here. So much for the facts. Now, I desire to say something in reference to the argument, the theory of this question.

Mr. Sanial, after his alleged recitation of the facts, or rather his recitation of the alleged facts, makes an argument and calls your attention to Austria, where the trade unions, he says, are the creation and branches of the Socialist Labor Party; also in Switzerland, Germany and France. In the course of a joint debate between Henry George and Sergius Schevitch[10] in the last part of the argument Schevitch said to George substantially "if Shantytown is your ideal of the solution of the problem, you ought to live in Shantytown," and I say to you, if the condition of the working people of Austria is your ideal of the labor movement go to Austria to live and you will find your ideal shattered. I measure the condition of the labor movement in the world by the material and physical and moral and mental condition of its people. Show me the country where the social, economic and mental condition of the people is poor and I will show you it is attributable to the lack of their labor organizations being based upon economic principles.

Mr. Morgan:[11] Oh, pshaw! that is all nonsense. It makes me tired.

Mr. Gompers: I desire to say this, that I am a gentleman and a man, and Mr. Morgan, in his remark just now, exhibits himself in any other character but that.

Chairman Daly: The chair desires to say this, that he does not want any interference. Let the speaker proceed, and I insist that he shall proceed with his line of argument.

A Delegate: I rise to a point of order.

Chairman Daly: State the point of order.

A Delegate: The speaker is not in order. He is not speaking to the matter before the house.

Chairman Daly: The president has a right to speak.

A Delegate: He speaks as a delegate and has spoken once before.

Chairman Daly: Not at all. Delegate Gompers spoke. The president of the American Federation of Labor is now speaking, and I so decide.

Mr. Gompers: In the proceedings here upon this question a gentleman arose to a point of order when Mr. Sanial was speaking and I refused to sustain the point of order. I said Mr. Sanial should be given all the latitude he desired, and I think it due the Executive Council, it is due the organization that what I have to say to this convention should be said fearlessly and above board.

Mr. Foster: I do not desire to interrupt the delegate who is speaking, but I do desire in behalf of delegates on this floor that the chair shall take back what he has said. I understand no one individual has any larger liberty on this floor than another. The chair decided that because the speaker was the president he had such liberty, and I hold that to be a misruling.

Chairman Daly: The chair will take it back. (Laughter.)

Mr. Gompers: I do not want anybody to go back from this country, I do not wish to be narrow and be understood to say that any one should go back, but what I do say is this, that we do not want that movement which has brought about the condition of affairs which has been pictured to us as the ideal. I heard some gentleman say something (pauses).

I say the facts are not as Mr. Sanial remarked in his paper, which he read yesterday, as to the condition of the labor movement in England. He says that the Socialists have organized half a million of workmen in the Trade Unions of England and have organized what is known as the New Trade Unionism. Conceding it, for the sake of this argument, but did you ever hear of John Burns, or of Tom Mann, or of Tillet, presenting themselves at the Trade Union Congress of England,[12] or at the London Trades Council or any Central Trade Union Organization of any part of England as the representatives of the Social Democratic Federation of England?[13] No. They came there as the representatives of Trade Unions, and that is what I answer to you. If you are Socialists, why I shake you by the hands. Do you hold any other opinions, are you an Anarchist, a Single Taxist, are you a Greenback reformer? Do you hold any other political or social belief? I do not care, but I say *if you want to be represented upon an equality with every other Trade Union in the American Federation of Labor, you must produce a card of membership in your trade union.* The condition precedent, I hold, to representation in a trade union movement is good standing membership of a trade union.

You heard Mr. Sanial's attacks upon what he termed the corrupt leaders of the labor movement of England, and I say here it does not come with elegant grace. It is easy to cry corruption. Why, the railroad men's organizations which refused to order a strike recently, were charged by the same parties with having received "boodle" from the Vanderbilts,[14] because they refused to sanction or order a wild-cat, unauthorized, impulsive strike,[15] because they refused to hurl their organization into the whirlpool.

I presume in the Trades Unions of England there has been some corruption, I suppose there are some corrupt men, but does the Socialist Labor Party claim exclusive propriety and purity, honesty and honor, or a monopoly of it? Has no member of the Socialist Labor Party ever gone wrong?

It is charged that some of the men in the trade union movement

of England have been corrupt, so have others, but that is no argument
for or against trade unions no more than it is against any other form
of organizations.

In reference to the charge that the leaders of the trade unions of
England bow and toady to the Liberals, I say it is not true. There is
no doubt in the politics of that country, the trade union leaders of
England lean toward the Liberals, but it is also true that the Socialists
of England lean toward the Tories and I refer you to their official
journals for a verification of this statement. As to the wisdom of the
action of both or the chances for corrupt influences to operate, I
would rather you than I judge.

It has been said that if we did not grant a charter to the Central
Labor Federation, notwithstanding the fact that it may have the S.L.P.
represented therein, that it is going to injure the labor movement.
Unless we do this they say we are to be antagonized. Is that the
boasted spirit of fraternity with which we are met? Is that the spirit
to build up?

Representative Skeffington, we heard this morning expressed the
fear that if no charter is granted, it would hurt every organization
in New York and we hear Representative Morgan saying, "No, not
unless the representative of the Central Labor Federation is refused
a seat." In other words, that if we do not recognize the Socialist Labor
Party as being entitled to representation here, it means war upon us.

A Voice: No.

Mr. Gompers: Well, I hope it won't be, I don't think it will, I know
though, that we have been challenged. The *Volkszeitung* last Saturday,
in an editorial, which I have clipped out and submit to you, says "If
the S.L.P. is not recognized it will be a question of who arrives first
at the meeting." The article asserts that we are not the only ones that
came in contact with the Socialist Labor Party; it calls attention to
the Henry George movement and other movements that have antagonized the Socialist Labor Party and have been killed themselves.
Now, I maintain that we do not antagonize the Socialist Labor Party.
I deny that any one has given utterance to a word that could be so
construed, but we ask that the trade unions be let alone. We ask that
we may be enabled to work as Trade Unionists. We declare that
Socialists, or any other organization of any shade of political, social,
economic or scientific belief, may be permitted to disseminate their
doctrines in this great labor movement as often, as loud and deep as
they possibly can. Spread the light, spread the light, but it must come
through the pure fountain of the Trade Unions.

I say to you, friends and delegates, that the man who would accuse
me or charge me with being an anti-Socialist, simply says that that

he don't know anything about, he does not know Sam. Gompers. I say here broadly and openly that there is not a noble hope that a Socialist may have that I do not hold as my ideal. There is not an inspiring and ennobling end that they are striving for that my heart does not beat in response to. But our methods are different. The Socialist Party and Trade Unions are different; inherently do they differ in their methods.

We want to go down into the dregs of society, into the lowest stratum, where the people are being eaten with vermin, if you please, where the children are eking out a miserable existence, we want to go to them and infuse into their minds and their hearts the first idea of progress, the recognition that they should organize to get out of that filth first, so that they may be enabled to appreciate cleanliness, and beauty, and grandeur and nobleness of character, and struggle for their achievement.

A few more words and I am done. I have spoken of the principle involved first. I have probably spoken of the first out of place, and now I shall speak of expediency.

We have grown immensely. There are some here who witnessed the birth of the American Federation of Labor, some were in its councils and know of its struggles, but I doubt there were many that would have credited the idea that it would grow into the proportions it has assumed to-day. We find national organizations growing and becoming a part of us. We find old organizations working for laudable objects, and we are gaining their confidence, they are coming with us and working for the benefit of each and all. There are a number of great labor organizations in this country, however, which are not yet affiliated with the American Federation of Labor, and it becomes our first duty, it seems to me, and it should appeal to the noblest impulses of the members of the Socialist Labor Party, to see that these great national organizations should be won, converted into the bond of fellowship in the American Federation of Labor before they should propose anything looking to a demand for recognition of their party.

The great railroad organizations, the brotherhoods of railroad men, the organizations of brick-layers, are not yet with us. Do you think it would have a tendency to win them over to the American Federation of Labor, if they knew that the American Section of the Socialist Party, or of any other party, would be recognized in our councils? Do you think the Brotherhood of Locomotive Engineers would be likely to affiliate with us with the Socialist Labor Party in it? Isn't it difficult enough to get these men to work hand in hand with the firemen, who stand upon the engine with them? I say we have a good deal before us. We have so much to do, our aims are so great, that we cannot afford to allow so much to be lost—in order to gain so little.

The Trade Unions of New York can form a grand central organization of *bona fide* Trade Unions, and let me add this much, that if they were [to] do it, they would find many *bona fide* Trade Unions in the Central Labor Union which would join with them but cannot now, because they do not agree with the Socialist Labor Party, or that it ought to be in the Central Labor Federation. If this course were pursued I think it would be best for all concerned and conducive to the best interests of the labor movement. I have said all I desire to say. I thank the delegates of the convention for listening to me as patiently as they have.

Chairman Daly: The question now recurs upon the report of the committee.

. . .

Mr. Morgan: I was going to say, that I, not being a gentleman, a mere factory hand, born and raised as near hell as you could get to it on this earth, and living in the conditions that pertain to such a climate some relics of the curse cling to me, and by impulse a word slips out sometimes and I said "Nonsense, you make me tired." I apologize, I am sorry I said it, but it appeared so unfair to me that that statement should be made to the prejudices of Knownothingism, that I am sorry to say has been acquired by long residence in this country that I felt insulted for myself and others who had, like myself to skip out from over there to save our lives—not from the hangman or the jail, but from the industrial system. The idea set forth by the president that the ideas common in Austria were the result of economic organization and work there—

Mr. Gompers: Lack of economic organization.

Mr. Morgan: You can put [it] in any shape you see fit—when he implied it was the result or non-result of organization in any shape, he was far from the truth. The conditions in the old country, whatever they may be, are the result of despotism that is gradually being eliminated in Europe, by the efforts of such men as are commonly called Socialists; that instead of the slightest imputation as to the ineffectiveness or lack of methods being implied or hurled against these men, they should be entitled to the greatest consideration. You of the United States, under a free flag, with all the chances to organize that you desire, are so abjectly subjugated to the power of monopoly, not monarchical rule, that you even shave off your whiskers when you are so ordered. (Applause.)

The idea that the Germans, the Austrians, the Italians have got any form of organization at all; the idea that they have in any shape lifted the yoke, is a credit to them. Just think, men, of being denied the right to speak, to talk, to vote, and yet they have labor unions; yet their effort to raise labor, to improve their condition has set at defiance the strongest despotism in Europe. I would like to ask my friends if this state of facts is due to lack of organization, or to landlordism, that they want to abolish. Of course, I was astonished that those references should have been made, that he should have overlooked the tyranny and the despotism of the old methods of the old institutions of the world, and taking the opportunity he had as president of the organization, to slap in the face the boys that "get from under" and come here to the United States, that he should slap those who have not the opportunity to get out, but stay at home and fight it out. I am sorry, indeed, that every word that is uttered in this shape will go out to be reiterated and exaggerated. I am sorry indeed that the president took advantage of his position to inject into this debate these ideas and utterances. I tell you, boys, that this question cannot be solved by stirring up personal or party animosities. It would have been of great value if the president of this body had done what he implied he would do last night. He said this matter is of such importance that I want every word down in writing,* and I expected he had put down every word in writing, and that when I made my motion for a reference that every word he wanted to utter was said deliberately, knowing it was going before the world and be subject to investigation and criticism. But instead of that, here, verbally, extemporaneously, he utters what he, Samuel Gompers, will be sorry for hereafter, and this Federation will be sorry also that these utterances were made. I regret exceedingly the episode that has occurred here. I hope the Socialists here will not participate further in the discussion. I hope they will be able, with my friend Riedel[16] here, whom I have been identified with in Chicago and Sheboygan—like him, I hope they will be able to boil this down and get it down where the rest is that we have had to swallow for so many years. And we will say, we will do the best under the circumstances. We will show the boys that though the world casts us out, Christ like, we forgive them, for they know not what they do, and go home and make up our minds that the best work that can be done is to go on like Christ did, not minding the utterances of those whom he passed when he was bearing the cross, no matter if they spat on him, no matter if

---

*An expert stenographer was present and took down every word as uttered. Mr. Morgan was evidently not aware of this.

they taunted him, and we can go on with this work knowing that we will fetch them after all.

I am a Socialist and I have been a trade unionist ever since I was a boy, and I have made the mistake that some of our friends have made, I left the trade union believing that that was the best thing to do, and I could see far away that I found myself all alone and I had to go back, I had to feel that I stood in touch with my fellow-men. (Applause.) But I don't like to remain in touch at the expense of being clubbed. But all reformers have to put up with a great deal that is not pleasant, and I stayed, and I intend to stay, no matter how sorry I may be or how much I regret what has been done.

Let me call your attention to two particular phases of this movement that seem to have been overlooked by those who do not thoroughly understand the question. There seems to be an honest, sincere fear in the minds of many great unionists, that the Socialists are dangerous enemies, and that their political movement should not be recognized or supported in any shape or form. Let me tell you there is a political movement in the labor movement, and has been ever since I knew about it, that is more insidious and dangerous than can come from any mistakes made by reformers like Socialists. Let me tell you that the labor unions in Chicago and other cities have been sold out periodically to the Democrats or Republicans in their respective towns.

A voice: That's right.

Mr. Morgan: That has been done repeatedly and never have I heard that form of political trickery arraigned. They have actually traded off the political power of this country for dollars and cents and offices, and how ready they are to get up and denounce socialism. Let me tell you what occurred in Chicago in 1879. The Socialists polled twelve thousand votes and put in four aldermen.[17] They introduced the inspection law in factories that guaranteed protection to every man, woman and child, that guaranteed protection to labor,[18] and the trade and labor unions of that town being dominated by Democrats and Republicans, they allowed that ordinance to stay on the municipal code unenforced and it has been so ever since 1879, being satisfied if twenty or thirty of their members had jobs as inspectors of tenement houses under this very law. Let me tell you that in 1886 the trade and labor unions in Chicago to the number of four hundred with the assemblies came together, and for once in the history of Chicago, cast aside all their prejudices and declared in the most emphatic manner that the continued dominance of the Republican and Democratic parties was ominous to the people of this country and rolled up 35,000 votes for the master workman,[19] and on that occasion, when labor was organized, political and economic together, Powderly, Powderly sent around orders that any Knight of Labor assembly that would aid, by the contribution of funds out of their assembly, this political labor movement, should be suspended and expelled. In less than two years after the Knights of Labor movement was dead in Chicago. Twenty-five thousand votes were cast for mayor and 35,000 in the county, and Mr. Powderly, in a public speech delivered in Philadelphia, did something near akin to what our president has done to-day; he appealed to the Knownothingism of his audience and drew out, during an impassioned speech, from underneath his coat a little United States flag and thanked God that the Anarchists' red flag had been snowed under by the votes of American citizens. The antagonism that that created has never been allayed and never will be allayed as long as T. V. Powderly lives. That being so nearly akin, as I said, to the remarks of our president, called to my attention the danger that he himself is placing himself in. I want it to be understood in all fairness that a man has not got to be insulted as a Socialist and be a trade unionist at the same time. You must not antagonize any man who knows anything about the labor movement. Any man who knows anything about that movement and the progress of civilization, knows that socialism is coming whether you will it or not. Be friendly to it if you cannot be fair and square.

. . .

Mr. Gompers: I want to reply to a few things that have been said, which are aspersions upon me. I think the delegate, Brother Morgan, will find it very difficult to place me in the position of trying to advocate Knownothingism. I think he will find it very difficult to convince either the foreign and American born workingmen that I am a "Knownothing.["] It is so preposterous. Myself a foreign born citizen. Myself a factory operative since I was ten years and a half old—I think it comes with pretty bad grace, the insinuation that the delegate made as far as I was concerned. I, a boy who worked in a factory for a living every day until I was thirty-seven years of age.

I must say that the worst insinuation and one that I feel most keenly, is his endeavor to compare me to Powderly. I thought my conduct in the labor movement would have at least spared me that. It is said I am opposed to socialism, or that I am doing all I can to antagonize socialism. Please remember the contrast I make between socialism and the Socialistic Labor Party, and I want to accentuate that with all the force and whatever little ability there may be within me. I did not say one word against the struggling men who are fighting the battles of the poor in Europe, but I did say and do say that it is wrong to hold up their movement as the ideal for the American workmen to follow. That is what I am controverting, that is what I dispute.

I maintain that the labor movements of Great Britain and America are far in advance of the labor movements of all other countries of the civilized world, regardless of all the opinions that may prevail in the minds of others to the contrary.

The gentleman has said the president will live to be sorry for what he has said. Well, I am just now nearly forty-one. I have been a fairly active boy and a rather active man, and there is not one word in my whole life that I have uttered in my connection with the labor movement, or one act that I have done or one step that I have taken, that I would take back, or which I am sorry for; I would not unsay it except to say it stronger, nor take back that step but to make it more emphatic. To tell me that I will be sorry; you don't know me. Do you say that it will drive me from the position of president of the American Federation of Labor? You don't know me. The position is in my estimation the most honorable in the labor movements of this age, and the highest honor in the world, the greatest gift at the command of man; but I have deep-seated convictions and when I am asked to prove false to them, there is no one on, under or above earth, or anyone living or dead, seen or unseen, who could swerve me one jot, when I know I am right. (Applause.)

A delegate has said there is no difference between the organizations, there is no necessity for making "fish of one and flesh of the other," but is there not a difference between a Knight of Labor assembly and a trade union, and would he have us grant a charter to a K. of L. assembly as such?

I want to say a word about the charge of being acrimonious. Let me say this to Mr. Morgan and others. He has heard the speeches that have been made here under the guise of friendship, and for the purpose of converting or of winning the delegates of this convention to the admission in some way of the delegate from the Central Labor Federation, or practically speaking the Socialist Labor Party. But did he notice in any way the very acrid, the very bitter attacks made upon the trade unionists, or did he say one word when Mr. Sanial upon this floor made the terrible charge against the trade unions of Great Britain? Why did not his indignation rise then? Why did he not criticize those who slandered, upon the floor of this convention, the honored names of the leaders of the trades unions of England? I am a trade unionist, simple, unvarnished, wherever it tends, wherever it goes, wherever it leads, there will I follow. Mr. Morgan probably does not know because of the expression of an opinion that I made in reference to this matter that it was the delegate from the Socialist Labor Party to the Central Labor Federation who said upon that floor, in answer to my letter of criticism, that they would cram socialism down the throats of American workmen. I will say this, I am exceedingly fond of ice cream, but any fellow that attempts to cram ice cream down my throat will get it in his eye.

I am willing to give credit to the members of the socialist party for the work they have done. I would not detract from it by one word, nor have I ever said a word against them, except as to their admission into the trade union movement. I say this, however, please, please remember that there was a labor movement before the Socialistic Labor Party was ever in existence. Please remember that John Burns, of England, is a graduate from the Engineers' Union. Please remember that Tillet and Mann are graduates from the trade unions of Great Britain, and that they never made so preposterous a claim to representation in the trades union central organization, as is here presented, never. I challenge proof to the contrary. They organized unions. Why, here are men on this floor that I can name, Robert Bandlow,[20] and others that I cannot just see—Abrams,[21] Clark,[22] Sullivan[23]—men who do not belong to the Socialist Labor Party and who have spent days and nights for years in organizing unions not of their trades. Is it essential that a man must be a member of the socialist party before he can do some good in the labor movement? I say it is not so, that is all. I deny the claim that is made of the work being exclusively done by the Socialist Labor Party. I say it is the trades unions from which the social evolution of this movement must come. I believe the trade union movement is the movement of the trade unionists, hence the stand I take, but I think we can afford to cultivate the friendship of the Socialist Labor Party, as well as of every other element, radical or conservative, regardless of the opinions that may be held upon the labor movement, or upon the labor question. I want you to give us all the advice you can, but I appeal to you, don't propose to lead us, don't propose to force us.

I prefer that my acts and work in the labor movement should speak for me rather than to deal in braggadocio about myself. When men pose for effect and at every opportunity profess to be extraordinarily self-sacrificing, when they call attention to their Christ-like qualities, I believe the time has arrived to pause and think. To call attention to the fact that others have claimed to be modern Christs, but upon closer examination or investigation, their divine attributes were hardly so palpable and plain. We are neither Gods nor Goddesses, we are plain men and women of labor, proposing to deal with the questions that are before us in a spirit of fairness, and to conduct our movement for the benefit of our men, women and children. The trade union movement for trade unionists. While declaring for and acting upon this principle, we court the friendship of all and cultivate in our organization the discussion of the broadest principles, the highest ideas that the human mind can conceive. If we go on in this way, we can carry our movement to success, and not wreck the hopes and aspirations of the toiling masses upon the rocks of dissension that will inevitably be in our way.

. . .

The roll call was then proceeded with and the secretary made the following announcement:

Secretary: Mr. President. Total number of votes cast 2,070. The result of the vote is 1,574 for, 496 against, majority 1,078.

President Gompers: In accordance wherewith I declare the report of the committee adopted.

. . .

AFL, *An Interesting Discussion at the Tenth Annual Convention*[24] *of the American Federation of Labor Held at Detroit, Michigan, December 8-13, 1890, Upon the Question: "Should a Charter Be Issued by the American Federation of Labor to a Central Labor Union Which Has a Political Party Represented Therein." Reported by an Expert Stenographer* (New York, 1891), pp. 3-8, 15-23, 26-28, 35-37, 40.

1. The German Central Labor Union (CLU) was organized in Baltimore about 1885.

2. Gottlieb (variously Gustav) A. HOEHN, a socialist editor, worked for the *Chicagoer Arbeiter-Zeitung* between 1888 and 1891.

3. August Waldinger, who represented the United Machinists of New York, ran for New York City comptroller on the SLP ticket in the fall 1890 elections.

4. Frank Leonard RIST was a leader in International Typographical Union 3 of Cincinnati and the Cincinnati Central Labor Council.

5. The pamphlet erroneously dates this discussion as having taken place the afternoon of December 10.

6. James J. Daly of New York City, who represented the Tile Layers' National Union.

7. Ale and Porter Brewers' Union 33.

8. Charles F. BECHTOLD was secretary of local 6 of St. Louis of the National Union of the United Brewery Workmen of the United States from 1888 to 1892.

9. Ernst Kurzenknabe.

10. The debate, entitled "Single Land Tax as a Basis of the Political Labor Movement," took place on Oct. 22, 1887, in New York City; SG presided.

11. Thomas John MORGAN was a Chicago machinist and brass finisher and a leader in the SLP.

12. The TRADES Union Congress of Great Britain.

13. The Democratic Federation, founded in 1881, changed its name to the Social Democratic Federation (SDF) in 1884. Originally organized as a political party that called for the nationalization of railroads and banks, after 1887 the SDF urged members to join unions and played an active role in labor agitation. It became the Social Democratic party in 1907.

14. A reference to the family of Cornelius Vanderbilt, president of the New York and Harlem Railroad and chairman of the board of directors of the New York Central and Hudson River Railroad.

15. A reference to the New York Central and Hudson River Railroad strike of August and September 1890. See "An Article by Samuel Gompers in the *Carpenter*," Nov. 15, 1890, n. 1, above.

16. John G. Riedel, a furniture worker, represented the Sheboygan, Wis., CLU.

17. Dr. Ernst Schmidt polled nearly 12,000 votes, approximately 20 percent of the total, as the SLP candidate for mayor of Chicago in 1879. He lost to Democrat Carter Harrison. Three socialist aldermen were elected, joining one socialist incumbent on the city council.

18. The Chicago city council passed an ordinance in October 1879, originally drafted by Morgan, providing for inspectors to enforce standards of workplace cleanliness, health, and safety, and establishing fines for noncompliance or refusal to permit inspection.

19. On Sept. 23, 1886, a coalition of Knights and trade unionists in Chicago launched the United Labor party (ULP), which called for an eight-hour day for government employees and employees of "special privilege" corporations, government ownership of means of communication, monetary and land reform, and an end to convict labor and private police forces. The party elected seven state assemblymen and one senator in the fall elections. In 1887, however, internal conflict wracked the ULP and it elected only one alderman. Robert Nelson, master workman of District Assembly 24, ran unsuccessfully for mayor in the 1887 campaign.

20. Robert BANDLOW was an AFL organizer, secretary of the Cleveland CLU, and a member of Deutsch-Amerikanische Typographia 6.

21. Henry Abrahams.

22. George W. CLARK, a carpenter, was treasurer of the Massachusetts State Branch of the AFL.

23. John O'SULLIVAN was a reporter and labor editor for the *Boston Globe* and general president of the Sailors' and Firemen's Union.

24. That is, counting the 1881-85 FOTLU conventions as the first five annual meetings, and the 1886 FOTLU convention and founding session of the AFL as the sixth.

[December 11, 1890]

. . .

UNION COLOR LINE IN THE SOUTH.

. . . At this point the colored delegate, Moxley,[1] was called to the chair to a burst of applause, a modest and awkward fellow; black as a black cat in a coal scuttle at the bottom of a coal shaft. Curiously enough, while he was in the chair, a grievance was read from a southern machinists' union[2] regarding proposed affiliation, and one of the delegates arose to denounce a section of their constitution which confined admission to white men. Another delegate said that the Federation cannot recognize the southern machinists who draw the color line, as that was not the policy of trade unionists. Delegate Lennan offered a resolution excluding such locals as draw the color or race lines, and to organize the machinists in a national body who do not inject the race clause in the constitution. Delegate Abrams argued against this resolution as ordering locals what to do and thus taking away their home rule character. Delegate Mench thought the convention had a right to say what locals must not do, and the color question was one of those things. Delegate Morgan, ignoring the special point raised, urged the formation of a committee to bring the machinists of the United States into a national union. The chairman on labels and boycotts[3] thought it inadvisable to force the southern machinists to eliminate the obnoxious clause. He thought that ultimate education would eliminate it. Chairman Gompers said that while the convention could not force the point, it could express its conviction on the question looking to the influencing of the machinists by argument to strike the clause from southern constitutions. A respectful request was added to the resolution to that effect, and the whole referred to the executive council for action on that basis.

LABOR LOBBYISTS AT WASHINGTON.

Delegate Foster favored the creation of a special committee, whose business it would be to look after federal legislature [legislation?], and the executive council was given the power, by the convention, to direct the committee with favorable recommendations from the convention. Delegate Morgan intimated that the committee sent to Washington to overlook legislation would be apt to fall into the pool of corruption. He thought communications direct from the Federation would have more influence than paid lobbyists. The speech reversed the current of thought on the subject of watching legislation. Delegate Daly took the floor in the interest of the Washington delegation, but the noon adjournment left his speech in the air.

· · ·

At the afternoon session debate was resumed on the formation of a committee on federal legislation, and Delegate Daly continued his speech in favor of it because the employers of labor had their agents and the boodle at Washington.

· · ·

Detroit Evening News, Dec. 11, 1890.

1. James Frank Moxley, a bricklayer, represented AFL Sewer and Building Bricklayers' 5245 of Cleveland.
2. The National Association of Machinists.
3. James J. Daly.

GET DOWN TO BUSINESS.

Yesterday afternoon debate continued in the labor convention on the motion to send a committee on legislation to Washington. Delegate Foster urged the formation of the committee on the ground that it was by this means the sons of St. Crispin,[1] of Massachusetts, procured a reduction of hours. He did not want the committee to reside at Washington in the midst of corruption; but to go there when necessity demanded it. Communications would be useless, the congressmen must be met face to face. P. J. Maguire opposed the measure. He did not favor an imitation of the crude ideas of the Knights of Labor. The influence of the Federation, unless backed up by an enormous voting power, would be all wind. A committee will be only a little gang of politicians among us. We ought to go on as we are doing. Other delegates followed in similar strain. Delegate McBride had served, he said, both as a lobbyist and a legislator, and his experience taught him it is far more pleasant to be a legislator than to knock at the doors of the legislature. The coal miners tried a committee and secured a few crumbs, but when they went in irrespective of party, placed in nomination legislators and elected them, they got the required legislation. He said that boodle should not control, but that the trades could discount boodle by placing men in the state and national halls of legislation. That can be done, he said, when we forget we are democrats, republicans and socialists.

At the close of McBride's speech the vote was taken and the legislative committee question was put into the hands of the executive committee for investigation and report at the next convention. A motion to reconsider was voted down.

On motion of Delegate Morgan the action on the machinists' unions was reconsidered and his resolution calling for a convention of the machinists[2] was passed.

. . . The committee on constitution reported that they deemed it inexpedient to legislate on the Morgan resolution to change the presidential term, making it possible to serve but two terms of one year each. The proposition to form an executive committee of five, with the president as a member without a vote—the executive committee being now composed entirely of the officers—met with favor, although an attempt was made by motion to make it read: "The executive committee shall consist of four elective members and the president shall be a member, with the casting vote in cases of tie." The motion was lost, and the new amendment not receiving a two-thirds vote was also lost. This was regarded as a victory for Gompers. . . .

. . .

. . . A provision was introduced looking to the erection of four new officers, against which P. J. McGuire argued on the ground of expense and that no reasons for the changes had been advanced. He protested against hampering the president. Delegate McBride kicked against McGuire, and said the latter had not read the report of the constitutional committee, or he would have seen that no expense attached. The argument was far-fetched: the amendment had no design for tying the president's hands, but to procure the proper intermediary between the unions and the presidency.

President Gompers Wins Every Time.

Personal explanations were the rule this forenoon. On the question of the readjustment of the executive board and the power of the president, the committee reported back an amendment regarded by the friends of the president as of a restrictive tendency. Mr. McGuire opposed it in a fiery speech as having a tendency to tie the hands of the president, and Mr. McBride advocated the amendment in strong terms. Delegate Morgan spoke in favor of the amendment and said something plain in regard to restricting the authority of the president and to keep the power in the hands of the unions. Delegate Skeffington followed, and said that Morgan's insinuation against the president satisfied him that the amendment ought to be defeated. Morgan followed in a personal explanation that a certain newspaper's statement that he was an assailant of Gompers was false. He was long opposed to the centralization of power in the hands of the president, long before he personally knew Gompers. But if this amendment passed it would serve to save errors of the one man power. As it stood all of the errors of Powderly were attributed to the Knights of Labor, and it might come to pass that the errors of Gompers might have the same effect.

President Gompers arose to a personal explanation in which he said he was not affected with [a] big head and besides he knew the men on the executive board were not capable of crawling on their stomachs to Sam Gompers. As for Mr. Morgan, he deeply respected him as a man of independent mind and conscientious impulse and believed he could respect others, however much they might differ from himself. He wished to say, however, that Mr. Morgan was in error in attributing to him an expression which his speech on Sanial a few days ago failed to carry out.

At this juncture a point of order was raised that President Gompers must explain out of the chair. This he yielded to and called P. J. McGuire, who ruled in favor of taking a vote on the new amendment. A vote was taken and while it was being taken President Gompers resumed his personal explanation and read the heading of a German New York paper in which Gompers was charged with petty tricks in cutting off debates in favor of Sanial, and that in every way Gompers was against the socialists. He would ask if these things were true and whether he deserved the abuse. He would not quote socialist papers that said he was a fit candidate for a lunatic asylum. He claimed to have acted impartially, but he would not ask the convention to take any action.

Here a delegate arose to say he would object to further explanations of a personal character on newspaper articles.

On the count of the vote it was found that the amendment did not have the necessary two-thirds vote, and was declared lost. This was regarded as a success for Gompers.

. . .

Detroit Evening News, Dec. 12, 1890.

1. The Knights of St. Crispin (KOSC) was formed on Mar. 7, 1867, at Milwaukee, Wis., as a national organization of shoemakers. It attained its greatest strength between 1868 and 1871 when it became the largest labor organization in the country. Thereafter it declined; an attempt to revive it in 1875 failed and the KOSC finally collapsed in 1878.

2. The International Machinists' Union of America held its founding convention in New York City, June 22-24, 1891.

[December 13, 1890]

. . .

THE BATTLE FOR EIGHT HOURS.

Chairman Foster, of the special committee on the 8 hour day, reported that they re-affirmed the idea of the 8-hour day, that the campaign adopted in 1890 be followed and that the Federation assess the unions 2 cents per week per capita for five weeks to procure the funds. Delegate McNeil followed the recommendation in a generalization on the merits of the eight-hour day. They left the choice of the unions to the executive committee, but recommended the coal miners as the proper people to follow the carpenters. Delegate John McBride, of the mine workers, said that the united mine workers were chosen by the late executive committee, and that all the convention had to do was to have the present council ratify the choice of the old board.

Delegate Shields looked over the position and said that all the carpenters got was $12,000 and thought that this was not enough. Therefore the assessments ought to be seen to and so the question ought to go to the new executive council.

Delegate Foster said the coal miners were selected last year, and owing to circumstances the arrangements of the executive council were upset. As the preceding speaker had dimly outlined that the carpenters ought to have another try at it, it must be seen that the choice ought to lie with the executive board.

Delegate John McBride said that next May was definitely chosen by the miners and if the convention says the matter must be deferred indefinitely it will upset the instructions issued to the miners already. Therefore the convention must hold up the hands of the miners, who demand to lead in the eight hour battle. Delegate McNeil said that the committee shaped their report so that the carpenters could go in with the miners, as the carpenters had not finished their fight.

After some further debate the committee retired for conference, and shortly after reported in favor of the selection of the coal miners to lead the eight hour fight. An unanimous vote adopted the report.

A delegate took occasion to remark that the miners' fight would not be like that of the carpenters, the iron and steel workers would be affected and so also the engineers, something might be done by those trades, not in the way of money, but in other ways. Delegate McBride said there was now 7,000 miners on strike in Alabama[1] and nothing would give them greater pleasure than to cooperate with the iron and steel workers. Delegate Prosser[2] said the iron and steel workers were ready to go out with the miners.

President Gompers said both employers and employes would feel the importance of the demand for eight hours by the coal miners.

On the adoption of the amended constitution the convention proceeded to fix the salaries. Present salaries—President, $1,500; secretary, $1,200; treasurer, $100. There was some little effort to increase these figures by a few of the delegates, but it was fiercely opposed, and the case of Powderly was brought in by Delegate Daly, who said that Powderly was made a god of, and hoped that the convention would not make the same mistake. After the convention got in and out of a parliamentary snarl the convention fixed the salaries at the present figures. . . .

Detroit Evening News, Dec. 13, 1890.

1. On Nov. 29, 1890, coal miners in Jefferson and Bibb counties, Ala., under the leadership of District 20 of the United Mine Workers of America, struck for an increase in wages. The mine owners hired replacements and evicted miners from company houses and property; the strike ended unsuccessfully on Jan. 13, 1891.

2. Rees W. Prosser of New Albany, Ind., was vice-president of the Third District of the National Amalgamated Association of Iron and Steel Workers.

[December 14, 1890]

SECOND MAY-DAY BATTLE.

. . .

The principal piece of work done by the convention was the selection of the coal miners to lead in the May-day strike next spring, in which, as it appeared from the discussion, the typographers desired to take a hand. It must not be understood that by the selection of the coal miners that no other trade is to participate in the strike since, as developed by the convention debate, the carpenters are still in it, and that their selection last year was not for a sporadic effort, but a continuous fight, so long as it could be endured. Hence, as will be seen, the carpenters and joiners of the country, inclusive, of course, of Detroit, will strike again on the first of next May and so continue until all win, who have not won, the eight-hour day, for it is not supposed that those who have won the eight hours will find it necessary to strike. There has also been drawn from the debates the plain inference that in the event of the adjustment of misunderstandings among the steel and iron workers they, too, will also join in the strike of next May.

As will be seen by the closing hours of the convention, the struggle with the socialists, which promised to assume such vast proportions, when reduced as it was to a simple point by the very able debates of the convention in which the socialist delegates participated freely, did not amount to much and the onset of the radicals lost force. The simple point was that the Federation of Labor would not admit socialists in their capacity of practical party politicians. This was the point on which Gompers stood pat and upon which the convention acted. But it was Gompers whom the socialists assailed and it was a socialist who appeared against him as a candidate for president, Thomas Morgan, of Chicago.

It is, perhaps, needless to say that the Federation, while giving attention to the mass of work that comes before the body, are keeping in view as their principal object the gaining of the eight-hour day and that their attention cannot be drawn from that object by anything whatsoever. That point they never tire of, and its mention, even incidentally, is received with steadfast approval and enthusiasm.

It is needless to say also that the address of Miss Van Etten on the work of women[1] met with the heartiest approval, and resulted in the instant adoption of her views of amelioration, since the lady's main cure for the horrible industrial disease of tenement house sweating work was the adoption of the eight-hour working day. While the well-sustained debates showed manly independence, and while no delegate hesitated to strike a blow at anything which did not appear to jibe with the measure of his views, absolute unanimity prevailed on the question of the eight-hour day's work, and all argument went to strengthen every detail of the plan of battle. Instead of any hesitation being expressed by the representatives of the coal miners, they actually resented any suggestion looking to the possible choice for the lead in the strike of any other occupation. It had been an affair over which they had pondered for two years, and their conclusion was fixed and immutable. They spoke like men for whom any change could not be for the worse.

. . . President Gompers closed the service of thanksgiving by saying that had he consulted his own feelings and interests, he would not have been a candidate for the presidency. He believed, however, that a labor man owes his first allegiance to the movement. He said to the socialists that if they regarded him as any enemy to their views they were mistaken. He believed they were honest and he wanted the credit of the same motive. He believed good, honest criticism does a man good and that he comes out all the better for it. He believed that there was no place broader than the floor of the Federation convention. He had said the radicals did great service in preventing the conservatives getting fossilized and that the conservatives prevented the radicals rushing headlong into the abyss of error. He was glad of the spirit in which the convention closed, and he promised for the officers the very best administration of which they were capable. All must concentrate to assist the miners in their coming great work, on which so much depended.

Delegate Morgan took the stage and said: "You are the pleasantest set of boys I have ever met. (Cheers.) I have spent the pleasantest week in my life with you, except one week; that week I got married." (Cheers and laughter.) The speaker then informed them that he was broadened by contact there with others, and said that, though a socialist, he would be a promoter of the success of the Federation. Delegate McNeil closed with a few remarks. The convention then adjourned sine die at 4:30 o'clock.

Thus the convention, which opened with the radicals or socialists arrayed in hostile attitude to the conservatives, closed in the most perfect harmony of expression, and with every indication of a closing instead of a widening of a breach that threatened for a time to disorganize, if not to disrupt, the organization.

Detroit Evening News, Dec. 14, 1890.

1. The AFL published the address as a pamphlet entitled *The Condition of Women Workers under the Present Industrial System* (Washington, D.C., 1891).

From John Elliott

Baltimore, Md., Dec 20 1890

Dear Gompers

Please send me the hand book issued for the Detroit Session A.F of L.

Willard[1] is a fraud & went to Detroit on Fleischmans money. At the last moment it looked as if our delegate "Lipe"[2] on account of trouble in his Union would not act. If such had been the case our Ex. Bd would have urged me to attend. I am glad I was spared the fatigue as well as the inconvenience of absence from my work. You would have had one additional delegate, had I come, opposed to the stand taken against the C.F of L. If however the friction will add to a further spread of the principles of the S.L. Party it will be well but I would rather see them advanced and promulgated in a different manner. Tery V.[3] has now an opportunity, it remains to be seen if he will use it.

I dont understand how my last payment is for Oct. I will overlook the account later. A merry Xmas & happy New Year to your self & household.

From your Sincere friend   J. T. Elliott

Stamp for book postage. enclosed.

ALS, Brotherhood of Painters and Decorators of America Records, reel 141, *AFL Records*.

1. The AFL's Detroit convention rejected the credentials of John F. Willard, a member of Brotherhood of Painters and Decorators of America (BPDA) local 75 of Fall River, Mass., on the grounds that his national union had not authorized him to act as its delegate. According to Elliott, the BPDA's Executive Board had declined to appoint Willard despite his offer to pay his own expenses to the convention. Elliott subsequently heard from August Delabar, secretary of the Journeymen Bakers' and Confectioners' International Union of America (JBCIU), that Willard was an agent of Fleischmann and Co., a manufacturer of compressed yeast and the object of a boycott instituted by the JBCIU and the AFL in 1889. The JBCIU claimed that Charles Fleischmann's yeast company had a business interest in his brother Louis Fleischmann's Vienna Bakery, one of fourteen New York City and Brooklyn firms that locked out their workers in August 1889. The bakery owners refused to negotiate wages and hours and asserted their right to hire and fire workers at their own discretion. In response, the JBCIU boycotted all fourteen firms. Charles Fleischmann protested that the boycott of his company was unjustified and attempted to have it

removed. The union's boycott of Fleischmann and Co. continued until April 1893, however; the AFL officially lifted its boycott at the end of May.

2. Morris Lipe was a member of BPDA 37 of Detroit.

3. Terence V. Powderly.

A News Account of a Mass Meeting in Detroit

[December 20, 1890]

THE MEETING.

The mass-meeting called by Lucien Sanial, as representative of the Central Labor Federation, took place Friday evening, Dec. 12, at Jahn's Hall.

Charles Erb, cigarmaker and organizer of the Detroit Section, S.L.P., presided. Before 8 P.M. the hall was already full to overflowing and presented in this respect a striking contrast with the meeting called on the previous day by Gompers and his arrangement committee. The Brewers' Union came in a body with a band of music and their handsome banner, which was placed on the platform by the side of the chairman amid great applause. Many of the delegates were present.

After reading the instructions which he had received from the C.L.F., Sanial sailed into Gompers. He said he regretted the necessity in which he was of taking some notice of that pompous and theatrical gentleman.

But while the position which Gompers occupied as President of the American Federation would not enable him, or any other mediocrity vested with similar powers, to side track the Labor movement, it might enable him for some time to obstruct and retard its advance. It was therefore important that every member of the Federation be thoroughly posted and vigilant. The speaker then reviewed the issue between Gompers and the C.L.F., and after a concise statement of fact, which showed that even the technicalities of the case, however befogged by Gompers, were plainly in favor of the C.L.F., he took up the real question involved, i.e. — Socialism in the Labor movement. Gompers, and with him some gentlemen on the floor of the convention who were anxious to be sent to Washington by the great Federation as a lobbying committee, had claimed that they admired Socialism very much, nay — that they were Socialists, but were opposed to Socialist methods, to the Socialist party, and, in fact, to every agency through which Socialism could be advanced. Trade unionism, they said, was broad enough for them. They would not interfere with the right of any one to vote as he pleased, or to shout himself hoarse for any of the plutocratic parties. They had, indeed, asserted this right for themselves by shouting themselves hoarse for the Governor of Michigan at the opening of the convention.

Of course, should a big strike take place here by order of the Federation, this same Governor, who gave you such nice taffy last Monday, will call out his plutocratic militia and give you the rifle diet. The usual appeals had been made by Mr. Gompers to the old prejudices against socialism, nursed by the plutocratic press. One of the most heinous and hypocritical charges is that the Socialists preach the class struggle; whereas, in reality, they merely state the obvious fact of its existence; a fact that meets us at every step; a struggle that is forced day and night and everywhere upon the wage-workers by the plutocracy and from which trade unionism has sprung.

The Socialists merely say to you workingmen: Open your eyes; see the struggle in which you are engaged; see the weapons that the plutocratic class is using against you. These weapons are, wealth, which you produce for that class, and political power, which you resign into the hands of that class by voting against each other for its plutocratic parties.

The speaker then depicted the class struggle, showing how the plutocracy was using the political power to disinherit and enslave the workers by appropriating to itself the public property, public franchises, public functions, all the agencies of production and distribution, in a word, all the means of life. He gave statistics, showing the growing concentration of wealth in this country, and demonstrating that in those industries where such concentration was greatest the workmen's power of resistance was smallest, although their trades unions were largest and apparently strongest. All this concentration and its disastrous effects, economic and moral, were the products of a system which could only be maintained or destroyed by the use of political power. He reviewed the labor movement in Europe, showed its Socialist character and the inconsistency or presumption of Gompers in inviting this thoroughly Socialist movement to send representatives to his proposed Anti-Socialist show in 1893. He earnestly thanked the many delegates who had personally expressed to him either their concurrence with his views or their desire to study the question and to advance its discussion in their respective organizations, but who under the present circumstances were in duty bound to vote as they did. He assured them that while his constituents would probably not forgive Gompers for his behavior toward them, they would be the last to foment discord, but would go on sustaining and reinforcing Organized Labor.

In conclusion, he made a strong appeal for unity, education and independent political action. The next Convention of this body he said, will unquestionably show that the seed dropped in this has germinated, and that the time is not distant when the workers of America, united to a man, will claim their own and take it. Then will the class struggle be at an end, class rule be abolished, and trade unionism, as an organization born from war and for war, be a thing of the past.

Thomas J. Morgan, of Chicago, was the next speaker. The remarkable ability which he had displayed in the Convention had concentrated upon him the public attention, and many had come to hear his address. They were not disappointed. He spoke nearly an hour and a half and never for a moment allowed his hearers to lose interest or grow impatient. Frequently humorous, sometimes pathetic, and always eloquent, he gave them a lesson in social economy which they carried home that night and from there to the shop, where, the following day, it was the general topic of discussion. He first narrated how he had come from England to this country of "freedom," voted the Republican ticket and a few days later found himself a wage-slave, without work, without opportunity to work, therefore without bread, without coal, without any of the necessities of life, although the storehouses were full, the productive capacity of land and machinery unlimited, and his own willingness to labor unquestioned. We have no king here, no emperor, no czar, but we have the plutocrat, who owns the means of life, tells us when we can work, when we must be idle, when we can eat and when we must starve, and even makes us shave our whiskers if he fancies that we should have none. He gave instances of such dictation in various establishments, and of the necessary compliance of "free" citizens with the orders of their despotic masters. His statistical treatment of the productive machinery was full of striking illustrations and comments, which made the dry figures speak humorously and eloquently. He then defined Socialism, explained its object, considered its practical application, and showed that all the tendencies of the labor movement were in its direction. He concluded with a strong appeal to the workingmen for union and presented the following

RESOLUTIONS

which were unanimously adopted:

Resolved, That we, workingmen of Detroit in mass meeting assembled, endorse the position of the New York C.L.F. and recognize the necessity of merging into one comprehensive movement the economic and political forces of labor upon the ground that political power is indispensable to the accomplishment of the object contemplated by the labor movement.

Resolved, That notwithstanding the action of the Convention in refusing to admit Delegate Sanial, we hereby accept the action of said body in a friendly and fraternal spirit and pledge our support to the American Federation of Labor, hoping and believing that the kind and fraternal consideration given by the delegates to this important matter and to its representatives upon the floor of the Convention, must in the near future result in a practical recognition of the Socialists.

Resolved, That we urge our fellow Socialists everywhere to so act as to improve the present good feeling felt by the Convention of the American Federation of Labor toward Socialism, and to avoid everything that will cause antagonism.

August Delabar and Richard Braunschweig spoke in German, after which the meeting adjourned.

Workmen's Advocate (New York), Dec. 20, 1890.

An Editorial in the *Workmen's Advocate*

[December 20, 1890]

THE DETROIT CONVENTION.

For the views hastily expressed here as we go to press the editor[1] alone can be held responsible. He has just returned from the Detroit convention and had no opportunity of either rendering to his constituents an account of his mission as representative of the New York Central Labor Federation or ascertaining the general drift of opinion among them.

The sum of his personal impressions of men and things in Detroit may best be expressed by the term, "satisfaction." True, he found there—as he expected to find—that the case which it devolved upon him to present had already been prejudged by a majority of the organizations represented in the Convention, and that many of the delegates had been instructed to vote against his admission. As Socialism was more or less directly involved, the capitalistic press throughout the country had not been idle, it had done its work with its usual effectiveness. Yet, upon the question of giving the C.L.F. representative a hearing on the floor of the convention, thirty-three delegates only voted in the negative, whereas forty-nine proclaimed their sense of fair play by granting him this important privilege.

From that moment the pending issue became clearer and clearer every hour in the minds of the delegates; not that the brief statement made by the New York representative was in itself sufficiently plain and exhaustive, but that in the great debate which followed, thanks chiefly to the ability displayed by Thos. J. Morgan, of Chicago, and to the courageous standing of influential delegates from the miners, glass workers and other powerful trades, a flood of light was cast upon the true nature of the labor movement, such as had never before illuminated the subject in a labor convention on this side of the Atlantic. The fierce and actually desperate opposition of Mr. Gompers served only to emphasize the issue, and, by affording our outspoken friends an opportunity of exploding antiquated notions or exposing the sophistry of "conservatism," so-called, gained us many sympathies. For reasons already stated, the New York delegate could not, under any circumstances, have been seated. But the effect of the debate was subsequently made plain by the overwhelming defeat of Mr. Gompers in all his pet schemes — among which the issue of an official journal and the appointment of a lobbying committee. The Convention had vividly realized (1) that in the hands of any President of the American Federation of Labor, and especially in those of such a passionate man as Mr. Gompers (who had just shown that he did not even scruple to misquote and otherwise distort the language of an opponent in his very face), an official journal might prove a dangerous weapon, and (2) that if representatives of labor were sent to Washington, they should not appear there in the attitude of political intriguers or contemptible beggars, but as Members of Congress, elected by their fellow wage-workers.

We believe, and in fact we know, that many of the delegates will go back to their constituents with an understanding of Socialism very different from that which they formerly had, and that the light which they received in Detroit will not be kept by them under the bushel. It now rests with both the Central Labor Federation and the Socialist Labor party, not only to preserve the advantage gained, but to follow it up with steady progress under a wise and firm policy.

In our opinion, then, the position taken by the Central Labor Federation, and upon which the fight has been made in the Detroit Convention against political scabbism, must be maintained: 1 — because it is right and unassailable; 2 — because its soundness, already now conceded by many, cannot fail to be soon recognized by all; 3 — because it cannot under any circumstances interfere with the protection which the American Federation is in duty bound to extend to those of its affiliated unions that are represented in the New York central body; and 4 — because it is the only position actually consistent with the best interests of the American Federation itself, which require the active co-operation of the most earnest and advanced workers in the labor movement.

Of course, this position can only be maintained by carrying out the vigorous policy which it logically involves—that is, by demonstrating, in the light of practical achievements, that the combined action of the Central Labor Federation and the Socialist Labor party is a most potent factor in organization.

Workmen's Advocate (New York), Dec. 20, 1890.

1. Lucien Sanial.

A Translation of an Interview in the *New Yorker Volkszeitung*

[December 21, 1890]

AN INTERVIEW ABOUT THE RESULT OF THE DETROIT CONVENTION.

Returning from the convention in Detroit, President Gompers entered the office of the American Federation of Labor at 10:30 yesterday morning. On the way he had stopped in Rochester on account of the shoemakers' lockout,[1] as is already known. A reporter from the *Volkszeitung* was the first to greet him and submitted a series of questions, the answers to which Gompers dictated to his typist in the course of the day. The questions and answers were as follows:

Are you satisfied with the result of the convention?

Gompers: Yes, certainly. It was an excellent convention, full of good material, common sense, clear convictions, and the honest desire to achieve the best results in the interest of labor.

Is it your opinion that you have won a victory against the socialists?

Gompers: I don't think that the question of socialists or socialism was a point of discussion at the convention at all. I am convinced that there are more socialists outside the Socialist Labor party than within it, and therefore any talk about a victory over the socialists is meaningless.

In Detroit you said the issue of the Central Labor Federation was no longer in your hands since it had been handed over to the Executive Council, whereas P. J. McGuire has told one of our reporters the Executive Council had never made a decision in the matter, but had advised you to come to terms with the C.L.F.

Gompers: As far as it concerns me, your question is based on an incorrect interpretation of the facts, since I never said this; and with reference to what Mr. McGuire is supposed to have said, it is my opinion that there is some mistake.

Why did you take such a decisive stand against Sanial's admittance after the matter was put before the convention to decide? As president you should actually have taken an impartial stand.

Gompers: It is my opinion that the trade union movement should remain purely a trade union movement. The question was not whether to admit Sanial, for whom I personally have always had the highest respect, but a more important one. If Sanial had been admitted as a representative of the Socialist Labor party, we would have had to admit the representatives of all other political reform parties as well, whether they be socialists, anarchists, single taxers, Greenbackers, etc. Furthermore, I must say that I was absolutely impartial as I always am when I preside; regardless of my personal views I keep strictly to the subject at hand and am completely impartial, and I am prepared to submit my decisions for examination to any expert or anybody with experience in parliamentary procedure.

Unfavorable Impressions.

Hasn't it occurred to you that your persistent demand not to admit the C.L.F., must have made an unfavorable impression of you personally on the delegates?

Gompers: No, I am convinced that this was not the case. Quite the contrary, everybody agreed about the important points of the movement.

How do you explain the fact that after your apparent triumph over the socialists all other important suggestions that you made were rejected by the convention?

Gompers: Since I did not try to triumph over the socialists, the first part of your question is superfluous. My chief desire was to concentrate all energies on the eight-hour agitation and that suggestion of mine was accepted.

What was your purpose in appointing the committee that is to be stationed in Washington?

Gompers: I have never called for a committee to be sent to Washington and did not even know a resolution for that purpose existed until it was presented to the convention. I have never said a word for or against it, neither at the convention nor in conversation with the delegates, and therefore all the talk about it is completely unjustified and without foundation.

For what purpose did you want to have an official organ?

Gompers: I have not called for one and have not recommended it to the convention, but I think that an official organ, not edited by the president but by a competent staff, could do a great deal to clear up mistaken notions about the labor movement as it is being led by the trade unions, to disseminate correct ideas about economic and social questions, to defend the American Federation of Labor against the attacks of its enemies, and to make it self-sufficient.

Wouldn't you have attacked the socialists or their party in this newspaper?

Gompers: Since I have never attacked either the socialists or their party, who I think can do and are doing a lot of good in their own way, I would never have attacked them personally nor have permitted attacks against them.

How could you honestly maintain that you have no objection to socialism when you fight them and their methods so vigorously?

Gompers: I have neither opposed socialism nor the socialists and their methods, because I believe that there are more socialists in the trade unions who follow trade union methods in order to reach the goals of the socialists than there are in the Socialist Labor party.

Do you think that a purely trade unionist struggle without unified political action can achieve the goals that the American Federation of Labor has set?

Gompers: Yes, I believe that the trade unions will bring about both the improvement of conditions and the ultimate emancipation of workers.

THE PURE FOUNTAIN.

What did you mean by the phrase that the light shall be shed only from the pure fountain of trade unionism?

Gompers: I think that the emancipation of the working classes has to be achieved by the workers themselves. Trade unions are the pure, unadulterated organizations of the working classes.

What did you actually mean by the following words in your annual report: "There are those who, failing to comprehend the economic, politic, and social tendencies of the Trade Union movement regard it as entirely 'too slow,' 'too conservative,' and desire to hurl it headlong into a path which, while struggling and hoping for the end, will leave us stranded and losing the practical and beneficial results of our efforts"?

Gompers: That is like the fable of the dog who ran over a bridge with a piece of meat in his mouth, and who thought he saw another dog with an even bigger piece in the water. When he tried to snatch this one too, he lost both. There are many people who encourage such a policy.

You have also said Burns developed from the trade union movement. Did you mean by this that workers become socialists in the school of the trade unions?

Gompers: This statement speaks for itself and I'm sure I don't need to add anything further to it.

THE GREATEST ECONOMIST.

How did you get the idea that Ira Steward[2] was the most important of all economic and social thinkers, as you stated in your annual report?

Gompers: Because in my opinion he and Marx in the English and German languages, respectively, are the greatest minds on these matters.

What policies are you going to pursue with respect to the Central Labor Federation, and will you protect and defend the local unions represented in it that are associated with the American Federation of Labor against attacks from the Knights of Labor?

Gompers: I will pursue a policy of fairness, justice, and fraternity as always, and I trust that the Socialist Labor party will rise to the occasion in the interest of the labor movement, and since I have always protected and defended the trade union movement, the second part of your question is completely superfluous.

Don't you feel that it was wrong to use the capitalist argument against Sanial that if he liked it better in Austria, he should go to Austria?

Gompers: Your question is based on an erroneous interpretation of the facts. Mr. Sanial talked about the labor movement in Austria, Germany, France, and Switzerland as an ideal that the workers of America should take as a model. I, on the other hand, represented the opinion that the labor movement in England and America has advanced further than in any other country in the world toward bringing about the final resolution of the labor question.

What do you think of Morgan, and why did you say that he was no man and no gentleman?

Gompers: I think Morgan is a very clear thinker, an intelligent and serious man. During the convention he once used language that I described as unworthy of a man and gentleman. Later he apologized for his remarks, and I accepted the apology in good faith. That settled the matter.

Socialists Welcome.

Don't you admit that the socialists, wherever they might go, serve the labor movement well as agitators and organizers, and, therefore, shouldn't everyone who is struggling for the emancipation of the working classes welcome the aid of the socialists?

Gompers: Certainly! And I have never missed an opportunity to say precisely that. But I add, as I did at the convention, that the socialists should not force themselves on the trade unions as a party, because in this way they will achieve just the opposite of what they want to achieve.

Are you willing to make peace with the socialists, and haven't you suggested that the socialists would be welcome in the American Federation of Labor if they wanted to organize themselves as federal unions?

Gompers: Since I have no quarrel with the socialists at all, with the exception of a few who call themselves socialists and object to my standing firm on the trade union issue, it is not necessary for me to make peace. I am sure that if they wanted to organize themselves as federal labor unions and allow the trade union movement to take its natural course of development, peace would come about. It is not necessary that we quarrel with each other. We have so much to do in assisting our fellow workers in this great fight against wrong and injustice that all honest and upright men can contribute their assistance without quarrelling with each other on either a personal or official level.

. . .

New Yorker Volkszeitung, Dec. 21, 1890. Translated from the German by Patrick McGrath.

1. Seven hundred and fifty members of the Boot and Shoe Workers' International Union (BSWIU) were involved in a strike that began at the factory of the P. Cox Shoe Co. at Fairport, N.Y., on May 31, 1890, and spread to its Rochester, N.Y., plant a few days later. The workers were challenging wage rates related to the introduction of new machinery. The strike, supported by a boycott that began in August, sustained itself despite the company's resort to strikebreakers, lawsuits, and injunctions. The New York Supreme Court in November enjoined the distribution of strike relief. On Dec. 1 shoe manufacturers in the Rochester Boot and Shoe Manufacturers' Association locked out 3,000 union members in twenty-one shops, demanding that the BSWIU end the Cox strike. During the first weeks in December the New York State Board of Mediation and Arbitration tried unsuccessfully to settle the conflict. SG went to Rochester where, on Dec. 17, he, Henry J. Skeffington, and Rochester Shoe Council Secretary Frank Sieverman attempted to negotiate an end to the strike; the effort faltered on the manufacturers' refusal to discharge strikebreakers. In January, however, the lockout ended as BSWIU members returned to work under an agreement recognizing their local organizations but not the BSWIU. On Jan. 27, Cox signed an

agreement ending the strike at his factories. It provided for the reemployment of the strikers at the wage scale that existed on May 1—that rate to continue until January 1892—and the settling of all future disagreements though arbitration. Cox guaranteed the right of workers to belong to their union and they accepted his right to hire and fire workers at his discretion.

2. Ira STEWARD formulated the theoretical basis for the eight-hour movement in the United States.

To John Elliott

Dec. 22d [1890]

Mr. John T. Elliott,
Sec. Bro. Painters and Decorators of America.
1314 N. Fulton Ave, Baltimore, Md
Dear Sir and Friend:—

As per your request a souvenir[1] will be forwarded to you with this, and I am sure you will find the reading matter therein of a first class quality. Let me know your opinion of it. Much of it will do to reprint.

Of course I should have regretted to have seen you oppose the stand I took but I am sure, first that I am right and secondly that much more good will come to the advancement of correct ideas of the labor and social questions than to allow the trade union movement to be engrafted upon with an organized element that must of necessity ultimately clash with the pure trade union methods. Then it would have opened up the doors to and justified all other political reform parties of whatever stripe clamoring for admission.

At the meeting of the C.L.F. on Sunday Sanial proposed to call a mass-meeting for the purpose of denouncing us and because he was defeated in that proposition he turned his denunciation upon the delegates who dared vote against his proposition and used such covert threats what would be done through the papers under the control of the Socialist Party that they were glad to bask in the sunshine of his good will by reconsidering the vote and decided to hold the meeting. Such a state of affairs in the National conventions of the American Federation of Labor would be a pretty sort of a movement of the Trade Unions. For one I have the courage of my convictions and dare to stand up for them, even when I know I shall be knocked down. As for Mr. Powderly I cannot see how he can gain any advantage from the dispute. The trade union movement is a clear cut one and the man who would be elected as its President who would trim his sail for every breeze would be unworthy of the position. Let me tell you this that I am sure that socialists as a rule both in and out of the party are opposed to their methods and opposed to the interjection of the party as a party in the American Federation of Labor. I have just been reliably informed that no lesser men than John Swinton, and Thaddeus B. Wakeman concur in the stand I took.

Tom Morgan of Chicago criticised the socialists of New York very severely in the same direction.

I tell you Jack, I know I am right and I would rather be driven from the honorable position I hold, yes entirely out of the labor movement than to prove false to my convictions. That the trade unions are the best form of organization to protect and advance the interest of the wage workers and to secure their final emancipation.

With earnest hopes for success and wishing you the compliments of the season I am,

Fraternally Yours   Saml Gompers.
President American Federation of Labor.

TLpS, reel 4, vol. 5, pp. 290-91, SG Letterbooks, DLC.

1. See "From John Elliott," Dec. 20, 1890, above.

To William Martin

New York. Dec. 23rd 1890.

Mr. William Martin,
963 Liberty St. Pittsburgh, Pa
Dear Friend Bill:—

Your favor of the 18th came duly to hand and I am free to say that I have my doubts as to whether I should be congratulated or condoled with on my reelection, but after the fight that was made upon me and the ideas I represent as a trade unionist and having been the one to stand the brunt of the battle thus far and the covert threats of these people to make war upon the American Federation of Labor it would have been rank cowardice in me to have declined a reelection.

In the matter of salary I can assure you that I feel it is an injustice to me, since it leaves me at the end of the year just proportionately poorer as I hold the office, but I could not and would not say one word upon the subject and followed the course that I usually pursue at the convention, of leaving the hall while the subject was under discussion, in order to give the delegates free opportunity to express themselves without regard to my feelings upon the matter.[1]

There are some men in the labor movement whom it seems I cannot and never will suit, whose enmity through some cause unknown to me I have incurred. Be that as it may there is too much work ahead of me to allow an opportunity to attend to personal affairs or to endeavor to placate men who never allow me to know what grievance they have against me.

That my [motives?] in the labor movement have been and are pure and honorable I do not wish to discuss here but prefer that my record of twenty-five years shall stand as the best answer. Of course, man is liable to err in judgement, but I have yet to learn of the move I have made or the word I have said in our cause that I regret.

Yes, Harry Layton[2] was in constant attendance at the convention and said that his experience there he would not have lost in $500.00. It was indeed a great convention, not a personal one, but a convention of organized labor differing upon things at times, but in all doing the best kind of work.

I suppose you know that the Miners have been selected to make the demand for eight hours next May and thus the continuance of the policy I outlined for the concentration of all our efforts on the eight hour workday is again the watchword. That that policy is bound to lead to unlimate [ultimate?] success I am more than satisfied. I am convinced and it was that move which untimately [ultimately] prevented the socialists from declaring open war, but that they will endeavor to make my bed anything but that of roses you may rest assured; that it will swerve me from my purpose of keeping the trade union undefiled I answer, never!

With this I shall mail a souvenir and am sure you will find it interesting reading. Give me your opinion of it?

Your cut is an excellent one and I think for about $1.00 I could secure an electro of it.

The wife has been very dangerously ill since I left New York and is still confined to her bed receiving daily medical attendance. All our other friends are well and desire to be remembered to you.

I am somewhat recovering and wish you the compliments of the season and ask you to write as frequently as possible to

Your Friend. Saml Gompers

N.B. Your telegram was very well received.

S. G.

TLpS, reel 4, vol. 5, pp. 288-89, SG Letterbooks, DLC.

1. SG's annual salary was increased from $1,200 to $1,500 in 1889 but the 1890 convention failed to raise it further.
2. Harry B. Layton was a reporter for the *Pittsburgh Chronicle-Telegraph*.

GLOSSARY

Individuals

Abrahams, Henry (1855-1923), was born in Buffalo and moved to Boston in 1868 where he worked for a dry-goods merchant. At the age of eighteen he became a cigarmaker, serving as secretary of CMIU 70 of Cambridgeport, Mass. (1879), and as corresponding secretary of CMIU 97 of Boston (1885, 1892-1923). He helped found the Boston Workingmen's Central Union (later Boston Central Trades and Labor Union) in 1878 and served as its secretary from 1901 until his death. He served as a delegate from District Assembly 30 to the KOL General Assembly in 1886 and was president of the Massachusetts State Branch of the AFL from 1889 to 1890.

Adler, Felix (1851-1933), a German immigrant, was a philosopher, educator, and social reformer. After receiving his B.A. from Columbia University and his Ph.D. from the University of Heidelberg, he established the New York Society for Ethical Culture in 1876. SG became a member of this organization, which emphasized the importance of moral activism and supported many reform causes. Adler was instrumental in the 1880s in the successful drives leading to the investigation of tenement-house conditions and the enactment of the first anti-sweatshop legislation. During the next decade he arbitrated several labor disputes while a member of the New York Council of Mediation and Conciliation (established by the Church Association for the Advancement of the Interests of Labor). From 1902 until his death Adler held the position of professor of political and social ethics at Columbia University. Between 1904 and 1921 he chaired the National Child Labor Committee, which he and others founded to study and improve the conditions of child labor in the United States.

Altgeld, John Peter (1847-1902), was born in Germany and immigrated with his family to Ohio in 1848. After service in the Union army he worked as a teacher in Missouri, practiced law, and in 1874 was elected state's attorney for Andrew County, Mo. In 1875 he moved to Chicago where he became active in Democratic politics, running

431

unsuccessfully for Congress in 1884. He served as judge of the Superior Court of Cook County between 1886 and 1891, retiring as chief justice. Altgeld was elected governor of Illinois in 1892, and in 1893 pardoned the three surviving Haymarket defendants. He also opposed President Grover Cleveland's use of federal troops in the Pullman strike in 1894. Altgeld was not reelected in 1896 and ran unsuccessfully as an independent candidate for mayor of Chicago in 1899.

APPEL, George W. (b. 1860?), served as the general secretary of the Metal Workers' National Union of North America from 1886 to 1889. Born in Maryland, he worked as a silver plater and brass finisher in Baltimore.

ARCHIBALD, James Patrick (1860-1913), an Irish-born paperhanger and member of the Irish National Land League, was an officer in the New York City Central Labor Union and its successor, the Central Federated Union, from 1882 to 1904, with the exception of one year. He was prominent in the KOL in the late 1880s, representing District Assembly 49 and paperhangers' National Trade Assembly (NTA) 210 in the General Assembly and organizing for the Knights in England, Scotland, and Ireland. He served as district master workman of NTA 210 from 1888 to 1890. In 1895 he helped found the National Paperhangers' Protective and Beneficial Association, serving for seven years as its president. When this union was unable to compete with the AFL's affiliate in the trade, the Brotherhood of Painters, Decorators, and Paperhangers of America, and merged with it in 1902, Archibald served the Brotherhood as general organizer, local and district officer, and AFL delegate. In politics Archibald moved from leadership in the Henry George New York City mayoralty campaign in 1886 and other activities as an independent to support of Grover Cleveland and a leading place in the New York state Democratic party. He served as warden of the Ludlow Street Jail in 1895, was active after the turn of the century in the New York City Civic Federation, was president of the Democratic Association of Workingmen of Greater New York, and for several years was the city's deputy commissioner of licenses. Archibald served as a lobbyist and officer of the Workingmen's Federation of the State of New York and the New York State Federation of Labor.

ARTHUR, Peter M. (1831-1903), a Scottish immigrant, was grand chief engineer of the Brotherhood of Locomotive Engineers (BLE) from 1874 until his death. He was a charter member of BLE Division 46 in Albany, N.Y., was its chief engineer in 1868, and represented it in BLE conventions from 1866 to 1874. Arthur served as second grand assistant engineer of the BLE from 1869 to 1874. As grand chief engineer he maintained the BLE's independence from the AFL and other labor organizations.

BACON, Henry J., a carpenter from Meriden, Conn., was elected the first president of the Connecticut State Branch of the AFL in March 1887, and treasurer at its October 1887 session. In 1888 he went into business first as a car builder, and then as an architect. In the 1890s he returned to carpentry and moved to New Britain. He returned to Meriden in 1913 where he lived at least until 1923.

BAILEY, William H., a miner, was born in Hamilton, Ontario, and lived in Shawnee, Ohio. He served as a member of the KOL General Executive Board (1884-87) and was master workman of the miners' National Trade Assembly 135 (1886-87).

BANDLOW, Robert (1852-1911), manager of the *Cleveland Citizen* from 1891 to 1910, was the son of German immigrants who came to America in 1854. Trained as a printer, he helped organize the Cleveland Gutenberg Society, which became Deutsch-Amerikanische Typographia 6 shortly after its founding in 1873. Bandlow held various posts in the Cleveland Central Labor Union (CLU): secretary from the late 1880s to 1893, president in 1893-94, and treasurer from 1898 to 1902. He served as treasurer of the CLU's successor, the United Trades and Labor Council of Cuyahoga County, from 1902 to 1910. Bandlow became a socialist in the mid-1890s, served on the national committee of the Socialist Party of America from 1908 to 1909, and ran regularly, though unsuccessfully, for city and state office on the socialist ticket.

BANFORD, Lawrence H. (1842-1915), a cigarmaker, was born in Pennsylvania and served as a general organizer for the AFL. In January 1888, as vice-president of the Syracuse Central Trade and Labor Assembly, he attended the first convention of the New York State Branch of the AFL and was elected treasurer.

BARR, Matthew (b. 1840), a Scottish-born sheet metal worker, arrived in New York in 1868 where he worked at his trade until about 1907. He founded the Tin and Sheet Iron Workers' Union in 1887, and became its walking delegate and president. He was a member of the New York City Central Labor Union Board of Trustees in 1886 and 1887. As a member of Tin and Sheet Iron Workers' Local Assembly 1654 in 1887, he was involved in a dispute with District Assembly 49 that resulted in the local's suspension and was active in the United Labor party.

BEAUMONT, Ralph (b. 1844), was born in England and immigrated to Massachusetts about 1848. He was apprenticed to a shoemaker at the age of ten and practiced that trade until 1881 when he became a newspaper correspondent. In the 1870s he was a leader of the Utica, N.Y., Knights of St. Crispin and later was prominent in KOL Local Assembly 1965 of Elmira, N.Y. He represented KOL District Assembly 15 in several general assemblies and was elected to two terms as KOL grand worthy foreman (1878-79, 1882-83). Beaumont ran unsuccessfully on the Greenback-Labor ticket for the New York state senate in 1877 and for Congress in 1878. He served as chairman of the KOL's National Legislative Committee in the late 1880s and was a KOL lecturer in the early 1890s. In 1890 he became secretary of the Citizen's Alliance and represented that organization in the founding of the Confederation of Industrial Organizations in 1891. He also served on the executive committee of the National Reform Press Association. Beaumont accepted an appointment as a U.S. immigrant inspector in 1901 and served in various Canadian ports.

BECHTOLD, Charles F., was secretary of St. Louis local 6 of the National Union of the United Brewery Workmen of the United States (NUUBW) from 1888 to 1892. In 1892 he was elected secretary of the NUUBW, holding the position jointly with Ernst Kurzenknabe until 1899 and with Julius Zorn from 1899 to 1901.

BECKLER, George H., a Peoria, Ill., cigarmaker, served as president of CMIU 118 (1885-88) and as an officer of the Illinois State Federation of Labor (1888-90). During the 1890s he moved to Kewanee, Ill., where he was an AFL organizer and officer of Federal Labor Union 6925.

BLOCK, George G. (1848-1925), secretary of the Journeymen Bakers' National Union (JBNU) from 1886 to 1888, was born in Bohemia and immigrated to New York City in 1870. Moving to Philadelphia in the 1870s, he worked as a pocketbook maker and a journalist, joined the Social Democratic Workingmen's Party of North America, and, during 1877, was organizer for the Philadelphia American-speaking section of the Workingmen's Party of the United States. Block returned to New York City in the early 1880s where he joined the staff of the *New Yorker Volkszeitung*. He helped found the New York City Central Labor Union and was secretary of the Executive Committee of the Henry George campaign. In 1885 he established the *Deutsch-Amerikanische Bäcker-Zeitung* through which he helped generate interest in organizing the JBNU in 1886. He served as secretary of the union until 1888 and editor of the journal until 1889. Around 1889 he went into the liquor business.

BOHM, Ernest (1860-1936), secretary of the Central Labor Federation of New York City from 1889 to 1899 and of the Central Federated Union of New York City from 1899 to 1921, was born and educated in New York. He was a compositor, clerk, and manager of a cloak operators' union early in his career, becoming secretary of the Excelsior Club of the KOL in 1881 and corresponding secretary of the Central Labor Union in 1882. During the 1880s and 1890s he was active in the organization of the brewery workers. He supported Henry George in his campaign for the mayoralty of New York City in 1886, participated in the formation of the United Labor party, and served as secretary of the Progressive Labor party in 1887. Bohm was a member of the SLP and from 1896 to 1898 secretary of the General Executive Board of the Socialist Trade and Labor Alliance. During World War I he worked with the American Peace League, but then allied with SG in the prowar effort. After the war he served as secretary of the New York City Farmer-Labor party (1919-21). From 1921 he was a leader of the Bookkeepers', Stenographers', and Accountants' Union — AFL Federal Labor Union 12646 — holding several positions including the presidency.

BOYER, David P. (1842-1931), a Columbus printer, was born in Ohio. During the 1870s and 1880s he held offices in International Typographical Union (ITU) 5, the Columbus Trades Assembly, and the Ohio State Trades and Labor Assembly. Boyer served as chief organizer for the ITU from 1885 to 1888.

BROCKMEYER, Herman F. (b. 1834?), apparently secretary of the Journeymen Barbers' International Union in 1889-90, was a New York City barber active in the Central Labor Federation.

BUCHANAN, Joseph Ray (1851-1924), was born in Missouri and moved to Denver in 1878, where he became an editor and an organizer of the International Typographical Union. In 1882 he helped organize KOL Local Assembly 2327 and began publishing the *Labor Enquirer.* The following year Buchanan helped form the Rocky Mountain division of the International Workingmen's Association. Between 1884 and 1886 he organized western railroad workers and led several successful railroad strikes. Buchanan was a member of the KOL General Executive Board from 1884 to 1885 and of the KOL auxiliary board in 1886. He served as district master workman of KOL District Assembly 89 from 1885 until he moved to Chicago in January 1887. In that year the KOL expelled him as a result of his disagreement with the decision to force CMIU members to leave the Knights. Buchanan moved to New Jersey in 1888 and twice ran unsuccessfully for Congress. In 1892 he helped organize the People's party, serving on its national committee during the 1892, 1896, and 1900 elections. He was labor editor of the *New York Evening Journal* (1904-15) and a member of the conciliation council of the U.S. Department of Labor (1918-21).

BULLOCK, Jacob C. (1850?-1933), was born in Wales and immigrated with his family to Cleveland at the age of thirteen. A steel worker, he moved to Milwaukee at the age of seventeen and worked as a puddler until 1889. Between 1885 and 1886 he served as vice-president for the fourth district of the National Amalgamated Association of Iron and Steel Workers. About 1890 he became city assessor for Milwaukee's seventeenth ward, a position he held for twenty-seven years. He ended his career as an operator of a real estate agency.

BURNS, John Elliott (1858-1943), a British engineer and a leader of the 1889 London dockers' strike, joined the Amalgamated Society of Engineers in 1879. He was a member of the Social Democratic Federation from 1884 to 1889, the year he was elected to the London County Council. In 1892 he was elected to Parliament as a Social Democrat, serving until 1918. He was one of the delegates from the Trades Union Congress of Great Britain to the 1894 AFL convention in Denver, and in 1895 SG helped him set up a speaking tour of American cities to promote the principles of trade unionism. In 1906 Burns became a cabinet member in the ruling Liberal government; he resigned his post in 1914, however, in protest against Britain's entry into World War I.

CARRICK, Michael Patrick (1857-1904), a painter, was born in Ireland and emigrated to the United States in 1872. A member of Pittsburgh KOL Local Assembly 1397, Carrick helped organize the Brotherhood of Painters and Decorators (BPDA) in 1887. He served as secretary of BPDA 15 in Allegheny, Pa., between 1887 and 1894. When factional struggles split the BPDA in 1894, Carrick supported what was known as the Lafayette (Ind.) Brotherhood or McKinney faction, serving as general organizer. Although Carrick was elected general president of the Lafayette Brotherhood in 1896, he resigned this post in 1897 in favor of unity in the BPDA. Carrick was also active in the United Labor League of Western Pennsylvania, serving as secretary in 1895 and agent in 1897, and in the National Building Trades Council, of which he was fourth vice-president in 1897. In 1901 Carrick was elected general secretary-treasurer of the BPDA.

CAVANAUGH, George (b. 1841), a New York City carpenter, immigrated to the United States from Canada in 1856. He was secretary of the American District of the Amalgamated Society of Carpenters and Joiners in 1890 and 1891.

CLARK, George W., a member of local 135 of the United Brotherhood of Carpenters and Joiners in Chelsea, Mass., was treasurer (1888-89, 1890-93) and president (1889-90) of the Massachusetts State Branch of the AFL.

COSTELLO, John (b. 1854), a member of the KOL General Executive Board from 1888 to 1890, was born in Scotland and worked in the mines before emigrating to Pittsburgh about 1868. He served as the president of the Pittsburgh District Miners' Union during the early 1880s, resigning in 1886 to become an organizer for KOL National Trade Assembly 135. In the early 1890s he organized for the United Mine Workers of America (UMWA) and served as president of UMWA District 5.

DALEY, Edward L. (1855-1904), was born in Danvers, Mass., and apprenticed in the shoemaker's trade at age thirteen. A member of KOL Local Assembly 715, Daley organized the Lynn, Mass., Lasters' Protective Union in 1878 and was its first secretary. He was the general secretary of the New England Lasters' Protective Union (subsequently the Lasters' Protective Union of America) from 1885 to 1895. In 1891 he was elected to a single term in Congress as a Democrat.

DARROW, Clarence Seward (1857-1938), son of a furniture maker, was born in Ohio where he studied law. He moved to Chicago in 1887 where he played an active role in Democratic reform politics, in association with law partner John P. Altgeld, and worked to secure amnesty for the Haymarket defendants in 1887. In 1889 Darrow was named special assessment attorney for Chicago and in 1890 became corporation counsel to the city. He was well known for his work against monopolies. He defended Eugene V. Debs in 1895, William D. Haywood in 1906-7, and the McNamara brothers in 1911, and was chief counsel for the miners in the arbitration of the 1902 coal strike. Darrow served as a Democrat in the Illinois legislature in 1903.

DEBS, Eugene Victor (1855-1926), born in Terre Haute, Ind., entered railroad work as an engine-house laborer and became a locomotive fireman. He was elected first secretary of Vigo Lodge 16 — the Terre Haute local of the Brotherhood of Locomotive Firemen (BLF) — in 1875 and became grand secretary and treasurer of the BLF and editor-in-chief of its journal, the *Firemen's Magazine,* in 1880. Debs resigned his offices in the Brotherhood in 1892 to begin building a single union for all workers employed in the industry; he resigned the editorship in 1894. He founded the American Railway Union

(ARU) in 1893 and served as its president, leading it in a victorious strike against the Great Northern Railroad in 1894. The same year he was arrested and imprisoned for defying a federal court order in connection with the refusal of ARU members to handle Pullman cars while Pullman Co. workers were on strike. The Pullman strike effectively destroyed the ARU.

During his six months in prison Debs studied socialist theory and upon his release turned his energies to political activity. He organized the Social Democratic Party of the United States (SDPUS) in 1897, and in 1900 he polled 100,000 votes as the presidential candidate of the SDPUS and a wing of the SLP led by Morris Hillquit. In 1901 Debs participated in the creation of the Socialist Party of America (SPA). He ran for president as the party's candidate in 1904, 1908, 1912, and 1920, making his best showing in 1912 with 6 percent of the vote. Debs joined with William D. Haywood and other radicals in 1905 to form the Industrial Workers of the World, a revolutionary syndicalist industrial union that he hoped would function as the economic arm of the SPA; he resigned three years later because of tactical differences.

During World War I, Debs became the most famous individual prosecuted under the Espionage Act, receiving a ten-year sentence because of a 1918 speech in which he questioned the sincerity of capitalist appeals to patriotism. SG supported the campaign for clemency that culminated in a presidential pardon in 1921. After his release, Debs attempted to rebuild the SPA, which had been devastated by government repression inspired by the party's pacifist position during World War I.

DELABAR, August, a German immigrant, was secretary of San Francisco Journeymen Bakers' National Union (JBNU) 24 from 1886 to 1887 and in 1888 was elected secretary of the JBNU (after 1890 the Journeymen Bakers' and Confectioners' International Union), serving until 1892. In 1890 he ran for mayor of New York City on the SLP ticket.

DEVLIN, John (1846-1918), a Pennsylvania-born Civil War veteran, operated a grocery business until 1879 when he moved to Detroit to work as a painter in the Pullman car works. In 1882 he was elected as a Democratic and Independent Labor party candidate to the Michigan legislature. He was then appointed deputy labor commissioner and in 1885, U.S. consul to Windsor, Canada, serving for five years. Devlin represented KOL District Assembly 50 at the Knights' general assemblies and was a member of the General Executive Board from 1888 to 1893.

DEWEY, Adelbert M. (b. 1856), a New York–born printer, moved to Detroit about 1878 and joined International Typographical Union 18, serving twice as its president. He also served as president of the Detroit Trades Council, master workman of KOL Local Assembly 901, and worthy foreman of District Assembly 50. Dewey moved to Philadelphia in 1888 to become editor and manager (1888-89) of the KOL official organ, the *Journal of United Labor,* and was chairman of the KOL Pennsylvania legislative committee from 1889 to 1891. During the 1890s he worked for the U.S. Government Printing Office and was a special agent for the Department of Labor in Washington, D.C.

DILLON, William J., secretary of the American Flint Glass Workers' Union (AFGWU) from 1886 to 1893, was born in Newark, N.J., and became a glass worker in Brooklyn. He served as president of Brooklyn local 1 of the AFGWU before assuming national office and moving to Pittsburgh. Dillon resigned his position in 1893 to become a glass manufacturer in Hyde Park, Pa.

DONNELLY, Patrick H. (b. 1857), was secretary of the Coal Miners' Benevolent and Protective Association of Illinois (CMBPA) from 1885 to 1888. Born in Pennsylvania, he moved to Springfield, Ill., in 1879 and served as a district president before becoming secretary of the CMBPA. He became chief clerk for the Illinois State Documentary Department in 1889.

DYER, Josiah Bennett (1843-1900), granite cutters' leader, was born in England and came to the United States in 1871. He was an early member of the KOL in Boston and helped organize a branch of the Granite Cutters' International Union in Graniteville, Mass., in 1877. The following year he was elected secretary of the Granite Cutters' International (later National) Union, serving in that office until 1895.

EBY, George M. (b. 1857), born in Illinois, was first president (1890-91) of the Retail Clerks' National Protective Association of America. He worked as a clerk and manager in Duluth, Minn. (1886-91), and in 1891 moved to Cedar Falls, Iowa. He later lived in Des Moines.

EDMONSTON, Gabriel (1839-1918), a founder and the first president of the Brotherhood of Carpenters and Joiners of America (1881-82), was born in Washington, D.C., and served in the Confederate army. He helped organize Washington carpenters in 1881 and was carpenter of the House of Representatives in the 1880s. A member of the FOTLU Legislative Committee from 1882 to 1886, he was elected its secretary in 1884. He introduced a series of resolutions at the FOTLU 1884 convention calling for the inauguration of the eight-hour movement. From 1886 to 1888 Edmonston served as treasurer of the AFL.

ELLIOTT, John T. (1836-1902), a founder of the Brotherhood of Painters and Decorators of America (BPDA), was born in Baltimore, Md. Following the Civil War he moved to Philadelphia and joined the International Workingmen's Association (IWA). The IWA General Council in New York City elected him general secretary for the United States for 1871-72, and this brought him actively into socialist and reform politics and relief efforts in the city during the depression of the 1870s. He was involved in organizing the Grand Lodge of Painters of America in 1871, the first national painters' union, which lasted until 1876.

Returning to Baltimore in 1879, Elliott organized KOL Local Assembly 1466 and served as secretary of District Assembly 41. He resigned from the Knights in 1882, and in 1887 helped organize the BPDA and was elected secretary. Elliott presided over years of factionalism, during which the painters divided into two groups, Elliott's based in Baltimore, and another in Lafayette, Ind. Poor health forced him to retire in 1900.

ELY, Richard Theodore (1854-1943), an economist at the Johns Hopkins University and from 1892 director of the University of Wisconsin's School of Economics, Political Science, and History, was a leader in the "new school" of reform-oriented economics and one of the founders of the American Economics Association. Ely was an advocate of trade unionism and believed in positive government intervention in the economy.

EMRICH, Henry (b. 1846?), a cabinetmaker born in Prussia, immigrated to New York in 1866 and joined the Cabinet Makers' Union two years later. Emrich was active in the political organization of the New York City Central Labor Union in the 1880s. He served as secretary of the International Furniture Workers' Union between 1882 and 1891 and was its delegate to the FOTLU and AFL conventions between 1885 and 1889. He was elected sixth vice-president of the FOTLU in 1885 and treasurer of the AFL in 1888 and 1889.

ENGEL, George (1836-87), a printer born in Cassel, Germany, immigrated to the United States in 1873, moved to Chicago in 1874, and was a member of the International Workingmen's Association, the SLP, and, after 1883, the anarchist International Working People's Association, or Black International. He wrote for the *Anarchist*. Engel was convicted of murder in connection with the Haymarket incident and was hanged on Nov. 11, 1887.

EVANS, Christopher (1841-1924), an Ohio miners' leader and AFL secretary from 1889 to 1894, was born in England and immigrated to the United States in 1869. He helped found the Ohio Miners' Amalgamated Association, serving as its president in 1889, and the National Federation of Miners and Mine Laborers (NFMML). As secretary of the NFMML from 1885 to 1888, he participated in joint conferences between miners and operators to establish annual scales of prices and wages in the Midwest coal region. After 1895 he became an organizer for the United Mine Workers of America (UMWA) and the AFL, and in 1901 he was appointed UMWA statistician.

FERRELL, Frank J. (b. 1852), was a prominent black trade unionist, socialist, and member of the KOL. Born in Virginia, he worked as a machinist and stationary engineer in New York City into the twentieth century. He became a member of the SLP and of the Eccentric Engineers Association, affiliated with District Assembly (DA) 49, and actively supported Henry George for the mayoralty of the city in 1886 and for secretary of state of New York in 1887. Within the KOL he was prominent in efforts to end segregation. He unsuccessfully advocated admitting Chinese workers to membership in the Knights. At the General Assembly in Richmond in 1886 he and fellow delegates from DA 49 were involved in an incident challenging segregationist practices in the host city, and he received national attention when he introduced Terence Powderly at the Assembly's opening ceremonies with the claim that the KOL was intent on ending racial divisions between workers. Ferrell joined in the denunciation of the death sentences for the Haymarket anarchists and went to Illinois as part of the delegation sent by the New York City Central Labor Union that asked Governor Richard J. Oglesby to commute the sentences.

FIELDEN, Samuel (b. 1847), born in Lancashire, was a cotton mill worker in England. After coming to the United States in 1868, he worked as an itinerant laborer, hauling stone and working the canals, railroads, and levees of the Midwest and South. He settled in Chicago in 1871, was involved in labor organization among teamsters, and by the early 1880s was a prominent labor agitator. He joined the anarchist International Working People's Association in 1884. Fielden was convicted of murder in connection with the Haymarket incident. His sentence was commuted to life imprisonment by Governor Richard J. Oglesby, and he was pardoned by Governor John P. Altgeld in 1893.

FINKELSTONE, Edward (1863-1927), president of the Journeymen Barbers' Protective Union of New York from 1886 to 1887, was born in Germany and immigrated to the United States in 1873. He led the movement that founded the Journeymen Barbers' National Union in December 1887 and served for one year as its first president.

FISCHER, Adolph (1858?-87), a compositor born in Bremen, Germany, immigrated to the United States about 1871. He worked in Little Rock, Ark., and St. Louis, Mo., before coming to Chicago in 1883 where he was employed by the *Chicagoer Arbeiter-Zeitung.* Fischer was convicted of murder in connection with the Haymarket incident and was hanged on Nov. 11, 1887.

FITZGIBBON, James H., was president of the Menominee River Laboring Men's Protective and Benevolent Union, editor of the Marinette, Wis., *Laborer* (1886-88), and statistician of KOL Local Assembly 3313. In 1888 he was appointed organizer for the AFL and worked for over ten years in northern Wisconsin and in northern Michigan. He was involved in an early but unsuccessful attempt to establish a state branch of the AFL in Wisconsin.

FITZPATRICK, Patrick Francis (1835-99), president of the Iron Molders' Union of North America (IMUNA), was born in County Caven, Ireland, and immigrated to the United States at the age of sixteen. Apprenticed to the trade of iron molding in Troy, N.Y., he eventually settled in Cincinnati, where he held offices in IMUNA 4 until 1898 and was one of the founders of the Building Trades Council. From 1879 to 1890 Fitzpatrick was president of the IMUNA and helped restore confidence in a union that had been shaken by charges of corruption and by the depression of the 1870s.

FORAN, Martin Ambrose (1844-1921), Democratic congressman from Ohio (1883-89), was a Cleveland cooper, an organizer in 1870 of the Coopers' International Union, and its president for three years. During the early 1870s he was active in the movement to form a federation of national trade unions. He became a lawyer in 1874 and served as prosecuting attorney of Cleveland between 1875 and 1877. As a congressman, he supported labor legislation, and in 1884 he introduced a bill to prevent the importation of contract labor.

FOSTER, Frank Keyes (1855-1909), was born in Massachusetts and worked as a printer in Connecticut before settling in Boston in 1880. He was active in the International Typographical Union and represented the Boston Central Trades and Labor Union at the 1883 FOTLU convention, where he was elected secretary of the Legislative Committee. A member of KOL Local Assembly 2006, he was elected secretary of District Assembly 30 and a member of the Knights' General Executive Board in 1883. In 1884 he began editing the KOL organ in Massachusetts, the *Laborer* (Haverhill). Foster ran unsuccessfully for lieutenant governor of Massachusetts in 1886 on the Democratic ticket. In 1887 he helped found the Massachusetts State Federation of Labor and served as treasurer (1887), secretary (1889-95), and chairman of the legislative committee (1892-93, 1900-1907). He founded the *Labor Leader* in 1887 in Boston and was its editor until 1897.

FOSTER, William Henry (1848?-86), an Irish-born printer who immigrated to the United States in 1873, was the founder of the *Cincinnati Exponent,* an officer of International Typographical Union (ITU) 3 of Cincinnati, and delegate from the Cincinnati Trades and Labor Assembly to the 1881 FOTLU convention. He was elected FOTLU Legislative Committee secretary in 1881, 1882, and 1885. In 1883 he joined the staff of the *Philadelphia Evening Call* and in 1884 became president of ITU 2 of Philadelphia. He helped found the city's Central Labor Union and served as its secretary. He joined KOL Local Assembly 3879 in 1886 and was its delegate to District Assembly 1.

FUHRMAN, Alfred (b. 1863), was active in the organization of seamen and brewers on the West Coast. Born in Germany, he immigrated to the United States in 1881. He organized local 16 of the National Union of the United Brewery Workmen of the United States (NUUBW) in San Francisco and served as its general secretary in 1889-90. He was also associated with the Coast Seamen's Union as a member and organizer. Fuhrman was secretary of the Representative Council of the Federated Trades and Labor Organizations of the Pacific Coast in 1889-90 and president in 1890. In 1890 the NUUBW suspended his local and the AFL suspended the Representative Council in a dispute that saw Fuhrman organize the rival United Brewery Workmen's Union of the Pacific Coast, of which he became general secretary. The San Francisco brewers rejoined the national organization in 1892. In 1891 Fuhrman helped organize and served as the first president (1891-92) of the Council of Federated Trades of the Pacific Coast. He later became a lawyer.

GEORGE, Henry (1839-97), a Philadelphia-born journalist, labor reformer, and anti-monopolist, began his newspaper career in 1860 as a printer and then worked as an editor for several San Francisco papers. George published *Progress and Poverty,* his most influential work, in 1879 and *The Irish Land Question* in 1881, and subsequently served in the British Isles as correspondent for the *Irish World.* In 1886 he ran second as the liberal and labor candidate in a three-way contest for mayor of New York City against Theodore Roosevelt and the victorious Abram S. Hewitt. His supporters gave serious consideration to a presidential race in 1888, but their hopes were dashed by his disappointing showing in the 1887 campaign for secretary of state of New York. In the campaign's aftermath supporters launched the single-tax movement, based on George's tax reform theories. George meanwhile continued his writing, edited the *Standard* from 1887 to 1890, undertook several speaking tours, and traveled extensively. In 1897, against medical advice, he again ran for mayor of New York City; he died four days before the election.

GOLDWATER, Samuel (1850-98), was born in Poland and immigrated to New York City in 1859, apprenticing as a cigarmaker and joining CMIU 15. He was active in the labor movement and the SLP in Chicago in the 1870s and 1880s, helping form the Chicago Trade and Labor Council (later the Trade and Labor Assembly of Chicago), serving as president of CMIU 11, and running for local offices on the SLP ticket. Moving to Detroit in 1886, he was twice elected president of the Detroit Trade and Labor Council and helped organize the Michigan Federation of Labor. He also served as a CMIU vice-president in 1895 and as a delegate to two AFL conventions. Goldwater was elected city alderman as an independent Democrat in 1894 and 1896, and twice ran unsuccessfully for mayor, dying in the midst of his second campaign.

GOMPERS, Samuel Julian (1868-1946), was the son of SG and Sophia Gompers. Born in New York City, he left school at the age of fourteen to work in a New York City print shop. He moved to Washington, D.C., about 1887 and worked as a printer in the Government Printing Office, a compositor in the U.S. Department of Commerce and Labor, and a clerk in the U.S. Census Office. He was a member of the Association of Union Printers and the Columbia Typographical Union. In 1913 he became chief of the Division of Publications and Supplies of the U.S. Department of Labor, and in 1918 he became chief clerk of the Department of Labor, a position he held until 1941. Gompers and his wife, Sophia Dampf Gompers, had one child, Florence.

GOMPERS, Simon (1849-96), SG's uncle and close childhood companion, was born in London and was a union shoemaker. Immigrating to the United States in 1868, he married Elizabeth Tate; they had six sons and two daughters.

HALLER, Frederick (b. 1853), was born in Augusta, Ga., and was later apprenticed to a Savannah cigar manufacturer. He moved to New York City in 1880, becoming a leader of the Cigarmakers' Progressive Union and the Central Labor Union. In 1886 he led a large group of Progressives into the CMIU, joined SG in the cigarmakers' struggle with the KOL, and was active in the Henry George mayoralty campaign. In 1888 Haller moved to Buffalo, N.Y., where he began studying law and was elected president of the New York State Branch of the AFL. He resigned at the end of 1890 to practice law, became assistant district attorney of Erie County in 1896, and five years later prosecuted Leon Czolgosz, the assassin of President William McKinley.

HANLY, Martin A. (b. 1851), emigrated from Ireland in 1870. A grocery salesman, insurance agent, and superintendent in Jersey City, N.J., Hanly was an active member of the KOL in the New York City vicinity. He represented District Assembly (DA) 49 at the Richmond General Assembly in 1886, and in 1887 was master workman of DA 197.

HARRIS, Daniel (1846-1915), a Civil War veteran and cigarmaker, was born in England and immigrated to the United States in the early 1860s. During the 1877-78 cigarmakers' strike the Central Organization of the Cigarmakers of New York appointed Harris to its Committee on Organization for Pennsylvania. In the late 1880s Harris was president of CMIU 144. He served as president of the New York State Workingmen's Assembly from 1892 to 1897 and of the New York Federation of Labor in 1899 and from 1906 until his death.

HARRIS, George (1853-1935), a Pennsylvania miners' leader, was born in England and immigrated to the United States in 1880, settling in Reynoldsville, Pa. He served as president of the Miners' Amalgamated Association of Pennsylvania (after 1886 the Miners' and Mine Laborers' Amalgamated Association of Pennsylvania) from 1883 until 1887, helped organize the National Federation of Miners and Mine Laborers (NFMML) in 1885, and was elected first vice-president of the AFL in 1886. The following year he resigned his position with the miners' federation to become an organizer for KOL National Trade Assembly 135, and in 1888 he participated in its merger with the NFMML to form the National Progressive Union of Miners and Mine Laborers, reorganized as the United Mine Workers of America (UMWA) in 1890. Harris was an organizer for the UMWA in the 1890s and in 1897 was elected president of UMWA Pennsylvania District 2 and vice-president of the newly organized UMWA Pennsylvania State Association, serving until 1899. He was an active campaigner for the Republican party in the 1880s and 1890s. In 1922 he moved to Wilmington, Del.

HARTMANN, Louis (d. 1896), a cigarmaker, served as general organizer for the AFL. He was secretary of the Illinois State Federation of Labor in 1888 and also secretary of the Trade and Labor Assembly of Chicago in the late 1880s.

HASKELL, Burnette G. (1857-1907), of San Francisco, a California-born lawyer, in 1881 founded the International Workingmen's Association (known as the Red International), a socialist organization with divisions on the Pacific Coast and the Rocky Mountain area. Shortly afterward it became the first American affiliate of the anarchist International Working People's Association. From 1882 to 1884 he published the *Truth* (San Francisco), a weekly paper devoted to labor and the anti-Chinese movement. Haskell subsequently became a follower of Edward Bellamy and Laurence Gronland, joining in the movement for the peaceful establishment of a cooperative commonwealth by sponsoring a Nationalist Club in San Francisco. In 1891 he unsuccessfully attempted to establish a cooperative colony in Hawaii.

HASSON, Samuel B. (1855-1921), a cigarmaker, joined CMIU 133 of Richmond in June 1879 and served as president of CMIU 1 of Baltimore from 1894 to 1895. He served as president of the Baltimore Federation of Labor from 1888 to 1889 and for several terms in the early 1890s. He was also sixth vice-president of the CMIU from 1897 to 1900.

HAYES, John William (1854-1942), was born in Philadelphia. By the 1870s he lived in New Jersey where he was initiated into the KOL while employed as a brakeman with the Pennsylvania Railroad in 1874. Soon after joining the Order he was commissioned as an organizer and, after the loss of his right arm in an 1878 railroad accident, became a telegrapher. Losing his position in 1883 because of union activities, he entered the grocery business. He was a member of the KOL General Executive Board from 1884 to 1916, serving as general secretary-treasurer from 1888 until 1902 and as the Knights' last general master workman from 1902 until the Order closed its central office in 1916. Hayes took an active part in the People's party in the early 1890s. He was manager of the Atlantic Gas Construction Co. in Philadelphia and, later, president of the North Chesapeake Beach Land and Improvement Co.

HERBRAND, Louis, immigrated to the United States from Germany in 1864. In the 1860s he was employed in Pittsburgh and Lancaster, Pa., and later he moved to New York where he held a variety of positions as a brewery worker. In 1884 he was a founder of the New York Brewers' Union, a local assembly of the KOL; he became the union's secretary in 1885. In 1886 he was elected secretary of the National Union of Brewers of the United States, subsequently the Brewers' National Union and then the National Union of the United Brewery Workmen of the United States. In April 1887 the newly formed Brewers' Pool locked out 4,000 men in an attempt to destroy the Brewers' union in New York, and in the fierce struggle that followed the union was defeated. Herbrand left New York during the lockout to settle his father's estate in Germany and, as a result, was stripped of his position in the union in 1888.

HILL, David Bennett (1843-1910), a Democrat, served as governor of New York from 1885 until 1892 and as a U.S. senator from 1892 until 1897.

HOEHN, Gottlieb (variously Gustav) A. (1865-1951), a socialist editor, was born in Germany and immigrated to the United States in 1884. He joined the Custom Shoeworkers' Union and the SLP in Baltimore in 1885 and was a delegate to the Baltimore Federation of Labor from 1886 to 1888. In 1888 he moved to Chicago where he worked for the *Chicagoer Arbeiter-Zeitung.* He moved to St. Louis in 1891 to edit the *St. Louis Tageblatt* and was active in the St. Louis Trades and Labor Assembly and the Missouri Federation of Labor. In 1893 Hoehn began a long-term editorship of the *St. Louis Labor,* a paper established in opposition to Daniel DeLeon's leadership of the SLP. He was a founder of the Social Democratic party in 1898, serving on its National Executive Committee. Hoehn edited other St. Louis papers at various times, including the *Abendpost und Tageblatt,* the *Arbeiter-Zeitung,* and the *Brauer-Zeitung.*

HOLLAND, James J. (b. 1844), a butcher, small businessman, lawyer, and local politician, was born in Ohio and came to Jacksonville, Fla., after serving with the Union army during the Civil War. A member of the Republican party in Jacksonville, Holland served as city clerk, alderman, fire chief, and sheriff of Duval County at various times in the 1880s. He was elected to the KOL General Executive Board in 1888 and again in 1890, but lost his position late in 1890 after the Florida assembly expelled him for his role in an internal political struggle.

HOWARD, Robert (1845-1902), a spinner and union organizer in Lancashire, England, immigrated to the United States in 1873. In 1878 he became secretary of the Fall River Mule Spinners' Association, serving until 1897. At the same time he played a leading role in national organizations of the trade—the Amalgamated Mule Spinners' Association, of which he was principal officer from 1878 to 1887, and the National Cotton Mule Spinners' Association. Howard campaigned for shorter-hour legislation and other labor measures. He was elected to a term in the Massachusetts House of Representatives in 1880 and to the Massachusetts Senate in 1885 and 1886.

He was treasurer of the FOTLU Legislative Committee in the early 1880s and was elected master workman of KOL District Assembly 30 in 1886. In the mid-1890s he conducted an organizing campaign among southern textile workers for the AFL.

HYSELL, Nial R. (b. 1854), was born in Ohio where he worked as a coal miner. In 1884 he was elected vice-president of the Ohio Miners' Amalgamated Association, a position he held for three years. He was also a member of the Executive Board of the National Federation of Miners and Mine Laborers (1886-87). He served in the Ohio General Assembly as a Democrat (1888-92) and as speaker of the house (1890-91). Hysell undertook the study of law in 1890 and was admitted to the bar in 1893.

IVES, Harry M. (b. 1856), born in Iowa, graduated from Iowa State Agricultural College and moved to Topeka, Kans., in 1881 where he worked as a printer. He was elected president of International Typographical Union 121 in 1889 and a director in 1890. In 1892 and 1893 he served as president of the short-lived Kansas State Federation of Labor and in 1893 worked as an organizer for the AFL. In 1905 Ives started a commercial printing establishment, H. M. Ives and Sons, where he worked until retirement in 1924.

JABLINOWSKI, Ludwig (b. 1856), a cigarmaker born in Germany, immigrated to the United States in 1880 and in 1885 became secretary of Cigarmakers' Progressive Union 1. Following the Progressives' amalgamation with the CMIU in 1886, he remained secretary of the local, renamed Cigar Makers' Progressive International Union 90, until 1889. Jablinowski was a financial secretary of the New York City Central Labor Union (CLU) between 1884 and 1886 and was active in the Henry George mayoralty campaign. He was one of the founders in 1889 of the New York City Central Labor Federation, which opposed the CLU during the following decade. In the 1890s he was a reporter for the SLP's organ, the *People,* and for the *New Yorker Volkszeitung;* he was later an editor of the *People.*

JUNIO, John Joseph (b. 1842), born in Boston, was president of the CMIU (1867), president of the New York Cigar Makers' State Union (1875-77), and an officer of local 6 of Syracuse, N.Y. He was active in labor reform, representing the Mechanical Order of the Sun at the National Labor Union congress in 1868, running for New York secretary of state on the Workingmen's Party of the United States ticket in 1877, serving as state chairman of the Greenback-Labor party, and representing District Assembly 152 at the KOL General Assembly in 1887. He was an organizer for the CMIU in the mid-

1880s and represented the New York State Federation of Labor at the 1895 AFL convention.

KEAN, Edward J. (b. 1851), a New York City printer, was born in Maryland. He served as president of the Amalgamated Trades and Labor Union of New York and Vicinity and as editor of International Typographical Union 6's organ, the *Boycotter*. Kean was chief clerk of the New York Bureau of Labor Statistics between 1885 and 1891.

KELLEY, Florence (1859-1932), was a prominent reformer in the areas of tenement-house manufacturing conditions and child labor. In 1884 she married Lazare Wischnewetzky, a fellow student and socialist; when the marriage ended in divorce in 1892, Kelley reassumed her maiden name. She translated several socialist publications, among them a work by Friedrich Engels that she published as *The Condition of the Working Class in England in 1844* (New York, 1887). In 1891 she moved to Chicago, residing at Hull-House until 1899. She served as chief state inspector of factories for Illinois from 1893 to 1897. In 1899 she became general secretary of the National Consumers' League, a position she held until her death. She also served on the boards of directors of the New York State and the National Child Labor Committees, was a founder and board member of the National Association for the Advancement of Colored People, and served as vice-president of the National American Woman Suffrage Association.

KEUFER, Auguste (1851-1924), was general secretary of the Fédération française des travailleurs du livre, the French typographical union, from 1885 to 1920. He was a leading positivist and in 1895 was one of the prime movers in the founding of the Confédération générale du travail, serving as its first treasurer. SG met with him on several occasions both in the United States and abroad.

KING, Edward (1846-1922), a type founder, immigrated from Scotland about 1870 and organized in his trade. He was one of a small group of New York City positivists. During the 1880s he served as a delegate to the New York City Central Labor Union and proved an ardent supporter of both trade unionism and independent political action on the part of the workers. In the late 1880s King became active with SG in the Social Reform Club which included trade unionists, employers, and members of the middle class who were interested in improving working conditions and the relationship between the classes. He was involved in the New York settlement movement from its beginning, living and working at the University Settlement House for many years, where he taught classes in Greek and Roman history.

He was also a member of the Advisory Council of the People's Institute, which organized clubs to discuss social problems.

KIRCHNER, John S. (1857-1912), a cigarmaker, was born in Maryland and became active in the labor movement in 1877 when he joined a Baltimore local assembly of the KOL. After moving to Philadelphia he helped organize CMIU 100, serving as its secretary (1881, 1884-90), and was CMIU fourth vice-president (1885-87) and organizer for Pennsylvania. In 1886 he was appointed secretary of the FOTLU Legislative Committee upon the death of William H. Foster.

KLIVER, William H. (1846-1914), an Ohio-born carpenter and Civil War veteran, came to Chicago in 1884 and became a member of KOL Local Assembly 1307 and Brotherhood of Carpenters and Joiners local 28. He was president of the Trade and Labor Assembly of Chicago in 1887 and first vice-president of the Illinois State Federation of Labor in 1888. In 1888 he became fifth vice-president of the United Brotherhood of Carpenters and Joiners and two years later was elected general president, serving until 1892. Kliver moved to Gary, Ind., in 1904 and was elected as a Republican to a two-year term in the Indiana legislature in 1908. He was building commissioner of Gary from 1909 until 1914.

KURZENKNABE, Ernst (1860?-1927), was national secretary of the National Union of the United Brewery Workmen of the United States (NUUBW) from 1888 to 1899 and held this position jointly with Charles Bechtold after 1892. A former secretary of NUUBW 1 of New York City, Kurzenknabe moved to St. Louis during his tenure as national secretary. Between 1900 and 1920 he worked variously as a saloon keeper, cashier, and bookkeeper before becoming a reporter for *Amerika*, a German-language paper, about 1921.

LABADIE, Joseph Antoine (1850-1933), born in Paw Paw, Mich., was apprenticed to a printer in South Bend, Ind., in 1866. After settling in Detroit in 1872 he joined International Typographical Union 18 and in 1878 became a KOL organizer. He was also active in politics, running unsuccessfully for mayor on the Workingmen's party ticket in 1879 and playing an active role in the SLP. In the early 1880s Labadie worked as a labor journalist for several papers and was one of the publishers of the *Labor Review* and the *Times*, a trade union paper. He played a major role in establishing the Detroit Trades and Labor Council in 1880, becoming its corresponding secretary, and was also a founder and first president (1889-90) of the Michigan Federation of Labor. Labadie became a philosophical anarchist in 1883 and was a close associate of Benjamin Tucker, a leading anarchist thinker; he frequently wrote for Tucker's journal, *Liberty*, until its demise in 1908. In 1893 Labadie was appointed clerk of the Detroit Water Works, a post he held until about 1920.

LAKE, Emmett J. (b. 1847), was a Troy, N.Y., carpenter. The AFL commissioned him in 1888 as its first general organizer. He served as the first secretary of the New York State Branch of the AFL during 1888-89.

LAKE, Obadaiah Read (1846-1923), a Canadian-born telegraph editor for the *St. Louis Globe-Democrat*, joined St. Louis International Typographical Union 8 in 1868 and thereafter regularly held offices in the local. He was master workman of KOL District Assembly 17 in 1889. In 1890 he married Leonora M. Barry, chief spokeswoman in the KOL for women workers. Lake was later a correspondent for the *New York Sun*.

LEAHY, Jeremiah J. (1850-1927), an Irish immigrant, was a charter member and master (1885-89) of Philadelphia Lafayette Lodge 293 of the Brotherhood of Locomotive Firemen (BLF). He served as a member of the BLF Grand Executive Board from 1886 to 1890 and as grand chaplain of the Brotherhood's conventions from 1904 to 1925.

LENNON, John Brown (1850-1923), president and subsequently general secretary of the national tailors' union, was born in Wisconsin and raised in Hannibal, Mo. He moved to Denver, Colo., in 1869 where he helped organize a tailors' union and the Denver Trades Assembly and held offices in both. In 1883 Lennon's local affiliated with the newly formed Journeymen Tailors' National Union of the United States (later renamed the Journeymen Tailors' Union of America) Lennon serving as president (1884-85), General Executive Board member (1885-87), and general secretary and editor of the *Tailor* (1887-1910). Lennon was treasurer of the AFL from 1890 to 1917. He was a member of the U.S. Commission on Industrial Relations (1912-15) and the Board of Mediators of the U.S. Department of Labor (1917).

LINGG, Louis (1864-87), a carpenter born in Baden, Germany, was active in the German labor movement before immigrating to Chicago in 1885. He was a member and organizer for the Brotherhood of Carpenters and Joiners and a delegate to the Chicago Central Labor Union. Lingg was convicted of murder in connection with the Haymarket incident and was sentenced to death. He committed suicide in jail.

LITCHMAN, Charles Henry (1849-1902), a general secretary of the

KOL, was born in Marblehead, Mass. He worked for his father, a shoe manufacturer, as a salesman until 1870 when he and his brother formed the shoe manufacturing firm of Litchman Brothers. In 1874 he left the company to study law, but after several months returned to the industry as a shoe worker. He joined Fraternity Lodge 38 of the Knights of St. Crispin in 1874, and between 1875 and 1878 was involved in efforts to revive the faltering national organization, serving successively as grand scribe of the Massachusetts Grand Lodge and grand scribe of the International Grand Lodge of America. Active in Republican politics in the mid-1870s, Litchman joined the Green-back-Labor party and was elected to the Massachusetts General Court in 1878, though not reelected in 1879. In 1877 he joined KOL Local Assembly 221 of New York City, and served as grand secretary of the KOL from 1878 to 1881 and general secretary, as the office was redesignated, from 1886 to 1888. In August 1888 he resigned to work in Benjamin Harrison's presidential campaign, and the following year was appointed special agent in the U.S. Treasury Department, serving until 1893. He also served as a Republican appointee to the U.S. Industrial Commission of 1900-1902.

LLOYD, Henry Demarest (1847-1903), was born in New York City where he became a lawyer in 1869. His opposition to monopoly power and special privilege drew him to the American Free-Trade League, and he served as league secretary as well as editor of its journal—the *Free Trader*—from 1869 to 1872. Moving to Chicago in 1872, he became financial editor and then chief editorial writer of the *Chicago Tribune*. His economic self-sufficiency, based largely on a financially advantageous marriage, enabled him to leave the *Tribune* in 1885 and devote himself independently to reform causes. Lloyd achieved prominence through his long campaign to reform the Chicago Board of Trade and through his exposé, published in the *Atlantic Monthly* in 1881, detailing the monopolistic practices of Standard Oil. Among his major works he later published an acclaimed book-length treatment of Standard Oil, *Wealth against Commonwealth* (1894). He was also associated closely with labor causes. He sought commutation for those convicted in connection with Chicago's 1886 Haymarket incident, became a central figure in the effort to build a labor-populist alliance in the early 1890s, defended Eugene Debs in the trial following the Pullman strike in 1894, and wrote extensively in sympathy with labor. Lloyd ran unsuccessfully for Congress as a People's party candidate in 1894.

McBRIDE, John (1854-1917), the only person to defeat SG for the presidency of the AFL, presided over the formation of the United

Mine Workers of America (UMWA) and was its second president. The son of an Ohio miner, he was elected president of the Ohio Miners' Protective Union in 1877 and master workman of KOL District Assembly 38 in 1880, and served as president of the Ohio Miners' Amalgamated Association from 1882 to 1889. In 1885 he was a founder and first president of the National Federation of Miners and Mine Laborers and in 1886 presided over the founding convention of the AFL, declining the Federation's nomination for president. He served as president of the National Progressive Union of Miners and Mine Laborers in 1889 and was a leader in merging that union with KOL National Trade Assembly 135 in 1890 to form the UMWA. He became president of the UMWA in 1892 and served until 1895.

McBride served as a Democrat in the Ohio legislature from 1884 to 1888, was commissioner of the Ohio Bureau of Labor Statistics from 1890 to 1891, and later became active in the populist movement. He was elected president of the AFL over SG in 1894 and narrowly lost to SG the next year. McBride purchased the *Columbus Record* in 1896, which he edited until 1917. He left that position in 1917 due to illness and moved to Arizona, where he served as a federal labor conciliator.

McBRYDE, Patrick (1848-1902?), secretary-treasurer of the United Mine Workers of America (UMWA) from 1891 to 1896, was born in Ireland and raised in Scotland, where he became active in local miners' organizations. He came to the United States in the late 1870s, working for several years before returning to the Scottish mines. About 1884 he immigrated to the United States, settling in the Pittsburgh area where he joined KOL Local Assembly 151. McBryde represented KOL National Trade Assembly 135 at the founding convention of the National Progressive Union of Miners and Mine Laborers, and served as its secretary-treasurer (1888-90). In 1890 he was elected to the National Executive Board of the newly founded UMWA. After retiring from the miners' union in 1896, he served as commissioner for mine operators in Ohio.

McDONNELL, Joseph Patrick (1847-1906), born in Ireland and active in the Fenian movement, joined the International Workingmen's Association (IWA) after moving to London in 1868 and served as Irish secretary of the IWA's General Council. Immigrating to New York City in 1872, he became a leading figure in the Association of United Workers of America and a member of the Economic and Sociological Club. He began editing the *Labor Standard*, an organ of the Workingmen's Party of the United States (WPUS), in 1876. Associated with the trade union faction of the WPUS, he moved the paper to Boston in 1877 in the midst of the WPUS's dissolution over the dispute between trade unionist and political tactics. In 1878 he moved the paper to Paterson, N.J., where he helped organize the International Labor Union. McDonnell was imprisoned twice between 1878 and 1880 for publishing libelous material against strikebreakers and manufacturers. In 1883 he helped organize the New Jersey Federation of Trades and Labor Unions; he served as its chairman until 1897. In 1884 he was a founder of the Paterson Trades Assembly. He became New Jersey's first factory inspector in 1884 and, in 1892, was appointed to the New Jersey Board of Arbitration. McDonnell continued to publish the *Labor Standard* until his death.

McGLYNN, Edward (1837-1900), a New York–born Catholic priest, was appointed pastor of St. Stephen's parish in 1866. He was a member of the American Land League and came into conflict with Archbishop Michael Corrigan for his outspoken support of Henry George in the 1886 mayoral campaign. As a result, early in 1887 he was transferred from St. Stephen's and later that year was excommunicated. During the next five years McGlynn regularly lectured about the single tax at meetings of the Anti-Poverty Society, of which he was the first president. In 1892 the papal representative in the United States reinstated McGlynn, and in 1894 he was named pastor of St. Mary's church in Newburgh, N.Y.

McGREGOR, Hugh (1840-1911), was an English-born jeweler. He served as a volunteer with Garibaldi's army and immigrated to the United States in 1865. During the 1870s he was a member of the International Workingmen's Association and a founder and active organizer of the Social Democratic Workingmen's Party of North America. He served as secretary of its New York branch in 1875 and its Philadelphia branch in 1876, returning to New York in the spring of that year to edit the new English-language organ of the party, the *Socialist.* A participant in the Economic and Sociological Club, he apparently left the socialist movement and became active in a small circle of New York City positivists. During the late 1880s he served as SG's secretary, directing the AFL office during the president's absence. He helped organize seamen on the Atlantic coast and between 1890 and 1892 served as secretary of the short-lived International Amalgamated Association of Sailors and Firemen. He later worked briefly in the AFL's Washington office.

McGUIRE, Peter James (1852-1906), chief executive officer of the United Brotherhood of Carpenters and Joiners of America (UBCJA), was born in New York City. He joined a local carpenters union there in 1872 and became a member of the International Workingmen's

Association. He was involved in relief efforts in New York City during the depression of the 1870s and played a major role in organizing the Tompkins Square demonstration of January 1874. In 1874 he helped organize the Social Democratic Workingmen's Party of North America and was elected to its Executive Board; that same year he joined the KOL. During the late 1870s McGuire traveled widely, organizing and campaigning first on behalf of the Workingmen's Party of the United States and then for the SLP. After living for a time in New Haven, Conn., he moved to St. Louis in 1878 and the following year was instrumental in the establishment of the Missouri Bureau of Labor Statistics, to which he was appointed deputy commissioner. He resigned in 1880 to campaign for the SLP and for the Greenback-Labor party. In 1881 he was elected secretary of the St. Louis Trades Assembly and, as a member of the provisional committee to organize a carpenters' national union, began editing the *Carpenter.* Through that journal he generated interest in organizing the Brotherhood of Carpenters and Joiners (later the UBCJA); he was elected secretary of the union at its founding convention later that year and held the position until 1901. McGuire moved to New York City in 1882, was a founder of the New York City Central Labor Union, and became a member of Spread the Light KOL Local Assembly 1562; he subsequently moved to Philadelphia. He served as secretary of the AFL from 1886 to 1889, second vice-president from 1889 to 1890, and first vice-president from 1890 to 1900.

McGuire, Thomas B. (b. 1849), a leader of KOL District Assembly (DA) 49 and a member of the Home Club, was a marble polisher and truck driver. Born in New York City, he served in the Union army during the Civil War. He became active in the labor movement in the early 1870s and subsequently served as an officer in KOL local assemblies 2234 and 1974. McGuire was master workman of DA 49 in 1886. He was a member of the Knights' General Executive Board from 1886 to 1888 and from 1892 to 1897, and lectured for the Order in the interim. In 1893 he was a member of the Advisory Committee of the People's party. During the 1890s he resided in Amsterdam, N.Y.

McLaughlin, Daniel (1831-1901), was first vice-president of the AFL for one term (1887-88). He was born in Lanarkshire, Scotland, and was involved with Alexander MacDonald in the Scottish miners movement before immigrating to Braidwood, Ill., in 1869. There he emerged as a leader of the KOL, served as a member of the KOL General Executive Board (1880-81), and successfully ran for town mayor on the Greenback ticket in 1877 and 1881.

McLaughlin was active in the Illinois State Federation of Labor and in several miners' unions. He served as president of the Coal Miners' Benevolent and Protective Association of Illinois (1885-88) and helped organize the National Federation of Miners and Mine Laborers in 1885. As its treasurer (1885-88) he proposed joint conferences between miners and operators to establish annual scales of prices and wages in the Midwest coal region. McLaughlin was elected to the state legislature on the Republican ticket in 1886 and 1888. Involved in the contest with the KOL for control of the coal fields, he helped organize the National Progressive Union of Miners and Mine Laborers in 1888. About 1890 he left Illinois to become a mine superintendent in Starkville, Colo.

McMackin, John (1852-1906), a painter and leader in the New York City Central Labor Union, was born in Ireland and immigrated to the United States in 1865. He was active in the Henry George mayoralty campaign and later, as a Republican, served as special inspector of customs for New York City (1889-94), deputy commissioner (1897-99) and commissioner (1899-1901) of the New York Bureau of Labor Statistics, and New York labor commissioner (1901-5).

McNeill, George Edwin (1837-1906), a Boston printer born in Massachusetts, was secretary of the Grand Eight-Hour League and president of the Boston Eight-Hour League. He helped lobby for the establishment of the Massachusetts Bureau of Statistics of Labor and served as its deputy director from 1869 to 1873. McNeill was an officer of the Sovereigns of Industry, president of the International Labor Union in 1878, and secretary-treasurer of KOL District Assembly 30 from 1884 to 1886. He was editor or associate editor of several papers including the *Labor Standard* in Boston, Fall River, Mass., and Paterson, N.J., and in 1887 published *The Labor Movement: The Problem of To-Day*. He helped organize the Massachusetts Mutual Accident Association in 1883 and was elected its secretary and manager in 1892. In 1897 he served as the AFL's fraternal delegate to the Trades Union Congress of Great Britain.

McVey, George H. (b. 1846), was president of the United Piano Makers' Union in 1887 and financial secretary of the New York City Central Labor Union in 1886 and 1887. He was active in the Henry George mayoralty campaign and was elected secretary of the New York State Workingmen's Assembly in 1887. McVey continued to work as a pianomaker and live in Brooklyn until the early twentieth century.

Mann, Thomas (1856-1941), a British engineer, was a member of the Amalgamated Society of Engineers (ASE) and, until 1889, of the Social Democratic Federation. A leader of the London dock strike of 1889, he became president of the Dock, Wharf, Riverside, and General Labourers' Union at its founding in mid-September of that year, serving until 1892. In 1891 he was one of seven trade unionists on the Royal Commission on Labour, which was formed to discuss the question of industrial relations. Mann was secretary of the Independent Labour party from 1894 to 1896. In 1916 he joined the British Socialist party and in 1920 helped found the British Communist party, remaining a member until his death. From 1919 to 1921 he was secretary of the Amalgamated Engineering Union, successor to the ASE. Mann stood unsuccessfully for Parliament four times.

MARDEN, William Henry (1843-1903), a leader of the Massachusetts shoemakers, was born in that state and served in the Union army. He was secretary of the Knights of St. Crispin Lodge in Stoneham, Mass., became a member of KOL Local Assembly 2340, and served as treasurer of the New England Lasters' Protective Union in the late 1880s. In 1893 he was elected fourth vice-president of the AFL. He was a member of the Massachusetts House of Representatives from 1895 to 1899.

MARTIN, William (1845-1923), who emigrated from Scotland in 1868, was secretary of the National Amalgamated Association of Iron and Steel Workers from 1878 to 1890. As secretary of the Columbus, Ohio, Lodge of the Iron and Steel Roll Hands' Union, he helped found the Amalgamated in 1876; he later moved to Pittsburgh. Martin served as second vice-president of the AFL from 1886 to 1888 and as first vice-president from 1889 to 1890. In 1891 he accepted a position as head of the Bureau of Labor of the Carnegie Steel Co. After leaving Carnegie in 1893, he became a varnish manufacturer and later held a variety of positions including insurance agent and night foreman.

MENCHE, Adam (b. 1849?), was born in Vermont and moved as a boy to Syracuse, N.Y., where he worked with his father in the salt works. He later became an apprentice cigarmaker and in 1865 joined the CMIU. Moving to Denver by 1890, he served as an AFL organizer and as the Denver Trade and Labor Assembly's delegate to AFL conventions. About 1896 he moved to Chicago and was president of CMIU 14, secretary-treasurer of the Chicago Union Label League, and, from 1901 to 1903, president of the Illinois State Federation of Labor.

MILLER, Hugo A. (1856-1926), secretary of the German-American

Typographia, was born in Freiberg, Saxony, and entered the printing trade at the age of fifteen. In 1873 he immigrated to New York City, joined the Typographia, and became active in union affairs. He represented the union at the 1882 FOTLU convention and served the Federation from 1882 until 1886 as its German-language secretary. Miller was secretary of his union from 1886 until 1894, when it amalgamated with the International Typographical Union (ITU) and moved its offices to Indianapolis. Thereafter he served as a vice-president of the ITU and secretary-treasurer of its German branch. From 1886 to 1926 he edited the Typographia's organ, the *Deutsch-Amerikanische Buchdrucker-Zeitung* (later, the *Buchdrucker-Zeitung*).

MORGAN, Elizabeth Chambers (b. 1850), a labor organizer and reformer, was a founder of AFL Ladies' Federal Labor Union (FLU) 2703. Born in Birmingham, England, and a mill worker from the age of eleven, she married Thomas J. Morgan in 1868 and they immigrated to Chicago in 1869. She and her husband became socialists during the depression of 1873. She was a charter member of the Sovereigns of Industry and in 1881 joined KOL Local Assembly 1789, later becoming its master workman. In 1886 she was elected delegate to the Trade and Labor Assembly (TLA) of Chicago and two years later helped organize Ladies' FLU 2703 and the Illinois Women's Alliance, a coalition of women's organizations working for woman suffrage and government protection of women and children from industrial exploitation. The report she wrote on sweatshop labor for the Chicago TLA served as a basis for the successful campaign for passage of the Illinois Factory and Workshop Inspection Act of 1893, and she subsequently testified before Congress on the sweating system. She later worked as a bookkeeper in her husband's law office.

MORGAN, Thomas John (1847-1912), a Chicago machinist and brass finisher, was born in Birmingham, England, where he married Elizabeth Chambers. They immigrated to the United States in 1869, and he worked for the Illinois Central Railroad, joining the International Machinists and Blacksmiths of North America in 1871 and serving as president of his local in 1874. Beginning in 1876 he was active in the Social Democratic Workingmen's Party of North America and its successor, the Workingmen's Party of the United States. He was an organizer of the Chicago American Section of the SLP (1878-81), running unsuccessfully for alderman in 1879 and 1881. He helped found the Council of Trades and Labor Unions of Chicago in 1877, joined Local Assembly 522 of the KOL in 1879, helped organize the Chicago Central Labor Union in 1884, founded the Machine Workers' Union of Chicago in 1886, and helped organize the International

Machinists' Union in 1891. In 1886 he was a founder of the United Labor party in Chicago, and he ran unsuccessfully for mayor of the city on the SLP ticket in 1891. Morgan left the Illinois Central in 1893 to study law, and in 1895 was admitted to the bar. In 1894 he took a leading role in forging a labor-People's party alliance. He helped launch the Social Democratic party in 1900, serving as secretary of its national campaign committee and running unsuccessfully as its nominee for state's attorney of Cook County. He became a leader in the Socialist Party of America, running unsuccessfully for a variety of offices including U.S. senator in 1909. From 1909 until his death he was editor and publisher of the *Provoker.*

MOST, Johann (1846-1906), a prominent anarchist born in Augsburg, Bavaria, was a bookbinder, editor, and amateur actor. He was elected as a Social Democrat to the German Reichstag in 1874 and 1877. During his second term German authorities arrested him for his anti-government pronouncements, exiling him in 1878. He moved to London, where he published *Die Freiheit,* and in 1879 he abandoned socialism for anarchism. In 1881 British authorities arrested him for his article applauding the assassination of Czar Alexander II, expelling him in 1882. He then came to the United States where he continued to publish *Die Freiheit* and in 1883 organized the American Federation of the International Working People's Association—the Black International—patterned after the London organization of the same name. Most made extensive speaking tours of the United States during the next two decades and served several jail terms for his activities and writings.

NEEBE, Oscar W. (b. 1850), a tinsmith born in New York City, became involved in the labor movement in Chicago after moving there in 1875. He was a member of the anarchist International Working People's Association and was operating a yeast business in 1886. He was convicted of murder in connection with the Haymarket incident and was sentenced to fifteen years in prison; he was pardoned by Governor John P. Altgeld in 1893.

O'DEA, Thomas (1846-1926), an Irish immigrant and Civil War veteran, served as secretary of the Bricklayers' and Masons' International Union (BMIU; 1884-87 and 1888-1900). After retirement from the BMIU, O'Dea worked in Cohoes, N.Y., as a contractor.

O'MALLEY, Timothy Thaddeus (1851-1930?), born in England, immigrated to the United States in 1871, settling in Salineville, Ohio, where he became a local KOL miners' leader in the late 1870s. In the early 1880s he was a delegate to the organizing conventions of the Ohio Miners' Amalgamated Association (1882), was elected vice-president of the fourth district of the Amalgamated Association of Miners of the United States (1883), and was secretary of KOL District Assembly (DA) 38 (1881-83). O'Malley was master workman of DA 38 in the late 1880s. He was expelled from the KOL by the 1889 General Assembly on charges that he was sympathetic to the National Progressive Union of Miners and Mine Laborers, a rival organization to coal miners' KOL National Trade Assembly 135. Beginning in 1884 he served as agent for a succession of labor journals including the *National Labor Tribune* of Pittsburgh and the *United Mine Workers Journal,* and, after 1895, he published the *Catholic Exponent* in Canton, Ohio, where he operated a printing business.

O'REILLY, Thomas (b. 1854), a onetime candidate for the priest-hood and a telegrapher from Edinburgh, Scotland, came to New York in 1882 and became a leader of the 1883 telegraphers' strike in New York City. In 1885 he was elected president of the Brotherhood of Telegraphers and in 1886 became master workman of KOL National District Assembly 45, the telegraphers' trade assembly. O'Reilly acted as Terence Powderly's representative in discussions with Catholic prel-ates who feared that the KOL posed a threat to the Catholic church. He was an editor of the *Journal of the Knights of Labor* from 1889 to 1893; in 1901 he became Powderly's confidential clerk at the Bureau of Immigration.

O'SULLIVAN, John F. (1857-1902), a Boston journalist and labor organizer, was born in Charlestown, Mass. He wrote on labor for the *Boston Labor Leader* and *Boston Herald* before joining the *Boston Globe* in 1890 as a reporter and labor editor. In the late 1880s he became active in organizing sailors, serving as treasurer of the Boston sailors' union. The first convention of the Sailors' and Firemen's Union (SFU) in 1890 elected him as general president, a position he held for several terms. He represented the SFU and the Atlantic Coast Seamen's Union in the Boston Central Trades and Labor Union (CTLU) and served two terms as president of the CTLU in the early 1890s. He also was active in the Massachusetts Federation of Labor as a member of the legislative committee. In 1894 he married Mary Kenney. O'-Sullivan was secretary of Newspaper Writers' Union 1 of Boston from 1896 until his death and served the International Typographical Union as an organizer, fifth vice-president (1897-1902), and fourth vice-president (1902).

OWENS, Charles E. (b. 1848), a New York–born carpenter, joined a carpenters' union in 1872 and in 1880 became a member of the United Order of American Carpenters and Joiners. He served as president and business agent of lodge 2 and president of the Order's Grand Executive Council. When the United Order merged with the Brotherhood of Carpenters and Joiners of America to form the United Brotherhood of Carpenters and Joiners of America (UBCJA) in 1888, Owens became a member of UBCJA local 382. The United Order lodges were slow to dismantle their old structure, however, and into the 1890s Owens continued to serve as president of the Order's Grand Executive Council. He became vice-president of District 4 of the UBCJA in 1890 and in 1894 was elected president of the UBCJA for one term ending in 1896.

OYLER, Charles P. (1855-99), born in Pennsylvania, was a Baltimore cigarmaker. He first participated in the labor movement in 1874 as a member of a mixed trades assembly of the KOL. Seven years later he became a member of CMIU 1, subsequently serving as recording and financial secretary. He served as seventh vice-president of the CMIU from 1888 to 1890. Later he moved to New Haven, Conn., where he was a member of CMIU 39.

PARSONS, Albert R. (1848-87), a Confederate army veteran from Montgomery, Ala., moved to Chicago after the war, working as a printer and joining International Typographical Union 16 and the KOL. He was active in the Workingmen's Party of the United States and the SLP. The SLP nominated him for the presidency of the United States in 1879, but he declined because he was underage. Parsons was a leader of the eight-hour movement and a founder and leader of the American affiliate of the anarchist International Working People's Association and edited its organ, the *Alarm*. He was convicted of murder in connection with the Haymarket incident and was hanged on Nov. 11, 1887.

POWDERLY, Terence Vincent (1849-1924), general master workman of the KOL, was born in Carbondale, Pa. Apprenticed as a machinist, he moved to Scranton and joined the International Machinists and Blacksmiths of North America in 1871, becoming president of his local and an organizer in Pennsylvania. After being dismissed and blacklisted for his labor activities, Powderly joined the KOL in Philadelphia in 1876 and shortly afterward founded a local assembly of machinists and was elected its master workman. In 1877 he helped organize District Assembly 5 (number changed to 16 in 1878) and was elected corresponding secretary. He was elected mayor of Scranton on the Greenback-Labor ticket in 1878 and served three consecutive two-year terms. At the same time he played an important role in calling the first General Assembly of the KOL in 1878, where he was chosen grand worthy foreman, the KOL's second highest office.

The September 1879 General Assembly elected him grand master workman, and he continued to hold the Order's leading position (title changed to general master workman in 1883) until 1893. Active in the secret Irish nationalist society, *Clan na Gael,* Powderly was elected to the Central Council of the American Land League in 1880 and was its vice-president in 1881. He became an ardent advocate of land reform and temperance and, as master workman, favored the organization of workers into mixed locals rather than craft unions, recommended that they avoid strikes, encouraged producers' cooperatives, and espoused political reform.

In 1894 Powderly was admitted to the Pennsylvania bar and in 1897 President William McKinley, for whom he had campaigned, appointed him commissioner general of immigration. President Theodore Roosevelt removed him from his position in 1902 but in 1906 appointed him special representative of the Department of Commerce and Labor to study European immigration problems. Powderly was chief of the Division of Information in the Bureau of Immigration and Naturalization from 1907 until his death.

PRYOR, Roger Atkinson (1828-1919), a Virginia Democratic congressman from 1858 to 1860, served as a Confederate general during the Civil War. He then moved to New York City where, as a lawyer, he advocated the rights of labor unions and challenged the validity of trusts. In 1886 he defended New York City eight-hour strikers and in 1887 represented the Haymarket anarchists before the U.S. Supreme Court. In the 1890s he was a judge and for a few years a justice of the New York Supreme Court.

QUINN, James E. (1836-1901), a bookbinder born in Boston, was elected master workman of KOL District Assembly (DA) 49 in New York City in 1883 and was active in the Central Labor Union. He was a leader of the inner circle of DA 49 known as the Home Club and an activist in the United Labor party. He served on the auxiliary General Executive Board of the KOL in 1886. In 1887 he defied the KOL leadership by publicly urging clemency for the condemned Haymarket defendants.

RIST, Frank Leonard (1858-1918), a printer born in Cincinnati, apprenticed with the *Cincinnati Volksfreund* and later worked for the *Cincinnati Enquirer.* He became a member of German-American Typographia 2 in 1878 and joined the KOL, subsequently becoming a leader of International Typographical Union 3 and the Cincinnati Central Labor Council (CLC). In 1892 he founded the *Chronicle,* official organ of the CLC, serving as editor and manager until his death. He was also a long-term organizer for the AFL.

ROBERTS, William T., was a member of American Lodge 29 of the National Amalgamated Association of Iron and Steel Workers (NAAISW) and vice-president of the NAAISW from the Pittsburgh region from 1888 to 1890.

RONEY, Frank (1841-1925), vice-president of the Iron Molders' Union of North America (1886-88) and a founder and president of the Representative Council of the Federated Trades and Labor Organizations of the Pacific Coast (1885-87), was an immigrant from Ireland who came to the United States to avoid imprisonment for his participation in the Fenian movement. He settled in Omaha, Neb., where he worked as an iron molder, served as an officer of his local union, and became active in reform politics. In 1875 he moved to San Francisco and was a leader of the Workingmen's party of California in 1878. He organized the Seamen's Protective Union in 1880, served as president of the San Francisco Representative Assembly of Trades and Labor Unions in 1881 and 1882, and was one of the promoters of the anti-Chinese label on cigars and shoes. He was a strong proponent of a national federation of trades. Blacklisted in his trade, Roney found work as a foundry worker in Vallejo, Calif., helped organize the town's Trades and Labor Council in 1899, and served one term as its president. In 1909 he moved to Los Angeles and in 1915 served as secretary-treasurer of the city's Iron Trades Council.

SANIAL, Lucien Delabarre (1836-1927), a French-born journalist, came to the United States in 1863 as a war correspondent for *Le Temps*. A prominent leader of the SLP, he drafted the party's platform in 1889, edited its organs, the *Workmen's Advocate* (1889-91) and the *People* (1891), and ran for mayor of New York on the SLP ticket in 1897. Around 1902 Sanial left the SLP; he later joined the Socialist Party of America, remaining an active member until breaking with the party in 1917 over its opposition to World War I. Sanial spoke at the founding convention of the American Alliance for Labor and Democracy in 1917.

SARGENT, Frank Pierce (1854-1908), grand master of the Brotherhood of Locomotive Firemen (BLF) from 1885 to 1902, was born in Vermont and was a textile operative, farm laborer, and a U.S. cavalryman before becoming a railroad worker. He joined Lodge 94 of the BLF in Tucson, Ariz., in 1881 and in 1883 was elected vice grand master of the Brotherhood. As grand master he urged moderation and negotiation with employers and refused to support sympathetic strikes. He was appointed to the U.S. Industrial Commission in 1898, and Theodore Roosevelt appointed him U.S. commissioner general of immigration in 1902. Sargent was active in the National

Civic Federation and was one of the labor representatives to its Division of Conciliation and Mediation.

SCHILLING, George Adam (1850-1938), a German-born cooper, emigrated with his parents and settled in Ohio in 1852. He worked as an itinerant cooper before moving to Chicago in 1875. There he was associated with the anarchist movement. He helped establish the Chicago English-speaking section of the Workingmen's Party of the United States in 1876, and with Thomas Morgan and Albert Parsons led the English-speaking branch of the SLP in the late 1870s, publishing the *Socialist* between 1878 and 1879. In 1878 he also was a member of the provisional committee that drew up the program of the International Labor Union. He ran unsuccessfully for alderman of Chicago in 1879 and 1880 and for mayor in 1881. After 1886 Schilling was an advocate of Henry George's single-tax movement, serving as president of the Chicago Single Tax Club. He helped organize a committee favoring amnesty for the Haymarket anarchists and led their defense before Governor Richard J. Oglesby of Illinois in 1887. A member of the executive board and master workman of KOL District Assembly 24 in the late 1880s, he led its secession from the KOL in 1889 in reaction to Terence Powderly's condemnation of the Haymarket defendants and failure to support the eight-hour movement. Between 1893 and 1897 he served as commissioner of the Illinois Bureau of Labor Statistics under Governor John P. Altgeld. In the late 1890s he was a member of the Chicago Civic Federation, and subsequently he served as a member (1903-5) and president (1905-7, 1911-15) of the Chicago Board of Local Improvements.

SCHILLING, Robert (1843-1922), was born in Osterburg, Saxony, and immigrated to St. Louis in 1846. After serving with the Union army, Schilling apprenticed as a cooper and joined the St. Louis coopers' union in 1863. In 1871 he was elected first vice-president of the Coopers of North America (CNA), a position he held until 1875. Moving to Cleveland Schilling was president of the Industrial Council of Cuyahoga County in 1874. He served as president of the Industrial Congress in 1873 and 1874, was president of the CNA in 1875, and joined the KOL the same year. Schilling was a founder of the Greenback party in 1875 and was a delegate to the founding convention of the Greenback-Labor party in 1878. Between 1878 and 1880 he edited the *Labor Advance*. About 1880 he moved to Milwaukee where he edited the *Volksblatt*, the *Reformer*, and the *Advance*. He ran unsuccessfully for Congress in 1888 and served as chairman of the state central committee of the United Labor party in 1889. He was national secretary of the National People's party in 1896. At the time of his death, Schilling was known as a spiritualist.

SCHWAB, Michael (b. 1853), a bookbinder born in Kitzingen, Germany, and a member of the Sozialdemokratische Arbeiterpartei, immigrated to the United States in 1879 where he became a member of the SLP. In the early 1880s he was a reporter in Chicago for the *Chicagoer Arbeiter-Zeitung* and organized the socialist clubs that participated in the founding of an American branch of the anarchist International Working People's Association in 1883. He was convicted of murder in connection with the Haymarket incident. His sentence was commuted to life imprisonment by Governor Richard J. Oglesby, and he was pardoned by Governor John P. Altgeld in 1893.

SEIDEL, Oscar G., secretary of the Textile Workers' Progressive Union of America, was a Philadelphia weaver who was born in Germany in 1852 and immigrated to the United States in 1878.

SHEVITCH, Sergius E. (variously Sergei E. Schewitsch; 1835-1912), was born in Russia and came to the United States in 1877. Because of his facility in three languages he was an important figure in the SLP in New York City during the 1880s. In 1884 he became editor of the *New Yorker Volkszeitung,* a post he retained until 1890. He also edited the *Leader* in 1887. In 1887 he ran for mayor of New York City on the Progressive Labor party ticket. Shevitch left the United States in 1890 and after an interlude in the Baltic provinces took up residence in Munich.

SHIELDS, William J. (1854-1918), general president of the Brotherhood of Carpenters and Joiners of America (BCJA) from 1886 to 1888, was born in Massachusetts and was a charter member in 1882 of local 33 of Boston. He served the local as secretary (1882-84), president (1884-86), delegate to the Boston Central Trades and Labor Union (1882-89), and business agent (1894). He was second vice-president of the BCJA from 1884 to 1886 and served on the General Executive Board of the renamed United Brotherhood of Carpenters and Joiners of America (UBCJA) from 1893 to 1896. In 1891 he ran unsuccessfully for lieutenant governor of Massachusetts on the People's party ticket. He was a general organizer for the UBCJA from 1900 until his death.

SIMSROTT, William A. (1861-97?), a Chicago railroad worker, helped organize the Switchmen's Mutual Aid Association in 1886. He was grand secretary and treasurer from 1887 to 1894, when, according to contemporary switchmen's sources, his defalcation contributed to the union's demise.

SKEFFINGTON, Henry J. (1858-1927), a shoemaker born in California, joined Philadelphia KOL Local Assembly (LA) 64 in 1878. He became master workman of LA 64, organized female carpet weavers in Philadelphia into the KOL's first assembly of women, and helped found the Executive Council of Shoe and Leather Workers, linking together various KOL shoe workers' trade districts. In 1887 he helped organize KOL shoe workers' National Trade Assembly 216, serving as its master workman and striving to establish its jurisdiction over shoeworkers within the Order. He led the secession of shoemakers from the KOL in 1889 and their amalgamation to form the Boot and Shoe Workers' International Union, serving as its secretary-treasurer in 1889, and as both general secretary and general treasurer from 1890 to 1894. He was also U.S. deputy immigration officer (1885-89) and chief immigration inspector (1894-97) for Boston and immigration commissioner for New England (1913-21). In the early 1920s he was a contract labor inspector in Providence, R.I., and a conciliation commissioner for the U.S. Department of Labor.

SMITH, James W. (1837-1903), a vice-president of the Journeymen Tailors' National Union (1885-87), was born in Ireland and immigrated to the United States in 1850, settling finally in Springfield, Ill. He served as first vice-president of the FOTLU Legislative Committee (1885-86), second vice-president of the AFL (1886-87), and president of the Illinois State Federation of Labor (1885-86, 1888-89).

SPEYER, Carl (b. 1845), was a German immigrant and leader of the New York City furniture workers' union. Speyer belonged to the General Council of the International Workingmen's Association after its transfer to New York from London in 1872. In the late 1870s he was a member of the Economic and Sociological Club, to which SG also belonged. As corresponding secretary of the United Cabinet Makers' Union of New York, he signed the call for the convention that founded the Gewerkschafts Union der Möbel-Arbeiter von Nord Amerika (Furniture Workers' Union of North America) in 1873. He helped organize the Amalgamated Trades and Labor Union of New York and Vicinity in 1878, serving as its first secretary, and was a founder of the short-lived International Labor Union in 1878, serving as its treasurer (1878-79) and general secretary (1880-82).

SPIES, August Vincent Theodore (1855-87), born in Landesberg, Germany, came to the United States in 1872 and moved to Chicago in 1873, joining the SLP and the KOL. He was a founder of an American affiliate of the International Working People's Association in 1883. Spies, who became editor of the *Chicagoer Arbeiter-Zeitung* in

1880, was convicted of murder in connection with the Haymarket incident and was hanged on Nov. 11, 1887.

STEWARD, Ira (1831-83), leader of the movement for the eight-hour workday, was born in Connecticut and apprenticed as a machinist, becoming a leading figure in the International Machinists and Blacksmiths of North America. During the mid-1860s in Boston he helped organize several associations devoted to the establishment of the eight-hour workday, and he successfully promoted the passage of a Massachusetts ten-hour law for women and children in 1874. During the 1870s he developed close ties with New York City trade unionists in the International Workingmen's Association and he helped found and served as an organizer for the International Labor Union. Steward formulated the theoretical basis for the eight-hour movement in the United States. He believed that freeing workers from long hours of labor would stimulate their desire for a better life and facilitate their education and organization, leading eventually to the abolition of the wage system. His ideas were disseminated in pamphlets and through the writings of his disciples, most notably George McNeill and George Gunton.

STRASSER, Adolph (1843-1939), was born in Hungary and immigrated to the United States about 1872. He became a cigarmaker, helped organize New York City cigar workers excluded from membership in the CMIU, and played a leading role in the United Cigarmakers. Strasser was a member of the International Workingmen's Association and, in 1874, helped organize the Social Democratic Workingmen's Party of North America, serving as its executive secretary. He was also a founder of the Economic and Sociological Club. In 1876 he was a delegate to the unity congress that organized the Workingmen's Party of the United States, and he aligned with the trade unionist faction of the party. During 1876 and 1877 he worked to establish a central organization of New York City trade unions, and his efforts culminated in the founding of the Amalgamated Trades and Labor Union of New York and Vicinity in the summer of 1877. Strasser was elected vice-president of the CMIU in 1876 and president in 1877 and successfully promoted the reorganization of the union in the late 1870s and early 1880s. After retiring as president in 1891, he continued to work for the CMIU as an organizer, auditor, and troubleshooter. In addition he served as an AFL lecturer, member of the Federation's legislative committee, and AFL arbitrator of jurisdictional disputes. He ended his labor career in 1914, becoming a real estate agent in Buffalo, and in 1919 he moved to Florida.

SWINTON, John (1830-1901), a Scottish-born journalist, emigrated in 1843 and apprenticed as a printer in Montreal. He was on the editorial board of the *New York Times* throughout the 1860s, and the *New York Sun* from 1875 to 1883 and again from 1892 to 1897. He published the influential New York City labor reform newspaper *John Swinton's Paper* between October 1883 and August 1887. Active in New York City politics, he ran for mayor in 1874 on the Industrial Political party ticket and worked in the mayoralty campaign of Henry George in 1886.

TALBOT, Thomas Wilson (1849-92), was born in South Carolina and went to work in a shoe factory when he was ten. In 1865 he became an apprentice in a Florence, S.C., railroad machine shop, and worked as a machinist and engineer before opening his own machine shop in Sumter, S.C., in 1874. Joining the KOL, he served as a master workman and state organizer. In 1887 he moved to Atlanta and in the following year helped organize the Order of United Machinists and Mechanical Engineers of America. In May 1889 Talbot was elected grand master machinist of the National Association of Machinists, as the Order was renamed, and he was reelected the following year. He resigned in July 1890.

THAYER, Walter Nelson (1849-1929), a leader of International Typographical Union 52 of Troy, N.Y., and an official in the Troy city government, served as president of the New York State Workingmen's Assembly in 1884-86. In 1892 he became warden of New York's Dannemora Prison.

TILLETT, Benjamin (1860-1943), a British seaman and dock worker, helped organize the Tea Operatives' and General Labourers' Association in 1887 and was a leader of the London dock strike of 1889. In its aftermath he was a founder of the Dock, Wharf, Riverside and General Labourers' Union of Great Britain and Ireland and its general secretary until 1922. In 1910 he helped organize the National Transport Workers' Federation. He was a member of the parliamentary committee of the Trades Union Congress (1892-95) and a founder of the Independent Labour party in 1893, serving on its executive council during its first year. In 1900 he helped establish the Labour Representation Committee, direct predecessor to the Labour party. Tillett stood unsuccessfully for Parliament four times before serving as a Labour Member from 1917 to 1924 and 1929 to 1931.

TURNER, Frederick (b. 1846), general secretary-treasurer of the KOL from 1883 to 1886, was born in England and immigrated to the United States in 1856, settling in Philadelphia. A Civil War veteran, he became a goldbeater and helped organize local assemblies of the KOL in that trade in Philadelphia, New York, and Boston in 1873 and 1874. As a result of his organizing activities, he was black-listed in 1877 and became a grocer. He served as financial secretary and recording secretary of Pennsylvania District Assembly 1 and from 1880 was a member of the Knights' General Executive Board. After the Order divided the secretary-treasurer's position in 1886, Turner served as general treasurer until 1888.

VAN ETTEN, Ida M. (1867?-94), was born in Van Ettenville, N.Y., and moved to New York City in 1887. In 1888 she helped organize the New York Working Women's Society, was elected secretary, and for several years was a leading figure in organizing women workers in New York. She frequently lectured and published articles on the industrial status of women, and she lobbied before the New York legislature for the abolition of the sweating system and for passage of the Fassett bill providing for female factory inspectors. In 1889 she helped organize women feather workers and women cloakmakers in New York City and at the 1891 AFL convention served as secretary of a women's committee that recommended commissioning a woman organizer. She went to Europe in 1893 to gather material for a series of articles and died the following year in Paris.

VOGT, Hugo, a notary public and later a lawyer, was a leader of the SLP in New York City. He served as acting secretary of the SLP in 1883, supported Henry George's mayoralty campaign, and was active in the United Labor party. In the 1880s and 1890s he ran for the New York assembly several times. Together with Daniel DeLeon and Lucien Sanial, Vogt led the SLP in the 1890s, serving as secretary of its New York American Section, editing the *Vorwärts*, and serving as manager of the *Daily People*. He was active in KOL District Assembly 49 and also was a founder in 1895 of the Socialist Trade and Labor Alliance. Vogt left the SLP about 1902 after a dispute with Daniel DeLeon.

WALTON, Henry (b. 1840?), born in England, was a member of the Brotherhood of Locomotive Firemen (BLF) Grand Executive Board from 1885 to 1894 and secretary of the BLF's Philadelphia Enterprise Lodge 75.

WEAVER, John G. (1838-1918?), an iron molder born in Ohio, was assistant secretary of the Iron Molders' Union (1886-1903) and secretary of the Covington, Ky., water works (1906-13).

WELTER, John M. (1857-1911), a New York–born painter, joined KOL Local Assembly 3629 in 1882 and in 1887 became a charter member of Brotherhood of Painters and Decorators of America (BPDA)

local 42 of Buffalo. He was secretary of the Buffalo Central Labor
Union and the Buffalo Building Trades Council during the late 1880s
and in 1890 was elected vice-president of the New York State Branch
of the AFL. Welter served as president of the BPDA between 1894
and 1896, siding with the Lafayette, Ind., faction against the Baltimore
group headed by John Elliott. About 1895 he moved to Chicago.

WHEATON, Calvin S. (b. 1846), born in New York, was grand chief
conductor of the Order of Railway Conductors from 1880 to 1890,
when he declined renomination because of the Order's decision to
drop its anti-strike clause. After the 1890 convention, Wheaton and
other dissident members formed a rival organization, the Independent
Order of Railway Conductors, and he briefly served as president.

WILKINSON, Joseph (b. 1856), was born in Ireland and immigrated
to the United States in 1872. A tailor, he helped found the Amalgamated Trades and Labor Union of New York and Vicinity in 1877.
He was secretary of the Journeymen Tailors' National Union of the
United States from 1884 to 1887.

WILKINSON, Stephen Edward (b. 1850), born in Ohio and a Civil
War veteran, was the first master of Enterprise Lodge 27 of the
Brotherhood of Railroad Brakemen in Peoria, Ill. He helped organize
the Brotherhood (name changed to Brotherhood of Railroad Trainmen in 1890) and served as grand master from 1885 to 1895.

WRIGHT, Alexander Whyte (1847?-1919), a Canadian labor leader,
was born in Ontario and briefly worked in the woolen business before
becoming a journalist in 1873 or 1874. He edited a variety of papers
in the 1870s and 1880s and was an advocate of land and currency
reform, labor legislation, and public ownership of the Canadian Pacific
Railway. He was elected secretary of the Canadian Currency Reform
League in 1879 and was a speaker for the Greenback-Labor party in
the 1880 elections. In 1882 he became secretary of the Canadian
Manufacturers' Association, serving until 1886. He joined the KOL
in 1883, helping to organize and serving as worthy foreman and
recording secretary of Toronto District Assembly 125 and master
workman of Hugo Assembly 7814 of Toronto. Wright became a KOL
lecturer in 1888, was a member of the General Executive Board from
1888 to 1893, and was an editor of the *Journal of the Knights of Labor*
between 1889 and 1893. He later was an organizer of the Conservative
party in Ontario and in 1914 was appointed vice-chairman of the
Workmen's Compensation Commission.

ORGANIZATIONS

The Journeymen BAKERS' National Union of the United States was organized in 1886, participated in the formation of the AFL that year, and was chartered by the AFL in 1887. In 1890 it adopted the name Journeymen Bakers' and Confectioners' International Union of America and, in 1903, became the Bakery and Confectionery Workers' International Union of America.

The Journeymen BARBERS' National Union, founded in 1887 by unions formerly affiliated with the KOL, affiliated with the AFL in 1888 as the Journeymen Barbers' International Union of America.

The National Boilermakers' and Helpers' Protective and Benevolent Union organized in 1881 and in 1884 changed its name to the International Brotherhood of Boiler Makers and Iron Ship Builders' Protective and Benevolent Union of the United States and Canada. In 1887 it affiliated with the AFL as the International Brotherhood of BOILER Makers. It withdrew in 1893 and merged with the National Brotherhood of Boiler Makers to form the Brotherhood of Boiler Makers and Iron Ship Builders of America, which affiliated with the AFL in 1896. In 1906 the boiler makers adopted the name International Brotherhood of Boiler Makers, Iron Ship Builders and Helpers of America.

The BOOT and Shoe Workers' International Union (BSWIU) was organized in 1889 by seceding locals of shoemakers' National Trade Assembly (NTA) 216 of the KOL; it affiliated that year with the AFL. The remnant of NTA 216 continued as a separate organization. In 1895 the BSWIU merged with another AFL affiliate, the Lasters' Protective Union of America, and with NTA 216 to form the Boot and Shoe Workers' Union.

The National Union of Brewers of the United States organized in 1886 and affiliated with the AFL as the BREWERS' National Union in March 1887. Later that year it changed its name to the National Union of the United Brewery Workmen of the United States, and it became the International Union of the United Brewery Workmen of America in 1903. After a prolonged series of jurisdictional disputes the AFL revoked the union's charter in 1907; it reinstated the Brewers in 1908. In 1917 the union became the International Union of United Brewery and Soft Drink Workers of America, and in 1918, the International Union of United Brewery, Flour, Cereal and Soft Drink Workers of America.

The BRICKLAYERS' and Masons' International Union of America was organized in 1865. It did not affiliate with the AFL until 1916.

The Amalgamated Society of CARPENTERS and Joiners (ASCJ), a

British trade union founded in 1860, established its American District in New York City in 1868. In 1888 the AFL rejected its application for affiliation upon the objection of the United Brotherhood of Carpenters and Joiners of America (UBCJA), but in 1890 the UBCJA dropped its protest and the ASCJ affiliated with the AFL. Beginning about 1900 the UBCJA and the ASCJ engaged in a series of jurisdictional disputes. The 1911 AFL convention ruled that the two unions must amalgamate, and the Federation revoked the ASCJ's charter two years later. The two organizations merged in January 1914.

The Brotherhood of CARPENTERS and Joiners of America was organized in 1881 and was chartered by the AFL in 1887. In 1888 the Brotherhood and the United Order of American Carpenters and Joiners merged, forming the United Brotherhood of Carpenters and Joiners of America.

The Cigar Makers' National Union of America was organized in 1864 and changed its name to the CIGAR Makers' International Union of America (CMIU) in 1867. It participated in the formation of the FOTLU in 1881. The following year, seceding New York City locals formed the Cigarmakers' Progressive Union of America; the Progressives rejoined the International in 1886. The AFL chartered the CMIU in March 1887.

The Retail CLERKS' National Protective Association of America was organized in Detroit in December 1890 as an AFL affiliate. It changed its name to the Retail Clerks' International Protective Association in 1899.

The American FLINT Glass Workers' Union of North America was organized in 1878 by locals formerly affiliated with the KOL. It joined the AFL in 1887.

The Gewerkschafts Union der Möbel-Arbeiter von Nord Amerika (Furniture Workers' Union of North America) was organized in 1873, and in 1882 it changed its name to the International FURNITURE Workers' Union of America. It affiliated with the AFL in 1887 and in 1896 merged with the Machine Wood Workers' International Union of America to form the Amalgamated Wood Workers' International Union of America.

The Granite Cutters' International Union of the United States and the British Provinces of America was formed in 1877. In 1880 it changed its name to the GRANITE Cutters' National Union of the United States of America, and in the following year participated in the formation of the FOTLU. It joined the AFL in 1888 and in 1905 adopted the name Granite Cutters' International Association of America.

The International HOD Carriers and Building Laborers Union of America was organized in 1903. It affiliated with the AFL during the same year.

The National Amalgamated Association of IRON and Steel Workers was organized in 1876 and in 1887 was chartered by the AFL. In 1897 it changed its name to the National Amalgamated Association of Iron, Steel, and Tin Workers and in 1908 dropped "National" from its name.

The National Union of Iron Molders (after 1874 the IRON MOLDERS' Union of North America) was organized in 1859 and in 1881 participated in the formation of the FOTLU. It was chartered by the AFL in 1887. In 1907 it changed its name to the International Molders' Union of North America.

The New England LASTERS' Protective Union was organized in 1878 and affiliated with the AFL in 1887. It changed its name to the Lasters' Protective Union of America in 1890, and in 1895 merged with KOL National Trade Assembly 216 and the Boot and Shoe Workers' International Union to form the Boot and Shoe Workers' Union.

The locomotive engineers organized the Brotherhood of the Footboard in 1863. In 1864 the organization became the Brotherhood of LOCOMOTIVE Engineers.

The Brotherhood of LOCOMOTIVE Firemen was organized in 1873, and in 1878 merged under its name with the International Firemen's Union. In 1906 it adopted the name Brotherhood of Locomotive Firemen and Enginemen.

The Order of United Machinists and Mechanical Engineers of America organized in 1888 and the following year changed its name to the National Association of MACHINISTS. It changed its name to the International Association of Machinists in 1891 and in 1895 affiliated with the AFL.

The International MACHINISTS' Union of America was established in 1891 and chartered that year by the AFL; it disbanded in 1895.

The METAL Workers' National Union of North America was organized in 1882 and was chartered by the AFL in 1887. It disbanded in 1889.

The National Federation of MINERS and Mine Laborers was or-

ganized in 1885. Beginning in 1886, it was involved in bitter jurisdictional disputes with KOL miners' National Trade Assembly (NTA)
135. In 1888 it merged with a faction of NTA 135 and the Miners'
and Mine Laborers' Amalgamated Association of Pennsylvania to form
the National Progressive Union of Miners and Mine Laborers
(NPUMML). The NPUMML merged with the remainder of NTA
135 in 1890, creating the United Mine Workers of America.

NATIONAL Trade Assembly (NTA) 135, the KOL miners' assembly,
was organized in May 1886, eight months after the founding of the
National Federation of Miners and Mine Laborers. The two organizations competed for jurisdiction. In December 1888 a minority of
NTA 135 seceded and joined the Miners Federation, which was reorganized as the National Progressive Union of Miners and Mine
Laborers. NTA 135 and the Progressives united in 1890 as the United
Mine Workers of America (UMWA), affiliated with both the AFL and
NTA 135 of the KOL. In 1894 the Knights' General Assembly ex-
cluded NTA 135 on the grounds that it was dominated and controlled
by the UMWA.

The Representative Council of the Federated Trades and Labor
Organizations of the PACIFIC Coast was organized in 1885. It originated at a Pacific Coast anti-Chinese convention called by the San
Francisco District Assembly of the KOL. As originally conceived, it
was to be a federation of all western unions with an authority over
them similar to that of a national trade union over its locals. It failed
to achieve significant influence outside San Francisco and in 1891
was superseded by the Council of Federated Trades of the Pacific
Coast.

The Brotherhood of PAINTERS and Decorators of America (BPDA)
was organized in 1887, affiliating with the AFL the same year. In
1891 the union withdrew from the Federation, but it reaffiliated the
following year. In 1894 the BPDA split between western and eastern
factions headquartered, respectively, in Lafayette, Ind., and Baltimore. The factions merged in 1900, becoming the Brotherhood of
Painters, Decorators and Paperhangers of America.

The QUARRYMEN'S National Union of the United States of America
was chartered by the AFL in 1890 and suspended in 1900.

The Brotherhood of RAILROAD Brakemen of the Western Hemi-
sphere organized in 1883. In 1886 it changed its name to the Brotherhood of Railroad Brakemen and in 1890 to the Brotherhood of
Railroad Trainmen.

The Conductors' Union, organized in 1868, changed its name to the Conductors' Brotherhood at its first annual convention in 1869. In 1878 the union became the Order of RAILWAY Conductors of America.

The SWITCHMEN'S Mutual Aid Association of the United States of America organized in 1886 and disbanded in 1894. It was succeeded by the Switchmen's Union of North America, founded later in 1894.

The Journeymen TAILORS' National Union of the United States, composed of custom tailors, was organized in 1883 and was chartered by the AFL in 1887. It changed its name in 1889 to the Journeymen Tailors' Union of America and in 1913 to the Tailors' Industrial Union. The following year it merged with the Amalgamated Clothing Workers of America (ACWA) but in 1915 seceded from the ACWA and again assumed the name of Journeymen Tailors' Union of America. The union's membership declined thereafter, and in 1938 the AFL revoked its charter.

The Brotherhood of TELEGRAPHERS, which became District Assembly 45 of the KOL, was organized in 1882 in New York.

The United Silk Workers organized in 1883 and the following year adopted the name TEXTILE Workers' Progressive Union of America (TWPUA). The TWPUA affiliated with the AFL in 1888 and withdrew three years later.

The TIN, Sheet Iron and Cornice Workers' International Association organized in 1888 and affiliated with the AFL the following year.

The TRADES Union Congress of Great Britain, the central organization of that country's trade union movement, was founded in 1868.

The German-American TYPOGRAPHIA was organized in 1873 and was chartered by the AFL in 1887. It merged with the International Typographical Union as an autonomous unit in 1894.

The National Typographical Union was organized in 1852 by a group of locals that had held national conventions in 1850 and 1851 under the name Journeymen Printers of the United States. In 1869 it adopted the name International TYPOGRAPHICAL Union (ITU). Although ITU members participated in the formation of the FOTLU in 1881 and in the organizing of the AFL in 1886, the union did not affiliate with the Federation until 1888.

INDEX

Names of persons or organizations for whom there are glossary entries are followed by an asterisk.

Italics indicate the location of detailed information. While this index is not cumulative, it does include references to substantive annotations in volume one that are relevant to this volume but are not repeated here; these appear first in the index entry. The reference to the Boston Central Trades and Labor Union's annotation in volume one, for example, appears in this index as *1:166n*.

Neebe, Oscar W.,* 53, *55n*

Nelson, Robert, 301, *304n*, 409n

Netherlandisch Isralitiche Sickefund:
letter to, 116-17

New York, Housesmith's Benevolent
and Protective Union of the City of.
See Housesmith's Benevolent and Protective Union of the City of New
York

New York, Independent Clothing Cutters' Union of. *See* Clothing Cutters'
Union of New York, Independent

New York, Mutual Musical Protective
Union of. *See* Musical Protective
Union of New York, Mutual

New York, Workingmen's Federation of
the State of, *96n*

New York and Vicinity, Bakers' Association of. *See* Bakers' Association of
New York and Vicinity

New York and Vicinity, Lager Beer
Brewers' Board of Trade of. *See*
Brewers' Board of Trade of New
York and Vicinity, Lager Beer

New York and Vicinity, United Order
of Carpenters of. *See* Carpenters and
Joiners, United Order of American

New York Board of Arbitration, 5, 7,
10n

New York Board of Mediation and Arbitration, 5, *10n*, 101n, 197n, 427

New York Bureau of Statistics of Labor,
1:364n, 5, *10n*

New York carpenters, mass meeting of:
letter to. *See* Carpenters, mass meeting of New York: letter to

New York Central and Hudson River
Railroad, 382n

New York City: cigar industry in, 124-
26; eight-hour conference, 183, 193

New York City, Co-operative Shirtmakers of. *See* Shirtmakers of New York
City, Co-operative

New York City Board of Walking Delegates. *See* Board of Walking Delegates, New York City

New York City Central Federated
Union, *1:379n*, 192

New York City Central Labor Federation, *1:379n*, 421-23, 426; news accounts of meetings of, 249-51, 367-
70, 382-83

— 1889: formation of, 191, 386,
392; conflict with Central Labor
Union (CLU), 193, 195, 206-7; chartering of, by American Federation of
Labor (AFL), 191, 195, 206-7, 213,
387, 392; and Gompers' nomination
for senator, 245, 247n, 249-51; and
merger with CLU, 191, 358, 387,
392-93

— 1890: formation of, 191-92, 387,
393; demand for return of 1889 AFL
charter, 192, 358-59, 387, 391, 393-
94; application for new AFL charter,
192, 362-63, 367-70, 377-78, 387,
391, 394-95; instructions to delegate
to 1890 AFL convention, 383, 418;
1890 AFL convention and, 192, 378,
386-408, 417, 421-24

— 1899: merger with CLU, 192

New York City Central Labor Union,
1:379n, 45, 114; and building trades
section, 120, 120n; and conflict with
Central Labor Federation, 193, 195,
206-7; corruption within, 191, 207,
392; and eight-hour movement
(1890), 183, *184n;* factions within,
191, 392-93; and Gompers' nomination for senator, 245; and Haymarket
clemency campaign, 55n, 58n, 61;
and Knights of Labor, 292-93; and
trade union party politics, 161

New Yorker Staats-Zeitung, 124, 126

New Yorker Volkszeitung, 191, 400; letter
to, 211-12

New York Press: letter to, 349-53

New York Railroad Commission, 4, *10n*

New York Society for Ethical Culture,
Workingmen's School of the. *See* Ethi-
cal Culture, New York Society for,
Workingmen's School of the

New York State: constitutional convention, 6, *11n;* jury duty in, 8

— legislation: arbitration law, 5, *10n;*
child labor law, 3-4, *10n;* contract
convict labor law, 4-5, *10n*, 320,
320n, 363; factory inspection law, 7,
11n, 288-89, 289n-90n; incorporation
of trade union law, 6, *11n;* industrial
conspiracy law, 6, 151, *152n;* Labor
Day law, 6, *11n;* mechanics' lien law,
5, *10n-11n;* railroad employees,